Street by Street

WEST KENT

PLUS BIGGIN HILL, GRAYS, ORPINGTON, TILBURY

Enlarged Areas Chatham, Gillingham, Maidstone, Rochester, Royal Tunbridge Wells, Sevenoaks

G000097876

1st edition May 2001

© Automobile Association Developments Limited 2001

This product includes map data licensed from Ordnance Survey® with the permission of the Controller of Her Majesty's Stationery Office. © Crown copyright 2000. All rights reserved. Licence No: 399221.

Published by AA Publishing (a trading name of Automobile Association Developments Limited, whose registered office is Norfolk House, Priestley Road, Basingstoke, Hampshire, RG24 9NY. Registered number 1878835).

Mapping produced by the Cartographic Department of The Automobile Association.

A CIP Catalogue record for this book is available from the British Library.

Printed by G. Canale & C. S.P.A., Torino, Italy

The contents of this atlas are believed to be correct at the time of the latest revision. However, the publishers cannot be held responsible for loss occasioned to any person acting or refraining from action as a result of any material in this atlas, nor for any errors, omissions or changes in such material. The publishers would welcome information to correct any errors or omissions and to keep this atlas up to date. Please write to Publishing, The Automobile Association, Fanum House, Basing View, Basingstoke, Hampshire, RG21 4EA.

Ref: MX098

Key to map pages	ii-iii
Key to map symbols	iv-1
Enlarged scale pages	2-11
Street by Street	12-209
Index – towns & villages	210-211
Index – streets	211-233
Index – featured places	233-236

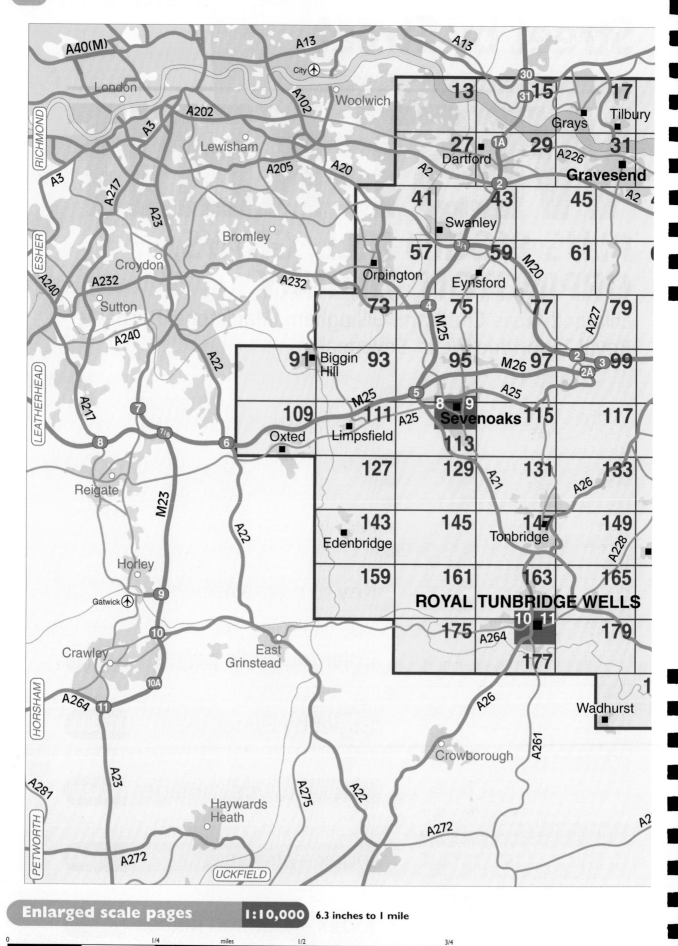

Enlarged scale pages | **1:10,000** | 6.3 inches to 1 mile

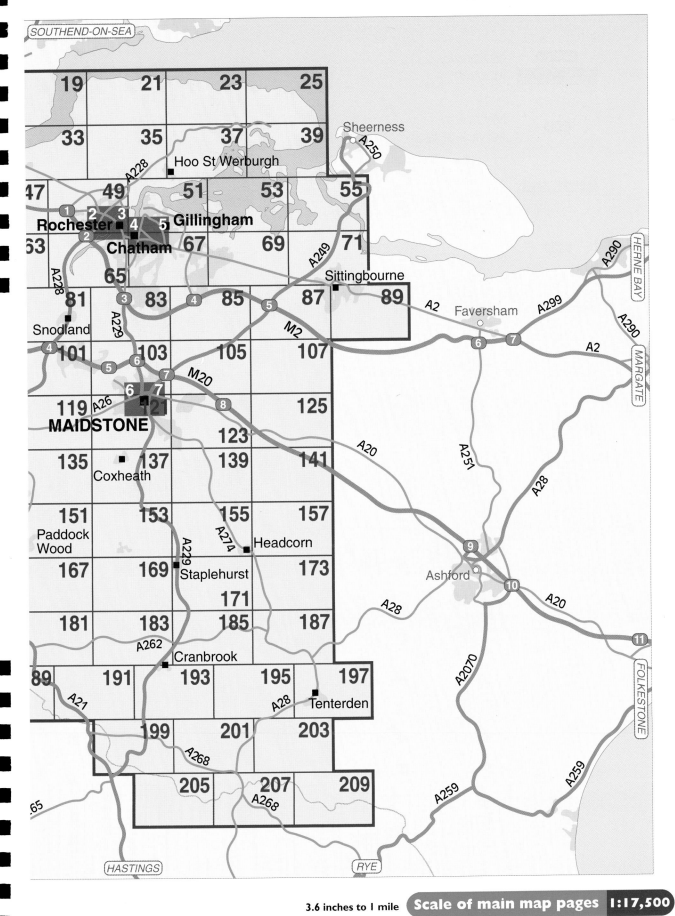

SOUTHEND-ON-SEA

| 19 | 21 | 23 | 25 |

Sheerness
A250

| 33 | 35 | 37 | 39 |

A228
Hoo St Werburgh

| 47 | 49 | 51 | 53 | 55 |

Rochester
Gillingham
Chatham

| 63 | 67 | 69 | 71 |

65
A228
A249
Sittingbourne

| 81 | 83 | 85 | 87 | 89 |

Snodland
A229
M2
Faversham
A2
A299
HERNE BAY
A290

| 101 | 103 | 105 | 107 |

MAIDSTONE
A26
M20
A2
A290
MARGATE

| 119 | 121 | 125 |

123

| 135 | 137 | 139 | 141 |

Coxheath
A20
A251
A28

| 151 | 153 | 155 | 157 |

Paddock Wood
A274
Headcorn
A229
Staplehurst

| 167 | 169 | 173 |

171
Ashford

| 181 | 183 | 185 | 187 |

A262
Cranbrook
A28
A20
FOLKESTONE

| 89 | 191 | 193 | 195 | 197 |

A21
A28
Tenterden
A2070

| 199 | 201 | 203 |

A268

| 205 | 207 | 209 |

A268
A259
A259

A65

HASTINGS
RYE

3.6 inches to 1 mile   **Scale of main map pages** 1:17,500

0   1/2   miles   1
0   1/2   1   kilometres   1 1/2   2

iv

Junction 9	Motorway & junction
Services	Motorway service area
	Primary road single/dual carriageway
Services	Primary road service area
	A road single/dual carriageway
	B road single/dual carriageway
	Other road single/dual carriageway
	Restricted road
	Private road
← ←	One way street
	Pedestrian street
	Track/ footpath
	Road under construction
⌐ = = = = ⌐	Road tunnel
P	Parking

P+	Park & Ride
	Bus/coach station
	Railway & main railway station
	Railway & minor railway station
⊖	Underground station
⊖	Light railway & station
++++++++++++	Preserved private railway
LC	Level crossing
•—•—•—•—•	Tramway
- - - - - - -	Ferry route
....	Airport runway
- · - · - · -	Boundaries- borough/ district
▼▼▼▼▼▼▼▼▼▼	Mounds
93	Page continuation 1:17,500
7	Page continuation to enlarged scale 1:10,000

River/canal lake, pier		Toilet with disabled facilities
Aqueduct lock, weir		Petrol station
465 ▲ Winter Hill — Peak (with height in metres)		PH — Public house
Beach		PO — Post Office
Coniferous woodland		Public library
Broadleaved woodland		i — Tourist Information Centre
Mixed woodland		Castle
Park		Historic house/ building
Cemetery		Wakehurst Place NT — National Trust property
Built-up area		M — Museum/ art gallery
Featured building		† — Church/chapel
City wall		Country park
A&E — Accident & Emergency hospital		Theatre/ performing arts
Toilet		Cinema

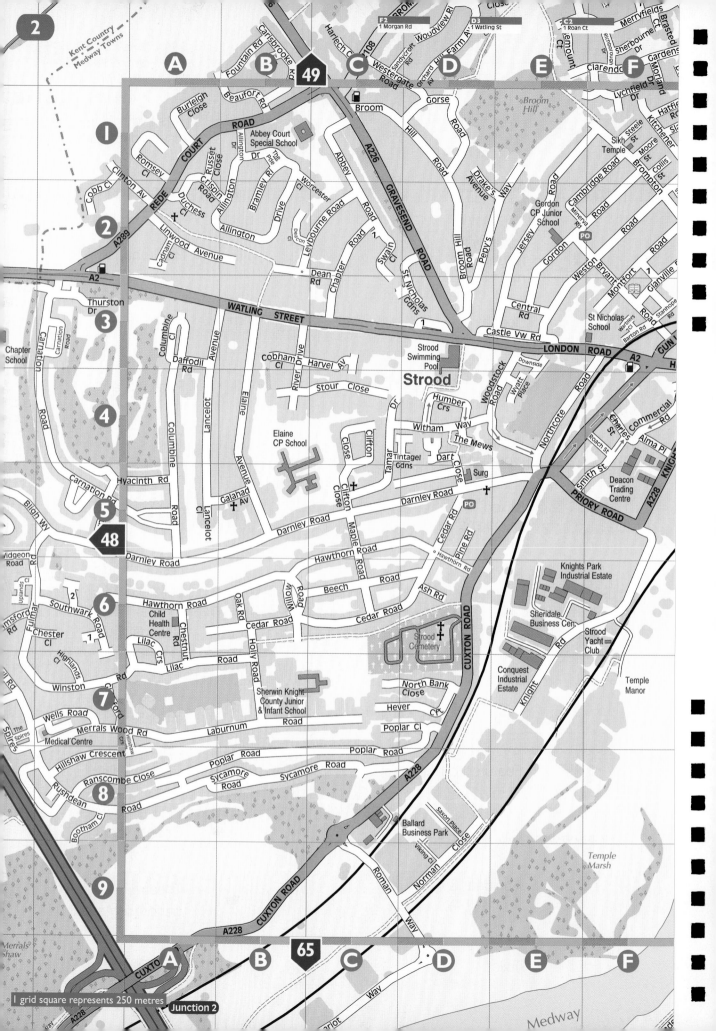

Kent Country
Medway Towns

A **B** **49** **C** **D** **E** **F**

F2 1 Morgan Rd   D3 1 Watling St   C2 1 Roan Ct

Merryfields
Brasted

Sherbourne Dr

Clarendon
Morland
Kitchener
Hatfield
Slade

Lychfield Dr

1

Burleigh Close
Beaufort Rd
Fountain Rd
Carisbrooke Rd
Harlech Cl
7108
Sandycroft Rd
Woodview Rd
Westgate Road
Orchard Av
Farm Av
Gorse
Broom Hill
Sikh Steele
Temple

Romsey Cl
REDE COURT ROAD
Russet Close
Crispin Road
Allington Dr
The Dr
Abbey Court Special School
Bramley Rd
Worcester Cl
Drive
Hill
Gorse Road
Broom Hill
Cambridge Road
Brompton
Moore
Collis St

2
Clinton Av
Cobb Cl
A289
Duchess Cl
Linwood Avenue
Cadnam Rd
Allington
Allington
Deacon
Leybourne Road
Chapter Road
Abbey Road
Swain Cl
A226 GRAVESEND ROAD
Drake's Avenue
Broom Hill Road
Pepy's
Way
Jersey Road
Gordon CP Junior School
Minerva Rd
Gordon
Weston
Bryant
Montfort
PO
7
Glanville
Rd
Road

Thurston Dr

3
A289
Carnation Road
Columbine Cl
WATLING STREET
Avenue
Cobham Cl
River Drive
Harvel Av
Dean Rd
St Nicholas Gdns
Castle Vw Rd
Central Rd
St Nicholas School
Warblers
Barton Rd
LONDON ROAD
A2
GUN
H

Chapter School
Carnation Road
Daffodil Rd
Columbine
Elaine
Stour Close
Strood Swimming Pool
Strood
Woodstock Road
Downside
Wyatt Place
Northcote Road
Charles St
Commercial Rd

4
Elaine CP School
Lancelot
Avenue
Clifton Close
Clifton
Tamar Dr
Humber Crs
Witham
Way
The Mews
Dart Close
Alma Pl
Deacon Trading Centre
A228
KNIGHT

Hyacinth Rd
Carnation Rd
Galanad
Lancelot Cl
Galahad Av
Clifton Close
Tintagel Gdns
Darnley Road
PO
Surg
Smith St
PRIORY ROAD
KNIGHT

5
Bligh Wy
48
Darnley Road
Darnley Road
Maple Road
Cedar Rd
Pine Rd
Hawthorn Rd

Widgeon Road
Uplands Cl
Hawthorn Road
Willow Road
Beech
Road
Cedar Road
Ash Rd
Hawthorn Rd
Knights Park Industrial Estate

6
Fulmar
Southwark Road
Child Health Centre
Chestnut Rd
Oak Rd
Cedar Road
Strood Cemetery
Sheridale Business Cen
Strood Yacht Club

Bramsford Rd
Chester Cl
2
7
Lilac Crs
Lilac
Road
Holly Road
CUXTON ROAD
Conquest Industrial Estate
Knight Rd
Temple Manor

Highlands Cl
Winston

7
Wells Road
Clifford
Sherwin Knight County Junior & Infant School
North Bank Close
Hever

The Spires
Merrals Wood Rd
Medical Centre
Laburnum Road
Poplar Cl
Poplar Cl

Hillshaw Crescent
Hillshaw Crs
A228

8
Ranscombe Close
Poplar Road
Sycamore Road
Poplar Road

Rushdean
Sycamore Road
Ballard Business Park
Saxon Place
Viking Cl
Norman Way
Temple Marsh

Bootham Cl
Roman Way
Medway

9

Merrals Shaw

A228 CUXTON ROAD

A CUXTO **B** **65** **C** **D** **E** **F**

1 grid square represents 250 metres

Junction 2

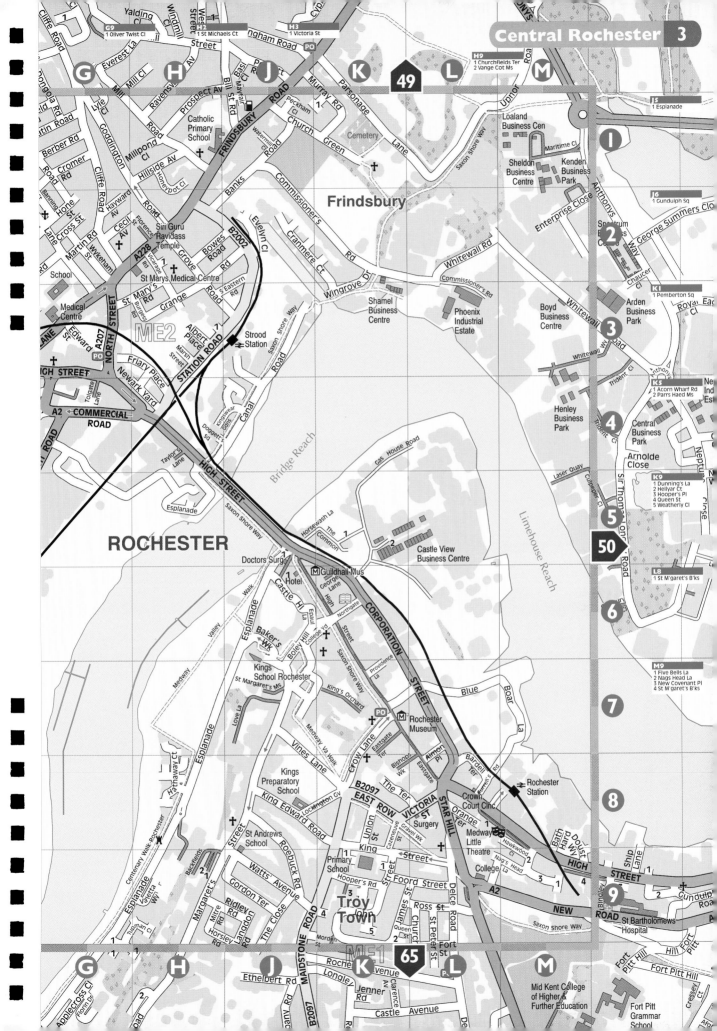

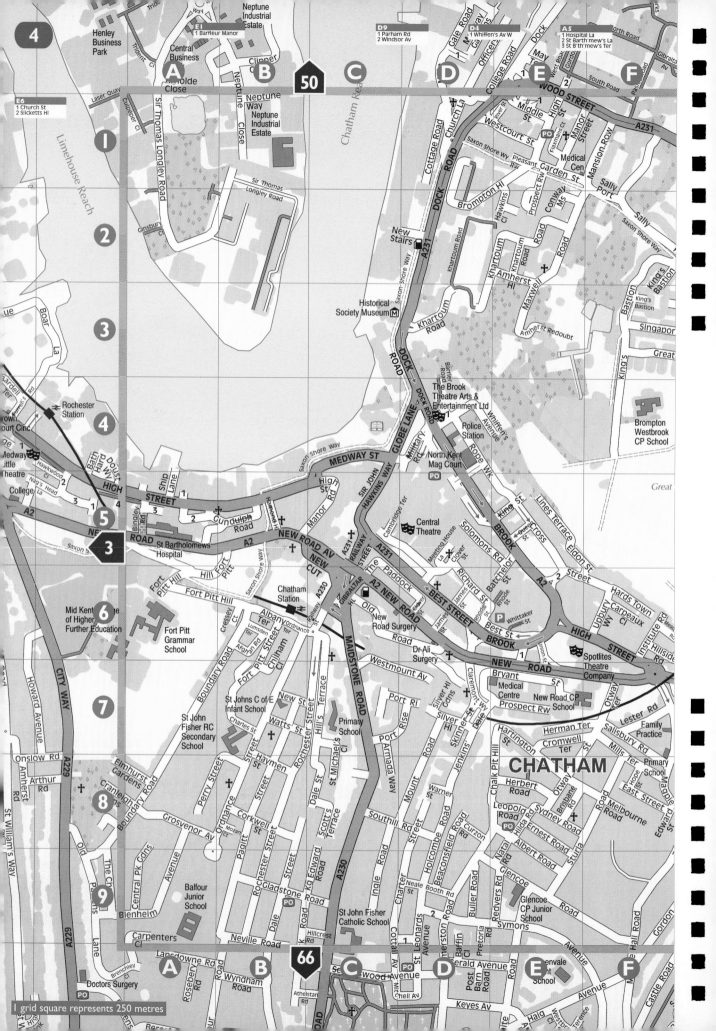

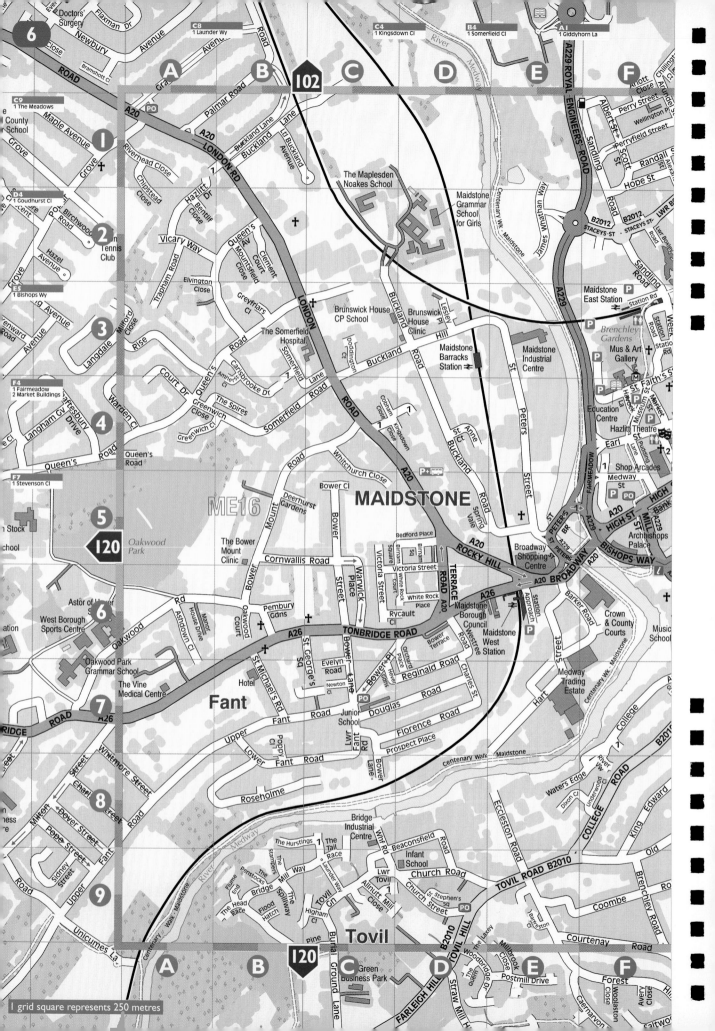

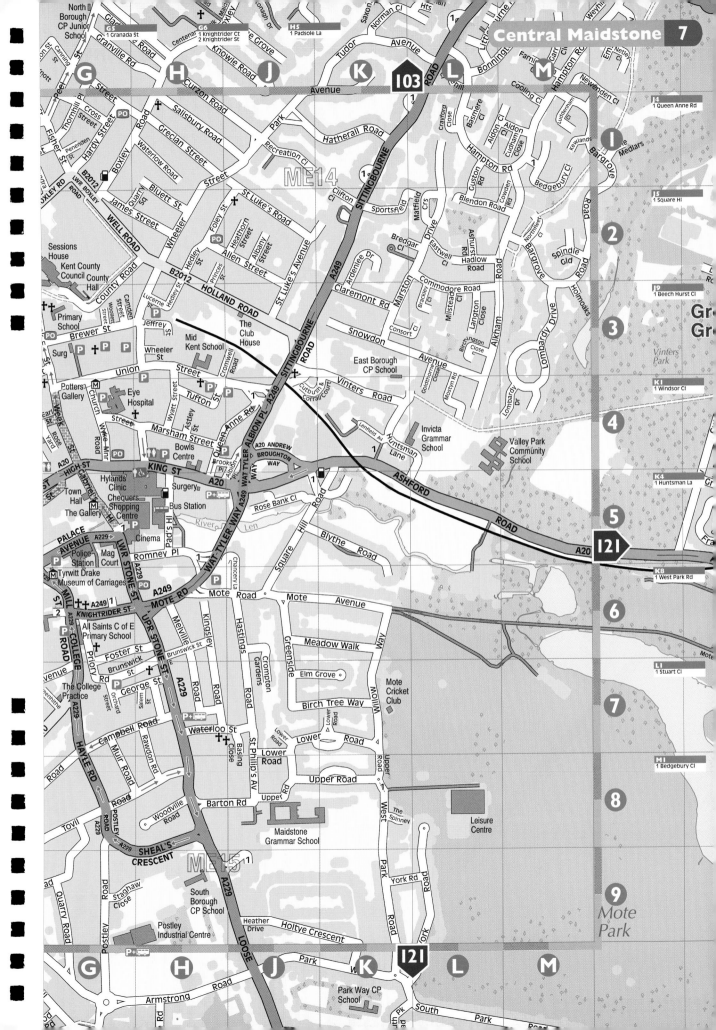

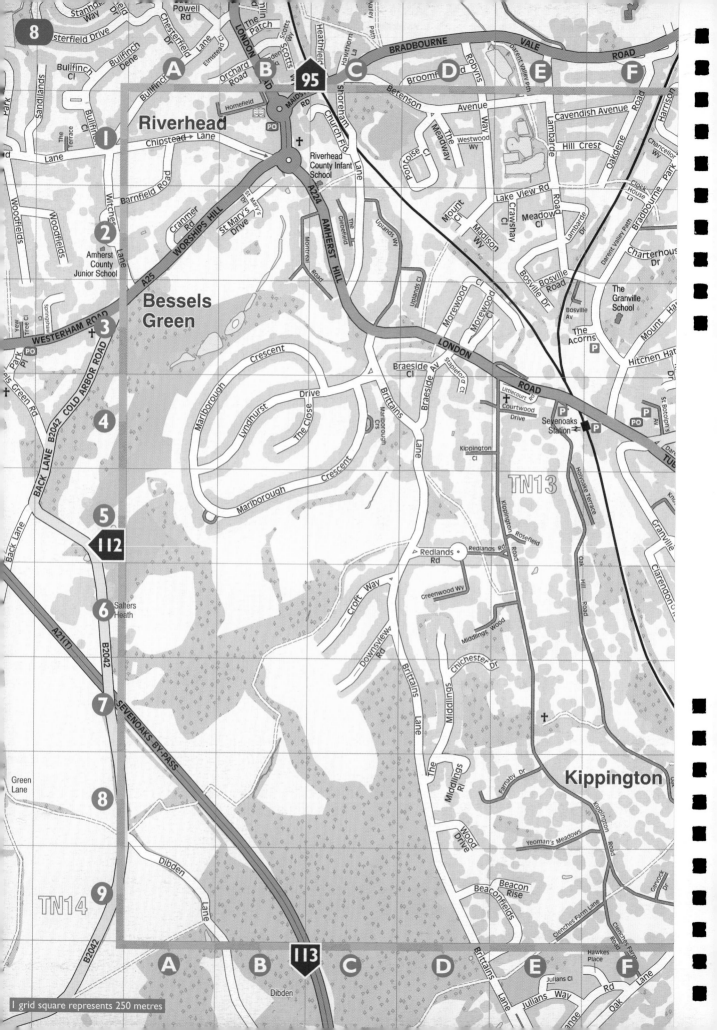

1 grid square represents 250 metres

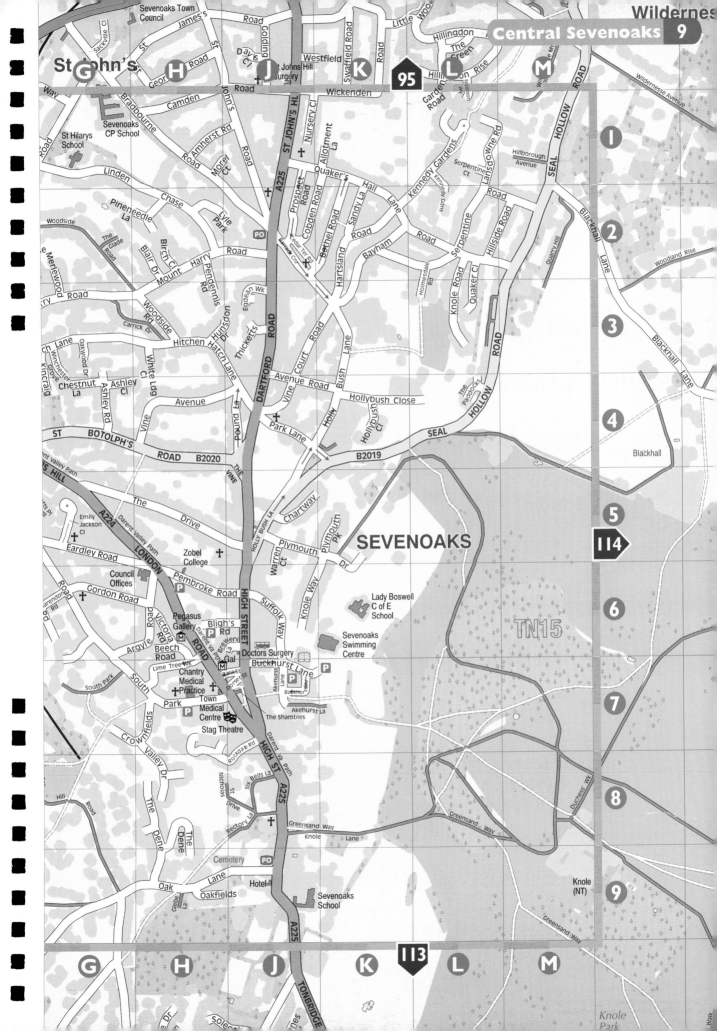

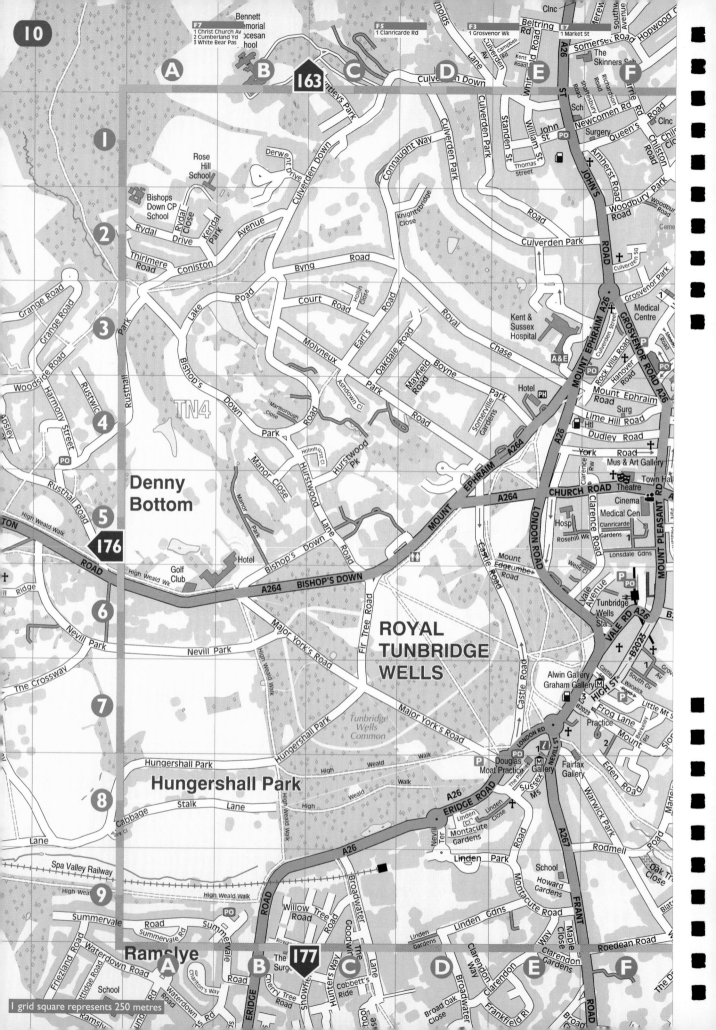

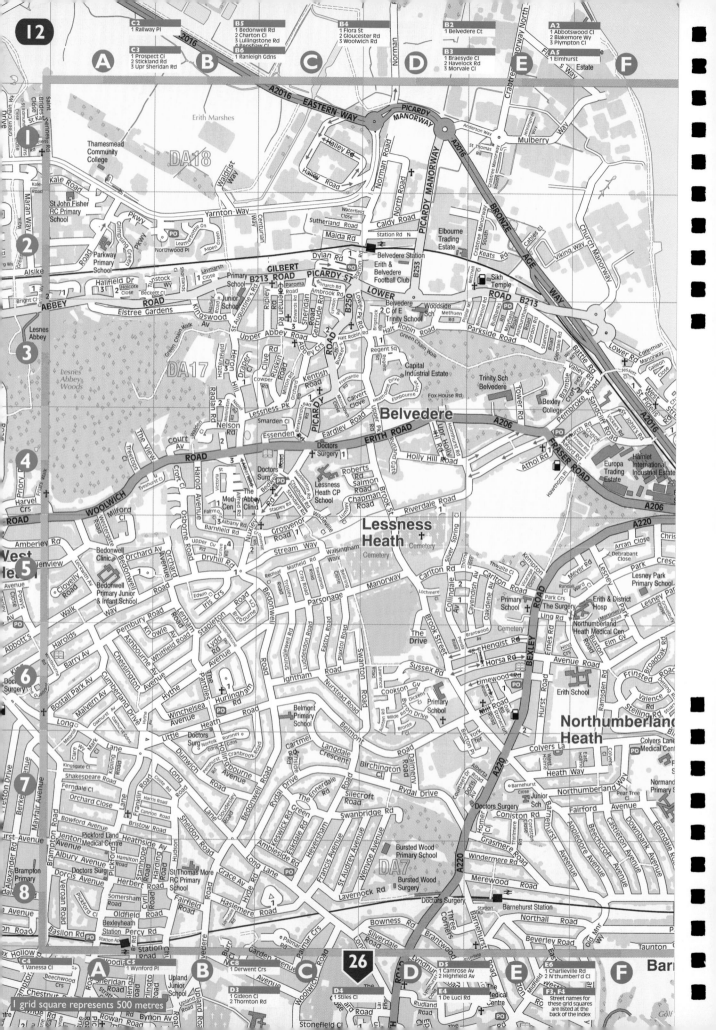

Coldharbour

Erith Rands

Havering
Bexley

Crayford
Ness

Erith

Riverside
Swimming
Centre

Erith High St

Erith
Theatre Guild

Erith
Library & Mus

Erith
Small Business
Centre

James Watt
Way

Wheatley Ter

Health
Centre

Crescent Road

Manor Road

Manford
Industrial Estate

Sports
Centre

DA8

Alexandra Rd

Springhead

Aperfield
Road

Frobisher Rd

Cornwallis
Close

Turpin
Lane

Reddy
Road

Raleigh
Close

Bilton Road

Canada Rd

Ray Lamb Way

Landau Way

Dayton Drive

Maypole
Crescent

Burnett Road

Ness Road

Wallhouse Road

Thanet
Road

Larner Rd

Festival
Close

Arthur St

Page
Crs

The
Nursery

Richmer Rd

Church
Trading
Estate

School

Green Road

Alderney
Road

Jennings Rd

Sheppey
Cl

Longreach
Way

Bacon Rd

Hilden Dr

Brompton Dr

Widgeon
Rd

Health
Centre

Colvers Lane

Pearswood Road

Slade Green
Road

Northend
CP Sch

Power
Ind.
Estate

Elm Road

Forest Road

Larkswood

Hazel Road

Hollywood
Wy

Fern Cl

Rodeo
Dr

Hazel Cl

Leycroft
Gdns

Slade Green
Football Club

Crayford
Marshes

Brendon
Close

Doyle
Close

Newbery
Road

Bridge
Road

Cloudesley Rd

Scott
Crs

Cedar Rd

Clark Cl

Willow
Road

Moat Lane

North
End

Slade Green
Station

Slade
Green

Whitehall Lane

Dale View

Howbury Lane

Oak Rd

Kent County
Bexley

Eversley Avenue

Cumbrian
Avenue

Wessex Dr

Venners Cl

Lincoln
Cl

Sun Ct

Lincoln Road

Ely Cl

Parkside Avenue

Doctors
Surgery

Holmsdale Gro

Howbury Rd

Crayside
Industrial Est

27

Darent Valley Path

Joyce Green Lane

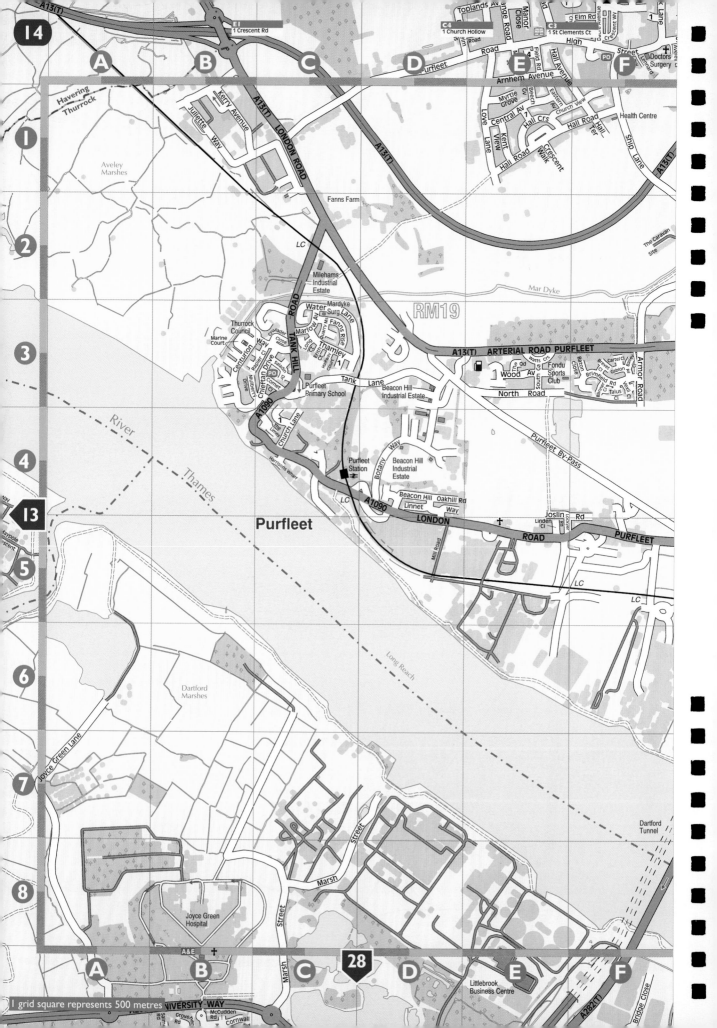

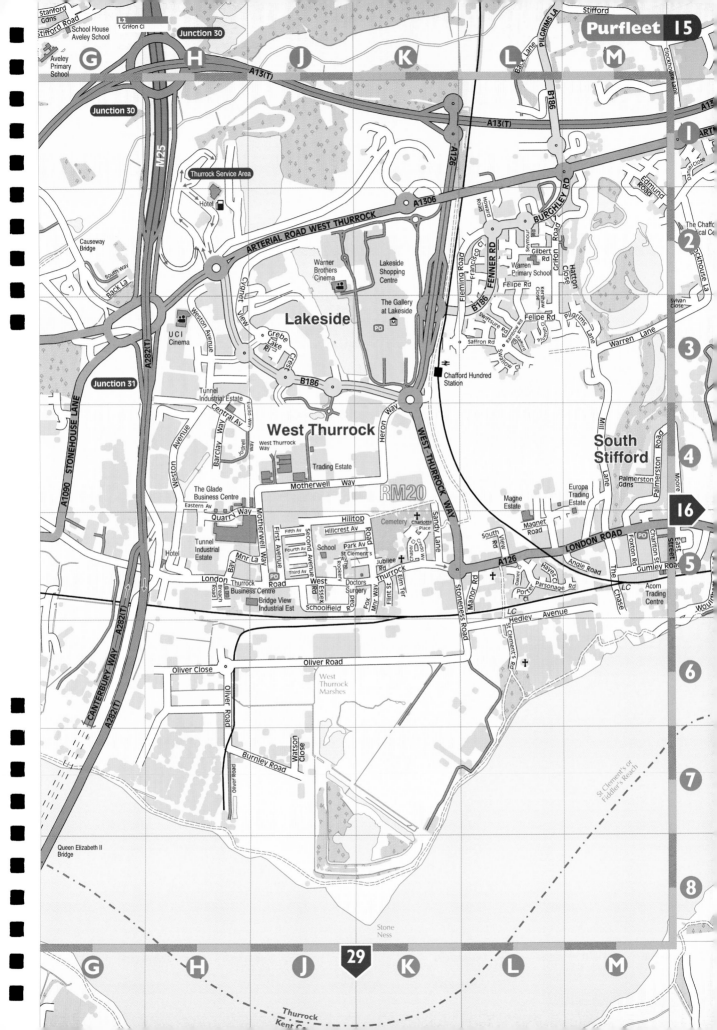

G H J K L M

Stanford Gdns
Stifford Road
School House
Aveley School
L2
1 Grifon Cl
Junction 30
Aveley Primary School
I
Stifford
Clockhouse La
A13

Junction 30
A13(T)
A13(T)
B186
The Chaffc dical Ce
2
Daniel Close
Edmund Road

Thurrock Service Area
Hotel
Causeway Bridge
South Way
Back La
M25
A1306
ARTERIAL ROAD WEST THURROCK
A126
Warner Brothers Cinema
Lakeside Shopping Centre
Fleming Road
Francisco Cl
Howard Road
FENNER RD
Seymour Rd
BURGHLEY RD
Gilbert Rd
Warren Primary School
Grifon Road
Hatton Close
Sylvan Close
3

Weston Avenue
UCI Cinema
Lakeside
Grebe Lake
The Gallery at Lakeside
PO
B186
Felipe Rd
Felipe Rd
Swiftsure Rd
Kershaw Close
Pilgrims Lane
Warren Lane

A282(T)
Cygnet View
Crest
Saffron Rd
Swallow Rd
Chafford Hundred Station

Junction 31
Tunnel Industrial Estate
Central Av
Euclid Way
B186
Heron Way
WEST THURROCK WAY
South Stifford
Mill Road
Moore Road
Palmerston Road
4

Weston Avenue
Sorrell
West Thurrock
West Thurrock Way
A1090 STONEHOUSE LANE
Barclay Way
Palmerston Gdns
16

The Glade Business Centre
Eastern Av
Motherwell Way
Trading Estate
RM20
Magne Estate
Europa Trading Estate
Magnet Road
London Road
PO
Charlton St
Foxton Rd
Gumley Road
East Street
5

Quarry Way
Tunnel Industrial Estate
Hotel
Motherwell Way
First Avenue
Fifth Av
Second Avenue
Fourth Av
Third Av
Hilltop
Hillcrest Av
School
Park Av
St Clement's
The Rookery
Cemetery
Charlotte Place
Credo Wy
Sandy Lane
South View
South Rd
Manor Rd
A126
Hayes Rd
Porter Cl
Parsonage Rd
Angle Road
The Chase
LC
Acorn Trading Centre
Wounl

Mnr La
Bay
Breach Road
London Thurrock Road
Jubilee Rd
West Essex
Flint St
Elm Ter
Fox
Mnr Way
Thurrock
Doctors Surgery
Schoolfield
Stoneness Road
LC
Hedley Avenue
St Clement's Rd

CANTERBURY WAY
A282(T)
London Business Centre
Bridge View Industrial Est

Oliver Close
Oliver Road
Oliver Road
West Thurrock Marshes
6

St Clement's or Fiddler's Reach

Oliver Road
Watson Close
Burnley Road
7

Queen Elizabeth II Bridge
8

Stone Ness

G H J K L M
29

Thurrock Kent C

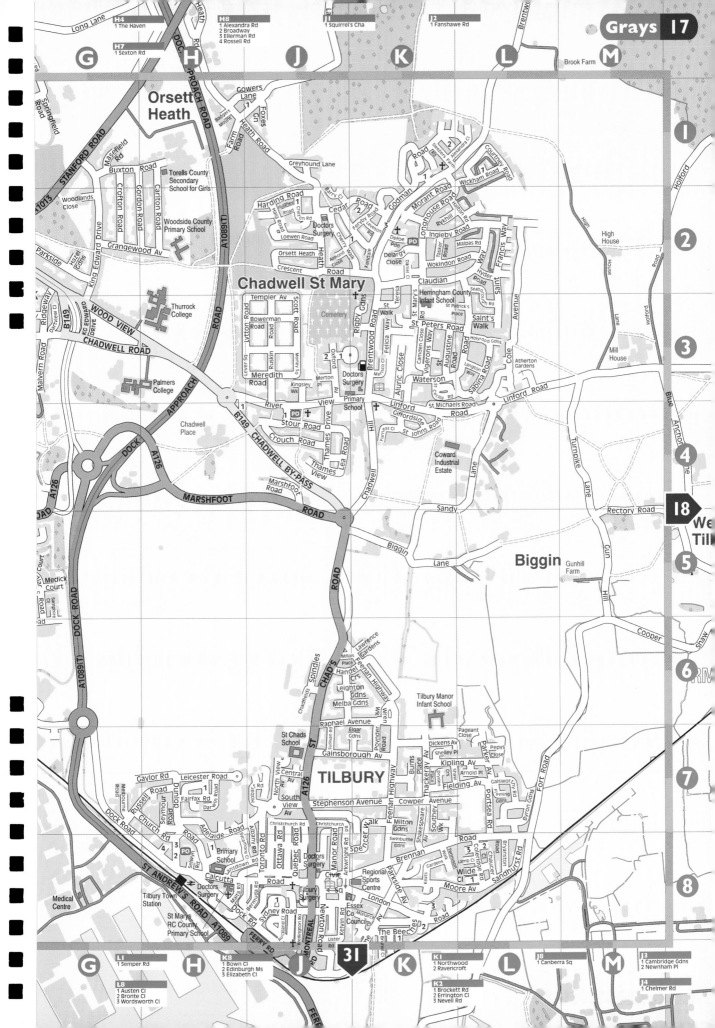

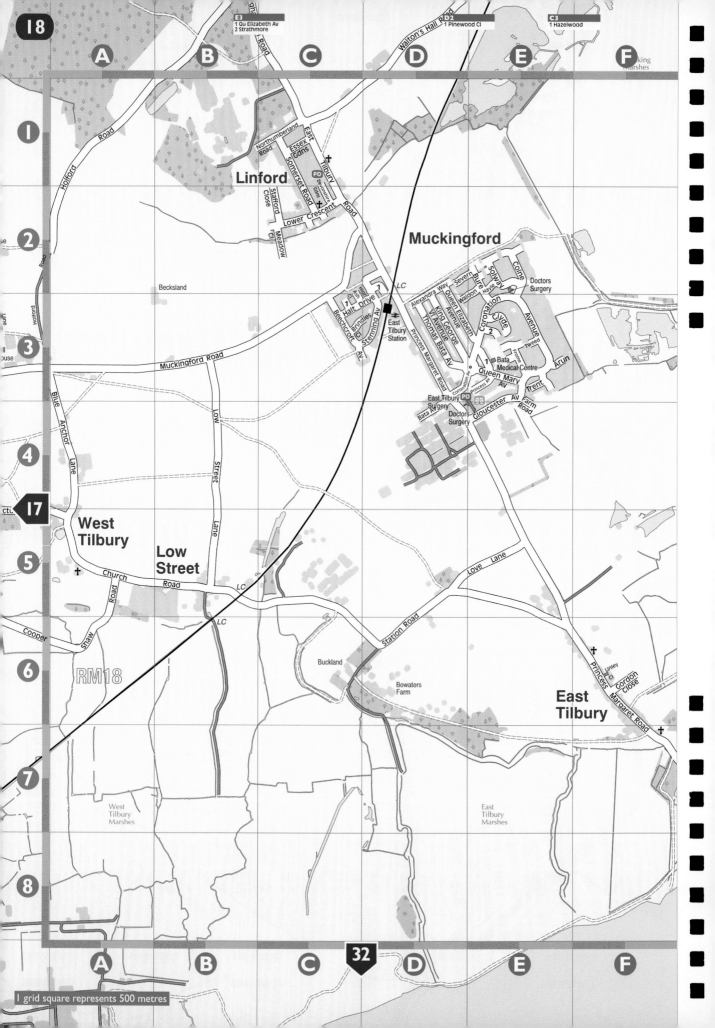

G H J K L M

1
2
3
4
20
5
6
7
8

Thurrock
Medway Towns

Lower
Hope Point

Mead Wall

Saxon Shore Way

Medway Towns
Kent County

Coalhouse
Point

G H J K L M

33

A   B   C   D   E   F

D8
1 Chesterton Rd

River   Thames

1

2

3

4

19

5

Cliffe
Marshes

6

Ryestreet Common

Boatrick
House

Mead Wall

7

Pickle's   Way
Church   North   Road
Close   Lane
Reed   Street   Wharf Lane
Marsh Lane
Cres
Saxon Shore Way   Rookery Crescent   Common   Lane
PO   PH   Cliffe
Buttway Lane   Swingate
Avenue
Manor   Efford   Wadlands   Rye Street
Farm   Quickrells   Road   Farm
West   Rd   Chancery Rd
Street   St Helens   Saxon Shore Way   Thatcher's Lane
Common Wall

8   St Helens Road   Saxon Shore Way

CHURCH STREET
St Helens C of E
Primary School

Turner Street
Millcroft
Road

A   B   C   34   D   E   F
New Rd   Norwood
Close
Cooling Road
Higham Road   Cooling   Road

G H J K L M

I
2
3
4
22
5
6
7
8

Blythe
Sands

Salt Fleet

Hope Fleet

Halstow
Marshes

Decoy Fleet

Cooling
Marshes

Buckland Fleet

Whalebone
Marshes

Saxon Shore Way

Bromhey
Farm

Saxon Shore Way

Cooling

Cooling Road

35

Buckhole
Farm

G H J K L M

Lipwell Hill

Buckhole Farm Road

Harrison
eden Rd

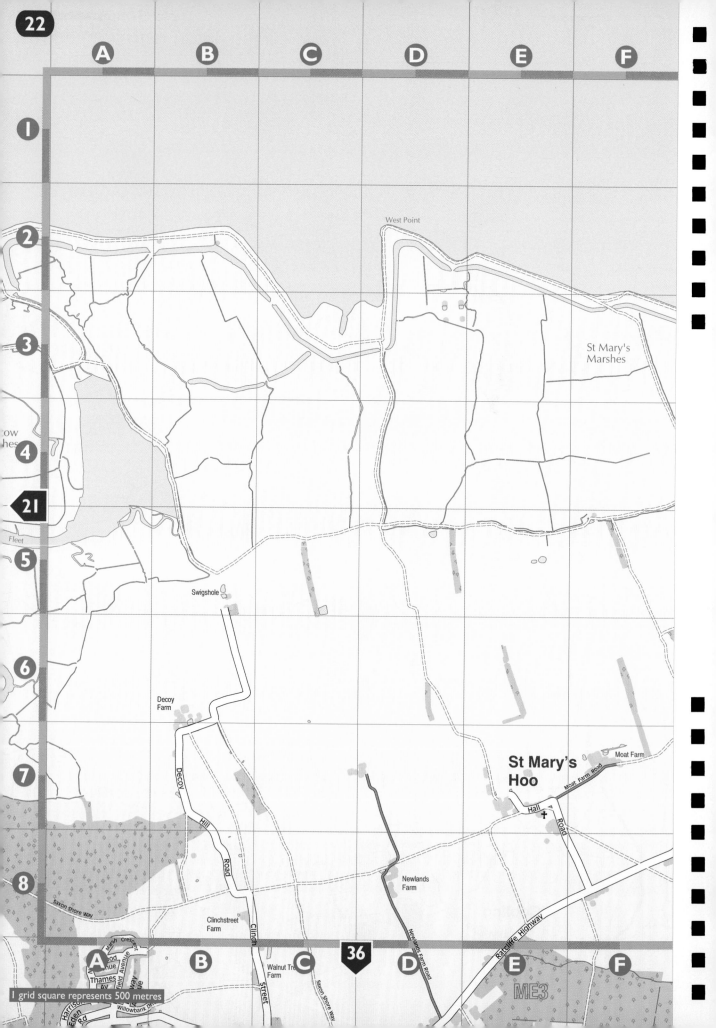

A   B   C   D   E   F

I

2

3

4

21

Fleet

5

6

7

8

West Point

St Mary's
Marshes

ow
hes

Swigshole

Decoy
Farm

Decoy

Hill

Road

Clinchstreet
Farm

Clinch

Street

Walnut Tr
Farm

Saxon shore Way

Newlands
Farm

Newlands Farm Road

St Mary's
Hoo

Hall   Road

Moat Farm Road

Moat Farm

Ratcliffe Highway

Saxon shore way

Marsh Crescent

Thames Av

Eden Rd

Harrison

Willowbank Dri

A   B   36   C   D   E   F

ME3

M5
1 Avery Cl
2 St Matthew's Wy

G H J K L M

I

River Thames

2

3

The Brimp

Queensway

4

The Elms
Medical
Practice

24

Avery Way

St Luke's
Way

Homewards Road

5

St David's Rd

Road

Dagnam
Farm

Binney

Ratcliffe Highway

Jutland
Close

PO 1 2

Allhallows

6

Shakespeare Farm Road

Brick
House
Farm

Stoke Road

Newhall
Farm

7

Coombe Farm Lane

New Hall Farm Lane

Marshland View

Hoopers Lane

Cuckold's
Green

Allhallows & Stoke
CP School

Button Drive

8 Sto
M.

Cuckolds Green Road

Allhallows Road

**Lower
Stoke**

G H J 37 K L M

Mallard Way

Heron Way

Mallard Way

Chapel Row
Shephe

A228

Mackay's

A **B** **C** **D** **E** **F**

1

River Thames

2

3

Allhallows-on-Sea

Brimp

Avery Way

PO

Avery Close

4

The Elms
Medical
Practice

23

Avery Way

St Luke's

David's

Rd

Binney

Road

5

llhallows

Allhallows
Marshes

Binney
Farm

6

North Level

Yantlet Creek

Southend-on-Sea
Medway Towns

7

Isle of Grain

8

Stoke
Marshes

A **B** **C** **38** **D** **E** **F**

GRAIN   ROAD

Kent Oil Refinery

J7
1 Fry Cl

K7
1 Doggetts Rw
2 Levett Cl
3 Pintail Cl

K8
1 Puffin Rd
2 Shelldrake Cl
3 Teal Cl

G H J K L M

I
2
3
4
5
6
7
8

Medway Towns

Lees Marshes

Grain Marsh

Peat Way

Peat Way

Rose Court Farm

West Lane

Pannell Road

HIGH STREET

St James C of E Primary School

Green Lane

St James Road

Grain

Perry's Farm

PO

B2001 Chapel Road

Edinburgh Road

Coronation Road

Puffin Road

Lapwing Road

St Werburgh Medical Practice

Chapel Road

Seaview

Port

Grayne Avenue

Victoria Road

Smithfield Road

GRAIN ROAD

G H J K L M

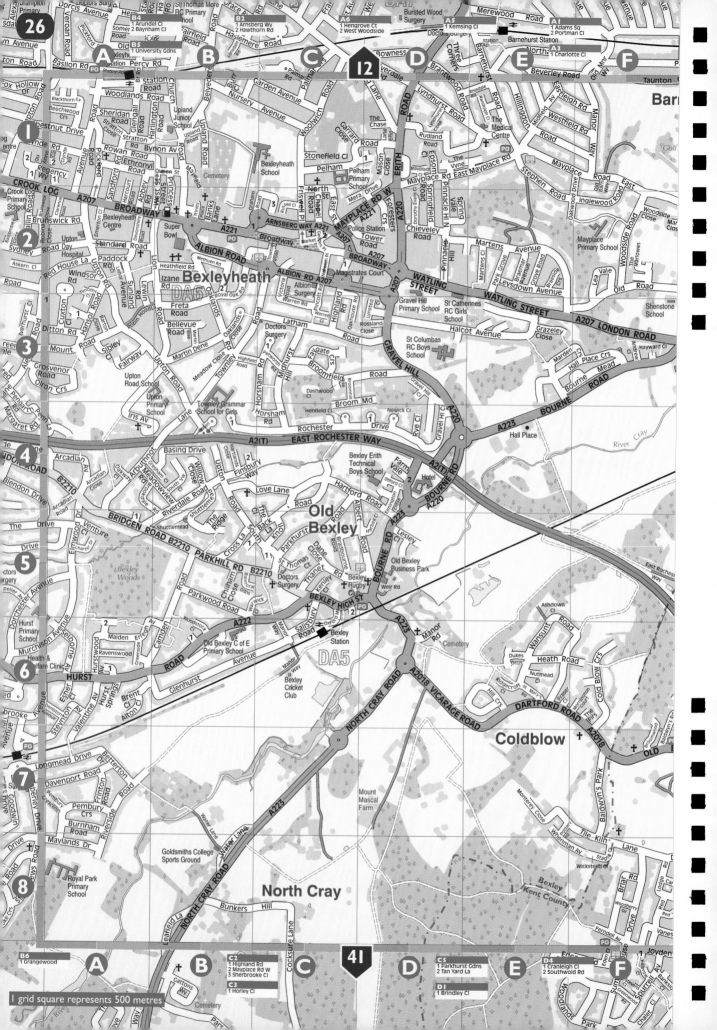

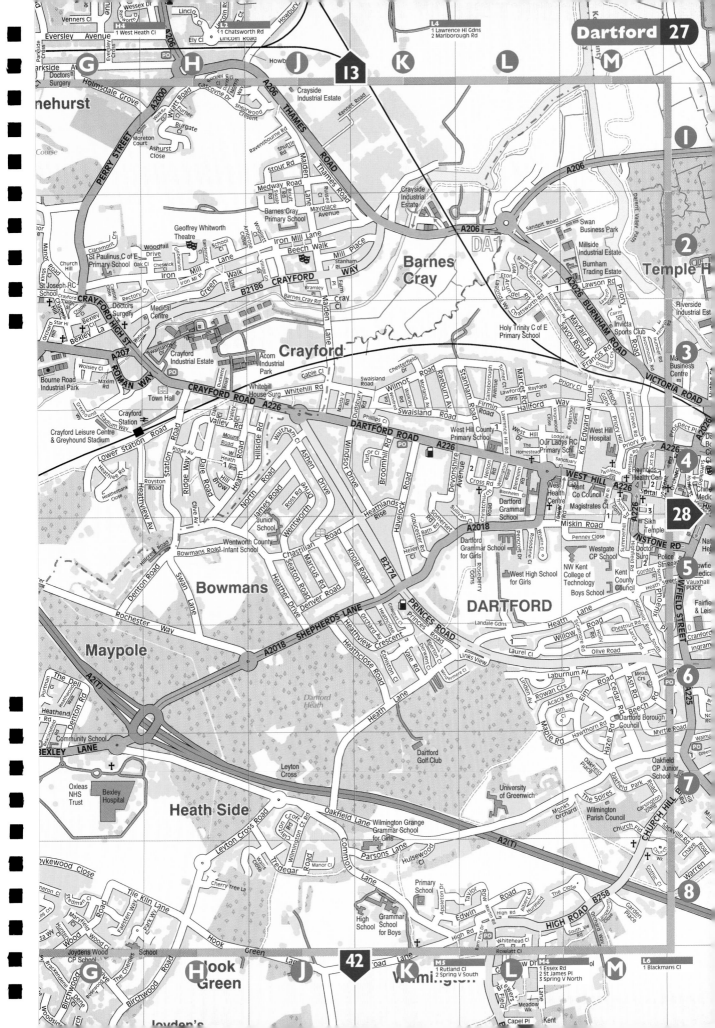

H3
1 Stafford Cl
2 Unicorn Wk

H4
1 Church Pth

J2
1 Crest Vw

G H J 15 Stone Ness K L M

I
2
3
30
4
5
6
7
8

Thurrock
Kent County

Clipper Bvd

St Mary's Road
A206 CROSSWAYS BOULEVARD
Charles Street
Stone Crossing Station LC
Elizabeth Street
Church Hill
Church Rd
Bell Close
Cooper Cl

King Edward Rd
Kestner Industrial Est
Chambers Cl
Jack Cl
Sayer
Cowley Av
Dawes
Bullfinch
Steele
Trivett
Low Cl
Castle St
K G Edward Rd
Providence St

Sara Crs
Frobisher Wy Pier
HIGH STREET
Fiddlers Cl
Eagles Road B255
Smugglers
Maritime Cl
Woodman Wy
Station Road
Hurst Dr
Ivy Bower
Breakneck Hill

Stone
DA9

Chalice Swallow Cl
Stone Place Rd
Chichester
Stanley
Bishops Ct
Branton Road
Winston Cl

Perkins
A226

A206
Station Road
A226
Greenhithe for Bluewater Stn
Ivy Bower Surgery

Knockhall
Park Terrace
Greenhithe Health Clinic
Greenhithe

Mounts Road
Bean Road
Port Av
The Cres
Avenue
Jubilee
Vale
Spring
Western Cross Cl
Whites
Kemsley Cl
Valley Vw
Valley
Pilgrims View
Alkerden Lane

Swanscombe

Eynsford Rd
Knockhall Crove
Abbey Rd
Knockhall Road
Hasted Cl

London Rd
A226
LONDON RD

Park Terrace
Wakefield Rd
Alexander Rd
Dial Cl

Cravlands Lane

Broomfield
Lewis
Milton St
Cravlands
Broad Rd
Treppl
Gilbert Cl
Childs Crs
Manor Road

Doctors Surgery
LONDON
Acacia Rd
Oak Rd
Elm Rd
Carlton Av
Woodward Ter
Birch
PO
B2174
ROAD
Horns Cross
Barnfield Road

HEDGE PLACE ROAD
Cliff Reach
Bluewater Parkway
Chestnut Av

Stone Castle

Stone B255

Morgan Drive
Louvain Road
Hayes Road
ST JAMES' LANE
B2174
Turnbull
Cemetery
Oak Tree Avenue
Kincade Gallery
Bluewater Park
The Artisan Gallery
Lime Tree Av

Bluewater Parkway
A296

Darenth Wood
Wood Lane
A2(T)
Redding Ford Cl
Darenth Wood Road

ROMAN ROAD
A296
A2(T)

Bean Lane
B255
Turner Rd
Fallowfield
Foxwood Way
Drudgeon Way
Bramble Av
The Beacon
The Surgery
Page Cl
Stonewood Lane
School
The Thrift

Stonewood

Bean
HIGH STREET
PO
Bea Primary
SOUTH FLEET ROAD

Sandy Lane
Claywood Lane

G M3
1 Craylands Sq
H L4
1 Austen Cl
2 Bevans Cl
3 Johnsons Wy
J 44 K K4
1 Starboard Av
L J3
1 Admirals Wk
2 Skippers Cl
M J3
1 Borland Cl
2 Cutty Sark Ct
3 Riverview Rd
4 Wheatley Cl

Lords Wood

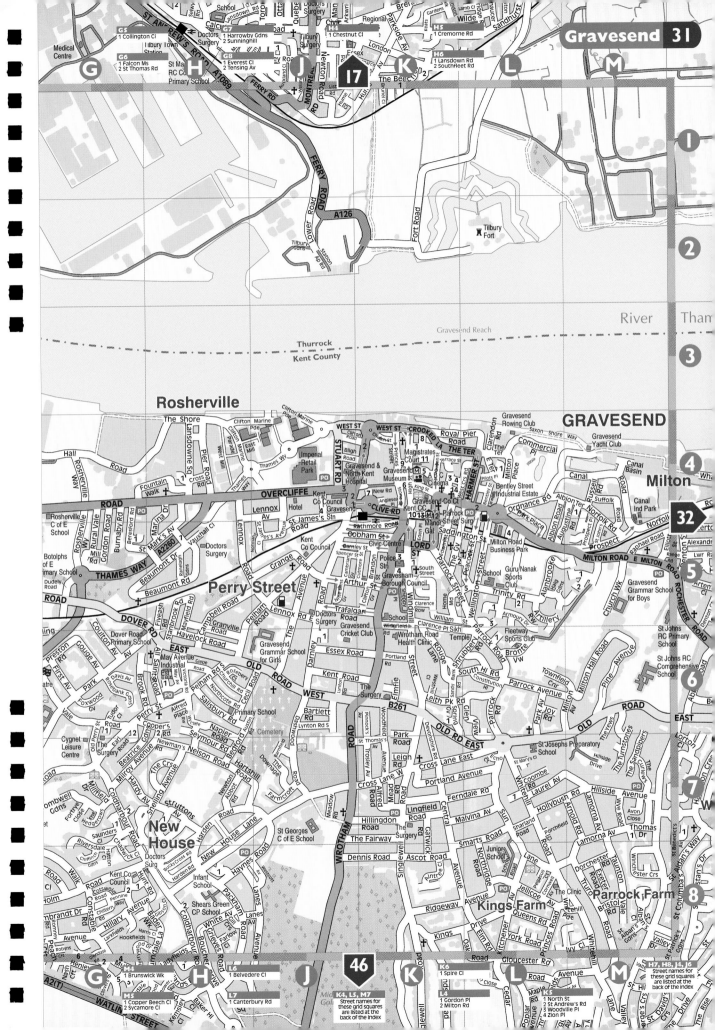

D7
1 Beckley Cl
2 Manor Cl
3 Shirley Cl
4 Sutherland Cl

B7
1 Oxford Cl
2 Terence Cl

B6
1 Barham Cl
2 Farriers Cl
3 Kingsdown Cl
4 Maypole Rd

A7
1 Lindisfarne Cl

River Thames

Saxon Shore Way

Milton
Wharf Road
Mark Lane
Road
Waterton Av
Alexandra Rd
Lwr Range Rd
Raphael Road
E MILTON
Empress Rd
Havengore Av
Denton
Shamrock Rd
Thistle Rd
Gravesend Grammar School for Boys
Artemis Cl
Gerald Rd
Dickens Rd
Farley Rd
Primary School
Dering Way
Damigos Rd
Megbury Rd
Ingoldsby Road
St Johns RC Primary School
Rose Av
North West Kent College
Chalk
St Johns RC Comprehensive School
Copperfield Cl
Lower Higham Road
Darenth Drive
Abbey Road
Bellman Av
Nickleby Rd
Orrick Road
Lapis Cl
Brooke Drive
Castle Lane
EAST B261
Lower Higham Road
Havisham Rd
Vicarage Lane
Chalk Road
Villa Cl
Lisle Cl
Lower Higham Road
Hampton Crescent
Jubilee Crescent
Forge Lane
Barr Road
Bourne Road
Thong Lane
A226 ROCHESTER ROAD
East Court Manor
Westcourt County Primary School
Cruden Road
Freeman Road
West Court
Doctors Surgery
Medhurst Crs
Medhurst Gdns
Hibernia Dr
Cervia Way
Church Lane
ROCHESTER ROAD
Raynehurst CP School
Thamesview School
St Benedicts Way
St Aidan's Dr
St Columba's Dr
St Dunstan's Dr
St Chad's Dr
St Hilda's Dr
St Margaret's Crs
Cambria Av
Beltana Dr
Verona Gdns
Windhover Drive
Kelso Drive
Clipper Crescent
Cascades Leisure Centre

Riverview

1 grid square represents 500 metres

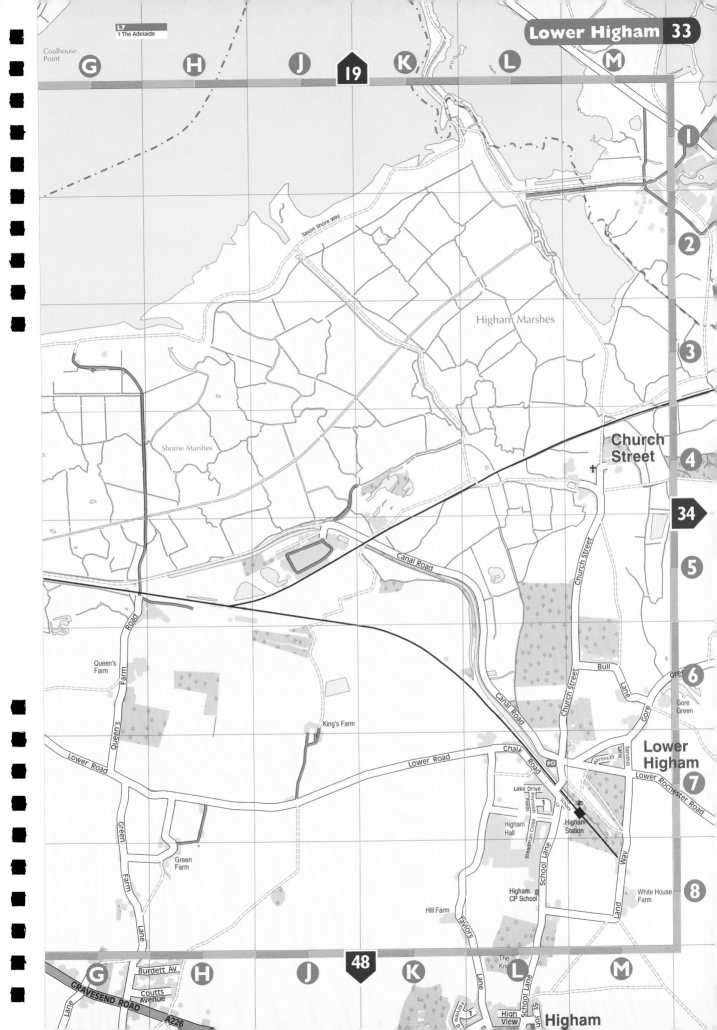

A8
1 Nursery Gdns

A   B   C   22   D   E   F

Newlands
Farm

I

Northwood
Avenue
Thames
Av
Longfield Avenue
Medway Avenue
Marsh Crescent
Willowbank Drive
Harrison Drive
Eden Street
Goodwood
Draper Close
Holmes Cl
Leaman Close
Rubbles Close
Valentine Drive

Walnut Tree
Farm

Clinch Street

Saxon Shore Way

Clinchstreet
Farm

Ratcliffe Highway

ME3

High Halstow
Primary School

The Street

Street

A228

Newlands Farm Road

Bellwood
Court

Turkey Hall
Farm

MALMAYNES

**High
Halstow**

2

Forge Lane
The

Christmas Lane
PO

Fenn
Street

Ratcliffe Highway

3

Solomons
Farm

Sharnal Street

35

**Sharnal
Street**

Cold Arbour

**Tunbridge
Hill**

4

35

Ratcliffe Highway

5

Roper's Green Lane

Roper's Lane

Stoke Road

LC

6

Bell's Lane

Tile Barn
Farm

Beluncle
Farm

Stoke Road

Alpha Close
Beta Rd
Jetty Road
Main Road
Gamma Road

Kingshill Drive
Grandsire Gardens
Walters Road
Wylie Road
Knights Close
Bell's Lane

Jacob's Lane

Eshcol Road

7

St Werburgh
Medical Centre

Kingsnorth

Wylie Rd
Miskin Road
Stoke Road
Peal Cl
Peal Cl

Saxon Shore Way

8

PO
Newitt Road
Coombe Road
Flack Gdns
Knott Rd
Trubridge Road
Main Road
The Elms
Medical Centre
Brookside
Church Street
Vicarage
Butchers Close
Badgin Close
Armytage Close
Abbot's
Court

Court Road

Abbots

Saxon Shore Way

A   B   C   **51**   D   E   F

1 grid square represents 500 metres

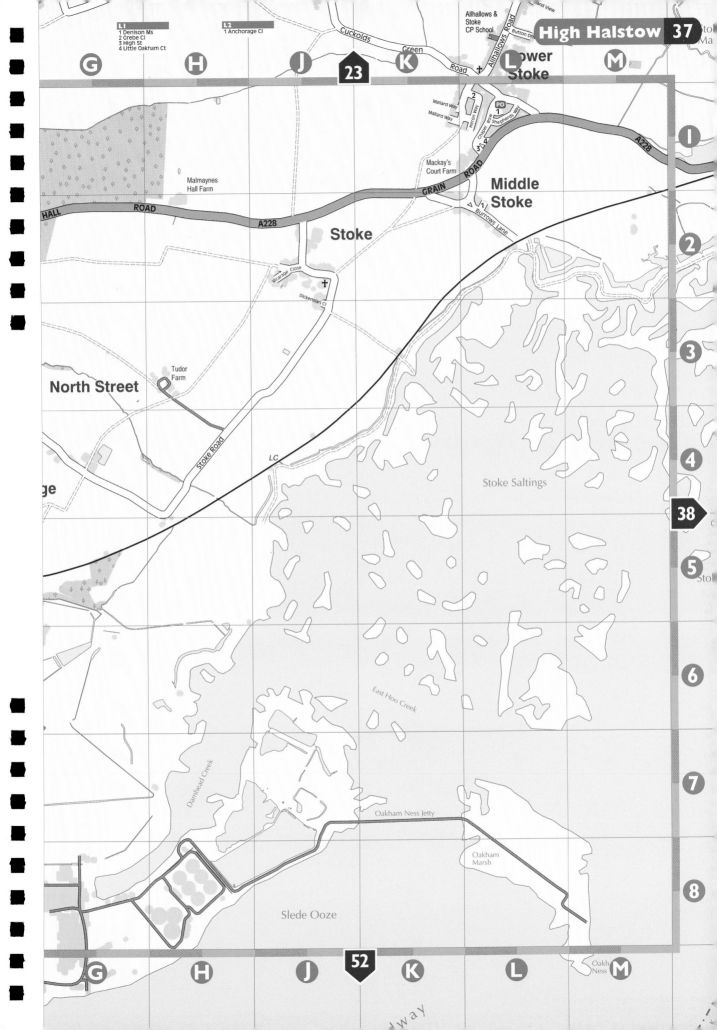

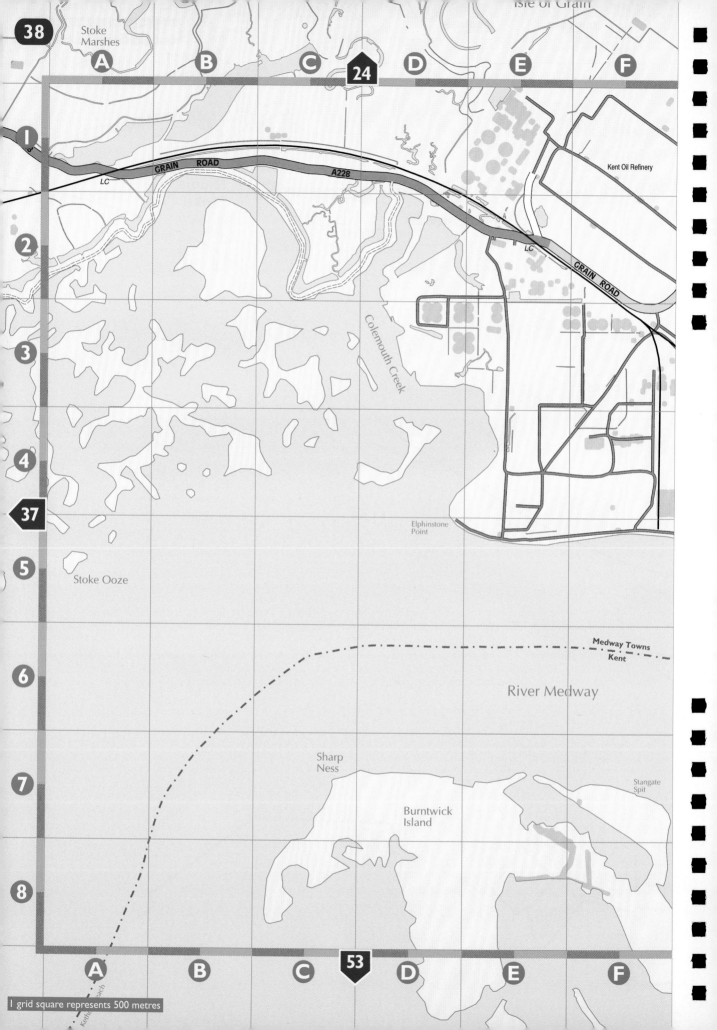

Isle of Grain

Stoke
Marshes

Ⓐ   Ⓑ   Ⓒ   **24**   Ⓓ   Ⓔ   Ⓕ

1

GRAIN ROAD   A228   GRAIN ROAD

LC

Kent Oil Refinery

2

LC

3

Colemouth Creek

4

37

Elphinstone
Point

5

Stoke Ooze

6

Medway Towns
Kent

River Medway

7

Sharp
Ness

Stangate
Spit

Burntwick
Island

8

Ⓐ   Ⓑ   Ⓒ   **53**   Ⓓ   Ⓔ   Ⓕ

1 grid square represents 500 metres

G H J 25 K L M

GRAIN ROAD

B2001

St Werburgh
Medical Practice

Grayne
Avenue

Coronation

Puffin Road
Lapwing Road

Port

Chapel Road
Seaview

Victoria
Road

Smithfield Road

Port Victoria Road

I

2

3

4

Riv

5

Saltpan Reach

6

Queenborough
Spit

Wes
Swale

Deadmans
Island

7

Stangate Creek

8

West
Point

G H J 54 K L M

Long Reach

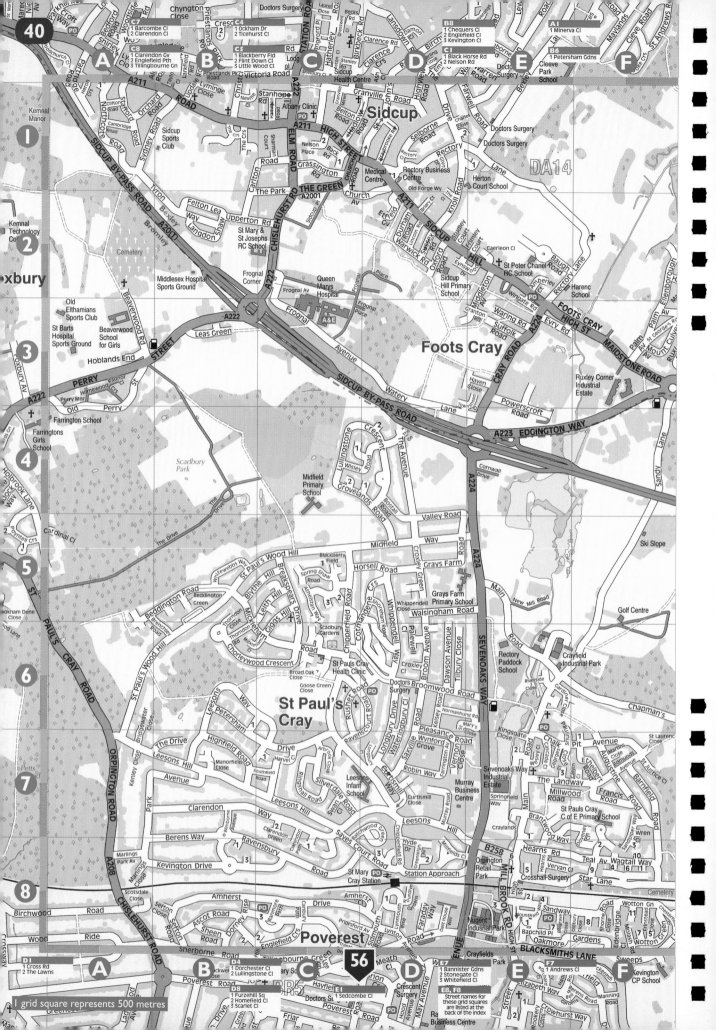

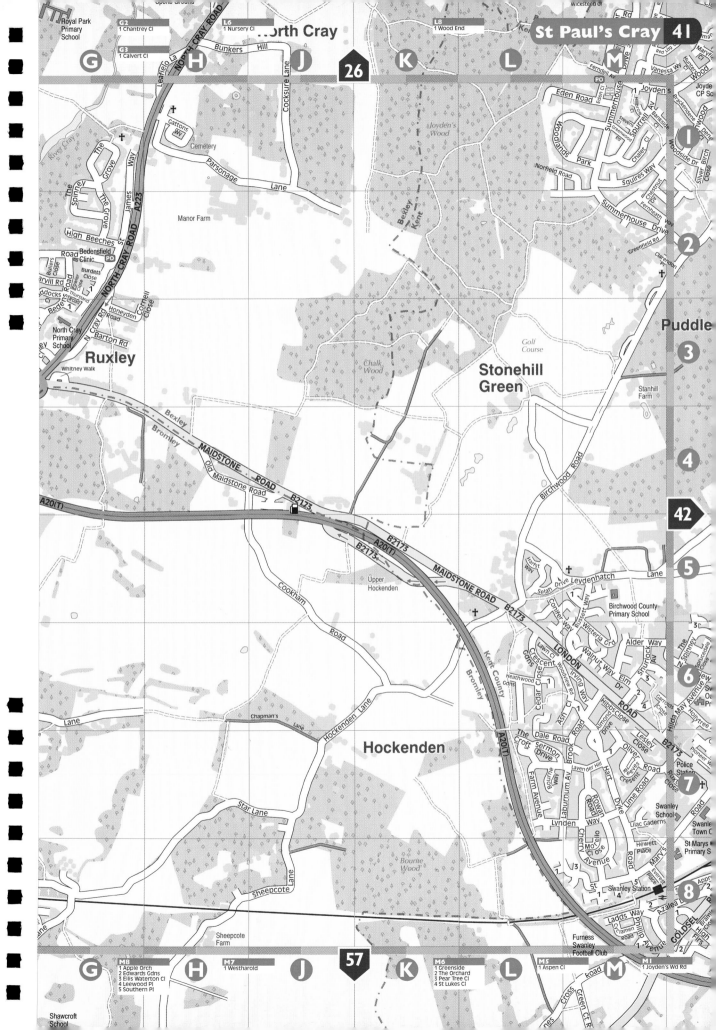

A B C 27 D E HIGH RO F

Hook
Green

Wilmington

Joyden's
Wood

Joydens Wood
CP School

Rowhill School

Kent County
Council

Shirehall Road

I

2

Puddledock

Hotel

3

Clement
Street

TOP DARTFORD ROAD

Hextable
CP School

Furness
School

Clement Street

Hextable

Lower Road

4

Gildenhill Road

St Pauls
C of E
School

Hotham
Close

41

Hextable
Comprehensive
School

Nutley
Close

Squires
Field

Highlands
Farm

5

New Barn Road

Highlands Hill

Swanley Village Road

Wood Street

Church Road

White Oak

Swanley Village

6

Swanley White
Oak County
Primary Sch

St Bartholomews
Hospital

M25

7

Police
Station

SWANLEY

Parkwood Hall
School

Swanley
School

Doctors
Surgery

Swanley
Town Council

Park Road
Industrial
Estate

Downsview
Junior School

St Marys C of E
Primary School

BR8

Farningham Woods
(Nature Reserve)

8

High Firs CP
School

Moreton
Industrial
Estate

A B 58 C D E F

Hill Farm

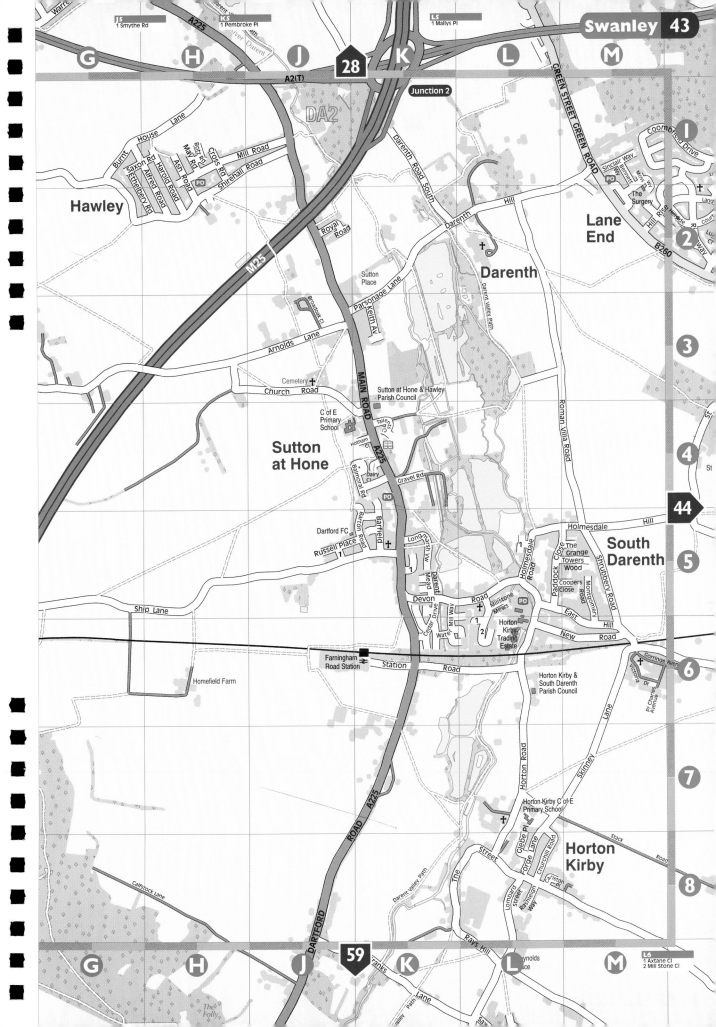

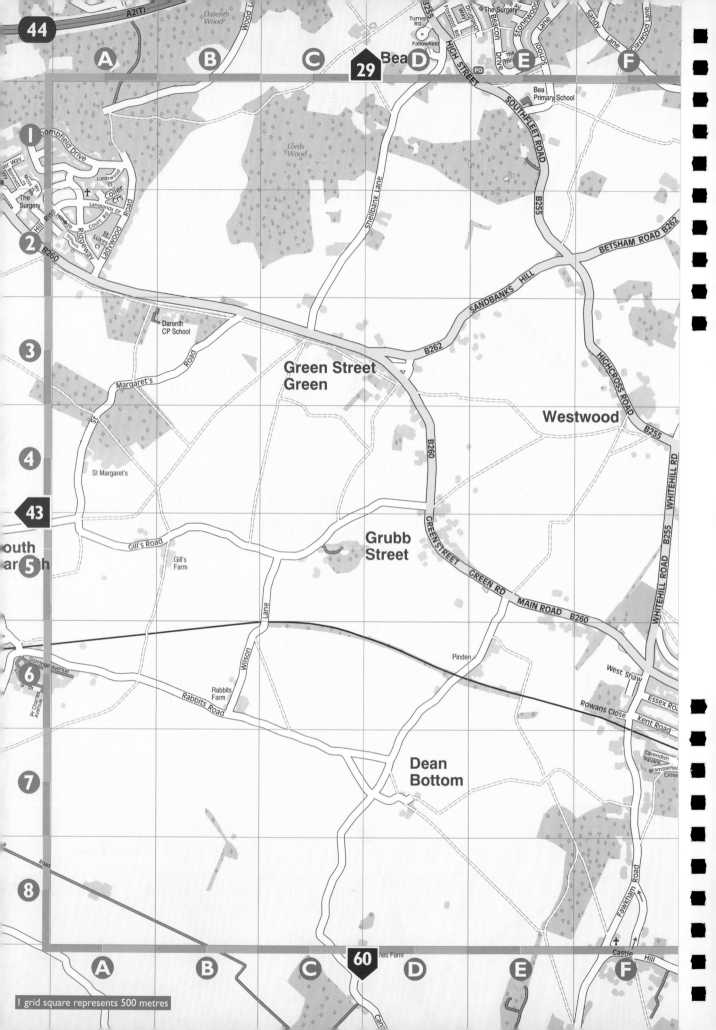

A B C **29** Bea D E F

I

Coombfield Drive

The Surgery

2 B260

Hill Rise Hillside

Lordswood Ct

Collier Crs

Langlands Dr

Court Rd

St Lukes Cl Ladywood Cl

Ridgeway

St Vincents

Darenth Wood

Wood L

Lords Wood

Shellbank Lane

Turner Rd

Fallowfield

HIGH STREET

PO

SOUTHFLEET ROAD

B255

Bea Primary School

The Beacon

Stonewood

Bridgeon Way

Forwood Rd

The Av

Sandy Lane

Claywood Lane

BETSHAM ROAD B262

SANDBANKS HILL

HIGHCROSS ROAD

B255

3

Margaret's Road

Darenth CP School

B262

Green Street Green

Westwood

4

St Margaret's

St Margaret's

B260

WHITEHILL RD

B255

WHITEHILL ROAD

43

South ar th

Gill's Road

Gill's Farm

Grubb Street

GREEN STREET

GREEN RD

MAIN ROAD B260

5

6 Gorringe Avenue

Victoria Dr

Pr Charles Avenue

Rabbits Road

Rabbits Farm

Wilson Lane

Pinden

West Shaw

Essex Rd

Rowans Close Kent Road

7

Dean Bottom

Cavendish Square

Bramblefie

Close

8

Road

Fawkham Road

Castle Hill

A B C **60** hes Farm D E F

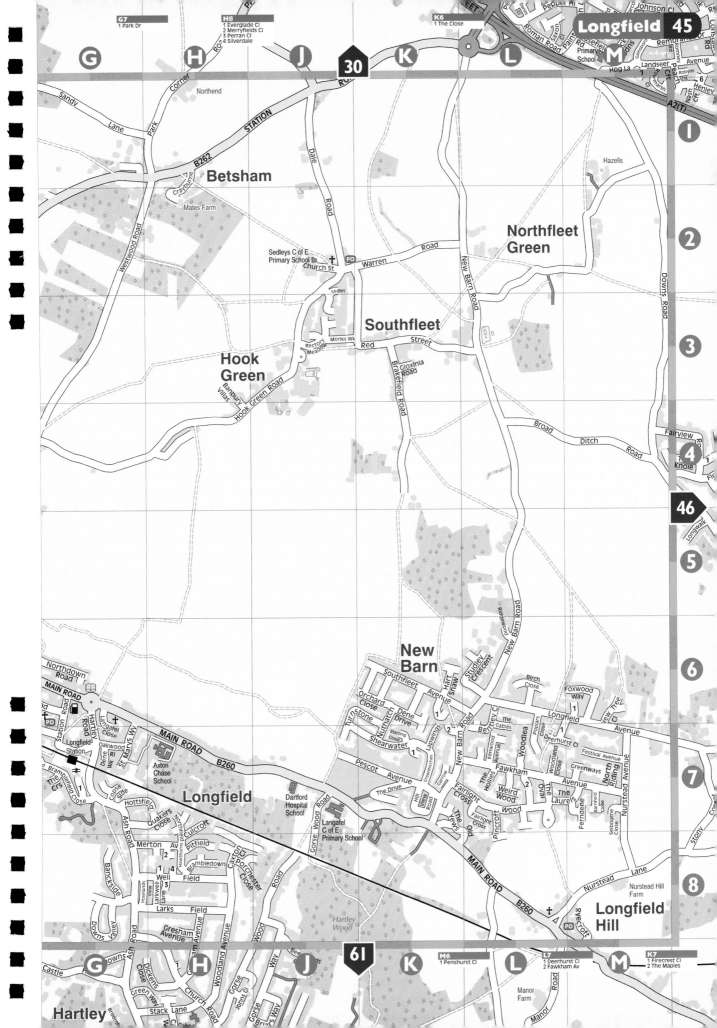

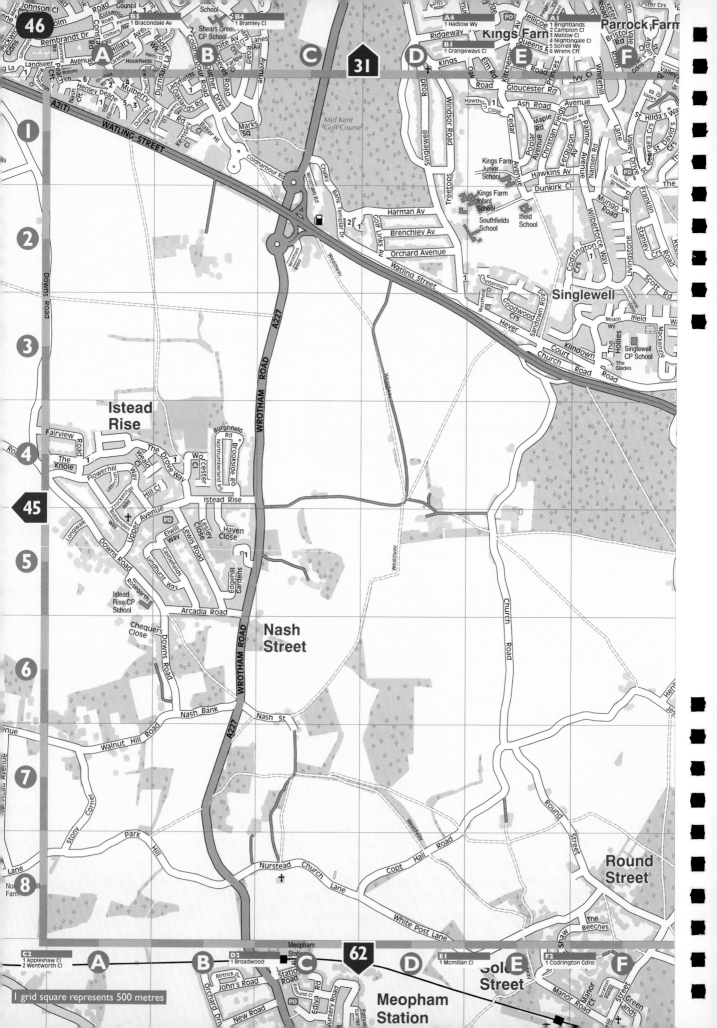

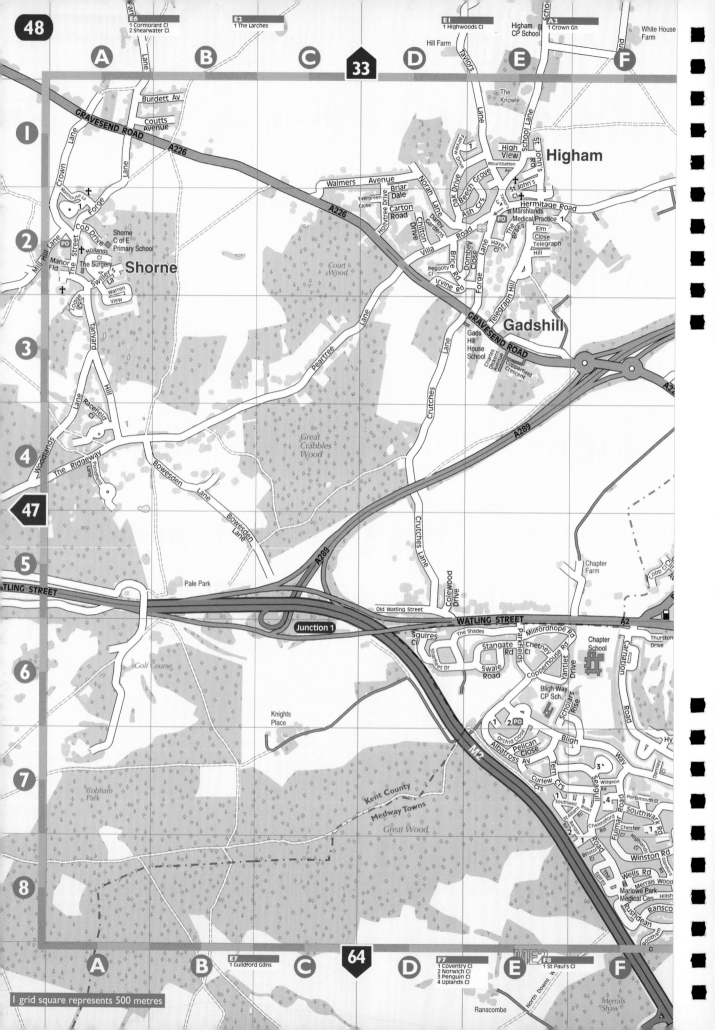

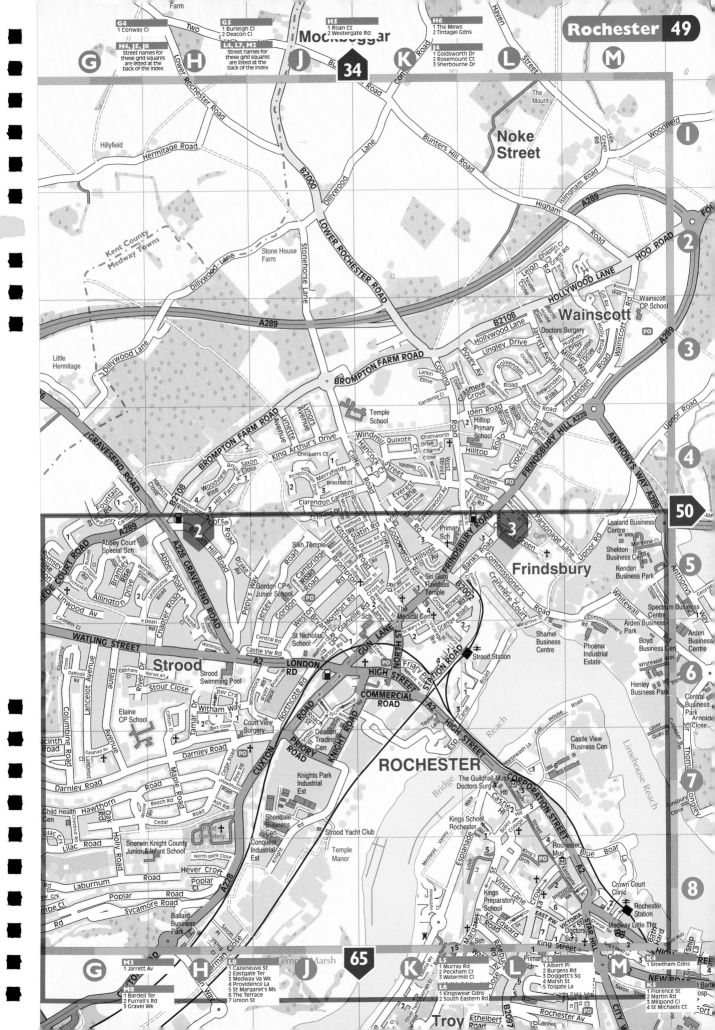

G H J K L M

Hoo Flats

Darnet Fort

South Ya...

Pinup Reach

Hoo Ness

52

RSPB Site

5

Nor... Ma...

Gillingham Reach

The Strand

Grange

LOWER RAINHAM ROAD B2004

East Court Farm

Lower Twydall

Riverside Country Park

G H J K L M

A   B   Slede Ooze   C   **37**   D   E   F

Marsh

Oakham
Ness

Medway

1

Long Reach

2   River   Bishop Spit

3
et

South Yantlet Creek   Bishop Ooze

4

51
RSł

Half A

5   Nor
Marsh

6   Bartlett Creek

7

•RSPB Site

Motney
Hill

ersid
untr
8   Rainham Creek   Otterham Creek   Horsham
Marsh

Saxon shore way   Road

A   B   C   **68**   D   E   F
B2004   Bloors
Wharf   Motney

G H J 38 K L M

I
2
3
54
5
6
7
8

Kethole Reach

Medway Towns
Kent

Ham Ooze

Sharfleet Creek

Greenborough
Marshes

Slayhills
Marsh

Millfordhope
Marsh

Twinney Creek

Halstow Creek

Bayford

Shoregate Lane

Poot Lane

Saxon Shore Way

**Ham
Green**

Saxon Shore Way

**Wetham
Green**

Shore Way

Street

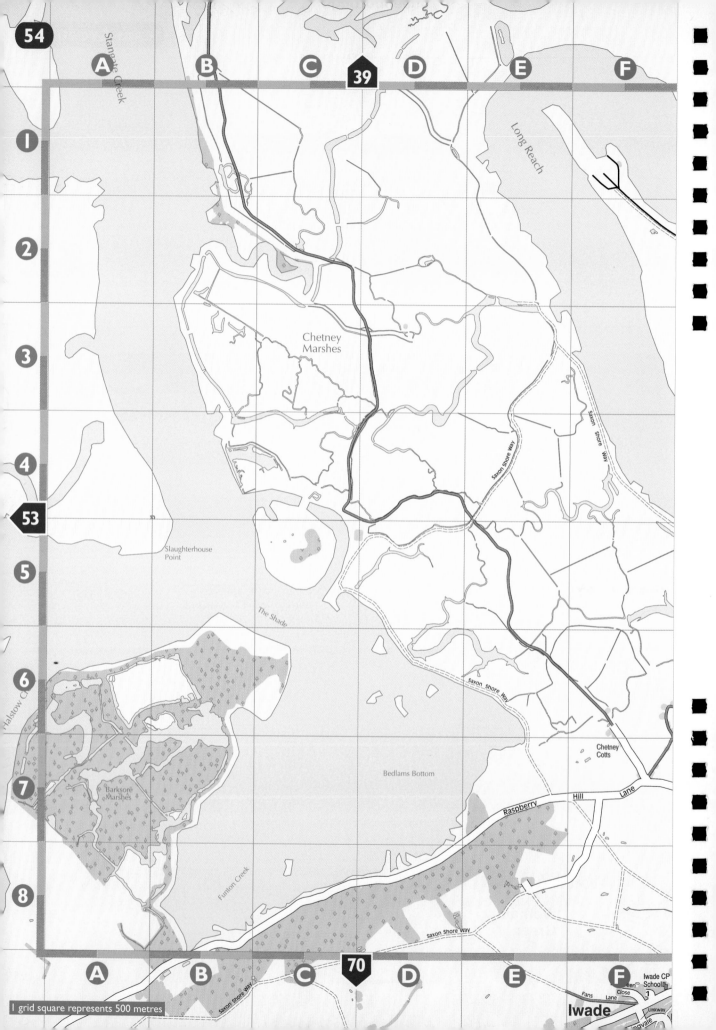

A B C **39** D E F

I

2

3

4

53

5

6

7

8

Stangate Creek

Long Reach

Chetney
Marshes

Saxon Shore Way

Saxon Shore Way

Slaughterhouse
Point

The Shade

saxon shore way

Chetney
Cotts

Halstow C

Barksore
Marshes

Bedlams Bottom

Raspberry Hill Lane

Funton Creek

Saxon Shore Way

A B **70** C D E F

Iwade CP
School

Fans Lane

Feen
Close

Iwade

Linkway

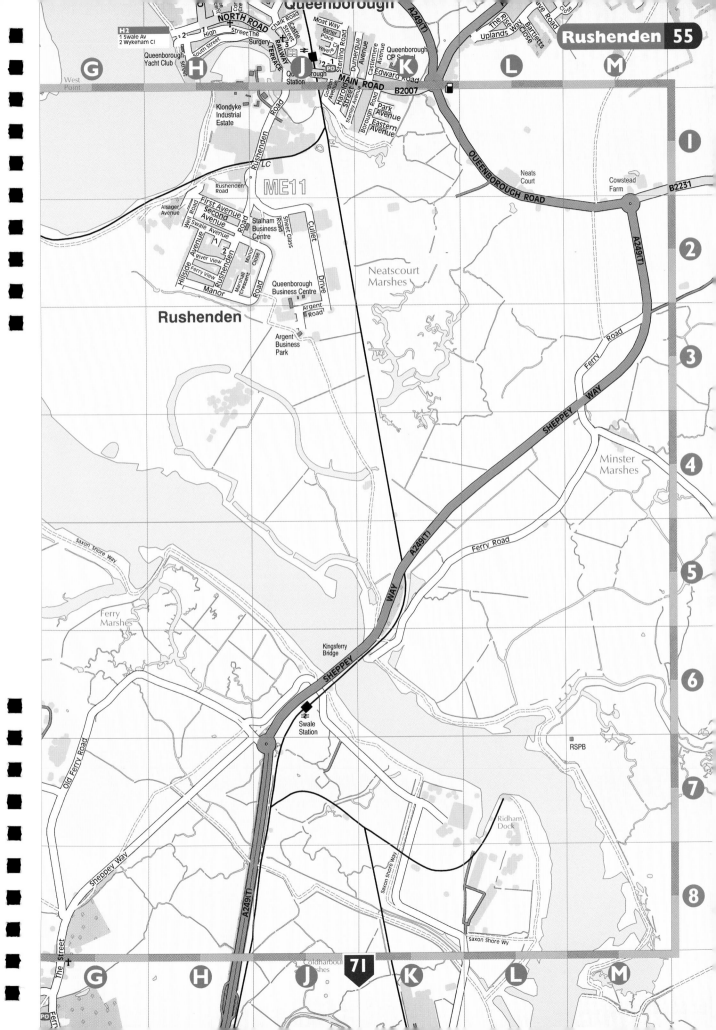

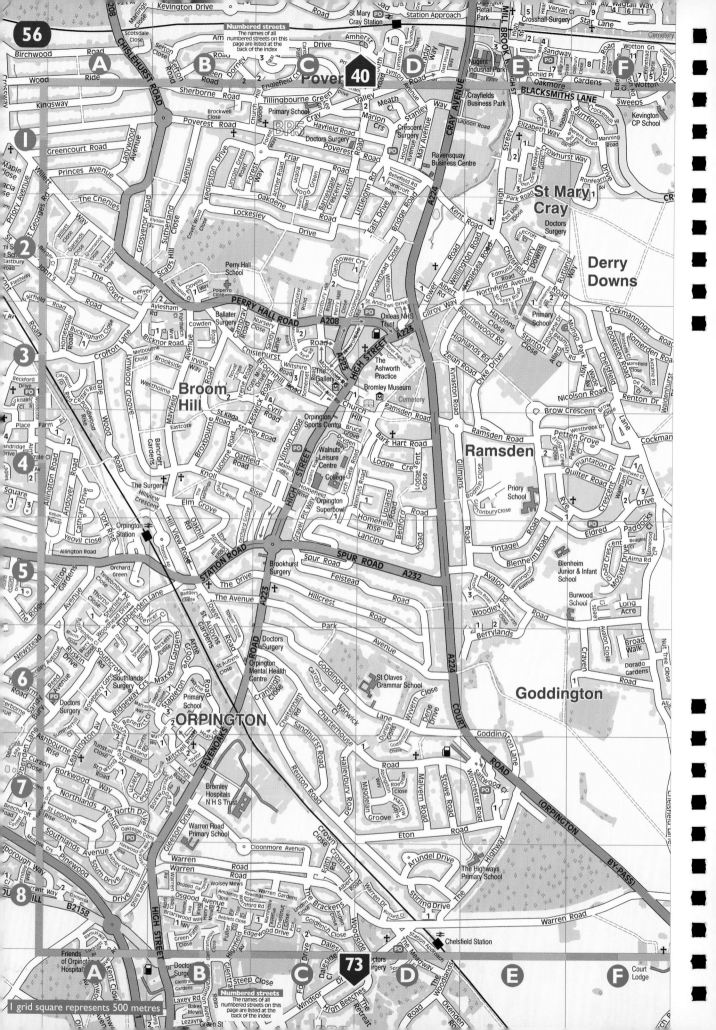

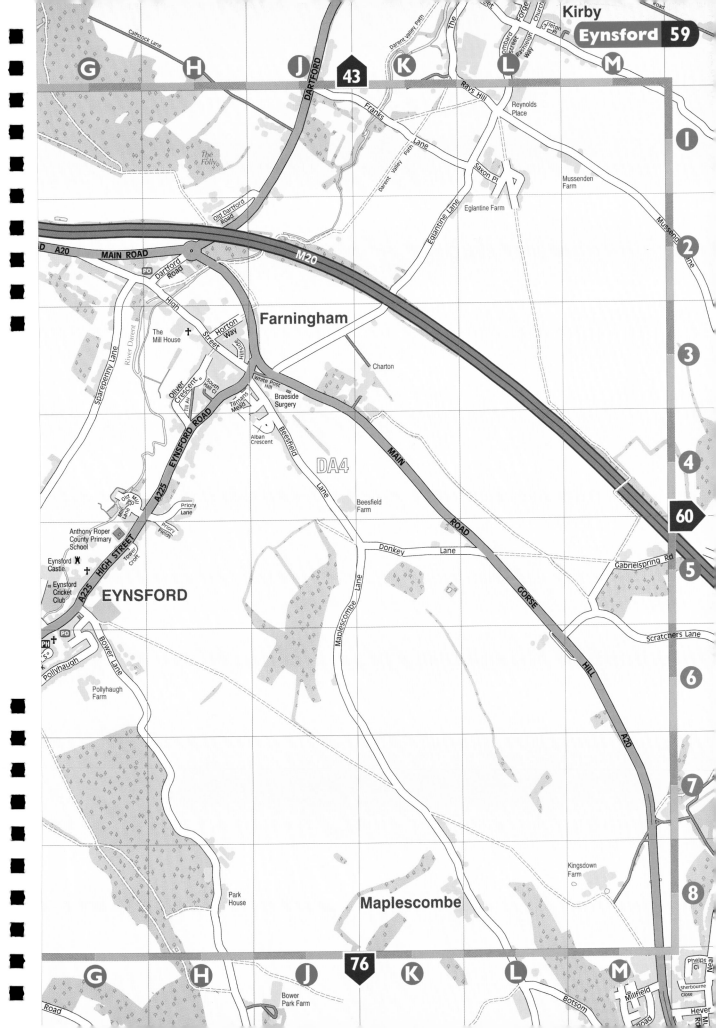

G H J **43** K L M

Calfstock Lane

The Folly

DARTFORD

Franks

Ravs Hill

Reynolds Place

Darent Valley Path

Eglantine Lane

Saxon Pl

Mussenden Farm

Eglantine Farm

Mussend... ...ne

I

Old Dartford Road

2

A20 **MAIN ROAD**

Dartford Road

PO

High

M20

Horton Way

Hillside

Farningham

3

The Mill House

Oliver Crescent

Till Av

Street

South Hall Cl

Charton

White Post Hill

Tilmans Mead

Braeside Surgery

Sparepenny Lane

River Darent

EYNSFORD ROAD

Alban Crescent

Beesfield

DA4

MAIN

4

A225

Priory Lane

Lane

Beesfield Farm

60

Old Mill Lane

Priory Fields

Anthony Roper County Primary School

Tower Croft

Donkey   Lane

ROAD

Gabrielspring Rd

5

Eynsford Castle

HIGH STREET

Maplescombe Lane

A225

EYNSFORD

Eynsford Cricket Club

CORSE

Scratchers Lane

PH

PO

Pollyhaugh

Bower Lane

HILL

6

Pollyhaugh Farm

A20

7

Park House

Kingsdown Farm

8

Phelps Cl

Maplescombe

Neal

G H J **76** K L M

Bower Park Farm

Botsom

Milfield

Sherbourne Close

Hever

Road

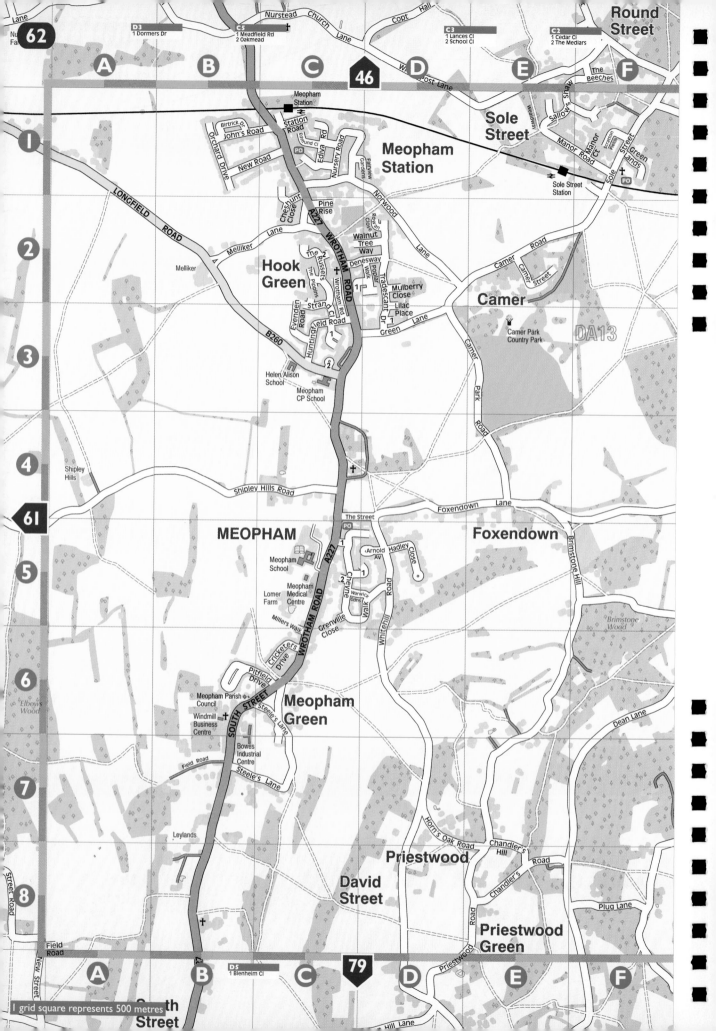

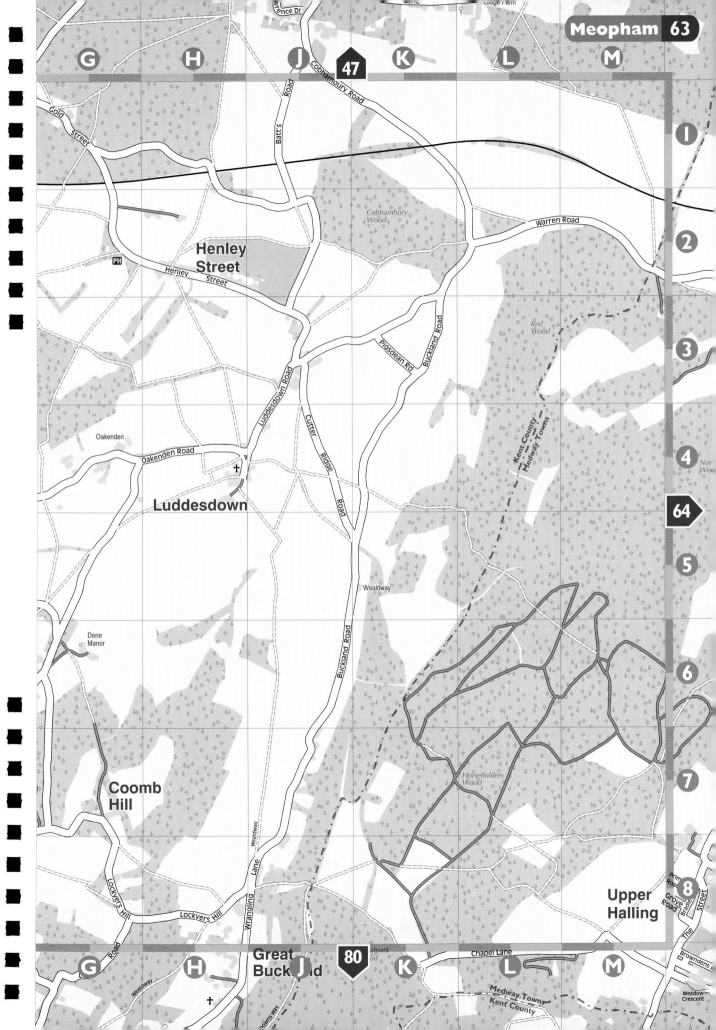

G H J 47 K L M

I

2

3

4

64

5

6

7

8

Gold Street

Batt's Road

Cobhambury Road

Cobhambury Wood

Henley Street

PH

Henley Street

Warren Road

Red Wood

Buckland Road

Pigsdean Rd

Luddesdown Road

Cutter Ridge Road

Oakenden

Oakenden Road

†

Luddesdown

Kent County Medway Towns

Nor Wo

Wealdway

Dene Manor

Buckland Road

Coomb Hill

Horseholders Wood

Lockyers Hill

Lockyers Hill

Wrangling Lane

Wealdway

Upper Halling

Grove Road

The Bridle

prim Road

Street

Browndens

G H **Great Buck...nd** J 80 K L Chapel Lane M

Meadow Crescent

Medway Towns
Kent County

A   B   C   **48**   D   E   F

ME2

Wells Rd

Merrals Wood

Marlowe Park
Medical Cen

Rushdean

Ransco

1

Ranscombe

Merrals
Shaw

2

Lower Bush

Bush   Road

North Downs Way

North Downs Way

Poplicans Road

Nine   Acres
Rd

Charles

Ladywood Rd

Whiteleaves

Harold
Rd

Reginald Av

Drive

Pilgrims Way

SUNDRIDGE HILL

ROCHESTER ROAD

Cuxton

3

Upper Bush
Road

**Upper
Bush**

Court
Lodge

Bush   Road

PO

Cuxton
CP Junior
School

Cuxton County
Infant School

Woodhurst
Cl

Wood
St

May St

Hayley
Cl

Stanford
Way

James Rd

The
Glebe

Hillcrest Dr

A228

Station
Road

LC

Cuxton Station

Cuxton
Industrial
Estate

Medway

Wouldham
Marshes

4

North
Wood

Dean
Farm

North Downs Way

River

63

Rings Hill
Farm

Wouldham Road

5

ROCHESTER   ROAD

Wingate
Wood

6

**North
Halling**

Pilgrims Road

A228

FORMBY RD

7

**New
Town**

Stake

Kent
Rd

School
Farm

School   Lane

Vicarage   Road

Essex Road

Halling
Station

Marsh Road

Marsh Road

Rectory Cl

Street

Wouldham

8

Primrose
Road

Bradley Rd

Grove
Road

Street

The

Vicarage
Cl

Vicarage
Cl

A228

High Street

Cem

Cemete
Rd

Low   Meadow

Halling

Trafalgar Rd

Nelson Rd

High

PO

School
Farm

Cornwall
Cres

Knowle

Browndens

Maximilian

rside Me
actice

Iison

Acre
CV

81

pp
alling

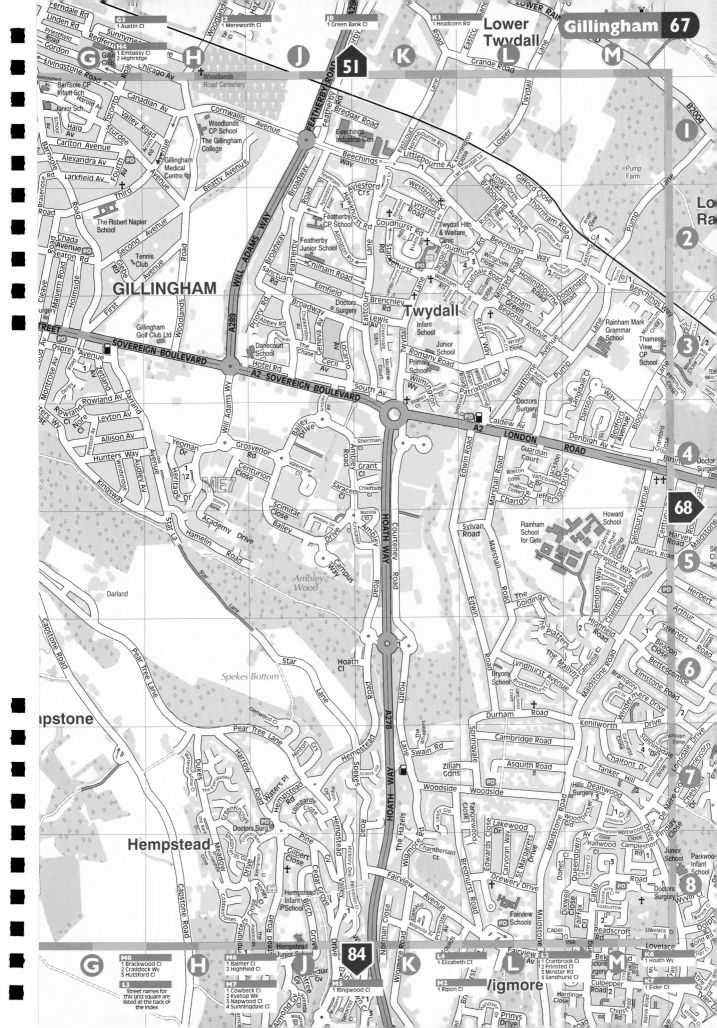

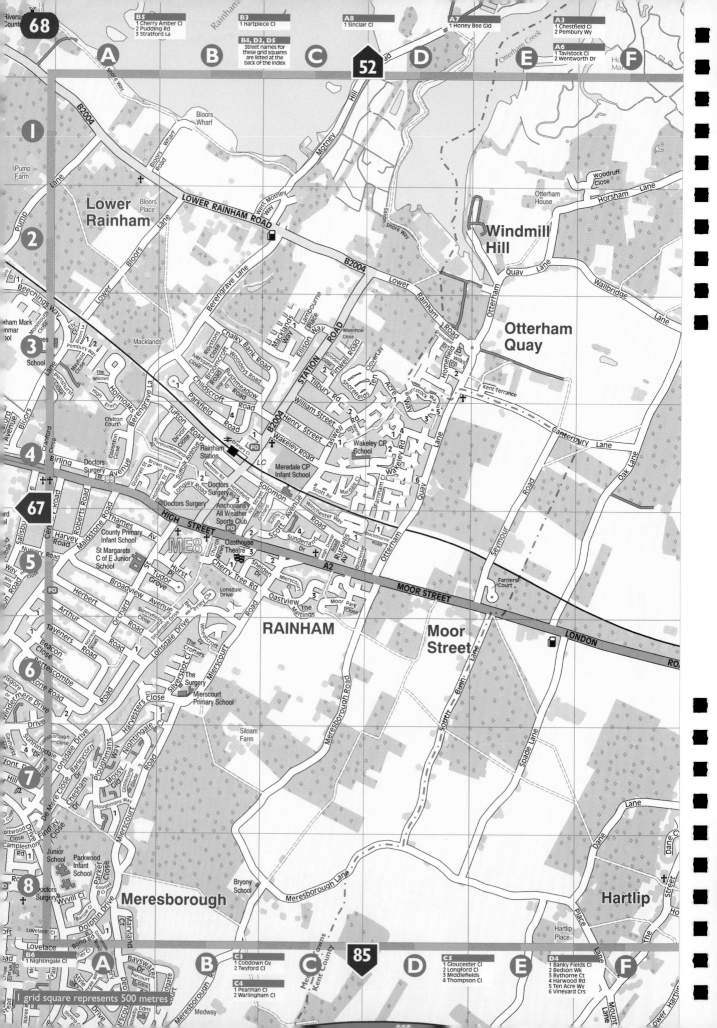

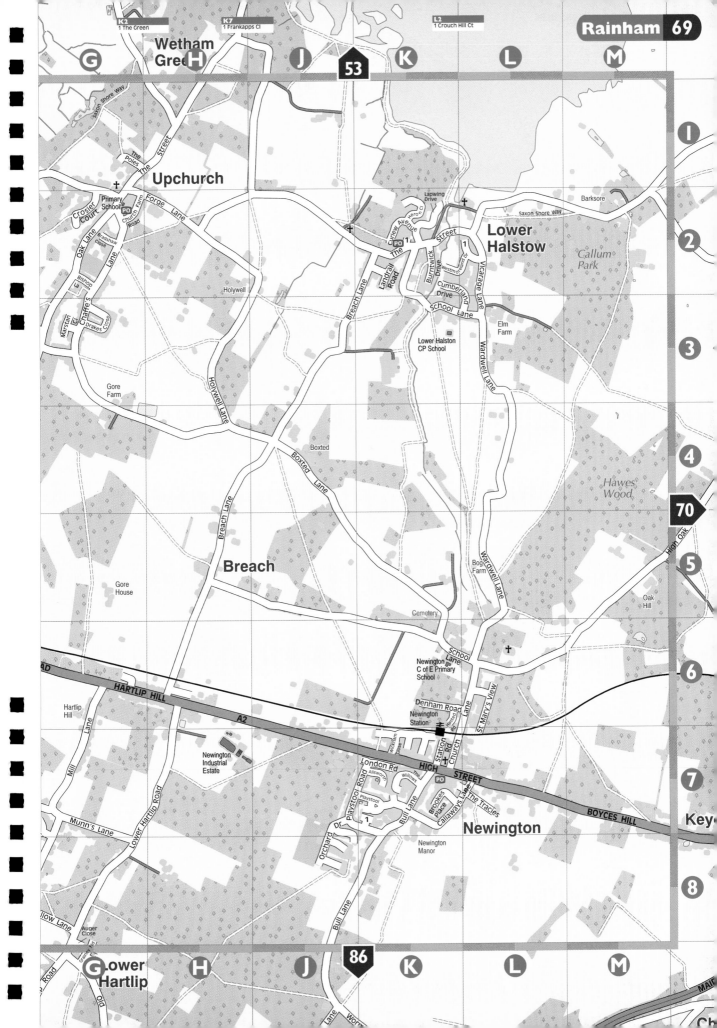

K2
1 The Green

K7
1 Frankapps Cl

L2
1 Crouch Hill Ct

Wetham Green

G **H** **J** 53 **K** **L** **M**

Saxon Shore Way

The Poles

The Street

Upchurch

Crosier Court

Primary School
PO

Church Farm Road

Forge Lane

Oak Lane

Bradshaw Close

Lane

Bishop La

Marstan

Chaffe's Cl

Drakes Close

Holywell

Lapwing Drive

Barksore

Saxon Shore Way

Curlew Avenue

Heron Cl

Lower Halstow

The Street

Burntwick Drive

Westmoor Dr

Vicarage Lane

Callum Park

Cumberland Drive

School Lane

Lower Halston CP School

Elm Farm

Wardwell Lane

I

2

3

Gore Farm

Holywell Lane

Boxted Lane

Boxted

Hawes Wood

4

70

Breach

Breach Lane

Cemetery

Wardwell Lane

Bog Farm

High Oak

Oak Hill

5

School Lane

Newington C of E Primary School

6

RD

HARTLIP HILL

A2

Hartlip Hill

Mill Lane

Newington Industrial Estate

Lower Hartlip Road

Munn's Lane

Denham Road

Newington Station

Wickham Close

London Rd

Aldsworth

Playstool Road

Bull Lane

Orchard Dr

Playstool

1

Brookes Place

Callaways Lane

St Mary's View

Warded Rd

HIGH STREET

Station Rd

Church

PO

The Willows

The Tracies

Newington

Newington Manor

BOYCES HILL

Key

7

8

Willow Lane

Auger Close

Orchard Gr

Old Road

G **Lower Hartlip** **H** **J** 86 **K** **L** **M**

MAI

Ch

A   B   C   54   D   E   F

F7
1 Pippin Cl
F1
1 Meadow Cl
E8
1 Ashington Cl
2 Wentworth Dr
D8
1 Gainsborough Cl

1

Iwade
Iwade CP School
Evergreen Close
Fans Lane
Springvale
Meadow Rise
Sheerstone
Linkway

Funton

2

Orchard Farm

Coleshall

Sheppey Way

3

Culnells

Stickfast Lane

Cambray Farm

Pheasant Farm

4

Belnor

Great Norwood

Howt Green

69

Avenue

Parsonage   Lane

Little Norwood

Nether Toes

A249(T)

5

High Oak Hill

Oak Hill

Parsonage

Parsonage

Lane

Lane

Sheppey Way

Upper Toes

Quinton   Road

6

Cold   Harbour   Lane

Bobbing

Bobbing CP School

The Meads Avenue
Roberts
Knightsfield Road
Vicarage Rd

7

Cold   Harbour

Cold Harbour Lane

Keycol

Rook   Hill

Grove Dairy Farm Business Centre

Bobbing Hill

Grove Park CP School

Hilton Dr

Laxton   Way
Worcester   Cherry Cl
Windmill   Road
Avenue

B2006

STAPLEHURST RD

Milton Regis

A2   KEYCOL   HILL

Ladyfields Close

MAIDSTONE

SHEPPEY WAY

Wellington   Rd

Key Street

Gore Court Cricket Club

Clive Road

PO

Gayhurst Drive

Sittingbourne Industrial Park

Hythe Rd
Warner
Road Eastwood   Gdns
Springfield Rd
Waterloo Rd

8

A249(T)

KEY STREET

Cherry Flds

Grove Pk Av

Brier   Rd

KEY STREET

Gibbons Rd
Sandford Road
Chatsworth Road

Cadby   Provender
Lonsdale   Drive
Warwick Cres

Kenilworth Ct   Road

A2   LONDON

Well Winch Rd
Staplehurst
Bourne   Cavell Way

Chalkwell

87

MAIDSTONE   ROAD

Chestnut   Street

Westlands Secondary School

Sydney Avenue

Somerset Close

Tryalls Lane
Canberra
Brisbane

Adelaide Drive

Lydbrook Close

Tavistock Close

London Road Trading Est

CHALKWELL   ROAD

PO
Barkers Rd

Doctors Surgery

Chestnut

A   B   C   87   D   E   F

1 grid square represents 500 metres

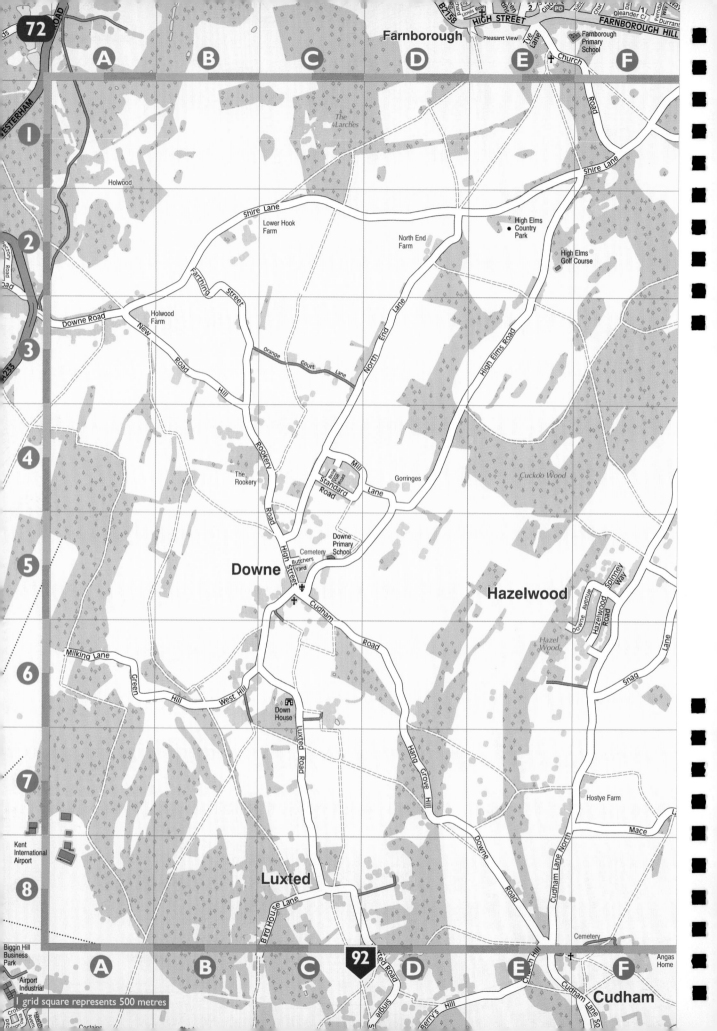

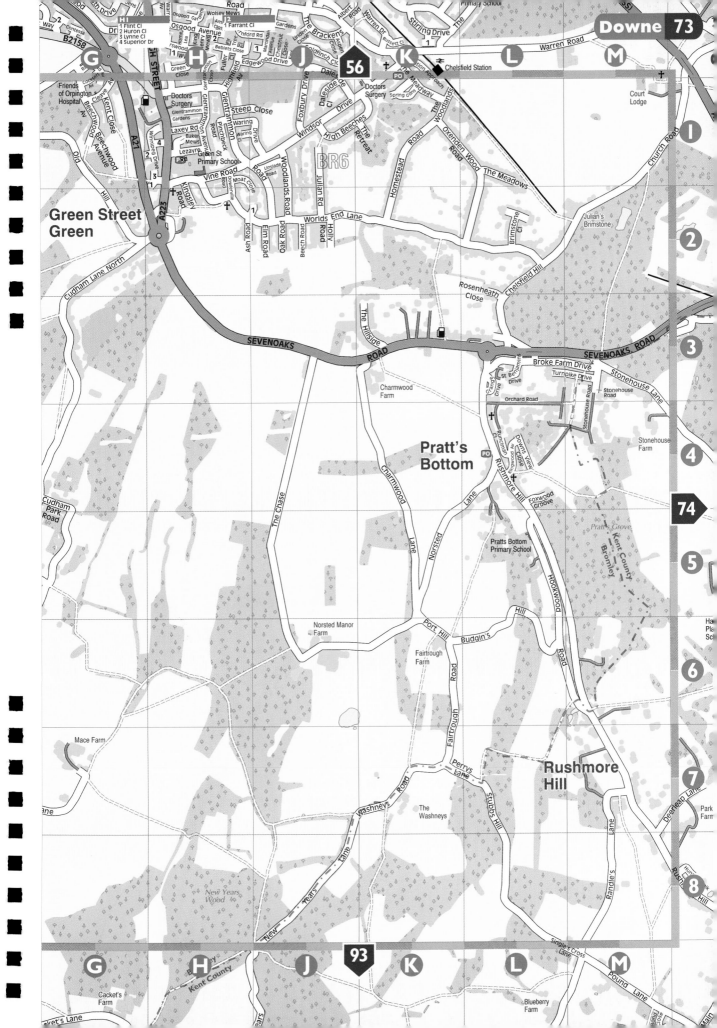

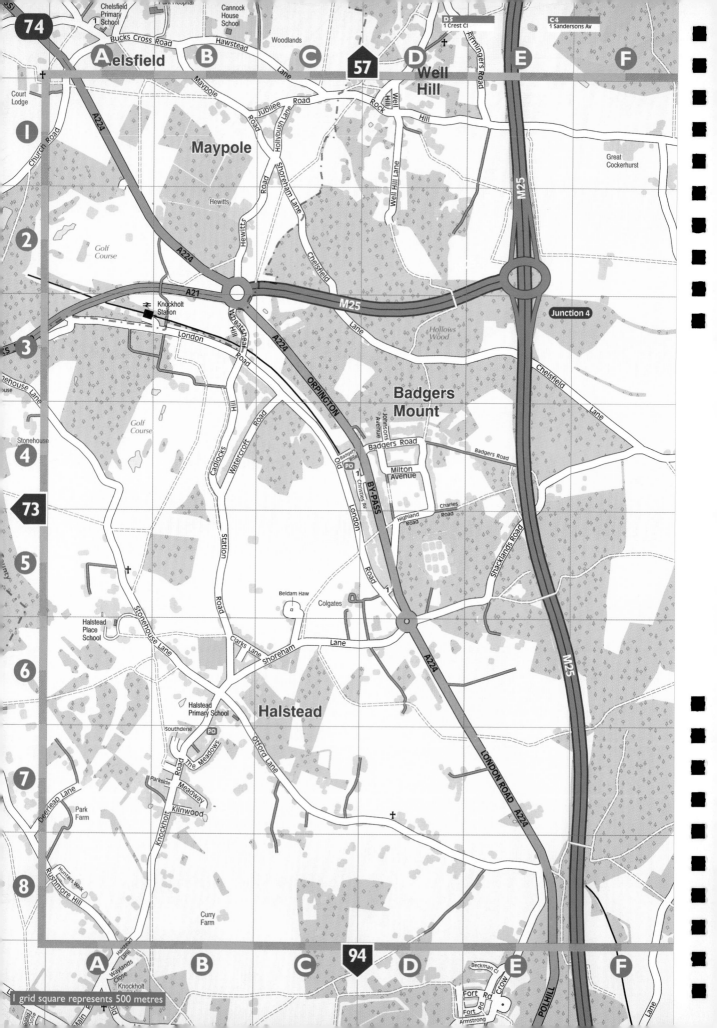

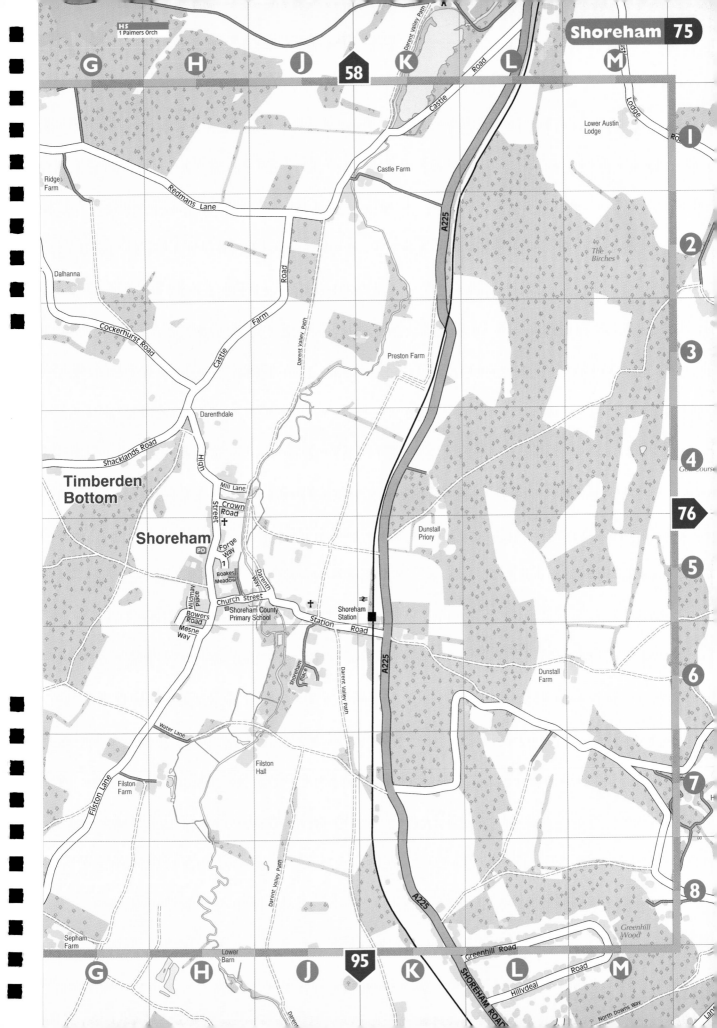

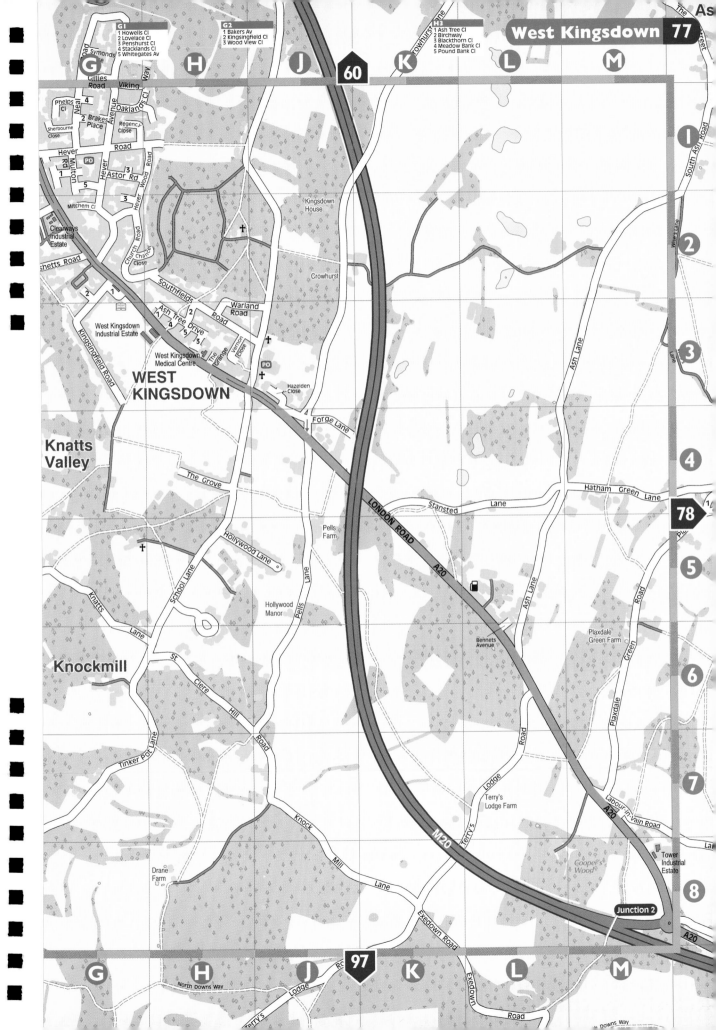

G1
1 Howells Cl
2 Lovelace Cl
3 Penshurst Cl
4 Stacklands Cl
5 Whitegates Av

G2
1 Bakers Av
2 Kingsingfield Cl
3 Wood View Cl

H3
1 Ash Tree Cl
2 Birchway
3 Blackthorn Cl
4 Meadow Bank Cl
5 Pound Bank Cl

As

G   H   J   60   K   L   M

I

2

3

78

4

5

6

7

8

Gillies Road
Viking Avenue
pen Symonds
Phelps Cl
Neal
Brakes Place
Regency Close
Sherbourne Close
Hever Rd
Multon
PO
Hever Road
Astor Rd
Mitchem Cl
Clearways Industrial Estate
shetts Road
Southfields
Church Road
Chancel Close
Warland Road
Vernon Close
Kingsdown House
Crowhurst
West Kingsdown Industrial Estate
Kingsingfield Road
Ash Tree Drive
West Kingsdown Medical Centre
The Grange
PO
Hazelden Close
WEST KINGSDOWN
Forge Lane

Knatts Valley

The Grove
Hollywood Lane
Pells Farm
LONDON ROAD
A20
Stansted Lane
Hatham Green Lane
Ash Lane

School Lane
Hollywood Manor
Pells Lane
Bennets Avenue
Plaxdale Green Farm
Ash Lane
Plaxdale Green Road

Knockmill

Knatts Lane
St Clere Hill Road
Tinker Pot Lane
Knock Mill Lane
Terry's Lodge Farm
Terry's Lodge Road
M20
Labour-in-vain Road
A20
Cooper's Wood
Tower Industrial Estate

Drane Farm
Exedown Road
Junction 2

G   H   J   97   K   L   M

North Downs Way
Terry's Lodge
Exedown Road
Downs Way

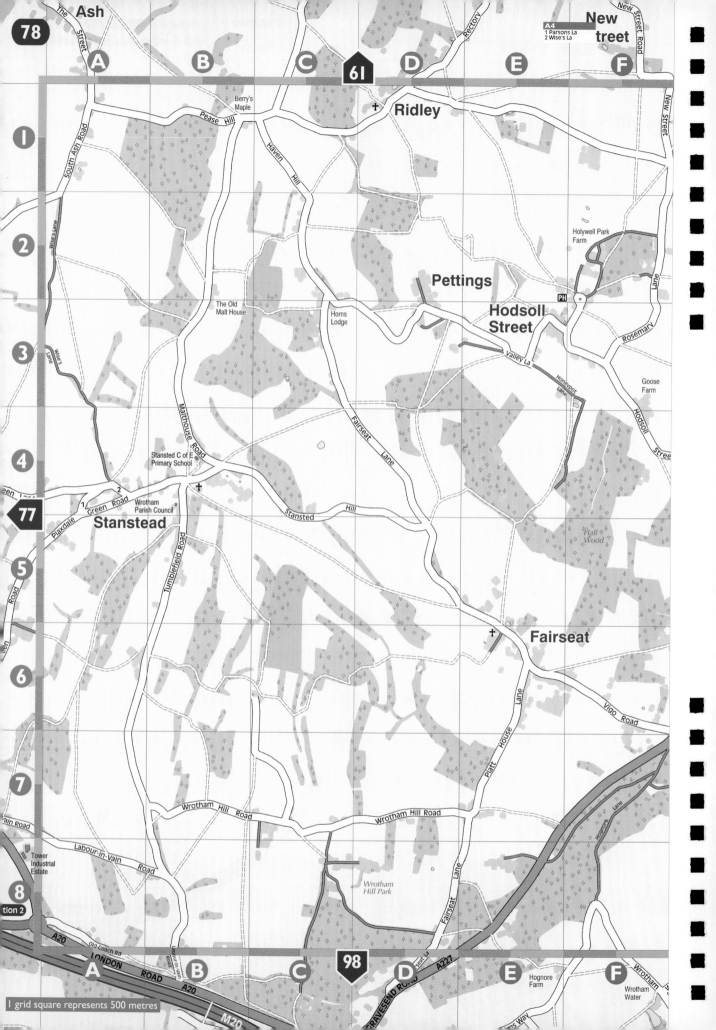

Upper Halling

Ⓐ   Ⓑ   Ⓒ   63   Ⓓ   Ⓔ   Ⓕ

Great
Buckland

Chapel Lane

Greatpark
Wood

Luxon

Wealdway

North Downs Way

Ⓘ

Medway Towns
Kent County

Holly Hill

Lockyers Hill

Lo...s Hill

Wrangling Lane

Leywood Road

Holly Hill

Wrangling Lane

Lad's Farm

Pilgrims Way

Ⓐ 2
Boughurs Street
Farm

Holly Hill

Ⓐ 3

Crookhorn
Wood

Horse Road

Ⓐ 4

Birling   Hill

Pilgrims Way

Paddlesworth

79

Holly Hill

Paddlesworth Road

Ⓐ 5
Birling
Place

Stangate   Road

rse

Ⓐ 6

Coney
Lodge

Snodland Road

Ledge Lane

Park Farm Road

Ⓐ 7
Birling Lodge

Birling

Birling Park

Snodland Road

Ledge Lane

Ⓐ 8

Workhouse Road

Chapel

Bull Road

Birling Road

The
Close

Birling Road

Chapel Cl

Street

Birling
Road

Ryarsh
CP Sch

Ryarsh   100

Birling Road

Masters Lane

Ryarsh Road

Birling Road

Birli
As...

ars

The Street   Old Scho

Ⓐ   Ⓑ   Ⓒ   Ⓓ   Ⓔ   Ⓕ

I grid square represents 500 metres

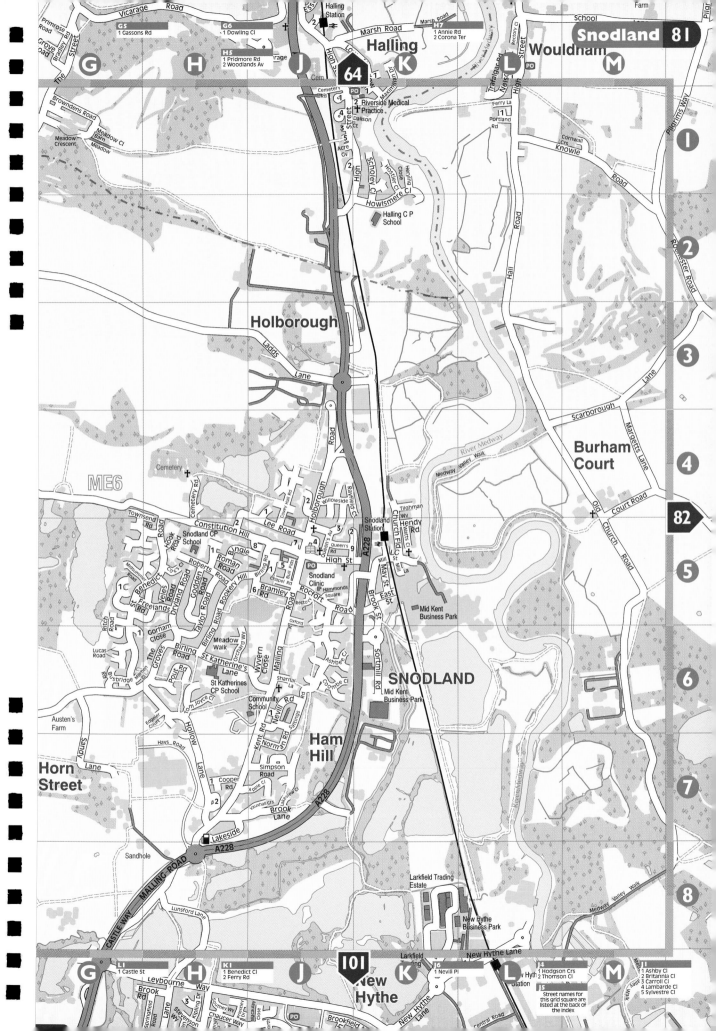

A   B   C   69   D   E   F

Lower Hartlip

I

Hollow Lane
The
Close
Galney Rd

Lower Hartlip Road

Old House Road

Bull Lane

Chesley

Wormdale Road

Wormdale

Maidstone Road

2

Cowstead Road

Bull Lane

Thrognall Farm

Wormdale Hill

A249(T)

Sittingbourne & Milton Regis Golf Club

Danaway

3

Cowstead

Bull Lane

Green Lane

M2

MAIDSTONE ROAD

Woodgate Lane

4

Bull Lane

Junction 5

†

South Street Rd

Church Lane

5

Road

PO

Sparrow Ct

Stockbury

Honeycrock Hill

A249

Pett Lane

M2

†

6

Church Hill

Amens Hill

South Green Lane

Pett Farm

Frid Wood

Norton Green

Little Pett Farm

7

Dead Lane

Hayes Lane

Magpie Hall

Deans Hill

Rumstead Rd

†

South Green

Deans Bottom

Bicknor Lane

8

Rumsted Court

A   B   C   **106**   D   E   F

South Green Lane

Kennel Barn Road

Street Road Lane

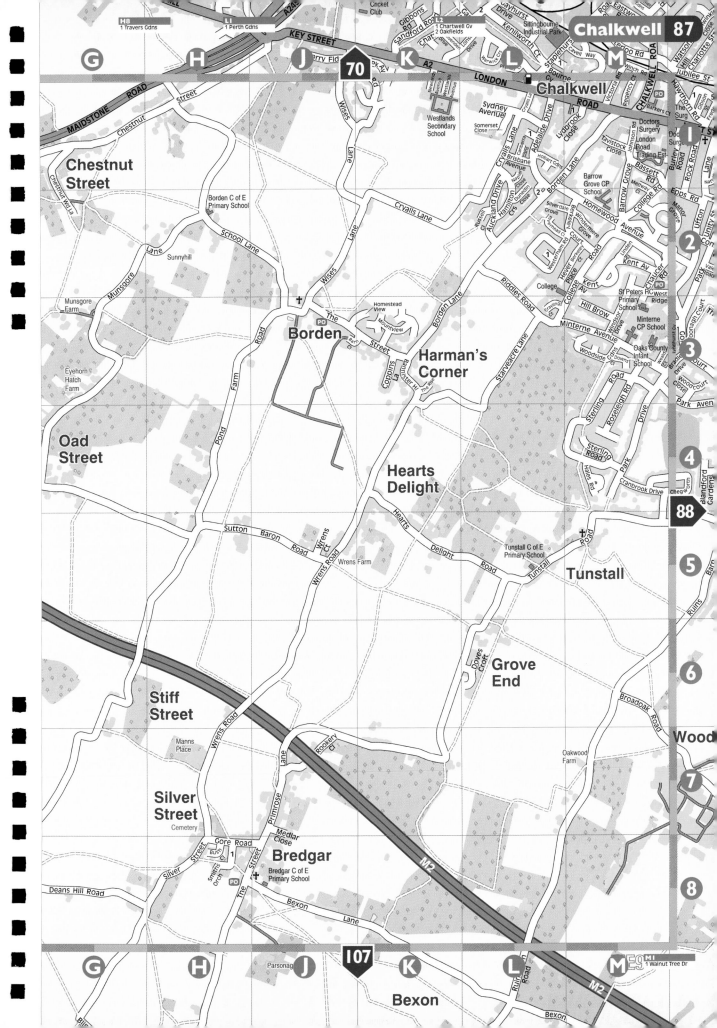

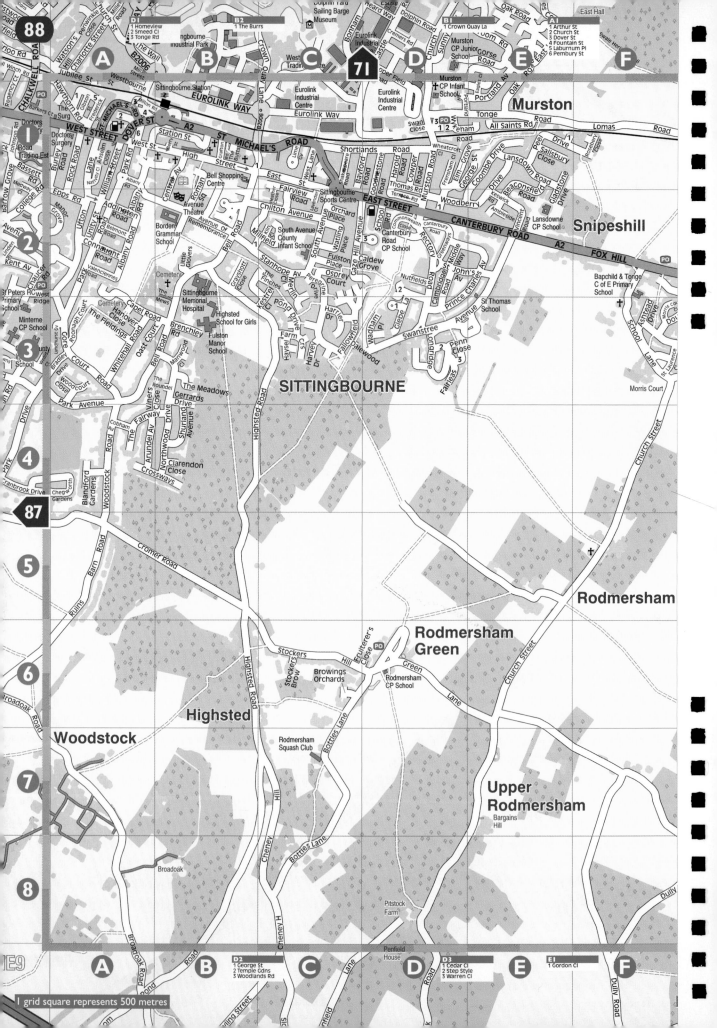

A B **Farleigh Court** C D E F

I

2

Old Farleigh Road

Farleigh Road

Farleigh Court
Road

Scotshall Lane

Farleigh Ct Rd

Cemetery

Farleigh Rovers
F C

Harrow Gdns

Parsonage Close

Harrow Road

Daniels Lane

Brennan Way

Vanguard Way

Warlingham
Park Hospital

*Holt
Wood*

Church Lane

Chelsham Common Road

Warlingham
Park
School

Ledgers Farm

†

3

Warlingham
County
Junior School

Farleigh Rd

Greenhill Lane

Cranmer Gdns

Sunny Bank

Alexandra Rd

Chelsham Road

Chelsham

Vanguard Way

The Mdw

Eglise Road

Cranmer Rd

Albert Rd

Alexandra Av

Warlingham
Rugby
Football Club

Chelsham
Lane

LIMPSFIELD ROAD

Bond

Upden

Marks Rd

Mavins Dr

Fernleigh Dr

†

Rogers Lane

Washpond Lane

Chelsham Court
Farm

4

John Fisher
Sports Club

Birch Way

Blanchman's Rd

Gresham Av

Eden Wy

B269

Chelsham Place
Farm

Ledgers Road

Warlingham

Warren Pk

Lime Cl

Cedar Cl

Larch

Farm Road

High La

LIMPSFIELD

ROAD

B269

Worms
Heath

Broom Bank

Beech Farm Road

5

Beechwood Lane

Plantation

Halliloo Farm

Haigh Lane

Slines Oak

Slines New Road

Barnard Road

Vanguard Way

6

Road

Slines New Road

Dukes Hill

Beulah Wk

Butlers Dene Road

Slines Oak Road

Upland Rd

Vanguard Way

Beech Farm

Beech Farm

7

Park

Beulah
Walk

Hilltop Walk

Camp Rd

Long Hill

**Woldingham
Garden Village**

Lunghurst Road

The
Wold

Vanguard Way

Long Hill

High Drive

Station Road

8

Church Road

Station Road

Southdown Road

Station Road

Woodlea
Primary
School

Croft Rd

†

Woldingham
Station

Lustin Ct

Nethern Ct

Southfields

CROYDON

A B C **108** D E F

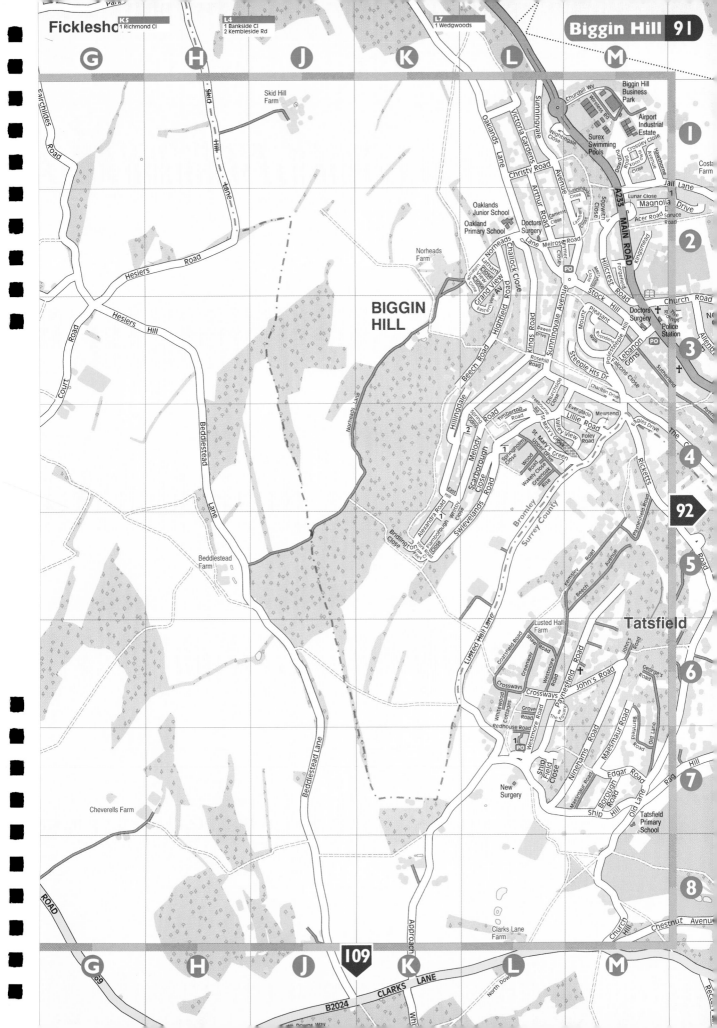

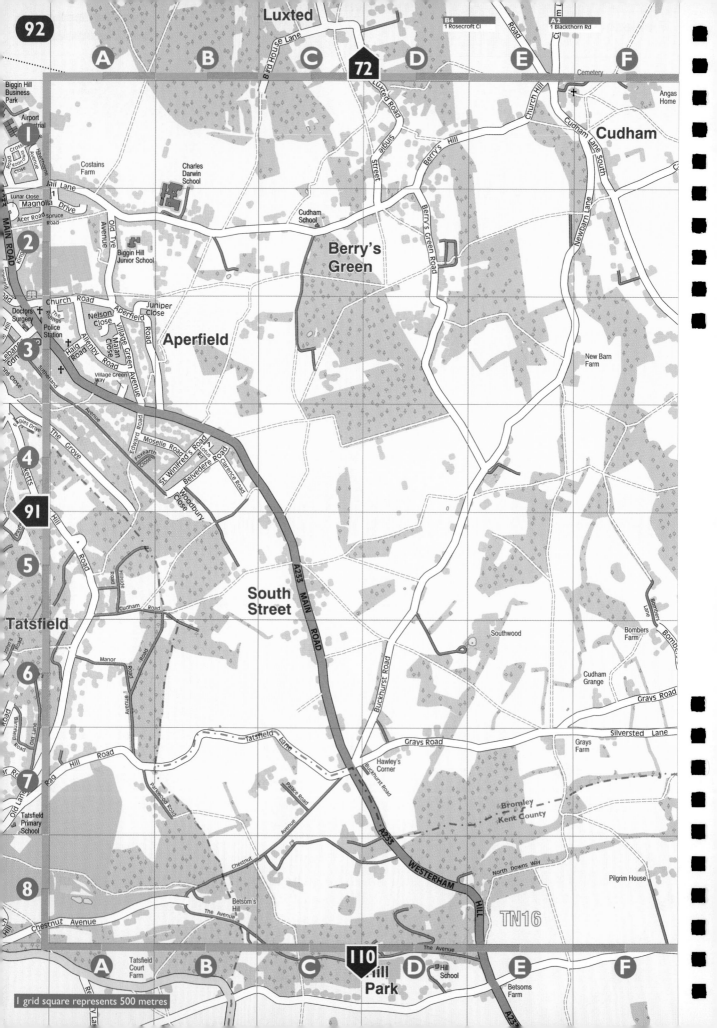

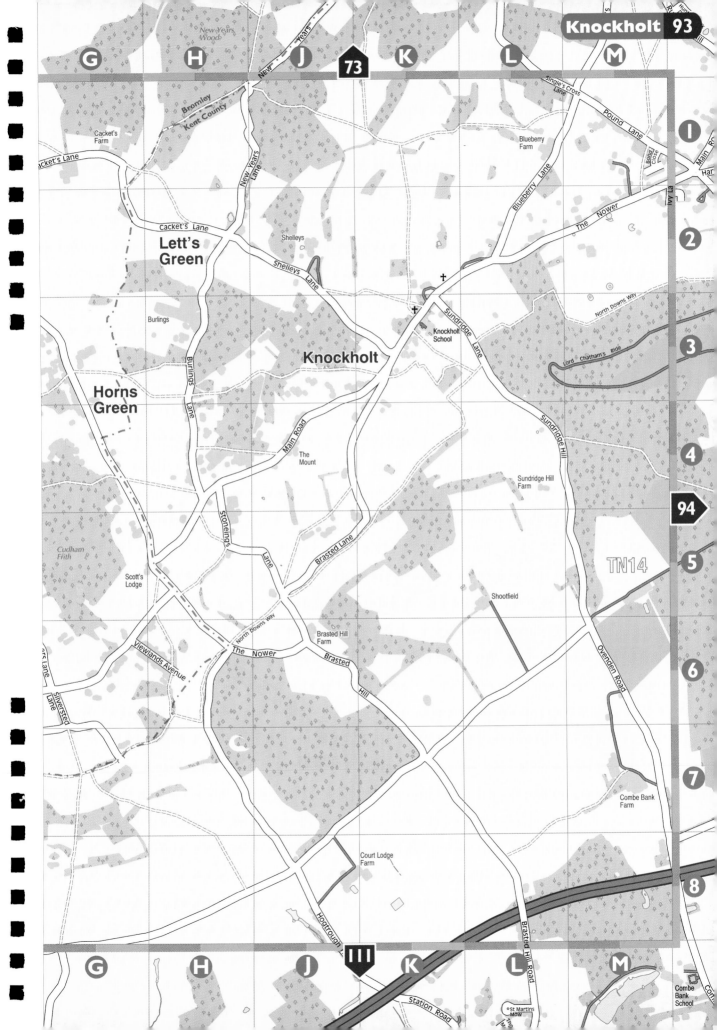

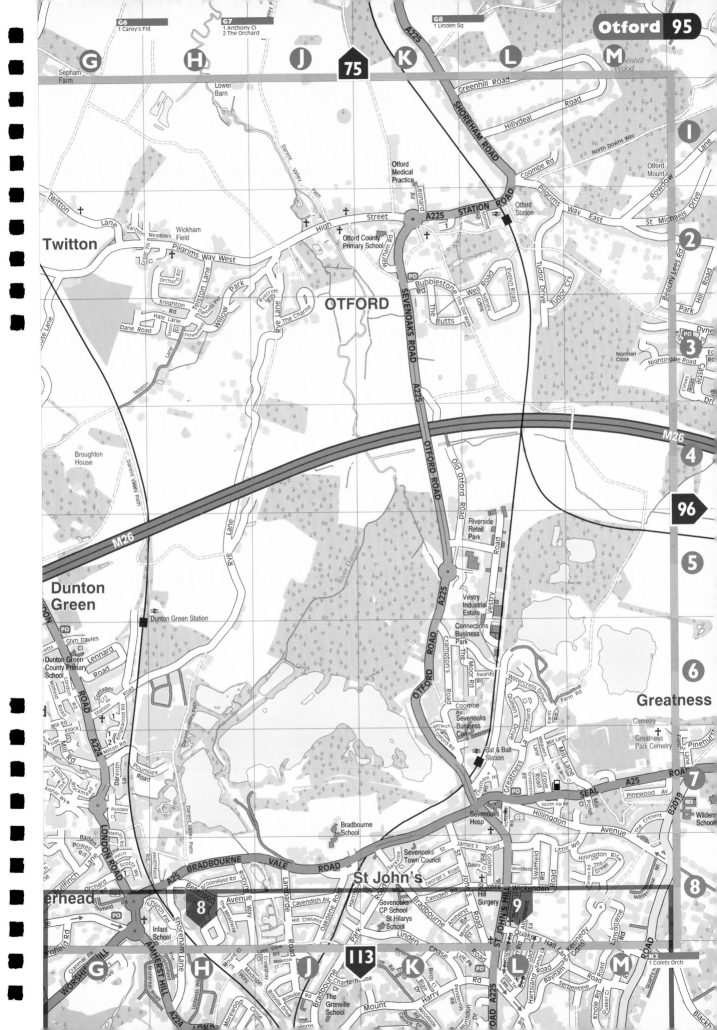

76

95

114

A B C D E F

1

2

3

4

5

6

7

8

KEMSING

Crowdleham

Childsbridge

Noah's Arks

Greatness

Seal

Wildernesse

Greenhill Wood

Otford Court

Otford Mount

Birchin Cross Road

North Downs Way

Shorehill Lane

Fernbank Farm

Orford Manor

Kester

Cotman's

Ash Lane

Rowdow Lane

St Michaels Drive

Beechy Lees Rd

Park Hill Road

Chalkways

Pilgrims Way

The Chase

Highfield Road

Northdown Rd

Collet

Barfield Crs

Hillside Rd

Copperfields Wk

Dippers Close

Orchard Way

The Landway

West End

Kemsing CP School

Kemsing Parish Council

Heaverham Road

Pilgrims Way

Dynes Rd

Knave Wood Rd

Edgar Rd

Castle Road

Brookfield

Oxenhill Road

Playfield

Greystones

Spring Head Rd

Copperfields

Nightingale Road

Cleves Road

Montfort

Boswell Drive

Childsbridge La

St Edith's Road

Old Barn Close

High Street

Wulfred Wy

Chart

PO

M26

Childsbridge Lane

Rushymead

Park Lane

Fawfield Close

Noah's Ark

M26

Chaucer Business Park

Kemsing Station

Honeypot Lane

Penfield

Close Bank

Mills Crs

Bentley's Meadow

Chipstead Way

The Shellings

Meadow Rd

Wickenden Rd

Zambra Way

Wilmot Rd

Landway

Church Street

Tanners Cross

Stonepitts

Cemetery

Greatness Park Cemetery

Pinehurst

Flints Lane

Highlands Pk

Ash Platt

Jubilee Ri

School La

Church Rd

Fullers Hill

Watery Lane

A25 Road

ROAD

B2019

Pinewood Av

The Cresent

Wilderness Sports Centre

Wildernesse School

Seal Drive

Wildernesse Avenue

HIGH STREET

PO

Grove Road

MAIDSTONE ROAD

A25

Saxbys Road

Dorton College of Further Education

Dorton House

Dorton Dr

Woodland Rise

Wildernesse Golf Club

The Grove

Woodland

Parkfield

Park Lane

Hall

Seal Chart

Blackf

Quarry Hill

I grid square represents 500 metres

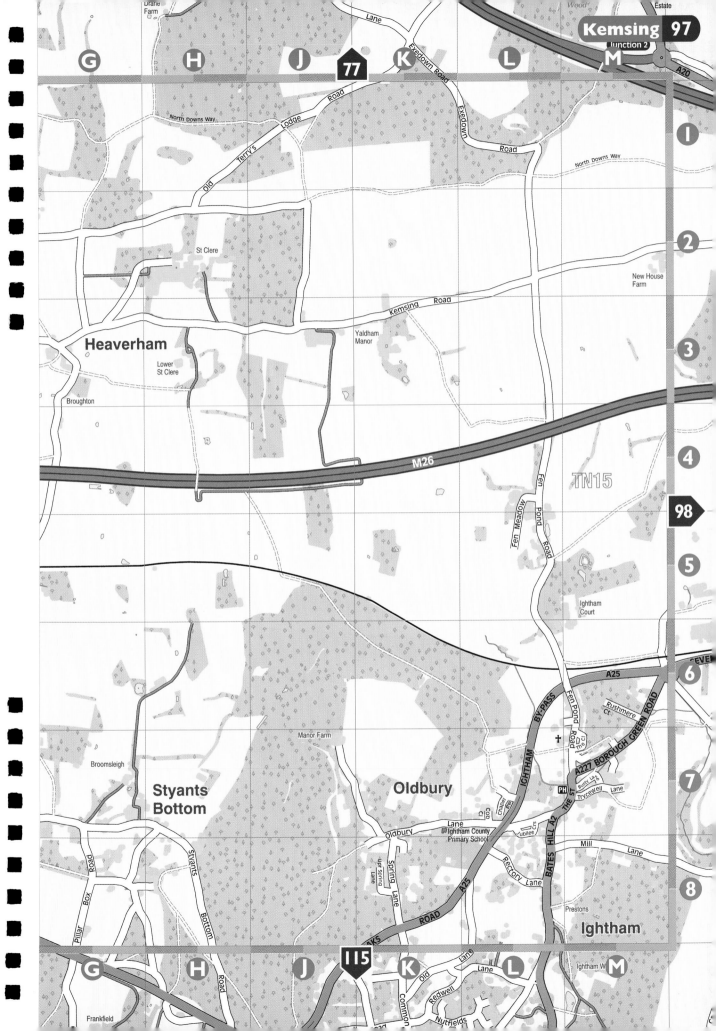

Junction 2

A20

G H J **77** K Exedown Road L M

North Downs Way

Lodge Road

Terry's

Old

St Clere

Kemsing Road

New House Farm

North Downs Way

Heaverham

Yaldham Manor

Lower St Clere

Broughton

M26

Fen Meadow

Fen Pond Road

TN15

98

Ightham Court

EVE

A25

Broomsleigh

Styants Bottom

Manor Farm

Oldbury

Fen Pond Road

A227 BOROUGH GREEN ROAD

Rushmere Ct

The Cl

Busty La

PH

The St

TryceWell Lane

IGHTHAM BY-PASS

Oldbury Lane

Chapel Fld

Cobb

Ightham County Primary School

Jubilee Crs

BATES HILL A2

RecTory Lane

Mill Lane

Pillar Box Road

Styants Bottom Road

Upr Spring Lane

Spring Lane

A25

ROAD

AKS

Prestons

Ightham

Ightham W

Redwell Lane

Old Lane

Lane

Frankfield

Common

Nutfields

I

2

3

4

5

6

7

8

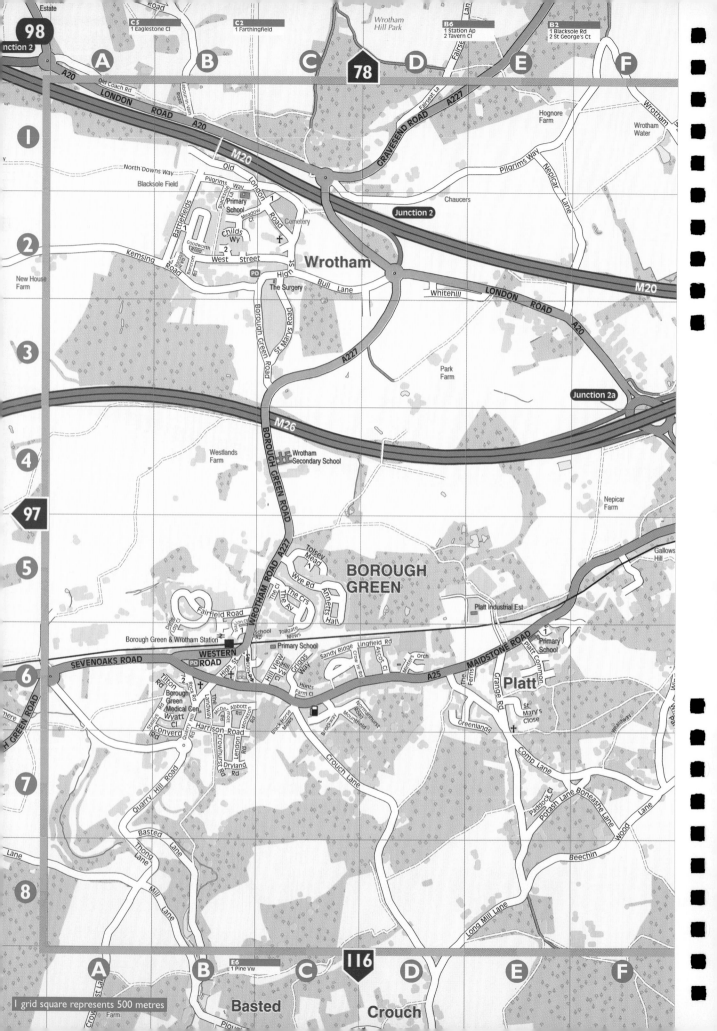

nction 2

A   **B**   **C**   78   **D**   **E**   **F**

C5
1 Eaglestone Cl

C2
1 Farthingfield

Wrotham
Hill Park

B6
1 Station Ap
2 Tavern Cl

B2
1 Blacksole Rd
2 St George's Ct

I

Estate

Old Coach Rd

A20

LONDON ROAD A20

M20

North Downs Way

Blacksole Field

Pilgrims Way

Old

London Road

Kemsing Road

Battlefields

Goodworth Road

Childs Wy

West Street

Meadow Ct

Cemetery

Primary School

Wrotham

GRAVESEND ROAD A227

Fairseat La

Pilgrims Way

Nepicar Lane

Chaucers

Hognore Farm

Wrotham Water

Junction 2

2

New House Farm

High St

PO

The Surgery

Bull Lane

Borough Green Road

St Marys Road

Whitehill

LONDON ROAD A20

M20

3

A227

Park Farm

4

Westlands Farm

BOROUGH GREEN ROAD A227

M26

Wrotham Secondary School

Junction 2a

Nepicar Farm

5

Tolsey Mead

Wye Rd

The Crs

The Av

Annetts Hall

BOROUGH GREEN

Gallows Hill

Fairfield Road

Platt Industrial Est

Primary School

Platt Common

Borough Green & Wrotham Station

WESTERN ROAD

School Ad

Tollgate Mews

Primary School

Sandy Ridge

Lingfield Rd

Ascot Cl

Minter's Orch

A25 MAIDSTONE ROAD

Platt

6

SEVENOAKS ROAD

PO

High St

Hill View Vw

Griggs Way

Hunts Farm Cl

Crouch Hill

The Ferns

Grange Rd

Greenlands

St Mary's Close

H GREEN ROAD

Tilton

Borough Green Medical Cen

Wyatt Cl

Conyerd Rd

Harrison Road

Crowhurst Rd

Dryland Rd

Rock Rd

The Landway

Abbott Rd

London Rd

Black Horse Mews

Brookway

Mountfield

Normanhurst

Comp Lane

7

here

Quarry Hill Road

Basted Lane

Thong Lane

Crouch Lane

Paddock Cl

Potash Lane

Boneashe Lane

Wood Lane

Wealdway

Beechin

8

Lane

Mill Lane

Long Mill Lane

1 grid square represents 500 metres

A   **B**   **C**   116   **D**   **E**   **F**

E6
1 Pine Vw

Basted   **Crouch**

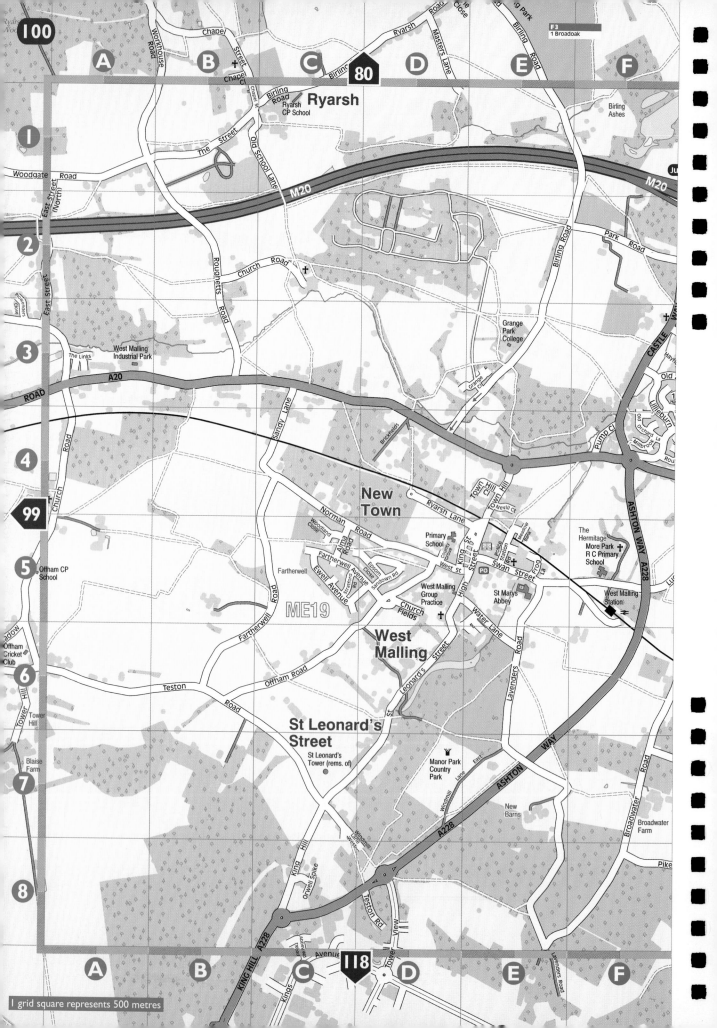

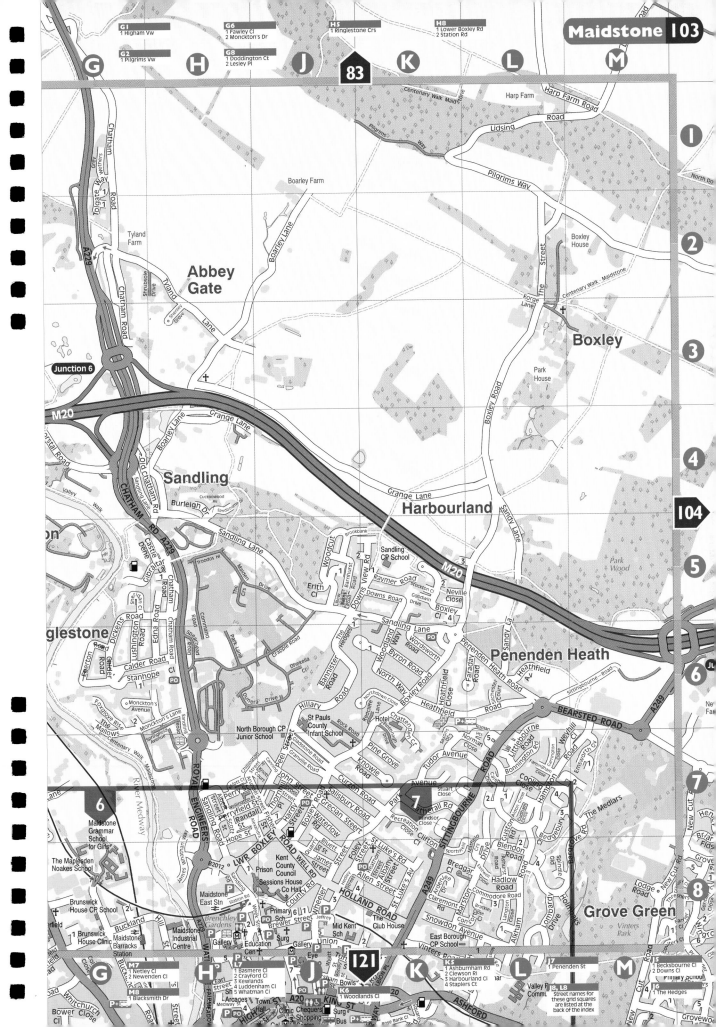

A B C 84 D E F

1

North Downs Way

2

Pilgrims Way

North Downs Way

Hermitage Lane

Mount House

Broader Lane

Scragged Oak Road

Stockings Wood

Cox Street

3

ME14

DETLING HILL

Pilgrims Way

East Court

Pilgrims Way

Castle Hill

4

Harpole

Harpole Lane

Detling C of E Primary School

The Street

PO

Princes Way

Queens Wy

Detling

North Downs Way

103

A249

ROAD

St Martin's Cl

Orchard View

Thurnham

Castle Hill

5

SITTINGBOURNE

Horish Wood

Hockers Close

Aldington Lane

6

Junction 7

A249

M20

Hockers Lane

Honeyhills Wood

Court Farm

Thurnham Farm

Newnham Court Farm

7

Bearsted Road

Coppice View

Henley Fields

Shepherds Gate Dr

Harrow Way

Exton Gdns

Wents

Weavering Street

Birling House

Chapel Lane

Ware Street

Bearsted Golf Club

M20

8

New Cut Rd

Briar Flds

Grovewood Drive

The Hedgerows

Rampion Cl

Maurice Cl

Grove Gn Rd

Greenways

Highdene

Shillingheld

Fulbert Rd

Averenches

Ware Street

Peverel Drive

Ware Street

Bearsted Station

PO

Bearsted Green Business Centre

The Maltings

Medical Centre

PO

New Grove Green Surgery

FitzWilliam Rd

Hill Brow

Mount Pleasant Drive

Bell Lane

Sandy Mt

Yeoman Lane

Windmill Hill Drive

Frenches Street

Primary School

Shearers Close

Threshers Dr

Couters Cl

Wingrove Dr

Grovewood

Birling Ave

Junior School

Spurway

Rossmore

1 grid square represents 500 metres

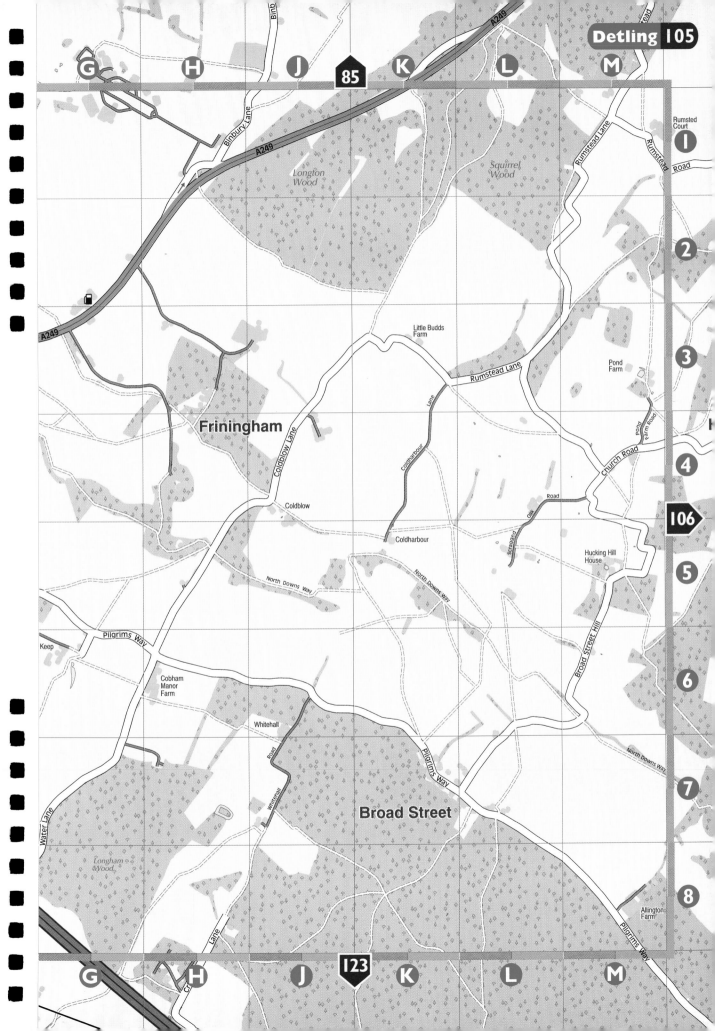

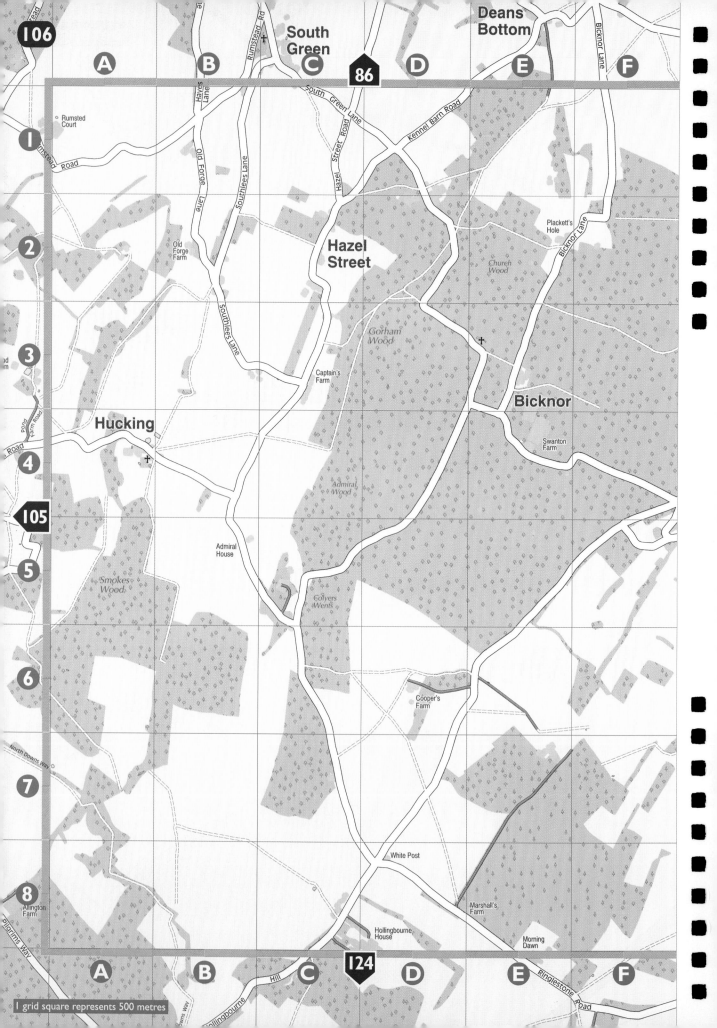

Deans Hill Road

Silver S

smiths orch

PO

The Str

Bredgar C of E
Primary School

Bexon

M2

G   H   J   **87**   K   L   M

Parsonage Farm

ME9

Bexon

Ruins Barn Road

Bexon   Lane

M2

I

Blind Mary's   Lane

Bashford Barn Lane

**Swanton
Street**

Bottom Pond Road

2

Hor

3

**Bottom
Pond**

Trundle
Wood

High
Wood

Bottom Pond Road

Norwood

Stock
Wood

4

Bedmonton

5

Saywell
Farm

Frinsted

The Street

Gray's
Field

Copes

6

Mattinson
Place

Wormshill

Kippen

Yewtree
Farm

7

Oorlair

Yoke's
Court

Park Farm

8

Madam's
Court

Lord's
Hill

Post

G   **Ring**H**tone**   J   **125**   K   L   M

Ringlestone   Road

PH

A B C 90 D E F

1

Marden Park Farm

Woodlea Primary School

Croft Rd

Clare Court

Ulstan Cl

Nethern Road

Station Road

Church Road

PO

The Crs

Sylves Oak Rd

Southfields

Woldingham

Park View Road

The Green

The Wold

Vanguard Way

2

Church Road

Upper Court Road

Southfields Road

Southview Road

Vanguard Way

3

Woldingham School

North Downs Golf Club

Northdown Road

Southfields Road

Chalkpit La

Flint House

4

North Downs Way

M25

5

North Downs Way

Gangers Hill

Chalkpit Lane

Westlands Way

Oakshaw

Barnett's

PO

Central Wy

Eastlands Wy

Wo shaw

Hamfield

Gordons Way

Eastlands Cl

Oxted & Limpsfield Hospital

6

Flinthall Farm

Tandridgehill Lane

N Downs Way

M25

Barrow Green Court

Hogtrough La

Wheeler Avenue

7

Flower Lane

Barrow Green Farm

Barrow Green Road

Sandy Lane

OXT

Peter Av

The Haywain

Church

WEST

8

Brooks Nest Farm

Streete Court School

The Priory

Meadowbrook

Brook

PH

High St

Godstone Rd

Bushey Croft

West Hill Bank

Fairley Pk

A B C D E F

ROAD

Nags Hall

A25

Godstone Road

GODSTONE ROAD

St Clair Cl

Beadles Lane

Springfield

Neb Lane

Spring

Tandridge Golf Club

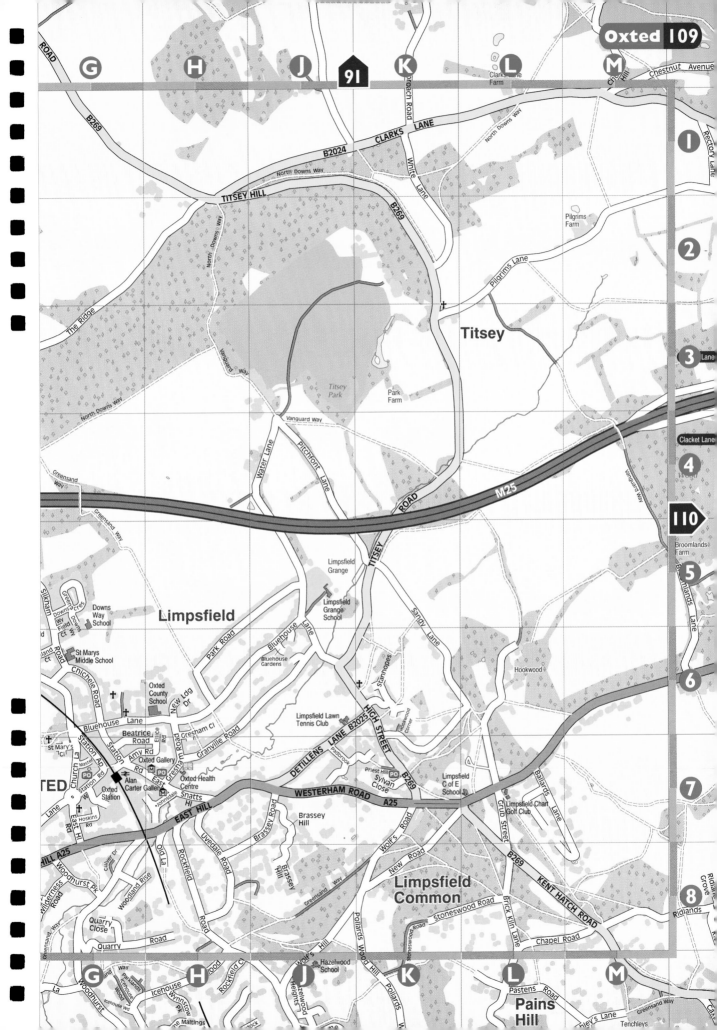

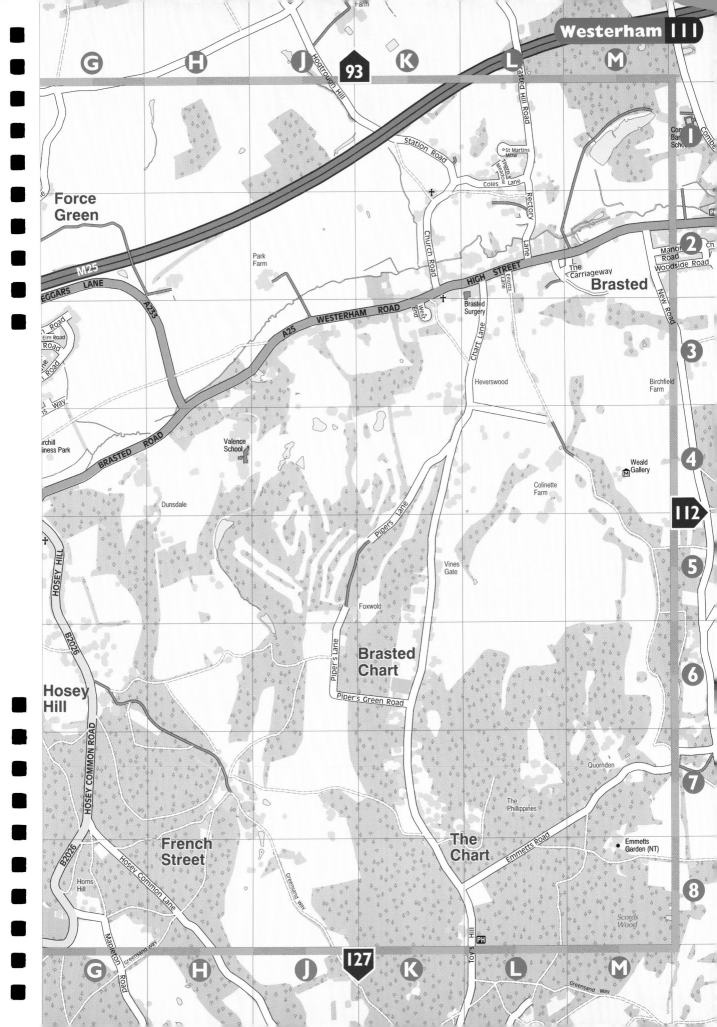

G H J **93** K L M

Force
Green

M25

BEGGARS LANE

A233

Elm Road

Road

Road

Way

Churchill
Business Park

BRASTED ROAD

Park
Farm

Valence
School

Dunsdale

A25 WESTERHAM ROAD

Hogtrough Hill

Station Road

St Martins
Mow

Horns
Meadow

Coles Lane

Church Road

HIGH STREET

West
End

Chart Lane

Brasted
Surgery

Rectory Lane

Elliotts
Lane

The
Carriageway

Brasted

Manor
Road

Woodside Road

New Road

Brasted Hill Road

Combe
Bank
School

I

2

3

Heverswood

Birchfield
Farm

Weald
Gallery

Colinette
Farm

4

112

HOSEY HILL

B2026

Hosey
Hill

HOSEY COMMON ROAD

B2026

Horns
Hill

Mapleton Road

Hosey Common Lane

Greensand Way

**French
Street**

Greensand Way

Pipers Lane

Piper's Lane

Foxwold

**Brasted
Chart**

Piper's Green Road

Vines
Gate

**The
Chart**

Emmetts Road

Toys Hill

PH

Quornden

The
Phillippines

Emmetts
Garden (NT)

Scords
Wood

5

6

7

8

G H J **127** K L M

Greensand Way

A   B   C   94   D   E   F

1

Combe Bank School

I

Combe Bank Drive

B2211

CHEVENING ROAD

M25

Willow Farm

Chipstead

Chipstead Park Close

Riv

Spanhook

Darent Cl   High Street

Martins Shaw

The Old Carriageway

Chipstead Pk

The Old's Gdn

Witches Lane

Woodfields

Chip

Homedean Rd

Westerham Rd

Packhorse

Nursery Place

New Tree Cl

Amherst County Junior School

WESTERHAM ROAD A25

Larkfield Rd

Bessels Green Rd

Bessels Meadow

COLD ARBOR RD

A25

2

PO   A25   MAIN   ROAD

Manor Road

Chapmans Road

Woodside Road

New Road

Sundridge

WESTERHAM ROAD A25

Dryhill Lane

Dryhill

Bessels Green

BACK LANE

B2042

3

Birchfield Farm

Sundridge Primary School

St Mary's Church Road

Greystone Park

Church Road

Sundridge Place

4

W Gallery M

III

Lodge Barn Farm

Manor Farm

Back Lane

Green Lane

TN14

5

Penn Lane

6

Penn Farm

Whitley Forest

7

Brook Place

Whitley Row

Apps Hollow

Great Norman Street Farm

Cordons Farm

Emmetts Garden (NT)

8

Norman Street

B2042

Nightingale Lane

Goathurst Common

ords ood

Everlands

A   **Ide Hill**   B   C   **128**   D   E   F

Ide Hill School

PO

Camp Lane

WHEATSHEAF HILL

Greensand Way

1 grid square represents 500 metres

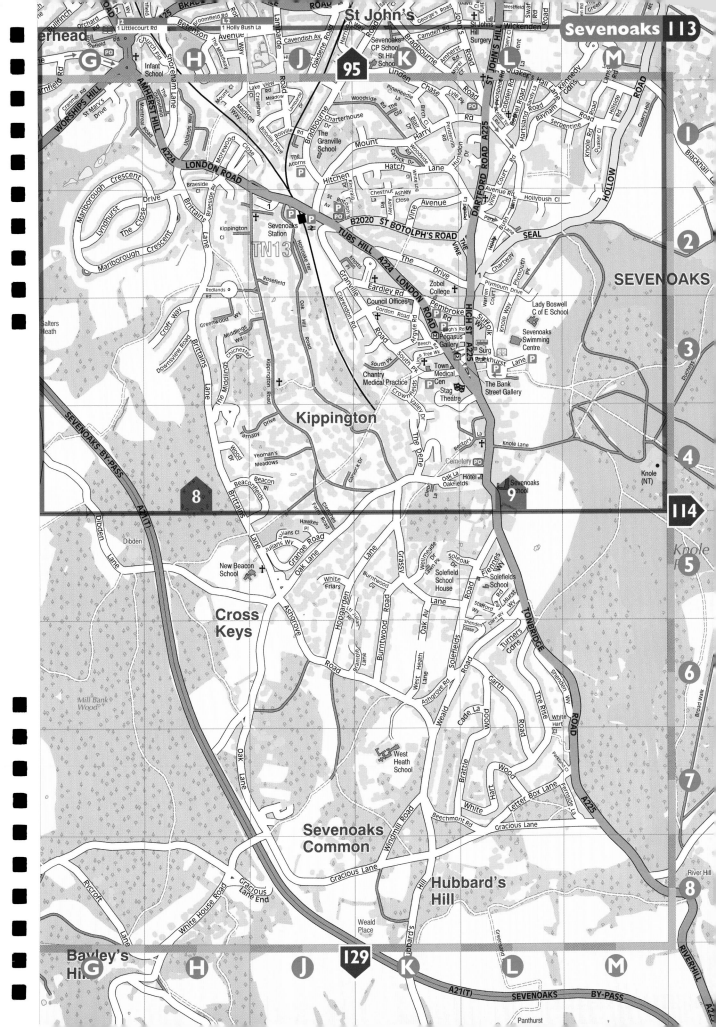

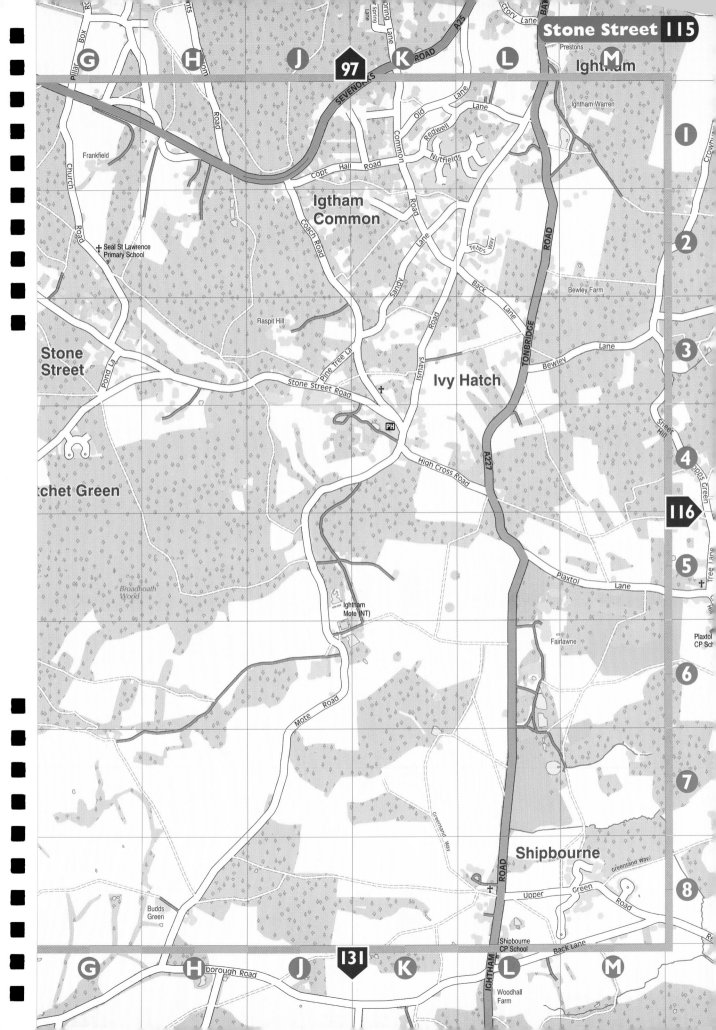

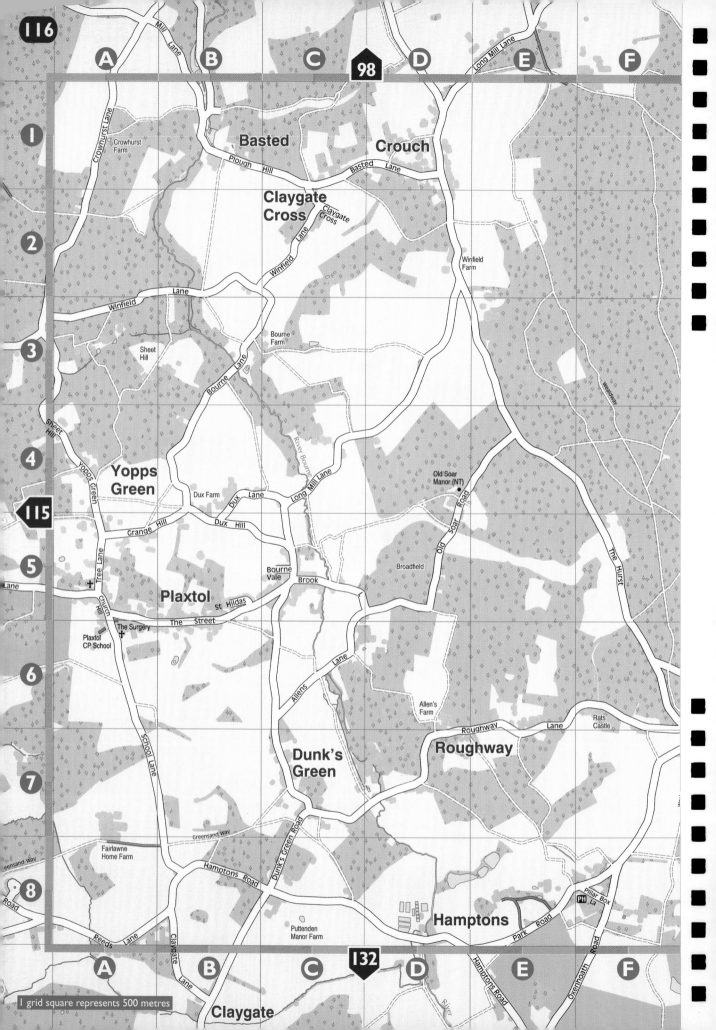

98

115

132

A B C D E F

1
2
3
4
5
6
7
8

Crowhurst Lane
Crowhurst Farm
Mill Lane

Basted

Crouch

Plough Hill
Basted Lane

Long Mill Lane

Claygate Cross

Claygate Cross Lane

Winfield Lane

Winfield Farm

Winfield Lane

Bourne Farm

Sheet Hill

Bourne Lane

River Bourne

Westway

Sheet Hill

Yopps Green

Yopps Green

Dux Farm
Dux Lane

Long Mill Lane

Old Soar Manor (NT)

Grange Hill

Dux Hill

Old Soar Road

The Hurst

Lane

Tree Lane

Bourne Vale

Brook

Broadfield

Plaxtol

St Hilda's

Church Hill

The Street

The Surgery

Plaxtol CP School

Allens Lane

Allen's Farm

Roughway Lane

Rats Castle

Dunk's Green

Roughway

School Lane

Greensand Way

Greensand Way

Fairlawne Home Farm

Hamptons Road

Dunk's Green Road

Reeds Lane

Claygate Lane

Puttenden Manor Farm

Hamptons

Park Road

Hamptons Road

Oxenhoath Road

Pillar Box La

PH

River

Claygate

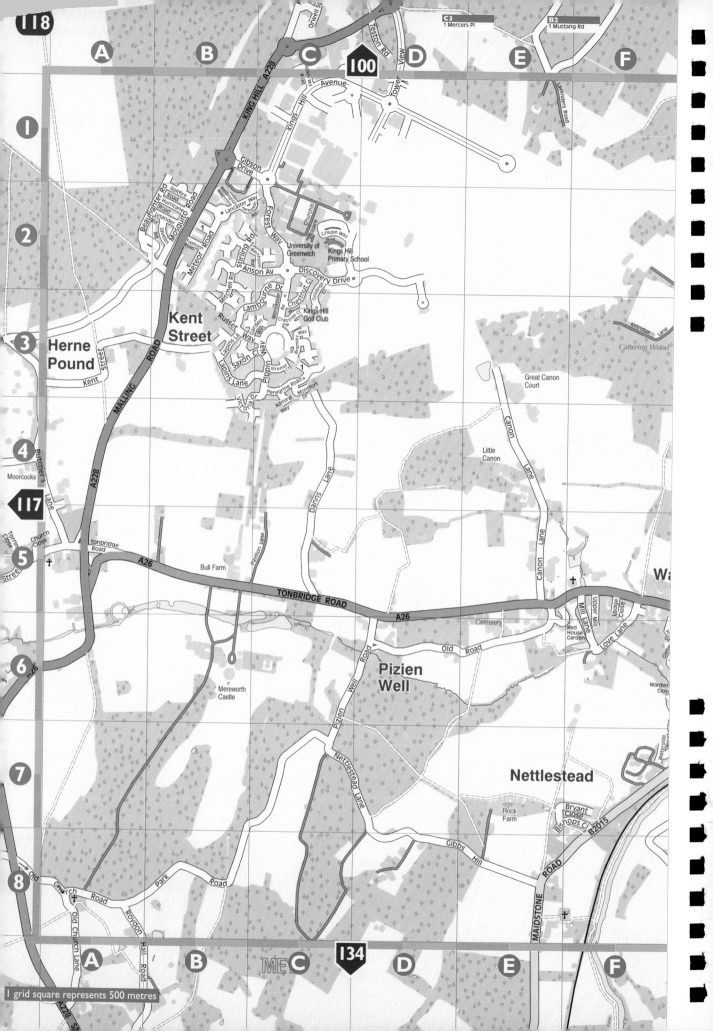

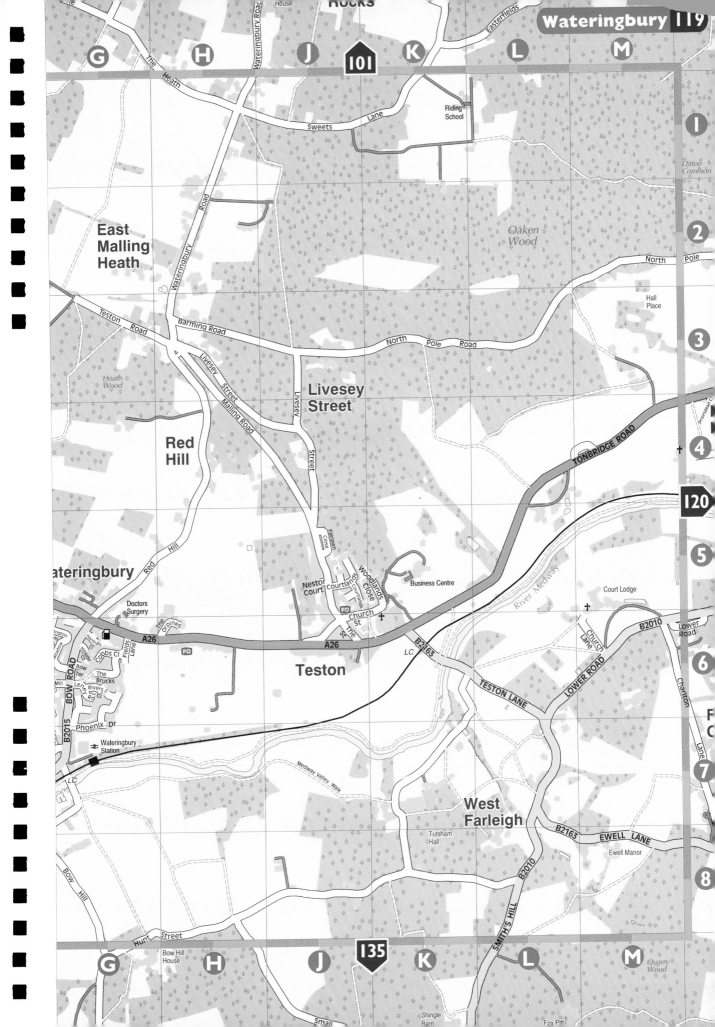

G H J 101 K L M

ROCKS

I

Ditton Common

East Malling Heath

2

North Pole

Oaken Wood

Hall Place

Wateringbury Road

Sweets Lane

Riding School

Teston Road

Barming Road

3

North Pole Road

Hoath Wood

Livesey Street

Red Hill

Livesey Street

Malling Road

TONBRIDGE ROAD

Progsean Cl

+ 4

120

River Medway

Court Lodge

5

Fairlawn Close

Business Centre

+

ateringbury

Red Hill

Doctors Surgery

Nestor Court

Woodlands Close

Courtland

Courtlands

The Cromes

Church St

+

B2010

Lower Road

6

Cobbs Cl

A26

A26

PO

The St

LC

B2163

Church Lane

Charlton Lane

Wimbury Lfields Lane

Fields Lane

PO

Teston

TESTON LANE

LOWER ROAD

BOW ROAD

Bow Ter

The Brucks

Rivers Cl

Rd

F C

B2015

Phoenix Dr

Wateringbury Station

7

Medway Valley Walk

West Farleigh

LC

B2010

B2163

EWELL LANE

Bow Hill

Tutsham Hall

Ewell Manor

8

Hunt Street

G H J 135 K L M

Bow Hill House

SMITH'S HILL

Quarry Wood

Small

Shingle Barn

Fox Pitt

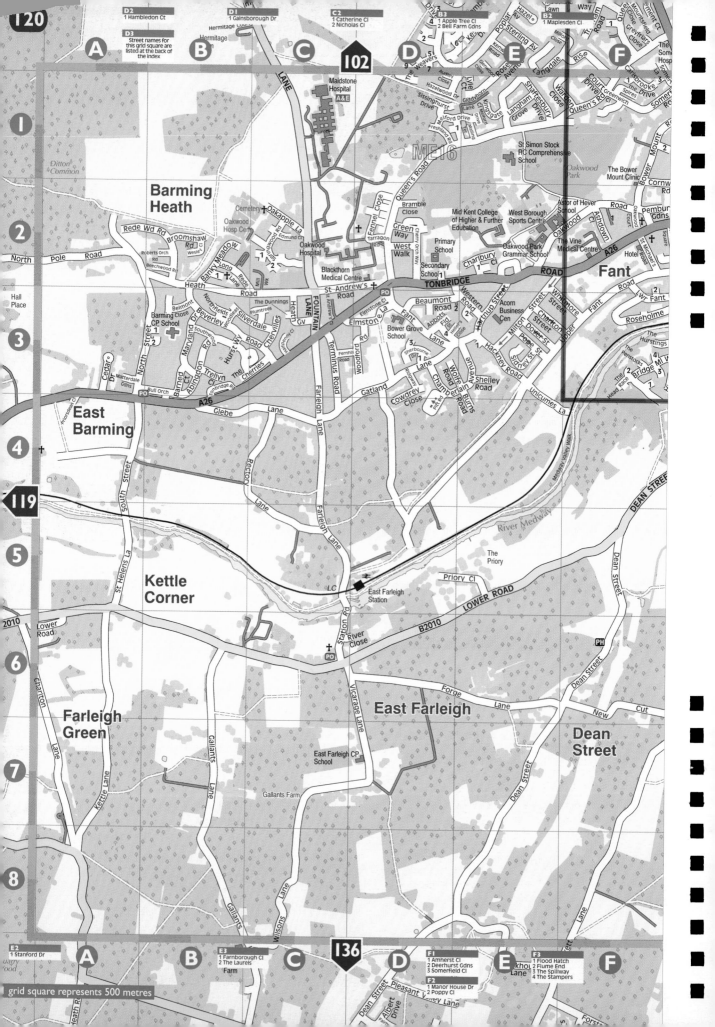

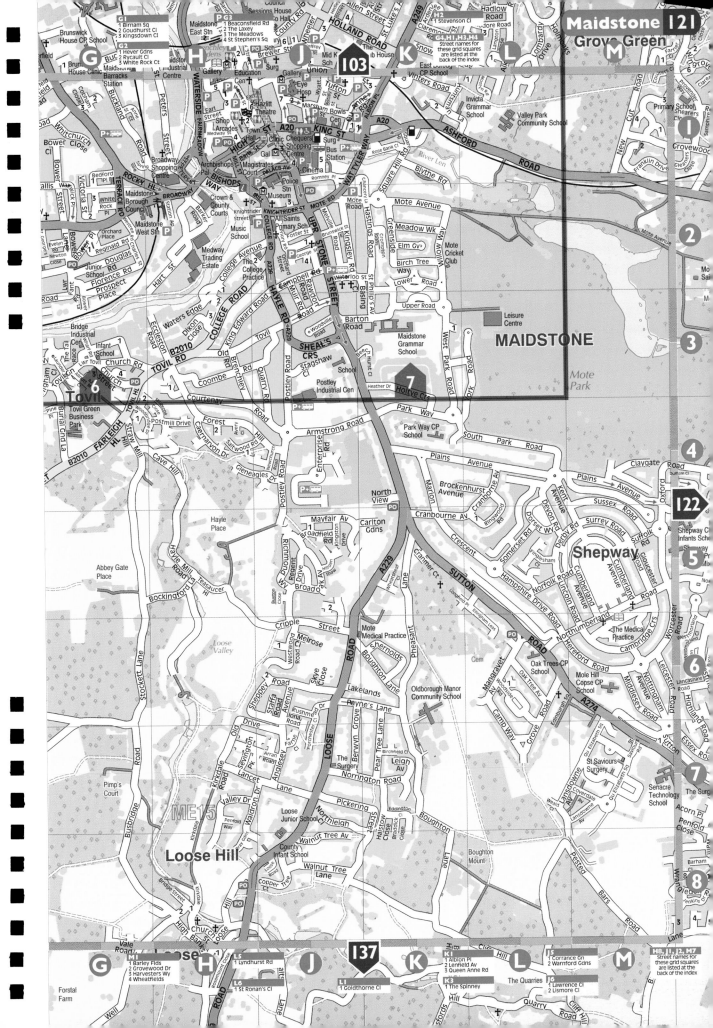

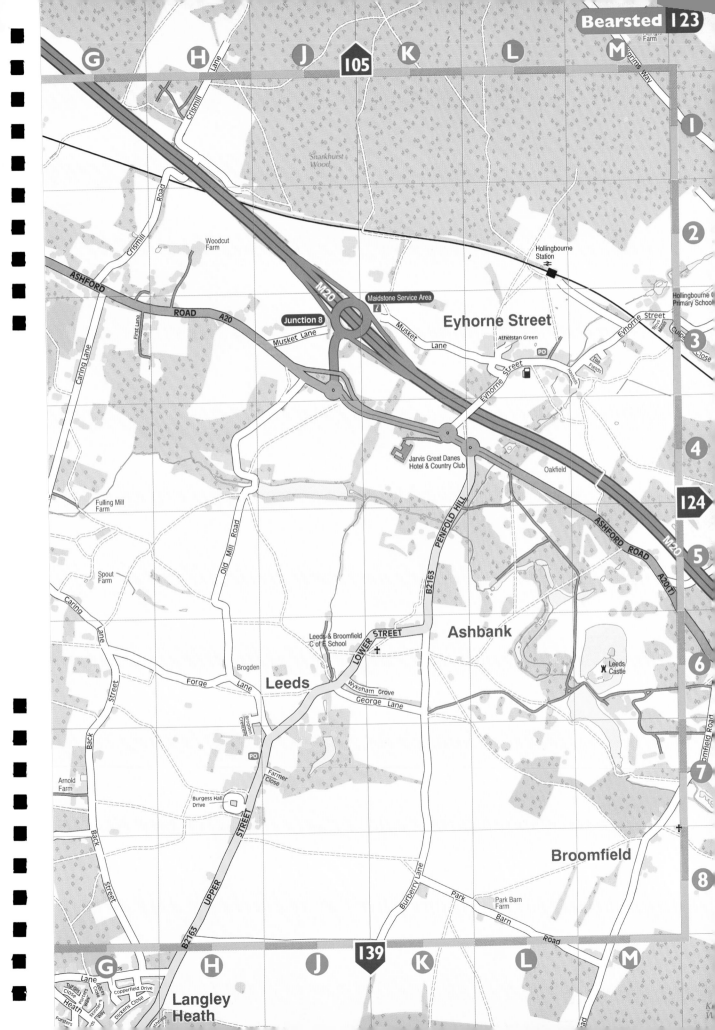

124

A B C D 106 Hollingbourne House E Morning Dawn F

Marshall's Farm

Ringlestone Road

1

North Downs Way

Hollingbourne Hill

2

Upper Street

PH

High Wood

Hollingbourne County Primary School

Pilgrims Way

Hollingbourne

3

Greenway

Culpeper Close

Court

Road

North Downs Way

4

Harpswood

Greenway Court

123

Hospital Road

Greenway Court Road

M20

5

Warren Wood

A20(T)

Court Road

Greenway

6

Greenway Forstal

Greenway Lane

Goddington

Court Lodge Farm

Chegworth Road

Goddington Lane

Broomfield Road

Holm Mill Lane

Harrietsham Station

Harrie

7

Chegworth Lane

ASHFORD ROAD

West Street

Station Road

Chippendayle Drive

Chegworth

M20

A20(T)

HOOK Lane

Quested Way

Forge Meadow

Cricketers Close

PO

Taylor Close

Pollhill

8

Waterlane Farm

Lane

A B 140 C D E F

grid square represents 500 metres

Kings Wood

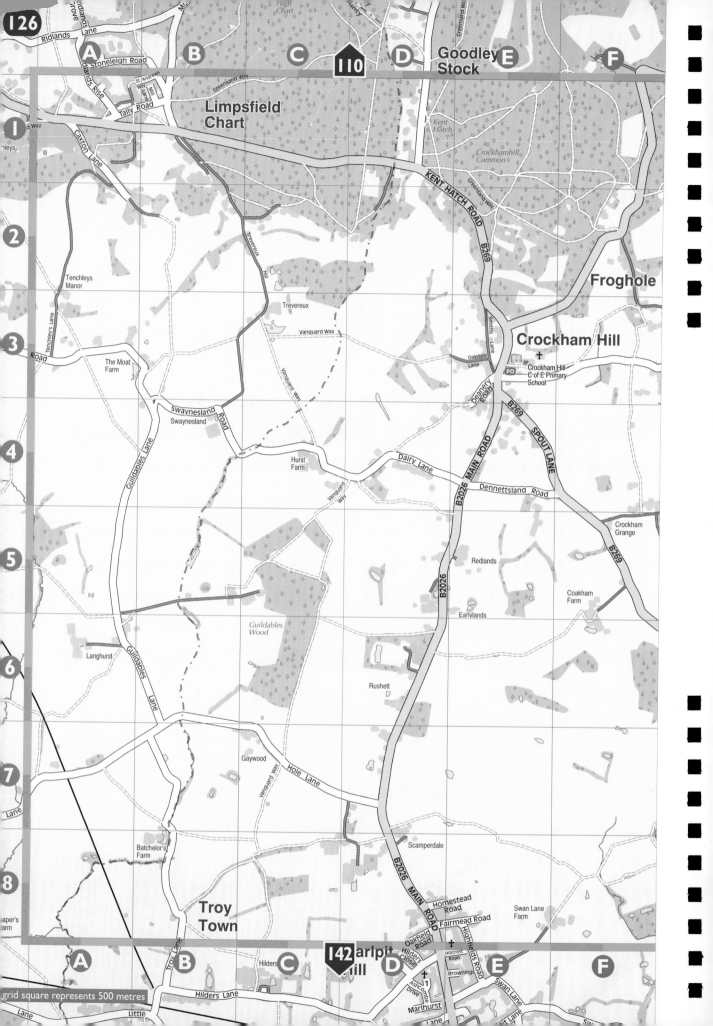

A   B   C   **110**   D   Goodley Stock   E   F

Limpsfield Chart

Ridlands Lane
Stoneleigh Road
St Andrews Way
Mill Lane
Tally Road
Caxton Lane

1

Greensand Way

Kent Hatch

Crockhamhill Common

KENT HATCH ROAD

Froghole

2

Tenchleys Manor

Trevereux Hill

B269

Smiths Lane

Crockham Hill

3

Road
Tenchley's Lane

The Moat Farm

Trevereux

Vanguard Way

Vanguard Way

Oakdale Lane

Crockham Hill C of E Primary School

Deanery Road

4

Swaynesland Road
Swaynesland

Hurst Farm

Dairy Lane

B269   SPOUT LANE

MAIN ROAD   B2026

Dennettsland Road

Guildables Lane

Crockham Grange

B269

5

Redlands

B2026

Coakham Farm

Earlylands

Guildables Wood

6

Langhurst

Guildables Lane

Rushett

7

Gaywood
Vanguard Way   Hole Lane

Scamperdale

B2026   MAIN ROAD

8

Batchelor's Farm

Homestead Road

Swan Lane Farm

Troy Town

Fairmead Road

Oakfield Road

Hilders Close

Highfields Road

Brownings

A   B   Hilders   C   **142** arlpit ill   D   E   F

Hilders Lane
Little
Lane

Ashronhar Drive

Marlhurst   Swan Lane

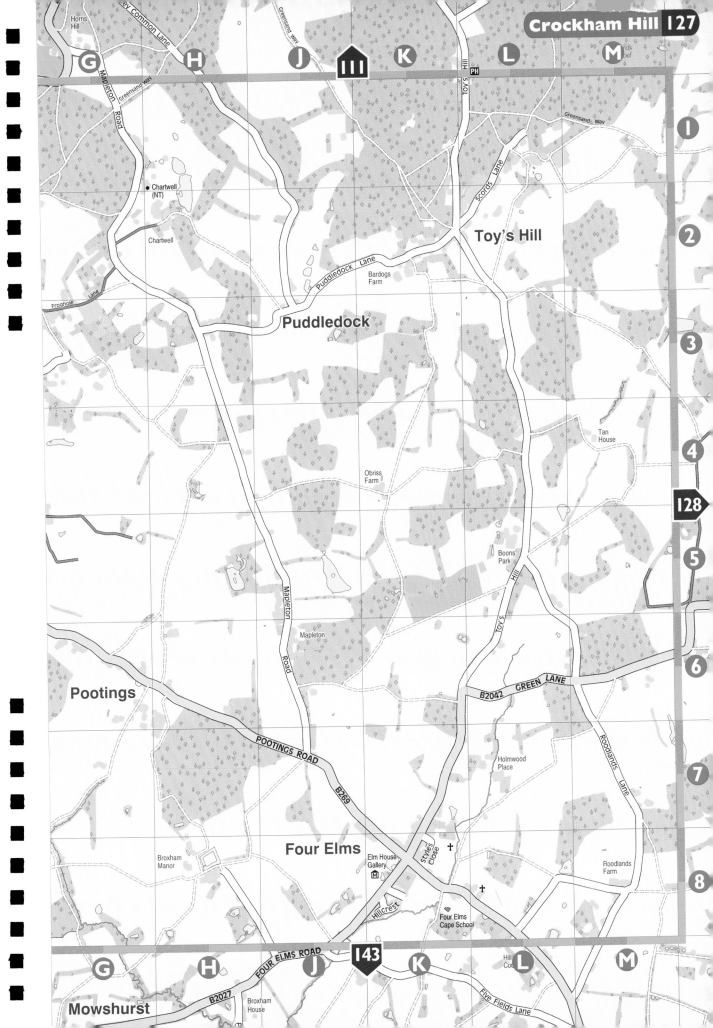

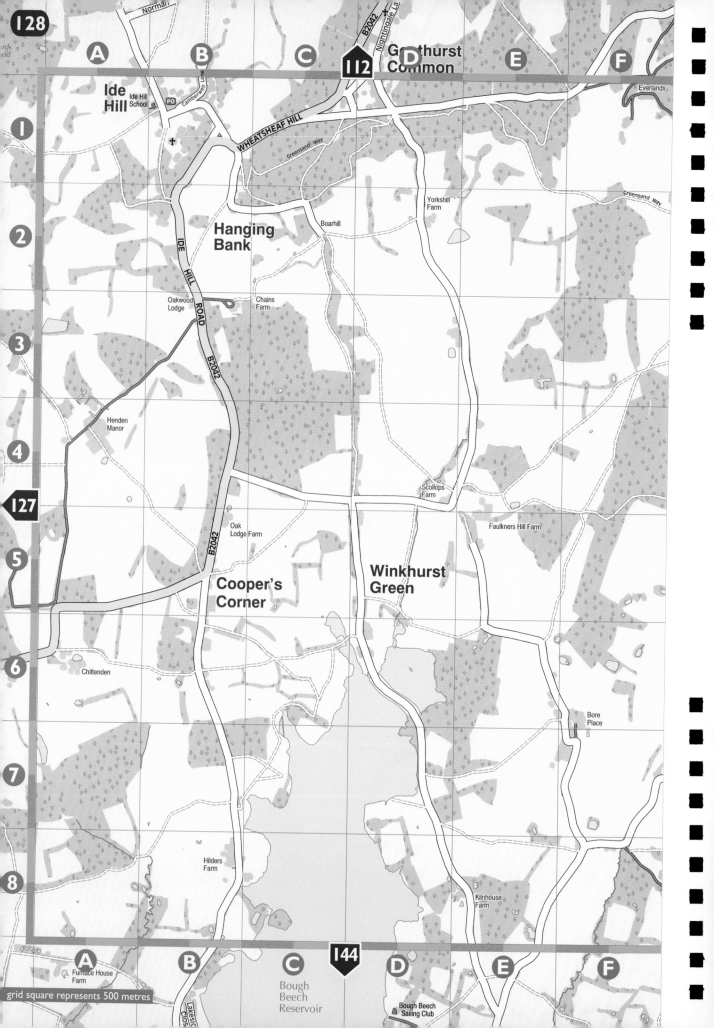

128

A **B** **C** **D** **E** **F**

112

Ide Hill School
PO
Ide Hill
†

WHEATSHEAF HILL

G̲thurst
Common

Everlands

Greensand Way

Greensand Way

1 · · · · · ·

Hanging Bank

Boarhill

Yorkshill Farm

2

Oakwood Lodge

Chains Farm

IDE HILL ROAD

B2042

3

Henden Manor

4

127

Scollops Farm

B2042

Oak Lodge Farm

Faulkners Hill Farm

5

Cooper's Corner

Winkhurst Green

6

Chittenden

Bore Place

7

Hilders Farm

8

A **B** **C** **D** **E** **F**

Furnace House Farm

Lakeside Close

144

Bough Beech Reservoir

Kilnhouse Farm

Bough Beech Sailing Club

grid square represents 500 metres

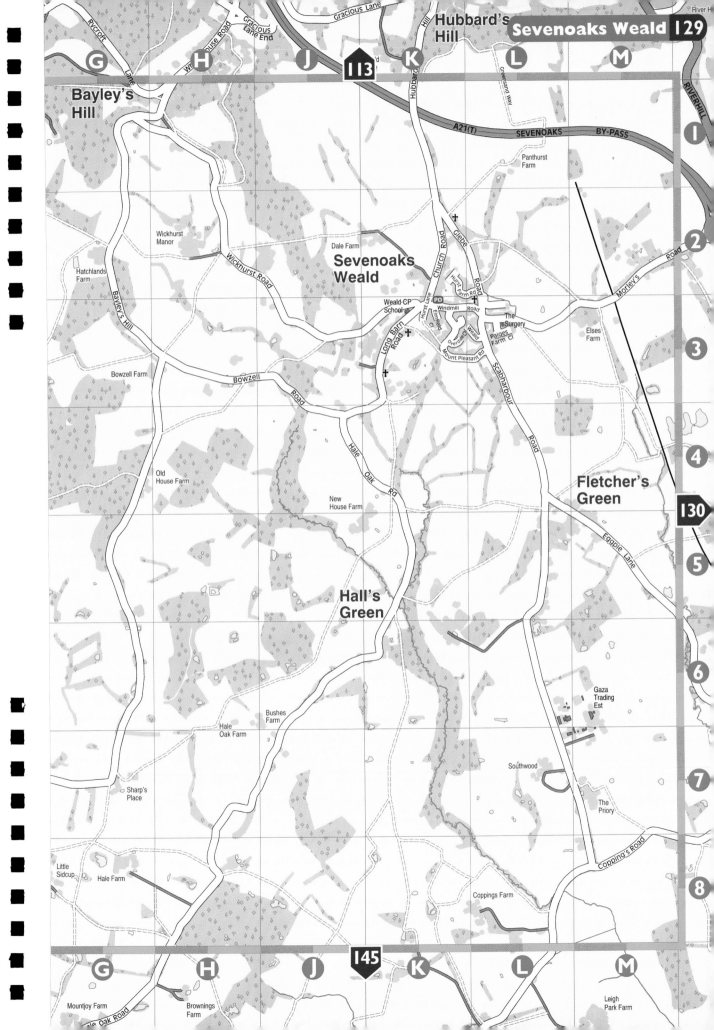

Gracious Lane

River H.

RIVERHILL

Hubbard's
Hill

Hill

RYCROFT

Lane

W'r
House Road

Gracious
Lane End

Hubbard's

Hill

Creesand Way

A21(T)   SEVENOAKS   BY-PASS

**Bayley's
Hill**

Panthurst
Farm

Morley's

Road

Wickhurst
Manor

Dale Farm

**Sevenoaks
Weald**

Church Road

Glebe

Road

Hurst Farm Rd

Panthurst
Farm

Hatchlands
Farm

Wickhurst Road

Weald CP
School

Hurst Lane

PO

Windmill

Elmfield
Cl

The

Surgery

Palges
Farm Cl

Elses
Farm

Bayley's Hill

Long Barn
Road

Overdale

Weald

Road

Mount Pleasant Rd

Bowzell Farm

Bowzell

Road

Scabharbour

Road

**Fletcher's
Green**

**Old
House Farm**

Hale

Oak

Rd

New
House Farm

Eggpie Lane

**Hall's
Green**

Gaza
Trading
Est

Bushes
Farm

Southwood

Hale
Oak Farm

Sharp's
Place

The
Priory

Copping's Road

Little
Sidcup

Hale Farm

Coppings Farm

Mountjoy Farm

Hale Oak Road

Brownings
Farm

Leigh
Park Farm

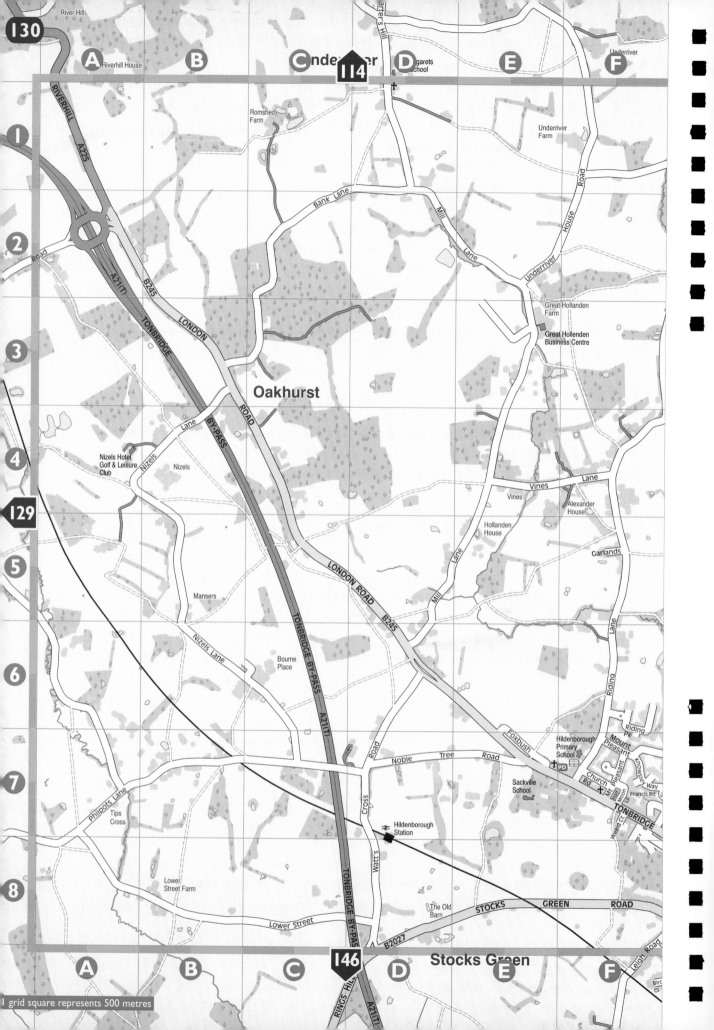

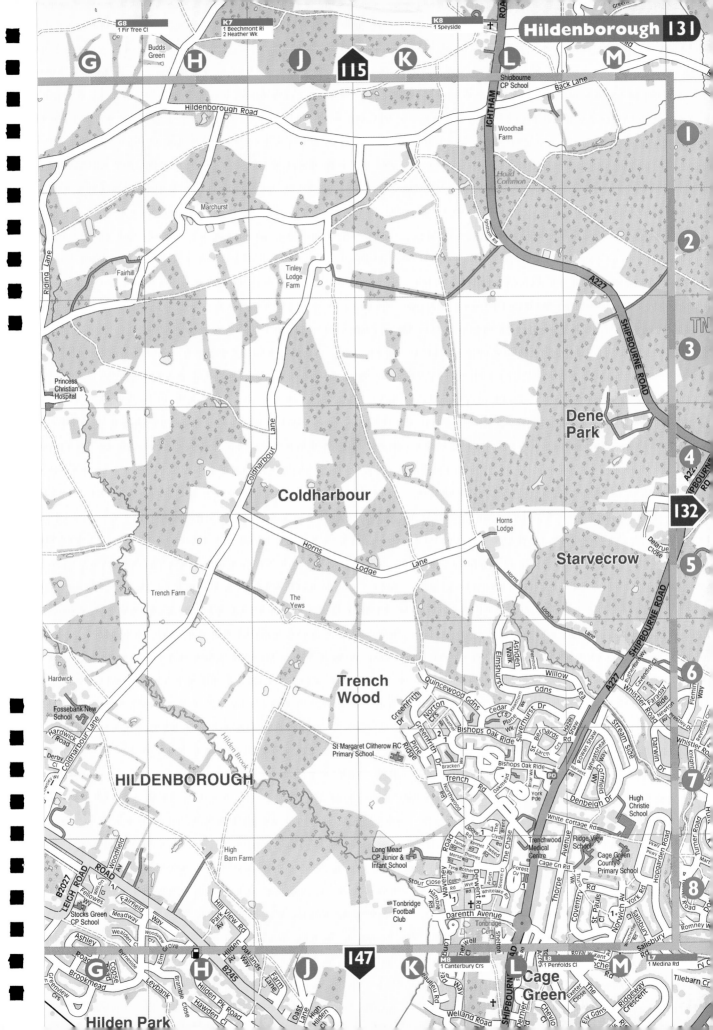

G8
1 Fir Tree Cl

K7
1 Beechmont Ri
2 Heather Wk

K8
1 Speyside

G **H** **J** **115** **K** **L** **M**

Shipbourne
CP School

Back Lane

Hildenborough Road

Woodhall
Farm

Marchurst

I

Ightham Rd

2

A227

Fairhill

Tinley
Lodge
Farm

TN

3

Princess
Christian's
Hospital

Coldharbour Lane

Coldharbour

Dene
Park

SHIPBOURNE ROAD

4

A2-
SHIPBOURNE RD

132

Horns
Lodge

Horns   Lodge   Lane

Starvecrow

Delarue
Close

5

Trench Farm

The
Yews

Horns

Lodge

Lane

SHIPBOURNE ROAD

Hardwick

**Trench
Wood**

Ashden
Walk

Elmshurst

Willow

Gdns

Lea

A227

Rutherford

Whistler Rd

Cavendish

Faraday
Ride

Fleming Way

Newton

Flemi

6

Fossebank New
School

Hardwick
Road

Coldharbour Lane

Hilden Brook

Greenfrith
Dr

Norton
Crs

Greenfrith Dr

Quincewood Gdns

Cedar
Crs

Silverhurst
Dr

Plate
Wk

Bernards

St
Larch

Hazel
Rd

Rowan Shaw

Harvest
Rd

Wheatsheaf
Way

Cornfield

Stream
Side

Darwin
Dr

Whistler Rd

7

Derby
Cl

Bracken

St Margaret Clitherow RC
Primary School

Pine
Ridge

Bishops Oak Ride

Trench
Rd

Northwood
Rd

York
Pde

Bishops Oak Ride

PO

Denbeigh Dr

Hugh
Christie
School

HILDENBOROUGH

The
Bretr

Clyde

Tamar

Kennet

Tweed

Mersey

White Cottage Rd

Ridge View
School

Cage Green
County
Primary School

Hopgarden Rd

Turner Road

8

B2027

LEIGH ROAD

Woodfield

ROAD

Fellowes

AV

Fairfield

Meadway

Way

Woodview

Elm Grove

Hill View Rd

Park View
AV

Hilden
Oaklands
Way

High
Barn Farm

Long Mead
CP Junior &
Infant School

Tyne

Rother

Stour Close

Colne

Severn
Rd

Wye
Rd

Whitelake

Derwent

Forest
Cv

Thuro

Thorpe
AV

Coventry
Rd

St Pauls

Norwich Av

York
Rd

Winchester

Salisbury
Rd

Ridgeway
Crescent

Tilebarn Cr

Ashley

Wealden

Byrneside

Greenview
Crs

Brookmead

Levbank

Copse

Bramble close

Hilden Pk Road

Coast
Lane

Farm
Lane

Tonbridge
Football
Club

Darenth Avenue

Tonbridge
Cem

Shelton

The
Well

Acres

Royal

Derrier

Penfolds Cl

Chevio

Ely Gdns

G **H** **147** **J** **K** **L** **M**

1 Canterbury Crs

1 Penfolds Cl

1 Medina Rd

**Cage
Green**

Hilden Park

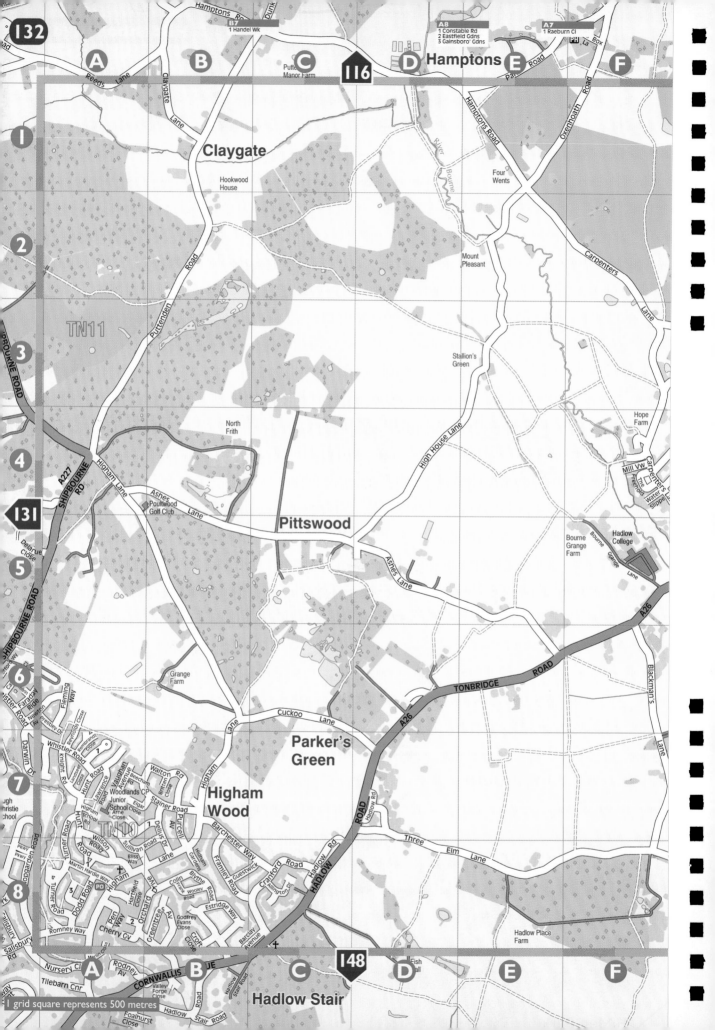

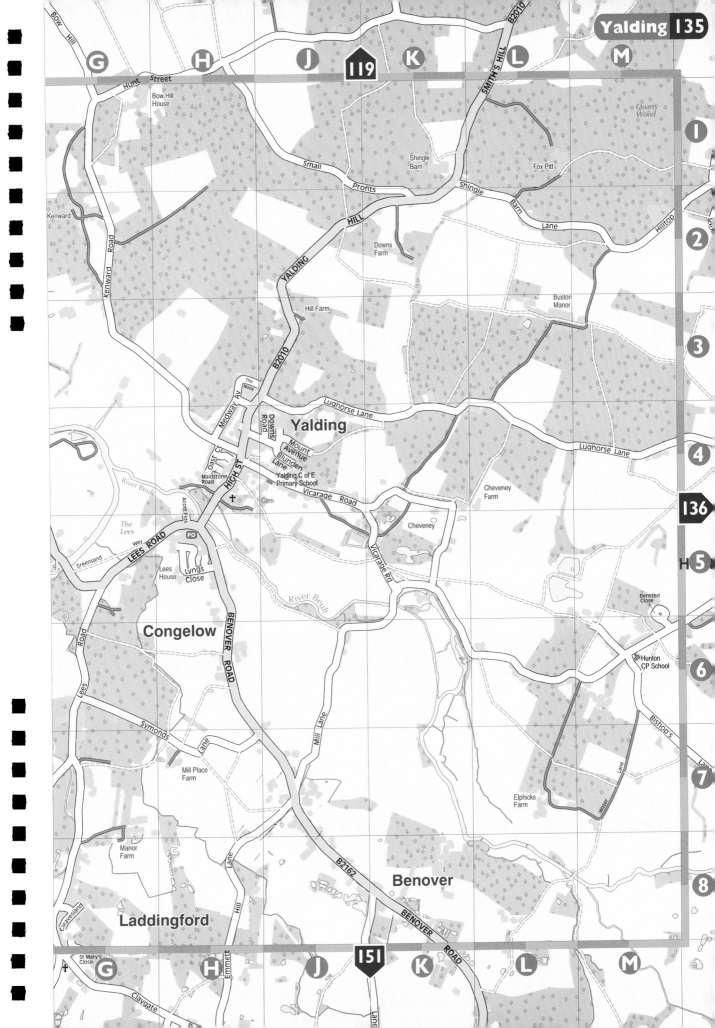

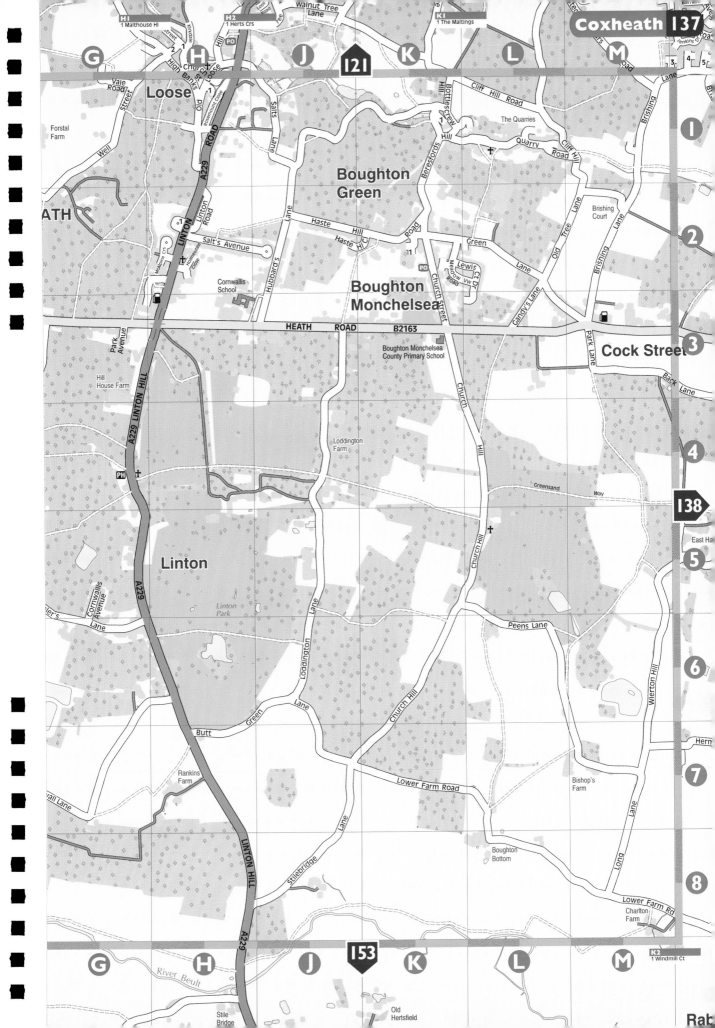

122

B1
1 Coldred Rd
2 Collington Ter
3 Lymington Ct
4 Somner Wk

D4
1 Mercer Wy

Barham
Bellwood Junior School
Avenue
Brishing Lane
Haslemere Industrial Est
Haslemere Trading Est
Rumwood Court
Langley

A B C D E F

Park Wood
Holy Family Catholic Primary School
Longshaw Road
Selby Rd
Bicknor Road
Cuxton Road
Birchott Road
Parkwood Industrial Estate
Wren Industrial Estate
Heronden Road
Langley Park Farm
Horseshoes

1

Pal Industrial Est
Target Business Cen Birchott Road
Boxmend Industrial Est
Orchard Industrial Est
Rectory Farm

2

Mount Pleasant Farm

Back Street

3

Back Lane
Wierton Lane
Brishing Road
Pleasant Farm
Fir Tree Farm
PLOUGH WENTS ROAD B2163
Norton Road

Cobfield
Lested Lane
Laxton Drive
Chart Corner
Warm

4

Amber Lane
Amberfield
PO
Warmlake Road
Marsham Crs
Chart Hl Road
Church Road

137

East Hall
Wierton Rd
Wierton
Chart Hill Road
Chart Hill
Underhill School
Cobtree Medical Ce
Sutton Valence CP School

5

Greensand Way
Greensand Way
Chart Road

Wierton
Heronden
Rectory Lane

6

East Hall Hill
Hermitage Lane
Lucks Lane
Chart Hill Road
Forsham Lane
Spark's Hall

7

Lamb's Cross
Forge Lane
Chart Sutton
Green Lane
Chart Bottom Farm
Charlton

8

er Farm Rd

A B C D E F

154

Holbrook
Moat Farm
Lake

1 grid square represents 500 metres

Rabbit's

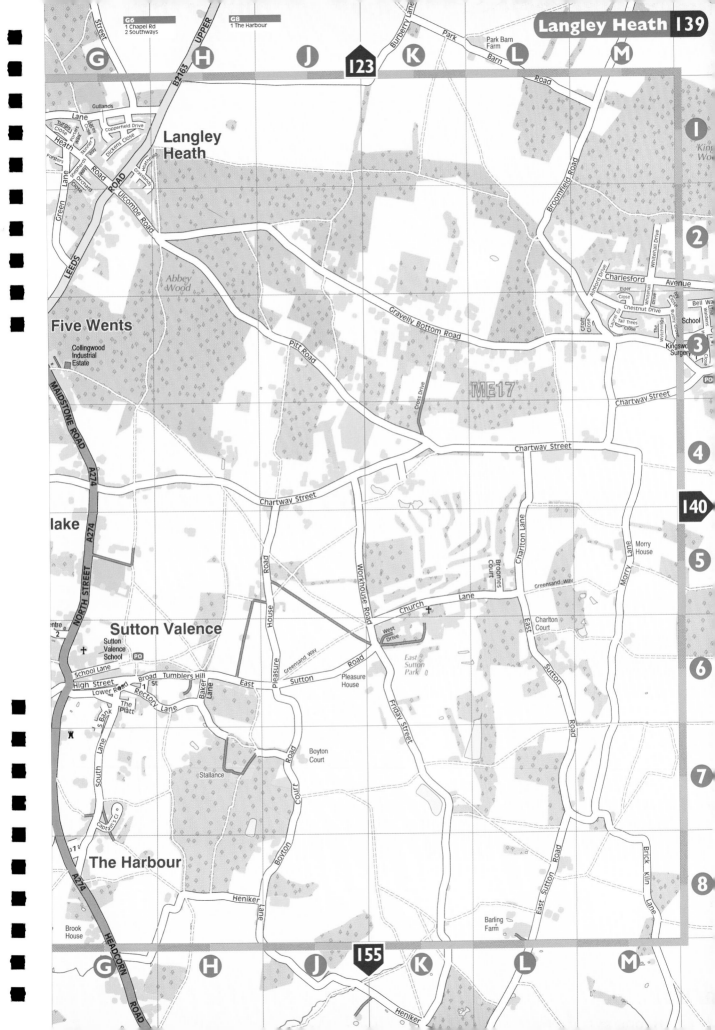

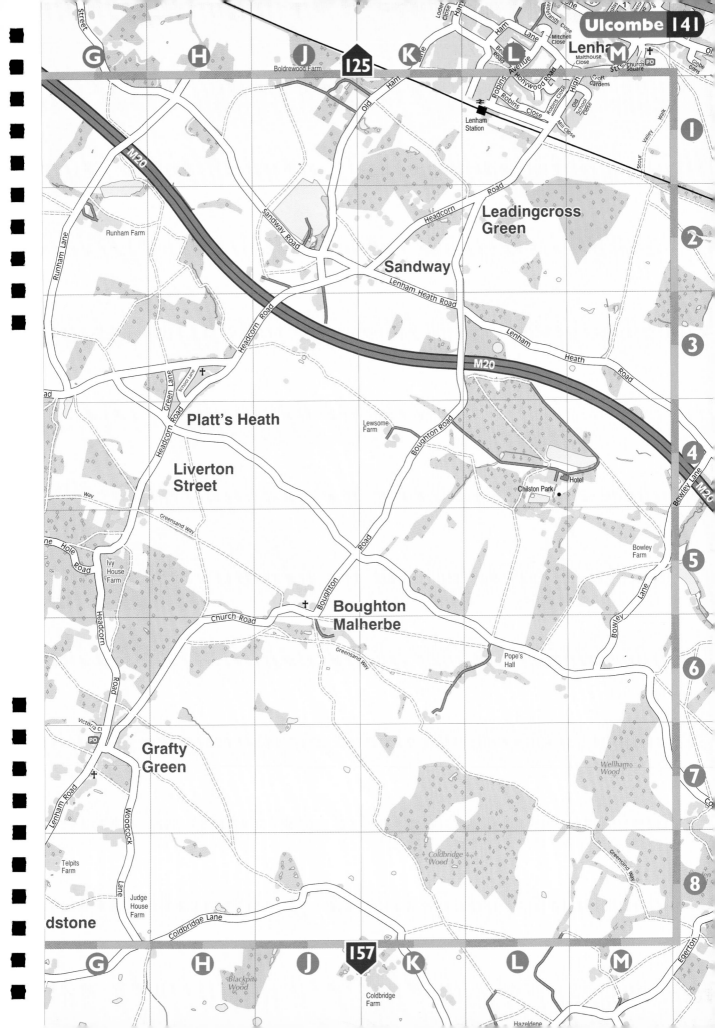

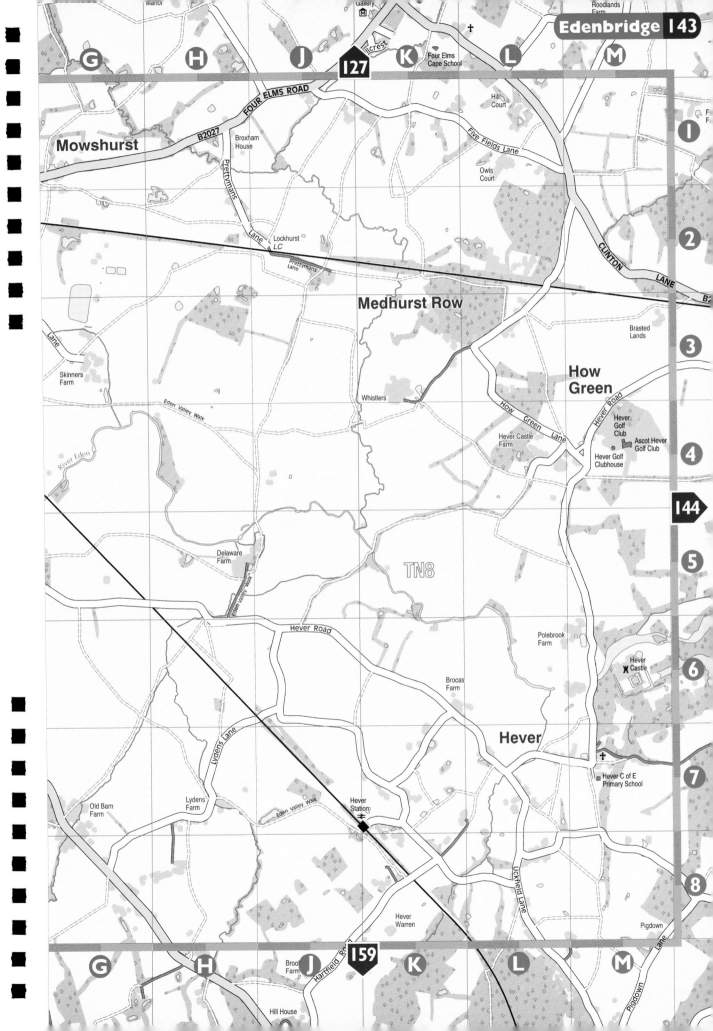

G H J K L M

127

I
2
3
4
144
5
6
7
8

Mowshurst

Four Elms
Cape School

Hillcrest

FOUR ELMS ROAD

B2027

Broxham
House

Prettymans
Lane

Lockhurst
LC

Prettymans
Lane

Hill
Court

Five Fields Lane

Owls
Court

CLINTON LANE

Medhurst Row

Brasted
Lands

How
Green

Skinners
Farm

Lane

Whistlers

How Green Lane

Hever Road

Hever Castle
Farm

Hever
Golf
Club

Ascot Hever
Golf Club

Hever Golf
Clubhouse

River Eden

Eden Valley Walk

Delaware
Farm

Eden Valley Walk

TN8

Hever Road

Polebrook
Farm

Hever
Castle

Brocas
Farm

Hever

Lydens Lane

Old Barn
Farm

Lydens
Farm

Eden Valley Walk

Hever
Station

Hever C of E
Primary School

Hever
Warren

Uckfield Lane

Pigdown

G H J K L M

159

Brook
Farm

Hartfield Road

Hill House

Pigdown Lane

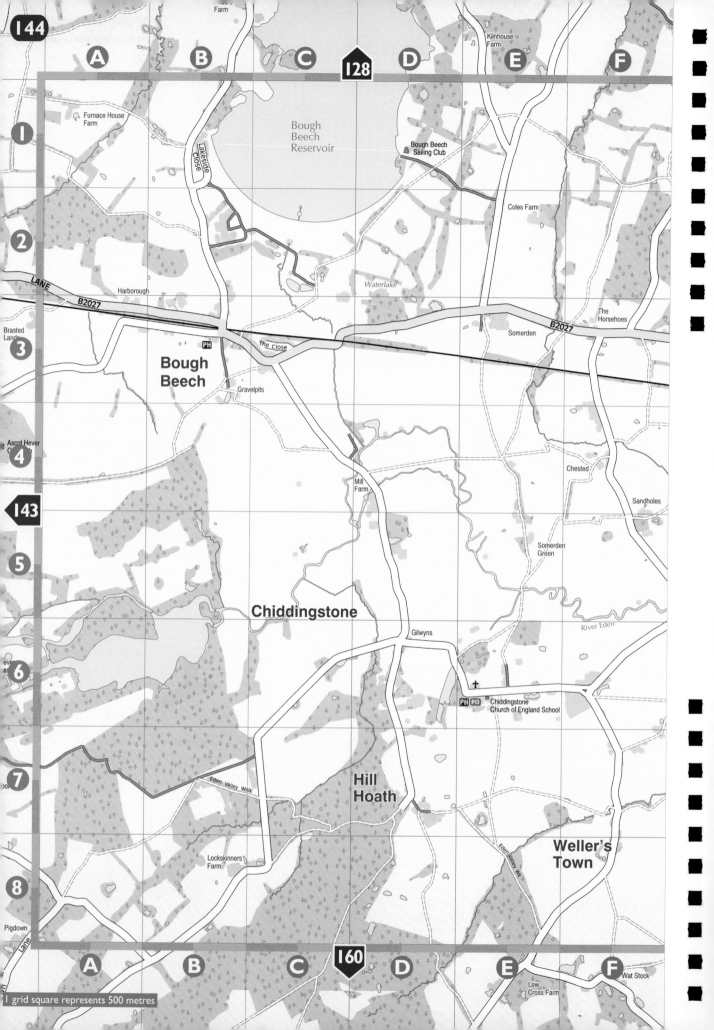

144

A   B   **128**   C   D   E   F

I

Furnace House
Farm

Bough
Beech
Reservoir

Kilnhouse
Farm

Bough Beech
Sailing Club

Coles Farm

2

LANE

Harborough

B2027

Waterlake

B2027

The Horsehoes

Somerden

3

Brasted
Lande

PH

The Close

**Bough
Beech**

Gravelpits

Ascot Hever
G Club

4

Mill
Farm

Chested

Sandholes

143

5

Somerden
Green

Chiddingstone

Gilwyns

River Eden

6

eve
as

PH PO

Chiddingstone
Church of England School

7

Eden Valley Walk

**Hill
Hoath**

**Weller's
Town**

Lockskinners
Farm

Eden Valley Wk

8

Pigdown

Lane

A   B   **160**   C   D   E   Wat Stock   F

Lew
Cross Farm

I grid square represents 500 metres

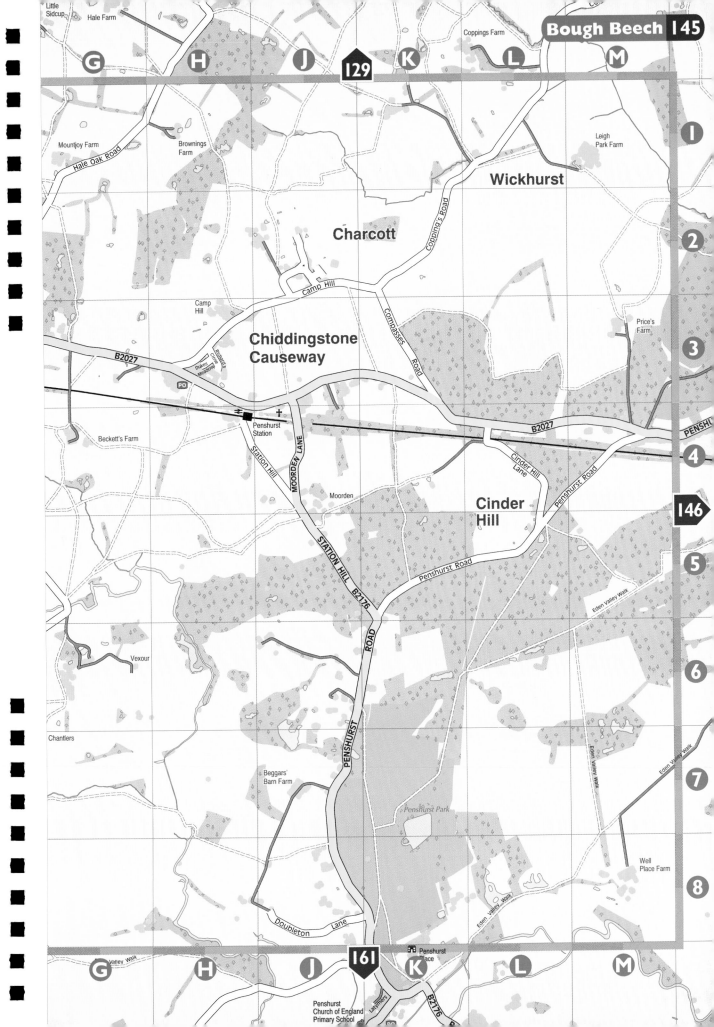

Little
Sidcup

Hale Farm

Coppings Farm

G   H   J   **129**   K   L   M

Mountjoy Farm

Brownings
Farm

Leigh
Park Farm

1

Wickhurst

Hale Oak Road

Charcott

Coppings Road

Camp Hill

2

Price's
Farm

Camp
Hill

**Chiddingstone
Causeway**

Compasses Road

3

B2027

Dukes Meadow

Richard's Close

PO

B2027

PENSH

Beckett's Farm

Penshurst
Station

Moorden Lane

Cinder Hill
Lane

4

Station Hill

Moorden

Penshurst Road

**Cinder
Hill**

146

STATION HILL B2176

Penshurst Road

5

Eden Valley Walk

Vexour

6

Chantlers

Eden Valley Walk

PENSHURST ROAD

Beggars'
Barn Farm

Eden Valley Walk

7

Penshurst Park

Well
Place Farm

8

Valley Walk

Doubleton   Lane

G   H   J   **161**   K   L   M

Penshurst
Place

B2176

Penshurst
Church of England
Primary School

Latymers

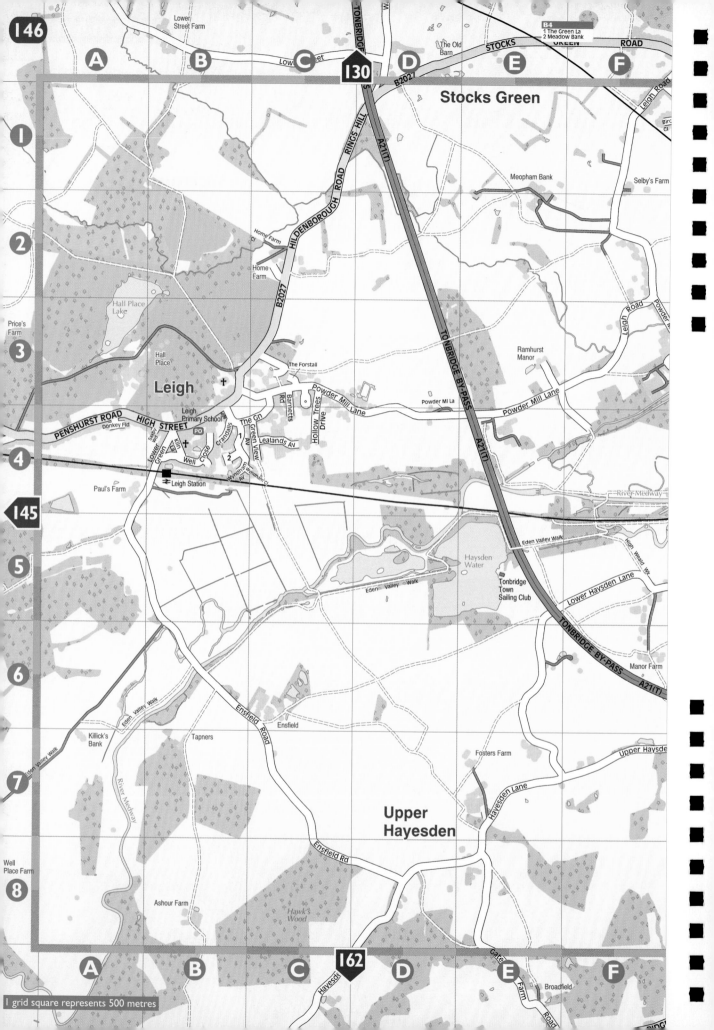

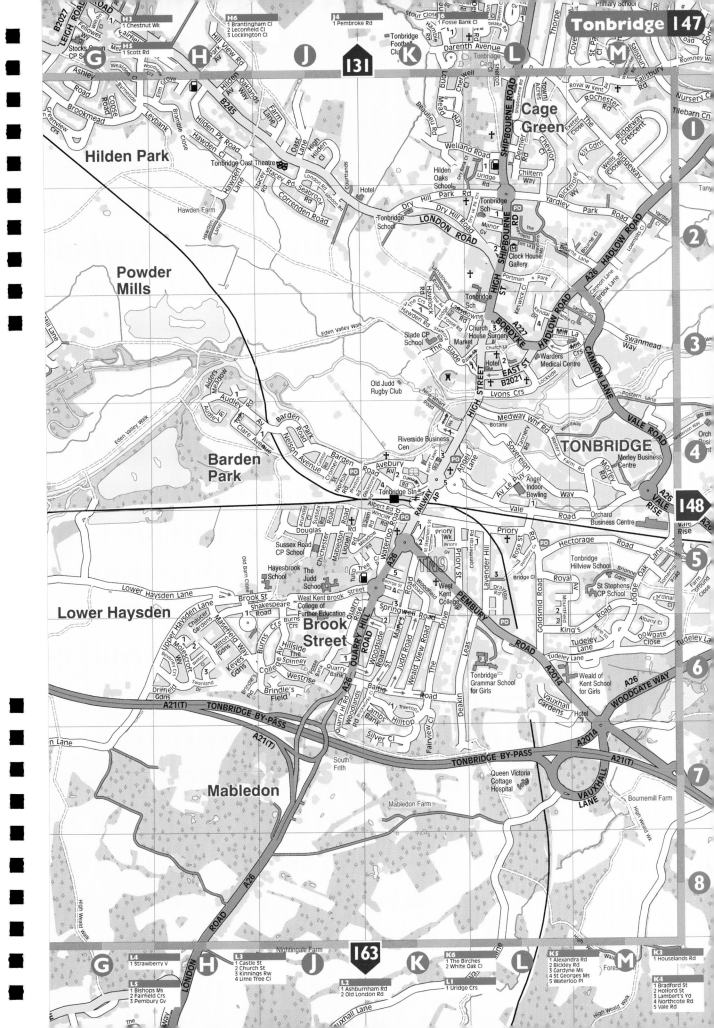

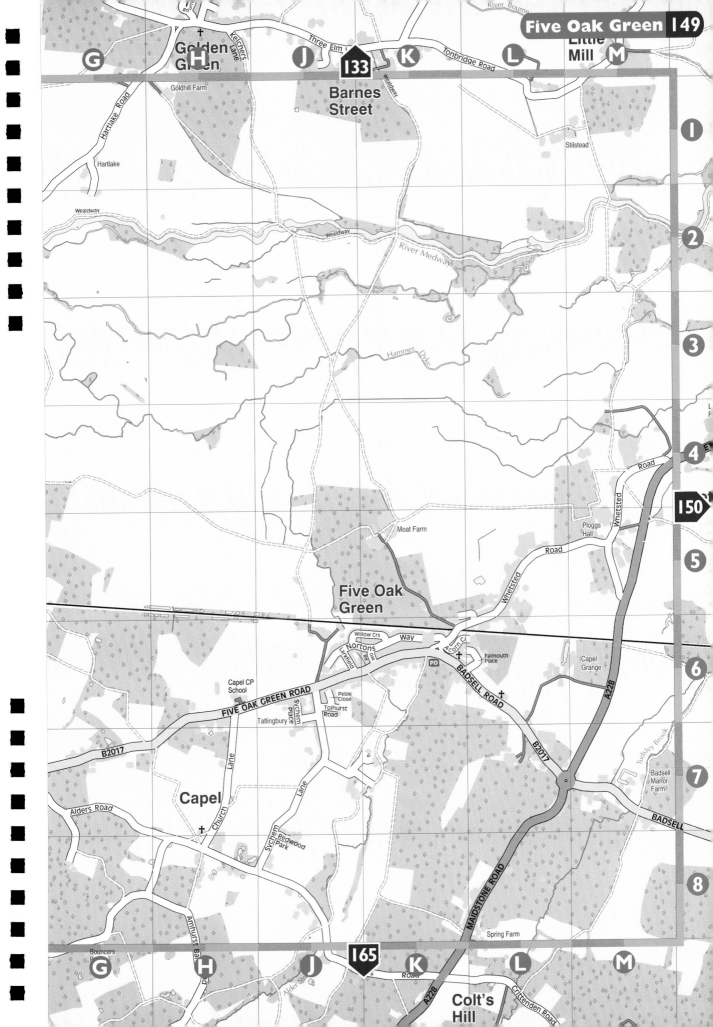

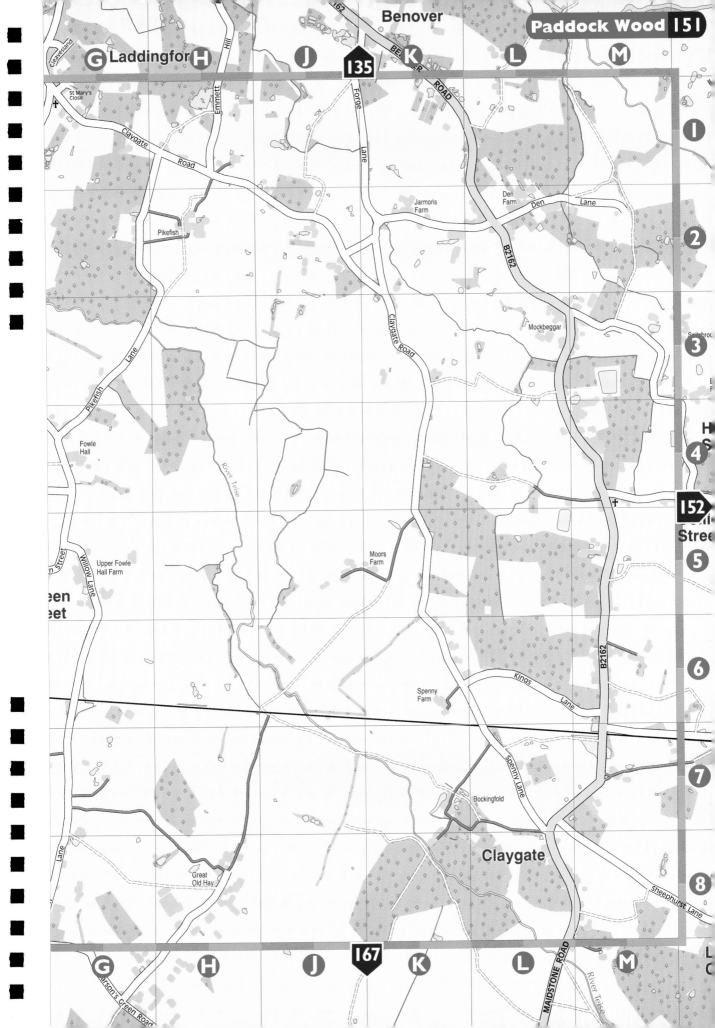

A B C **136** D E F

F8
1 Jewell Gv
2 Napoleon Dr
3 Oak Tree Cl
4 Stella Cl
5 Sunburst Cl

F7
1 Merchant Pl

E7
1 Barrel Arch Cl
2 Lime Cl

1

2

3

4

151

5

6

7

8

Chainhurst

Dairy Lane
Dairy House
Reed Court Farm

Great Tilden
Tilden Lane
Chain Dene Farm

New Lodge House

Hunton Road

Spitzbrook

Bradenbury Farm

Haviker Street

Lesser Teise

Murzie Farm

Broad Forstal Farm

Green Lane

Collier Street

Gatehouse Farm

Tilden Lane

Underlyn Lane

Hunton Road

Little Pattenden

Pattenden Lane

Little Pattenden

Brook Farm

Longend Farm

Wheelbarrow Park Estate

Guardian Industrial Estate

Church Farm

Great Pattenden

TN12

Turkey Farmhouse

Crest Industrial Estate

Marden Station

Sovereigns Way

B2079

CHURCH GREEN

HIGH ST

enden Cl

Hgh

Way

Marden Medical Centre

Marden CP School

Coudhurst Road

Sutton Ct

Sutton Forge

Roundel Wy

Albion Road

Barnes Walk

South Road

MARDEN

Little Cheveney Farm

Gravelpit Farm Cotts

Westfield House

Little Cheveney

A B **168** C D E F

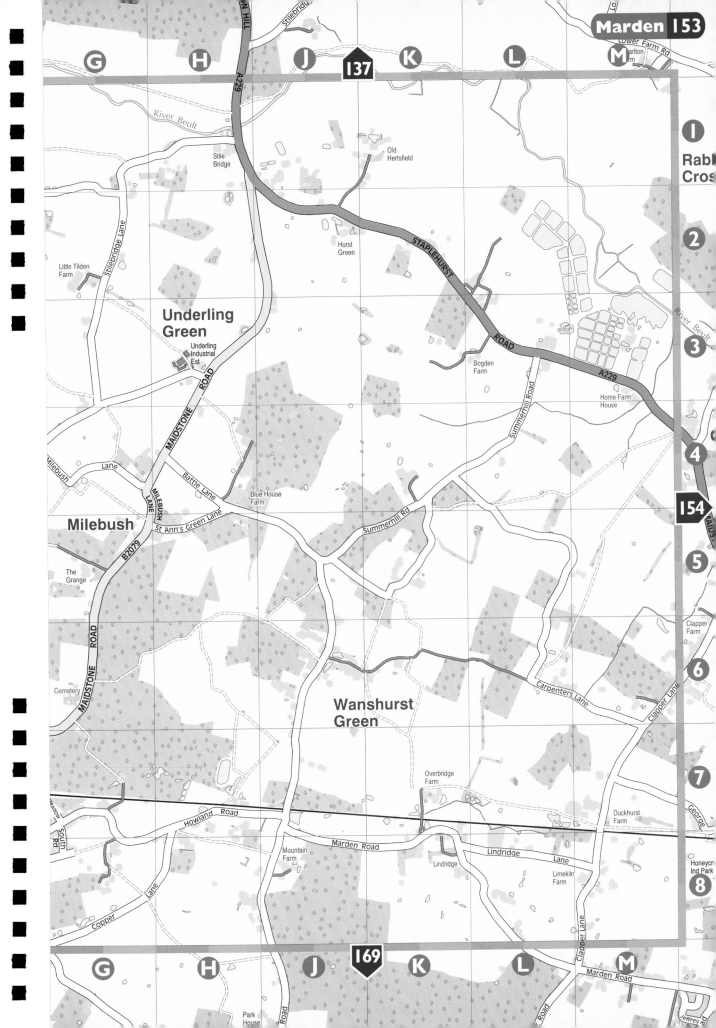

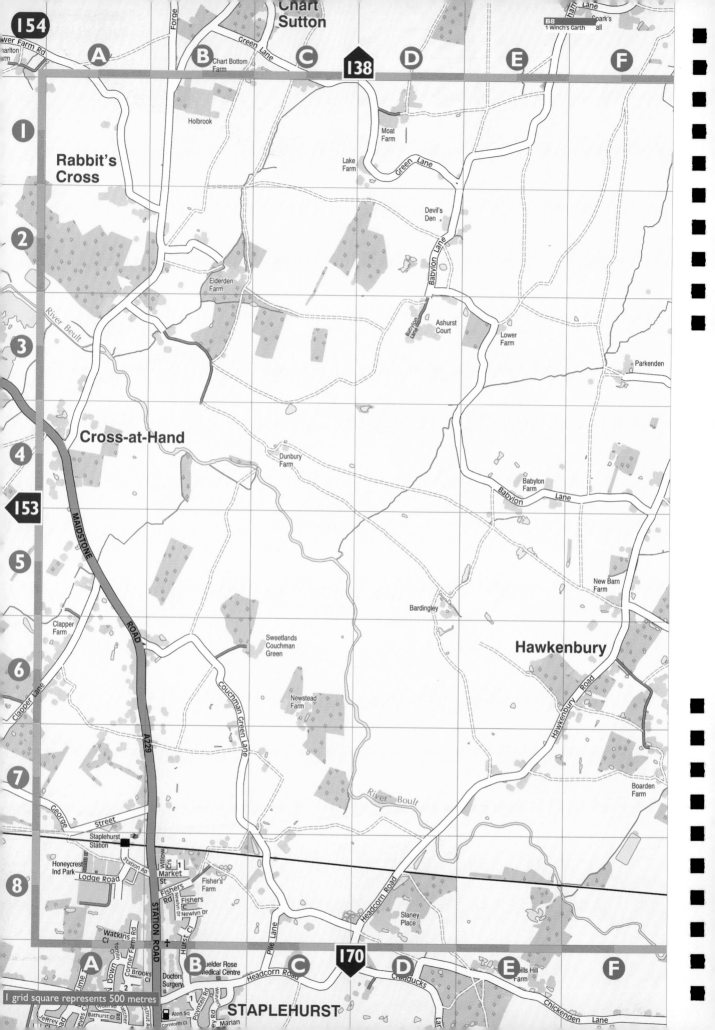

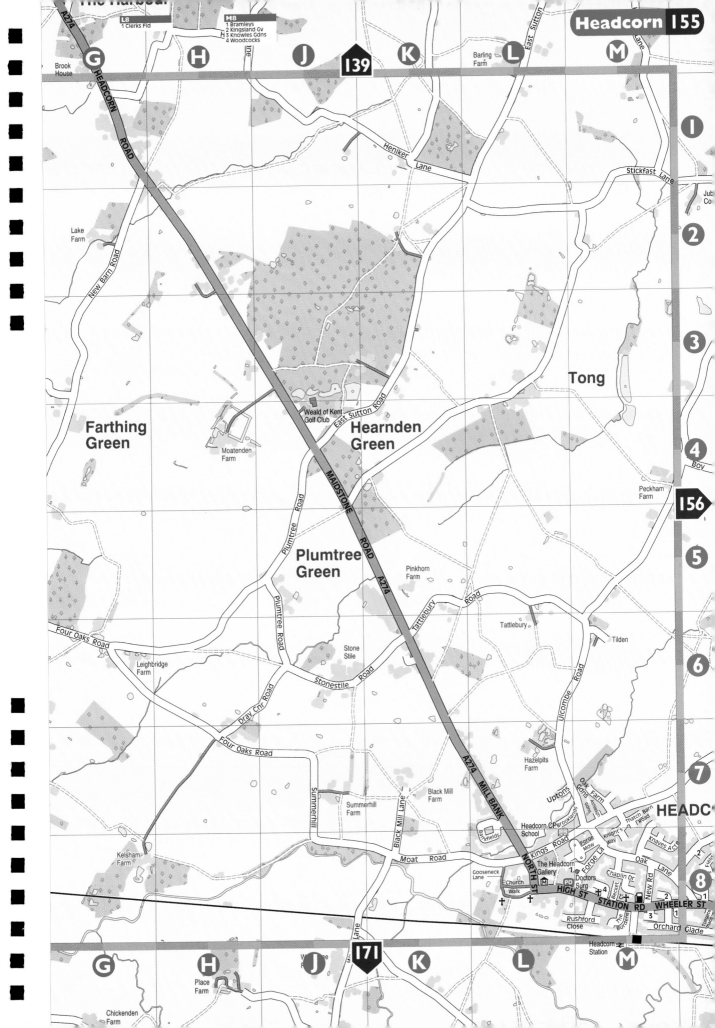

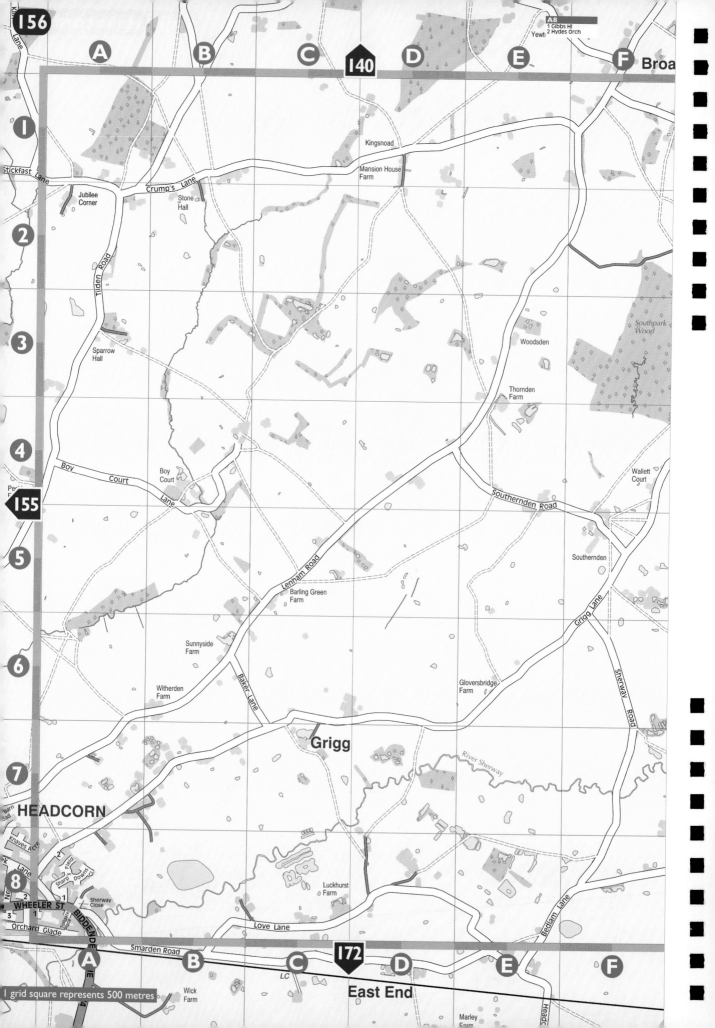

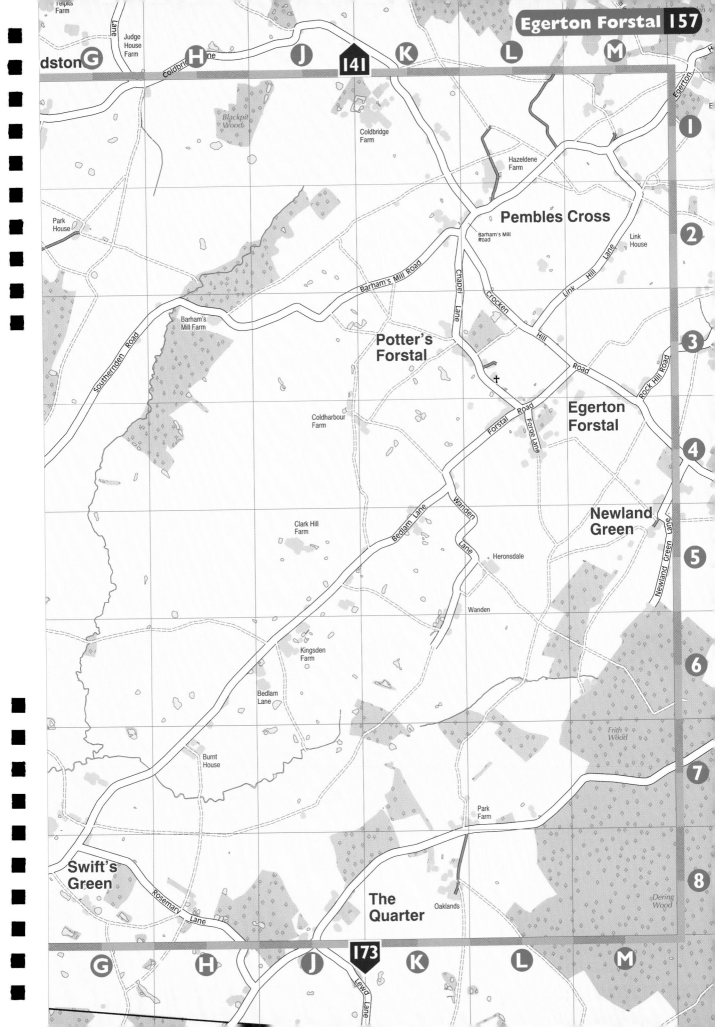

G H J **141** K L M

I

Judge
House
Farm

Coldbrid ne

*Blackpit
Wood*

Coldbridge
Farm

Hazeldene
Farm

2

Pembles Cross

Park
House

Barham's Mill
Road

Link
House

Barham's Mill Road

Chapel Lane

Crocken

Link Hill Lane

Southernden Road

Barham's
Mill Farm

**Potter's
Forstal**

Hill

Road

3

Rock Hill Road

+

Coldharbour
Farm

Forstal Road

**Egerton
Forstal**

4

Forge Lane

**Newland
Green**

Clark Hill
Farm

Wanden Lane

Bedlam Lane

Heronsdale

Newland Green Lane

5

Wanden

6

*Frith
Wood*

Kingsden
Farm

Bedlam
Lane

Burnt
House

7

Park
Farm

**Swift's
Green**

8

Rosemary Lane

**The
Quarter**

Oaklands

*Dering
Wood*

G H J **173** K L M

Lewd Lane

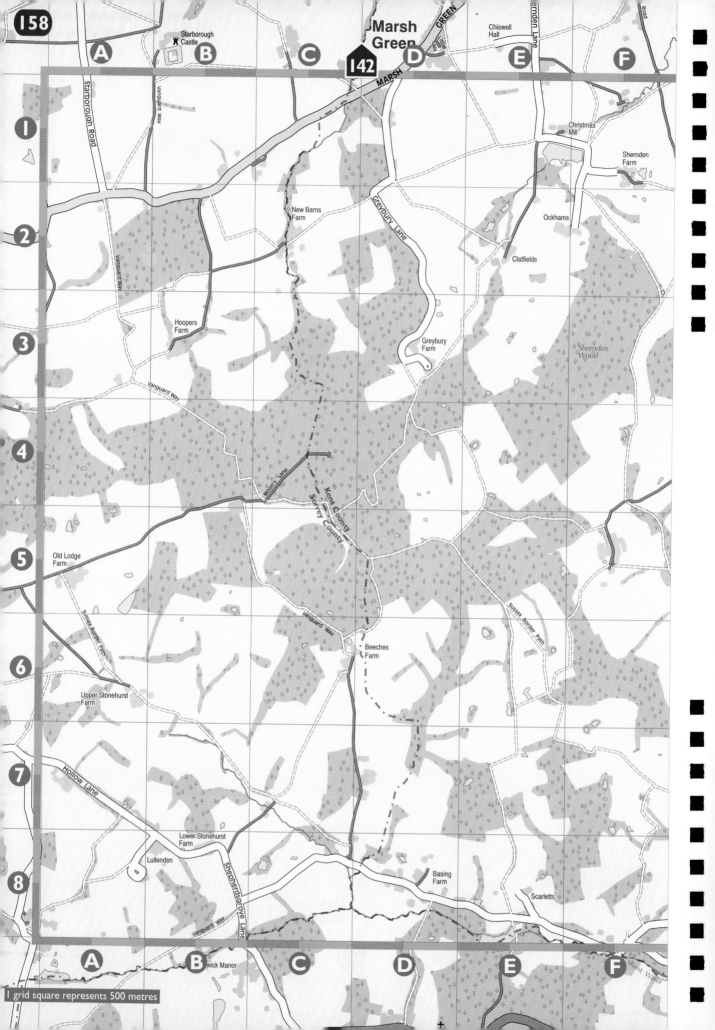

A **B** **C** **D** Marsh Green **E** **F**

Marsh Green

MARSH

GREEN

Chiswell
Hall

rnden Lane

Road

I

Starborough
Castle

Starborough Road

Vanguard Way

Christmas
Mill

Shernden
Farm

2

Vanguard Way

New Barns
Farm

Greybury Lane

Ockhams

Clatfields

Hoopers
Farm

3

Vanguard Way

Greybury
Farm

Shernden
Wood

4

Moon's Lane

Kent County
Surrey County

5

Old Lodge
Farm

Sussex Border Path

Vanguard Way

Sussex Border Path

6

Upper Stonehurst
Farm

Beeches
Farm

7

Hollow Lane

8

Lower Stonehurst
Farm

Lullenden

Shepherdsgrove Lane

Vanguard Way

Basing
Farm

Scarletts

A **B** wick Manor **C** **D** **E** **F** Kent Water

I grid square represents 500 metres

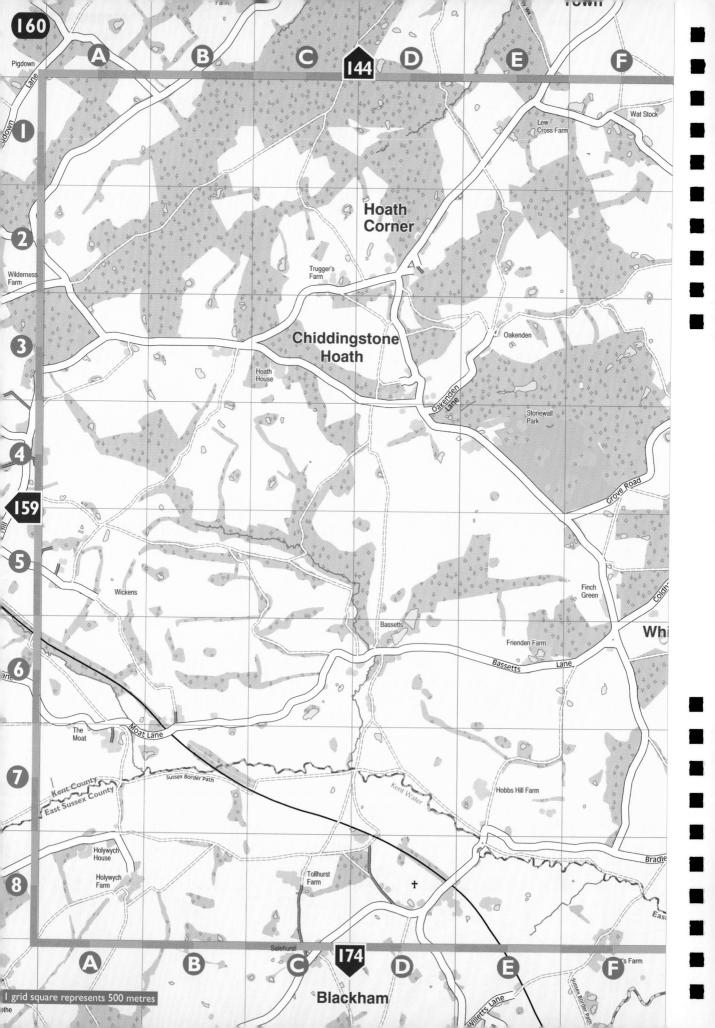

A　　　　B　　　　C　　**144**　　D　　　　E　　　　F

Pigdown

1

2

Wilderness
Farm

Hoath
Corner

Trugger's
Farm

3

Chiddingstone
Hoath

Hoath
House

Oakenden

Lew
Cross Farm

Wat Stock

Stonewall
Park

4

159

Grove Road

5

Wickens

Finch
Green

Coldh

Bassetts

Frienden Farm

Bassetts   Lane

Whi

6

The
Moat

Moat Lane

7

Kent County

East Sussex County

Sussex Border Path

Kent Water

Hobbs Hill Farm

Bradle

8

Holywych
House

Holywych
Farm

Tollhurst
Farm

†

Eas

A　　　　B　　　　C　　**174**　　D　　　　E　　　　F

Blackham

Willetts Lane

Sussex Border Path

's Farm

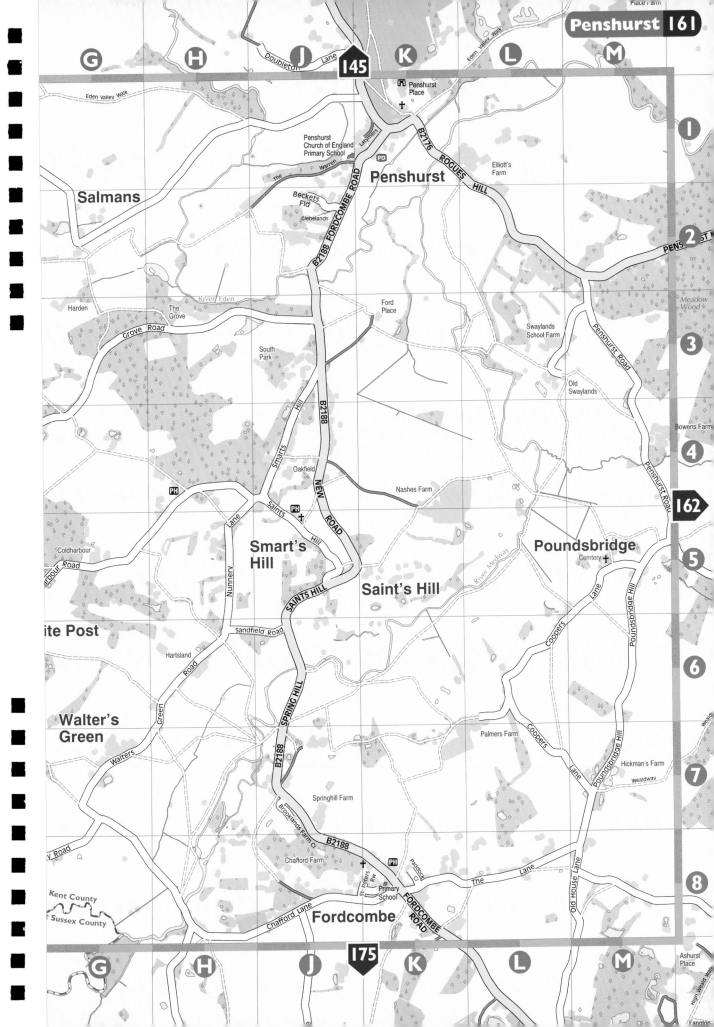

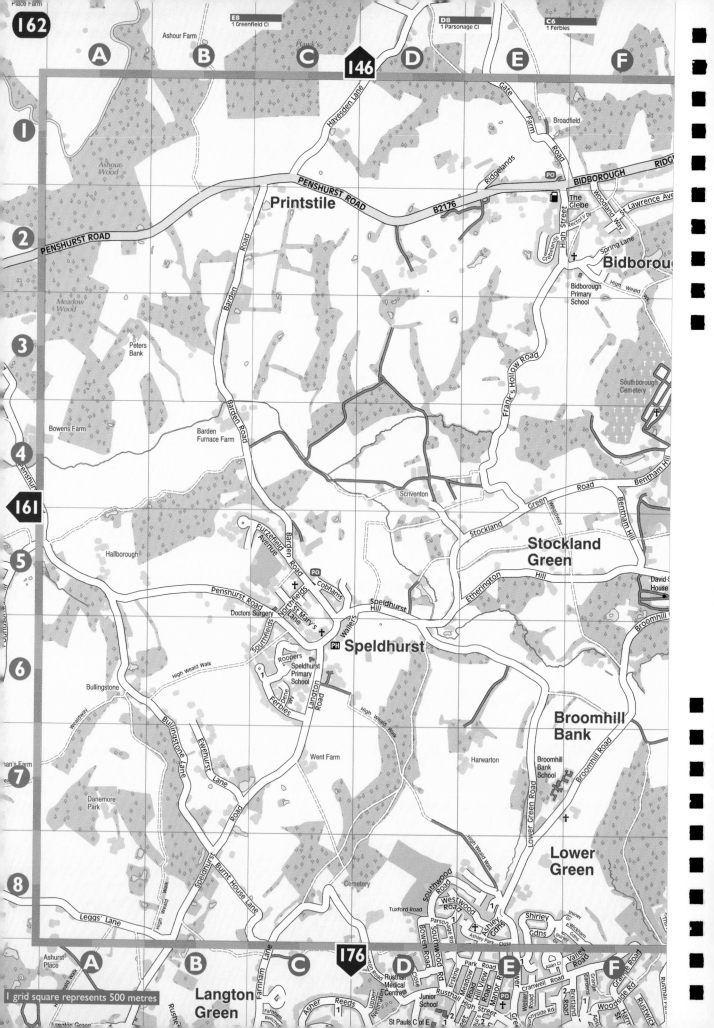

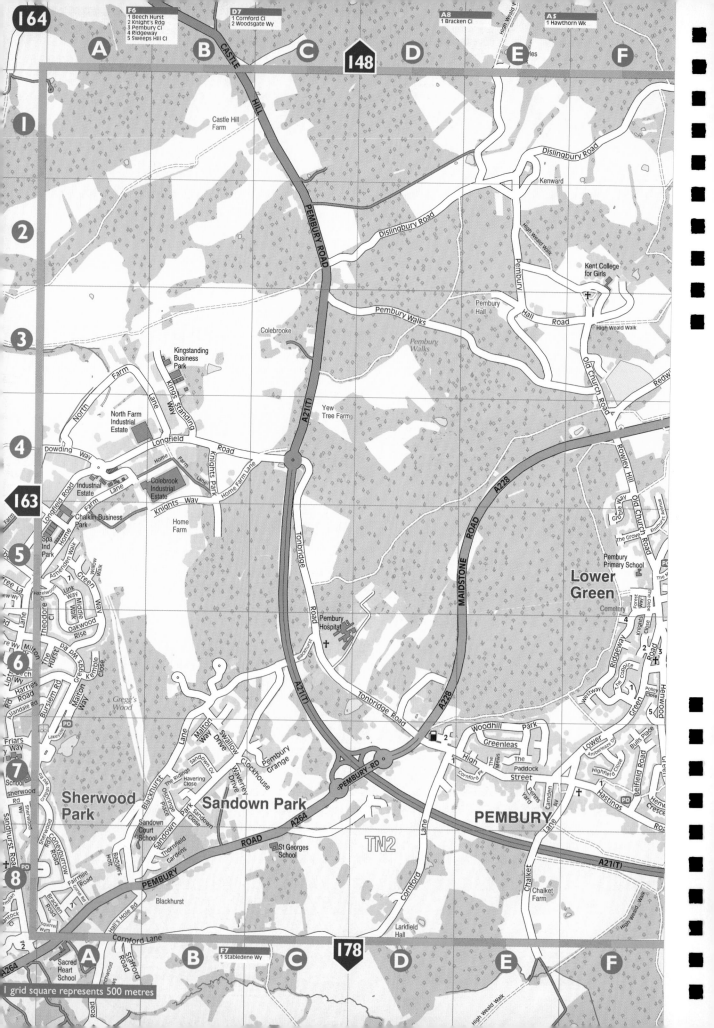

F6
1 Beech Hurst
2 Knight's Rdg
3 Pembury Cl
4 Ridgeway
5 Sweeps Hill Cl

D7
1 Cornford Cl
2 Woodsgate Wy

A8
1 Bracken Cl

A5
1 Hawthorn Wk

A   B   C   D   E   F

Castle Hill Farm

Dislingbury Road

Kenward

Dislingbury Road

Kent College for Girls

Pembury Hall Road

Pembury Walks

Pembury Hall

High Weald Walk

Colebrooke

Pembury Walks

Old Church Road

Redw

Kingstanding Business Park

Yew Tree Farm

A21(T)

Kings Standing Way

North Farm Industrial Estate

Longfield Road

North Farm

Home Farm Lane

Knights Park Lane

A228

Maidstone Road

Rowley Hill

Dowding Way

Home Farm Lane

Knights Way

Colebrook Industrial Estate

Industrial Estate

Home Farm

Lower Green

Pembury Primary School

The Grove

Chalklin Business Park

Home Farm

Tonbridge Road

Pembury Hospital

Cemetery

Spa Ind Park

Ashenden Walk

Willow Walk

Green Way

Link Way

Middle Walk

Oakwood Rise

Ridgeway

Knights Close

Tonbridge Road

A228

Gregg's Wood

Malton Way

Swallow Drive

Clockhouse

Waverley Drive

Pembury Grange

Woodhill Park

Greenleas

High Street

The Paddock Street

Hastings

PEMBURY

Sherwood Park

Blackhurst

Sandown Park

A264

PEMBURY ROAD

St Georges School

TN2

Cornford Lane

A21(T)

Chalket Lane

Belfield Road

Henwood Cresce

Sandown Court School

Thornfield Gardens

Badgers Holt

Blackhurst

Larkfield Hall

Chalket Farm

High Weald Walk

Cornford Lane

Sacred Heart School

Stafford Road

F7
1 Stabledene Wy

A   B   C   D   E   F

1 grid square represents 500 metres

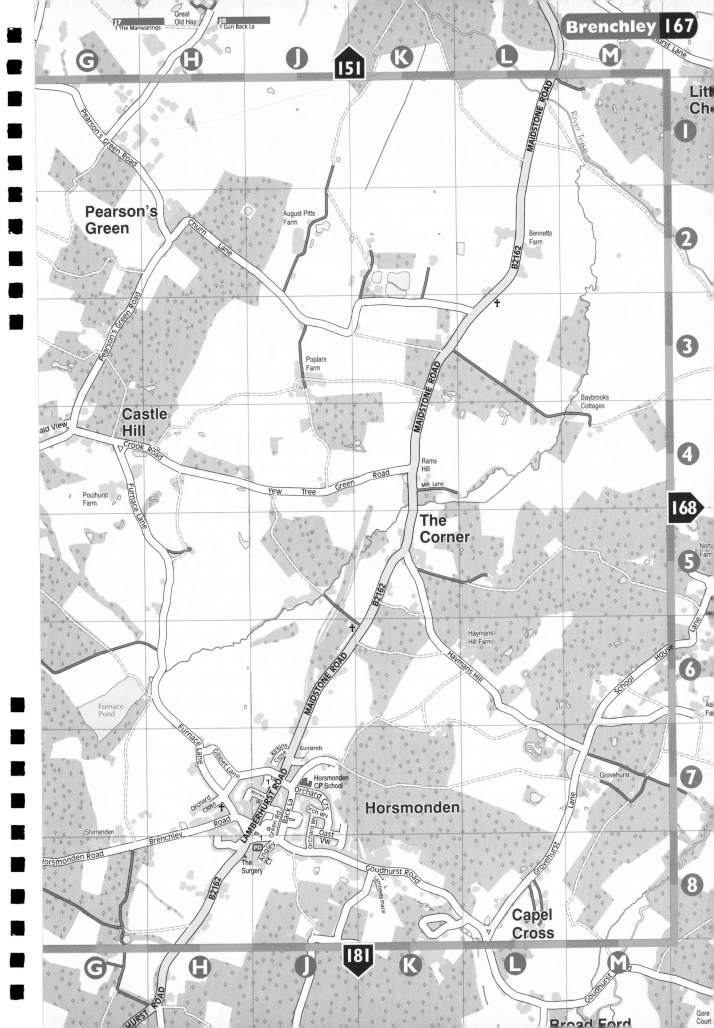

G   H   J   **151**   K   L   M

J7 1 The Manwarings
Great Old Hay
J8 1 Gun Back La

Litt
Che

1

Pearson's Green

Pearson's Green Road

August Pitts Farm

Bennetts Farm

2

B2162

MAIDSTONE ROAD

River Teise

Churn Lane

Poplars Farm

3

MAIDSTONE ROAD

Baybrooks Cottages

Castle Hill

eald View

Crook Road

Rams Hill

Mill Lane

4

Furnace Lane

Yew Tree Green Road

168

Poulhurst Farm

The Corner

Nort
Farm

5

B2162

House

Lane

Haymans Hill Farm

6

Furnace Pond

Haymans Hill

School

As
Fa

Furnace Lane

Gibbet Lane

Kirkins Close

Gunlands

Grovehurst

7

Morley
Orchard Rd
Orchard Crs
Horsmonden CP School

Orchard Close

LAMBERHURST ROAD
Green Rd
Back La
Orch Wy
Orch VW
Oast VW

Horsmonden

Grovehurst Lane

Shirrenden

Brenchley Road

PO
Andley Ct
The Surgery

Goudhurst Road

8

Horsmonden Road

B2162

Lamberts Place

Capel Cross

G   H   J   **181**   K   L   M

LAMBERHURST ROAD

Goudhurst

Gore
Court

Broad Ford

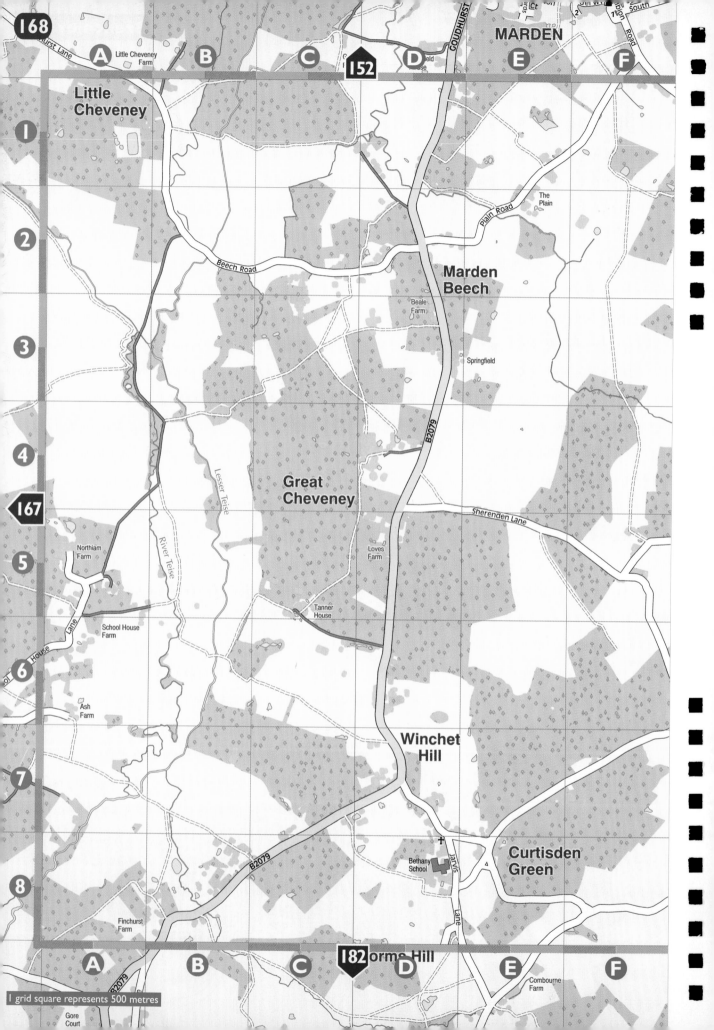

A   Little Cheveney Farm   B   C   152   D   MARDEN   E   F

Little
Cheveney

I

Beech Road

2

Marden
Beech

Beale
Farm

3

Springfield

4

Great
Cheveney

167

Sherenden Lane

Lesser Teise

River Teise

Loves
Farm

5

Northiam
Farm

School House
Farm

Tanner
House

6

Ash
Farm

Winchet
Hill

7

B2079

Bethany
School

Curtisden
Green

8

Finchurst
Farm

Jarvis Lane

B2079

A   B   C   **182** orms Hill   D   E   F

Plain Road

The
Plain

GOUDHURST

Combourne
Farm

Gore
Court

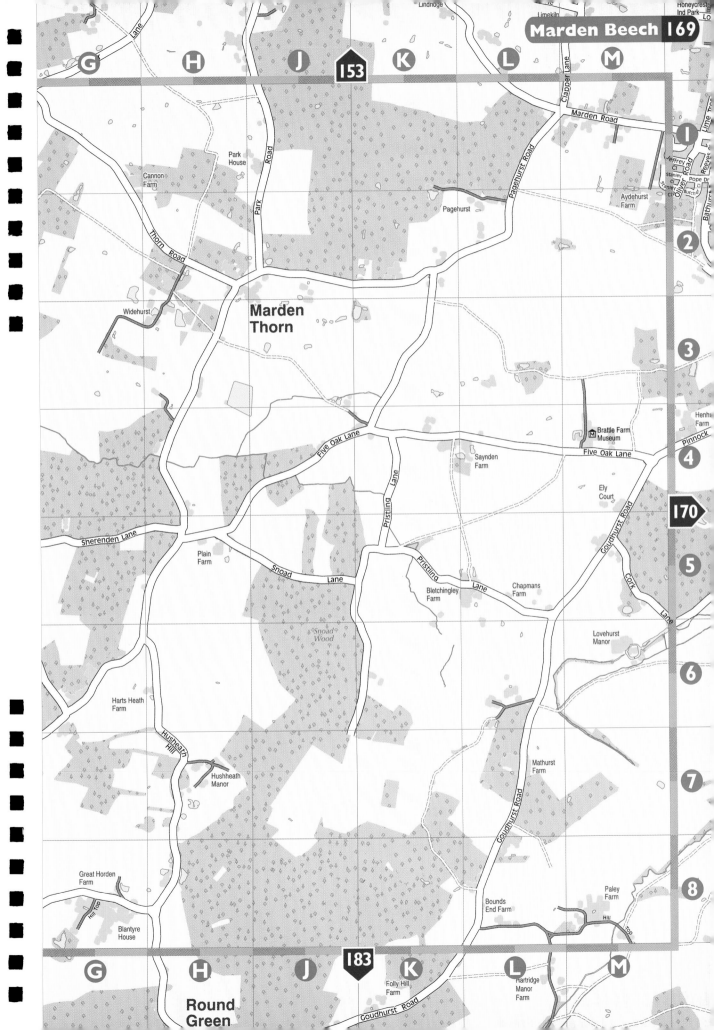

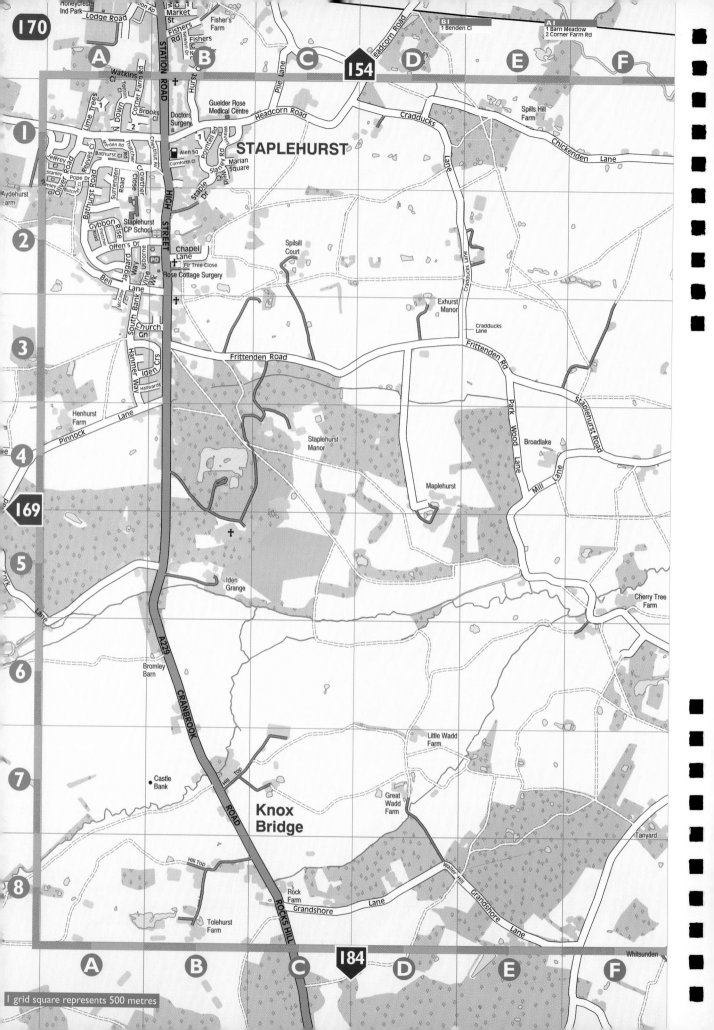

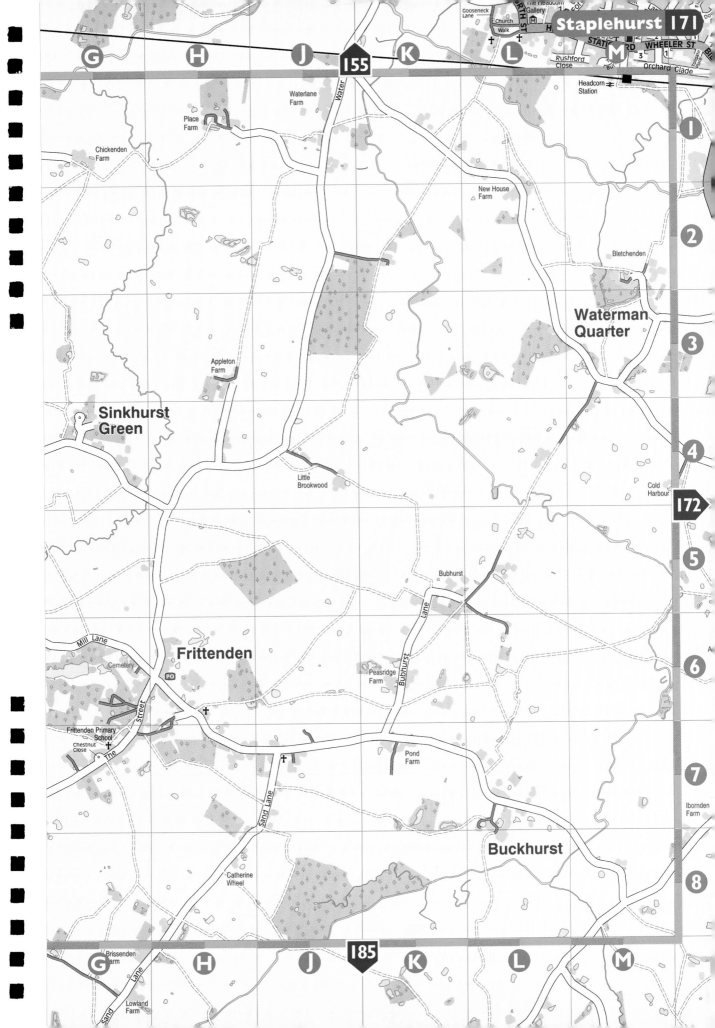

G H J **155** K L **M**

STATION RD WHEELER ST

Gooseneck Lane

The Headcorn Gallery

Church Walk

RTH ST

Rushford Close

Orchard Glade

Headcorn Station

1

Waterlane Farm

Place Farm

Chickenden Farm

New House Farm

Bletchenden

2

Waterman Quarter

3

Sinkhurst Green

Appleton Farm

4

Cold Harbour

172

Little Brookwood

5

Bubhurst

Mill Lane

Frittenden

Cemetery

PO

Peasridge Farm

Bubhurst Lane

6

The Street

Frittenden Primary School

Chestnut Close

Pond Farm

7

Ibornden Farm

Sand Lane

The

Catherine Wheel

Buckhurst

8

Brissenden Farm

Sand Lane

Lowland Farm

G H J **185** K L **M**

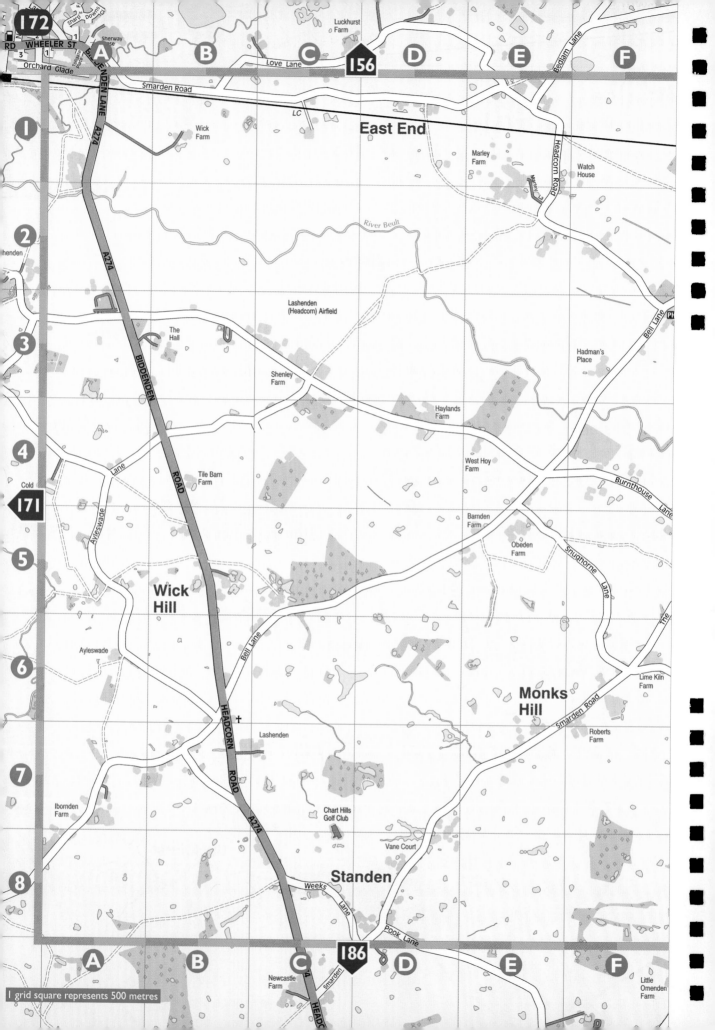

172

RD | WHEELER ST

A BIDDENDEN LANE

Orchard Glade

Smarden Road

I

henden

2

3

Cold

171

5

Wick Hill

Ayleswade

6

Ayleswade

7

Ibornden Farm

8

A274 BIDDENDEN ROAD

A274 HEADCORN ROAD

Lane

Tile Barn Farm

Wick Farm

The Hall

Shenley Farm

Lashenden (Headcorn) Airfield

Love Lane

LC

156

East End

River Beult

Haylands Farm

West Hoy Farm

Barnden Farm

Obeden Farm

Bell Lane

†

Lashenden

Chart Hills Golf Club

Vane Court

Newcastle Farm

Weeks Lane

Standen

Smarden

186

Pook Lane

HEADC

Luckhurst Farm

Marley Farm

Marley La

Watch House

Bedlam Lane

Headcorn Road

Hadman's Place

Bell Lane

PH

Burnthouse Lane

Snughorne Lane

Monks Hill

Smarden Road

Roberts Farm

Lime Kiln Farm

The

Little Omenden Farm

A **B** **C** **D** **E** **F**

I grid square represents 500 metres

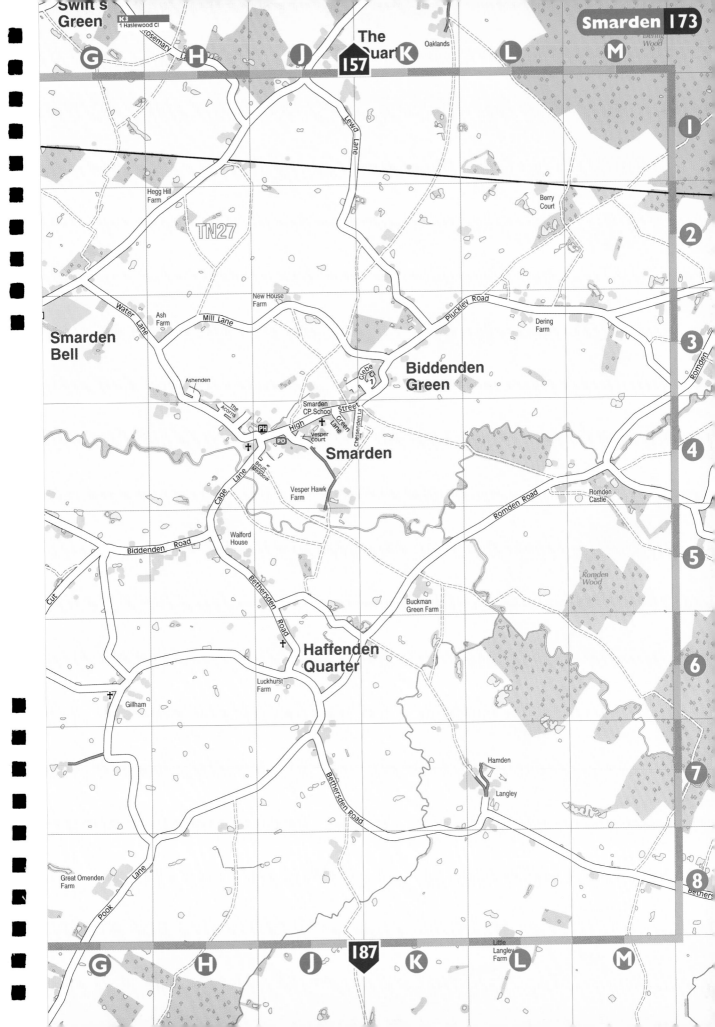

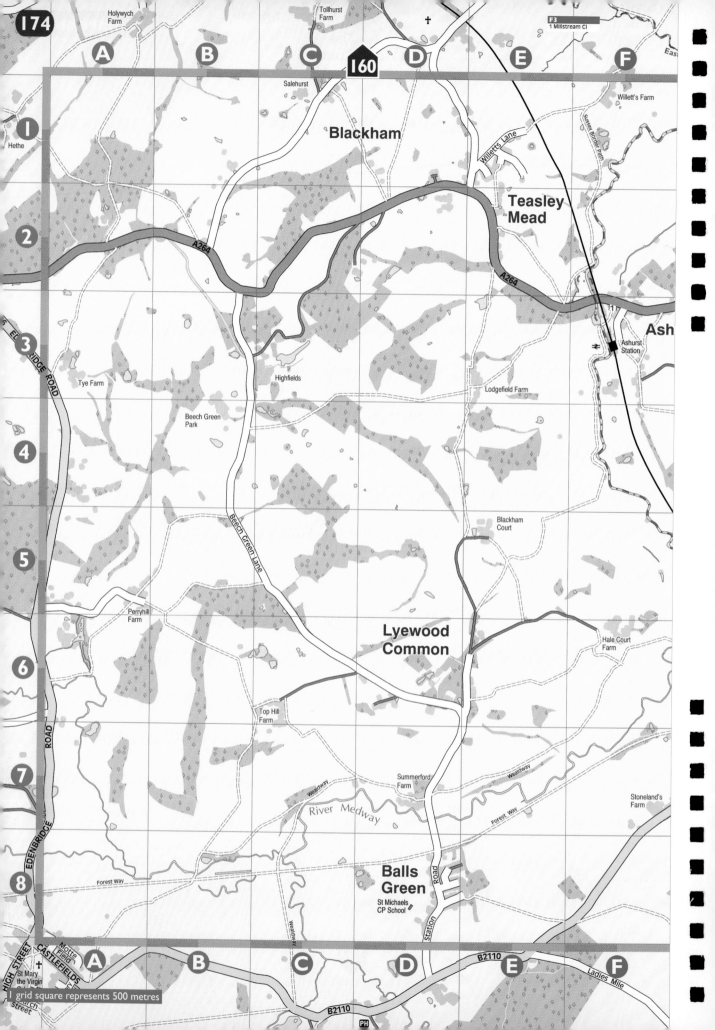

A B C **160** D E F

I Hethe

Holywych Farm

Tollhurst Farm

F3 1 Millstream Cl

Willett's Farm

Salehurst

Blackham

Willett's Lane

Sussex Border Path

2 A264

Teasley Mead

A264

East

3 EDENBRIDGE ROAD

Tye Farm

Highfields

A264

Ashurst Station

Ash

Lodgefield Farm

4 Beech Green Park

5 Beech Green Lane

Blackham Court

6 Perryhill Farm

Lyewood Common

Hale Court Farm

Top Hill Farm

7 EDENBRIDGE ROAD

Wealdway

Summerford Farm

Wealdway

Stoneland's Farm

River Medway

Forest Way

8 Forest Way

Wealdway

Balls Green

Station Road

St Michaels CP School

HIGH STREET

CASTLEFIELDS

Motte Field

St Mary the Virgin

Church Street

A B B2110 PH C D B2110 E Ladies Mile F

1 grid square represents 500 metres

B2110

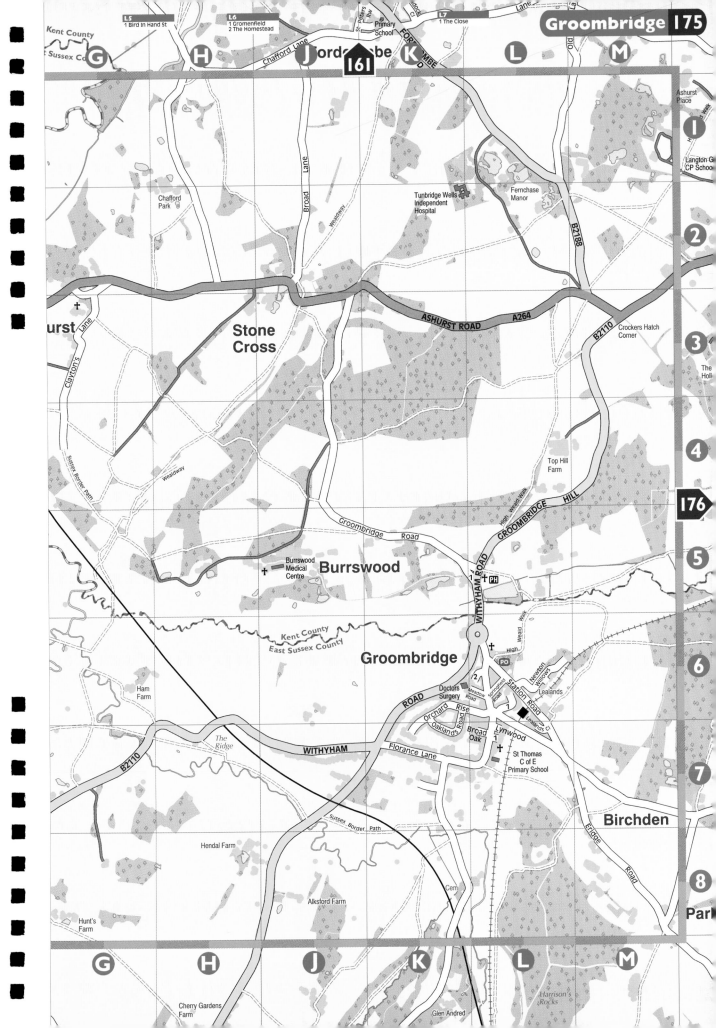

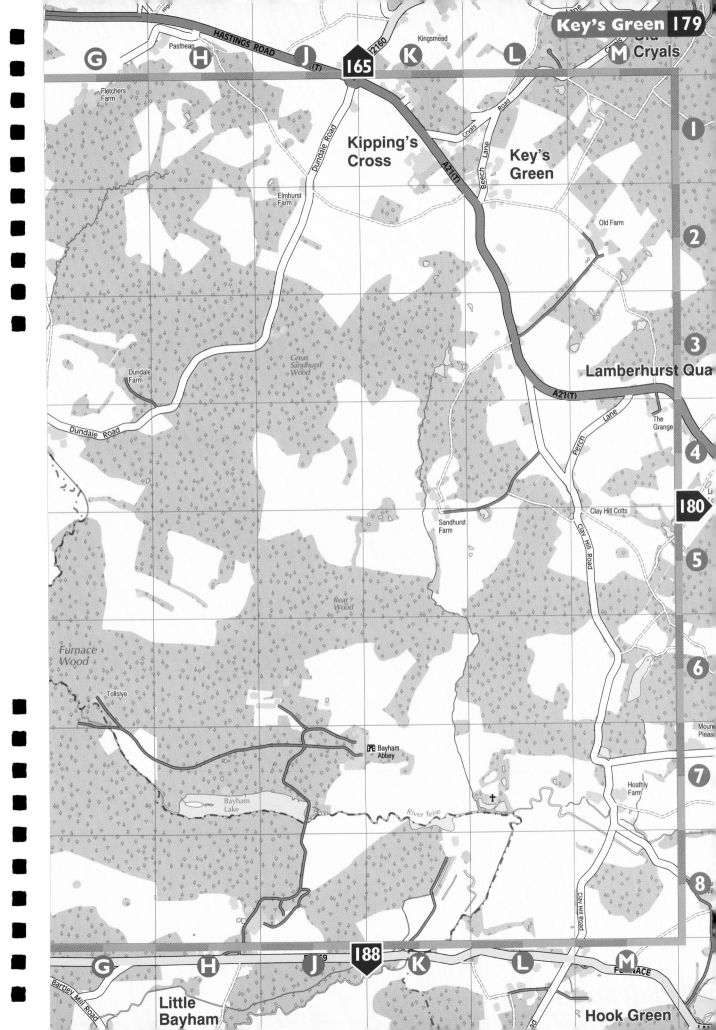

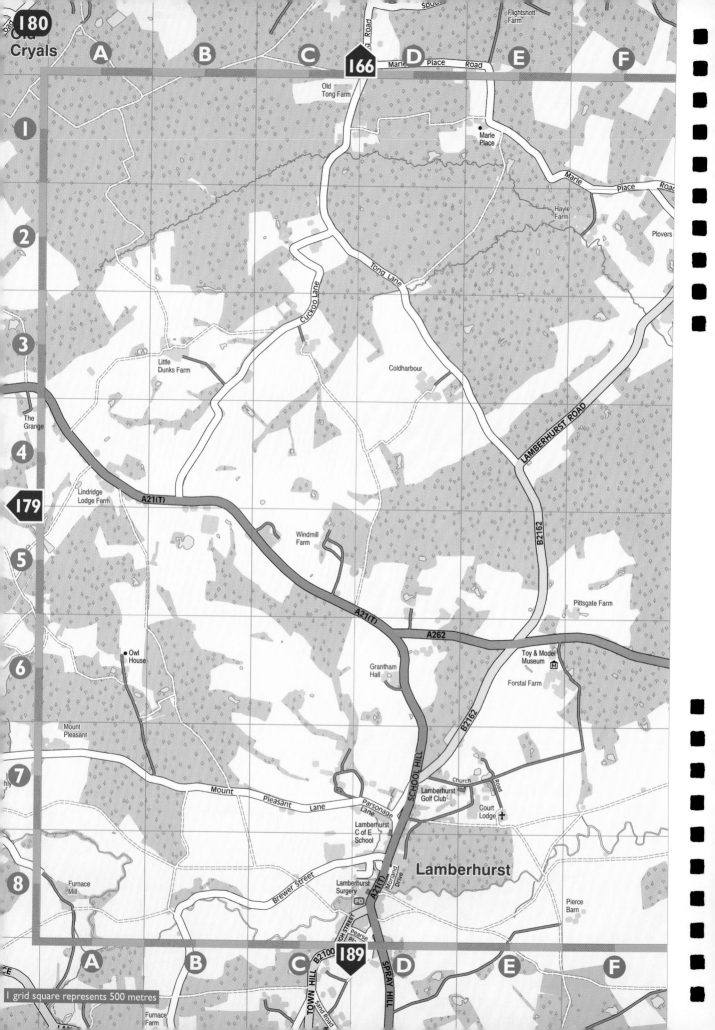

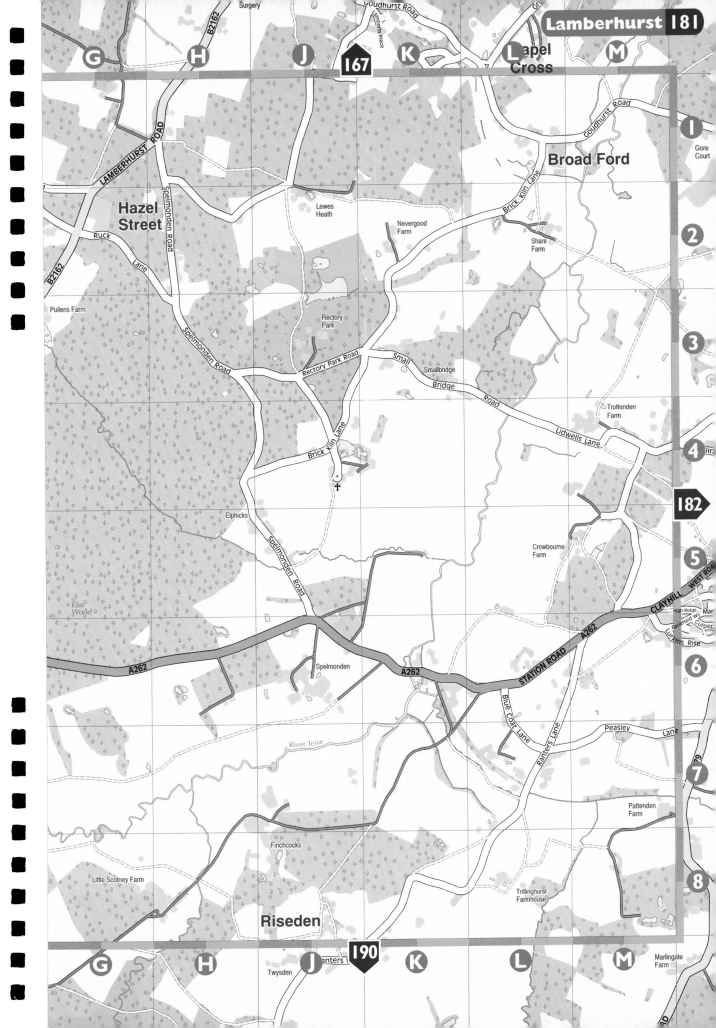

G H J **167** K L **apel Cross** M

1

Gore Court

Broad Ford

Surgery

Goudhurst Road

B2162

LAMBERHURST ROAD

Spelmonden Road

Hazel Street

Ruck Lane

B2162

Pullens Farm

Lewes Heath

Rectory Park

Spelmonden Road

Rectory Park Road

Brick Kiln Lane

Elphicks

Spelmonden Road

East Wood

Brick Kiln Lane

Nevergood Farm

Share Farm

Small

Smallbridge

Bridge Road

Lidwells Lane

Trottenden Farm

2

3

4

182

Crowbourne Farm

5

CLAYHILL WEST RO

High Ridge Mar

Barkfield W

Lurkins Rise

Culper

A262

STATION ROAD

6

A262

Spelmonden

A262

River Teise

Blue Coat Lane

Ranters Lane

Peasley Lane

7

Pattenden Farm

Finchcocks

Little Scotney Farm

8

Trillinghurst Farmhouse

Riseden

G H J **190** K L M

Twysden anters Marlingate Farm

A B C **168** D E F

Worms Hill

1 2 3 4 5 6 7 8

Finchurst Farm

Gore Court

Gore Lane

B2079

Swan Farm

Swan Lane

Bockingfold Farm

Combourne Farm

Brandfold

Lidwells House

Ladham House

Ladham Road

Jarvis Lane

Blue Barn Farm

Blind Lane

NORTH ROAD

Lovers Lane

Trowswell

B2084

Tattlebury Lane

Beresford Road

Jarvis Lane

Mile Lane

Frog's Hole

B2079

CHURCH ROAD

A262

Beaman Close

Goudhurst and Kilndown C of E Primary School

CRANBROOK ROAD

Iden Green

PO WEST ROAD HIGH ST Back Lane PH

CLAYHILL

BALCOMBES HILL

Maypole

Goudhurst

Lime Tree Farm

A262 PH

High Ridge Mary Day's

Bankfield Wy Culpepers

Lurkins Rise

Trigg's Farm

B2079

Lane

Smugley Farm

Glassenbury House

Marlingate Farm

A B **191** C D E F

Blackbush

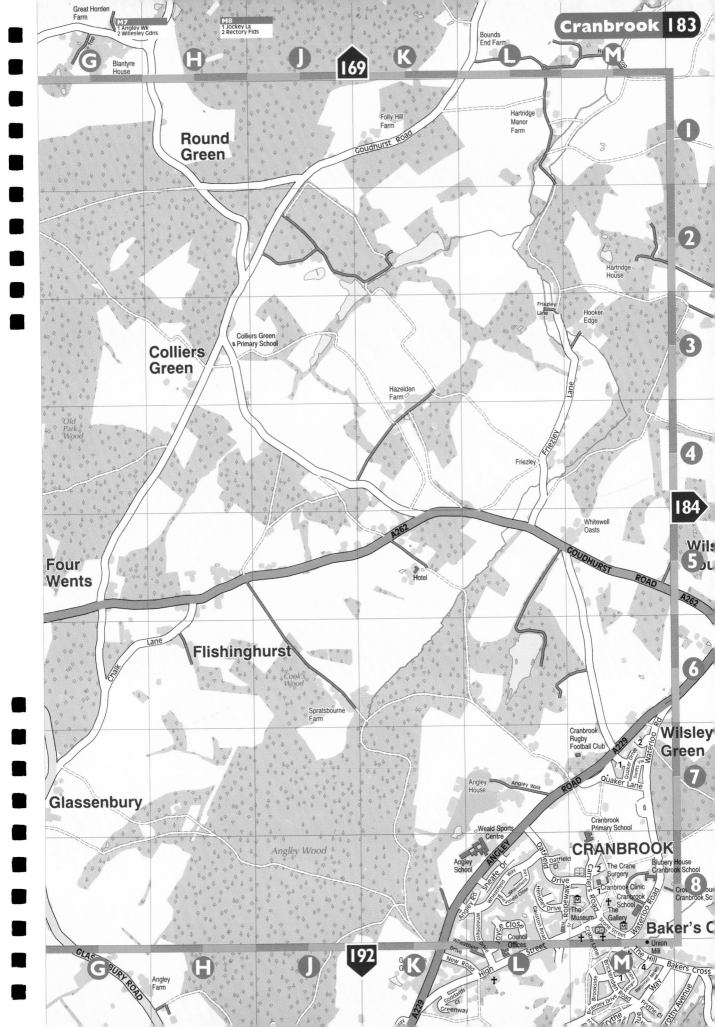

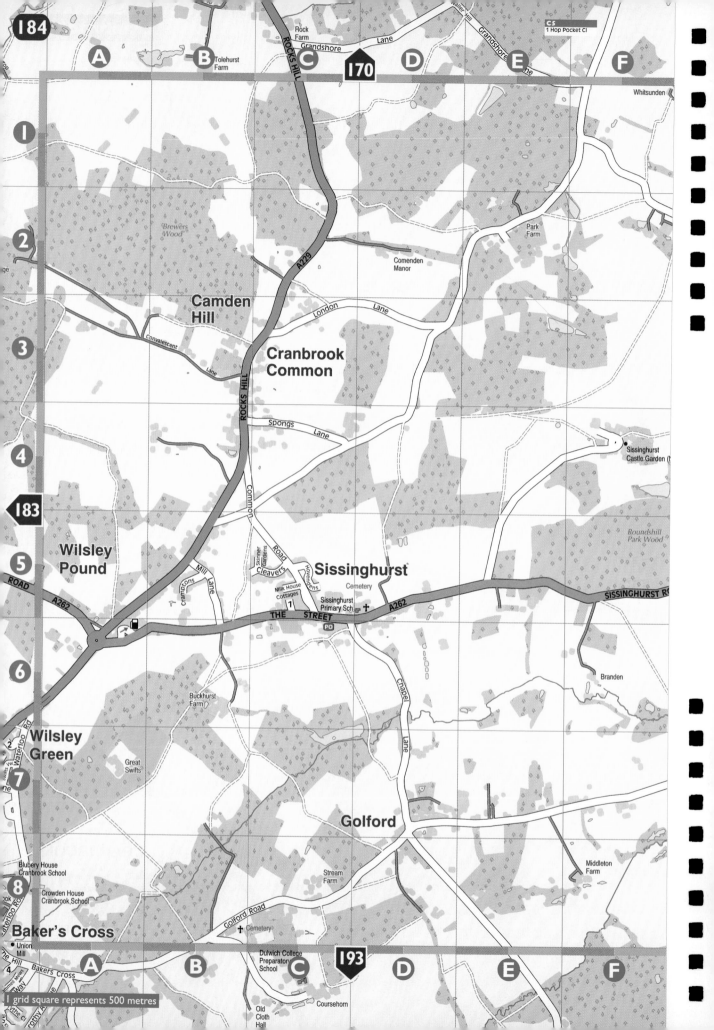

A   B   Tolehurst Farm   Rock Farm   C   D   E   F

Grandshore   Lane   Grandshore   ne

170   Whitsunden

C5
1 Hop Pocket Cl

1

Brewers Wood   Park Farm

2   A229   Comenden Manor

Camden Hill   London   Lane

3   Convalescent   Lane   **Cranbrook Common**

Spongs   Lane   Sissinghurst Castle Garden (N

4

183   Common   Roundshill Park Wood

5   **Wilsley Pound**   Skinner Gardens   **Sissinghurst**   Cemetery   SISSINGHURST RC

ROAD   Cleavers   Hovenens   Mill House Cottages   Sissinghurst Primary Sch   A262

A262   Cramptons   Mill Lane   **1**   THE   STREET   PO

6   Buckhurst Farm   Branden

Waterloo Rd   Chapel   Lane

2   **Wilsley Green**   Great Swifts

7   Golford   Middleton Farm

Blubery House Cranbrook School   Stream Farm

8   Crowden House Cranbrook School   Cemetery

Baker's Cross   Golford Road

Union Mill   Dulwich College Preparatory School   **193**

A   Bakers Cross   B   C   Coursehorn   D   E   F

Old Cloth Hall

I grid square represents 500 metres

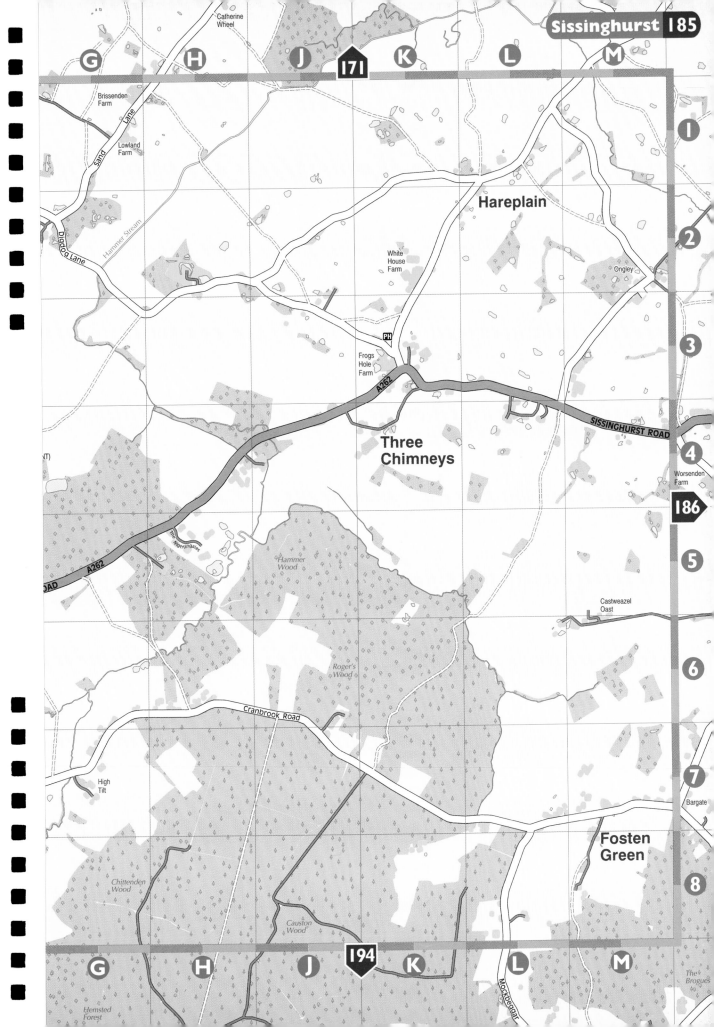

G H J **171** K L M

I

2

3

4

186

5

6

7

8

Catherine Wheel

Brissenden Farm

Sand Lane

Lowland Farm

Diddog Lane

Hammer Stream

Hareplain

White House Farm

Ongley

PH

Frogs Hole Farm

A262

SISSINGHURST ROAD

Three Chimneys

Worsenden Farm

(NT)

ROAD

A262

The Nightingales

Hammer Wood

Castweazel Oast

Roger's Wood

Cranbrook Road

High Tilt

Bargate

Fosten Green

Chittenden Wood

Causton Wood

Hemsted Forest

Mockbeggar

The Brogues

G H J **194** K L M

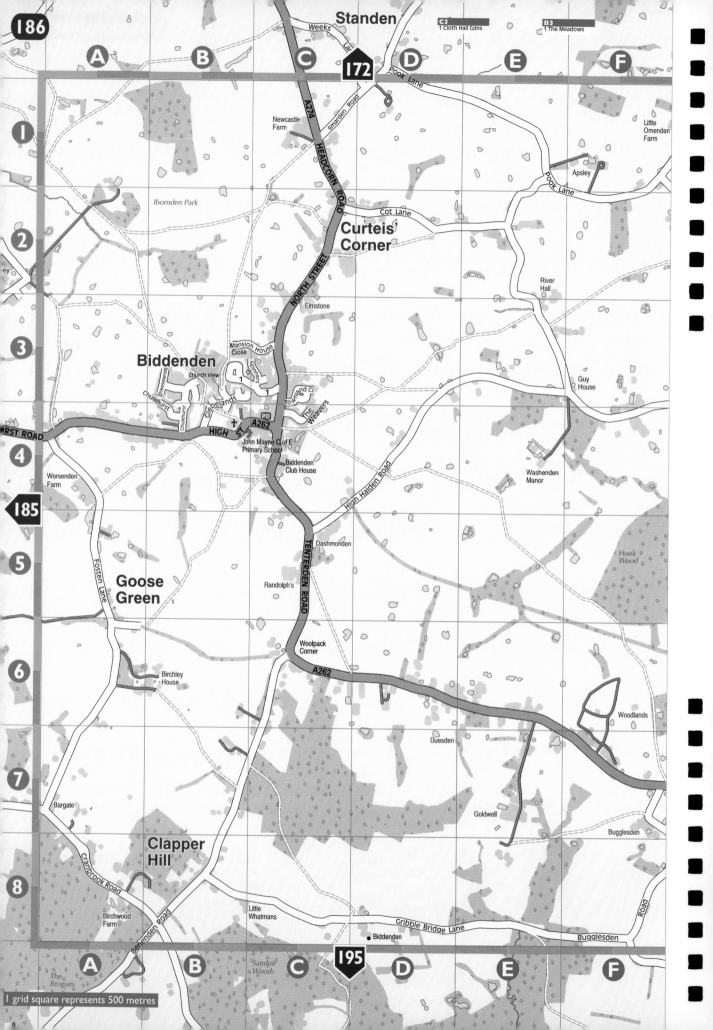

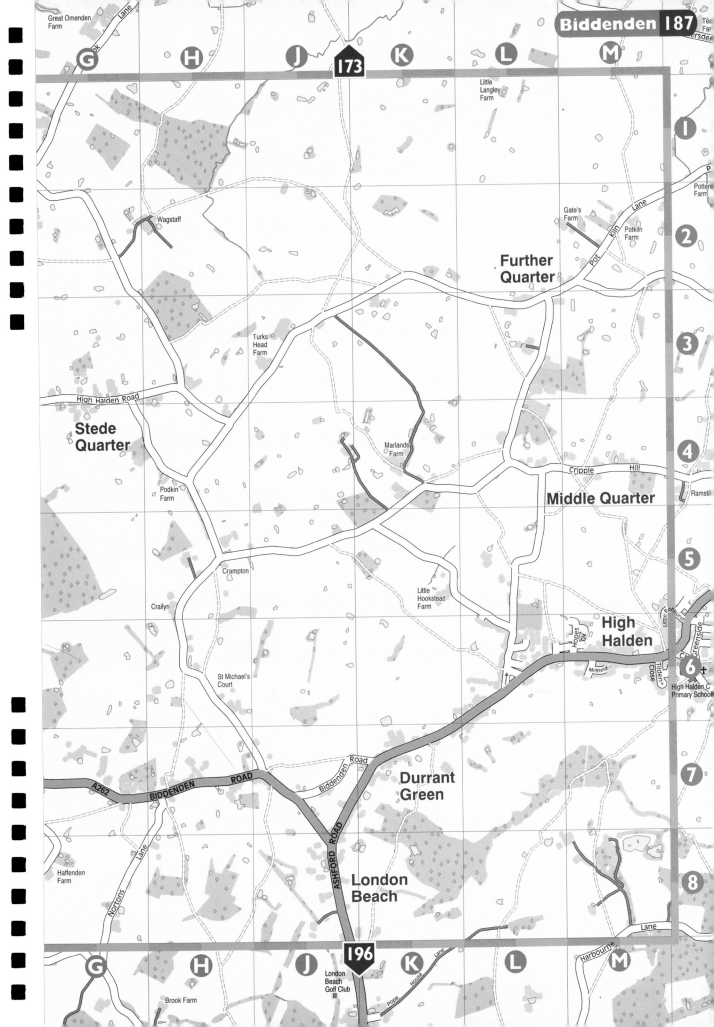

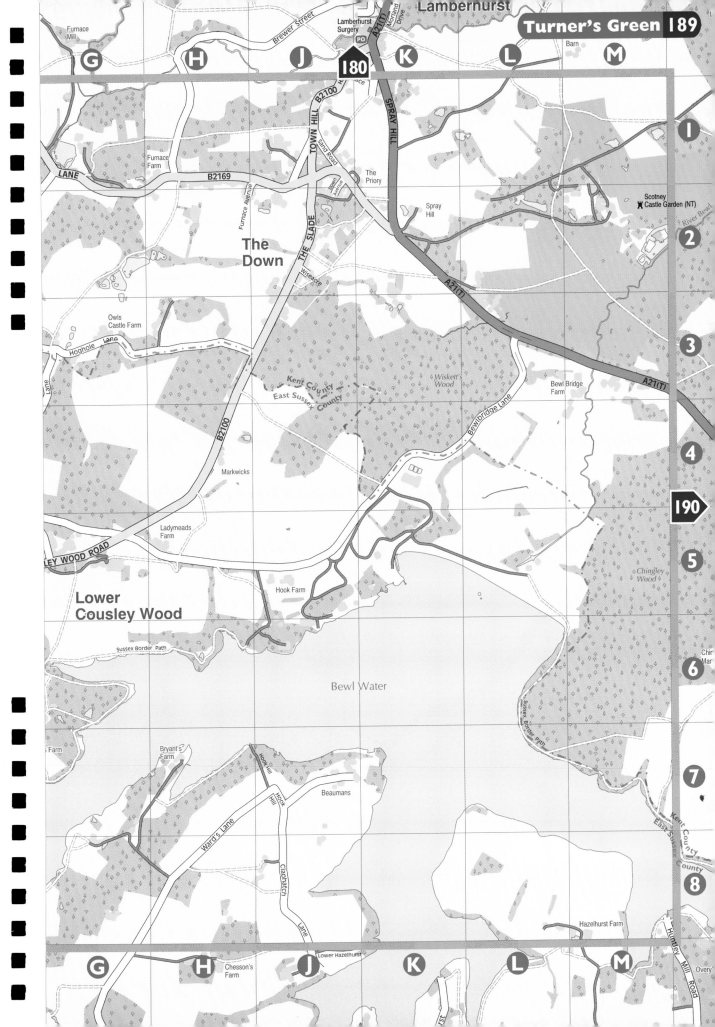

Lambernurst

Furnace
Mill

Brewer Street

Lamberhurst
Surgery

PO

180

Morland
Drive

Barn

G   H   J   K   L   M

Furnace
Farm

LANE

B2169

Furnace Avenue

The Slade

TOWN HILL

B2100

Sand Road

Town
Avenue

The Priory

SPRAY HILL

The
Down

Wiseacre

Spray
Hill

A21(T)

Scotney
Castle Garden (NT)

River Bewl

I

2

Owls
Castle Farm

Hoghole   Lane

Lane

B2100

Kent County

East Sussex County

Wiskett's
Wood

Bewlbridge Lane

Bewl Bridge
Farm

A21(T)

3

Markwicks

190

4

Ladymeads
Farm

Chingley
Wood

5

..LEY WOOD ROAD

Hook Farm

**Lower
Cousley Wood**

Sussex Border Path

Chir
Mar

6

Bewl Water

Sussex Border Path

..Farm

Bryant's
Farm

Hook Hill

Beaumans

Ward's Lane

Hook Hill

Claphatch Lane

7

Kent County

East Sussex County

Hazelhurst Farm

Huntley Mill Road

8

Overy'

G   H   Chesson's
Farm   J   Lower Hazelhurst   K   L   M

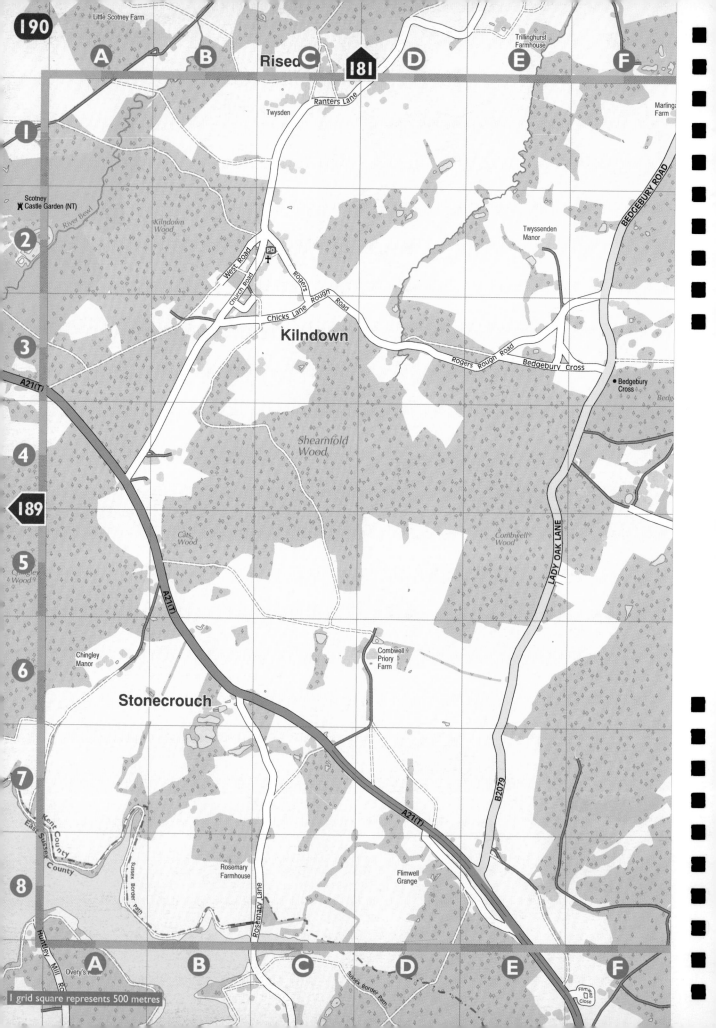

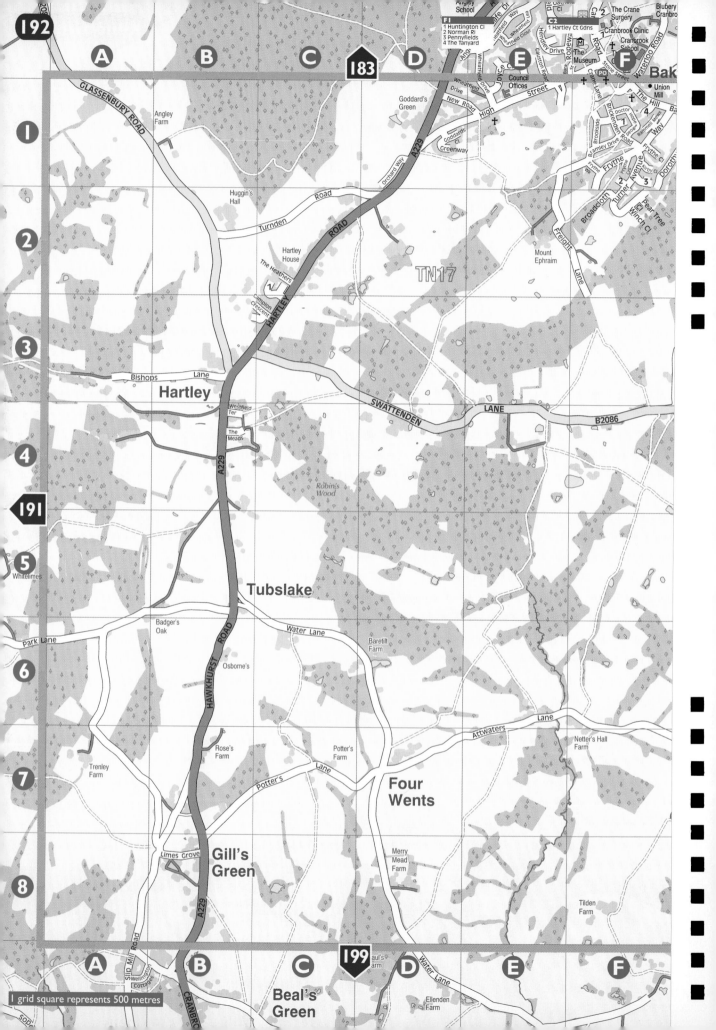

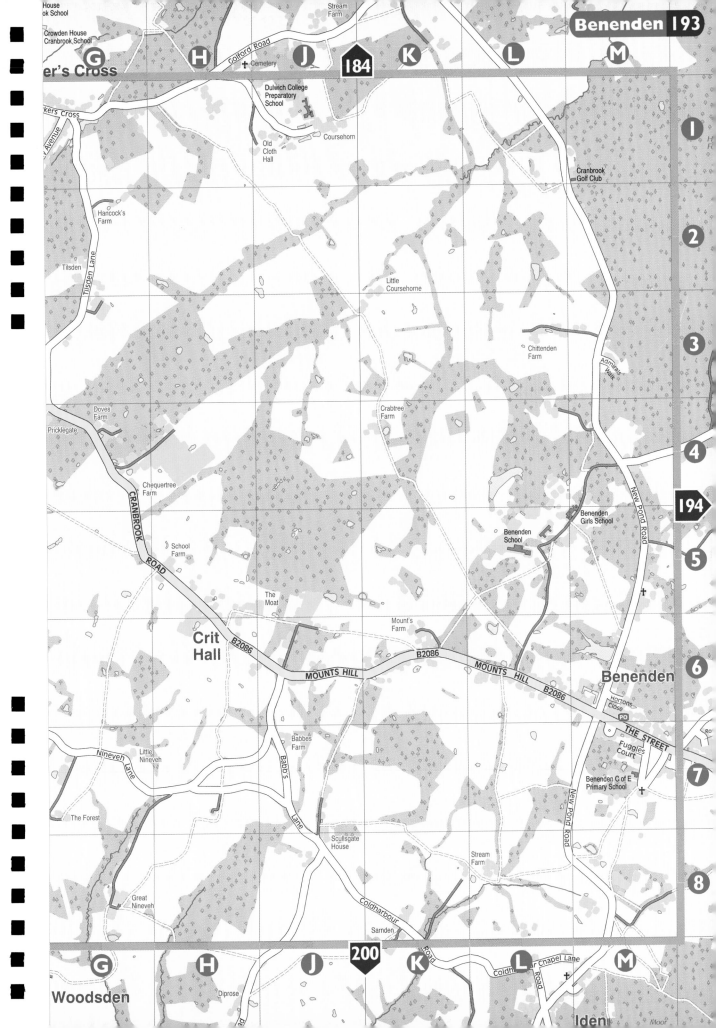

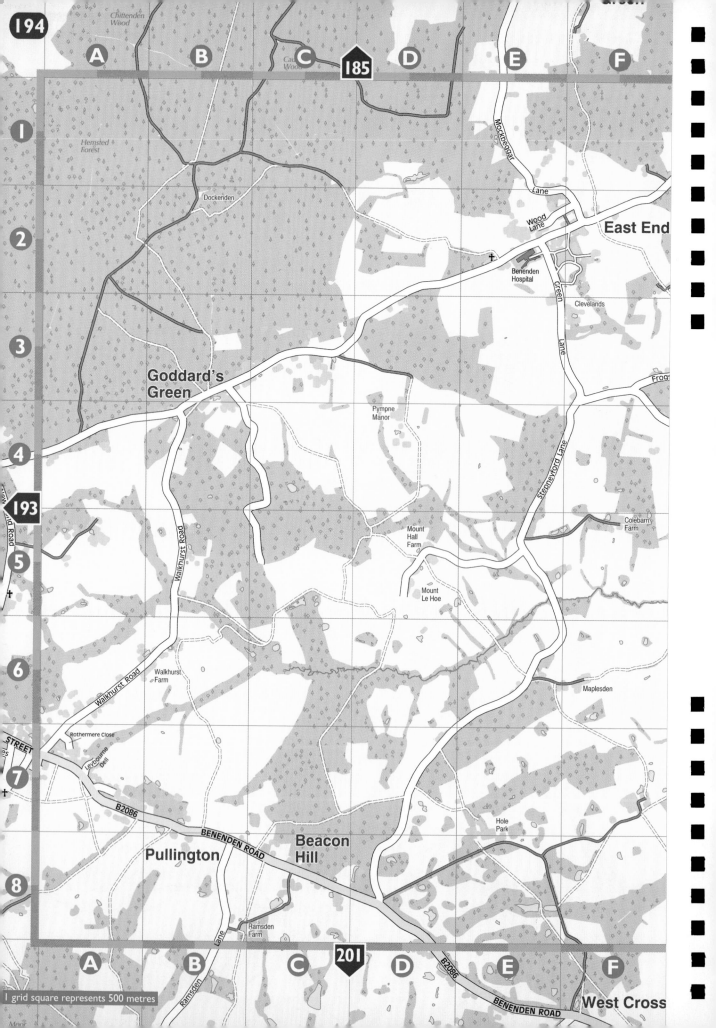

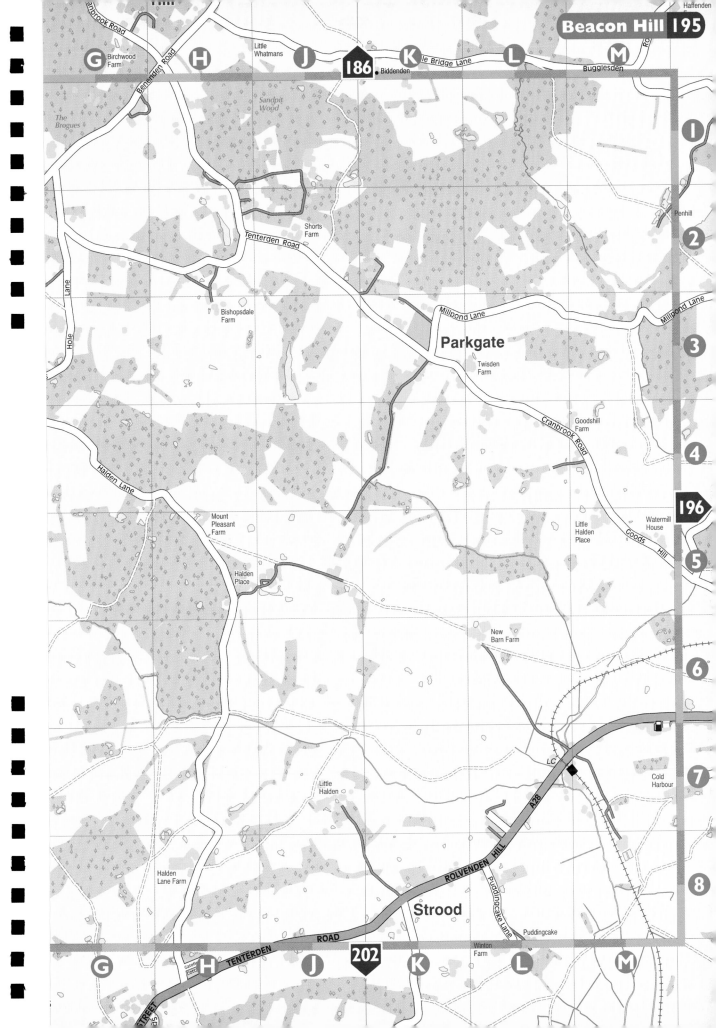

G Birchwood Farm

H

Little Whatmans

J

186 Biddenden

le Bridge Lane

K

L

M Bugglesden

Haffenden

I

Penhill

2

Benenden Road

Cranbrook Road

The Brogues

Sandpit Wood

Tenterden Road

Shorts Farm

Lane

Hole

Bishopsdale Farm

Millpond Lane

Parkgate

Twisden Farm

Millpond Lane

3

Goodshill Farm

Cranbrook Road

4

Halden Lane

Mount Pleasant Farm

Little Halden Place

Watermill House

196

Goods Hill

5

Halden Place

New Barn Farm

6

Little Halden

LC

Cold Harbour

7

A28

Halden Lane Farm

ROLVENDEN HILL

Puddingcake Lane

Strood

Winton Farm

Puddingcake

8

Gaten Cott

TENTERDEN ROAD

STREET

G

H

J

202

K

L

M

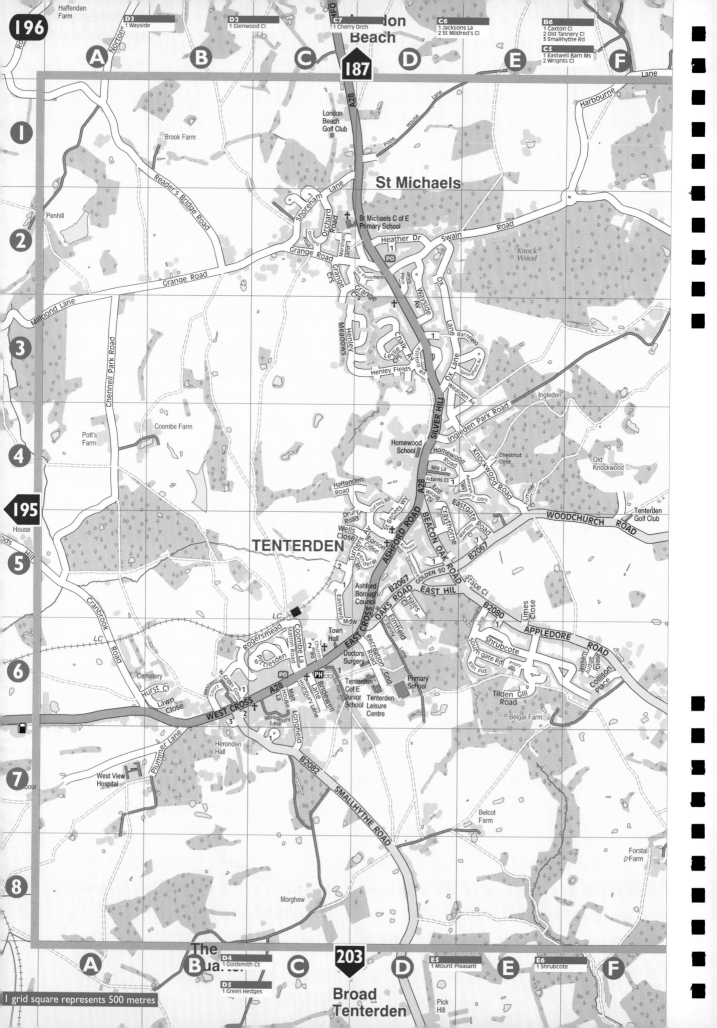

A   B   C   D   E   F

187

D3 1 Wayside
D2 1 Glenwood Cl
C7 1 Cherry Orch
C6 1 Jacksons La
2 St Mildred's Cl
B6 1 Caxton Cl
2 Old Tannery Cl
3 Smallhythe Rd
C5 1 Eastwell Barn Ms
2 Wrights Cl

I

Haffenden
Farm

Brook Farm

London
Beach
Golf Club

St Michaels

Harbourne
Lane

2

Penhill

Reader's Bridge Road

Grange Road

Shoreham Lane

St Michaels C of E
Primary School

Heather Dr

Swain
Road

Knock
Wood

3

Millpond Lane

Chennell Park Road

Grange Road

Grange Crs

Grange Crs

Henley Meadows

Henley Fields

Chalk Av

Leslie Crs

Ashford Rd

Ox Lane

Wayside Av

Barnfield

Wealden Av

Springhead Av

Ingleden

4

Pott's Farm

Coombe Farm

Haffenden Road

Homewood School

Homewood Road

Silver Hill

Ingleden Park Road

Knockwood Road

Chestnut Close

Old Knockwood

Tenterden Golf Club

195
House

5

Drury Road

Wells Close

Turners Av

St Benets Wy

Ashford Road

Beacon Oak Road

Craythorne Road

Martins Road

WOODCHURCH ROAD

TENTERDEN

Cranbrook Road

B2067

East Hill

B2067

Golden Sq

Grace Cl

B2080

Limes Close

APPLEDORE ROAD

Collison Place

William Judge Close

6

Cemetery

Hurst Cl

Lawn Close

WEST CROSS

Rodersmead

Station Road

Coombe La

Pittlesden

A28

Hanbury Lane

Bidewell Lane

Town Hall

Doctors Surgery

Recreation Gnd

Tenterden C of E Junior School

Tenterden Leisure Centre

Primary School

Shrubcote

Southgate Rd

Kiln Fld

Priory Way

Tilden Gill Road

Belgar Farm

7

Plummer Lane

Heronden Hall

Malt House

Woodbury Lane

Longfield

B2082

SMALLHYTHE ROAD

West View Hospital

Belcot Farm

Forstal Farm

8

Morghew

The Bua...

203

A   B   C   D   E   F

D4 1 Goldsmith Ct
D5 1 Green Hedges
E5 1 Mount Pleasant
E6 1 Shrubcote

Broad Tenterden

Pick Hill

1 grid square represents 500 metres

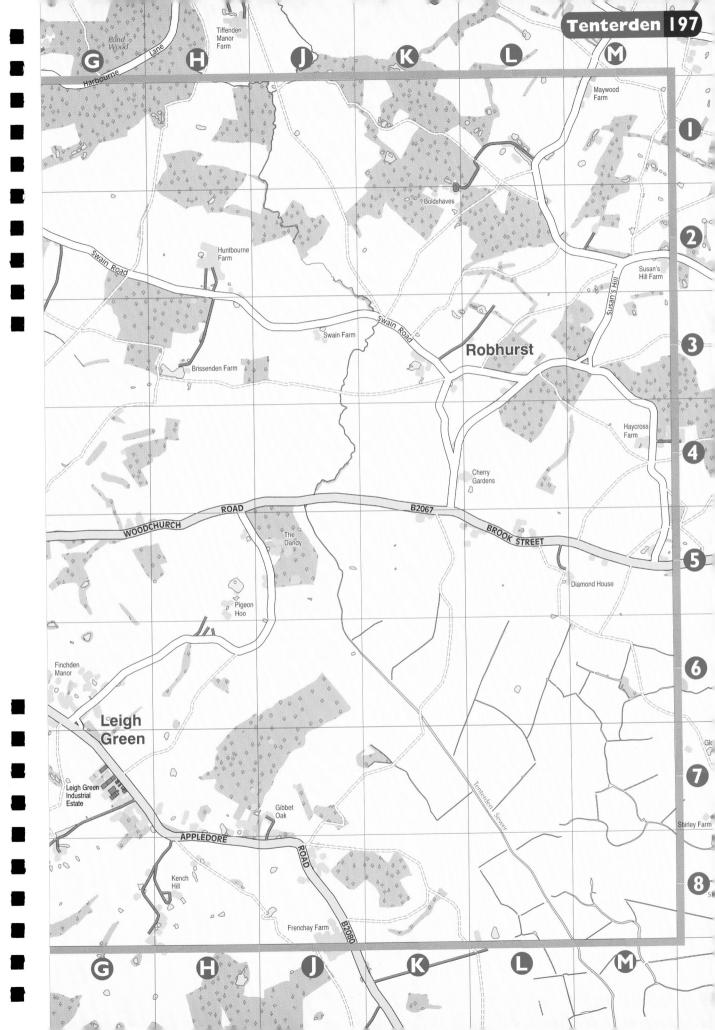

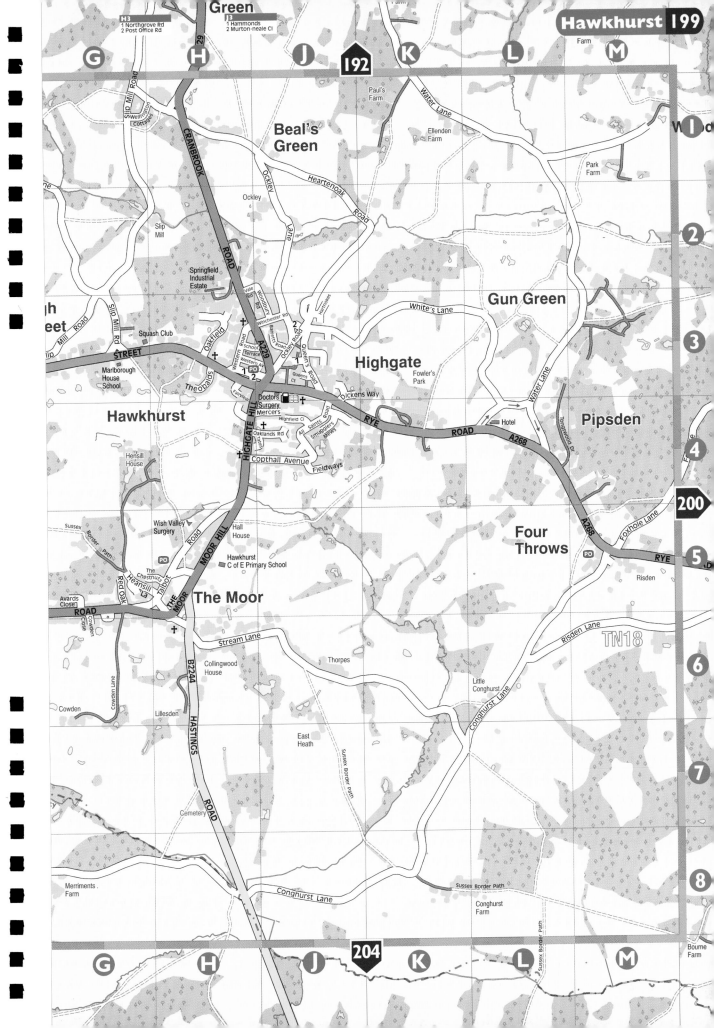

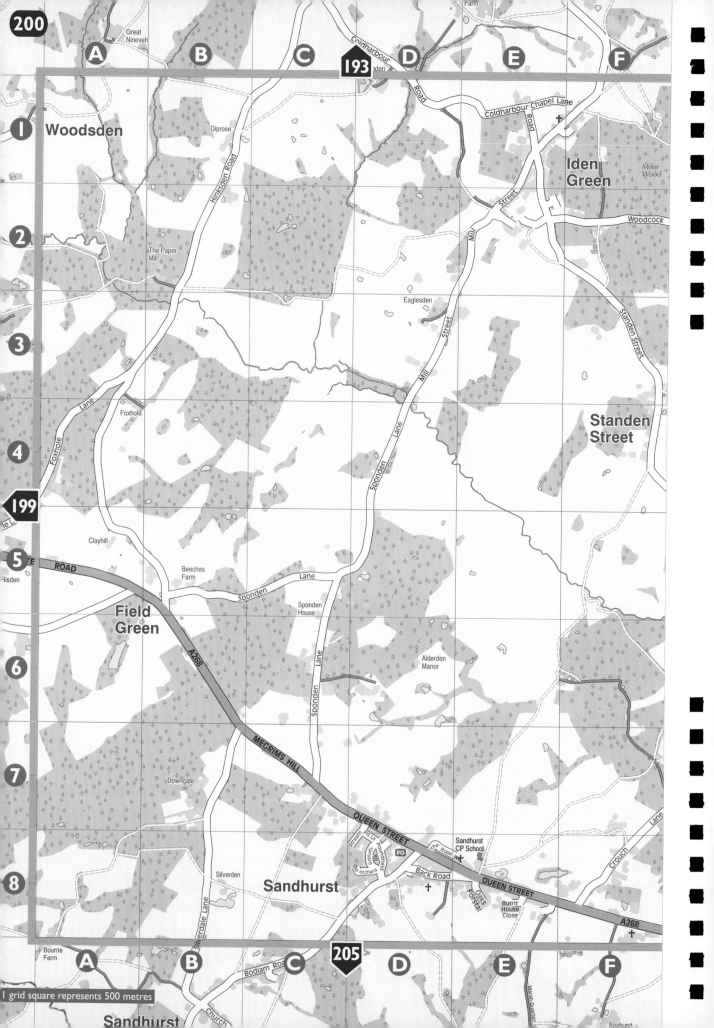

A   B   C   193   D   E   F

I   Woodsden   Great Nineveh   Diprose   Coldharbour   Coldharbour Chapel Lane   †   **Iden Green**   Moor Wood

2   The Paper Mill   Eaglesden   Street   Woodcock

3   Lane   Foxhole   Mill Street   Sponden Lane   **Standen Street**

4   Foxhole   Foxhole   Mill   Standen Street

Clayhill

5   ROAD   Beeches Farm   Sponden   Lane   Sponden House

Risden   **Field Green**   A268   Sponden Lane   Alderden Manor

6

7   Downgate   MEGRIMS HILL

8   Silverden   **Sandhurst**   QUEEN STREET   Stream Pit La   Poundfield   PO   The   Rope   Wk   Sandhurst CP School   †   Back Road   QUEEN STREET   Crouch Lane

Bourne Farm   Silverdale Lane   Bodiam Road   †   Oaks Forstal   Burnt House Close   A268   †

A   B   C   **205**   D   E   F

1 grid square represents 500 metres

Sandhurst   Church   Boxhurst

G H J 194 K L M

West Cross 1

REGENT

Old'R
Drive

2

B2086

BENENDEN ROAD

Sandhurst Road

Kemsdale

Ramsden
Farm

Ramsden   Lane

Standen Wood

Lane

Dingleden

Merrington
Place

3

R

Cornhill

HASTINGS

4

Old
Standen

Dingleden Lane

Cattsford

Sandhurst Road

Devenden

202

Springhill
Farm

Hopehouse
Lane

Kensham
Farm

Great Job's
Cross

5

Standen Street

Crouch
Lane

Hope
House

A28

Forsham
Farm

6

Hopehouse Lane

HASTINGS

Hexden
Farm

7

Hoad's
Farm

ROAD

HASTINGS

Stone Pit Lane

Lomas   Lane

Lomas
Lane

8

Lane

rden

Lossenh

G H A268 J 206 K L M

Linkhill

Heronden
Farm

Frogs Hill

Lossenham
Lane

Lossenham

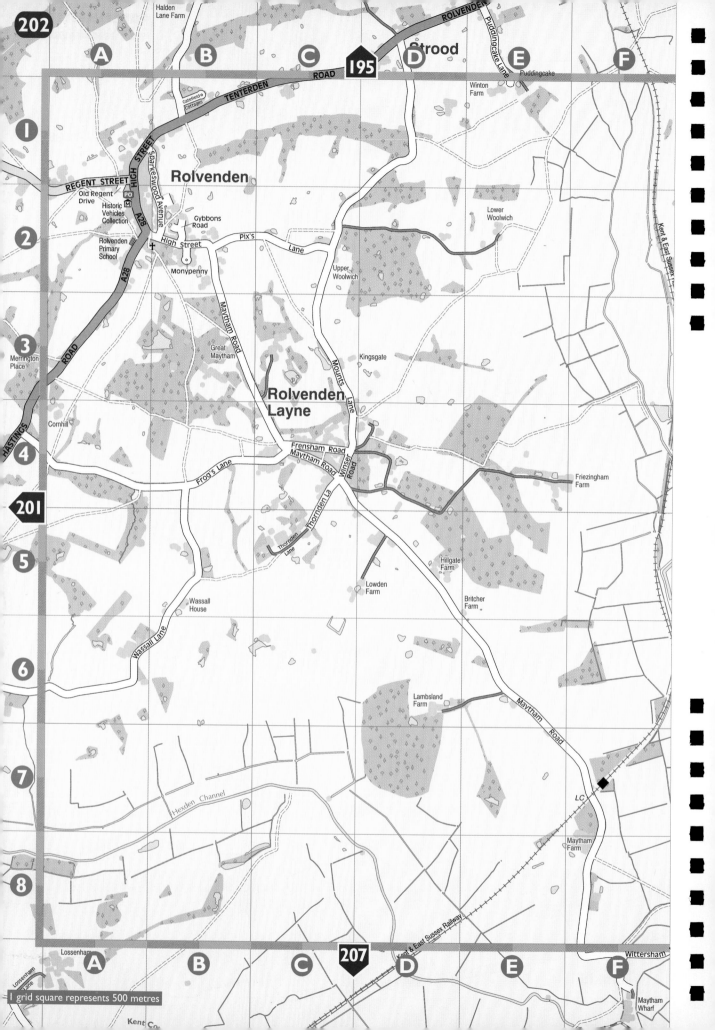

A   B   C   195   D   Strood   E   F

Halden Lane Farm

ROLVENDEN
Puddingcake Lane
Puddingcake

Winton Farm

TENTERDEN   ROAD
Gatefield Cottages

1

HIGH STREET
Sparkeswood Avenue

Rolvenden

REGENT STREET
Old Regent Drive
Historic Vehicles Collection
PO
M

Gybbons Road

Lower Woolwich

Pix's   Lane

2

A28
Rolvenden Primary School
High Street
Monypenny

Upper Woolwich

Maytham Road

3
Merrington Place

Great Maytham

Kingsgate

Mounts Lane

Rolvenden Layne

Cornhill

HASTINGS

4

Frensham Road
Maytham Road

Winser Road

Friezingham Farm

Frog's Lane

201

Thornden La

Thornden Lane

Hillgate Farm

5

Wassall House

Lowden Farm

Britcher Farm

Wassall Lane

6

Lambsland Farm

Maytham   Road

7

Hexden Channel

LC

Maytham Farm

8

Kent & East Sussex Railway

Lossenham

A   B   C   207   D   E   F   Wittersham

Lossenham Lane

Maytham Wharf

Kent & East Sussex Railway

Kent Co.

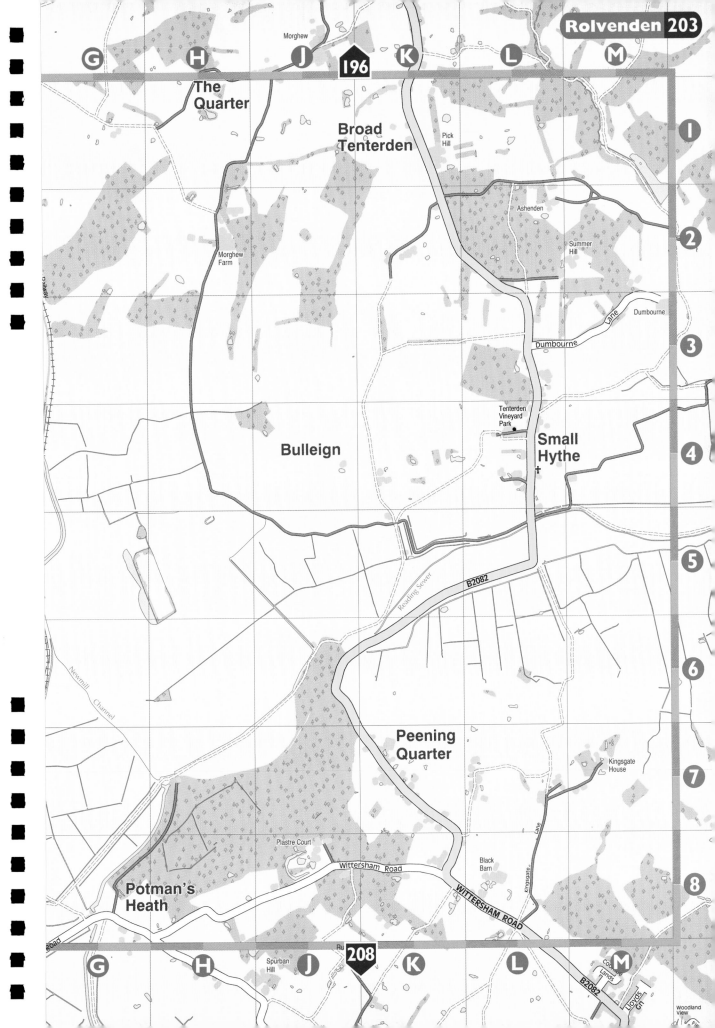

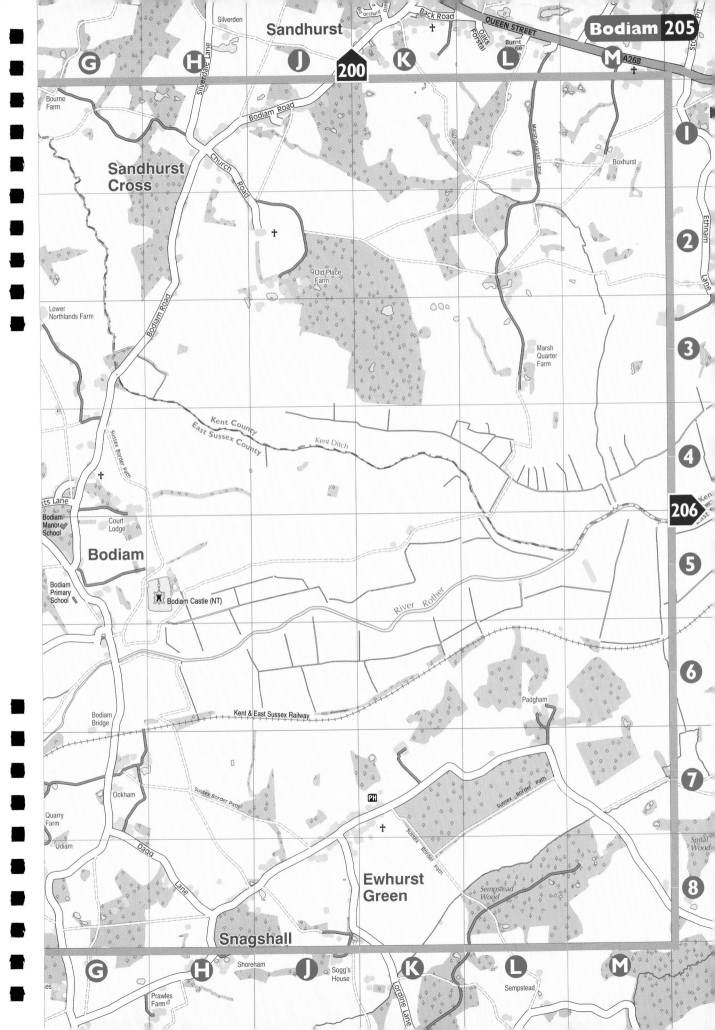

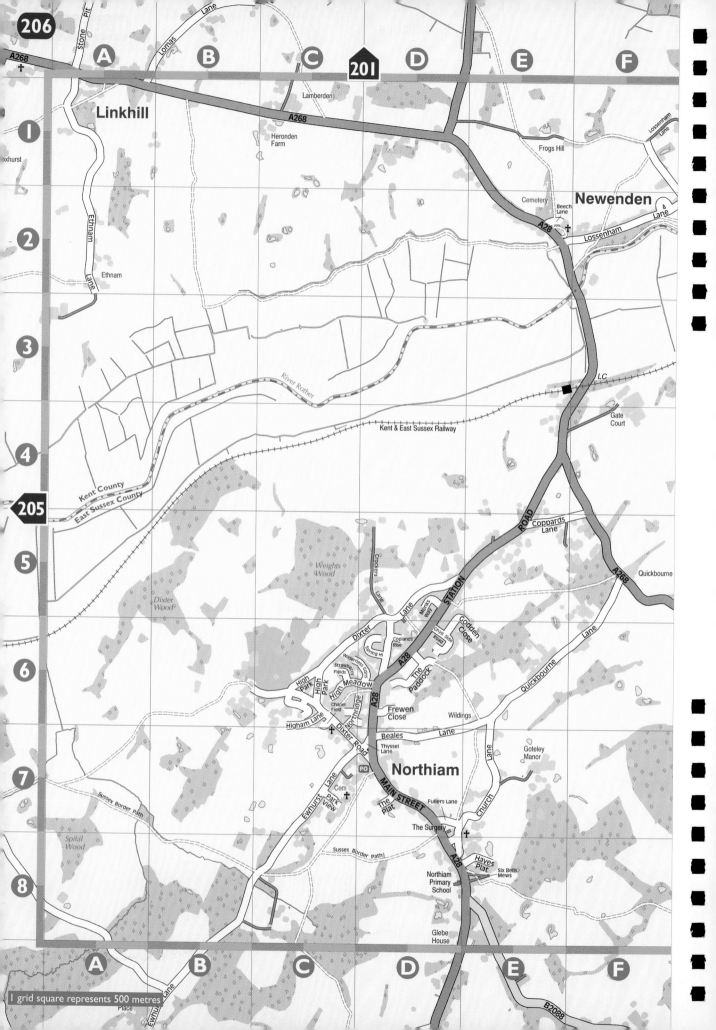

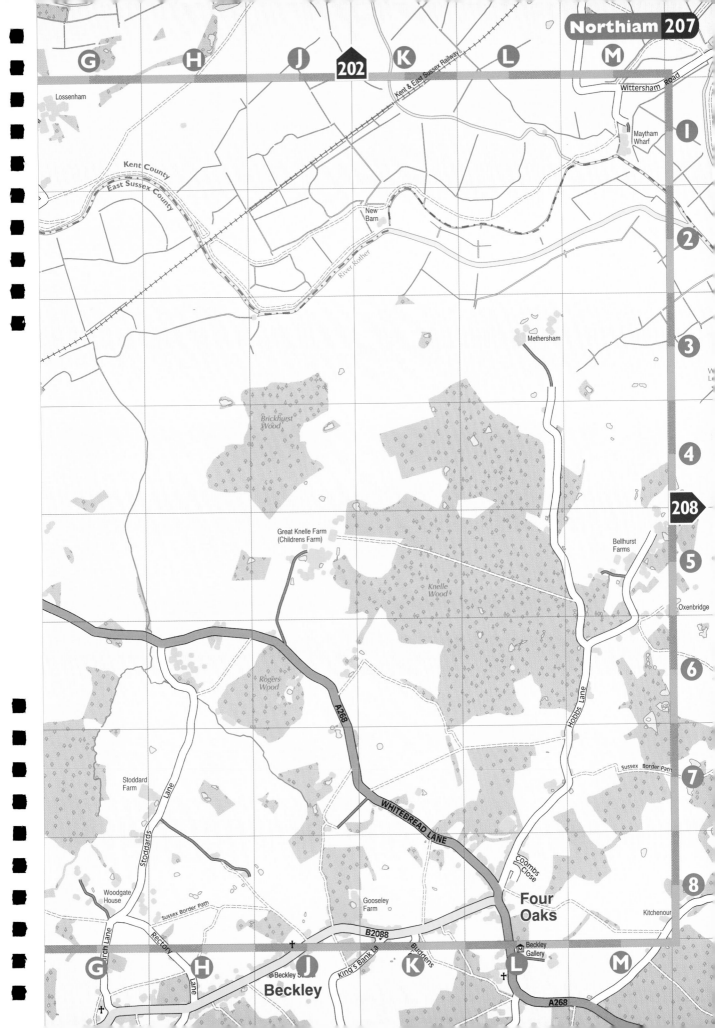

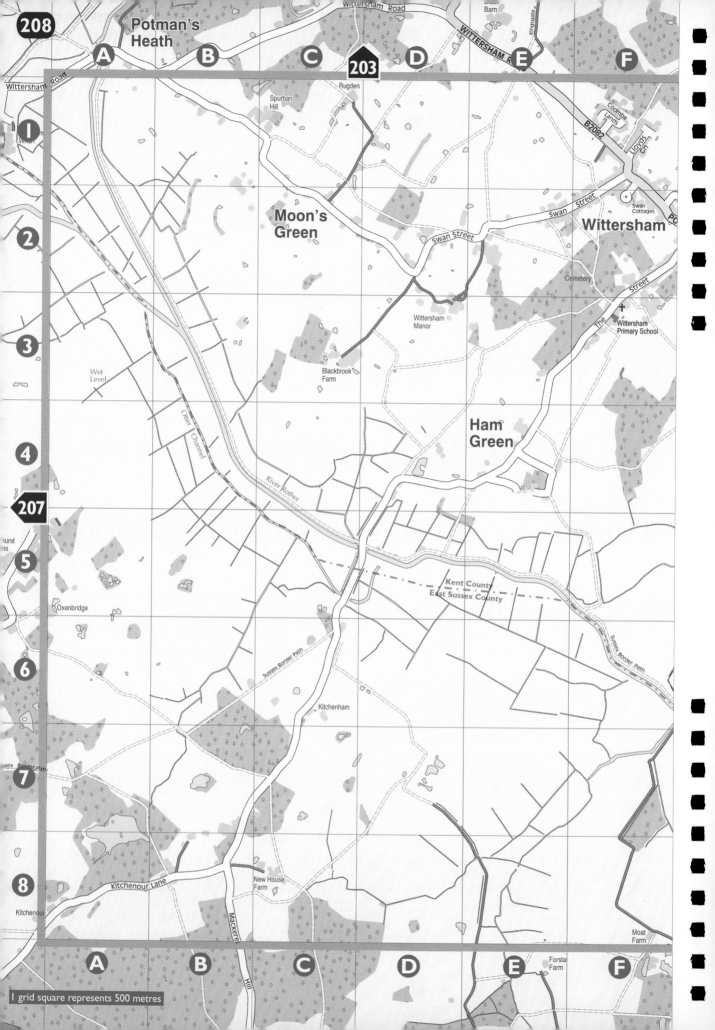

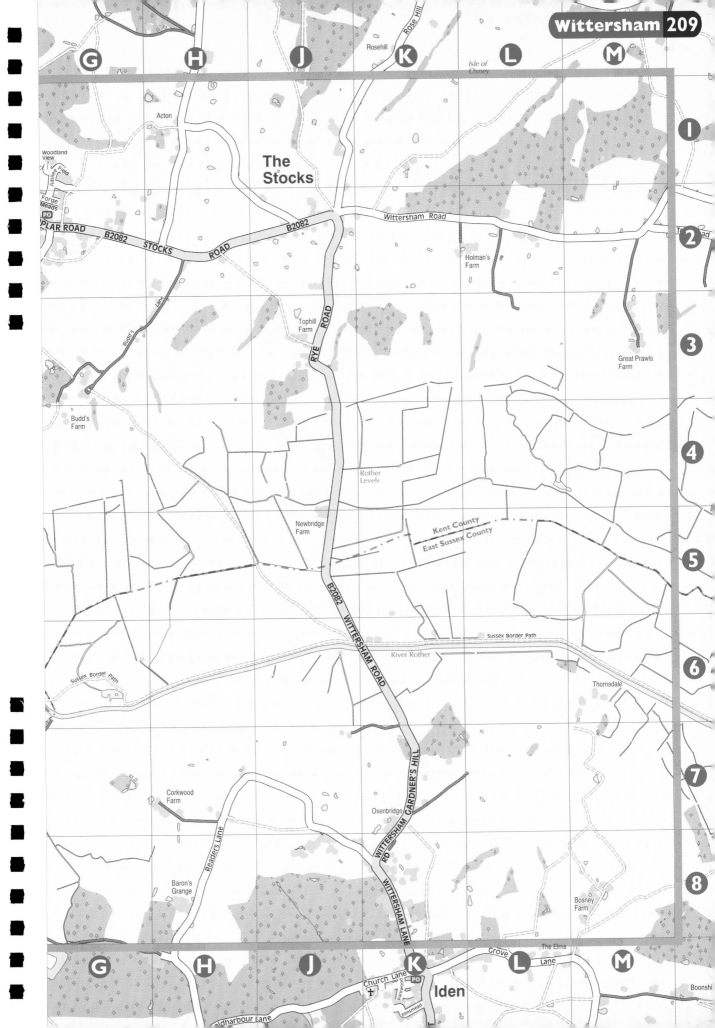

Abbey Gate	103 H2	Coldharbour	13 J3
Addington	99 M3	Coldharbour	131 J4
Allhallows	23 M6	Colliers Green	183 H3
Allhallows-on-Sea	24 B3	Collier Street	152 B3
Allington	102 F5	Colt's Hill	165 K1
Aperfield	92 B3	Comp	99 H7
Ash	61 G8	Congelow	135 G6
Ashbank	123 K6	Cooling	21 H8
Ashurst	174 F3	Cooling Street	34 F4
Aylesford	102 B2	Coomb Hill	63 G7
Badgers Mount	74 D3	Cooper's Corner	128 B5
Baker's Cross	183 M8	The Corner	167 K5
Balls Green	174 C8	Cousley Wood	188 E6
Bapchild	89 G2	Cowden	159 J7
Barden Park	147 H4	Coxheath	136 F2
Barming Heath	120 B2	Cranbrook	183 M8
Barnehurst	26 F1	Cranbrook Common	184 C3
Barnes Cray	27 K2	Crayford	27 J3
Barnes Street	149 J1	Crit Hall	193 H6
Barrow Green	89 M2	Crockenhill	57 M3
Basted	116 B1	Crockham Hill	126 E3
Bayley's Hill	129 G1	Crockhurst Street	148 D7
Beacon Hill	194 C8	Cross-at-Hand	154 A4
Beal's Green	199 J1	Cross Keys	113 H5
Bean	29 K8	Crouch	116 D1
Bearsted	122 D3	Crowdleham	96 F3
Bells Yew Green	178 D8	Cudham	92 F1
Beltring	150 D1	Culverstone Green	79 G3
Belvedere	12 D4	Curteis' Corner	186 C2
Benenden	193 M6	Curtisden Green	168 E8
Benover	135 K8	Cuxton	64 E3
Berry's Green	92 C2	Danaway	86 E3
Bessels Green	8 A3	Darenth	43 L2
Betsham	45 H1	Dartford	27 L5
Bexleyheath	26 B2	David Street	62 C8
Bexon	107 K1	Dean Bottom	44 D7
Bicknor	106 E3	Deans Bottom	86 E8
Bidborough	162 F2	Deans Hill	86 F7
Biddenden	186 A3	Dean Street	120 F7
Biddenden Green	173 K3	Dene Park	131 M4
Biggin	17 L5	Denny Bottom	10 A3
Biggin Hill	91 K3	Denton	32 A5
Birchden	175 M7	Derry Downs	56 F2
Birling	80 D7	Detling	104 D4
Bitchet Green	114 F4	Dingleden	201 H2
Blackham	174 C1	Ditton	101 L3
Blue Bell Hill	82 E4	Downe	72 B5
Bobbing	70 D6	The Down	189 H2
Bodiam	205 G5	Dryhill	112 D2
Borden	87 J3	Dunk's Green	116 C7
Borough Green	98 C5	Dunn Street	84 C5
Borstal	65 K3	Dunton Green	95 G5
Bottom Pond	107 M3	Durgates	188 A8
Bough Beech	144 B3	Durrant Green	187 K7
Boughton Green	137 J1	East Barming	120 A4
Boughton Malherbe	141 J8	East End	172 C1
Boughton Monchelsea	137 J2	East End	194 F2
Bowmans	27 H5	East Farleigh	120 D6
Boxley	103 M3	East Hill	76 D3
Branbridges	134 D7	East Malling	101 K7
Brasted	111 M2	East Malling Heath	119 G3
Brasted Chart	111 K6	East Peckham	134 B7
Breach	69 H5	East Tilbury	18 E6
Bredgar	87 J8	Eccles	82 C8
Bredhurst	84 D4	Edenbridge	142 F3
Brenchley	166 E5	Egerton Forstal	157 M4
Broad Ford	181 L1	Erith	13 H4
Broadstone	140 F8	Ewhurst Green	205 K8
Broad Street	50 E1	Eyhorne Street	123 K3
Broad Street	105 K7	Eynsford	59 G5
Broad Tenterden	203 C4	Fairbourne Heath	140 C4
Broadwater Down	177 H5	Fairseat	78 E6
Brompton	5 G2	Fant	6 A7
Brook Street	147 J6	Farleigh Green	120 A7
Broomfield	123 L8	Farningham	59 J3
Broom Hill	56 B3	Farthing Corner	85 G2
Broomhill Bank	162 E6	Farthing Green	155 G4
Buckhurst	171 L8	Fawkham Green	60 D6
Bulleign	203 J4	Fenn Street	36 C2
Burham	82 B4	Ferndale	11 K2
Burham Court	81 M4	Field Green	200 A6
Burrswood	175 J5	Five Oak Green	149 J5
Cage Green	147 L1	Five Wents	139 G3
Camden Hill	184 B3	Fleet Downs	28 D7
Camden Park	11 K6	Fletcher's Green	129 M4
Camer	62 E2	Flishinghurst	183 H6
Capel	149 H7	Foots Cray	40 D3
Capel Cross	167 L8	Force Green	111 G2
Capstone	66 F6	Fordcombe	161 J8
Castle Hill	167 G4	Forstal	102 E3
Cellarhill	89 L4	Fosten Green	185 M8
Chadwell St Mary	17 H2	Four Elms	127 J8
Chainhurst	152 C1	Four Oaks	207 L8
Chalk	32 C6	Four Throws	199 L5
Chalkwell	87 L1	Four Wents	183 G5
Charcott	145 J2	Four Wents	192 D7
Chart Corner	138 D4	Foxendown	62 E5
Chart Hill	138 D5	French Street	111 H8
Chart Sutton	138 C8	Frindsbury	3 K2
The Chart	111 K8	Friningham	105 H4
Chatham	4 E8	Frinsted	107 L6
Chattenden	35 G8	Frittenden	171 H6
Chegworth	124 B7	Frogholt	126 F2
Chelsfield	57 G8	Further Quarter	187 L2
Chelsham	90 E3	Gadshill	48 E3
Chesley	86 C2	Gillingham	67 G2
Chestnut Street	87 G1	Gill's Green	192 B8
Chevening	94 B5	Glassenbury	183 G7
Chiddingstone	144 C5	Goathurst Common	112 D8
Chiddingstone Causeway	145 H3	Goddard's Green	194 B3
Chiddingstone Hoath	160 C3	Godden Green	114 D3
Childsbridge	96 B5	Goddington	56 E6
Chillmill	166 C7	Golden Green	133 H8
Chipstead	94 E8	Golford	184 C7
Church Street	33 M4	Goodley Stock	110 D8
Cinder Hill	145 L4	Goose Green	133 K3
Clapper Hill	186 B8	Goose Green	186 A5
Claygate	132 B1	Goudhurst	182 B5
Claygate	151 L8	Gover Hill	117 G7
Claygate Cross	116 C2	Grafty Green	141 G7
Clement Street	42 F3	Grain	25 L7
Cliffe	20 E7	Grange	51 K7
Cliffe Woods	34 E6	Gravesend	31 L4
Cobham	47 H8	Grays	16 C6
Cock Street	137 M3	Great Buckland	80 C1
Coldblow	26 E7	Great Cheveney	168 C4
Coldblow	42 B1	Greatness	95 M6
Cold Harbour	70 B7	Great Pattenden	152 C7

Green Hill	122 D5	Langton Green	176 B1
Greenhithe	29 K3	Larkfield	101 J3
Green Street Green	44 C3	Leadingcross Green	141 L2
Green Street Green	73 G2	Leeds	123 J8
Grigg	156 C7	Leigh	146 B3
Groombridge	175 J6	Leigh Green	197 G6
Grove End	87 L6	Lenham	125 M8
Grove Green	103 M8	Lessness Heath	12 D5
Grubb Street	44 D5	Lett's Green	93 H2
Gun Green	199 L3	Leybourne	101 G2
Hadlow	133 H4	Lidsing	84 A4
Hadlow Stair	148 C1	Limpsfield	109 H5
Haffenden Quarter	173 J6	Limpsfield Chart	126 B1
Hale	66 F5	Limpsfield Common	109 K8
Hale Street	134 C6	Linford	18 B1
Halling	64 D8	Linkhill	206 A1
Hall's Green	129 J5	Linton	137 H5
Halstead	74 C6	Little Bayham	188 B1
Ham Green	53 H7	Little Cheveney Fm	168 A1
Ham Green	208 E4	Little Mill	133 M8
Ham Hill	81 J7	Little Pattenden	152 E5
Hamptons	116 D8	Little Preston	102 C4
Hanging Bank	128 B2	Little Thurrock	16 E3
Harbourland	103 K4	Liverton Street	141 H4
The Harbour	139 C8	Livesey Street	119 J3
Hareplain	185 L2	London Beach	187 J8
Harman's Corner	87 K3	Longfield	45 H7
Harrietsham	124 F7	Longfield Hill	45 M8
Hartley	61 H1	Longford	94 F6
Hartley	192 B3	Loose	137 H1
Hartley Green	61 G1	Loose Hill	121 H8
Hartlip	68 F8	Lords Wood	83 L3
Harvel	79 L2	Lower Bitchet	114 E4
Haviker Street	152 A4	Lower Bush	64 B2
Hawkenbury	11 L8	Lower Cousley Wood	189 G5
Hawkenbury	154 E6	Lower Cox Street	84 F7
Hawkhurst	199 G4	Lower Green	162 E8
Hawley	43 G2	Lower Green	164 F5
Haxted	142 B5	Lower Halstow	69 L2
Hazel Street	106 C2	Lower Hartlip	86 A1
Hazel Street	181 G2	Lower Haysden	147 G5
Hazelwood	72 E5	Lower Higham	33 M7
Headcorn	155 M7	Lower Rainham	68 A2
Hearnden Green	155 J4	Lower Stoke	23 L8
Hearts Delight	87 K4	Lower Twydall	51 L8
Heath Side	27 H7	Lower Upnor	50 B2
Heaverham	97 G3	Low Street	18 B5
Hempstead	67 G8	Loyterton	89 M8
Henhurst	47 L5	Luddesdown	63 H4
Henley Street	63 H2	Lunsford	101 G1
Henwood Green	165 H7	Luton	66 D4
Herne Pound	118 A3	Luxted	72 C8
Hever	143 L7	Lywood Common	174 D6
Hextable	42 C4	Lynsted	89 J7
Higham	48 E1	Mabledon	147 H7
Higham Wood	132 B7	Maidstone	6 C5
High Brooms	163 L5	Maplescombe	59 K8
Highgate	199 J3	Marden	152 E8
High Halden	187 M6	Marden Beech	168 D2
High Halstow	36 A2	Marden Thorn	169 J3
Highsted	88 B6	Markbeech	159 M3
High Street	198 F3	Marlpit Hill	142 D1
Hildenborough	131 G7	Marsh Green	142 D8
Hilden Park	147 G1	Matfield	166 A5
Hill Green	85 L4	Maypole	27 G6
Hill Hoath	144 D7	Maypole	74 B1
Hill Park	110 D1	Medhurst Row	143 K3
Hoath Corner	160 D2	Meopham	62 B5
Hockenden	41 K7	Meopham Green	62 C6
Hodsoll Street	78 E3	Meopham Station	62 D1
Holborough	81 J3	Meresborough	68 A8
Hollingbourne	124 A3	Mereworth	117 L5
Holt Hill	101 M5	Middle Quarter	187 L4
Hook Green	42 B1	Middle Stoke	37 L1
Hook Green	45 H3	Milebush	153 G5
Hook Green	62 C2	Mile Oak	166 E1
Hook Green	188 F1	Millhall	101 L3
Hoo St Werburgh	35 L7	Mill Street	101 G6
Horns Green	93 G3	Milton	31 M4
Horn Street	81 C7	Milton Regis	70 E8
Horsalls	125 H3	Mockbeggar	34 C8
Horshoe Green	159 M4	Modest Corner	163 G3
Horsmonden	167 K7	Monks Hill	172 E6
Horton Kirby	43 M8	Moon's Green	208 C2
Hosey Hill	111 G6	Moorhouse Bank	110 C6
How Green	143 M3	Moor Street	68 D6
Howt Green	70 F4	The Moor	199 H5
Hubbard's Hill	113 K8	Mowshurst	143 G1
Hucking	106 A4	Mundy Bois	157 M5
Hulberry	58 D5	Murston	88 E1
Hungershall Park	10 A8	Nash Street	46 C6
Hunton	136 A5	Nettlestead	118 E7
Ide Hill	128 A1	Nettlestead Green	134 D3
Iden Green	182 E5	New Barn	45 K6
Iden Green	200 F1	Newenden	206 F2
Ightham	97 M8	New House	31 G7
Ightham Common	115 J2	New Hythe	101 K1
Istead Rise	46 A4	Newington	69 L2
Ivy Hatch	115 K3	New Street	61 M8
Iwade	70 F1	New Town	28 B4
Kemsing	96 B3	New Town	64 C7
Kemsley	71 H4	New Town	100 D4
Kemsley Street	84 E4	Noah's Ark	96 C5
Kent Street	118 B3	Noke Street	49 L1
Kettle Corner	120 B5	North Cray	26 C8
Kevingtown	70 A7	North End	13 H7
Keycol	70 A7	Northfleet	30 E3
Key's Green	179 L1	Northfleet Green	45 L2
Key Street	70 C8	North Halling	64 C6
Kildown	190 C3	Northiam	206 D7
Kings Farm	31 L8	North Street	37 G3
Kingswood	140 A3	Northumberland Heath	12 E6
Kipping's Cross	179 J1	Oad Street	87 G4
Kippington	8 C7	Oakhurst	130 C3
Kit's Coty	82 E5	Offham	99 M5
Knatts Valley	77 C4	Old Bexley	26 C5
Knockhall	29 K3	Oldbury	97 K7
Knockholt	97 K7	Old Cryals	165 M8
Knockmill	77 C6	Orpington	56 B6
Knox Bridge	170 C7	Orsett Heath	17 H1
Laddingford	135 G8	Otford	95 J3
Lakeside	15 J3	Otham	122 C6
Lamberhurst	180 D8	Otham Hole	122 E7
Lamberhurst Quarter	179 M3	Otterham Quay	68 G3
Lamb's Cross	138 B7	Oxted	108 F7
Lane End	43 M2	Paddlesworth	80 F4
Langley	138 E1	Paddock Wood	150 D7
Langley Heath	139 H1		

Palmer's Green	166 F5
Park Corner	176 A8
Parker's Green	132 C7
Parkgate	195 K3
Park Wood	84 E2
Park Wood	138 A1
Parrock Farm	31 M8
Pearson's Green	167 G2
Peckham Bush	133 M5
Peening Quarter	203 K7
Pell Green	188 D6
Pembles Cross	157 L2
Pembury	164 E7
Penenden Heath	103 L6
Penshurst	161 K1
Perry Street	31 H5
Petteridge	166 B7
Pettings	78 D2
Pipsden	199 M4
Pittswood	132 C5
Pizien Well	118 D6
Platt	98 E6
Platt's Heath	141 H4
Plaxtol	116 B5
Plumtree Green	155 J5
Pollhill	124 D8
Pootings	127 G6
Potman's Heath	203 G8
Potter's Forstal	157 K3
Poundsbridge	161 L5
Poverest	40 C8
Powder Mills	147 G2
Pratling Street	102 D1
Pratt's Bottom	73 K4
Priestwood	62 D8
Priestwood Green	62 E8
Printstile	162 C2
Puddledock	41 M3
Puddledock	127 J3
Pullington	194 B8
Purfleet	14 C1
Pye Corner	140 C7
The Quarter	157 K8
The Quarter	203 H1
Queen Street	150 F5
Rabbit's Cross	154 A1
Radfield	89 J3
Rainham	68 C6
Ramsden	56 E4
Ramslye	176 F4
Red Hill	119 H4
Ridley	78 D1
Ringlestone	102 F6
Ringlestone	125 H1
Riseden	181 J8
Riverhead	8 A1
Riverview Park	47 J1
Robhurst	197 L3
Rochester	3 G5
The Rocks	101 J8
Rodmersham	88 F5
Rodmersham Green	88 D6
Rolvenden	202 B1
Rolvenden Layne	202 C3
Romford	165 H6
Romney Street	76 B6
Rooks Hill	114 E6
Roseacre	122 C3
Rosherville	31 H3
Roughway	116 D7
Round Green	183 H1
Round Street	46 F8
Royal British Legion Village	102 B5
Royal Tunbridge Wells	10 C6
Rushenden	55 H3
Rushmore Hill	73 L7
Rusthall	176 E1
Ruxley	41 G3
Ryarsh	100 C1
St John's	95 J8
St John's	163 H7
St Leonard's Street	100 C1
St Mary Cray	56 E1
St Mary's Hoo	22 E7
St Michaels	196 D1
St Paul's Cray	40 C6
Saint's Hill	161 K5
Salmans	161 G2
Sandhurst	200 C8
Sandhurst Cross	205 G1
Sandling	103 H4
Sandown Park	164 B7
Sandway	141 K2
Scragged Oak	84 F6
Seacox Heath	198 A3
Seal	96 C7
Sevenoaks	9 K5
Sevenoaks Common	113 J7
Sevenoaks Weald	129 J2
Sharnal Street	36 C4
Shepway	121 M5
Sherwood Park	164 A7
Shipbourne	115 L8
Shoreham	75 G5
Shorne	48 A2
Shorne Ridgeway	47 M4
Sidcup	40 D1
Silver Street	87 H7
Singlewell	46 E3
Sinkhurst Green	171 G4
Sissinghurst	184 C5
Sittingbourne	88 C3
Slade Green	13 J8
Small Hythe	203 L4
Smarden	173 J4
Smarden Bell	173 G3
Smart's Hill	161 K5
Snagshall	205 H8
Snipeshill	88 E2
Snodland	81 K6
Sole Street	62 L1
Southborough	163 J4
South Darenth	43 M5
Southfleet	45 K3
South Green	86 C8
South Stifford	15 M4
South Street	79 G1
South Street	85 M6

South Street	92 B5	Styants Bottom	97 H7	Troy Town	3 K9
Sparrow's Green	188 B8	Sundridge	112 B2	Troy Town	126 B8
Speed Gate	60 B5	Sutton at Hone	43 J4	Tubslake	192 B5
Speldhurst	162 C6	Sutton Valence	139 G6	Tudeley	148 E6
Spitals Cross	142 E2	Swanley	42 C7	Tudeley Hale	148 E4
Standen	172 C8	Swanley Village	42 C6	Tunbridge Hill	36 F4
Standen Street	200 F4	Swanscombe	29 M4	Tunstall	87 M5
Stanstead	78 A5	Swanton Street	107 H2	Turner's Green	188 A7
Staplehurst	170 B1	Swift's Green	157 G8	Twitton	95 G2
Starvecrow	131 L5	Tatsfield	91 M6	Twydall	67 K3
Stede Quarter	187 G4	Teasley Mead	174 E2	Ulcombe	140 A6
Stick Hill	159 K2	Temple Hill	27 M2	Underlining Green	153 H3
Stiff Street	87 H6	Tenterden	196 C5	Underriver	114 C8
Stockbury	86 A5	Teston	119 J6	Upchurch	69 H1
Stockland Green	162 E5	Teynham	89 L2	Upper Bush	64 B3
Stocks Green	146 D1	Thong	47 J3	Upper Halling	63 M8
The Stocks	209 J1	Three Chimneys	185 K4	Upper Hayesden	146 D7
Stoke	37 J2	Thurnham	104 E5	Upper Rodmersham	88 E7
Stone	29 H3	Tilbury	17 J7	Upper Upnor	50 A4
Stone Cross	175 M1	Timberden Bottom	75 G4	Vigo Village	79 H5
Stonecrouch	190 A6	Titsey	109 L3	Wainscott	49 L3
Stonehill Green	115 C3	Tonbridge	147 L4	Walderslade	83 H2
Stone Street	115 C3	Tong	155 L3	Walter's Green	161 G6
Stonewood	29 M8	Tovil	6 C9	Wanshurst Green	153 L6
Strawberry Hill	176 F5	Toy's Hill	127 L2	Ware Street	104 D8
Strood	2 D4	Trench Wood	131 J6	Warmlake	138 F5
Strood	195 K8	Trottiscliffe	79 J8	Wateringbury	118 F5

Waterman Quarter	171 M3	Wierton	138 B5
Wayfield	66 D6	Wigmore	84 E1
Weavering Street	122 B1	Wildernesse	96 A8
Weller's Town	144 E8	Willington	122 B4
Well Hill	57 K8	Wilmington	42 D1
Well Street	101 G7	Wilsley Green	183 M7
West Court	32 A7	Wilsley Pound	184 A5
West Cross	201 M1	Winchet Hill	168 D7
Wested Fm	58 A3	Windmill Hill	68 E2
Westerham	110 F5	Winkhurst Green	128 D5
West Farleigh	119 K7	Wittersham	208 F2
Westfield Sole	83 L6	Woldingham	108 C1
West Kingsdown	77 G3	Woldingham Garden Village	90 B7
West Malling	100 D6	Woodlands	76 E7
West Peckham	117 K7	Woodsden	200 A1
West Street	20 C8	Wood's Green	188 B5
West Thurrock	15 J4	Woodstock	88 A7
West Tilbury	18 A5	Worms Hill	182 D1
Westwood	44 E4	Wormshill	107 J6
West Yoke	60 F6	Wouldham	64 E8
Wetham Green	53 H8	Wrotham	98 C2
Whetsted	150 A4	Wrotham Heath	99 G3
White Oak	42 A6	Yalding	135 J4
White Post	160 F6	Yelsted	85 J4
Whitley Row	112 D7	Yopps Green	116 A4
Wick Hill	172 B5		
Wickhurst	145 L1		

USING THE STREET INDEX

Street names are listed alphabetically. Each street name is followed by its postal town or area locality, the Postcode District, the page number, and the reference to the square in which the name is found.

Example: **Abbotswood Cl** *BELV* DA17 .... **12** A2 🗓

Some entries are followed by a number in a blue box. This number indicates the location of the street within the referenced grid square. The full street name is listed at the side of the map page.

GENERAL ABBREVIATIONS

ACC	ACCESS	CUTT	CUTTINGS	HOL	HOLLOW	NW	NORTH WEST	SKWY	SKYWAY

ACC	ACCESS	CUTT	CUTTINGS	HOL	HOLLOW	NW	NORTH WEST	SKWY	SKYWAY
ALY	ALLEY	CV	COVE	HOSP	HOSPITAL	O/P	OVERPASS	SMT	SUMMIT
AP	APPROACH	CYN	CANYON	HRB	HARBOUR	OFF	OFFICE	SOC	SOCIETY
AR	ARCADE	DEPT	DEPARTMENT	HTH	HEATH	ORCH	ORCHARD	SP	SPUR
ASS	ASSOCIATION	DL	DALE	HTS	HEIGHTS	OV	OVAL	SPR	SPRING
AV	AVENUE	DM	DAM	HVN	HAVEN	PAL	PALACE	SQ	SQUARE
BCH	BEACH	DR	DRIVE	HWY	HIGHWAY	PAS	PASSAGE	ST	STREET
BLDS	BUILDINGS	DRO	DROVE	IMP	IMPERIAL	PAV	PAVILION	STN	STATION
BND	BEND	DRY	DRIVEWAY	IN	INLET	PDE	PARADE	STR	STREAM
BNK	BANK	DWGS	DWELLINGS	IND EST	INDUSTRIAL ESTATE	PH	PUBLIC HOUSE	STRD	STRAND
BR	BRIDGE	E	EAST	INF	INFIRMARY	PK	PARK	SW	SOUTH WEST
BRK	BROOK	EMB	EMBANKMENT	INFO	INFORMATION	PKWY	PARKWAY	TDG	TRADING
BTM	BOTTOM	EMBY	EMBASSY	INT	INTERCHANGE	PL	PLACE	TER	TERRACE
BUS	BUSINESS	ESP	ESPLANADE	IS	ISLAND	PLN	PLAIN	THWY	THROUGHWAY
BVD	BOULEVARD	EST	ESTATE	JCT	JUNCTION	PLNS	PLAINS	TNL	TUNNEL
BY	BYPASS	EX	EXCHANGE	JTY	JETTY	PLZ	PLAZA	TOLL	TOLLWAY
CATH	CATHEDRAL	EXPY	EXPRESSWAY	KG	KING	POL	POLICE STATION	TPK	TURNPIKE
CEM	CEMETERY	EXT	EXTENSION	KNL	KNOLL	PR	PRINCE	TR	TRACK
CEN	CENTRE	F/O	FLYOVER	L	LAKE	PREC	PRECINCT	TRL	TRAIL
CFT	CROFT	FC	FOOTBALL CLUB	LA	LANE	PREP	PREPARATORY	TWR	TOWER
CH	CHURCH	FK	FORK	LDG	LODGE	PRIM	PRIMARY	U/P	UNDERPASS
CHA	CHASE	FLD	FIELD	LGT	LIGHT	PROM	PROMENADE	UNI	UNIVERSITY
CHYD	CHURCHYARD	FLDS	FIELDS	LK	LOCK	PRS	PRINCESS	UPR	UPPER
CIR	CIRCLE	FLS	FALLS	LKS	LAKES	PRT	PORT	V	VALE
CIRC	CIRCUS	FLS	FLATS	LNDG	LANDING	PT	POINT	VA	VALLEY
CL	CLOSE	FM	FARM	LTL	LITTLE	PTH	PATH	VIAD	VIADUCT
CLFS	CLIFFS	FT	FORT	LWR	LOWER	PZ	PIAZZA	VIL	VILLA
CMP	CAMP	FWY	FREEWAY	MAG	MAGISTRATE	QD	QUADRANT	VIS	VISTA
CNR	CORNER	FY	FERRY	MAN	MANSIONS	QU	QUEEN	VLG	VILLAGE
CO	COUNTY	GA	GATE	MD	MEAD	QY	QUAY	VLS	VILLAS
COLL	COLLEGE	GAL	GALLERY	MDW	MEADOWS	R	RIVER	VW	VIEW
COM	COMMON	GDN	GARDEN	MEM	MEMORIAL	RBT	ROUNDABOUT	W	WEST
COMM	COMMISSION	GDNS	GARDENS	MKT	MARKET	RD	ROAD	WD	WOOD
CON	CONVENT	GLD	GLADE	MKTS	MARKETS	RDG	RIDGE	WHF	WHARF
COT	COTTAGE	GLN	GLEN	ML	MALL	REP	REPUBLIC	WK	WALK
COTS	COTTAGES	GN	GREEN	ML	MILL	RES	RESERVOIR	WKS	WALKS
CP	CAPE	GND	GROUND	MNR	MANOR	RFC	RUGBY FOOTBALL CLUB	WLS	WELLS
CPS	COPSE	GRA	GRANGE	MS	MEWS	RI	RISE	WY	WAY
CR	CREEK	GRG	GARAGE	MSN	MISSION	RP	RAMP	YD	YARD
CREM	CREMATORIUM	GT	GREAT	MT	MOUNT	RW	ROW	YHA	YOUTH HOSTEL
CRS	CRESCENT	GTWY	GATEWAY	MTN	MOUNTAIN	S	SOUTH		
CSWY	CAUSEWAY	GV	GROVE	MTS	MOUNTAINS	SCH	SCHOOL		
CT	COURT	HGR	HIGHER	MUS	MUSEUM	SE	SOUTH EAST		
CTRL	CENTRAL	HL	HILL	MWY	MOTORWAY	SER	SERVICE AREA		
CTS	COURTS	HLS	HILLS	N	NORTH	SH	SHORE		
CTYD	COURTYARD	HO	HOUSE	NE	NORTH EAST	SHOP	SHOPPING		

POSTCODE TOWNS AND AREA ABBREVIATIONS

ABYW	Abbey Wood	DIT/AY	Ditton/Aylesford	HOO/HM	Hoo St Werburgh/Higham	RMAID	Rural Maidstone	STH/RUST	Southborough/Rusthall
BELV	Belvedere	E/WMAL	East & West Malling	HRTF	Hartfield	ROCH	Rochester	STMC/STPC	St Mary Cray/St Paul's Cray
BFN/LL	Blackfen/Longlands	EDEN	Edenbridge	IOS	Isle of Sheppey	RRTW	Rural Royal Tunbridge Wells	STPH/PW	Staplehurst/Paddock Wood
BGR/WK	Borough Green/West Kingsdown	EGRIN	East Grinstead	LING	Lingfield	RSEV	Rural Sevenoaks	STRD	Strood
BH/WHM	Biggin Hill/Westerham	ERITH	Erith	MAID/BEAR	Maidstone/Bearsted	RSIT	Rural Sittingbourne	SWCM	Swanscombe
BUR/ETCH	Burwash/Etchingham	ERITHM	Erith Marshes	MAID/SHEP	Maidstone/Shepway	RTON	Rural Tonbridge	SWLY	Swanley
BXLY	Bexley	EYN	Eynsford	MAIDW	Maidstone west	RTWE	Royal Tunbridge Wells	TENT	Tenterden
BXLYHN	Bexleyheath north	GDST	Godstone	MEO	Meopham	RTWE/PEM	Royal Tunbridge Wells east/Pembury	TIL	Tilbury
BXLYHS	Bexleyheath south	GILL	Gillingham	ORP	Orpington	RYE	Rye	TON	Tonbridge
CDW/CHF	Chadwell St Mary/Chafford Hundred	GRAYS	Grays	OXTED	Oxted	SCUP	Sidcup	TONN	Tonbridge north
CHAT	Chatham	GRH	Greenhithe	PUR	Purfleet	SEV	Sevenoaks	WADH	Wadhurst
CHST	Chislehurst	GVE	Gravesend east	QBOR	Queenborough	SIT	Sittingbourne	WALD	Walderslade
CRBK	Cranbrook	GVW	Gravesend west	RAIN	Rainham (Gt Lon)	SLH/COR	Stanford-le-Hope/Corringham	WARL	Warlingham
CTHM	Caterham	HART	Hartley	RASHW	Rural Ashford west	SNOD	Snodland	WBY/YAL	Wateringbury/Yalding
DART	Dartford	HAWK	Hawkhurst	RBTBR	Robertsbridge	SOCK/AV	South Ockendon/Aveley	WTHK	West Thurrock
		HAYES	Hayes	RDART	Rural Dartford				
		HDCN	Headcorn	RHAM	Rainham (Kent)				

A

Abbey Crs *BELV* DA17	12 C3	Abigail Crs *WALD* ME5	83 J4
Abbey Rd *BXLYHS* DA6	26 A2	Abingdon Rd *MAIDW* ME16	120 B3
GRH DA9	29 L3	Abingdon Wy *ORP* BR6	56 D7
GVE DA12	32 A6	Abinger Dr *WALD* ME5	83 M3
RHAM ME8	67 J3	Acacia Rd *DART* DA1	27 L6
STRD ME2	2 C1	GRH DA9	29 C4
Abbey Wood Rd *E/WMAL* ME19	100 C8	Academy Dr *GILL* ME7	67 H5
Abbots Court Rd *HOO/HM* ME3	51 H1	Acer Av *RTWE/PEM* TN2	177 L5
Abbots Fld *MAIDW* ME16	120 D3	Acer Rd *BH/WHM* TN16	91 M2
Abbotswood Cl *BELV* DA17	12 A2 🗓	Achilles Rd *WALD* ME5	83 L3
Abbott Rd *BGR/WK* TN15	98 B6	Acorn Cl *STPH/PW* TN12	149 K6
Abbotts Cl *ROCH* ME1	65 K2	Acorn Gv *DIT/AY* ME20	101 M5
SWLY BR8	42 C8	Acorn Pl *MAID/SHEP* ME15	122 A7
Acorn Rd *GILL* ME7	67 H1		
The Acorns *HDCN* TN27	173 H4		
SEV TN13	8 E3		
Acorn Wharf Rd *ROCH* ME1	3 K5 🗓		

Acott Flds *WBY/YAL* ME18	135 H4	Admers Wy *MEO* DA13	79 K5 🗓
Acre Cl *CHAT* ME4	66 A4	Admiral Cl *STMC/STPC* BR5	40 F8 🗓
Acre Gv *STRD* ME2	81 J1	Admirals Wk *CRBK* TN17	193 M3
Adam Cl *RMAID* ME17	136 F2	GRH DA9	29 K3 🗓
Adams Cl *TENT* TN30	196 D4	TENT TN30	196 E4
Adams Sq *BXLYHN* DA7	26 A1 🗓	Admiralty Rd *STRD* ME2	50 B4 🗓
Addington Rd *SIT* ME10	88 A2	Admiralty Ter *STRD* ME2	50 B4 🗓
Addison Cl *E/WMAL* ME19	101 H4	Admiral Wy *WBY/YAL* ME18	118 C4
Addison Gdns *GRAYS* RM17	16 E3 🗓	Adstock Wy *GRAYS* RM17	16 B3
Addlestead Rd *STPH/PW* TN12	134 A7	Advice Av *CDH/CHF* RM16	16 C1
Adelaide Dr *SIT* ME10	87 L1	Afghan Rd *CHAT* ME4	4 B6
Adelaide Rd *GILL* ME7	5 K6	Aintree Cl *GVE* DA12	31 K8
TIL RM18	17 H7	Aintree Rd *WALD* ME5	83 L2
The Adelaide *HOO/HM* ME3	33 L7 🗓	Airedale Cl *RDART* DA2	28 E6
Adisham Dr *MAIDW* ME16	102 D6	Aisher Wy *SEV* TN13	95 G7
Adisham Gn *SIT* ME10	71 H5	Ajax Rd *ROCH* ME1	65 L6
		Akehurst La *BGR/WK* TN15	9 J7

Alamein Av *WALD* ME5	66 B6	
Alamein Gdns *RDART* DA2	28 F5	
Alamein Rd *SWCM* DA10	29 M4	
Alanbrooke *GVE* DA12	31 L5	
Alan Cl *DART* DA1	27 L2	
Alban Crs *EYN* DA4	60 D3	
Albany Cl *TON* TN9	147 M6	
Albany Hl *RTWE/PEM* TN2	11 K2	
Albany Rd *BELV* DA17	12 B5	
CHAT ME4	66 D3	
GILL ME7	5 M6	
ROCH ME1	65 L1	
SIT ME10	88 A2	
TIL RM18	17 J7	
Albany St *MAID/BEAR* ME14	7 J2	
Albany Ter *CHAT* ME4	4 B6	
Albatross Av *STRD* ME2	48 C7	

Albemarle Cl GRAYS RM17 16 C1
Albemarle Rd WALD ME5 83 L3
Alberta Rd BXLYHN DA7 12 E7
Albert Cl CDH/CHF RM16 16 E2
Albert Dr MAID/SHEP ME15 136 D1
Albert Murray Cl GVE DA12 31 L5 ❶
Albert Pl STRD ME2 3 H3
Albert Rd BELV DA17 12 B4
BXLY DA5 26 C4
CHAT ME4 4 E8
GILL ME7 5 J5
ORP BR6 56 C8
RDART DA2 27 L8
ROCH ME1 65 L2
STMC/STPC BR5 56 D2
SWCM DA10 30 B4
TON TN9 147 K4
WARL CR6 90 A3
Albert St MAID/BEAR ME14 6 F1
RTW TN1 11 G3
Albion Pl MAID/BEAR ME14 7 J4
MAID/SHEP ME15 7 J5
Albion Rd BXLYHS DA6 26 B2
GVE DA12 31 L5
RTW TN1 11 H2
STPH/PW TN12 152 F8
WALD ME5 83 K3
Albion Ter GVE DA12 31 L4
Albion Wy EDEN TN8 142 E1
Albury Av BXLYHN DA7 12 A8
Albury Cl WALD ME5 83 M3
Alder Cl RTWE/PEM TN2 163 L4
Alderney Rd ERITH DA8 13 J6
Aldershot Rd WALD ME5 66 C6
Alders Meadow TON TN9 147 H3
Alders Rd RTON TN11 149 G7
The Alders WBY/YAL ME18 117 M6
Alder Wy SWLY BR8 41 M6
Aldington Cl WALD ME5 66 D8
Aldington La MAID/BEAR ME14 104 F5
Aldington Rd MAID/BEAR ME14 122 B1
Aldon Cl MAID/BEAR ME14 7 L1
Aldon La E/WMAL ME19 99 K5
Alen Sq STPH/PW TN12 170 B1
Alexander Rd GRH DA9 29 L3
Alexandra Av GILL ME7 67 G1
WARL CR6 90 B3
Alexandra Cl CDH/CHF RM16 17 K1
SIT ME10 71 G6 ❶
SWLY BR8 42 A6
Alexandra Gln WALD ME5 83 J4
Alexandra Rd BH/WHM TN16 91 K5
CHAT ME4 66 D3
ERITH DA8 13 H5
GVE DA12 32 A5
TIL RM18 17 H8 ❶
TON TN9 147 K5 ❶
WARL CR6 90 A3
Alexandra St MAID/BEAR ME14 6 F1
Alexandra Wy TIL RM18 18 D3
Alford Rd ERITH DA8 12 E4
Alfred Cl CHAT ME4 66 D3
Alfred Pl GVW DA11 31 H6
Alfred Rd BELV DA17 12 B4
GVW DA11 31 K7
RDART DA2 43 H1
Alfred St GRAYS RM17 16 E5
Alkerden La GRH DA9 29 L4
Alkham Rd MAID/BEAR ME14 7 L3
Allan Cl STH/RUST TN4 176 E1
Allandale Pl ORP BR6 56 F6
Allandale Rd RTWE/PEM TN2 163 M7
Allard Cl STMC/STPC BR5 56 E3
Allenby Crs GRAYS RM17 16 D4
Allenby Rd BH/WHM TN16 92 A3
Allen Cl WALD ME5 66 E7 ❶
Allendale Cl RDART DA2 28 F6 ❶
Allens La BGR/WK TN15 116 C6
Allen St MAID/BEAR ME14 7 H2
Allhallows Rd HOO/HM ME3 23 L8
Alliance Wy STPH/PW TN12 150 B7
Allington Dr STRD ME2 2 B2
TONN TN10 132 C8
Allington Gdns WBY/YAL ME18 118 F6
Allington Rd ORP BR6 56 A4
RHAM ME8 67 J2
STPH/PW TN12 150 B6
Allington Wy MAIDW ME16 102 D7
Allison Av GILL ME7 67 G4
Allnutt Mill Cl MAID/SHEP ME15 6 C9
Allotment La SEV TN13 9 K1
All Saints Cl SWCM DA10 30 B3
All Saints' Rd GVW DA11 31 H6
HAWK TN18 199 J4
SIT ME10 88 E1
STH/RUST TN4 163 J7
Allsworth Cl RSIT ME9 69 K7
Alma Pl STRD ME2 2 F4
Alma Rd DIT/AY ME20 82 B7 ❶
E/WMAL ME19 100 C5
STMC/STPC BR5 56 F5
SWCM DA10 30 A3
Almond Cl CDH/CHF RM16 17 J2
Almond Dr SWLY BR8 41 M7
Almond Gv GILL ME7 84 C1
Almond Rd RDART DA2 28 E5
The Almonds MAID/BEAR ME14 122 C1
Almon Pl ROCH ME1 3 L8
Alpha Cl HOO/HM ME3 36 F6
Alsager Av QBOR ME11 55 H2
Alton Cl BXLY DA5 26 A6
Aluric Cl CDH/CHF RM16 17 K3
Amanda Cl WALD ME5 83 G2
Amber Cl RSIT ME9 89 M3
Amber La RMAID ME17 138 C4
Amberleaze Dr RTWE/PEM TN2 164 F7
Amberley Cl ORP BR6 56 B8
Amberley Ct SCUP DA14 40 E2
Ambleside SIT ME10 88 E2
Ambleside Rd BXLYHN DA7 12 C8
Ambley Gn GILL ME7 67 J5
Ambley Rd GILL ME7 67 J4
Ambrook Rd BELV DA17 12 C2
Ambrose Cl DART DA1 27 H2
ORP BR6 56 B6 ❶
Ambrose Hl WALD ME5 5 J9
Ames Av MAID/BEAR ME14 122 C1
Ames Rd SWCM DA10 30 A4
Amethyst Av WALD ME5 66 A7
Amherst Cl MAIDW ME16 6 B3
STMC/STPC BR5 40 C8
Amherst Dr STMC/STPC BR5 40 B8
Amherst Hl GILL ME7 4 E2
SEV TN13 8 C2
Amherst Redoubt GILL ME7 4 E3
Amherst Rd ROCH ME1 65 M2
SEV TN13 9 H1
STH/RUST TN4 10 F1
Amhurst Bank Rd
RTWE/PEM TN2 165 G2
Ampleforth Cl ORP BR6 56 E7 ❶
Amsbury Rd MAID/SHEP ME15 136 C3
Amy Rd OXTED RH8 109 G7
Anchorage Cl HOO/HM ME3 37 L2 ❶
Anchor Bvd GRH DA9 28 E2
Anchor Rd ROCH ME1 65 L4
Anderson Wy BELV DA17 12 D1
Andover Rd ORP BR6 56 A4
Andrea Av CDH/CHF RM16 16 B1
Andrew Broughton Wy
MAID/BEAR ME14 7 J4
Andrew Cl DART DA1 26 F3
Andrew Rd STH/RUST TN4 163 L5
Andrews Cl RTWE/PEM TN2 11 L1
STMC/STPC BR5 40 F7 ❶
Anerley Cl MAIDW ME16 102 F6
Angel La TON TN9 147 K4
Angle Rd WTHK RM20 15 M5
Anglesea Pl GVE DA12 31 K4
GVW DA11 31 K4
Anglesea Rd STMC/STPC BR5 56 E2
Anglesey Av MAID/SHEP ME15 121 J7
Anglesey Cl WALD ME5 66 D6
Angley Ct STPH/PW TN12 167 J8
Angley Rd CRBK TN17 183 L8
Angley Wk CRBK TN17 183 M7 ❶
Anne of Cleves Rd DART DA1 27 M3
Annetts Hall BGR/WK TN15 98 C5
Annie Rd SNOD ME6 81 H7 ❶
Ansell Av CHAT ME4 66 C3
Anselm Cl SIT ME10 88 A1
Anson Av E/WMAL ME19 118 B2
Anson Cl WALD ME5 66 E7
Antelope Av CDH/CHF RM16 16 C2
Anthony Cl SEV TN13 95 G7 ❶
Anthonys La SWLY BR8 42 C5
Anthonys Wy STRD ME2 50 A5
Aperfield Rd BH/WHM TN16 92 A3
ERITH DA8 13 H5
Appleby Cl ROCH ME1 65 M6
Apple Cl SNOD ME6 81 H7
Apple Ct STPH/PW TN12 150 B7 ❶
Applecross Cl ROCH ME1 65 K1
Appledore Av BXLYHN DA7 12 E7
Appledore Rd RHAM ME8 67 J2
TENT TN30 196 E6
Applegarth Dr DART DA1 28 A7
Apple Orch SWLY BR8 41 M8 ❶
Appleshaw Cl GVW DA11 46 C2 ❶
Appleton Dr RDART DA2 27 K8
Appletons RTON TN11 133 H5 ❶
Apple Tree Cl MAIDW ME16 120 B3 ❶
Apple Tree La RTWE/PEM TN2 163 M5
Appold St ERITH DA8 13 H5
Approach Rd WARL CR6 91 K8
The Approach ORP BR6 56 B5
April Cl ORP BR6 56 B8
Apsley St STH/RUST TN4 176 F1
Arbrook Cl STMC/STPC BR5 40 C7
Arbuthnot La BXLY DA5 26 A4
Arcadian Av BXLY DA5 26 A4
Arcadian Cl BXLY DA5 26 A4
Arcadian Rd BXLY DA5 26 A5
Arcadia Rd MEO DA13 46 B5
Archates Av CDH/CHF RM16 16 C2
Archer Rd STMC/STPC BR5 56 C2
WALD ME5 66 D7
Archer Wy SWLY BR8 42 B7
Archery Cl HOO/HM ME3 34 D6
Ardenlee Dr MAID/BEAR ME14 7 K3
Arden St GILL ME7 5 J2
Arethusa Rd ROCH ME1 65 L5
Argent Rd QBOR ME11 55 J3
Argent St GRAYS RM17 16 D6
WTHK RM20 16 A5
Argles Cl GRH DA9 29 J3
Argyle Cl ROCH ME1 66 A6
Argyle Rd SEV TN13 9 G6
STH/RUST TN4 163 J3
Argyll Rd GRAYS RM17 16 C4
Ariel Cl GVE DA12 47 H1
Ark Av CDH/CHF RM16 16 C2
Arkwright Rd TIL RM18 17 J8
Armada Wy CHAT ME4 4 C7
Armor Rd PUR RM19 14 F3
Armoury Dr GVE DA12 31 L5
Armstrong Cl RSEV TN14 94 D1
Armstrong Rd
MAID/SHEP ME15 121 J4
Armytage Cl HOO/HM ME3 51 G1
Arne Cl TONN TN10 132 A7
Arne Gv ORP BR6 56 B6
Arnhem Dr WALD ME5 66 B6
Arnold Av MEO DA13 62 D5
Arnolde Cl STRD ME2 50 A6
Arnold Pl TIL RM18 17 L7
Arnold Rd GVE DA12 31 L7
Arnolds La RDART DA2 43 J3
Arnsberg Wy BXLYHN DA7 26 C2
BXLYHS DA6 26 B2 ❶
Arnside Rd BXLYHN DA7 12 C7
Arran Cl ERITH DA8 12 F5
Arran Rd MAID/SHEP ME15 121 J7
Artemis Cl GVE DA12 32 A5
Arterial Road North Stifford
CDH/CHF RM16 16 A1
Arterial Road Purfleet
PUR RM19 14 E3
Arterial Road West Thurrock
WTHK RM20 15 H2
Arthur Rd BH/WHM TN16 91 L1
RHAM ME8 68 A5
ROCH ME1 65 M2
Arthur St ERITH DA8 13 H6
GRAYS RM17 16 E5
GVW DA11 31 J5
SIT ME10 88 A1 ❶
Artillery Rw GVE DA12 31 L5
Arun TIL RM18 18 E3
Arundel Av SIT ME10 88 A4
Arundel Cl BXLY DA5 26 B4 ❶
TON TN9 147 J5
WALD ME5 83 M4
Arundel Dr ORP BR6 56 D8
Arundel Rd DART DA1 27 L2
RTW TN1 11 G7
Arundel St MAID/BEAR ME14 103 H7
Ascot Cl BGR/WK TN15 98 D6
WALD ME5 83 L3
Ascot Rd GVW DA11 31 K8
STMC/STPC BR5 40 B8
Ashbee Cl SNOD ME6 81 J6
Ashbourne Av BXLYHN DA7 12 A6
Ashburnham Rd BELV DA17 12 E3
MAID/BEAR ME14 103 K5 ❶
TONN TN10 147 L2 ❶
Ashby Cl STRD ME2 81 J1 ❶
Ashby's Cl EDEN TN8 142 F5 ❶
Ash Cl DIT/AY ME20 102 A4
EDEN TN8 142 D4
RHAM ME8 67 K2
RTWE/PEM TN2 177 M5
SWLY BR8 41 L6
WALD ME5 66 E4
Ashcombe Dr EDEN TN8 142 D1
Ash Crs HOO/HM ME3 48 D2
Ashcroft Rd STPH/PW TN12 150 B8
Ashden Wk TONN TN10 131 L6
Ashdown Cl BXLY DA5 26 E5
MAIDW ME16 6 A6
STH/RUST TN4 10 C4
Ashenden HDCN TN27 173 H3
Ashenden Cl STRD ME2 49 L3
Ashenden Wk RTWE/PEM TN2 164 A5
Ashen Dr DART DA1 27 J4
Ashen Grove Rd EYN DA4 76 D4
Asher Reeds RRTW TN3 176 C1
Ashes La RTON TN11 132 D5
Ashford Dr RMAID ME17 139 M3
Ashford Rd MAID/BEAR ME14 7 K5
RMAID ME17 123 M5
TENT TN30 187 J8
Ash Gv MAIDW ME16 102 E7
Ashgrove Rd SEV TN13 113 J5
Ashington Cl SIT ME10 70 E8 ❶
Ash Keys MEO DA13 79 K5
Ash La BGR/WK TN15 77 L5
Ashleigh Cl MEO DA13 79 H4
Ashleigh Gdns HDCN TN27 155 M7
Ashley Cl SEV TN13 9 G4
Ashley Gdns ORP BR6 56 A8
STH/RUST TN4 162 E8
Ashley Park Cl STH/RUST TN4 162 E8
Ashley Rd RHAM ME8 67 L3
RTON TN11 131 G8
SEV TN13 9 G4
Ashmead Cl WALD ME5 83 L2
Ashmore Gdns GVW DA11 30 F8 ❶
Ash Platt Rd BGR/WK TN15 96 A7
Ash Rd BGR/WK TN15 60 F7
BH/WHM TN16 110 F3
DART DA1 27 M6
GVE DA12 46 E1
HART DA3 45 G7
HART DA3 61 G6
ORP BR6 73 J2
RDART DA2 43 H1
STRD ME2 2 D6
Ashtead Dr RSIT ME9 88 F3
Ashton Wy E/WMAL ME19 100 E7
Ash Tree Cl BGR/WK TN15 77 H3 ❶
Ash Tree Dr BGR/WK TN15 77 H3
Ash Tree La WALD ME5 66 F3
Ashurst Cl DART DA1 27 H1
Ashurst Rd MAID/BEAR ME14 7 L2
RRTW TN3 175 K3
Ashwood Cl HOO/HM ME3 34 E6
Askews Farm Rd GRAYS RM17 16 A4
Aspdin Rd GVW DA11 30 F8
Aspen Cl ORP BR6 56 C8
SWLY BR8 41 M5 ❶
Aspen Gn ERITHM DA18 12 B2
Aspen Wy RTWE/PEM TN2 163 L4
Aspian Dr RMAID ME17 136 F3
Asquith Rd RHAM ME8 67 L7
Aster Rd HOO/HM ME3 51 G2 ❶
Astley GRAYS RM17 16 B5
Astley St MAID/BEAR ME14 7 H4
Aston Cl WALD ME5 83 J3
Astor Rd BGR/WK TN15 77 G1
Astra Dr GVE DA12 47 G2
Athelstan Gn RMAID ME17 123 L3
Athelstan Rd CHAT ME4 66 B3 ❶
Athelstan Wy STMC/STPC BR5 40 C5
Atherton Gdns CDH/CHF RM16 17 L3
Athol Rd ERITH DA8 12 E4
Atkinson Cl ORP BR6 56 C8 ❶
Atlas Rd DART DA1 28 B1
Atterbury Cl BH/WHM TN16 110 F4
Attlee Ct GRAYS RM17 16 C2
Attlee Dr DART DA1 28 C3
Attlee Wy SIT ME10 71 G6
Attwaters La HAWK TN18 192 E7
Auckland Cl TIL RM18 17 J8
Auckland Dr SIT ME10 87 L2
Auckland Rd RTW TN1 163 L7
Auden Rd DIT/AY ME20 101 J1
Audley Av GILL ME7 67 G4
TON TN9 147 H3
Audley Cl MAIDW ME16 102 D8
Audley Ri TON TN9 147 H4
Auger Cl RSIT ME9 69 G8
Augusta Cl GILL ME7 50 E6 ❶
Augustine Rd GVE DA12 31 L5
STMC/STPC BR5 40 F7
Austen Cl GRH DA9 29 L4 ❶
TIL RM18 17 L8 ❶
Austen Rd ERITH DA8 12 D6
Austen Wy DIT/AY ME20 101 H1
Austin Cl GILL ME7 67 G3 ❶
SIT ME10 71 J5
Austin Rd GVW DA11 31 H6
STMC/STPC BR5 56 C2
Autumn Gld MAID/BEAR ME14 83 M5
Avalon Cl ORP BR6 56 F5
Avalon Rd ORP BR6 56 E5
Avards Cl HAWK TN18 199 G5
Avebury Av TON TN9 147 K4
Aveley Cl ERITH DA8 13 H5 ❶
Aveling Cl HOO/HM ME3 35 M7
Avenue La GRH DA9 29 L4
Avenue Le Puy TON TN9 147 L4
Avenue of Remembrance
SIT ME10 88 B2
Avenue Rd BH/WHM TN16 92 A6
BXLYHS DA6 26 A1
ERITH DA8 12 E6
SEV TN13 9 J4
The Avenue BGR/WK TN15 98 C5
BH/WHM TN16 92 B8
DIT/AY ME20 102 A4
GVW DA11 31 J6
ORP BR6 56 B5
STMC/STPC BR5 40 D4
TON TN9 147 K3
Averenches Rd
MAID/BEAR ME14 104 B8
Avery Cl HOO/HM ME3 23 M5 ❶
MAID/SHEP ME15 121 H4
Avery La MAID/SHEP ME15 122 E7
Avery Wy HOO/HM ME3 23 M5
Aviemore Gdns
MAID/BEAR ME14 122 B1
Avington Cl
MAID/SHEP ME15 121 H4 ❶
Avon Cl GVE DA12 31 M7
TONN TN10 131 L8
Avondale Rd GILL ME7 5 L3
Avonmouth Rd DART DA1 27 M3
Avon St RTW TN1 11 J1
Axtaine Rd STMC/STPC BR5 56 F3
Axtane Cl EYN DA4 43 L6 ❶
Ayelands HART DA3 61 G5 ❶
Ayelands La HART DA3 61 G6
Aylesford Crs RHAM ME8 67 J2
Aylesham Rd ORP BR6 56 A3
Ayleswade La HDCN TN27 172 A5
Aylewyn Gn SIT ME10 71 H5
Aynscombe Angle ORP BR6 56 C3 ❶
Azalea Dr SWLY BR8 41 M8

B

Babb's La CRBK TN17 193 J7
Babylon La RMAID ME17 154 D2
STPH/PW TN12 154 E4
Backfields ROCH ME1 3 H9
Back La BGR/WK TN15 114 C2
BGR/WK TN15 115 L2
BXLY DA5 26 C5
CRBK TN17 182 A5
PUR RM19 15 G3
RMAID ME17 137 M3
RSEV TN14 112 D6
RTON TN11 131 L1
SEV TN13 112 F2
STPH/PW TN12 167 J7
Back Rd HAWK TN18 200 D8
SCUP DA14 40 C1
Back St RMAID ME17 123 G7
Baden Powell Rd SEV TN13 95 G8
Baden Rd GILL ME7 50 F6
Bader Crs WALD ME5 66 C6
Bader Wk GVW DA11 31 G8
Badger Rd WALD ME5 83 L4
Badgers Copse ORP BR6 56 B5
Badgers Holt RTWE/PEM TN2 164 A8
Badgers Mt CDH/CHF RM16 17 H1
Badgers Ri RSEV TN14 74 C4
Badgers Rd RSEV TN14 74 D4
Badlow Cl ERITH DA8 13 G6
Badsell Rd STPH/PW TN12 149 K6
Baffin Cl CHAT ME4 66 B3
Bailey Cl PUR RM19 14 F3
Bailey Dr GILL ME7 67 J5
Baker Cl RSIT ME9 89 L2
Baker Hill Cl GVW DA11 46 B1
Baker La HDCN TN27 156 B6
RMAID ME17 139 H6
Baker Ms ORP BR6 73 H1
Bakers Av BGR/WK TN15 77 G2 ❶
Bakers Cross CRBK TN17 192 F1
Baker St ROCH ME1 65 L2
ROCH ME1 82 B4
Baker's Wk ROCH ME1 3 J6
Balaclava La WADH TN5 188 B6
Balcombes Hl CRBK TN17 182 A5
Baldwyn's Pk BXLY DA5 26 F7
Baldwyn's Rd BXLY DA5 26 F7
Balfour Rd CHAT ME4 66 A4
GRAYS RM17 16 E3
Ballard Cl STPH/PW TN12 152 E7
Ballards La OXTED RH8 109 L7
Ballard Wy STPH/PW TN12 150 D6
Ballens Rd WALD ME5 83 L2
Balmer Cl RHAM ME8 67 M6 ❶
Balmoral Gdns BXLY DA5 26 B5
Balmoral Rd EYN DA4 43 J4
GILL ME7 5 L3
Baltic Rd TON TN9 147 K6
Banbury Vls MEO DA13 45 H3
Banckside HART DA3 45 G8
Bancroft Gdns ORP BR6 56 B4
Bancroft Rd BGR/WK TN15 98 B2
Bangor Rd STRD ME2 48 F7
Bankfields HDCN TN27 155 L8
Bankfield Wy CRBK TN17 181 M6
Bankfoot GRAYS RM17 16 B3
Bank La BGR/WK TN15 130 C2
Bankside GVW DA11 30 E4
SEV TN13 94 F7
WADH TN5 188 A8
WALD ME5 66 D5
Bankside Cl BH/WHM TN16 91 L4 ❶
RDART DA2 41 M1
Banks La BXLYHS DA6 26 B2
Banks Rd STRD ME2 3 J2
Bank St CHAT ME4 5 G7
CRBK TN17 183 L8
GVE DA12 31 K4 ❶
MAID/SHEP ME15 6 F5
SEV TN13 9 H7
TON TN9 147 K3
Banky Fields Cl RHAM ME8 68 D4 ❶
Banky Meadow MAIDW ME16 120 B2
Banner Cl PUR RM19 14 F3
Banner Farm Rd
RTWE/PEM TN2 11 H8
Banning St STRD ME2 3 G2
Bannister Gdns
STMC/STPC BR5 40 E7 ❶
Bannister Hl RSIT ME9 87 K3
Bannister Rd MAID/BEAR ME14 103 J6
Bapchild Pl STMC/STPC BR5 40 E8
Barberry Av WALD ME5 65 M8
Barchester Wy TONN TN10 132 B7
Barclay Av TONN TN10 148 B1
Barclay Wy WTHK RM20 15 H4
Barcombe Cl CHST BR7 40 C7 ❶
Bardell Ter ROCH ME1 3 L8
Barden Park Rd TON TN9 147 J4
Barden Rd RRTW TN3 162 B3
TON TN9 147 J4
Bardsley Cl STPH/PW TN12 134 C6
Barfield EYN DA4 43 K5
Barfleur Mnr GILL ME7 4 E1 ❶
Barfreston Cl MAID/SHEP ME15 6 E9
Bargrove Rd MAID/BEAR ME14 7 M2
Barham Cl GVE DA12 32 B6 ❶
MAID/SHEP ME15 122 A8
Barham Rd DART DA1 28 C5
Barham's Mill Rd HDCN TN27 157 K3
Bark Burr Rd CDH/CHF RM16 16 B1
Barker Rd MAIDW ME16 6 E6
Barkers Ct SIT ME10 87 M1
Bark Hart Rd ORP BR6 56 D4
Barkis Cl ROCH ME1 65 M6
Barleycorn E/WMAL ME19 101 G4
Barleycorn Dr RHAM ME8 68 A7
Barley Flds
MAID/BEAR ME14 121 M1 ❶
Barleymow Cl WALD ME5 66 E7
Barling Cl WALD ME5 82 E4
Barlow Cl RHAM ME8 68 A8
Barming Rd E/WMAL ME19 119 H3
Barnaby Ter ROCH ME1 65 L3
Barnard Rd WARL CR6 90 D5
Barn Cl RSIT ME9 87 J3
Barncroft Cl
MAID/BEAR ME14 122 B1 ❶
Barncroft Dr GILL ME7 84 B1
Barned Ct MAIDW ME16 120 B4
Barnehurst Av BXLYHN DA7 12 E7
Barnehurst Cl ERITH DA8 12 E7
Barnehurst Rd BXLYHN DA7 12 E8
Barn End Dr RDART DA2 42 E1
Barn End La SWLY BR8 42 E3
Barnes Cray Rd DART DA1 27 J2
Barnesdale Crs STMC/STPC BR5 56 C2
Barnes La RMAID ME17 136 F5
Barnes Wk STPH/PW TN12 152 F8
Barnett Cl ERITH DA8 13 H8
Barnetts Cl RTWE/PEM TN2 163 L4
Barnetts Rd RTON TN11 146 C3
Barnett's Shaw OXTED RH8 108 F5
Barnetts Wy STH/RUST TN4 163 L4
Barnfield GVW DA11 31 J7
RTWE/PEM TN2 177 H6
TENT TN30 196 D3
WALD ME5 66 C5
Barnfield Cl GRH DA9 29 H4
HART DA3 45 M7
SWLY BR8 57 L3 ❶
Barnfield Crs RSEV TN14 96 A3
Barnfield Rd BELV DA17 12 B5
BH/WHM TN16 91 M6
SEV TN13 112 F1
STMC/STPC BR5 40 F7
Barn Hl MAID/SHEP ME15 136 A3
Barnhurst Rd
MAID/BEAR ME14 103 J5
Barn Meadow
STPH/PW TN12 170 A1 ❶
STRD ME2 81 G1
Barnsole Rd GILL ME7 5 M4
Barnwell Rd DART DA1 28 B1
Barnwood Cl ROCH ME1 65 K5 ❶
Baron Cl GILL ME7 51 G6
MAID/BEAR ME14 104 B8 ❶
Barrack Cnr SEV TN13 9 J2
Barrack Rd CHAT ME4 50 D5
Barrack Rw GVW DA11 31 J4 ❶
Barrel Arch Cl
STPH/PW TN12 152 E7 ❶
Barretts Rd HAWK TN18 199 J3
SEV TN13 94 F6
Barrie Dr DIT/AY ME20 101 H1 ❶
Barrier Rd CHAT ME4 4 D3
Barrington Cl WALD ME5 66 B8
Barrowfields WALD ME5 83 M4
Barrow Green Rd OXTED RH8 108 E7
Barrow Gv SIT ME10 87 M2
Barrow La RRTW TN3 176 B4
Barr Rd GVE DA12 32 B7
Barry Av BXLYHN DA7 12 A6
Barry Cl CDH/CHF RM16 17 J2
ORP BR6 56 A6
Bartholomew Wy SWLY BR8 42 A7
Bartlett Cl WALD ME5 83 L4
Bartlett Rd BH/WHM TN16 110 E4 ❶
GVW DA11 31 J6
Bartley Mill Rd RRTW TN3 188 A1
Barton Cl BXLYHS DA6 26 A3
Barton Rd EYN DA4 43 K5
MAID/SHEP ME15 7 H8
SCUP DA14 41 G3
STRD ME2 2 F3
Bashford Barn La RSIT ME9 107 J2
Basi Cl STRD ME2 49 L4
Basilon Rd BXLYHN DA7 12 A8
Basing Cl MAID/SHEP ME15 7 J7
Basing Dr BXLY DA5 26 B4
Basmere Cl MAID/BEAR ME14 7 L1
Bassett Rd SIT ME10 87 M1
Bassetts La EDEN TN8 160 E6
Basted La BGR/WK TN15 98 A7
Bata Av TIL RM18 18 D4
Batchelors RTWE/PEM TN2 165 G5
Batchelor St CHAT ME4 4 D6
Batchwood Gn STMC/STPC BR5 40 C8
Bates Cl DIT/AY ME20 101 J2
Bates Hl BGR/WK TN15 97 L8
Bath Hard ROCH ME1 3 M8
Bath Rd DART DA1 27 K5
Bath St GVW DA11 31 K4 ❷
Bathurst Cl STPH/PW TN12 170 A1
Bathurst Rd STPH/PW TN12 170 A2
Baton Cl PUR RM19 14 F3

Batteries Cl RSIT ME9 ... 89 K5
Battlefields BGR/WK TN15 ... 98 B2
Battle La STPH/PW TN12 ... 153 H4
Battlesmere Dr RHAM ME8 ... 34 D5
Battle Rd ERITH DA8 ... 12 E3
Battle St GVE DA12 ... 47 H7
Batt's Rd GVE DA12 ... 63 J1
Baugh Rd SCUP DA14 ... 40 E2
Bay Cl HOO/HM ME3 ... 51 G2
Bayford Rd SIT ME10 ... 88 C1
Bayhall Rd RTWE/PEM TN2 ... 11 J5
Bayham Rd RTWE/PEM TN2 ... 177 J5
  SEV TN13 ... 9 K2
Bayley's HI RSEV TN14 ... 129 C2
Bayly Rd DART DA1 ... 28 C4
Bay Manor La WTHK RM20 ... 15 H5
Baynham Cl BXLY DA5 ... 26 B4
Bayswater Dr RHAM ME8 ... 85 C1
Baywell DIT/AY ME20 ... 101 C4
  E/WMAL ME19 ... 101 G3
Bazes Shaw HART DA3 ... 61 H5
Beacon Cl RHAM ME8 ... 67 M6
Beacon Dr RDART DA2 ... 29 L8
Beaconfields SEV TN13 ... 8 D9
Beacon HI PUR RM19 ... 14 D4
  WALD ME5 ... 66 F3
Beacon Hill La HOO/HM ME3 ... 50 B1
Beacon Oak Rd TENT TN30 ... 196 D5
Beacon Ri SEV TN13 ... 8 E3
Beacon Rd ERITH DA8 ... 13 K6
  RMAID ME17 ... 125 L8
  WALD ME5 ... 5 J9
Beaconsfield Av GILL ME7 ... 5 M4
Beaconsfield Rd BXLY DA5 ... 27 C7
  CHAT ME4 ... 4 D9
  MAID/SHEP ME15 ... 6 C9
  SIT ME10 ... 88 C2
The Beacons RMAID ME17 ... 136 E5
Beadles La OXTED RH8 ... 108 F8
Beagles Cl STMC/STPC BR5 ... 56 F5
Beagles Wood Rd
  RTWE/PEM TN2 ... 165 G6
Beales La RYE TN31 ... 206 D7
Beaman Dr CRBK TN17 ... 182 B5
Beamish Cl STMC/STPC BR5 ... 56 E3
The Beams MAID/SHEP ME15.. 122 A4
Bean La RDART DA2 ... 29 K7
Bean Rd GRH DA9 ... 29 K2
Bearsted Cl RHAM ME8 ... 67 L3
Bearsted Rd MAID/BEAR ME14 .. 103 L6
Beaton Cl GRH DA9 ... 29 K2
Beatrice Gdns GVW DA11 ... 31 G7
Beatrice Rd OXTED RH8 ... 109 C6
Beatty Av GILL ME7 ... 67 H2
Beatty Rd WALD ME5 ... 65 M5
Beaufighter Rd E/WMAL ME19 .. 118 A4
Beaufort Cl CDH/CHF RM16 ... 16 B2
Beaufort Rd SWLY BR8 ... 2 B1
Beaufort Wk MAID/SHEP ME15 .. 138 A1
Beaulieu Ri ROCH ME1 ... 65 M4
Beaulieu Dr TONN TN10 ... 147 K1
Beaumont Dr GVW DA11 ... 31 G5
Beaumont Rd GVW DA11 ... 31 G5
  MAIDW ME16 ... 120 D3
Beau Nash Wy
  RTWE/PEM TN2 ... 177 K4
Beauvoir Dr SIT ME10 ... 71 J5
Beauworth Pk MAID/SHEP ME15.. 122 A5
Beaver Rd MAIDW ME16 ... 102 D6
Beaverwood Rd CHST BR7 ... 40 A2
Beblets Cl ORP BR6 ... 56 B8
Beckenham Dr MAIDW ME16 ... 102 F6
Becket Ct HDCN TN27 ... 155 M8
Beckets Fld RTON TN11 ... 161 J2
Beckett Cl BELV DA17 ... 12 A2
Becketts Cl ORP BR6 ... 56 B6
Beckley Cl GVE DA12 ... 32 D7
Beckley Ms WALD ME5 ... 66 B8
Beckman Cl RSEV TN14 ... 94 E1
Becksbourne Cl
  MAID/BEAR ME14 ... 103 J5
Becton Pl ERITH DA8 ... 12 D6
Beddington Gn STMC/STPC BR5 .. 40 B5
Beddington La WARL CR6 ... 91 H4
Beddlestead La WARL CR6 ... 91 H4
Beddow Wy DIT/AY ME20 ... 102 D3
Bedens Rd SCUP DA14 ... 41 G3
Bedford Av RHAM ME8 ... 67 M4
Bedford Pl MAIDW ME16 ... 6 C5
Bedford Rd DART DA1 ... 28 C5
  GRAYS RM17 ... 16 D4
  GVW DA11 ... 31 H7
  ORP BR6 ... 56 D5
  STH/RUST TN4 ... 163 J4
Bedgebury Cl
  MAID/BEAR ME14 ... 7 M1
  ROCH ME1 ... 65 M6
Bedgebury Cross CRBK TN17 ... 190 E5
Bedgebury Rd CRBK TN17 ... 190 F2
Bedlam La HDCN TN27 ... 156 E8
Bedonwell Rd BELV DA17 ... 12 A5
  BXLYHN DA7 ... 12 B5
Bedson Wk RHAM ME8 ... 68 D4
Bedwell Rd BELV DA17 ... 12 C4
Bedwin Cl ROCH ME1 ... 65 M6
Beecham Rd TONN TN10 ... 132 K7
Beech Av BH/WHM TN16 ... 91 M5
  SWLY BR8 ... 42 B8
Beechcroft Av BXLYHN DA7 ... 12 F7
  TIL RM18 ... 18 C3
Beech Dr MAIDW ME16 ... 102 E8
Beechen Bank Rd WALD ME5 ... 83 J4
Beechenlea La SWLY BR8 ... 42 C8
The Beeches DIT/AY ME20 ... 102 A4
  MEO DA13 ... 46 F8
  TIL RM18 ... 17 K8
  WALD ME5 ... 83 J1
Beech Farm Rd WARL CR6 ... 90 F6
Beechfield Rd ERITH DA8 ... 13 G6
Beech Green La HRTF TN7 ... 174 B5
Beech Gv HOO/HM ME3 ... 48 D2
  SOCK/AV RM15 ... 14 E1
Beech Hurst RTWE/PEM TN2 .. 164 F6
Beech Hurst Cl
  MAID/SHEP ME15 ... 7 J9
Beeching Rd WALD ME5 ... 83 K2
Beechings Gn RHAM ME8 ... 67 L2
Beechings Wy RHAM ME8 ... 67 H3
Beechin Wood La BGR/WK TN15 .. 98 E3
Beechlands Cl HART DA3 ... 61 J1

Beech La HAWK TN18 ... 206 E2
  STPH/PW TN12 ... 179 L2
Beechmont Ri TONN TN10 ... 131 K7
Beechmont Gv SEV TN13 ... 113 K7
Beechmore Dr WALD ME5 ... 83 J3
Beech Rd BH/WHM TN16 ... 91 L3
  DART DA1 ... 27 M6
  E/WMAL ME19 ... 101 H6
  HOO/HM ME3 ... 51 G2
  ORP BR6 ... 73 J2
  SEV TN13 ... 9 H6
  STPH/PW TN12 ... 168 B2
  STRD ME2 ... 2 C6
  WBY/YAL ME18 ... 117 M3
Beech St RTW TN1 ... 11 H5
Beech Wk DART DA1 ... 27 J2
Beechwood Av ORP BR6 ... 71 G7
  SIT ME10 ... 71 G7
  WALD ME5 ... 66 F3
Beechwood Dr MEO DA13 ... 79 J4
Beechwood Gdns MEO DA13 ... 79 J4
Beechwood Ms RTWE/PEM TN2 .. 178 A1
Beechwood Rd MAIDW ME16.. 120 B2
Beechy Lees Rd RSEV TN14 ... 95 M3
Beesfield La EYN DA4 ... 59 J4
Begonia Av RHAM ME8 ... 67 L3
Beke Rd RHAM ME8 ... 84 F1
Beldam Haw RSEV TN14 ... 74 C5
Belfield Rd RTWE/PEM TN2 .. 164 F7
Belgrave Cl STMC/STPC BR5 ... 40 E8
Belgrave Rd RTW TN1 ... 11 G3
Belgrave St DIT/AY ME20 ... 82 B7
Bell Cl GRH DA9 ... 29 H3
Bell Crs ROCH ME1 ... 82 B5
Bellefield Rd STMC/STPC BR5... 56 D1
Belle Friday Cl RSIT ME9 ... 89 L3
Bellevue Rd BXLYHS DA6 ... 26 B3
Belle Vue Rd ORP BR6 ... 72 C4
Bell Farm Gdns MAID/BEAR ME16 .. 120 B3
Bell Gdns STMC/STPC BR5 ... 56 E1
Bellgrove Ct WALD ME5 ... 83 J5
Bellingham Wy DIT/AY ME20 ... 101 K2
Bell La DIT/AY ME20 ... 101 K3
  HDCN TN27 ... 172 B6
  MAID/BEAR ME14 ... 83 J6
  MAID/BEAR ME14 ... 104 C8
  ROCH ME1 ... 82 B5
  STPH/PW TN12 ... 170 A2
Bellman Av GVE DA12 ... 32 A6
Bellmeadow MAID/SHEP ME15 .. 122 A7
Bellring Cl BELV DA17 ... 12 C5
Bell Rd MAID/SHEP ME15 ... 122 A8
  SIT ME10 ... 88 A3
Bells Farm Rd STPH/PW TN12 .. 133 M4
Bell's La HOO/HM ME3 ... 35 M6
Bell Wy RMAID ME17 ... 140 A3
Bellwood Ct HOO/HM ME3 ... 36 E2
Belmont Cl MAIDW ME16 ... 120 B3
Belmont Rd ERITH DA8 ... 12 C6
  GILL ME7 ... 5 J5
  GRAYS RM17 ... 16 B4
  SIT ME10 ... 88 A2
Belnor Av RSIT ME9 ... 70 A4
Beltana Dr GVE DA12 ... 47 G1
Belton Rd SCUP DA14 ... 40 C1
Beltring Rd STH/RUST TN4 ... 163 J7
  STPH/PW TN12 ... 150 D1
Beltwood Rd BELV DA17 ... 12 E3
Belvedere Cl GVE DA12 ... 31 L6
Belvedere Ct BELV DA17 ... 12 B2
Belvedere Rd BH/WHM TN16... 92 B4
  BXLYHN DA7 ... 26 B1
Benden Cl STPH/PW TN12 ... 170 B1
Bendon Wy RHAM ME8 ... 67 M5
Benedict Cl ORP BR6 ... 56 B8
  STRD ME2 ... 81 K1
Benenden Rd CRBK TN17 ... 194 B8
  HDCN TN27 ... 195 C1
  STRD ME2 ... 49 L3
Benhall Mill Rd RTWE/PEM TN2 .. 177 L5
Bennetts Av BGR/WK TN15.. 77 L6
Bennett Wy RDART DA2 ... 43 M1
Benover Rd WBY/YAL ME18 ... 135 H5
Benson Rd GRAYS RM17 ... 16 D5
Bensted Cl MAID/SHEP ME15 .. 135 M5
Bentham HI HART DA3 ... 162 F4
Bentley Cl HART DA3 ... 45 L7
  WALD ME5 ... 83 M3
Bentley's Meadow
  BGR/WK TN15 ... 96 B6
Bentley St GVE DA12 ... 31 L4
Bentlif Cl MAIDW ME16 ... 6 A2
Berber Rd STRD ME2 ... 3 G1
Berengrave La RHAM ME8 ... 68 A4
Berens Rd STMC/STPC BR5 ... 56 E1
Berens Wy CHST BR7 ... 40 B8
Beresford Rd CRBK TN17 ... 182 B5
  DIT/AY ME20 ... 82 E6
  GILL ME7 ... 5 L5
  GVW DA11 ... 31 G5
Beresfords HI RMAID ME17 ... 137 K1
Berkeley Ct ORP BR6 ... 56 A3
  ROCH ME1 ... 65 M5
  RTWE/PEM TN2 ... 165 G6
Berkeley Ct SIT ME10 ... 87 M2
Berkeley Crs DART DA1 ... 28 B6
Berkeley Rd RTW TN1 ... 10 F7
Berkhampstead Rd BELV DA17 .. 12 C4
Berkley Rd GVE DA12 ... 31 K4
Berkshire Cl WALD ME5 ... 66 E5
Bermuda Rd TIL RM18 ... 17 J8
Bernard St GVE DA12 ... 31 K4
Berrylands HART DA3 ... 61 J2
  ORP BR6 ... 56 C2
Berry Rd HOO/HM ME3 ... 51 G2
Berry's Green Rd BH/WHM TN16.. 92 D2
Berry's HI BH/WHM TN16 ... 92 D1
Berry St SIT ME10 ... 88 B1
Bersham La GRAYS RM17 ... 16 B3
Berwick Wy RSEV TN14 ... 95 K7
Berwyn Gv MAID/SHEP ME15.. 121 J7
Bessels Green Rd SEV TN13 ... 112 F1
Bessels Meadow SEV TN13 ... 112 F2
Best St CHAT ME4 ... 4 D6
Beta Rd HOO/HM ME3 ... 36 F4
Betenson Av SEV TN13 ... 95 H8
Bethel Rd SEV TN13 ... 9 H2
Bethersden Rd HDCN TN27 .. 173 H5

Betjeman Cl DIT/AY ME20 ... 101 H2
Betsham Rd ERITH DA8 ... 13 H6
  MAID/SHEP ME15 ... 122 B7
  MEO DA13 ... 44 F2
  SWCM DA10 ... 30 A5
Betterton Dr SCUP DA14 ... 26 A7
Bettescombe Rd RHAM ME8 ... 67 M6
Beulah Rd RTW TN1 ... 11 H2
Beulah Wk CTHM CR3 ... 90 A6
Beult Meadow HDCN TN27 ... 173 J4
Beult Rd DART DA1 ... 27 J1
Bevan Pl SWLY BR8 ... 42 B8
Bevans Cl GRH DA9 ... 29 L4
Beverley Cl RHAM ME8 ... 68 B5
Beverley Crs TON TN9 ... 147 H6
Beverley Rd BXLYHN DA7 ... 12 E8
  MAIDW ME16 ... 120 B3
Bevis Cl RDART DA2 ... 28 E5
Bewlbridge La RRTW TN3 ... 189 L4
Bewley La BGR/WK TN15 ... 115 L3
Bexhill Dr GRAYS RM17 ... 16 A5
Bexley Cl DART DA1 ... 27 G3
Bexley High St BXLY DA5 ... 27 G3
Bexley La DART DA1 ... 27 G3
  SCUP DA14 ... 40 E1
Bexley Rd ERITH DA8 ... 12 E6
  ERITH DA8 ... 13 H4
Bexon La RSIT ME9 ... 107 L1
Bickley Rd TON TN9 ... 147 K5
Bickmore Wy TON TN9 ... 147 L2
Bicknor La RSIT ME9 ... 106 E2
Bicknor Rd MAID/SHEP ME15... 138 B1
  ORP BR6 ... 56 A3
Bidborough Rdg
  STH/RUST TN4 ... 162 F1
Biddenden Cl DART DA1 ... 122 B2
Biddenden La HDCN TN27 ... 156 A8
Biddenden Rd HDCN TN27 ... 172 A3
  HDCN TN27 ... 187 H1
  RASHW TN26 ... 187 J7
Biddenden Wy MEO DA13 ... 46 A5
Biggin La GRAYS RM17 ... 17 L5
Bilberry Cl MAID/BEAR ME14 .. 104 A8
Billet HI DIT/AY ME20 ... 60 E7
Billings HART DA3 ... 61 H2
Bilsington Cl WALD ME5 ... 66 D8
Binbury La MAID/BEAR ME14.. 105 H1
The Bines STPH/PW TN12 ... 150 C8
Bingham Rd STRD ME2 ... 49 L4
Bingley Rd ROCH ME1 ... 4 A5
Bingley Rd SNOD ME6 ... 81 H5
Binland Gv WALD ME5 ... 65 M8
Binnacle Rd ROCH ME1 ... 65 L5
Binney Rd HOO/HM ME3 ... 23 M5
Birch Cl EYN DA4 ... 58 F6
  HART DA3 ... 45 L6
  RTON TN11 ... 146 F1
  RTWE/PEM TN2 ... 163 M6
  SEV TN13 ... 9 H2
  STPH/PW TN12 ... 165 M4
Birch Crs DIT/AY ME20 ... 101 M5
Birch Dr WALD ME5 ... 83 M4
The Birches SWLY BR8 ... 42 A4
  TON TN9 ... 147 K6
Birchetts Av RRTW TN3 ... 176 A2
Birchfield Cl MAID/SHEP ME15.. 121 K7
Birchfields WALD ME5 ... 83 J2
Birch Gv GILL ME7 ... 96 A1
Birchin Cross Rd RSEV TN14.... 95 M5
Birchington Cl BXLYHN DA7 ... 12 D7
  MAID/BEAR ME14 ... 7 L3
Bircholt Rd MAID/SHEP ME15 .. 138 B1
Birch Pl GRH DA9 ... 29 G4
Birch Rd HOO/HM ME3 ... 51 G2
  STPH/PW TN12 ... 150 C7
Birch Tree Wy MAID/SHEP ME15 .. 7 J7
Birchway BGR/WK TN15 ... 77 H3
Birch Wy RTWE/PEM TN2 ... 163 M6
  WARL CR6 ... 90 A4
Birchwood Av STH/RUST TN4.. 163 G2
Birchwood Dr RDART DA2 ... 42 A1
Birchwood Park Av SWLY BR8 ... 42 A7
Birchwood Rd MAIDW ME16 .. 102 E8
  RDART DA2 ... 41 L4
Bird House La ORP BR6 ... 72 C8
Bird in Hand St RTW TN1 ... 175 L5
Birken Rd RTWE/PEM TN2 ... 163 M7
Birkhall Cl WALD ME5 ... 66 C8
Birling Av MAID/BEAR ME14 .. 122 C1
  RHAM ME8 ... 67 M4
Birling Cl MAID/BEAR ME14... 122 B1
Birling Dr RTWE/PEM TN2 ... 177 J5
Birling HI MEO DA13 ... 80 C4
Birling Pk E/WMAL ME19 ... 80 E8
Birling Park Av RTWE/PEM TN2 .. 177 K5
Birling Rd E/WMAL ME19 ... 80 C8
  ERITH DA8 ... 12 F6
  RTWE/PEM TN2 ... 177 K5
  SNOD ME6 ... 81 H6
Birling Road Rookery HI
  SNOD ME6 ... 81 H6
Birnam Sq MAIDW ME16 ... 6 B5
Birtrick Dr MEO DA13 ... 62 B1
Bishop Butt Cl ORP BR6 ... 56 B6
Bishop La RSIT ME9 ... 69 G2
Bishops Cl WBY/YAL ME18 ... 118 E7
Bishops Ct GRH DA9 ... 29 G3
Bishop's Down STH/RUST TN4.. 10 B6
Bishop's Down Park Rd
  STH/RUST TN4 ... 10 A3
Bishop's Down Rd
  STH/RUST TN4 ... 10 B6
Bishops La CRBK TN17 ... 192 A3
  MAID/SHEP ME15 ... 135 M6
Bishops Ms TON TN9 ... 147 J3
Bishops Oak Ride TONN TN10 .. 131 K7
Bishops Wk ROCH ME1 ... 17 K5
Bishops Wy MAIDW ME16 ... 6 E5
Blackberry Fld STMC/STPC BR5 .. 40 C2
Blackberry Wy STPH/PW TN12 .. 150 C2
Black Eagle Cl BH/WHM TN16.. 110 E5
Blackhall La BGR/WK TN15 ... 9 M2
Black Horse Ms BH/WHM TN15 .. 98 C7
Black Horse Rd SCUP DA14 ... 40 C1
Blackhurst La RTWE/PEM TN2 .. 164 C6
Blacklands E/WMAL ME19 ... 101 H5
Blacklands Dr E/WMAL ME19 .. 101 H4
Blackman Cl HOO/HM ME3 ... 35 M6
Blackmans Cl DART DA1 ... 27 L6

Blackman's La RTON TN11 ... 132 F6
Blackmanstone Wy
  DIT/AY ME20 ... 102 D6
Blackmead SEV TN13 ... 95 G7
Black Mill La HDCN TN27 ... 155 K8
Blackmore Rd GRAYS RM17 ... 16 E4
Black Rock Gdns GILL ME7 ... 84 D1
Blackshots La CDH/CHF RM16 ... 16 F1
Blacksmith Dr
  MAID/BEAR ME14 ... 103 M8
Blacksmiths La STMC/STPC BR5 .. 56 E1
  WADH TN5 ... 188 C8
Blacksole Rd BGR/WK TN15 ... 98 B2
Blacksole Rd BGR/WK TN15 ... 98 B2
Blackthorn Av RTWE/PEM TN2 .. 163 L4
  WALD ME5 ... 83 J2
Blackthorn Dr BGR/WK TN15 .. 77 H3
Blackthorn Dr DIT/AY ME20 ... 101 K3
Blackthorne Rd RHAM ME8 ... 68 C5
Blackthorn Gv BXLYHN DA7 ... 26 A1
Blair Dr SEV TN13 ... 9 H2
Blake Dr DIT/AY ME20 ... 101 H1
Blake Gdns DART DA1 ... 28 B2
Blakemore Wy BELV DA17 ... 12 A2
Blaker Av ROCH ME1 ... 66 A4
Blake Wy RTWE/PEM TN2 ... 163 M6
Blanchard Cl E/WMAL ME19 ... 101 H4
Blandford Gdns SIT ME10 ... 88 A4
Blatchford Cl E/WMAL ME19 .. 101 H4
Blatchington Rd RTW TN1 ... 10 F9
Bleakwood Rd WALD ME5 ... 66 B8
Blean Rd RHAM ME8 ... 67 L3
Blendon Rd MAID/BEAR ME14 ... 7 L2
Blenheim Cl DART DA1 ... 27 L4
  MAID/SHEP ME15 ... 122 B2
  MEO DA13 ... 62 D5
Blenheim Rd DART DA1 ... 27 L4
  E/WMAL ME19 ... 118 B2
  ORP BR6 ... 56 E5
Bligh Rd GVW DA11 ... 31 J4
Bligh Wy STRD ME2 ... 48 E7
Blind La CRBK TN17 ... 182 A4
  GILL ME7 ... 84 B4
Blind Mary's La RSIT ME9 ... 107 G1
Bliss Wy TONN TN10 ... 132 A3
Blockhouse Rd GRAYS RM17 ... 16 E5
Blockmakers Ct CHAT ME4 ... 66 D4
Bloors La RHAM ME8 ... 67 M4
Bloors Wharf Rd GILL ME7 ... 68 A1
Blowers Grove Wd GILL ME7 ... 84 D2
Blowers HI EDEN TN8 ... 159 M5
Blue Anchor La TIL RM18 ... 18 A3
Bluebell Cl GILL ME7 ... 51 H7
Bluebell Wks STPH/PW TN12 .. 150 C7
Blueberry La RSEV TN14 ... 93 L2
Blue Boar La ROCH ME1 ... 3 L7
Blue Coat La CRBK TN17 ... 181 L6
Bluehouse Gdns OXTED RH8 ... 109 J6
Bluehouse La OXTED RH8 ... 109 C6
Bluett St MAID/BEAR ME14 ... 7 H1
Bluewater Pkwy GRH DA9 ... 29 J7
Blunden La WBY/YAL ME18... 135 J4
Blythe HI STMC/STPC BR5 ... 40 B5
Blythe Rd MAID/SHEP ME15 ... 7 K5
Boakes Meadow RSEV TN14 ... 75 H5
Boarley La MAID/BEAR ME14 ... 103 H4
Bobbing HI RSIT ME9 ... 70 C8
Bockingford La
  MAID/SHEP ME15 ... 121 G5
Bodell Cl CDH/CHF RM16 ... 16 D1
Bodiam Cl RHAM ME8 ... 67 L3
Bodiam Rd MAID/SHEP ME15... 122 D2
Bodkin HAWK TN18 ... 205 H3
Bodle Av SWCM DA10 ... 30 A4
Bodmin Cl STMC/STPC BR5 ... 56 E4
Bodsham Crs MAID/SHEP ME15.. 122 D2
Bogle Rd RSIT ME9 ... 89 L6
Boley HI ROCH ME1 ... 3 J6
Boleyn Cl CDH/CHF RM16 ... 16 B2
Boleyn Rd RSEV TN14 ... 96 A3
Boleyn Wy SWCM DA10 ... 30 A5
Bolner Cl WALD ME5 ... 83 H3
Bombers La BH/WHM TN16 ... 92 F6
Bonaventure Ct GVE DA12 ... 47 H1
Bond Cl RSEV TN14 ... 93 M1
Bondfield Cl STH/RUST TN4 ... 163 J4
Bondfield Rd E/WMAL ME19 .. 101 H4
Bond Rd RHAM ME8 ... 85 G1
Bond St GRAYS RM17 ... 16 E5
Boneashe La BGR/WK TN15 ... 98 F7
Bonflower La RMAID ME17 ... 136 E6
Bonham Dr SIT ME10 ... 71 J8
Bonner Wk CDH/CHF RM16 ... 16 B2
Bonney Wy SWLY BR8 ... 42 A6
Bonnington Rd
  MAID/BEAR ME14 ... 103 L7
Bootham Cl STRD ME2 ... 64 F1
Booth Rd CHAT ME4 ... 5 G8
Borden La RSIT ME9 ... 87 K3
Bordyke TON TN9 ... 147 L3
Borkwood Pk ORP BR6 ... 56 B7
Borkwood Wy ORP BR6 ... 56 A7
Borland Cl GRH DA9 ... 29 J3
Borough Green Rd
  BGR/WK TN15 ... 97 M7
Borough Rd BH/WHM TN16 ... 91 M7
  GILL ME7 ... 5 L6
  OBOR ME11 ... 55 K1
Borstal Rd ROCH ME1 ... 65 K2
Borstal St ROCH ME1 ... 65 J3
Boscombe Av GRAYS RM17 ... 16 F3
Bostall Park Av BXLYHN DA7... 12 A6
Bostall Rd STMC/STPC BR5 ... 40 D4
Boston Gdns RHAM ME8 ... 67 L4
Boston Rd WALD ME5 ... 83 K3
Bosville Av SEV TN13 ... 8 E3
Bosville Dr SEV TN13 ... 8 E3
Bosville Rd SEV TN13 ... 8 E3
Boswell Ct STMC/STPC BR5 ... 147 L4
Botany TON TN9 ... 147 L4
Botany Wy PUR RM19 ... 14 D4
Botsom La BGR/WK TN15 ... 76 E1
Bottlescrew HI RMAID ME17 ... 137 K1
Bottles La RSIT ME9 ... 88 C3
Bott Rd RDART DA2 ... 43 H1
Boucher Dr GVW DA11 ... 31 H8
Boughton La MAID/SHEP ME15.. 121 K6

Boughton Rd RMAID ME17 ... 141 K4
Boundary Rd RTWE/PEM TN2 ... 11 L9
Boundary St ERITH DA8 ... 13 H6
The Boundary RRTW TN3 ... 176 D2
Bounds Oak Wy STH/RUST TN4.. 163 G2
The Bounds DIT/AY ME20 ... 102 A4
Bourne Cl TON TN9 ... 147 M2
Bourne Grange La RTON TN11 .. 132 F2
Bourne Gv SIT ME10 ... 70 E8
Bourne La BGR/WK TN15 ... 116 B3
  RBTBR TN32 ... 204 B5
  TON TN9 ... 147 L2
Bourne Pk BXLY DA5 ... 26 E3
Bourne Rd RTON TN11 ... 133 H8
Bourne Rd BXLY DA5 ... 26 E3
  GVE DA12 ... 32 B7
Bourne V BGR/WK TN15 ... 116 C5
Bourne Wy SWLY BR8 ... 41 L7
Bournewood Cl
  MAID/SHEP ME15 ... 122 B4
Bournewood Rd
  STMC/STPC BR5... 56 D3
Bournville Av CHAT ME4 ... 66 C5
Bow Arrow La DART DA1 ... 28 C4
  RDART DA2 ... 28 D4
Bowen Rd STH/RUST TN4 ... 162 D8
Bower Cl MAIDW ME16 ... 6 C5
Bower La EYN DA4 ... 59 G6
  MAIDW ME16 ... 6 C5
Bowerman Rd CDH/CHF RM16... 17 J3
Bower Mount Rd MAIDW ME16 ... 6 B5
Bower Pl MAIDW ME16 ... 6 C7
Bower Rd SWLY BR8 ... 42 C4
Bowers Av GVW DA11 ... 46 B1
Bowers Rd RSEV TN14 ... 75 H5
Bower Ter MAIDW ME16 ... 6 D6
Bowesden La GVE DA12 ... 48 B4
  STRD ME2 ... 48 B5
Bowes Rd STRD ME2 ... 3 H2
Bowes Wd HART DA3 ... 61 H6
Bowford Av BXLYHN DA7 ... 12 E8
Bow HI WBY/YAL ME18 ... 119 G8
Bowls Pl STPH/PW TN12 ... 150 C6
Bowman Cl WALD ME5 ... 66 E8
Bowmans Rd DART DA1 ... 27 H5
Bown Cl TIL RM18 ... 17 K8
Bowness Rd BXLYHN DA7 ... 12 D8
Bow Rd WBY/YAL ME18 ... 119 G6
Bow Ter WBY/YAL ME18 ... 119 G6
Bowzell Rd RSEV TN14 ... 129 H3
Boxley Cl MAID/BEAR ME14 ... 103 K5
Boxley Rd MAID/BEAR ME14 ... 7 G1
  WALD ME5 ... 83 K4
Boxted La RSIT ME9 ... 69 J4
Boyces HI RSIT ME9 ... 69 M7
Boy Court La HDCN TN27 ... 156 A4
Boyne Pk STH/RUST TN4 ... 10 D3
Boyton Court Rd RMAID ME17... 139 J8
Brabourne Av RHAM ME8 ... 67 L1
Brabourne Crs BXLYHN DA7 ... 12 E5
Bracken Cl RTWE/PEM TN2 ... 164 A8
Brackendene BXLY DA5 ... 42 A1
Bracken HI WALD ME5 ... 83 J4
Bracken Lea WALD ME5 ... 66 E4
Bracken Rd RTWE/PEM TN2 ... 164 A8
The Brackens ORP BR6 ... 56 C8
Bracken Wk TONN TN10 ... 131 K7
Brackley Cl MAID/BEAR ME14.... 7 L3
Brackwood Cl RHAM ME8 ... 67 M8
Bracondale Av MEO DA13 ... 46 B5
Bradbourne La DIT/AY ME20 ... 101 K4
Bradbourne Park Rd SEV TN13 ... 8 F2
Bradbourne Pkwy DIT/AY ME20 ... 101 J4
Bradbourne Rd BXLY DA5 ... 26 C5
  GRAYS RM17 ... 16 E5
  SEV TN13 ... 9 G1
Bradbourne Vale Rd SEV TN13... 95 H8
Braddick Cl MAID/SHEP ME15 .. 121 K8
Bradfield Av RSEV TN14 ... 89 M3
Bradfields Av WALD ME5 ... 66 B7
Bradfields Av West
  WALD ME5 ... 66 B8
Bradford St TON TN9 ... 147 K4
Bradleigh Av GRAYS RM17 ... 16 E3
Bradley Dr SIT ME10 ... 88 A3
Bradley Rd RRTW TN3 ... 160 F8
  STRD ME2 ... 64 A8
Bradshaw Cl RSIT ME9 ... 69 G2
Braemar Av BXLYHN DA7 ... 26 E2
Braeside Av SEV TN13 ... 8 D4
Braeside Cl SEV TN13 ... 8 C5
Braeside Crs BXLYHN DA7 ... 26 E2
The Braes HOO/HM ME3 ... 48 E2
Braesyde Cl BELV DA17 ... 12 B3
Brake Av WALD ME5 ... 66 A8
Brakefield Rd MEO DA13 ... 45 K3
Brakes Pl BGR/WK TN15 ... 77 G1
Bramble Av RDART DA2 ... 29 L8
Bramble Bank MEO DA13 ... 79 H6
Bramble Cl MAIDW ME16 ... 120 D2
  RTON TN11 ... 147 H1
Bramble Cft ERITH DA8 ... 12 E3
Brambledown HART DA3 ... 45 H8
  WALD ME5 ... 66 D5
Bramblefield Cl HART DA3 ... 44 F7
Bramblefield La SIT ME10 ... 71 G4
Bramble La SEV TN13 ... 113 G6
Bramble Reed La
  STPH/PW TN12 ... 165 K6
Brambletree Crs ROCH ME1 ... 65 K6
Bramley Cl MEO DA13 ... 46 B4
  RHAM ME8 ... 68 D3
  SWLY BR8 ... 42 A4
Bramley Crs STPH/PW TN12 ..... 152 D7
Bramley Crs MAID/SHEP ME15.. 122 B2
Bramley Dr CRBK TN17 ... 192 F1
Bramley Gdns RMAID ME17 ... 136 F2
  STPH/PW TN12 ... 150 A6
Bramley Pl DART DA1 ... 27 J3
Bramley Ri STRD ME2 ... 2 B2
Bramley Rd SNOD ME6 ... 81 J3
  STPH/PW TN12 ... 134 D7
Bramley Wy WBY/YAL ME18 ... 118 C3
Bramshott Cl MAID/BEAR ME14 .. 7 K1
Branbridges Rd STPH/PW TN12.. 134 D8
Brandon Rd DART DA1 ... 28 C5
Brandon St GVW DA11 ... 31 K5
Brands Hatch Rd BGR/WK TN15.. 60 C6

Bransell Cl *SWLY* BR8 .... 57 L2
Bransgore Cl *RHAM* ME8 .... 67 M6
Brantingham Cl *TON* TN9 .... 147 H6
Branton *GRH* DA9 .... 29 H4
Brantwood Av *ERITH* DA8 .... 12 E6
Brantwood Rd *BXLYHN* DA7 .... 12 D8
Brantwood Wy *STMC/STPC* BR5 .. 67 G2
Brasenose Rd *GILL* ME7 .... 67 G2
Brassey Dr *DIT/AY* ME20 .... 101 M5
Brassey Hl *OXTED* RH8 .... 109 J7
Brassey Rd *OXTED* RH8 .... 109 J7
Brasted Ct *STRD* ME2 .... 49 J4
Brasted Hl *RSEV* TN14 .... 93 J6
Brasted Hill Rd *BH/WHM* TN16 . 93 L8
Brasted La *RSEV* TN14 .... 93 J5
Brasted Rd *BH/WHM* TN16 ..... 111 G4
    ERITH DA8 .... 13 G6
Brattle Wd *SEV* TN13 .... 113 L7
Braunstone Dr *MAIDW* ME16 .. 102 F6
Bray Gdns *MAID/SHEP* ME15 .. 121 H8
Breach La *RSIT* ME9 .... 69 H5
Breach Rd *WTHK* RM20 .... 15 H5
Breakneck Hl *GRH* DA9 .... 29 K3
Breakspears Dr *STMC/STPC* BR5 .. 40 C5
Bredgar Cl *MAID/BEAR* ME14 .... 7 K2
Bredgar Rd *RHAM* ME8 .... 67 J1
Bredhurst Rd *RHAM* ME8 .... 84 D2
Breedon Av *STH/RUST* TN4 .... 163 H4
Bremner Cl *SWLY* BR8 .... 42 C8
Brenchley Av *GVW* DA11 .... 46 D2
Brenchley Rd *ROCH* ME1 .... 65 M5
Brenchley Rd *MAID/SHEP* ME15 ... 6 F9
    RHAM ME8 .... 67 K3
    SIT ME10 .... 88 B3
    STMC/STPC BR5 .... 40 A5
    STPH/PW TN12 .... 166 A4
Brendon Av *WALD* ME5 .... 83 J1
Brendon Cl *BXLYHN* DA7 .... 13 G7
    RTWE/PEM TN2 .... 11 L2
Brennan Rd *TIL* RM18 .... 17 K8
Brent Cl *BXLY* DA5 .... 26 A4
    RDART DA2 .... 28 D4
    WALD ME5 .... 66 A8
Brentfield Rd *DART* DA1 .... 28 C4
Brentlands Dr *DART* DA1 .... 28 C6
Brent La *DART* DA1 .... 28 B5
The Brent *DART* DA1 .... 28 D5
    TONN TN10 .... 131 L7
Brent Wy *DART* DA1 .... 28 D4
Brentwood Rd *CDH/CHF* RM16 .. 17 K3
Brenzett Cl *WALD* ME5 .... 66 D8
Bretland Rd *STH/RUST* TN4 ... 176 F1
Breton Rd *ROCH* ME1 .... 65 L3
Brevet Cl *PUR* RM19 .... 14 F3
Brewer Rd *CDH/CHF* RM16 ..... 34 D6
Brewers Rd *GVE* DA12 .... 47 L5
Brewer St *MAID/BEAR* ME14 .... 7 G3
    RRTW TN3 .... 180 C8
Brewery La *SEV* TN13 .... 9 H6
Brewery Rd *SIT* ME10 .... 71 G7
Brewhouse Yd *GVE* DA12 .... 31 K4
Brian Crs *STH/RUST* TN4 .... 163 K5
Briar Cl *DIT/AY* ME20 .... 101 J3
Briar Dl *HOO/HM* ME3 .... 48 D2
Briar Flds *MAID/BEAR* ME14 .. 104 A8
Briar Rd *BXLY* DA5 .... 26 F8
The Briars *BGR/WK* TN15 .... 76 F1
Briars Wy *HART* DA3 .... 61 J1
Briarswood Wy *ORP* BR6 .... 56 B4
Briar Wk *TONN* TN10 .... 131 L7
Briary Ct *SCUP* DA14 .... 40 D2
Brice Rd *HOO/HM* ME3 .... 48 D2
Brickenden Rd *CRBK* TN17 .... 192 F1
Brickfields *E/WMAL* ME19 .... 100 D4
    RTWE/PEM TN2 .... 165 G5
Brick Field Vw *STRD* ME2 .... 49 L4
Brick Kiln La *OXTED* RH8 ...... 109 L8
    RMAID ME17 .... 139 M8
    STPH/PW TN12 .... 181 J4
Brickworks Cl *TON* TN9 .... 147 J6
Bridewell La *TENT* TN30 .... 196 C6
Bridge Cl *GRH* DA9 .... 28 F1
    TON TN9 .... 147 L5
Bridge Mill Wy *MAID/SHEP* ME15 .. 6 B9
Bridgen Rd *BXLY* DA5 .... 26 A5
Bridge Rd *BXLYHN* DA7 .... 26 A1
    ERITH DA8 .... 13 J7
    GILL ME7 .... 50 E6
    GRAYS RM17 .... 16 D5
    ROCH ME1 .... 65 L3
    STMC/STPC BR5 .... 56 D2
Bridges Dr *DART* DA1 .... 28 C3
Bridge St *MAID/SHEP* ME15 .. 121 H8
Bridgewater Cl *CHST* BR7 ...... 40 A7
Bridgewater Pl *E/WMAL* ME19 .. 101 G3
Bridlington Cl *BH/WHM* TN16 .. 91 K5
Brier Cl *WALD* ME5 .... 66 D8
Brier Rd *SIT* ME10 .... 70 C8
Brightlands *GVW* DA11 .... 46 A1
Bright Rdg *STH/RUST* TN4 .... 163 G5
Bright Rd *CHAT* ME4 .... 5 G9
Brigstock Rd *BELV* DA17 .... 5 J4
Brimfield Cl *PUR* RM19 .... 14 F3
The Brimp *HOO/HM* ME3 .... 23 M4
Brimstone Cl *ORP* BR6 .... 73 L2
Brimstone Hl *MEO* DA13 .... 62 E5
Brindles *TIL* RM18 .... 18 C3
Brindle's Fld *TON* TN9 .... 147 H6
Brindle Wy *WALD* ME5 .... 83 L4
Brindley Cl *BXLYHN* DA7 .... 26 D1
Brionne Gdns *TON* TN9 .... 147 M5
Brisbane Av *SIT* ME10 .... 87 L1
Brisbane Rd *CHAT* ME4 .... 5 K9
Brishing Cl *MAID/SHEP* ME15 . 122 A8
Brishing La *MAID/SHEP* ME15 . 122 A8
    RMAID ME17 .... 137 M2
Brishing Rd *RMAID* ME17 ..... 138 A1
Brissenden Cl *STRD* ME2 .... 50 C2
Bristol Cl *STRD* ME2 .... 48 F8
Bristol Rd *GVE* DA12 .... 31 M8
Bristow Rd *BH/WHM* TN16 ..... 91 J2
Britannia Cl *SIT* ME10 .... 71 G6
    STRD ME2 .... 81 J1
Britannia Dr *GVE* DA12 .... 47 H2
Brittains La *SEV* TN13 .... 8 C4
Britten Cl *TONN* TN10 .... 132 B7
Britton St *GILL* ME7 .... 5 K1
Broadacre *RSIT* ME9 .... 89 M3
Broadcloth *CRBK* TN17 .... 192 F2

Broadcroft *RTWE/PEM* TN2 .. 177 H5
Broad Ditch Rd *MEO* DA13 ..... 45 L4
Broad La *RDART* DA2 .... 42 D1
Broade La *MAID/BEAR* ME14 .. 104 D3
Broadfield Rd
    MAID/SHEP ME15 .... 121 J5
Broad Gv *RTWE/PEM* TN2 .... 177 J4
Broadlands Dr *WALD* ME5 ...... 83 K1
Broadlands Dr *GRAYS* RM17 ... 16 B4
Broad La *RDART* DA2 .... 42 D1
    RRTW TN3 .... 175 J2
Broadmead Av
    RTWE/PEM TN2 .... 177 H5
Broadoak *E/WMAL* ME19 ...... 100 F5
Broad Oak *RRTW* TN3 .... 175 K7
    STPH/PW TN12 .... 166 E5
Broadoak Av *MAID/SHEP* ME15 .. 121 J5
Broadoak Cl *RDART* DA2 .... 43 J3
Broad Oak Cl *RTWE/PEM* TN2 .. 177 H4
    STMC/STPC BR5 .... 40 C5
    STPH/PW TN12 .... 166 E5
    RSIT ME9 .... 87 M6
Broad Oak Rd *ERITH* DA8 ..... 12 F6
Broad St *SWCM* DA10 .... 30 A4
Broad Street HI *RMAID* ME17 . 105 M6
Broadview Av *CDH/CHF* RM16 . 16 F1
    RHAM ME8 .... 68 A5
Broad Wk *BGR/WK* TN15 ..... 114 A6
    ORP BR6 .... 56 F6
Broadwater Down
    RTWE/PEM TN2 .... 177 H5
Broadwater La *RTWE/PEM* TN2 . 10 C9
Broadwater Rd *RTWE/PEM* TN2 . 177 H7
Broadwater Rd *E/WMAL* ME19 . 100 F7
    GRAYS RM17 .... 16 E5
    RHAM ME8 .... 6 E6
    RHAM ME8 .... 67 J3
    TIL RM18 .... 17 H8
The Broadway *RRTW* TN3 ..... 180 C8
Broadwood *GVW* DA11 .... 46 D2
Broadwood Rd *HOO/HM* ME3 .. 50 B1
Brockenhurst Av
    MAID/SHEP ME15 .... 121 K4
Brockenhurst Cl *RHAM* ME8 ... 67 L6
Brockett Rd *CDH/CHF* RM16 .. 17 K2
Brockway *BGR/WK* TN15 .... 98 C7
Brockwell Cl *STMC/STPC* BR5 . 56 B1
Brogden Crs *RMAID* ME17 .... 123 H6
Broke Farm Dr *ORP* BR6 .... 73 L3
Brokes Wy *STH/RUST* TN4 .... 163 L4
Bromley *GRAYS* RM17 .... 16 B5
Bromley Cl *WALD* ME5 .... 83 K1
Brompton Dr *ERITH* DA8 .... 13 K6
Brompton Farm Rd *STRD* ME2 . 49 H4
Brompton HI *STRD* ME2 .... 2 F1
Brompton Rd *GILL* ME7 .... 5 G2
Bronington Cl *WALD* ME5 .... 66 C8
Bronte Cl *DIT/AY* ME20 .... 101 H2
    ERITH DA8 .... 13 L8
Bronte Gv *DART* DA1 .... 28 B2
Bronte Vw *GVE* DA12 .... 31 L6
Bronze Age Wy *BELV* DA17 .... 12 E2
Brook *CHAT* ME4 .... 4 D6
Brookbank *MAID/BEAR* ME14 . 103 J5
Brookdale Rd *BXLY* DA5 .... 26 A4
Brooke Dr *GVE* DA12 .... 32 D6
Brooke Rd *GRAYS* RM17 .... 16 C4
Brookes Pl *RSIT* ME9 .... 69 K7
Brookfield *RSEV* TN14 .... 96 A3
Brookfield Av *DIT/AY* ME20 ... 101 J1
Brookfields *RTON* TN11 .... 133 G4
Brook Hl *OXTED* RH8 .... 108 E8
Brookhurst Gdns
    STH/RUST TN4 .... 163 G2
Brooklands *DART* DA1 .... 28 A6
    HDCN TN27 .... 155 L7
    RTWE/PEM TN2 .... 163 M6
Brooklands Farm *RRTW* TN3 . 161 J7
Brooklands Dr *DIT/AY* ME20 .. 101 J2
Brook La *BGR/WK* TN15 .... 116 C5
    SNOD ME6 .... 52 A7
    TON TN9 .... 147 M3
Brooklyn Paddock *GILL* ME7 ... 5 L1
Brookmead *RTON* TN11 .... 147 G1
Brookmead Cl *ORP* BR6 .... 56 D3
Brookmead Rd *HOO/HM* ME3 . 34 D6
Brookmead Wy *ORP* BR6 .... 56 D2
Brook Rd *DIT/AY* ME20 .... 101 G1
    GVW DA11 .... 31 G6
    RTWE/PEM TN2 .... 163 L6
    SWLY BR8 .... 41 M7
Brookside *CRBK* TN17 .... 192 F1
    HOO/HM ME3 .... 36 A8
    ORP BR6 .... 56 B3
Brookside Rd *MEO* DA13 .... 46 B4
Brooks Pl *MAID/BEAR* ME14 ... 7 H4
Brook St *BELV* DA17 .... 12 D4
    RASHW TN26 .... 197 L5
    SNOD ME6 .... 52 A7
    TON TN9 .... 147 H5
Broom Av *STMC/STPC* BR5 .... 40 D6
Broom Bank *WARL* CR6 .... 90 E5
Broomcroft Rd *RHAM* ME8 ..... 68 B3
Broomes Ct *RMAID* ME17 ...... 139 L5
Broomfield *BXLYHS* DA6 .... 26 C3
    RMAID ME17 .... 139 L2
    SEV TN13 .... 95 H8
    SWCM DA10 .... 30 A4
Broomfields *HART* DA3 .... 61 G1
Broomhill Park Rd
    STH/RUST TN4 .... 163 G5
Broomhill Rd *BXLYHS* DA6 .... 26 C5
Broomhill Rd *DART* DA1 .... 27 K4
    ORP BR6 .... 56 B3
    RRTW TN3 .... 162 F7
Broom Hill Rd *STRD* ME2 .... 2 C1
Broomlands La *OXTED* RH8 ... 110 A5
Broom La *RRTW* TN3 .... 176 B4
Broom Md *BXLYHS* DA6 .... 26 C4
Broom Pk *RRTW* TN3 .... 176 A2
Broom Rd *SIT* ME10 .... 71 L8
Broomshaw Rd *MAIDW* ME16 . 120 B2
Broomwood Cl *BXLY* DA5 ...... 26 F7
Broomwood Rd *STMC/STPC* BR5 . 40 D6
Brow *STMC/STPC* BR5 .... 56 F3

Brow Crs *STMC/STPC* BR5 ..... 56 E4
Browndens Rd *STRD* ME2 .... 81 G1
Brownelow Copse *WALD* ME5 .. 83 J4
Brownhill Cl *WALD* ME5 .... 83 J1
Browning Cl *DIT/AY* ME20 .... 101 H1
Browning Rd *DART* DA1 .... 28 B2
Brownings *EDEN* TN8 .... 142 E1
Brownings Orch *RSIT* ME9 ...... 88 C6
Brown Rd *GVE* DA12 .... 32 A7
Brown St *RHAM* ME8 .... 68 A4
Broxbourne Rd *ORP* BR6 .... 56 B4
Bruce Gv *ORP* BR6 .... 56 C4
Bruces Wharf Rd *GRAYS* RM17 . 16 C5
The Brucks *WBY/YAL* ME18 .. 119 G6
Brunel Cl *TIL* RM18 .... 17 K8
Brunel Wy *CHAT* ME4 .... 50 C5
Brunswick St *MAID/SHEP* ME15 . 7 G7
Brunswick St East
    MAID/SHEP ME15 .... 7 H6
Brunswick Wk *GVE* DA12 ...... 31 M4
Bryanston Rd *TIL* RM18 .... 17 L8
Bryant Cl *WBY/YAL* ME18 .... 118 F7
Bryant Rd *STRD* ME2 .... 2 F2
Bryant St *CHAT* ME4 .... 4 E7
Bubblestone Rd *RSEV* TN14 .. 95 K3
Bulhurst La *CRBK* TN17 .... 171 K6
Buckham Thorns Rd
    BH/WHM TN16 .... 110 E4
Buckhurst Av *BGR/WK* TN15 ... 9 J7
Buckhurst La *SEV* TN13 .... 9 J7
Buckhurst Rd *BH/WHM* TN16 . 92 D6
Buckingham Rd *STMC/STPC* BR5 . 56 A3
Buckingham Rd *GILL* ME7 .... 5 M3
    GVW DA11 .... 30 F5
    RTW TN1 .... 11 G7
Buckingham Rw
    MAID/SHEP ME15 .... 122 A6
Buckland Cl *WALD* ME5 .... 83 J5
Buckland HI *MAIDW* ME16 .... 6 C3
Buckland La *MAIDW* ME16 .... 6 B1
Buckland Rd *HOO/HM* ME3 .... 34 B6
    MAIDW ME16 .... 6 C3
    MEO DA13 .... 63 J6
    ORP BR6 .... 56 A7
Bucklers Cl *RTWE/PEM* TN2 ... 11 K5
Buckley Cl *DART* DA1 .... 13 H8
Bucks Cross Rd *GVW* DA11 .... 31 H8
    ORP BR6 .... 57 C8
Budd's La *TENT* TN30 .... 209 G3
Budgin's HI *ORP* BR6 .... 73 K6
Bugglesden Rd *HDCN* TN27 .. 186 F8
Bull Cl *CDH/CHF* RM16 .... 16 B1
Bulldog Rd *WALD* ME5 .... 83 K3
Buller Rd *CHAT* ME4 .... 4 D9
Bullers Cl *SCUP* DA14 .... 41 G2
Bull Flds *SNOD* ME6 .... 81 J5
Bullfinch Cl *SEV* TN13 .... 94 F8
    STPH/PW TN12 .... 150 C8
Bullfinch Dene *SEV* TN13 .... 94 F8
Bullfinch La *SEV* TN13 .... 8 A1
Bullingstone La *RRTW* TN3 .. 162 B6
Bullion *STPH/PW* TN12 .... 150 A7
Bullivant Cl *GRH* DA9 .... 29 J3
Bull La *BGR/WK* TN15 .... 98 C2
    DIT/AY ME20 .... 82 C7
    HOO/HM ME3 .... 33 M6
    RSIT ME9 .... 86 A4
Bull Orch *MAIDW* ME16 .... 120 B3
Bull Rd *E/WMAL* ME19 .... 80 E8
Bulls Pl *RTWE/PEM* TN2 ...... 164 F7
Bulrush Cl *WALD* ME5 .... 83 H2
Bumbles Cl *ROCH* ME1 .... 65 M5
Bunkers HI *SCUP* DA14 .... 26 B8
Bunters Hill Rd *HOO/HM* ME3 . 34 C8
Bunyard La *RMAID* ME17 ..... 123 K4
Burdett Av *GVE* DA12 .... 48 A1
Burdett Cl *SCUP* DA14 .... 41 G2
Burdett Rd *STH/RUST* TN4 ... 176 D1
Bure *TIL* RM18 .... 18 E2
Burgate *DART* DA1 .... 27 H1
Burgess Hall Dr *RMAID* ME17 . 123 H7
Burgess Rd *STRD* ME2 .... 3 H1
Burghclere Dr *MAIDW* ME16 . 120 D3
Burghfield Rd *MEO* DA13 .... 46 B4
Burghley Rd *CDH/CHF* RM16 .. 15 L2
Burham Rd *ROCH* ME1 .... 65 G6
Burial Ground La
    MAID/SHEP ME15 .... 6 C9
Burkeston Cl *SIT* ME10 .... 71 J5
Burleigh Cl *STRD* ME2 .... 2 A1
Burleigh Dr *MAID/BEAR* ME14 . 103 H4
Burley Rd *SIT* ME10 .... 88 A1
Burlings La *RSEV* TN14 .... 93 H3
Burman Cl *RDART* DA2 .... 28 E5
Burmarsh Cl *WALD* ME5 .... 66 D8
Burma Wy *WALD* ME5 .... 66 B7
Burnaby Rd *GVW* DA11 .... 31 G5
Burnett Rd *ERITH* DA8 .... 13 M5
Burnham Cl *SIT* ME10 .... 71 G5
Burnham Crs *DART* DA1 .... 27 L2
Burnham Rd *DART* DA1 .... 27 M3
    SCUP DA14 .... 26 A7
Burnham Wk *RHAM* ME8 .... 85 G2
Burnley Rd *WTHK* RM20 .... 15 H7
Burns Cl *ERITH* DA8 .... 13 H7
Burns Crs *TON* TN9 .... 147 J6
Burns Pl *TIL* RM18 .... 17 K7
Burn's Rd *GILL* ME7 .... 50 E6
Burnt House Cl *HAWK* TN18 . 200 E8
Burnt House La *RDART* DA2 ... 43 G1
    RRTW TN3 .... 162 B8
Burnthouse Rd *HDCN* TN27 .. 172 F4
Burntwick Dr *RSIT* ME9 .... 69 K2
Burntwood Gv *SEV* TN13 ..... 113 K5
Burntwood Rd *SEV* TN13 ..... 113 K6
Burr Cl *BXLYHN* DA7 .... 26 B1
Burrfield Dr *STMC/STPC* BR5 . 56 F1
Burrows La *HOO/HM* ME3 ...... 36 A2
The Burrs *SIT* ME10 .... 88 B2
Burrstock Wy *RHAM* ME8 ...... 67 M6
Burslem Rd *RTWE/PEM* TN2 . 164 A7
Burston Rd *RMAID* ME17 ..... 136 D3
Burton Cl *HOO/HM* ME3 .... 49 L2

Burwash Cl *STMC/STPC* BR5 .. 56 E1
Busbridge Rd
    MAID/SHEP ME15 .... 121 G8
    SNOD ME6 .... 81 G6
Bush *CHAT* ME4 .... 87 H8
Bushey Cft *OXTED* RH8 .... 108 E8
Bushmeadow Rd *RHAM* ME8 .. 68 B3
Bush Rd *STPH/PW* TN12 ...... 134 A5
    STRD ME2 .... 64 B2
Bush Rw *DIT/AY* ME20 .... 102 C3
Bushy Gill *RRTW* TN3 .... 176 C2
Bushy Gv *RMAID* ME17 .... 139 M3
Busty La *BGR/WK* TN15 .... 97 M7
Butcher Cl *STPH/PW* TN12 ... 170 A2
Butchers La *BGR/WK* TN15 .... 60 F5
    WBY/YAL ME18 .... 117 M4
Butchers Yd *ORP* BR6 .... 72 C5
Butlers Dene Rd *CTHM* CR3 ... 90 B6
Buttercup Cl *STPH/PW* TN12 . 150 C8
Butterfly Av *DART* DA1 .... 28 B7
Buttermere Cl *GILL* ME7 .... 51 H8
Buttermere Rd
    STMC/STPC BR5 .... 40 F8
Butt Green La *RMAID* ME17 .. 137 H7
Butt Haw Cl *HOO/HM* ME3 .... 36 A8
Button Dr *HOO/HM* ME3 .... 23 L8
Button La *MAID/SHEP* ME15 . 122 D3
Button Rd *CDH/CHF* RM16 .... 16 B3
Button St *SWLY* BR8 .... 42 E8
Butts La *WADH* TN5 .... 188 E6
The Butts *RSEV* TN14 .... 95 K3
    SIT ME10 .... 88 B1
Buttway La *HOO/HM* ME3 ...... 20 C7
Buxton Cl *MAID/SHEP* ME15 . 121 J5
    WALD ME5 .... 83 M4
Buxton Rd *CDH/CHF* RM16 .... 17 G1
    ERITH DA8 .... 12 F6
Byng Rd *STH/RUST* TN4 .... 10 B2
Bynon Av *BXLYHN* DA7 .... 26 A1
Byrneside *RTON* TN11 .... 147 G1
Byron Dr *ERITH* DA8 .... 12 D6
Byron Gdns *TIL* RM18 .... 17 L7
Byron Rd *DART* DA1 .... 28 D2
    GILL ME7 .... 5 J7
    MAID/BEAR ME14 .... 103 K6
Bythorne Ct *RHAM* ME8 .... 68 D4

C

Cables Cl *BELV* DA17 .... 12 E2
Cacket's La *RSEV* TN14 .... 92 F1
Cade La *SEV* TN13 .... 113 L6
Cadlocks HI *RSEV* TN14 .... 74 B4
Cadnam Cl *STRD* ME2 .... 2 A2
Cadogan Av *RDART* DA2 .... 28 F5
Cadogan Gdns *RTW* TN1 .... 11 G4
Caerleon Cl *SCUP* DA14 .... 40 E2
Caernarvon Dr
    MAID/SHEP ME15 .... 121 H4
Cage Green Rd *TONN* TN10 .. 131 L8
Cage La *HDCN* TN27 .... 173 H4
Cairns Cl *DART* DA1 .... 27 M3
Caistor Rd *TON* TN9 .... 147 J4
Calcutta Rd *TIL* RM18 .... 17 H8
Caldecote Cl *RHAM* ME8 .... 68 D3
Calder Rd *MAID/BEAR* ME14 . 103 G6
Calderwood *GVE* DA12 .... 47 G3
Caldew Av *RHAM* ME8 .... 67 L4
Caldew Gv *SIT* ME10 .... 88 C2
Caldy Rd *BELV* DA17 .... 12 D2
Calehill Cl *MAID/BEAR* ME14 . 103 L7
Caley Rd *RTWE/PEM* TN2 .... 163 M5
Calfstock La *EYN* DA4 .... 43 G8
Caling Cft *HART* DA3 .... 61 H4
Caliph Cl *GVE* DA12 .... 32 B8
Callaways La *RSIT* ME9 .... 69 K7
Calshot Av *CDH/CHF* RM16 ... 16 B1
Calverley Ct *RTWE/PEM* TN2 . 11 H4
Calverley Pk *RTWE/PEM* TN2 . 11 H5
Calverley Park Crs
    RTWE/PEM TN2 .... 11 H5
Calverley Park Gdns *RTW* TN1 . 11 H4
Calverley Rd *RTW* TN1 .... 11 G4
    RTWE/PEM TN2 .... 11 H5
Calverley St *RTW* TN1 .... 11 G4
Calvert Cl *BELV* DA17 .... 12 C3
    SCUP DA14 .... 41 G3
Calvin Cl *STMC/STPC* BR5 ..... 40 F7
Camberwell La *RSEV* TN14 ... 128 B1
Cambray Rd *ORP* BR6 .... 56 B3
Cambria Av *ROCH* ME1 .... 65 H3
Cambria Crs *GVE* DA12 .... 47 J5
Cambrian Gv *GVW* DA11 .... 31 J5
Cambrian Rd *STH/RUST* TN4 . 163 L6
Cambridge Crs
    MAID/SHEP ME15 .... 121 M6
Cambridge Gdns
    CDH/CHF RM16 .... 17 J3
    RTWE/PEM TN2 .... 11 H7
    SCUP DA14 .... 40 A1
    SIT ME10 .... 88 D3
    STRD ME2 .... 2 E2
Cambridge St *RTWE/PEM* TN2 . 11 J6
Cambridge Ter *CHAT* ME4 .... 4 C5
Camden Av *RTWE/PEM* TN2 . 164 E7
Camden Cl *CDH/CHF* RM16 .... 17 K3
    GVW DA11 .... 30 E6
    WALD ME5 .... 66 D8
Camden HI *RTWE/PEM* TN2 ... 11 J7
Camden Pk *RTW* TN1 .... 11 G5
Camden Rd *BXLY* DA5 .... 26 B6
    CDH/CHF RM16 .... 16 A2
    GILL ME7 .... 50 F6
    RTW TN1 .... 11 G4
    STH/RUST TN4 .... 163 H3
    STRD ME2 .... 50 A4
    SWCM DA10 .... 30 B4
    TON TN9 .... 147 L3
Camden St *MAID/BEAR* ME14 . 12 F7
Camelia Cl *RHAM* ME8 .... 67 M6
Camelot Cl *BH/WHM* TN16 .... 91 L2
Cameron Cl *BXLY* DA5 .... 26 F8
Camer Park Rd *MEO* DA13 ..... 62 D3
Camer Rd *MEO* DA13 .... 62 E3
Camer St *MEO* DA13 .... 62 E2
Campbell Rd *GVW* DA11 .... 31 H6
    MAID/SHEP ME15 .... 7 G7

    STH/RUST TN4 .... 163 J7
Camp HI *RTON* TN11 .... 145 J2
Campion Cl *GVW* DA11 .... 46 A1
    WALD ME5 .... 83 G2
Campion Crs *CRBK* TN17 ...... 192 B3
Campleshon Rd *RHAM* ME8 ... 84 C5
Camp Rd *CTHM* CR3 .... 90 A7
Campus Wy *GILL* ME7 .... 67 J5
Camrose Av *CDH/CHF* RM16 .. 12 C5
Camrose Av *ERITH* DA8 .... 13 K6
Canada Farm Rd *EYN* DA4 ...... 60 D1
Canada Rd *ERITH* DA8 .... 13 K6
Canadian Av *GILL* ME7 .... 67 G1
Canal Basin *GVE* DA12 .... 31 M4
Canal Rd *GVE* DA12 .... 31 M4
    HOO/HM ME3 .... 33 K5
    STRD ME2 .... 3 J4
Canberra Gdns *SIT* ME10 .... 87 L1
Canberra Sq *TIL* RM18 .... 17 J8
Canbury Pth *STMC/STPC* BR5 .. 40 D8
Canning St *MAID/BEAR* ME14 . 103 J7
Cannon La *TON* TN9 .... 147 M3
Cannon Rd *BXLYHN* DA7 .... 12 A7
Canon La *ROCH* ME1 .... 65 K3
Canon La *WBY/YAL* ME18 .... 118 E4
Canterbury Cl *DART* DA1 .... 28 C5
Canterbury Crs *TONN* TN10 .. 131 M8
Canterbury La *MAID/BEAR* ME14 . 68 C4
Canterbury Rd *GVE* DA12 ...... 31 L7
    RTWE/PEM TN2 .... 165 G7
    SIT ME10 .... 88 D2
Canterbury St *GILL* ME7 .... 5 J4
Capel Cl *RHAM* ME8 .... 67 L8
Capel Cl *RMAID* ME17 .... 136 E2
Capel Pl *RDART* DA2 .... 42 E1
Capel Rd *SIT* ME10 .... 88 A3
Capstan Ct *GRH* DA9 .... 28 E2
Capstone Rd *GILL* ME7 .... 67 G6
    WALD ME5 .... 66 F4
Captain's Cl *RMAID* ME17 ..... 139 G7
The Caravan Site *SOCK/AV* RM15 . 14 F2
Caravel Cl *CDH/CHF* RM16 .... 16 B1
Cardens Rd *HOO/HM* ME3 ...... 34 D5
Cardinal Cl *TON* TN9 .... 147 M5
Cardine Cl *SIT* ME10 .... 71 G6
Carey's Fld *SEV* TN13 .... 95 G6
Caring La *RMAID* ME17 .... 122 F5
Caring Rd *MAID/BEAR* ME14 . 122 F4
Carisbrooke Dr *MAIDW* ME16 .. 6 B3
Carleton Pl *EYN* DA4 .... 43 L8
Carleton Rd *DART* DA1 .... 28 C5
Carlisle Rd *DART* DA1 .... 28 C4
Carlton Av *GILL* ME7 .... 67 G1
    GRH DA9 .... 29 G4
Carlton Crs *RTWE/PEM* TN2 ... 11 J4
    WALD ME5 .... 66 F5
Carlton Gdns *MAID/SHEP* ME15 . 121 K5
Carlton Rd *CDH/CHF* RM16 .... 17 H1
    ERITH DA8 .... 12 D5
    RTWE/PEM TN2 .... 11 J4
    SCUP DA14 .... 40 B2
Carmelite Wy *HART* DA3 .... 61 H1
Carnation Cl *E/WMAL* ME19 . 101 J4
Carnation Crs *E/WMAL* ME19 . 101 H5
Carnation Rd *STRD* ME2 .... 48 F6
Caroline Crs *MAIDW* ME16 .... 102 F6
Carolyn Dr *ORP* BR6 .... 56 C6
Carpeaux Cl *CHAT* ME4 .... 4 F6
Carpenters Cl *ROCH* ME1 .... 4 A9
Carpenters La *RTON* TN11 .... 132 F2
    STPH/PW TN12 .... 153 L6
Carpinus Cl *WALD* ME5 .... 83 K4
The Carriageway *RSEV* TN14 . 111 M2
Carrick Dr *SEV* TN13 .... 9 G3
Carriers Rd *CRBK* TN17 .... 183 M8
Carrington Cl *GILL* ME7 .... 51 H7
Carrington Rd *DART* DA1 .... 28 B4
Carroll Cl *STRD* ME2 .... 81 J1
Carroll Gdns *DIT/AY* ME20 ... 101 H2
Carsington Gdns *DART* DA1 ... 27 M7
Cartel Cl *PUR* RM19 .... 14 F3
Carter's HI *BGR/WK* TN15 .... 114 D8
Carter's Hill La *MEO* DA13 ..... 79 H3
Cartmel Rd *BXLYHN* DA7 ...... 12 C7
Carton Cl *ROCH* ME1 .... 65 M3
Carton Rd *HOO/HM* ME3 .... 48 D2
Carville Av *STH/RUST* TN4 ... 163 H4
Carvoran Wy *RHAM* ME8 .... 67 L8
Cascade Cl *STMC/STPC* BR5 .. 40 E7
Casstine Cl *SWLY* BR8 .... 42 B5
Castle Av *ROCH* ME1 .... 65 L1
Castle Dene *MAID/BEAR* ME14 . 103 G5
Castle Dr *RSEV* TN14 .... 96 A3
Castle Farm Rd *RSEV* TN14 .... 75 H3
Castlefields *MEO* DA13 .... 46 B5
Castle HI *HART* DA3 .... 60 F1
    MAID/BEAR ME14 .... 104 A3
    ROCH ME1 .... 3 J6
    RTON TN11 .... 148 B7
Castle Hurst *RBTBR* TN32 ... 204 D5
Castle La *GVE* DA12 .... 32 D7
Castlemaine Av *GILL* ME7 ...... 51 G7
Castle Rd *CHAT* ME4 .... 66 C3
    EYN DA4 .... 75 K1
    GRAYS RM17 .... 16 A5
    MAIDW ME16 .... 102 F5
    SIT ME10 .... 71 K8
    STH/RUST TN4 .... 10 D5
    SWCM DA10 .... 30 B4
    TON TN9 .... 147 L3
Castleton Av *BXLYHN* DA7 .... 12 F7
Castle View Rd *STRD* ME2 ...... 2 C1
Castle Wy *DIT/AY* ME20 .... 81 G8
    E/WMAL ME19 .... 101 G2
Catalina Av *CDH/CHF* RM16 .. 16 B1
Catharine Cl *MAIDW* ME16 .. 120 C2
Catherine Pl *RTW* TN1 .... 11 G4
Catherine St *ROCH* ME1 .... 65 M2
Catkin Cl *WALD* ME5 .... 83 H4

Catlyn Cl E/WMAL ME19 ... 101 J5
Catterick Rd WALD ME5 ... 83 M3
Causeway Br SOCK/AV RM15 ... 15 G2
Causton Rd CRBK TN17 ... 183 L8
Cave Hl MAID/SHEP ME15 ... 121 H4
Cavell Crs DART DA1 ... 28 C2
Cavell Wy SIT ME10 ... 70 F8
Cavendish Av ERITH DA8 ... 12 E5
GILL ME7 ... 51 G7
SEV TN13 ... 8 E1
Cavendish Cl TONN TN10 ... 131 M6
Cavendish Dr RTWE/PEM TN2 ... 11 H8
Cavendish Rd ROCH ME1 ... 65 M2
Cavendish Sq HART DA3 ... 44 F7
Cavendish Wy
MAID/SHEP ME15 ... 122 C2
Caversham Cl RHAM ME8 ... 68 B4
Caxton Cl HART DA3 ... 45 H8
TENT TN30 ... 196 B6
Caxton La OXTED RH8 ... 126 A1
RTON TN11 ... 133 C5
Cayser Dr RMAID ME17 ... 140 A3
Cazeneuve St ROCH ME1 ... 3 K9
Cecil Av CDH/CHF RM16 ... 16 B1
RHAM ME8 ... 67 J3
STRD ME2 ... 3 G2
Cecil Rd GVW DA11 ... 31 H6
ROCH ME1 ... 65 L2
Cedar Av TENT TN30 ... 46 E1
Cedar Cl DIT/AY ME20 ... 101 M5
MEO DA13 ... 62 C2
SIT ME10 ... 88 D3
SWLY BR8 ... 41 L6
WARL CR6 ... 90 A4
Cedar Crs TONN TN10 ... 131 L6
Cedar Dr EDEN TN8 ... 142 D3
EYN DA4 ... 43 K6
MAIDW ME16 ... 120 A3
Cedar Gv GILL ME7 ... 67 J8
Cedar Rdg RTWE/PEM TN2 ... 163 M7
Cedar Rd CDH/CHF RM16 ... 17 J2
DART DA1 ... 27 M6
ERITH DA8 ... 13 J7
HOO/HM ME3 ... 51 G2
STRD ME2 ... 2 B6
The Cedars STPH/PW TN12 ... 150 C6
Cedar Terrace Rd SEV TN13 ... 9 J2
Celedon Cl CDH/CHF RM16 ... 16 A1
Celestine Cl WALD ME5 ... 83 J4
Cellar Hl MET ME9 ... 89 L5
Celt Cl SIT ME10 ... 71 H5
Cement Block Cottages
GRAYS RM17 ... 16 E4
Cemetery La RTON TN11 ... 133 J5
Cemetery Rd SNOD ME6 ... 81 H4
STRD ME2 ... 81 J1
Centenary Walk - Maidstone
DIT/AY ME20 ... 82 C7
MAID/BEAR ME14 ... 6 E1
Centenary Walk - Rochester
ROCH ME1 ... 65 J2
Central Av GVE DA12 ... 31 K7
SIT ME10 ... 88 B2
SOCK/AV RM15 ... 14 E1
TIL RM18 ... 17 J7
WTHK RM20 ... 15 H4
Central Park Gdns ROCH ME1 ... 4 A9
Central Rd DART DA1 ... 28 A3
DIT/AY ME20 ... 101 K1
STRD ME2 ... 2 E3
Central Ter HOO/HM ME3 ... 35 H7
Central Wy OXTED RH8 ... 108 F5
Centre Rd DART DA1 ... 61 G6
Centurian Wy ERITHM DA18 ... 12 B2
Centurion Cl GILL ME7 ... 67 H4
Centurion Wy PUR RM19 ... 14 B3
Century Rd RHAM ME8 ... 67 M5
Cerne Rd GVE DA12 ... 47 G1
Cervia Wy GVE DA12 ... 32 B8
Chada Av GILL ME7 ... 67 G2
Chadfields TIL RM18 ... 17 J6
Chadwell By-pass GRAYS RM17 ... 17 J4
Chadwell Hl CDH/CHF RM16 ... 17 K4
Chadwell Rd GRAYS RM17 ... 16 E3
Chadwick Cl GVE DA11 ... 31 G7
Chaffe's La RSIT ME9 ... 69 G3
Chaffinch Cl WALD ME5 ... 66 C6
Chaffinch Wy STPH/PW TN12 ... 150 B8
Chafford La RRTW TN3 ... 161 J8
Chalet Cl RDART DA2 ... 41 M1
Chalfont Dr RHAM ME8 ... 67 M7
Chalice Wy GRH DA9 ... 29 G3
Chalk Av TENT TN30 ... 196 D3
Chalkenden Av RHAM ME8 ... 67 J3
Chalket La RTWE/PEM TN2 ... 164 E8
Chalk La CRBK TN17 ... 183 G6
Chalk Pit Av STMC/STPC BR5 ... 40 E7
Chalk Pit Hl CHAT ME4 ... 4 E8
Chalkpit La OXTED RH8 ... 108 L5
Chalkpit Wd OXTED RH8 ... 108 F5
Chalk Rd GVE DA12 ... 32 C6
HOO/HM ME3 ... 33 L7
Chalkways RSEV TN14 ... 96 A2
Chalkwell Rd SIT ME10 ... 87 M1
Chalky Bank GVW DA11 ... 46 C1
Chalky Bank Rd RHAM ME8 ... 68 B3
Chalky Rd RSIT ME9 ... 85 L7
Challenge Cl GVE DA12 ... 47 H1
Challenger Cl SIT ME10 ... 71 G6
STPH/PW TN12 ... 150 B7
Challock Cl BH/WHM ME16 ... 91 L2
Chamberlain Av MAIDW ME16 ... 120 D3
Chamberlain Cl RHAM ME8 ... 67 K8
Chamberlain Rd CHAT ME4 ... 5 C9
Chambers Cl GRH DA9 ... 29 H3
Chance Cl CDH/CHF RM16 ... 16 B2
Chancel Cl BGR/WK TN15 ... 77 C2
Chancellor Wy SEV TN13 ... 8 F1
Chancery La MAID/SHEP ME15 ... 7 J2
Chancery Rd HOO/HM ME3 ... 20 D8
Chandlers Dr ERITH DA8 ... 12 F3
Chandler's Hl MEO DA13 ... 62 E7
Chandler's Rd MEO DA13 ... 62 E8
Chandos Rd RTW TN1 ... 11 J2
Chantler's Hl STPH/PW TN12 ... 166 B2
Chantlers Md EDEN TN8 ... 159 J8
Chantrey Cl SCUP DA14 ... 41 G2
Chantry Av HART DA3 ... 61 G2
Chantry Pl STPH/PW TN12 ... 152 E8
Chantry Rd STPH/PW TN12 ... 152 E8

Chapel Cl DART DA1 ... 27 G3
E/WMAL ME19 ... 80 B8
WTHK RM20 ... 15 K5
Chapel Fld RYE TN31 ... 206 A1
Chapel Hl DART DA1 ... 27 G2
Chapel La CRBK TN17 ... 184 D6
CRBK TN17 ... 200 E1
GILL ME7 ... 84 C1
HDCN TN27 ... 157 K2
MAID/BEAR ME14 ... 104 C8
STPH/PW TN12 ... 170 B2
STRD ME2 ... 80 E1
Chapel Rd BXLYHN DA7 ... 26 C2
HOO/HM ME3 ... 25 J8
OXTED RH8 ... 109 L8
RMAID ME17 ... 139 C6
SNOD ME6 ... 81 J5
Chapel Rw BGR/WK TN15 ... 97 L7
HOO/HM ME3 ... 37 L1
Chapel St E/WMAL ME19 ... 80 B8
E/WMAL ME19 ... 100 B1
E/WMAL ME19 ... 101 J7
Chapel Wd HART DA3 ... 61 G5
Chapel Wood Rd HART DA3 ... 61 G5
Chaplin Cl HOO/HM ME3 ... 49 L2
Chaplin Dr HDCN TN27 ... 155 M8
Chapman Av MAID/SHEP ME15 ... 122 B4
Chapman Rd BELV DA17 ... 12 G1
Chapman's Hl BGR/WK TN15 ... 79 C1
Chapman's La STMC/STPC BR5 ... 40 F6
SWLY BR8 ... 41 J6
Chapmans Rd RSEV TN14 ... 112 A2
Chapman Wy E/WMAL ME19 ... 101 H5
RTWE/PEM TN2 ... 163 L5
Chappell Wy SIT ME10 ... 70 F7
Chapter Rd STRD ME2 ... 2 C3
Charing Cl ORP BR6 ... 56 B7
Charing Rd RHAM ME8 ... 67 K2
Chariot Wy STRD ME2 ... 65 G2
Charlbury Cl MAIDW ME16 ... 120 E2
Charles Cl SCUP DA14 ... 40 D1
SNOD ME6 ... 81 J5
Charles Dickens Av STRD ME2 ... 48 E3
Charles Dr STRD ME2 ... 64 D2
Charlesford Av RMAID ME17 ... 139 M2
Charles Rd RSEV TN14 ... 74 D4
Charles St CHAT ME4 ... 4 B7
GRAYS RM17 ... 16 E5
GRH DA9 ... 29 H3
MAIDW ME16 ... 6 D7
STH/RUST TN4 ... 163 J5
STRD ME2 ... 2 F4
Charlieville Rd ERITH DA8 ... 12 E6
Charlock Cl MAIDW ME16 ... 102 F5
Charlotte Cl BXLYHS DA6 ... 26 A3
WALD ME5 ... 66 D7
Charlotte Dr RHAM ME8 ... 67 L4
Charlotte Pl WTHK RM20 ... 15 K5
Charlotte St SIT ME10 ... 71 G8
Charlton Dr BH/WHM TN16 ... 91 M3
Charlton La MAID/SHEP ME15 ... 119M6
RMAID ME17 ... 139 L5
Charlton St MAIDW ME16 ... 120 E3
WTHK RM20 ... 15 M5
Charlton's Wy
STH/RUST TN4 ... 177 G4
Charmwood La ORP BR6 ... 73 K4
The Charne RSEV TN14 ... 95 J3
Charnock SWLY BR8 ... 42 A8
Charter Dr BXLY DA5 ... 26 A5
Charterhouse Dr SEV TN13 ... 8 F2
Charterhouse Rd ORP BR6 ... 56 C6
Charter St CHAT ME4 ... 4 D9
GILL ME7 ... 50 E6
Chart Hill Rd RMAID ME17 ... 138 C7
Chart La RTON TN11 ... 111 L3
Charton Cl BELV DA17 ... 12 B5
Chart Pl RHAM ME8 ... 84 E2
Chart Rd RMAID ME17 ... 138 E6
Chart Vw BGR/WK TN15 ... 96 C3
Chartway SEV TN13 ... 9 J5
Chartway St RMAID ME17 ... 139 H4
Chartwell Cl STRD ME2 ... 47 K4
Chartwell Gv SIT ME10 ... 87 L2
Chase Sq GVE DA12 ... 31 K4
The Chase BXLYHN DA7 ... 26 D1
ORP BR6 ... 73 J5
RHAM ME8 ... 67 J3
ROCH ME1 ... 65 M3
RSEV TN14 ... 96 A2
TONN TN10 ... 131 L8
WTHK RM20 ... 15 M5
Chastilian Rd DART DA1 ... 27 J5
Chatfield Wy DIT/AY ME20 ... 101 K4
Chatham Gv CHAT ME4 ... 66 B4
Chatham Hl CHAT ME4 ... 5 G7
Chatham Hill Rd RSEV TN14 ... 95 L7
Chatham Rd DIT/AY ME20 ... 82 F7
MAID/BEAR ME14 ... 103 G1
WALD ME5 ... 82 F4
Chatsworth Dr SIT ME10 ... 70 D8
STRD ME2 ... 49 K4
Chatsworth Rd DART DA1 ... 27 L2
GILL ME7 ... 5 K1
Chattenden Ct
MAID/BEAR ME14 ... 103 K6
Chattenden La HOO/HM ME3 ... 50 B1
Chaucer Cl STRD ME2 ... 50 A5
TIL RM18 ... 17 L8
Chaucer Gdns TON TN9 ... 147 H6
Chaucer Pk DART DA1 ... 28 B5
Chaucer Rd GILL ME7 ... 5 K7
GVW DA11 ... 30 F8
SIT ME10 ... 87M2
Chaucer Wy DART DA1 ... 28 C2
DIT/AY ME20 ... 101 H2
Chave Rd DART DA1 ... 28 A8
Cheeselands HDCN TN27 ... 186 B3
Chegwell Dr WALD ME5 ... 83 K1
Chegworth Gdns SIT ME10 ... 88 A4
Chegworth La RMAID ME17 ... 124 D7
Chegworth Rd RMAID ME17 ... 124 B6
Chelmar Rd CHAT ME4 ... 5 G6
Chelmer Rd CDH/CHF RM16 ... 17 J4
Chelmsford Rd STRD ME2 ... 48 F7
Chelsfield Hl ORP BR6 ... 73 L3
Chelsfield La ORP BR6 ... 56 F7
ORP BR6 ... 74 C2
RSEV TN14 ... 56 G5
STMC/STPC BR5 ... 56 E2

Chelsfield Rd STMC/STPC BR5 ... 56 E2
Chelsham Common Rd
WARL CR6 ... 90 C2
Chelsham Court Rd WARL CR6 ... 90 F4
Chelsham Rd WARL CR6 ... 90 B3
Cheltenham Cl GVE DA12 ... 46 E2
MAID/SHEP ME15 ... 122 B7
Cheltenham Rd ORP BR6 ... 56 C6
Cheney Cl RSIT ME9 ... 67 M8
Cheney Hl RSIT ME9 ... 88 C8
Chenies Cl RTWE/PEM TN2 ... 177 J5
The Chenies ORP BR6 ... 56 A2
RDART DA2 ... 42 A1
Chennell Park Rd TON TN30 ... 196 A4
Chequers Cl MEO DA13 ... 46 A6
STMC/STPC BR5 ... 40 B8
WALD ME5 ... 83 J4
Chequers St RTON TN11 ... 49 J4
Cherbourg Crs WALD ME5 ... 66 B6
Cheriton Rd RHAM ME8 ... 67 M6
Cheriton Wy MAIDW ME16 ... 102 E6
The Cherries MAID/SHEP ME15 ... 120 B3
Cherry Amber Cl RHAM ME8 ... 68 B5
Cherry Av SWLY BR8 ... 41 M7
Cherry Cl SIT ME10 ... 70 F7
Cherry Flds SIT ME10 ... 70 C8
Cherry Gdns RSIT ME9 ... 89 L3
Cherry Gv TONN TN10 ... 132 A8
Cherry Orch DIT/AY ME20 ... 101 L5
TENT TN30 ... 196 C7
Cherry Orchard Cl
STMC/STPC BR5 ... 56 E1
The Cherry Orch RTON TN11 ... 133 C4
Cherry Orchard Wy
MAIDW ME16 ... 120 D2
Cherry Rd HOO/HM ME3 ... 51 G2
Cherry Tree Cl RSIT ME9 ... 89 M3
Cherry Tree Gv EYN DA4 ... 76 D4
Cherry Tree La RDART DA2 ... 27 H8
Cherry Tree Rd RHAM ME8 ... 68 B5
RTWE/PEM TN2 ... 177 G4
Cherry Trees HART DA3 ... 61 H2
Cherry Wk CDH/CHF RM16 ... 17 J2
Cherrywood Dr GVW DA11 ... 46 A4
Chervilles MAIDW ME16 ... 120 C3
Cherwell Cl TONN TN10 ... 147 K1
Chesham Dr RHAM ME8 ... 68 A7
Cheshire Rd MAID/SHEP ME15 ... 122 A3
Cheshunt Cl MEO DA13 ... 62 C2
Cheshunt Rd BELV DA17 ... 12 C4
Chessenden La RSIT ME9 ... 173 J4
Chessington Av BXLYHN DA7 ... 12 A6
Chester Av RTWE/PEM TN2 ... 11 M7
Chester Cl STRD ME2 ... 48 F7
Chesterfield Cl STMC/STPC BR5 ... 40 F8
Chesterfield Dr DART DA1 ... 27 K3
SEV TN13 ... 94 F8
Chester Rd GILL ME7 ... 5 M9
Chesterton Rd DIT/AY ME20 ... 101 H1
HOO/HM ME3 ... 20 D8
STH/RUST TN4 ... 163 K5
STPH/PW TN12 ... 170 A1
WALD ME5 ... 83 G2
Chestnut Av BH/WHM TN16 ... 91 M8
CDH/CHF RM16 ... 16 D1
GRH DA9 ... 29 H5
STH/RUST TN4 ... 163 K5
STPH/PW TN12 ... 170 A1
WALD ME5 ... 83 G2
Chestnut Cl CRBK TN17 ... 171 G7
E/WMAL ME19 ... 118 C3
EDEN TN8 ... 142 D3
GVW DA11 ... 31 H4
ORP BR6 ... 56 C8
RMAID ME17 ... 140 B7
STH/RUST TN4 ... 163 K5
TENT TN30 ... 196 A4
Chestnut Dr RMAID ME17 ... 136 D2
RMAID ME17 ... 139M3
Chestnut Gv RDART DA2 ... 41 M2
Chestnut La MEO DA13 ... 79 K5
SEV TN13 ... 9 G4
STPH/PW TN12 ... 166 A4
Chestnut Rd DART DA1 ... 27 M6
STRD ME2 ... 2 A6
The Chestnuts E/WMAL ME19 ... 99 L2
HAWK TN18 ... 199 G5
Chestnut St RSIT ME9 ... 87 G1
Chestnut Wk BGR/WK TN15 ... 114 B6
TON TN9 ... 147 H5
Chestnut Wood La RSIT ME9 ... 87 G1
Cheswick Cl DART DA1 ... 27 H2
Chesworth Cl ERITH DA8 ... 13 G7
Chetney Cl STRD ME2 ... 48 E6
Chevening Cl WALD ME5 ... 66 C8
Chevening La RSEV TN14 ... 94 A2
Chevening Rd RSEV TN14 ... 94 B5
RSEV TN14 ... 112 B1
Cheviot Cl BXLYHN DA7 ... 13 G8
TON TN9 ... 147 L1
Cheviot Gdns MAID/SHEP ME15... 122 C4
Cheyne Cl SIT ME10 ... 71 H5
Cheyne Wk MEO DA13 ... 62 C5
Chicago Av GILL ME7 ... 51 G8
Chichele Rd OXTED RH8 ... 109 G6
Chichester Cl RHAM ME8 ... 68 C5
Chichester Dr SEV TN13 ... 8 D7
Chichester Ri GVE DA12 ... 46 F1
Chichester Rd GRH DA9 ... 29 H3
Chickenden La STPH/PW TN12 ... 170 E1
Chickfield Gdns WALD ME5 ... 66 E3
Chicks La CRBK TN17 ... 190 C3
Chiddingstone Av BXLYHN DA7 ... 12 B5
Chiddingstone Cl
MAID/SHEP ME15 ... 122 B7
Chidley Cross Rd
STPH/PW TN12 ... 134 A7
Chieftain Cl GILL ME7 ... 67 K4
Chieftan Dr PUR RM19 ... 14 C3
Chieveley Dr RTWE/PEM TN2... 177 L4
Chieveley Rd BXLYHN DA7 ... 13 H4
Chiffinch Gdns GVW DA11 ... 31 G8
Childbridge La RSEV TN14 ... 96 A4
Childsbridge La BGR/WK TN15 ... 96 B6
Childsbridge Wy BGR/WK TN15 ... 96 B6
Childs Crs SWCM DA10 ... 29M4
Childs Wd BGR/WK TN15 ... 98 B2
Chilham Cl BXLY DA5 ... 26 A5
CHAT ME4 ... 4 B7
Chilham Rd MAIDW ME16 ... 102 E6
RHAM ME8 ... 67 J2

Chillington St
MAID/BEAR ME14 ... 103 H7
Chilliwack Rd HOO/HM ME3 ... 35 H8
Chilston Cl STH/RUST TN4 ... 10 F1
Chilston Rd RMAID ME17 ... 125M8
STH/RUST TN4 ... 10 F1
Chiltern Cl BXLYHN DA7 ... 13 G7
MAID/SHEP ME15 ... 122 B6
Chiltern Rd GVW DA11 ... 31 G8
Chilton Av SIT ME10 ... 88 C2
Chilton Ct RHAM ME8 ... 68 A4
Chilton Dr HOO/HM ME3 ... 48 D2
Chilton Rd CDH/CHF RM16 ... 17 J2
Chippendale Cl MAIDW ME16 ... 83 H4
Chippendayle Dr RMAID ME17 ... 124 F7
Chipperfield Rd STMC/STPC BR5 .. 40 C6
Chipstead Cl MAIDW ME16 ... 6 A1
Chipstead La SEV TN13 ... 94 F8
Chipstead Pk SEV TN13 ... 94 F8
Chipstead Park Cl SEV TN13 ... 94 F8
Chipstead Rd ERITH DA8 ... 13 C6
RHAM ME8 ... 84 F1
Chislehurst Cl
MAID/SHEP ME15 ... 122 B7
Chislehurst Rd ORP BR6 ... 56 C3
SCUP DA14 ... 40 C2
STMC/STPC BR5 ... 40 A8
Chorleywood Crs
STMC/STPC BR5 ... 40 B6
Christ Church Av ERITH DA8 ... 12 F5
RTW TN1 ... 10 F7
Christchurch Rd DART DA1 ... 27 L5
Christ Church Rd GVE DA12 ... 31 L5
Christchurch Rd TIL RM18 ... 17 J7
Christian Fields Av GVE DA12 ... 46 E1
Christie Cl WALD ME5 ... 66 D7
Christie Dr DIT/AY ME20 ... 101 H1
Christies Av RSEV TN14 ... 74 C4
Christmas La HOO/HM ME3 ... 36 A2
Christmas St GILL ME7 ... 51 C6
Christy Rd BH/WHM TN16 ... 91 L1
Chulkhurst HDCN TN27 ... 186 A3
Church Av SCUP DA14 ... 40 C2
Church Cl HOO/HM ME3 ... 20 D7
RSIT ME9 ... 166 E5
WBY/YAL ME18 ... 117M5
Church Crs RMAID ME17 ... 125 H7
Church Farm Cl HOO/HM ME3 ... 51 G1
Church Farm Rd RSIT ME9 ... 69 G2
Church Fld DART DA1 ... 27M7
EDEN TN8 ... 142 F4
SEV TN13 ... 8 C1
SNOD ME6 ... 81 K4
Church Flds E/WMAL ME19... 100 D5
Churchfields Ter ROCH ME1 ... 3 H9
Church Gn STPH/PW TN12 ... 152 E7
STPH/PW TN12 ... 170 A3
STRD ME2 ... 3 J1
Church Hl BGR/WK TN15 ... 116 A5
BH/WHM TN16 ... 91M8
DART DA1 ... 27M8
DART DA1 ... 27M8
GRH DA9 ... 29 G3
ORP BR6 ... 56 C3
RMAID ME17 ... 137 K6
RMAID ME17 ... 137 K3
RSEV TN14 ... 92 E1
RSIT ME9 ... 86 B6
WALD ME5 ... 66 E3
Church Hill Wd STMC/STPC BR5.... 56 B1
Church Hollow PUR RM19 ... 14 C4
Churchill Av WALD ME5 ... 66 B7
GRAYS RM17 ... 16 F5
GVW DA11 ... 31 H6
Churchill Cl DART DA1 ... 28 D6
Churchill Rd EYN DA4 ... 43 L8
Churchill Sq E/WMAL ME19... 118 C2
Church La BGR/WK TN15 ... 96 D3
CHAT ME4 ... 4 D1
E/WMAL ME19 ... 79 J8
GVE DA12 ... 32 E7
MAID/SHEP ME15 ... 119M6
OXTED RH8 ... 109 G7
PUR RM19 ... 14 C4
RMAID ME17 ... 125 C7
RMAID ME17 ... 139 K5
RSIT ME9 ... 69 K7
RSIT ME9 ... 86 A5
RTON TN11 ... 149 H7
RYE TN31 ... 206 E7
STPH/PW TN12 ... 134 B6
TON TN9 ... 147 L3
WARL CR6 ... 90 E2
Church Manorway ERITH DA8 ... 12 F2
Church Ms RHAM ME8 ... 68 B4
Church Pth GILL ME7 ... 51 G7
GRH DA9 ... 29 H4
GVW DA11 ... 30 E4
Church Rd BGR/WK TN15 ... 77 G2
BGR/WK TN15 ... 96 B7
BGR/WK TN15 ... 115 G1
BH/WHM TN16 ... 91M3
BH/WHM TN16 ... 111 K2
BXLYHN DA7 ... 12 B8
CRBK TN17 ... 183 A5
CRBK TN17 ... 190 B3
CTHM CR3 ... 108 A1
E/WMAL ME19 ... 100 B2
E/WMAL ME19 ... 100 B2
ERITH DA8 ... 13 G6
EYN DA4 ... 43 J3
GRH DA9 ... 29 G3
GVE DA12 ... 46 E5
HART DA3 ... 61 H1
HAWK TN18 ... 205 H1
MAID/BEAR ME14 ... 105M4
MAID/SHEP ME15 ... 6 D9
MAID/SHEP ME15 ... 122 B5
MEO DA13 ... 46 E5
ORP BR6 ... 73 G1
RMAID ME17 ... 125 C6
RMAID ME17 ... 138 C5
RMAID ME17 ... 141 H6
RHAM ME8 ... 180 D7
RRTW TN3 ... 112 A4
RSEV TN14 ... 129 K2
RSIT ME9 ... 89 G1
RTON TN11 ... 130 F7

RTW TN1 ... 10 E5
SCUP DA14 ... 40 C1
SIT ME10 ... 71 K8
STH/RUST TN4 ... 163 H3
STPH/PW TN12 ... 150 D7
SWCM DA10 ... 30 B4
SWLY BR8 ... 42 B5
SWLY BR8 ... 57 M3
TENT TN30 ... 196 C6
TIL RM18 ... 17 G7
TIL RM18 ... 18 A5
WBY/YAL ME18 ... 117 J7
Churchside MEO DA13 ... 79 J5
Churchside Cl BH/WHM TN16 ... 91 L4
Church Sq RMAID ME17 ... 125M8
Church St BGR/WK TN15 ... 96 C6
CHAT ME4 ... 4 E6
EDEN TN8 ... 142 F4
EDEN TN8 ... 159 K8
GILL ME7 ... 51 G7
GRAYS RM17 ... 16 E5
GVW DA11 ... 31 K4
HOO/HM ME3 ... 33 L6
HOO/HM ME3 ... 33 L6
HOO/HM ME3 ... 36 A8
MAID/BEAR ME14 ... 7 G4
MAID/SHEP ME15 ... 6 D9
MAID/SHEP ME15 ... 121 H8
MEO DA13 ... 45 J3
RMAID ME17 ... 137 G2
ROCH ME1 ... 3 L9
ROCH ME1 ... 82 A5
RSEV TN14 ... 75 H5
RSIT ME9 ... 88 E6
RTON TN11 ... 133 G5
SIT ME10 ... 71 K8
SIT ME10 ... 88 A1
TON TN9 ... 147 L3
WBY/YAL ME18 ... 119 J6
Church Ter WALD ME5 ... 66 E3
Church Vw HDCN TN27 ... 186 B3
SOCK/AV RM15 ... 14 E1
Church Wk DART DA1 ... 27M8
E/WMAL ME19 ... 101 J6
GVE DA12 ... 31M5
HDCN TN27 ... 155 L8
Churn La STPH/PW TN12 ... 167 H2
Chute Cl RHAM ME8 ... 84 F1
Cimba Wd GVE DA12 ... 47 G1
Cinder Hill La RTON TN11 ... 145 L4
Cinnabar Cl WALD ME5 ... 83 J4
Cirrus Crs GVE DA12 ... 47 G2
City Wy ROCH ME1 ... 65M1
Civic Sq TIL RM18 ... 17 J8
Civic Wy RTW TN1 ... 11 C5
Clacket La BH/WHM TN16 ... 110 A2
Clandon Rd WALD ME5 ... 83M4
Clanricarde Gdns RTW TN1 ... 10 F5
Clanricarde Rd RTW TN1 ... 10 F5
Claphatch La WADH TN5 ... 189 J4
Clapper La STPH/PW TN12 ... 169M1
Clare Av TON TN9 ... 147 H4
Clare Ct CTHM CR3 ... 108 C1
Clare La E/WMAL ME19 ... 101 G5
Claremont Cl CDH/CHF RM16 ... 16 E2
Claremont Crs DART DA1 ... 27 G2
Claremont Gdns RTW TN1 ... 11 H7
Claremont Rd MAID/BEAR ME14 ... 7 K3
RTW TN1 ... 11 C7
SWLY BR8 ... 42 A4
Claremont Wy CHAT ME4 ... 4 D7
Clarence Ct MAID/BEAR ME14 ... 122 A1
Clarence Pl GVE DA12 ... 31 K5
Clarence Rd BH/WHM TN16 ... 92 B4
BXLYHS DA6 ... 26 A2
GRAYS RM17 ... 16 D5
RTW TN1 ... 10 F5
Clarence Rw GVE DA12 ... 31 K5
RTW TN1 ... 10 F5
Clarendon Cl MAID/BEAR ME14 ... 122 C1
SIT ME10 ... 88 B4
STMC/STPC BR5 ... 40 C7
Clarendon Gdns RDART DA2 ... 28 F6
RTWE/PEM TN2 ... 177 J4
STRD ME2 ... 49 J4
Clarendon Gn STMC/STPC BR5 .... 40 C7
Clarendon Ms STMC/STPC BR5 .... 40 C8
Clarendon Pth STMC/STPC BR5 ... 40 C8
Clarendon Pl RDART DA2 ... 41M2
Clarendon Rd GVE DA12 ... 31 L4
SEV TN13 ... 8 F6
Clarendon Wy CHST BR7 ... 40 B7
RTWE/PEM TN2 ... 177 H4
Clare Wy BXLYHN DA7 ... 12 A7
SEV TN13 ... 113 L6
Clarewood Dr E/WMAL ME19 ... 101 G5
Claridge Cl GILL ME7 ... 84 B1
Clarkbourne Dr GRAYS RM17 ... 16 F5
Clark Cl ERITH DA8 ... 12 F3
Clarkes Green Rd BGR/WK TN15 .. 76 C3
Clark Ms DIT/AY ME20 ... 102 B4
Clarks La RSEV TN14 ... 74 B6
WARL CR6 ... 109 K1
Claston Cl DART DA1 ... 27 G2
Claudian Wy CDH/CHF RM16 ... 17 K2
Clavadal Rd STPH/PW TN12 ... 150 C6
Clavell Cl RHAM ME8 ... 84 F2
Claxfield Rd RSIT ME9 ... 89 H4
Claygate MAID/SHEP ME15 ... 121 M4
Claygate Cross BGR/WK TN15 ... 116 C2
Claygate La RTON TN11 ... 116 B8
Claygate Rd STPH/PW TN12 ... 151 K3
WBY/YAL ME18 ... 151 G1
Clayhill CRBK TN17 ... 181 M4
Clay Hill Rd RRTW TN3 ... 179 M5
Clayton Croft Rd RDART DA2 ... 27 J7
Clayton's La RRTW TN3 ... 175 G3
Clay Wood Cl ORP BR6 ... 56 A3
Claywood La RDART DA2 ... 29 M4
Clearway GVE DA12 ... 99 J4
Cleave Av ORP BR6 ... 73 G1
Cleave Rd GILL ME7 ... 67 G3
Cleavers CRBK TN17 ... 184 C6
Cleavesland WBY/YAL ME18 ... 135 G8
Cleeve Av RTWE/PEM TN2 ... 11 M8
Clematis Av RHAM ME8 ... 67 K8
Clement Ct MAIDW ME16 ... 6 B2
Clement St SWLY BR8 ... 42 F5
Clenches Farm La SEV TN13 ... 8 E9
Clenches Farm Rd SEV TN13 ... 8 F9

Clerke Dr SIT ME10 .... 71 J5
Clerks Fld HDCN TN27 .... 155 L8 🛙
Clermont Cl GILL ME7 .... 84 C1
Cleveland RTWE/PEM TN2 .... 11 L3
Cleveland Av GILL ME7 .... 5 M1 🛙
Cleves Rd RSEV TN14 .... 96 A3
Clewson Ri MAID/BEAR ME14 .... 103 K5 🛙
Cliff Hl RMAID ME17 .... 137 L1
Cliff Hill Rd RMAID ME17 .... 137 L1
Clifford Rd CDH/CHF ME16 .... 16 B1
Cliff Reach GRH DA9 .... 29 C4
Clifton Cl MAID/BEAR ME14 .... 7 K2
  STRD ME2 .... 2 C5
Clifton Gv GVW DA11 .... 31 K5
Clifton Marine Pde GVW DA11 .... 31 J4
Clifton Pl RTW TN1 .... 11 G7
Clifton Rd GILL ME7 .... 50 E6
  GVW DA11 .... 31 J4
  RTWE/PEM TN2 .... 163 L6
  SCUP DA14 .... 40 A1
Clinch St HOO/HM ME3 .... 22 B8
Clinton Av STRD ME2 .... 48 F5
Clinton Cl RMAID ME17 .... 136 D2
Clinton La EDEN TN8 .... 143 M2
Clipper Bvd GRH DA9 .... 29 G2
Clipper Bvd West GRH DA9 .... 28 F1
Clipper Cl STRD ME2 .... 50 A6
Clipper Crs GVE DA12 .... 47 H1
Clive Av DART DA1 .... 27 H4
Clive Rd BELV DA17 .... 12 C3
  GVW DA11 .... 31 K4
  ROCH ME1 .... 65 L2
  SIT ME10 .... 70 D8
Clockhouse RTWE/PEM TN2 .... 164 B7
Clockhouse La CDH/CHF RM16 .... 16 A2
Clock House La SEV TN13 .... 8 F1
Cloisterham Rd ROCH ME1 .... 65 H6
Cloonmore Av ORP BR6 .... 56 B8
The Close BGR/WK TN15 .... 97 M7
  BGR/WK TN15 .... 98 C5
  BXLY DA5 .... 26 C4
  CDH/CHF RM16 .... 16 D1
  E/WMAL ME19 .... 80 D8
  EDEN TN8 .... 144 C3
  HART DA3 .... 45 K6 🛙
  RDART DA2 .... 27 L8
  ROCH ME1 .... 3 J9
  RRTW TN3 .... 175 L7 🛙
  SCUP DA14 .... 40 D2
  SEV TN13 .... 8 B2
  STMC/STPC BR5 .... 56 A2
Cloth Hall Gdns HDCN TN27 .... 186 C5 🛙
Cloudesley Av RSEV TN14 .... 65 K4
Cloudesley Rd BXLYHN DA7 .... 12 B7
  ERITH DA8 .... 13 H7
Clovelly Rd BXLYHN DA7 .... 12 L5
Clovelly Wy ORP BR6 .... 56 B2
Clover Bank Vw WALD ME5 .... 66 D7
Clover Lay RHAM ME8 .... 68 D3
Clover Rd HOO/HM ME3 .... 51 C2 🛙
The Clovers GVW DA11 .... 46 A1
Clover St CHAT ME4 .... 4 D6
Clover Wy STPH/PW TN12 .... 150 C8
Clyde TIL RM18 .... 18 E3
Clyde Rd TONN TN10 .... 131 L8
Clydon Cl ERITH DA8 .... 13 G5
The Coach Dr MEO DA13 .... 79 G6 🛙
Coach Rd BGR/WK TN15 .... 115 J2
Cobb Cl STRD ME2 .... 48 F5
Cobbets Wy EDEN TN8 .... 142 E5
Cobbett Cl E/WMAL ME19 .... 101 H5 🛙
Cobbett's Ride
  RTWE/PEM TN2 .... 177 H4 🛙
Cobblestones GILL ME7 .... 67 G6
Cobbs St STPH/PW TN12 .... 150 B7
  WBY/YAL ME18 .... 119 C6
Cob Cl BGR/WK TN15 .... 97 L7
Cobden Rd SEV TN13 .... 9 J2
Cobdown Cl DIT/AY ME20 .... 101 K3
Cobdown Gv RHAM ME8 .... 68 C3 🛙
Cob Dr GVE DA12 .... 48 A2
Cobfield RMAID ME17 .... 138 C4
Cobham Av SIT ME10 .... 88 A4
Cobhambury Rd GVE DA12 .... 47 J8 🛙
Cobham Cl MAIDW ME16 .... 6 C4
  STRD ME2 .... 2 B3
Cobhams RRTW TN3 .... 162 C5
Cobham St GVW DA11 .... 31 J5
Cobtree Cl WALD ME5 .... 66 E5
Cobtree Rd RMAID ME17 .... 136 E2
Cockerhurst Rd RSEV TN14 .... 75 G3
Cockmannings La
  STMC/STPC BR5 .... 56 F4
Cockmannings Rd
  STMC/STPC BR5 .... 56 F3
Cockmount La WADH TN5 .... 188 A7
Cocksure La SCUP DA14 .... 41 J1
Codrington Crs GVE DA12 .... 46 E2
Codrington Gdns GVE DA12 .... 46 F2 🛙
Cogate Rd STPH/PW TN12 .... 150 A7
Colchester Cl WALD ME5 .... 66 B6
Cold Arbor Rd SEV TN13 .... 112 F2
Cold Blow Crs BXLY DA5 .... 26 F6
Coldarbour La MAID/BEAR ME14 .... 105 J3
Coldbridge La RMAID ME17 .... 141 H8
Coldharbour La DIT/AY ME20 .... 102 C4
  MAID/BEAR ME14 .... 105 K4
Cold Harbour La RSIT ME9 .... 70 B7
Coldharbour Rd RTON TN11 .... 131 G7
  SIT ME10 .... 71 J4
Coldharbour Rd CRBK TN17 .... 193 J8
  GVW DA11 .... 31 G7
  RTON TN11 .... 160 F5
Coldred Rd
  MAID/BEAR ME14 .... 138 B1 🛙
Coldrum La E/WMAL ME19 .... 79 L8 🛙
Cole Av CDH/CHF ME16 .... 17 L3
Colebrook Rd STH/RUST TN4 .... 11 G4
Colegate Dr MAID/BEAR ME14 .... 122 E1
Coleman Rd BELV DA17 .... 12 C2
Coleridge Cl DIT/AY ME20 .... 101 J1 🛙
Coleridge Rd DART DA1 .... 28 C2
  TIL RM18 .... 17 L8
Coleridge Wy ORP BR6 .... 56 C7 🛙
Coleshall Cl MAID/SHEP ME15 .... 122 B7
Coles La BH/WHM TN16 .... 111 L1 🛙
Colets Orch RSEV TN14 .... 95 K2 🛙
Colewood Dr STRD ME2 .... 48 D5

Colfe Wy SIT ME10 .... 71 J5
Colin Blythe Rd TONN TN10 .... 132 B8
Colin Chapman Wy HART DA3 .... 23 G7
Colin Rd RDART DA2 .... 28 D4
College Av GILL ME7 .... 5 H5
College Dr RTWE/PEM TN2 .... 11 L3
College Rd CHAT ME4 .... 50 C6
  DIT/AY ME20 .... 101 K2
  GRAYS RM17 .... 16 E3
  GVW DA11 .... 30 D3
  MAID/SHEP ME15 .... 6 F8
  SIT ME10 .... 87 M2
  SWLY BR8 .... 42 A4
Collet Yd RDART DA2 .... 3 J6
Coller Crs RDART DA2 .... 44 A2
Collet Rd RSEV TN14 .... 96 A3
Collet Wk RHAM ME8 .... 84 F1
Collindale Av ERITH DA8 .... 12 D5
Collingdon Cl GVW DA11 .... 31 G5 🛙
Collington Ter
  MAID/SHEP ME15 .... 138 B1 🛙
Collingwood Rd DIT/AY ME20 .... 82 E6
Collison Pl TENT TN30 .... 196 H6
Collis St STRD ME2 .... 2 F1
Colne TIL RM18 .... 18 E2
Colne Rd TONN TN10 .... 131 K8
Colney Rd DART DA1 .... 28 B4
Colonel's Wy STH/RUST TN4 .... 163 J3
Coltsfoot Ct GRAYS RM17 .... 16 F5
Coltsfoot Dr
  MAID/BEAR ME14 .... 122 B1 🛙
Coltstead HART DA3 .... 61 G5 🛙
Columbia Wharf Rd
  GRAYS RM17 .... 16 C5
Columbine Cl E/WMAL ME19 .... 101 H4 🛙
  STRD ME2 .... 2 A3
Columbine Rd E/WMAL ME19 .... 101 H4 🛙
  STRD ME2 .... 2 A4
Colyer Rd GVW DA11 .... 30 F7
Colyers Cl ERITH DA8 .... 12 F7
Colyers La ERITH DA8 .... 12 E7
Combe Bank Dr RSEV TN14 .... 112 A1
Comet Cl PUR RM19 .... 14 C3
Comfrey Ct GRAYS RM17 .... 16 F5
Command Rd
  MAID/BEAR ME14 .... 103 H5
Commercial Pl GVE DA12 .... 31 L4
Commercial Rd RTW TN1 .... 11 H2
  STPH/PW TN12 .... 150 B7
  STRD ME2 .... 2 F4
  TON TN9 .... 147 J5
Commissioner's Rd STRD ME2 .... 3 J1
Commodore Rd
  MAID/BEAR ME14 .... 7 L2
Common La HOO/HM ME3 .... 20 E7
  RDART DA2 .... 27 J7
Common Rd BGR/WK TN15 .... 115 K1
  CRBK TN17 .... 184 B4
  HOO/HM ME3 .... 49 K1
  ROCH ME1 .... 82 D3
  RTON TN11 .... 133 G3
Common Vw STH/RUST TN4 .... 176 E2
Common Wall HOO/HM ME3 .... 20 F7
Commonwealth Cl SIT ME10 .... 88 D2
Commority Rd MEO DA13 .... 79 K5
Compass Cl ROCH ME1 .... 65 L4
Compasses Rd RTON TN11 .... 145 K3
Comp La BGR/WK TN15 .... 98 C2
  E/WMAL ME19 .... 99 J6
Compton Cl WALD ME5 .... 83 M3 🛙
Compton Pl E/WMAL ME19 .... 13 H5
Concord Av WALD ME5 .... 66 A8
Concord Cl RTWE/PEM TN2 .... 11 K3 🛙
  STPH/PW TN12 .... 150 A8
Coneyburrow Rd
  RTWE/PEM TN2 .... 164 A8
Conghurst La HAWK TN18 .... 199 J8
Conifer Av HART DA3 .... 61 G2
Conifer Dr MEO DA13 .... 79 H3
  WALD ME5 .... 83 M4
Conifer Wy SWLY BR8 .... 41 L5
Coniston Av STH/RUST TN4 .... 10 A2
Coniston Cl BXLYHN DA7 .... 12 E7
  DART DA1 .... 27 K6
  ERITH DA8 .... 13 G4
  GILL ME7 .... 51 J7
Coniston Rd BXLYHN DA7 .... 12 E7
Connaught Av CDH/CHF RM16 .... 16 D1
Connaught Cl
  MAID/SHEP ME15 .... 122 B8 🛙
Connaught Rd CHAT ME4 .... 66 D3
  GILL ME7 .... 5 L3
  SIT ME10 .... 88 A2
Connaught Wy STH/RUST TN4 .... 10 C1
Conrad Cl CDH/CHF RM16 .... 16 D1
  RHAM ME8 .... 84 F7 🛙
Conrad Gdns CDH/CHF RM16 .... 16 C1
Consort Cl MAID/BEAR ME14 .... 7 K3
Constable Rd GVW DA11 .... 31 G8
  TONN TN10 .... 132 A8 🛙
Constitutional Hill Rd
  STH/RUST TN4 .... 163 G4
Constitution Hl CHAT ME4 .... 5 G9
  GVE DA12 .... 31 L6
  SNOD ME6 ....
Constitution Rd WALD ME5 .... 5 H8
Contessa Cl ORP BR6 ....
Convalescent La CRBK TN17 .... 184 A3
Conway Cl STRD ME2 .... 49 G4 🛙
Conway Gdns GRAYS RM17 .... 16 D6
Conway Ms SIT ME10 .... 34 F3
Conway Rd MAIDW ME16 .... 102 E7
Conyerd Rd BGR/WK TN15 .... 98 B6
Cooden Cl RHAM ME8 .... 68 C3
Cook Cl WALD ME5 .... 66 F7
Cookham Hl ROCH ME1 .... 65 J3
Cookham Rd SWLY BR8 .... 41 K7
Cookham Wood Rd ROCH ME1 .... 65 K5
Cooks La SIT ME10 .... 71 K8
Cookson Gv ERITH DA8 .... 12 D6
Cooling Cl MAID/BEAR ME14 .... 103 L2
Cooling Rd HOO/HM ME3 .... 34 F1
  STRD ME2 .... 49 K3
Cooling St HOO/HM ME3 .... 34 F3 🛙
Coombe Av RSEV TN14 .... 95 K6 🛙
Coombe Cl SNOD ME6 .... 81 J6 🛙

  WALD ME5 .... 83 K2
Coombe Dr SIT ME10 .... 88 B1
Coombe Farm La HOO/HM ME3 .... 23 G7
Coombe Lands TENT TN30 .... 208 F1
Coombe La TENT TN30 .... 196 C6
Coombe Rd GVE DA12 .... 31 L7
  HOO/HM ME3 .... 36 A8
  MAID/SHEP ME15 .... 6 F9
  RSEV TN14 .... 95 L1
Coomb Fld EDEN TN8 .... 142 E5
Coombfield Dr RDART DA2 .... 43 M1
Coombs La RYE TN31 .... 207 L8
Cooper Cl GRH DA9 .... 29 C3
Cooper Rd SNOD ME6 .... 81 H7
  WALD ME5 .... 83 J2
Coopers Cl EYN DA4 .... 43 L5
Cooper Shaw Rd TIL RM18 .... 17 M6
Coopers La RRTW TN3 .... 161 L7
Cooper's Rd GVW DA11 .... 31 G6
Coote Rd BXLYHN DA7 .... 12 B7
Copenhagen Rd GILL ME7 .... 5 J4
Coppards La RYE TN31 .... 206 D6
Copper Beech Cl GVE DA12 .... 31 M5 🛙
  STMC/STPC BR5 .... 56 E1 🛙
Copperfield Cl STRD ME2 .... 48 E3
Copperfield Crs STRD ME2 .... 48 E3
Copperfield Dr RMAID ME17 .... 139 G1
Copperfield Rd ROCH ME1 .... 65 L3
Copperfields BGR/WK TN15 .... 96 B3
Copperfields Wk BGR/WK TN15 .... 96 B3 🛙
Coppergate GILL ME7 .... 67 H8
Copperhouse La GILL ME7 .... 51 K7 🛙
Copperhouse Rd STRD ME2 .... 48 E6
Copper La STPH/PW TN12 .... 153 G8
Copperpenny Dr GILL ME7 .... 84 D2
Copper Tree Ct
  MAID/SHEP ME15 .... 121 J8
Coppice Ct GILL ME7 .... 84 D1 🛙
Coppice Rd WALD ME5 .... 83 L3
The Coppice BGR/WK TN15 .... 114 F4
  DIT/AY ME20 .... 102 A4
  MEO DA13 .... 79 K5
  RTWE/PEM TN2 .... 164 F6
Coppice Vw MAID/BEAR ME14 .... 104 A7
Copping's Rd RTON TN11 .... 145 K2
Coppins La RSIT ME9 .... 87 K3
Copse Bank BGR/WK TN15 .... 96 B6
Copse Cl CHAT ME4 .... 66 A4
Copsehill DIT/AY ME20 .... 101 G3
Copse Rd RTON TN11 .... 147 G1
Copse Side HART DA3 .... 45 G7
The Copse HOO/HM ME3 .... 51 G2
Copsewood Wy
  MAID/SHEP ME15 .... 122 C2
Copthall Av HAWK TN18 .... 199 H4
Copt Hall Rd BGR/WK TN15 .... 115 J1 🛙
  MEO DA13 .... 46 D8
Cordelia Crs ROCH ME1 .... 65 H3
Corinthian Manorway
  ERITH DA8 .... 12 F3
Corinthian Rd ERITH DA8 .... 12 F3 🛙
Cork La STPH/PW TN12 .... 169 M5
Cork St DIT/AY ME20 .... 82 B7
Corkwell St CHAT ME4 .... 4 B8
Cormorant Cl STRD ME2 .... 48 E6 🛙
Cornell Cl SCUP DA14 .... 41 G3
Corner Farm Rd
  STPH/PW TN12 .... 170 A1 🛙
Cornfield Wy TONN TN10 .... 131 M7
Cornflower Cl
  MAID/SHEP ME14 .... 122 A1 🛙
Cornford Cl RTWE/PEM TN2 .... 164 D7 🛙
Cornford La RTWE/PEM TN2 .... 164 D8
Cornford Pk RTWE/PEM TN2 .... 164 D7
Cornforth Cl STPH/PW TN12 .... 170 B1
Corn Mill Dr ORP BR6 .... 56 B3
Cornwall Cl MAID/SHEP ME15 .... 122 A6
Cornwall Crs ROCH ME1 .... 81 L1
Cornwall Dr STMC/STPC BR5 .... 40 E4
Cornwallis Av CHAT ME4 .... 66 A4
  GILL ME7 .... 67 H1
  RMAID ME17 .... 137 C5
  TONN TN10 .... 148 A1
Cornwallis Cl ERITH DA8 .... 13 H5
Cornwallis Rd MAIDW ME16 .... 6 B5
Cornwall Rd DART DA1 .... 28 B1
  GILL ME7 .... 5 K1
  ROCH ME1 .... 65 L2
Cornwell Av GVE DA12 .... 31 L8
Corona Ter SNOD ME6 .... 81 H7 🛙
Coronation Av TIL RM18 .... 18 D3
Coronation Rd HOO/HM ME3 .... 25 K8
  WALD ME5 .... 5 K9
Corporation Rd GILL ME7 .... 5 M1
Corporation St ROCH ME1 .... 3 K6
Corral Cl WALD ME5 .... 83 K4
Corrance Gn
  MAID/SHEP ME15 .... 121 J5 🛙
Correnden Rd RTON TN11 .... 147 J2
Cortland Cl SIT ME10 .... 71 G7 🛙
Cortland Ms SIT ME10 .... 71 G7 🛙
Cossack St ROCH ME1 .... 65 L2
Cossington Rd WALD ME5 .... 83 K4
Costells Meadow
  BH/WHM TN16 .... 110 F4
Cot La HDCN TN27 .... 186 D2
Cotmandene Crs
  STMC/STPC BR5 .... 40 D6
Cotman's Ash La BGR/WK TN15 .... 96 F1
Cotman Wy STPH/PW TN12 .... 134 V2
Cotswold Av BXLYHN DA7 .... 13 G7
Cotswold Gdns
  MAID/SHEP ME15 .... 122 C2
Cotswold Ri ORP BR6 .... 56 B2 🛙
Cotswold Rd GVW DA11 .... 31 G8
Cottage Rd CHAT ME4 .... 4 D1
Cottages Rd SEV TN13 .... 95 G6
Cottall Av CHAT ME4 .... 4 C9
Cottenham La E/WMAL ME19 .... 101 H6
Cotton La GRH DA9 .... 28 E3
Couchman Green La
  STPH/PW TN12 .... 154 B6
Coulman St GILL ME7 .... 5 M4
Coulters Cl MAID/BEAR ME14 .... 121 M1
Coulton Av GVW DA11 .... 31 G5
Council Av GVW DA11 .... 30 E4
County Gv E/WMAL ME19 .... 100 D5
County Rd MAID/BEAR ME14 .... 7 G3
Court Av BELV DA17 .... 12 B4

Court Crs SWLY BR8 .... 42 A8
Court Dr MAIDW ME16 .... 6 A3
Courtenay Dr RTWE/PEM RM16 .... 16 B2 🛙
Courtenay Rd MAID/SHEP ME15 .... 6 E9
Courteney Rd RHAM ME8 .... 67 K5
Courtfield Av WALD ME5 .... 83 L2
Courthope STPH/PW TN12 .... 150 C7
Courtlands RTON TN11 .... 147 J2
  WBY/YAL ME18 .... 119 J5
Court La MAID/BEAR ME14 .... 84 E8
  RTON TN11 .... 133 J5
Courtleet Dr BXLYHN DA7 .... 12 D7
Courtney Rd CDH/CHF RM16 .... 17 L1
Court Rd RDART DA2 .... 44 A2
  ROCH ME1 .... 81 M4
  SIT ME10 .... 71 G6
  STH/RUST TN4 .... 10 B3
Court Road
  (Orpington By-pass)
  ORP BR6 .... 56 D6
The Court WARL CR6 .... 90 A4
Courtwood Dr SEV TN13 .... 8 E4
Cousley Wood Rd WADH TN5 .... 188 C7
Coutts Av GVE DA12 .... 48 A1
Coventry Cl STRD ME2 .... 48 F7 🛙
Coventry Rd TONN TN10 .... 131 M8
Coverdale Av MAID/SHEP ME15 .... 121 M7
Coverdale Cl WALD ME5 .... 66 D6
The Covert MEO DA13 .... 79 G6
  ORP BR6 .... 56 A2
  WALD ME5 .... 83 K4 🛙
Covet Wood Cl STMC/STPC BR5 .... 56 B2
Covey Hall Rd SNOD ME6 .... 81 J5
Cowbeck Cl RHAM ME8 .... 67 M7 🛙
Cowden Cl HAWK TN18 .... 199 G5
Cowden La HAWK TN18 .... 199 G6
Cowden Ms EDEN TN8 .... 159 J8
Cowden MAID/BEAR ME14 .... 7 M2 🛙
  ORP BR6 .... 56 B3
Cowdrey Cl MAIDW ME16 .... 120 D4
  ROCH ME1 .... 65 K3
Cowdrey Ct DART DA1 .... 27 K5
Cow La EDEN TN8 .... 159 M3
Cowley Av GRH DA9 .... 29 H3
Cowper Av TIL RM18 .... 17 K7
Cowper Rd BELV DA17 .... 12 B3
  GILL ME7 .... 5 L7
  SIT ME10 .... 88 D1
Cowstead Rd RSIT ME9 .... 85 M2
Cox's Cl SNOD ME6 .... 81 H5
Cox St MAID/BEAR ME14 .... 84 E8
Cozenton Cl RHAM ME8 .... 68 A4
Crabtree Cl E/WMAL ME19 .... 118 C3
Crabtree Manorway North
  BELV DA17 .... 12 E1
Crabtree Manorway South
  BELV DA17 .... 12 E1
Crabtree Rd RHAM ME8 .... 67 M5
Craddock Wy RHAM ME8 .... 67 M8 🛙
Cradducks La STPH/PW TN12 .... 170 D1
Cradles Rd RSIT ME9 .... 85 L4
Cramptons CRBK TN17 .... 184 B5
Crampton's Rd RSEV TN14 .... 95 K6
Cranborne Av
  MAID/SHEP ME15 .... 121 L5
Cranbourne Av
  STPH/PW TN12 .... 170 A1 🛙
Cranbrook Cl MAID/SHEP ME15 .... 122 B6
  RHAM ME8 .... 67 L2 🛙
Cranbrook Dr SIT ME10 .... 87 M4
Cranbrook Rd BXLYHN DA7 .... 12 B7
  CRBK TN17 .... 182 C5
  CRBK TN17 .... 193 G4
  HAWK TN18 .... 199 H1
  HDCN TN27 .... 185 H6
  STPH/PW TN12 .... 170 B6
  TENT TN30 .... 196 A5
Crandalls RTON TN11 .... 146 B4
Crane La CRBK TN17 .... 183 M8
Cranford Cl RHAM ME8 .... 67 M4
Cranford Rd DART DA1 .... 28 A6
Cranleigh Cl BXLY DA5 .... 26 D4 🛙
  ORP BR6 .... 56 C6
Cranleigh Dr SWLY BR8 .... 42 A8
Cranleigh Gdns MAIDW ME16 .... 102 E6 🛙
  ROCH ME1 .... 65 M2
Cranmer Cl WARL CR6 .... 90 A3
Cranmer Ct MAID/SHEP ME15 .... 121 K5
Cranmere Ct STRD ME2 .... 3 J2
Cranmer Gdns WARL CR6 .... 90 A3
Cranmer Rd SEV TN13 .... 8 A2
Cranwell Rd STH/RUST TN4 .... 176 E1
Craven Rd ORP BR6 .... 56 F6
Crawfords SWLY BR8 .... 42 A4
Crawshay Cl SEV TN13 .... 8 E2
Cray Av STMC/STPC BR5 .... 56 D1
Craybrooke Rd SCUP DA14 .... 40 D1
Crayburne MEO DA13 .... 45 H2
Cray Cl DART DA1 .... 27 J3
Craydene Rd ERITH DA8 .... 13 J5
Crayford Rd MAID/BEAR ME14 .... 7 L1
Crayford High St DART DA1 .... 27 H3
Crayford Rd DART DA1 .... 27 H3
  MAID/BEAR ME14 .... 7 L1
Crayford Wy DART DA1 .... 27 J2
Craylands STMC/STPC BR5 .... 40 E7
Craylands La SWCM DA10 .... 30 A3
Craylands Sq SWCM DA10 .... 29 M3 🛙
Cray Rd BELV DA17 .... 12 C5
  SCUP DA14 .... 40 E3
  SWLY BR8 .... 57 L2
Craythorne TENT TN30 .... 196 D4
Cray Valley Rd STMC/STPC BR5 .... 56 C1
Credo Wy WTHK WM20 .... 15 K5
The Creek GVW DA11 .... 30 D3
Cremers Rd SIT ME10 .... 71 K8
Cremorne Rd DART DA1 .... 31 H5 🛙
Crendon Pk STH/RUST TN4 .... 163 J4
Crescent Av GRAYS RM17 .... 16 F4
Crescent Gdns SWLY BR8 .... 41 L6
Crescent Rd ERITH DA8 .... 13 H5
  RTWE/PEM TN2 .... 11 G5
  SOCK/AV RM15 .... 14 L1 🛙
The Crescent BGR/WK TN15 .... 98 C5
  CHAT ME4 .... 50 D4
  CTHM CR3 .... 108 C1
  GRH DA9 .... 29 L4
  GVW DA11 .... 31 H7
  HART DA3 .... 45 G7

  MAID/BEAR ME14 .... 103 H5
  RSIT ME9 .... 89 M2
  SCUP DA14 .... 40 B1
  SEV TN13 .... 95 M8
  SIT ME10 .... 71 H4
  STH/RUST TN4 .... 163 L1
  TON TN9 .... 147 K3
Crescent Wk SOCK/AV RM15 .... 14 E1
Crescent Wy ORP BR6 .... 56 A8
  RSIT ME9 .... 65 M8
Cressey Ct CHAT ME4 .... 4 B6
Crest Av GRAYS RM17 .... 16 D6
Crest Cl RSEV TN14 .... 74 D5 🛙
Crest Rd ROCH ME1 .... 65 L4
Cresthill Av GRAYS RM17 .... 16 C5
Crest Vw GRH DA9 .... 29 J2 🛙
Crestway WALD ME5 .... 66 D5
Crete Hall Rd GVW DA11 .... 30 F4
Creve Coeur Cl
  MAID/BEAR ME14 .... 104 C3 🛙
Cricketers Cl ERITH DA8 .... 13 G4
  RMAID ME17 .... 124 F7
  SIT ME10 .... 71 H5 🛙
Cricketers Dr MEO DA13 .... 62 C6
Cripple Hl RASHW TN26 .... 187 M4
Cripps Ct MAID/SHEP ME15 .... 121 J6 🛙
Crismill La MAID/BEAR ME14 .... 123 H1
Crismill Rd MAID/BEAR ME14 .... 123 G2
Crispe Cl RHAM ME8 .... 84 F1
Crispin Cl RMAID ME17 .... 136 E2 🛙
Crispin Rd STRD ME2 .... 2 A2
Crispin Wy E/WMAL ME19 .... 118 C2
Crittenden Rd STPH/PW TN12 .... 165 L1
Crockenhill Wy MEO DA13 .... 46 A5
Crockenhill Hl STMC/STPC BR5 .... 56 F1
Crockenhill La SWLY BR8 .... 58 C3
Crockenhill Rd STMC/STPC BR5 .... 56 F2
Crockers La RYE TN31 .... 206 D5
Croft Cl BELV DA17 .... 12 B4
  RMAID ME17 .... 139 M3
  TONN TN10 .... 132 B8
  WALD ME5 .... 83 L4
Croft Ct EDEN TN8 .... 142 E4
The Crofters RHAM ME8 .... 68 B6
Croft Gdns RMAID ME17 .... 125 M8
Croft La EDEN TN8 .... 142 E4
Crofton Rd CDH/CHF RM16 .... 17 G1
Croft Rd BH/WHM TN16 .... 110 D4
  CTHM CR3 ....
Croftside MEO DA13 .... 79 J5 🛙
The Croft E/WMAL ME19 .... 101 G3
  SWLY BR8 .... 41 L7
Croft Wy SEV TN13 .... 8 C6
Cromer Rd SIT ME10 .... 88 A5
  STRD ME2 .... 3 G1
Cromer St TON TN9 .... 147 J4
Cromford Cl ORP BR6 .... 56 A6 🛙
Crompton Gdns
  MAID/SHEP ME15 .... 7 J6
Cromwell Rd GRAYS RM17 .... 16 C3
  MAID/BEAR ME14 .... 7 H3
  RTWE/PEM TN2 .... 11 K6
Cromwell Ter CHAT ME4 .... 4 E7
Cronin Cl DIT/AY ME20 .... 101 H1
Crooked La GVE DA12 .... 31 K4
Crook Rd STPH/PW TN12 .... 166 E4
Crosier Ct RSIT ME9 .... 69 G2
Cross Dr RMAID ME17 .... 139 K4
Cross Keys MAID/BEAR ME14 .... 122 E1
Cross La BXLY DA5 .... 26 B5
  SIT ME10 .... 71 G7 🛙
Cross La East GVE DA12 .... 31 K7
Cross La West GVE DA12 .... 31 K7
Crossley Cl BH/WHM TN16 .... 91 M1
Cross Rd DART DA1 .... 27 L4
  GVW DA11 .... 31 H4
  RDART DA2 .... 43 H1
  SCUP DA14 .... 40 D1
  STMC/STPC BR5 .... 56 D1 🛙
Cross St CHAT ME4 .... 4 D5
  ERITH DA8 .... 13 G5
  GILL ME7 .... 5 J1
  MAID/BEAR ME14 .... 7 G1
  STRD ME2 .... 3 G2
Cross Wy ROCH ME1 .... 65 K2
Crossway WALD ME5 .... 66 A7
Crossways BH/WHM TN16 .... 91 L6
  SIT ME10 .... 88 A4
Crossways Bvd GRH DA9 .... 29 G3
Crouch Hill Ct RSIT ME9 .... 69 L2 🛙
Crouch House Rd EDEN TN8 .... 142 C2
Crouch La BGR/WK TN15 .... 98 C2
  HAWK TN18 .... 201 H5 🛙
Crouch Rd GRAYS RM17 .... 17 J4
Crowborough Cl WARL CR6 .... 90 A4 🛙
Crowborough Dr WARL CR6 .... 90 A4
Crow Dr RSEV TN14 .... 94 E1
Crow Hill Rd BGR/WK TN15 .... 98 C6
Crowhurst La MAID/BEAR ME14 .... 60 D8
  BGR/WK TN15 .... 116 A1
Crowhurst Rd BGR/WK TN15 .... 98 B7
Crowhurst Wy STMC/STPC BR5 .... 56 E1
Crow La ROCH ME1 .... 3 K8
Crown Acres STPH/PW TN12 .... 134 C7
Crown Cl ORP BR6 .... 56 C7
Crownfields
  MAID/BEAR ME14 .... 122 A1
  SEV TN13 .... 9 G7
Crown Gn GVE DA12 .... 48 A2 🛙
Crown La GVE DA12 .... 48 A1
Crown Quay La SIT ME10 .... 88 B1 🛙
Crown Rd EDEN TN8 .... 142 F2
  GRAYS RM17 .... 16 C5
  ORP BR6 .... 56 C8
  RSEV TN14 .... 75 H4
  SIT ME10 .... 16 E1
Crown St GILL ME7 .... 5 L2
Crowstone Rd GRAYS RM17 .... 16 E1
Crowther Rd STPH/PW TN12 .... 170 A1
Croxley Cl STMC/STPC BR5 .... 40 D6
Croxley Gn STMC/STPC BR5 .... 40 D5
Croydon Cl WALD ME5 .... 83 L1
Croydon Rd BH/WHM TN16 .... 110 D4
  WARL CR6 .... 90 F8
Cruden Rd GVE DA12 .... 32 B8
Crump's La RMAID ME17 .... 156 A2
Crundale Rd RHAM ME8 .... 67 L2

Crundwell Rd STH/RUST TN4 163 H4
Crusader Cl GILL ME7 67 J5
PUR RM19 14 C3
Crusoe Rd ERITH DA8 12 F4
Crutches La STRD ME2 48 D5
Cryalls La RSIT ME9 87 K2
SIT ME10 87 L1
Cryals Rd STPH/PW TN12 179 L1
Cuckolds Green Rd
HOO/HM ME3 23 J8
Cuckoo La RTON TN11 132 C6
STPH/PW TN12 180 C3
Cuckoowood Av
MAID/BEAR ME14 103 H4
Cudham Cl MAID/BEAR ME14 7 M1
Cudham La North RSEV TN14 72 E8
Cudham La South RSEV TN14 92 E1
Cudham Park Rd RSEV TN14 73 G4
Cudham Rd BH/WHM TN16 92 A5
ORP BR6 72 C5
Cugley Rd RDART DA2 28 E5
Culcroft HART DA3 45 H8
Culford Rd CDH/CHF RM16 16 E1
Cullet Dr QBOR ME11 55 J2
Culpeper Cl RMAID ME17 123 M3
STRD ME2 3 M5
Culpepers CRBK TN17 182 A6
Culpepper Rd RHAM ME8 84 F1
RMAID ME17 136 D2
Culverden Av STH/RUST TN4 163 H7
Culverden Down STH/RUST TN4 10 B2
Culverden Pk STH/RUST TN4 10 D1
Culverden Park Rd
STH/RUST TN4 10 D1
Culverden Sq RTW TN1 10 F2
Culverden St RTW TN1 10 F3
Culver Dr OXTED RH8 109 G8
Culvey Cl HART DA3 61 G1
Cumberland Av GVE DA12 31 L5 4
MAID/SHEP ME15 121 M5
Cumberland Dr BXLYHN DA7 12 A6
DART DA1 28 B5
RSIT ME9 69 K2
Cumberland Rd GILL ME7 50 E6
Cumberland Yd RTW TN1 10 F7 2
Cumbrian Av BXLYHN DA7 13 G8
Cunningham Cl
STH/RUST TN4 163 K6 1
Cunningham Crs WALD ME5 66 C5
Cunningham Rd STH/RUST TN4 163 K6
Curlew Av RSIT ME9 69 K2
Curlew Crs STRD ME2 48 E7
The Curlews GVE DA12 31 M7
Curling La GRAYS RM17 16 B4
Currie Rd STH/RUST TN4 163 J7
Curteis Rd TENT TN30 196 D5
Curtismill Cl STMC/STPC BR5 40 D7
Curtismill Wy STMC/STPC BR5 40 D7
Curzon Dr GRAYS RM17 16 E6
Curzon Rd CHAT ME4 4 D8
MAID/BEAR ME14 103 J7
Cutbush & Corrall Ct
MAID/BEAR ME14 7 J4
Cutmore St GVW DA11 31 K5
Cutter Ridge Rd MEO DA13 63 J4
The Cut HDCN TN27 172 F6
Cutty Sark Ct GRH DA9 29 J3 2
Cuxton Cl BXLYHS DA6 26 A3
Cuxton Rd MAID/SHEP ME15 122 B8
STRD ME2 2 B9
Cyclamen Rd SWLY BR8 41 M8
Cygnet Cl DIT/AY ME20 101 J3
Cygnet Rd WALD ME5 83 L3
Cygnet Vw WTHK RM20 15 H2
Cypress Av HOO/HM ME3 51 G2 7
Cypress Cl GILL ME7 51 H7
Cypress Gv RTWE/PEM TN2 177 L5 1
Cypress Rd STRD ME2 49 L4
Cyril Rd BXLYHN DA7 12 A8
ORP BR6 56 C3

D

Dabbling Cl ERITH DA8 13 K6 1
Daffodil Rd STRD ME2 2 A3
Dagg La RBTBR TN32 205 G8
Dagmar Rd CHAT ME4 66 D3
Dahlia Dr SWLY BR8 42 B6
Dairy Cl EYN DA4 43 K4
Dairy La EDEN TN8 126 D4
STPH/PW TN12 152 B1
Dale Cl DART DA1 27 H4
Dale Rd DART DA1 27 H4
MEO DA13 45 J1
ROCH ME1 65 L2
SWLY BR8 41 L7
Daleside ORP BR6 56 C8
Daleside Cl ORP BR6 73 J1
Dale St CHAT ME4 4 B9
RTW TN1 11 H3
Dale Vw ERITH DA8 13 J8
Dalewood SIT ME10 88 C3
Dale Wood Rd ORP BR6 56 A3
Dalison Ct STRD ME2 81 K1
Dalmeny Rd ERITH DA8 12 D7
Dalton Cl ORP BR6 56 A6
Daltons Rd SWLY BR8 57 L5
Dalton St GILL ME7 5 J2
Damiem Cl CHAT ME4 66 C3 1
Damigos Rd GVE DA12 32 B6
Damson Dr HOO/HM ME3 51 G2 8
Dane Cl BXLY DA5 26 C5
RSIT ME9 68 F8
WALD ME5 83 L3
Dane Ct RMAID ME17 136 E3
Dane La RSIT ME9 68 F8
Danemore TENT TN30 196 D5
Dane Rd SEV TN13 95 G3
Danes Cl GVW DA11 30 E8
Danes Hl GILL ME7 51 J7
Danes Md SIT ME10 71 G3
Daniel Cl CDH/CHF RM16 16 A1
CDH/CHF RM16 17 K2
Daniels La WARL CR6 90 B2
Danns La WBY/YAL ME18 118 C5
Danson Wy RHAM ME8 67 M4
Danvers Rd TON TN9 147 K4
Darby Gdns HOO/HM ME3 48 D2
Darent Cl SEV TN13 94 E8
Darenth Av TONN TN10 131 K8
Darenth Dr GVE DA12 32 D6
Darenth Gdns BH/WHM
TN16 110 F4 1
Darenth Hl RDART DA2 43 K2
Darenth La SEV TN13 95 G7
Darenth Park Av RDART DA2 28 F7
Darenth Ri WALD ME5 83 K2
Darenth Rd DART DA1 28 B6
Darenth Rd South RDART DA2 43 K1
Darenth Wy RSEV TN14 75 J5
Darenth Wood Rd RDART DA2 29 G6
Darent Md EYN DA4 43 K5
Darent Valley Pth DART DA1 13 M7
EYN DA4 59 K1
RSEV TN14 95 J1
SEV TN13 8 F2
Dargate Cl MAIDW ME16 102 E6
Dargets Rd WALD ME5 83 J2
Darland Av GILL ME7 67 G3
Darlton Cl DART DA1 13 H8
Darman La STPH/PW TN12 150 F2
Darnets Fld RSEV TN14 95 H3
Darnley Cl STRD ME2 48 F7
Darnley Dr STH/RUST TN4 163 G1
Darnley Rd GRAYS RM17 16 D5 2
GVW DA11 31 J4 2
Darnley St GVW DA11 31 J5
Darns Hl SWLY BR8 57 L3
Dart Cl STRD ME2 2 D4
Dartford Rd BXLY DA5 26 E6
DART DA1 27 J4
EYN DA4 59 H2
SEV TN13 9 J4
Dartview Cl GRAYS RM17 17 G3
Darwin Dr TONN TN10 131 M7
Darwin Rd TIL RM18 17 H7
Dashmonden Cl STRD ME2 49 L3
Dashwood Cl BXLYHS DA6 26 C3
Dashwood Rd GVW DA11 31 J6
Davenport Av GILL ME7 51 G7
Davis Av GVW DA11 31 G6
Davis Cl SEV TN13 95 L8
Davis Rd CDH/CHF RM16 16 B2
Davy's Pl GVE DA12 47 G3
Dawell Dr BH/WHM TN16 91 L3
Dawes Cl GRH DA9 29 H3
Dawes St GILL ME7 5 J3
Dawson Av STMC/STPC BR5 40 D6
Dawson Dr SWLY BR8 42 A4
Dayton Dr ERITH DA8 13 M4
Deacon Cl STRD ME2 2 B2
Deakin Leas TON TN9 147 K6
Deakins Ter ORP BR6 56 C3 2
Deanery Rd EDEN TN8 126 E4
Dean La MEO DA13 62 F6
Dean Rd SIT ME10 71 G7
STRD ME2 2 C3
Deans Hill Rd RSIT ME9 87 G8
Dean St MAID/SHEP ME15 120 F5
Deanwood Dr RHAM ME8 67 M7
Debrabant Cl ERITH DA8 12 F5
Decoy Hill Rd HOO/HM ME3 22 B7
Deepdene WADH TN5 188 B7
Deerhurst Cl HART DA3 45 L7 1
Deerhurst Gdns MAIDW ME16 6 B5
Deerleap La RSEV TN14 73 M7
Defiant Cl WALD ME5 66 D7
Defoe Cl WALD ME5 66 D7 1
Defoe Pde CDH/CHF RM16 17 K2
Delafield Rd GRAYS RM17 16 F4
Delagarde Rd BH/WHM TN16 110 E4
De Lapre Cl STMC/STPC BR5 56 F3
Delargy Cl CDH/CHF RM16 17 K2
Delarue Cl RTON TN11 131 M5
Delce Rd ROCH ME1 3 L9
Del Gdns SNOD ME6 81 J5 2
Delius Dr TONN TN10 132 B7
Dell Dr RTWE/PEM TN2 11 L3
Dell Rd GRAYS RM17 16 D3
The Dell BXLY DA5 27 G6
Delmonden Rd HAWK TN18 198 E5
De Luci Rd ERITH DA8 12 E4 1
Delves Av RTWE/PEM TN2 11 J9
De Mere Cl RHAM ME8 67 M7
Denbeigh Dr TONN TN10 131 M7
Denbigh Av RHAM ME8 67 M4
Denbigh Cl SIT ME10 71 G6
Denbigh Rd STH/RUST TN4 163 L6 1
Dene Cl RDART DA2 42 A1
Denecroft Gdns GRAYS RM17 16 F2
Dene Dr HART DA3 45 K6
ORP BR6 56 D6
Dene Holm Rd GVW DA11 30 F8
Dene Lodge Cl BGR/WK TN15 98 B6
Dene Rd DART DA1 28 B5
Denesway MEO DA13 62 C2
The Dene SEV TN13 9 H8
Dene Wk HART DA3 45 G7
Dene Wy RRTW TN3 162 C6
Denham Rd RSIT ME9 69 K6
Denison Ms HOO/HM ME3 37 L1 1
Den La STPH/PW TN12 151 L2
Dennettsland Rd EDEN TN8 126 E4
Dennis Rd GVW DA11 31 J8
Denton Cl MAID/SHEP ME15 122 A5
Denton Court Rd GVE DA12 32 A6
Denton Rd BXLY DA5 27 G6
DART DA1 27 G5
Denton St GVE DA12 32 A5
Denver Cl ORP BR6 56 A2
Denver Rd DART DA1 27 J5
Derby Cl RTON TN11 131 G7
SIT ME10 70 F7
Derby Rd MAID/SHEP ME15 121 L5
WALD ME5 67 G3
Derby Road Br GRAYS RM17 16 D4
Dering Wy GVE DA12 32 B6
Deringwood Dr
MAID/SHEP ME15 122 B4
Dernier Rd TON TN9 147 L1
Derry Downs STMC/STPC BR5 56 E2
Derwent Cl DART DA1 27 K6
Derwent Crs BXLYHN DA7 12 C8 1
Derwent Dr STH/RUST TN4 10 B1
Derwent Rd TONN TN10 131 L8
Derwent Wy RHAM ME8 67 M5
Detillens La OXTED RH8 109 J7
Detling Cl RHAM ME8 67 L3
Detling Hl MAID/BEAR ME14 104 C4
Detling Rd ERITH DA8 12 F6
GVW DA11 30 F6
Devereux Rd CDH/CHF RM16 16 B2
Devon Cl RHAM ME8 68 B4
WALD ME5 66 E6
Devon Rd EYN DA4 43 K5
MAID/SHEP ME15 121 L4
Devonshire Av DART DA1 27 K4
Devonshire Cl
RTWE/PEM TN2 177 H5 2
Devonshire Gdns SLH/COR SS17 18 C2
Devonshire Rd BXLYHS DA6 26 A2
CDH/CHF RM16 16 A3
GILL ME7 50 F6 2
GVW DA11 31 K6
ORP BR6 56 C3 3
Dewlands Av RDART DA2 28 D5
Dexter Cl GRAYS RM17 16 C2
Dhekelia Cl MAID/BEAR ME14 103 J6
Dial Cl GILL ME7 51 H7
GRH DA9 29 L3
Dial Rd GILL ME7 51 H7
Diamond Cl CDH/CHF RM16 16 B2
Diana Cl CDH/CHF RM16 16 B2
Dibden La RSEV TN14 8 A9
Dickens Av DART DA1 28 C2
TIL RM18 17 K7
Dickens Cl ERITH DA8 12 D6
HART DA3 61 G1
RMAID ME17 139 G1
Dickens Dr E/WMAL ME19 101 H4
Dickensian Cl HOO/HM ME3 37 J2
Dickens Rd GVE DA12 32 A6
MAID/BEAR ME14 103 G6
ROCH ME1 65 L3
Dickens Wy HAWK TN18 199 J4
Dickley La RMAID ME17 125 J7
Digdog La CRBK TN17 185 G2
Dignals Cl RHAM ME8 68 B3
Diligent Dr SIT ME10 71 H6
Dillon Wy RTWE/PEM TN2 163 M7
Dillywood La HOO/HM ME3 49 G3
Dimmock Cl STPH/PW TN12 150 D7
Dingleden La CRBK TN17 201 H3
Dippers Cl BGR/WK TN15 96 B3
Discovery Dr E/WMAL ME19 118 C2
Dislingbury Rd RTON TN11 164 D2
Disraeli Cl MAID/SHEP ME15 122 A8 2
Ditton Court Cl DIT/AY ME20 101 K4 1
Ditton Pl DIT/AY ME20 101 K4
Dixon Cl MAID/SHEP ME15 6 E8
Dixter La RYE TN31 206 C6
Dixter Rd RYE TN31 206 C6
Dixwell Cl RHAM ME8 67 M8
Dobbie Cl SIT ME10 71 G7
Dobson Rd GVE DA12 47 G2
Dock Approach Rd GRAYS RM17 17 G4
Dock Rd CHAT ME4 4 C3
GRAYS RM17 16 F5
TIL RM18 17 G7
Doctor Hope's Rd CRBK TN17 192 F1
Doddington Ct MAIDW ME16 6 C3
Doddington Rd RHAM ME8 67 L3
Dodd Rd TONN TN10 132 A8
Doggets Cl EDEN TN8 142 E5 1
Doggetts Rw HOO/HM ME3 25 K7 1
Doggett's Sq STRD ME2 3 H4
Dogwood Cl GVW DA11 46 B1
WALD ME5 83 M4 1
Dolphin Dr RHAM ME8 68 A8
Dolphin Rd SIT ME10 71 K8
Dombey Cl HOO/HM ME3 48 E2
ROCH ME1 65 L2 1
Donald Moor Av RSIT ME9 89 L3
Doncaster Cl
MAID/SHEP ME15 122 B7 5
Donemowe Dr SIT ME10 71 H5
Donet Cl RHAM ME8 67 L8
Dongola Rd STRD ME2 49 J4
Donkey Fld RTON TN11 146 A4
Donkey La EYN DA4 59 K5
Doon Brae STH/RUST TN4 163 J3
Dorado Gdns ORP BR6 56 F6
Dorchester Cl DART DA1 28 B5
HOO/HM ME3 34 D6 1
STMC/STPC BR5 40 D4 1
Dorchester Rd GVE DA12 31 M8
Dorcis Av BXLYHN DA7 12 A8
Doric Av STH/RUST TN4 163 H4
Doric Cl STH/RUST TN4 163 H4
Doris Av BXLYHN DA7 12 E7
Dorking Rd RTW TN1 163 L7
Dormers Dr MEO DA13 62 D3 1
Dornden Dr RRTW TN3 176 C1
Dornden Gdns WALD ME5 83 K3
Dorney Ri STMC/STPC BR5 40 B8
Dorothy Av CRBK TN17 192 F1
Dorothy Evans Cl BXLYHN DA7 26 D2
Dorrit Wy ROCH ME1 65 M3
Dorset Crs GVE DA12 47 G1
Dorset Rd RTWE/PEM TN2 11 M7
Dorset Sq RHAM ME8 67 M4
Dorset St SEV TN13 9 J7
Dorset Wy MAID/SHEP ME15 121 L5
Dotterel Cl WALD ME5 83 M4
Doubleday Dr RSIT ME9 88 F3
Doubleton La RTON TN11 145 J8
Douglas Cl CDH/CHF RM16 16 A2
Douglas Rd MAIDW ME16 6 C7
RMAID ME17 125 M8 1
TON TN9 147 J5
Doug Siddons Ct GRAYS RM17 16 E5 2
Doust Wy ROCH ME1 3 M8
Dove Cl WALD ME5 66 D7
Dovedale Rd RDART DA2 28 E6 1
Doveney Cl STMC/STPC BR5 40 F8
Dove Rd TONN TN10 131 L7
Dover Rd GVW DA11 30 F5
Dover Rd East GVW DA11 31 G5
Dover St MAIDW ME16 120 E3
SIT ME10 88 A1 3
Doves Cft RSIT ME9 87 L6
Dowding Rd BH/WHM TN16 91 M1
Dowding Wy RTWE/PEM TN2 164 A4
Dower House Crs STH/RUST TN4 163 G2
Dowgate Cl TON TN9 147 M6
Dowlerville Rd ORP BR6 73 H1
Dowling Cl SNOD ME6 81 G6 1
The Downage GVW DA11 31 J7
Down Av RRTW TN3 189 J2
Downbank Av BXLYHN DA7 12 F7
Downderry Wy DIT/AY ME20 101 K4
Downe Av RSEV TN14 72 E6
Downer Ct ROCH ME1 66 A5
Downe Rd HAYES BR2 72 A3
RSEV TN14 72 E8
Downlands RMAID ME17 125 H7
Downs Av DART DA1 28 C5
Downs Cl HDCN TN27 156 A8
MAID/BEAR ME14 103 J5 2
SIT ME10 87 M3
Downside STRD ME2 2 E3
Downs Rd MAID/BEAR ME14 103 K5
MEO DA13 45 M2
WBY/YAL ME18 135 J4
The Downs WALD ME5 82 F4
Downs Va HART DA3 45 G8
Downs Vw ROCH ME1 82 B4
Downsview E/WMAL ME19 79 J7
WALD ME5 66 E5
Downs View Cl ORP BR6 73 L4
Downsview Cl SWLY BR8 42 B7 1
Downs View Rd
MAID/BEAR ME14 103 J5
Downsview Rd SEV TN13 8 C7
Downsway ORP BR6 56 A8 1
Downs Wy OXTED RH8 109 G5
Downs Wd MEO DA13 79 H5
Doyle Cl ERITH DA8 13 G7
Drage Rd STPH/PW TN12 134 A7
Drake Rd CDH/CHF RM16 16 A1
Drake's Av STRD ME2 2 D1
Drakes Cl RSIT ME9 69 G3
Draper Cl BELV DA17 12 B3
Draper St STH/RUST TN4 163 H3
Dray Corner Rd HDCN TN27 155 H6
Dray Ct RTON TN11 133 G5 1
Dray's Fld RSIT ME9 107 J6
Drayton Cl HOO/HM ME3 36 A2
Drayton Rd TON TN9 147 L5
Drewery Dr RHAM ME8 67 L8
Driffield Gdns STH/RUST TN4 147 G6
The Drive CHST BR7 40 B5
ERITH DA8 12 D6
GVE DA12 46 F1
HART DA3 45 K7
ORP BR6 56 B5
RTWE/PEM TN2 177 J4
SEV TN13 9 G5
TON TN9 147 K6
The Drove Wy MEO DA13 46 A4
Drudgeon Wy RDART DA2 29 K8
Drummond Cl ERITH DA8 13 G7
Drury Rd TENT TN30 196 C5
Dry Bank Ct TONN TN10 147 K1
Dryden Pl TIL RM18 17 K7
Dryden Wy ORP BR6 56 C4
Dryhill La RSEV TN14 112 D1
Dry Hill Park Crs TONN TN10 147 L2
Dry Hill Park Rd TONN TN10 147 K2
Dryhill Rd BELV DA17 12 B5
Dry Hill Rd TONN TN10 147 K2
Dryland Av ORP BR6 56 B7
Dryland Rd BGR/WK TN15 98 B7
SNOD ME6 81 H5
Duarte Pl CDH/CHF RM16 16 B2
Duchess Cl STRD ME2 2 A2
Duchess of Kent Dr WALD ME5 83 K2
Duchess' Wk BGR/WK TN15 9 M8
Ducketts Rd DART DA1 27 H3
Dudely Rd GVW DA11 31 G5
Dudley Cl CDH/CHF RM16 16 A1
Dudley Rd RTW TN1 10 F4
Dudsbury Rd DART DA1 27 K4
Duffield Cl CDH/CHF RM16 16 B2
Dukes Av CDH/CHF RM16 16 C2
Dukes Hl CTHM CR3 90 A6
Dukes Meadow RTON TN11 145 H3
Dukes Meadow Dr GILL ME7 67 H7
Dukes Orch BXLY DA5 26 E6
Dukes Rd RTW TN1 11 J2
Dully Rd RSIT ME9 88 F8
Dumbourne La TENT TN30 203 L3
Duncan Rd GILL ME7 5 L4
Dundale Rd RRTW TN3 179 G4
Dunedin Cl SIT ME10 87 L2
Dunera Dr MAID/BEAR ME14 103 H6
Dunkin Rd DART DA1 28 C2
Dunkirk Cl GVE DA12 46 E2
Dunkirk Dr WALD ME5 66 B7
Dunk's Green Rd RTON TN11 116 C8
Dunlop Rd TIL RM18 17 H7
Dunning's La ROCH ME1 3 K9 1
ROCH ME1 3 K9 1
The Dunnings MAIDW ME16 120 C3
Dunn Street Rd GILL ME7 84 C5
Dunstan Rd STH/RUST TN4 163 K7
Dunwich Rd BXLYHN DA7 12 B7
Durant Rd SWLY BR8 42 C3
Durham Cl MAID/SHEP ME15 121 M4
Durham Rd RHAM ME8 67 L6
SCUP DA14 40 D2
Duriun Wy ERITH DA8 13 K6
Durley Gdns ORP BR6 56 D7
Durndale La GVW DA11 46 A1
Durrant Wy SWCM DA10 30 A5
Durrell Gdns WALD ME5 66 E4 1
Duval Dr ROCH ME1 66 A5
Dux Court Rd HOO/HM ME3 35 L5
Dux Hl BGR/WK TN15 116 B5
Dux La BGR/WK TN15 116 B4
Dyke Dr STMC/STPC BR5 56 E3
Dykewood Cl BXLY DA5 26 F8
Dylan Rd BELV DA17 12 C2
Dymchurch Cl ORP BR6 56 A7 1
Dynes Rd RSEV TN14 96 A3
Dynevor Rd STH/RUST TN4 163 L6
Dyngley Cl SIT ME10 71 G7 4

E

Eagle Cl DIT/AY ME20 101 J3
Eagles Cl SIT ME10 88 E1
Eagles Dr BH/WHM TN16 91 M4
Eagles Rd GRH DA9 29 K2
Eaglestone Cl BGR/WK TN15 98 C5 1
Eagle Wy GVW DA11 30 C3
Ealing Cl WALD ME5 83 K1
Eardemont Cl DART DA1 27 H2
Eardley Rd BELV DA17 12 C4
SEV TN13 9 G5
Earl Cl WALD ME5 83 K1
Earl Rd GVW DA11 31 G7
Earl's Rd STH/RUST TN4 10 C3
Earl St MAID/BEAR ME14 6 F4
East Cliff Rd STH/RUST TN4 163 J7
Eastcote ORP BR6 56 B4
Eastcourt Gn RHAM ME8 67 K2
Eastcourt La GILL ME7 51 L8
RHAM ME8 67 K3
East Cross TENT TN30 196 C6
East Dr STMC/STPC BR5 56 D2
Easterfields E/WMAL ME19 101 L8
Eastern Av QBOR ME11 55 K1
SOCK/AV RM15 14 E1
WTHK RM20 15 H4
Eastern Rd GILL ME7 51 H7
GRAYS RM17 16 F3 1
Eastern Vw BH/WHM TN16 91 L3
Eastern Wy ERITHM DA18 12 C1
GRAYS RM17 16 C5
Eastfield Gdns TONN TN10 132 A8 2
Eastgate ROCH ME1 3 L8
Eastgate Rd TENT TN30 196 D4
Eastgate Ter ROCH ME1 3 K7
East Gn SIT ME10 71 J4
East Hall Hl RMAID ME17 138 A7
East Hall La SIT ME10 71 L8
East Hall Rd STMC/STPC BR5 57 G3
East Hl BH/WHM TN16 91 K4
DART DA1 28 B5
EYN DA4 43 M5
OXTED RH8 109 H7
TENT TN30 196 D5
East Hill Dr DART DA1 28 B5 1
East Hill Rd BGR/WK TN15 76 D6
OXTED RH8 109 G7
East Holme ERITH DA8 12 F7
East Kent Av GVW DA11 30 E4
Eastlands Cl OXTED RH8 108 F5
STH/RUST TN4 177 G5
Eastlands Rd STH/RUST TN4 177 G5 1
Eastlands Wy OXTED RH8 108 F5
Eastleigh Rd BXLYHN DA7 12 E8
Eastling Cl RHAM ME8 67 M2
East Milton Rd GVE DA12 31 M5
East Park Rd DIT/AY ME20 102 C4
East Rochester Wy DART DA1 26 F5
East Rw ROCH ME1 3 K8
Eastry Cl MAIDW ME16 102 E6
Eastry Rd ERITH DA8 12 C6
East St BXLYHN DA7 26 C2
CHAT ME4 4 F8
E/WMAL ME19 99 M3
GILL ME7 5 L2
MAID/SHEP ME15 136 B5
RMAID ME17 125 G8
SIT ME10 88 C1
SNOD ME6 81 K5
TON TN9 147 L3
WTHK RM20 16 A5
East St (North) E/WMAL ME19 99 M2
East Sutton Rd HDCN TN27 155 J4
RMAID ME17 139 H6
East Ter GVE DA12 31 L4
East Thurrock Rd GRAYS RM17 16 D5
East Tilbury Rd SLH/COR SS17 18 C1
East Weald Dr TENT TN30 196 D4
Eastwell Barn Ms TENT TN30 196 C5 1
Eastwell Cl MAID/BEAR ME14 7 L2
STPH/PW TN12 150 A6
Eastwell Mdw TENT TN30 196 C5
Eastwood Rd SIT ME10 70 F8
Eccles Rw DIT/AY ME20 82 B7
Eccleston Rd MAIDW ME16 6 E8
Echo Cl MAID/SHEP ME15 122 B7
Echo Ct GVE DA12 31 L7
Eclipse Dr SIT ME10 71 G5
Eddington Cl MAID/SHEP ME15 121 K7
Eden Av WALD ME5 66 B6
Edenbridge Cl STMC/STPC BR5 56 F1
Eden Cl BXLY DA5 41 M1
Edendale Rd BXLYHN DA7 12 F7
Eden Pl GVE DA12 31 K5
Eden Rd BXLY DA5 41 L1
HOO/HM ME3 36 A1
RTW TN1 10 F8
Eden Valley Wk EDEN TN8 142 B7
RTON TN11 146 A6
Eden Wy WARL CR6 90 A4
Edgar Cl SWLY BR8 42 B7
Edgar Rd BH/WHM TN16 91 M7
RSEV TN14 96 A3
Edgefield Cl DART DA1 28 D6 2
Edgehill Gdns MEO DA13 46 B5
Edgeler Ct SNOD ME6 81 H6
Edgewood Dr ORP BR6 56 B8
Edgington Wy SCUP DA14 40 E4
Edinburgh Ms TIL RM18 17 K8 2
Edinburgh Rd CHAT ME4 66 E3
GILL ME7 5 K4
HOO/HM ME3 25 J8
Edinburgh Sq
MAID/SHEP ME15 121 L7
Edith Rd ORP BR6 56 C8
Ediva Rd MEO DA13 62 C1
Edmund Cl MAIDW ME16 120 C2
MEO DA13 62 C1
Edmund Rd CDH/CHF RM16 15 M1
STMC/STPC BR5 56 E2
Edmunds Av STMC/STPC BR5 40 F7
Edna Rd MAID/BEAR ME14 103 H6
Edward Rd BH/WHM TN16 92 A4
Edwards Cl RHAM ME8 67 L8
Edwards Gdns SWLY BR8 41 M8 2
Edwards Rd BELV DA17 12 C3
Edward St CHAT ME4 4 F8
STH/RUST TN4 163 H4
STRD ME2 3 G3
Edward Wk E/WMAL ME19 101 H5
Edwin Cl BXLYHN DA7 12 B5
Edwin Petty Pl RDART DA2 28 E5 1
Edwin Rd RDART DA2 27 K8
RHAM ME8 67 L4
Edwin St GVE DA12 31 K5
Edyngham Cl SIT ME10 71 J5
Egdean Wk SEV TN13 9 J3

Egerton Av SWLY BR8 .... 42 B5
Egerton Cl DART DA1 .... 27 K6
Egerton Rd MAID/BEAR ME14 .... 103 G6
Eggpie La RTON TN11 .... 129 M5
Eglantine La EYN DA4 .... 59 K2
Eglinton Rd SWCM DA10 .... 30 B4
Eglise Rd WARL CR6 .... 90 A3
Egremont Rd
MAID/SHEP ME15 .... 122 B3
Egret Cl CHAT ME4 .... 50 D3
Elaine Av STRD ME2 .... 2 B4
Elder Cl HOO/HM ME3 .... 51 G2 9
RMAID ME17 .... 139 M3
Elder Ct RHAM ME8 .... 67 K7 1
Eldon St CHAT ME4 .... 4 E5
Eldon Wy STPH/PW TN12 .... 150 B6
Eldred Dr STMC/STPC BR5 .... 56 F5
Eleanor Dr SIT ME10 .... 71 H5
Elford Rd HOO/HM ME3 .... 20 D8
Elgar Cl TONN TN10 .... 132 A7
Elgar Gdns TIL RM18 .... 17 J7
Elham Cl RHAM ME8 .... 67 K3
Eliot Rd DART DA1 .... 28 D3
Elizabeth Cl TIL RM18 .... 17 K8 3
Elizabeth Ct RHAM ME8 .... 67 L4 1
Elizabeth Rd CDH/CHF RM16 .... 16 B2
Elizabeth St GRH DA9 .... 29 G3
Elizabeth Wy STMC/STPC BR5 .... 56 E1
Ellenborough Rd SCUP DA14 .... 40 F3
Ellenswood Cl
MAID/SHEP ME15 .... 122 C4 1
Ellerman Rd TIL RM18 .... 17 H8 3
Ellice Rd OXTED RH8 .... 109 H7
Ellingham Leas
MAID/SHEP ME15 .... 121 L5
Elliotts La BH/WHM TN16 .... 111 L2
Elliott St GVE DA12 .... 31 M5
Ellison Wy RHAM ME8 .... 68 C3
Ellis Waterton Cl SWLY BR8 .... 41 M8 3
Ellis Wy DART DA1 .... 28 B7 1
Elm Av CHAT ME4 .... 66 A4
HOO/HM ME3 .... 50 C1
Elmbourne Dr BELV DA17 .... 12 D3
Elm Cl DART DA1 .... 27 L6
HOO/HM ME3 .... 48 E2
Elm Crs E/WMAL ME19 .... 101 H5
Elmcroft Rd ORP BR6 .... 56 C3
Elm Dr SWLY BR8 .... 41 M6
Elmfield RHAM ME8 .... 67 J2
TENT TN30 .... 196 D5
Elmfield Cl GVW DA11 .... 31 K6
RSEV TN14 .... 129 K3
Elm Gv ERITH DA8 .... 12 F6
MAID/SHEP ME15 .... 7 J7
ORP BR6 .... 56 B4
RTON TN11 .... 147 H1
SIT ME10 .... 88 D1
Elmhurst BELV DA17 .... 12 A5 1
Elmhurst Av RTWE/PEM TN2 .... 164 F5
Elmhurst Gdns ROCH ME1 .... 65 M2
Elmington Cl BXLY DA5 .... 26 D5
Elm La TON TN9 .... 147 L2
Elm Rd BH/WHM TN16 .... 111 G3
DART DA1 .... 27 M6
ERITH DA8 .... 13 J7
GILL ME7 .... 51 G7
GRAYS RM17 .... 16 E5
GRH DA9 .... 29 G4
GVE DA12 .... 31 L8
HOO/HM ME3 .... 51 G2 10
ORP BR6 .... 73 J2
SCUP DA14 .... 40 C1
STH/RUST TN4 .... 163 H4
Elmshurst Gdns TONN TN10 .... 131 L6
Elmstead Rd ERITH DA8 .... 13 G7
Elmstone Cl MAIDW ME16 .... 120 D3
Elmstone Hole Rd RMAID ME17 .... 140 F5
Elmstone La MAIDW ME16 .... 120 C3
Elmstone Rd RHAM ME8 .... 67 M6
Elm Ter WTHK RM20 .... 15 K5
Elm Tree Dr ROCH ME1 .... 65 J3
Elm Wk DIT/AY ME20 .... 102 A4
Elmwood Dr BXLY DA5 .... 26 A5
Elmwood Rd HOO/HM ME3 .... 35 H7
Elphick's Pl RTWE/PEM TN2 .... 177 K5 1
Elrick Cl ERITH DA8 .... 13 G5
Elstree Gdns BELV DA17 .... 12 A3
Elvington Cl MAIDW ME16 .... 6 A3
Elwill Wy MEO DA13 .... 46 B5
Ely Cl ERITH DA8 .... 13 H8
RHAM ME8 .... 68 A3
Ely Gdns TON TN9 .... 147 M1
Elysian Av STMC/STPC BR5 .... 56 A2
Embassy Cl GILL ME7 .... 67 H4 1
Emerald Cl ROCH ME1 .... 65 M6
Emersons Av SWLY BR8 .... 42 B4
Emerton Cl BXLYHS DA6 .... 26 A2
Emes Rd ERITH DA8 .... 12 E6
Emily Jackson Cl SEV TN13 .... 9 G5
Emily Rd WALD ME5 .... 66 D7
Emmett Hill La WBY/YAL ME18 .... 151 H1
Emmetts Rd BH/WHM TN16 .... 111 L8
Empress Rd GVE DA12 .... 32 A5
Emsworth Gv
MAID/BEAR ME14 .... 103 M7
Englefield Cl STMC/STPC BR5 .... 40 B8 2
Englefield Crs HOO/HM ME3 .... 34 D6
STMC/STPC BR5 .... 56 C1
Englefield Pth
STMC/STPC BR5 .... 40 C8 2
Ennerdale Rd BXLYHN DA7 .... 12 C7
Ensfield Rd RTON TN11 .... 146 B6
Enterprise Cl STRD ME2 .... 3 M2
Enterprise Rd
MAID/SHEP ME15 .... 121 J4
Epaul La ROCH ME1 .... 3 J6
Epps Rd SIT ME10 .... 88 A2
Epsom Cl BXLYHN DA7 .... 26 D1
E/WMAL ME19 .... 100 D5
MAID/SHEP ME15 .... 122 B7 6
Eridge Green Cl STMC/STPC BR5 .... 56 E4
Eridge Rd RRTW TN3 .... 175 M7
Erith Cl MAID/BEAR ME14 .... 103 J5
Erith Ct PUR RM19 .... 14 C3
Erith High St ERITH DA8 .... 13 G4
Erith Rd BELV DA17 .... 12 D4
BXLYHN DA7 .... 12 D8
Ernest Dr MAIDW ME16 .... 102 D8
Ernest Rd CHAT ME4 .... 4 E8
Errington Cl CDH/CHF RM16 .... 17 K2 2
Erskine Park Rd STH/RUST TN4 .... 176 D1
Erskine Rd MEO DA13 .... 79 K5
Eshcol Rd HOO/HM ME3 .... 36 E7
Esher Cl BXLY DA5 .... 26 A6
Eskdale Cl RDART DA2 .... 28 A6
Eskdale Rd BXLYHN DA7 .... 12 C8
Esplanade ROCH ME1 .... 3 J5 1
STRD ME2 .... 3 H5
Essenden Rd BELV DA17 .... 12 C4
Essex Cl RTWE/PEM TN2 .... 177 H5
Essex Gdns SLH/COR SS17 .... 18 C1
Essex Rd DART DA1 .... 27 M4 1
GVW DA11 .... 31 J6
HART DA3 .... 44 F6
MAID/SHEP ME15 .... 122 A7
STRD ME2 .... 64 C8
WTHK RM20 .... 15 J5
Estelle Cl ROCH ME1 .... 65 M6
Esther Ct SIT ME10 .... 71 G5
Estridge Wy TONN TN10 .... 132 B8
Etfield Gv SCUP DA14 .... 40 D2
Ethelbert Rd ERITH DA8 .... 12 E6
ROCH ME1 .... 65 L1
STMC/STPC BR5 .... 40 F7
Ethelbery Rd RDART DA2 .... 43 G1
Etherington Hl RRTW TN3 .... 162 E5
Ethnam La HAWK TN18 .... 206 A2
Ethronvi Rd BXLYHN DA7 .... 26 A1
Eton Cl WALD ME5 .... 83 H1
Eton Rd ORP BR6 .... 56 D7
Eton Wy DART DA1 .... 27 L2
Euclid Wy WTHK RM20 .... 15 H3
Eurolink Wy SIT ME10 .... 88 C1
Evans Cl GRH DA9 .... 29 J3
Eva Rd GILL ME7 .... 5 L8
Evelyn Cl STRD ME2 .... 3 J2
Evelyn Rd MAIDW ME16 .... 6 C7
RSEV TN14 .... 95 L2
Evenden Rd MEO DA13 .... 62 C3
Everest Cl GVW DA11 .... 31 G8 1
Everest Dr HOO/HM ME3 .... 51 G1
Everest La STRD ME2 .... 49 K4
Everest Ms HOO/HM ME3 .... 51 G1
Everest Pl SWLY BR8 .... 41 M8
Everglade BH/WHM TN16 .... 91 M4
Everglade Cl HART DA3 .... 45 H8 1
The Everglades GILL ME7 .... 67 H7
Evergreen Cl E/WMAL ME19 .... 101 G3 1
GILL ME7 .... 67 J8
HOO/HM ME3 .... 48 C2
RSIT ME9 .... 70 F1
Eversley Av BXLYHN DA7 .... 13 G8
Eversley Cl MAIDW ME16 .... 102 E7 2
Eversley Cross BXLYHN DA7 .... 13 G8
Evesham Rd GVE DA12 .... 31 M7 1
Evry Rd SCUP DA14 .... 40 E3
Ewart Rd CHAT ME4 .... 66 A4
Ewehurst La RRTW TN3 .... 162 B7
Ewell Av E/WMAL ME19 .... 100 C5
Ewell La MAID/SHEP ME15 .... 119 M8
Ewins Cl STPH/PW TN12 .... 150 C7
Exedown Rd BGR/WK TN15 .... 97 L1
Exeter Cl TON TN9 .... 147 M1
Exeter Rd GVE DA12 .... 31 M8
Exmouth Rd GILL ME7 .... 50 E6 2
GRAYS RM17 .... 16 D5
Exton Cl WALD ME5 .... 83 L3
Exton Gdns MAID/BEAR ME14 .... 103 L8
Eyhorne St RMAID ME17 .... 123 L4
Eynsford Ri EYN DA4 .... 58 F7
Eynsford Rd EYN DA4 .... 59 H4
GRH DA9 .... 29 L3
MAIDW ME16 .... 102 F6
SWLY BR8 .... 58 A2
Eynswood Dr SCUP DA14 .... 40 D2

F

Fackenden La BGR/WK TN15 .... 76 C7
Factory Rd GVW DA11 .... 30 E4
Faesten Wy BXLY DA5 .... 27 G8
Fagus Cl WALD ME5 .... 83 K4
Fairbourne La RMAID ME17 .... 140 E2
Fairby La HART DA3 .... 61 G2
Fairchildes Rd WARL CR6 .... 90 F1
Fairfax Cl RHAM ME8 .... 67 M8
Fairfax Rd GRAYS RM17 .... 16 D4 2
TIL RM18 .... 17 H7
Fairfield GVE DA12 .... 47 G2
Fairfield Av RTW TN1 .... 11 K1
Fairfield Cl BGR/WK TN15 .... 96 C4
Fairfield Crs TON TN9 .... 147 L5 2
Fairfield Rd BGR/WK TN15 .... 98 B5
BXLYHN DA7 .... 12 B8
Fairfield Wy RTON TN11 .... 131 G8
Fairford Av BXLYHN DA7 .... 12 E7
Fairhurst Dr MAID/SHEP ME15 .... 136 D1
Fairlawn Cl WBY/YAL ME18 .... 119 J5
Fairlead Rd ROCH ME1 .... 65 M4
Fairleas SIT ME10 .... 88 D3
Fairlight Cl STH/RUST TN4 .... 163 J3
Fairlight Cross HART DA3 .... 45 K7
Fairman's La STPH/PW TN12 .... 166 D7
Fairmeadow MAID/BEAR ME14 .... 6 F4 1
MAIDW ME16 .... 6 F5
Fairmead Rd EDEN TN8 .... 126 D8
Fairmile Rd RTWE/PEM TN2 .... 164 A8
Fairmont Cl BELV DA17 .... 12 B4
Fairseat La BGR/WK TN15 .... 78 D8
Fairtrough Rd ORP BR6 .... 73 K7
Fairview ERITH DA8 .... 13 H6 1
HAWK TN18 .... 199 H3
Fairview Av RHAM ME8 .... 67 K8
Fairview Cl RTON TN11 .... 147 K7
Fairview Dr HOO/HM ME3 .... 48 D1
Fairview Gdns MEO DA13 .... 62 D1
Fairview Rd MEO DA13 .... 45 M4
SIT ME10 .... 88 C2
Fairway BXLYHS DA6 .... 26 A3
CDH/CHF RM16 .... 16 D1
Fairway Cl ROCH ME1 .... 65 L4
Fairway Dr RDART DA2 .... 28 D5
The Fairways STH/RUST TN4 .... 163 J6 1
The Fairway GVW DA11 .... 31 J7
ROCH ME1 .... 65 L4
SIT ME10 .... 88 A4
Falcon Av GRAYS RM17 .... 16 D6
Falcon Cl DART DA1 .... 28 B3
Falcon Ms GVW DA11 .... 31 G6 1
Falcons Cl BH/WHM TN16 .... 91 M3
Falkland Pl WALD ME5 .... 83 G4
Fallowfield RDART DA2 .... 29 K8
SIT ME10 .... 88 C3
WALD ME5 .... 66 D5
Fallowfield Cl
MAID/BEAR ME14 .... 122 A1 2
Falmouth Pl STPH/PW TN12 .... 149 L6
Fanconi Rd WALD ME5 .... 83 K2
Fane Wy RHAM ME8 .... 84 F1
Fanns Ri PUR RM19 .... 14 C3
Fanshawe Rd CDH/CHF RM16 .... 17 J2 1
Fans La RSIT ME9 .... 70 F1
Fant La MAIDW ME16 .... 120 D3
Faraday Ride TONN TN10 .... 131 M6
Faraday Rd MAID/BEAR ME14 .... 103 L6
Faraday Wy STMC/STPC BR5 .... 40 D8
Farleigh Court Rd WARL CR6 .... 90 E1
Farleigh Hl MAID/SHEP ME15 .... 121 G4
Farleigh La MAIDW ME16 .... 120 C3
Farleigh Rd WARL CR6 .... 90 A3
Farley Cl WALD ME5 .... 83 M3
Farleycroft BH/WHM TN16 .... 110 D4
Farley La BH/WHM TN16 .... 110 D5
Farley Nursery BH/WHM TN16 .... 110 E5
Farley Pk OXTED RH8 .... 108 F8
Farley Rd GVE DA12 .... 32 B5
Farlow Cl GVW DA11 .... 31 H8
Farm Av SWLY BR8 .... 41 L7
Farmcombe Cl RTW TN1 .... 11 H8
Farmcombe La RTW TN1 .... 11 G7
Farmcombe Rd RTW TN1 .... 11 H8
Farm Crs SIT ME10 .... 88 C3
Farmcroft GVW DA11 .... 31 J7
Farmdale ROCH ME1 .... 65 H2 1
Farmdale Av ROCH ME1 .... 65 H3
Farmer Cl RMAID ME17 .... 123 J7
Farm Ground Cl TON TN9 .... 148 A5
Farm Holt HART DA3 .... 61 H4
Farm La RTON TN11 .... 147 J1
WTHK RM20 .... 16 A5
Farm Pl DART DA1 .... 27 J2
Farm Rd CDH/CHF RM16 .... 17 H1
RSEV TN14 .... 95 L6
TIL RM18 .... 18 E3
WALD ME5 .... 83 G2
WARL CR6 .... 90 A5
Farmstead Dr EDEN TN8 .... 142 F2
Farm V BXLY DA5 .... 26 D4
Farnaby Dr SEV TN13 .... 8 E8
Farnborough Cl MAIDW ME16 .... 120 E3 1
Farnborough Wy ORP BR6 .... 73 G1
Farne Cl MAID/SHEP ME15 .... 121 J7
Farnham Beeches RRTW TN3 .... 176 C1
Farnham Cl RHAM ME8 .... 68 D4
RRTW TN3 .... 176 C2 1
Farnham La RRTW TN3 .... 176 C1
Farnham Pl RRTW TN3 .... 176 C2
Farningham Cl
MAID/BEAR ME14 .... 103 L7
Farningham Hill Rd SWLY BR8 .... 58 E1
Farnol Rd DART DA1 .... 28 C3 1
Faraday Cl ROCH ME1 .... 65 M5
Farrant Cl ORP BR6 .... 73 J2 1
Farrier Cl MAID/BEAR ME14 .... 103 M8
Farriers Cl GVE DA12 .... 32 B6 2
Farriers Ct RHAM ME8 .... 68 E5
Farrington Av STMC/STPC BR5 .... 40 D7
Fartherwell Av E/WMAL ME19 .... 100 C5
Fartherwell Rd E/WMAL ME19 .... 100 B6
Farthingfield BGR/WK TN15 .... 98 C2 1
Farthing St ORP BR6 .... 72 B2
Farwell Rd SCUP DA14 .... 40 D1
Fauchon's Cl MAID/BEAR ME14 .... 122 B2
Fauchon's La MAID/BEAR ME14 .... 122 B2
Fawkes Av DART DA1 .... 28 B7
Fawkham Av HART DA3 .... 45 L7 2
Fawkham Green Rd HART DA3 .... 60 D6
Fawkham Rd BGR/WK TN15 .... 60 B7
HART DA3 .... 44 F8
Fawley Cl MAID/BEAR ME14 .... 103 G6 1
Faygate Crs BXLYHS DA6 .... 26 C3
Featherbed La RSIT ME9 .... 71 G3
Featherby Rd GILL ME7 .... 51 J8
RHAM ME8 .... 67 J2
Feenan Hwy TIL RM18 .... 17 K6
Felderland Cl RMAID ME17 .... 122 A8 3
Felderland Dr RMAID ME17 .... 122 A8 4
Felderland Rd RMAID ME17 .... 122 A8 5
Feldspar Cl WALD ME5 .... 83 H4 1
Felicia Wy CDH/CHF RM16 .... 17 K3
Felipe Rd CDH/CHF RM16 .... 15 L3
Fell Md STPH/PW TN12 .... 134 B7
Fellowes Wy RTON TN11 .... 131 G8
Felstead Rd ORP BR6 .... 56 C5
Felton Lea SCUP DA14 .... 40 B2
Fen Meadow BGR/WK TN15 .... 97 L5
Fennel Cl MAIDW ME16 .... 120 D2
ROCH ME1 .... 65 K2
Fenner Rd CDH/CHF RM16 .... 15 L2
Fen Pond Rd BGR/WK TN15 .... 97 M6
Fens Wy SWLY BR8 .... 42 C3
Ferbies RRTW TN3 .... 162 C6 1
Ferguson Av GVE DA12 .... 46 E1
Fernbank Cl WALD ME5 .... 83 G4
Fern Cl ERITH DA8 .... 13 K7
WARL CR6 .... 90 A4
Ferndale RTWE/PEM TN2 .... 11 K3
Ferndale Cl BXLYHN DA7 .... 12 A7
RTWE/PEM TN2 .... 11 K3
Ferndale Rd GILL ME7 .... 51 G8
GVE DA12 .... 31 K7
Ferndell Av BXLY DA5 .... 26 F8
Ferndene HART DA3 .... 45 M7
Fern Down MEO DA13 .... 79 K5
Ferndown Cl GILL ME7 .... 67 J8
Fernheath Wy RDART DA2 .... 41 M2
Fernhill Rd MAIDW ME16 .... 120 C3
Fernholt TONN TN10 .... 131 L6
Fernhurst Crs STH/RUST TN4 .... 163 J3
Fernleigh Ri DIT/AY ME20 .... 101 K3
Fernside La SEV TN13 .... 113 L7
The Ferns BGR/WK TN15 .... 98 E6
DIT/AY ME20 .... 101 K4
RTW TN1 .... 11 J4
Ferrier Cl RHAM ME8 .... 85 G1
Ferry La ROCH ME1 .... 81 L1
Ferry Rd IOS ME12 .... 55 M3
RSIT ME9 .... 71 G1
STRD ME2 .... 81 K1 2
TIL RM18 .... 17 J8
Ferry Vw QBOR ME11 .... 55 H2
Feryby Rd CDH/CHF RM16 .... 17 K2
Festival Av HART DA3 .... 45 M7
Festival Cl ERITH DA8 .... 13 H6
Ffinch Cl DIT/AY ME20 .... 101 M5
Fiddlers Cl GRH DA9 .... 29 K2
Field Cl WALD ME5 .... 66 A7
Field Ct OXTED RH8 .... 109 G6
Field Dr EDEN TN8 .... 142 F2
Fielding Av TIL RM18 .... 17 K7
Fielding Dr DIT/AY ME20 .... 101 J2
The Fieldings SIT ME10 .... 88 A3
Field Rd BGR/WK TN15 .... 62 A8
MEO DA13 .... 62 B7
Fields La WBY/YAL ME18 .... 119 G6
Fieldways HAWK TN18 .... 199 J4
Fieldworks Rd CHAT ME4 .... 50 C6
Fiennes Wy SEV TN13 .... 113 L5
Fifth Av WTHK RM20 .... 15 J5
Filborough Wy GVE DA12 .... 32 D6
Filey Cl BH/WHM TN16 .... 91 K5
Filmer La RSEV TN14 .... 96 A7
Filston La RSEV TN14 .... 75 G7
The Finches SIT ME10 .... 88 C2
Finchley Cl DART DA1 .... 28 C4
Finchley Rd GRAYS RM17 .... 16 D5
Findlay Cl RHAM ME8 .... 67 M8
Finglesham Cl
STMC/STPC BR5 .... 56 F4 1
Finglesham Ct
MAID/SHEP ME15 .... 121 L5
Finsbury Wy BXLY DA5 .... 26 B4
Fintonagh Dr
MAID/BEAR ME14 .... 103 K6
Finucane Dr STMC/STPC BR5 .... 56 E3
Finwell Rd RHAM ME8 .... 68 C3
Fircroft Wy EDEN TN8 .... 142 E2
Firecrest Cl HART DA3 .... 45 K7 1
Firethorn Cl GILL ME7 .... 51 G7 1
Firmingers Rd ORP BR6 .... 57 K8
Firmin Rd DART DA1 .... 27 L3
Firs Cl DIT/AY ME20 .... 102 A4
First Av CHAT ME4 .... 66 E3
GILL ME7 .... 67 G3
GVW DA11 .... 31 G6
QBOR ME11 .... 55 H2
WTHK RM20 .... 15 J5
The Firs BXLY DA5 .... 26 F6
First La MAID/SHEP ME15 .... 123 G3
First St RRTW TN3 .... 176 B2
Fir Tree Cl ORP BR6 .... 56 B8
RTON TN11 .... 131 G8 1
STPH/PW TN12 .... 170 B2
Fir Tree Gv GILL ME7 .... 84 D4
WALD ME5 .... 83 M4
Fir Tree Rd STH/RUST TN4 .... 10 C6
Fishermen's Hl GVW DA11 .... 30 D3 1
Fisher Rd WALD ME5 .... 66 D6
Fishers Cl STPH/PW TN12 .... 154 B8
Fishers Rd STPH/PW TN12 .... 154 B8
Fisher St MAID/BEAR ME14 .... 7 G1
Fitzwilliam Rd
MAID/BEAR ME14 .... 104 B8
Fiveash Rd GVW DA11 .... 31 H5
Five Bells La ROCH ME1 .... 3 M9 1
Five Fields La EDEN TN8 .... 143 L1
Five Oak Green Rd RTON TN11 .... 148 E7
TON TN9 .... 148 B6
Five Oak La STPH/PW TN12 .... 169 J4
Five Wents SWLY BR8 .... 42 C6
Flack Gdns HOO/HM ME3 .... 36 A8
Flamborough Cl BH/WHM TN16 .... 91 K5
Flamingo Cl WALD ME5 .... 66 C6 1
Flanders Cl SIT ME10 .... 71 H4
Flaxman Dr MAIDW ME16 .... 102 E7
Flaxmans Ct GILL ME7 .... 4 E1
Flaxmore Pl STH/RUST TN4 .... 163 J3 1
Fleet Av RDART DA2 .... 28 E6
Fleet Rd GVW DA11 .... 30 E8
RDART DA2 .... 28 E6
ROCH ME1 .... 65 M4
Fleming Gdns TIL RM18 .... 17 L7
Fleming Rd CDH/CHF RM16 .... 15 L3
Fleming Wy TONN TN10 .... 132 A6
Fletcher Rd STPH/PW TN12 .... 170 A2
Flint Cl ORP BR6 .... 73 H1 1
Flint Down Cl STMC/STPC BR5 .... 40 C5 2
Flint Gn WALD ME5 .... 83 L3
Flint La RMAID ME17 .... 125 M5
Flint St WTHK RM20 .... 15 K5
The Floats SEV TN13 .... 95 G7
Flood Hatch MAID/SHEP ME15 .... 6 B9
Florance La RRTW TN3 .... 175 K7
Flora St BELV DA17 .... 12 B4 1
Florence Cl WTHK RM20 .... 16 A5
Florence Rd MAIDW ME16 .... 6 D7
Florence St STRD ME2 .... 3 H2
Florin Dr ROCH ME1 .... 65 K1
Flowerfield RSEV TN14 .... 95 H3
Flowerhill Wy MEO DA13 .... 46 A4
Flume End MAIDW ME16 .... 6 B9
The Flyers Wy BH/WHM TN16 .... 110 F4
Foalhurst Cl TONN TN10 .... 148 A1
Foley Rd BH/WHM TN16 .... 91 M4
Foley St MAID/BEAR ME14 .... 7 H2
Fontwell Cl
MAID/SHEP ME15 .... 122 B7 7
Foord Cl RDART DA2 .... 29 G7
Foord Rd RMAID ME17 .... 125 M8
Foord St ROCH ME1 .... 3 K9
Footbury Hill Rd ORP BR6 .... 56 C3
Foots Cray High St SCUP DA14 .... 40 E3
Force Green La BH/WHM TN16 .... 110 F2
Fordcombe Cl
MAID/SHEP ME15 .... 122 B6 1
Fordcombe Rd RRTW TN3 .... 161 K8
RTON TN11 .... 161 J2
Fordcroft Rd STMC/STPC BR5 .... 56 D1
Fordingbridge Cl
MAIDW ME16 .... 102 D8 1
Ford La BGR/WK TN15 .... 99 H3
Ford Rd GVW DA11 .... 30 D3 2
Fordwich Cl MAIDW ME16 .... 102 D6
ORP BR6 .... 56 B3
Foremans Barn Rd
MAID/SHEP ME15 .... 136 B2
Forestdale Rd WALD ME5 .... 83 J5
Forest Dr WALD ME5 .... 83 H3
Foresters Cl WALD ME5 .... 83 H3
Foresters Crs BXLYHN DA7 .... 26 D2
Forest Gv TONN TN10 .... 131 L8
Forest Hl MAID/SHEP ME15 .... 121 H4
Forest Rd ERITH DA8 .... 13 J7
RTWE/PEM TN2 .... 11 M7
STPH/PW TN12 .... 150 B7
Forest Wy E/WMAL ME19 .... 118 C2
HRTF TN7 .... 174 E7
RTWE/PEM TN2 .... 164 F5
RTWE/PEM TN2 .... 177 L4
STMC/STPC BR5 .... 56 C1
Forge Cft EDEN TN8 .... 142 E4
Forgefield BH/WHM TN16 .... 91 M2
Forge La BGR/WK TN15 .... 77 J4
EYN DA4 .... 43 L8
GILL ME7 .... 51 G7
GILL ME7 .... 84 C4
GVE DA12 .... 32 B7
GVE DA12 .... 48 A2
HDCN TN27 .... 155 M8
HDCN TN27 .... 157 L4
HOO/HM ME3 .... 35 M2
HOO/HM ME3 .... 48 E2
MAID/BEAR ME14 .... 103 L2
MAID/SHEP ME15 .... 120 D6
RMAID ME17 .... 123 H6
RMAID ME17 .... 138 B8
RSIT ME9 .... 69 H2
WBY/YAL ME18 .... 117 J7
WBY/YAL ME18 .... 151 J1
Forge Meadow RMAID ME17 .... 124 F7
Forge Mdw HDCN TN27 .... 155 M8
Forge Meads TENT TN30 .... 209 G2
Forge Rd SIT ME10 .... 71 G7
STH/RUST TN4 .... 163 H4
Forge Wy RSEV TN14 .... 75 H5
STPH/PW TN12 .... 150 C6
Formby Rd STRD ME2 .... 64 C7
Forsham La RMAID ME17 .... 138 E8
Forson Cl TENT TN30 .... 196 D5
Forstall RRTW TN3 .... 176 C1 1
Forstal La RMAID ME17 .... 136 F1
The Forstall RTON TN11 .... 146 C3
Forstal Rd DIT/AY ME20 .... 102 C3
HDCN TN27 .... 157 L4
The Forstal RTON TN11 .... 133 G5
RTWE/PEM TN2 .... 165 G5 1
Forsters RMAID ME17 .... 139 G1
Forsyth Cl DIT/AY ME20 .... 101 J4 2
Fort Pitt Hl CHAT ME4 .... 4 A6
ROCH ME1 .... 4 A6
Fort Pitt St CHAT ME4 .... 4 B7
Fort Rd RSEV TN14 .... 94 E1
TIL RM18 .... 31 K2
Fortrye Cl GVW DA11 .... 31 G7
Fort St ROCH ME1 .... 65 M1
Forward Wy ROCH ME1 .... 65 L7
Fosse Bank TON TN9 .... 147 J6
Fosse Bank Cl TON TN9 .... 147 J6 1
Fosse Rd TON TN9 .... 147 K3
Fosten La HDCN TN27 .... 186 A5
Foster St MAID/SHEP ME15 .... 7 G6
Fostington Wy WALD ME5 .... 83 H4
Foulds Cl RHAM ME8 .... 84 D1
Fountain La MAIDW ME16 .... 120 C3
Fountain Rd STRD ME2 .... 49 G4
Fountain St SIT ME10 .... 88 A1 4
Fountain Wk GVW DA11 .... 31 G4
Four Elms Hl HOO/HM ME3 .... 50 A2
Four Elms Rd EDEN TN8 .... 143 H1
Four Oaks Rd STPH/PW TN12 .... 155 G6
Fourth Av GILL ME7 .... 67 G1
WTHK RM20 .... 15 J5
Fourwents Rd HOO/HM ME3 .... 35 M7
Fowey Cl WALD ME5 .... 66 E8
Fowler Cl RHAM ME8 .... 84 E2
SCUP DA14 .... 41 G2
Foxburrow Cl RHAM ME8 .... 67 M8
Foxbury Cl ORP BR6 .... 56 C8 2
Foxbury Dr ORP BR6 .... 73 J1
Foxbush RTON TN11 .... 130 E7
Fox Cl ORP BR6 .... 56 C8
Foxden Dr MAID/SHEP ME15 .... 122 B4
Foxearth Cl BH/WHM TN16 .... 92 A4
Foxendown La MEO DA13 .... 62 D4
Foxes Gn CDH/CHF RM16 .... 17 J1
Foxglove Crs WALD ME5 .... 83 G1
Foxglove Ri MAID/BEAR ME14 .... 103 G6
Foxgrove SIT ME10 .... 71 G6
Fox Hl SIT ME10 .... 88 F2
Foxhole La HAWK TN18 .... 199 M5
STPH/PW TN12 .... 165 L5
Fox House Rd BELV DA17 .... 12 D3
Fox Manor Wy WTHK RM20 .... 15 K5
Fox St GILL ME7 .... 5 J2
Foxton Rd WTHK RM20 .... 15 M5
Foxwood Gv GVW DA11 .... 31 G6
ORP BR6 .... 73 L4
Foxwood Rd RDART DA2 .... 29 K8
Foxwood Wy HART DA3 .... 45 L6
Framley Rd TONN TN10 .... 132 B8
Francis Av BXLYHN DA7 .... 12 C8
Francisco Cl CDH/CHF RM16 .... 15 L2
Francis Dr WALD ME5 .... 83 J3
Francis La MAID/SHEP ME15 .... 122 B8
Francis Rd DART DA1 .... 27 M3
RTON TN11 .... 130 F7
STMC/STPC BR5 .... 40 F7
Frankapps Cl RSIT ME9 .... 69 K7 1
Frankfield Ri RTWE/PEM TN2 .... 177 H4
Franklin Dr MAID/BEAR ME14 .... 121 M1
Franklin Rd BXLYHN DA7 .... 12 A7
GILL ME7 .... 5 L4
GVE DA12 .... 46 F2
Franks Ct RHAM ME8 .... 67 K4
Frank's Hollow Rd RRTW TN3 .... 162 E4
Franks La EYN DA4 .... 59 K1
Frank Woolley Rd TONN TN10 .... 132 B8
Frant Fld EDEN TN8 .... 142 F4
Frant Rd RTWE/PEM TN2 .... 10 E9
Fraser Cl BXLY DA5 .... 26 E6
Fraser Rd ERITH DA8 .... 12 E4
Frederick Rd GILL ME7 .... 5 J6
Frederick St SIT ME10 .... 88 A1
Free Heath Rd RRTW TN3 .... 188 E2
The Freehold RTON TN11 .... 132 F4
STPH/PW TN12 .... 134 B7
Freelands Rd SNOD ME6 .... 81 G5
Freeland Wy ERITH DA8 .... 13 J7

Freeman Gdns *CHAT* ME4 .... 66 B3
Freeman Rd *GVE* DA12 .... 32 A8
Freeman Wy *MAID/SHEP* ME15 .. 122 A6
Freesia Cl *GILL* ME7 .... 51 H7
　ORP BR6 .... 56 B1
Freight La *CRBK* TN17 .... 192 C2
Fremlin Cl *STH/RUST* TN4 .... 176 D1
Fremlins Rd *MAID/BEAR* ME14 .. 122 E1
Frensham La *SIT* ME10 .... 88 D1
Frensham Rd *CRBK* TN17 .... 202 C4
Frensham Wk *WALD* ME5 .... 83 H4
Freshland Rd *MAIDW* ME16 .... 120 D1
Freshwater Rd *WALD* ME5 .... 66 D6
Freta Rd *BXLYHS* DA6 .... 26 B3
Frewen Cl *RYE* TN31 .... 206 D6
Friar Rd *STMC/STPC* BR5 .... 56 C1
Friars Av *WALD* ME5 .... 83 H3
Friars Wy *RTWE/PEM* TN2 .... 163 M7
Friary Pl *SEV* TN13 .... 3 C3
Friday Rd *ERITH* DA8 .... 12 F4
Friday St *RMAID* ME17 .... 139 K6
Friezland Rd *STH/RUST* TN4 .... 176 F4
Friezley La *CRBK* TN17 .... 183 L3
Frimley Ct *SCUP* DA14 .... 40 E2
Frindsbury HI *STRD* ME2 .... 3 J1
Frindsbury Rd *STRD* ME2 .... 3 J1
Frinstead Cl *STMC/STPC* BR5 .... 56 C1
Frinstead Wk *MAIDW* ME16 .... 102 D6
Frinsted Cl *RHAM* ME8 .... 67 L2
Frinsted Rd *ERITH* DA8 .... 12 F6
Frinton Rd *SCUP* DA14 .... 26 A7
Friston Wy *ROCH* ME1 .... 65 M5
Friswell Pl *BXLYN* DA7 .... 26 C1
Frithwood Cl *MAID/SHEP* ME15 .. 122 B4
Frittenden Rd *STPH/PW* TN12 .. 170 B3
　STRD ME2 .... 49 M4
Frobisher Cl *SIT* ME10 .... 71 G7
Frobisher Gdns *ROCH* ME1 .... 65 L3
Frobisher Rd *ERITH* DA8 .... 13 J6
Frobisher Wy *GRH* DA9 .... 29 K2
　GVE DA12 .... 47 G2
Froghole La *EDEN* TN8 .... 127 C2
Frog La *E/WMAL* ME19 .... 100 E5
　RTW TN1 .... 10 F7
Frognal Av *SCUP* DA14 .... 40 C3
Frognal Cl *RSIT* ME9 .... 89 K3
Frognal Gdns *RSIT* ME9 .... 89 K3
Frognal La *RSIT* ME9 .... 89 K3
Frognal Pl *SCUP* DA14 .... 40 C2
Frogs Hole La *CRBK* TN17 .... 194 F3
Frog's La *CRBK* TN17 .... 202 B4
Frome *TIL* RM18 .... 18 E3
Frost Crs *WALD* ME5 .... 66 C6
Froyle Cl *MAIDW* ME16 .... 102 E7
Fruiterer's Cl *RSIT* ME9 .... 88 C6
Fry Cl *HOO/HM* ME3 .... 25 J7
Frythe Cl *CRBK* TN17 .... 192 F1
Frythe Crs *CRBK* TN17 .... 192 F1
Frythe Wk *CRBK* TN17 .... 192 F1
Frythe Wy *CRBK* TN17 .... 192 F1
Fuggles Pl *STPH/PW* TN12 .... 150 A7
Fuggles Rd *CRBK* TN17 .... 193 M7
　WBY/YAL ME18 .... 118 D8
Fulbert Dr *MAID/BEAR* ME14 .... 104 B8
Fuller Cl *ORP* BR6 .... 56 B8
　WADH TN5 .... 188 A8
Fullers Cl *MAID/BEAR* ME14 .. 122 C1
Fullers HI *MAID/SHEP* TN16 .... 110 F4
Fullers La *RYE* TN31 .... 206 D7
Fulmar Rd *STRD* ME2 .... 48 F8
Fulston Pl *SIT* ME10 .... 88 C2
Fulwich Rd *DART* DA1 .... 28 B4
Furfield Cl *MAID/SHEP* ME15 .. 122 A8
Furnace Av *RRTW* TN3 .... 189 H2
Furnace La *RRTW* TN3 .... 188 F1
　STPH/PW TN12 .... 167 G4
Furner Cl *DART* DA1 .... 27 H1
Furness Cl *CDH/CHF* RM16 .... 17 K4
Furrell's Rd *ROCH* ME1 .... 3 L8
Furzefield Av *RRTW* TN3 .... 162 C5
Furzehill Sq *STMC/STPC* BR5 .. 40 D8

G

Gabion Av *PUR* RM19 .... 14 F3
Gable Cl *DART* DA1 .... 27 J3
The Gables *HART* DA3 .... 45 L6
Gabriel Gdns *GVE* DA12 .... 47 G2
Gabriel's HI *MAID/BEAR* ME14 .... 7 A4
Gabriel Spring Rd *EYN* DA4 .... 59 M5
Gabriel Spring Rd (East)
　EYN DA4 .... 60 A5
Gadby Rd *SIT* ME10 .... 70 E8
Gainsborough Av *DART* DA1 .... 27 L3
　TIL RM18 .... 17 J7
Gainsborough Cl *RHAM* ME8 .... 67 M7
　SIT ME10 .... 70 D8
Gainsborough Dr *GVW* DA11 .... 30 F8
　MAIDW ME16 .... 120 D1
Gainsborough Gdns
　TONN TN10 .... 132 A8
Galahad Av *STRD* ME2 .... 2 B5
Galena Cl *WALD* ME5 .... 83 J4
Gallants La *MAID/SHEP* ME15 .. 120 B7
Galleon Bvd *GRH* DA9 .... 28 F2
Galleon Cl *ERITH* DA8 .... 12 F3
　ROCH ME1 .... 65 L5
Galley Hill Rd *SWCM* DA10 .... 30 B3
The Gallops *MEO* DA13 .... 79 H5
Galsworthy Rd *TIL* RM18 .... 17 L7
Gamma Rd *HOO/HM* ME3 .... 36 F6
Gandy's La *RMAID* ME17 .... 137 L3
Gangers HI *GDST* RH9 .... 108 B5
Garden Av *BXLYHS* DA7 .... 26 B1
Garden Cl *MAID/SHEP* ME15 .. 122 A6
Gardenia Cl *STRD* ME2 .... 49 K4
Garden Pl *DART* DA2 .... 27 M8
Garden Rd *RTW* TN1 .... 11 H3
　SEV TN13 .... 9 L1
　TON TN9 .... 147 M5
Garden Rw *GVW* DA11 .... 31 H8
Garden St *GILL* ME7 .... 4 E1
　RTW TN1 .... 11 H4
Garden Wy *WBY/YAL* ME18 .. 118 D3
Gardiner Cl *STMC/STPC* BR5 .. 40 E6
Gardiner St *GILL* ME7 .... 5 K2
Gardner's HI *RYE* TN31 .... 209 K7
Gardyne Ms *TON* TN9 .... 147 K5

Garfield Rd *GILL* ME7 .... 5 M1
Garlands *RTON* TN11 .... 130 F5
Garlinge Rd *STH/RUST* TN4 .... 163 J4
Garner Dr *E/WMAL* ME19 .... 101 J4
Garrard Cl *BXLYHN* DA7 .... 26 C1
Garrick St *GVW* DA11 .... 31 K4
Garrington Cl
　MAID/BEAR ME14 .... 103 L7
Garrolds Cl *SWLY* BR8 .... 41 M6
Garrow *HART* DA3 .... 45 K7
Garth Rd *SEV* TN15 .... 113 L6
Garvock Dr *SEV* TN13 .... 8 F9
Gascoyne Dr *DART* DA1 .... 27 H1
Gas Rd *SIT* ME10 .... 71 K7
Gasson Rd *SWCM* DA10 .... 30 A4
Gassons Rd *SNOD* ME6 .... 81 C5
Gatcombe Cl *MAIDW* ME16 .... 102 D8
　WALD ME5 .... 66 C8
Gate Farm Rd *RRTW* TN3 .... 162 E1
Gatefield Cottages *CRBK* TN17 .. 202 B1
Gatland La *MAIDW* ME16 .... 120 D3
Gattons Wy *SCUP* DA14 .... 41 H1
Gatwick Rd *GVE* DA12 .... 31 K7
Gault Rd *MAID/SHEP* ME15 .... 122 C3
Gayhurst Cl *RHAM* ME8 .... 67 M7
Gayhurst Dr *SIT* ME10 .... 70 E8
Gaylor Rd *TIL* RM18 .... 17 G7
Gaze Hill Av *SIT* ME10 .... 88 C2
Gazelle Gld *GVE* DA12 .... 47 H2
Gean Cl *WALD* ME5 .... 83 J4
Geddes Pl *BXLYHN* DA7 .... 26 C2
Gedge's HI *STPH/PW* TN12 .... 166 B3
Genesta Cl *SIT* ME10 .... 71 G6
Genesta Gld *GVE* DA12 .... 47 J2
Geneva Av *RHAM* ME8 .... 67 J3
Gentian Cl *MAID/BEAR* ME14 .. 104 A8
George La *RMAID* ME17 .... 123 J6
　ROCH ME1 .... 3 K6
Georges *STMC/STPC* BR5 .... 40 E7
George's Rd *BH/WHM* TN16 .... 91 M6
George St *GRAYS* RM17 .... 16 C5
　MAID/SHEP ME15 .... 7 G7
　MAID/SHEP ME15 .... 136 C7
　RTWE/PEM TN2 .... 11 J6
　SIT ME10 .... 88 D2
　STPH/PW TN12 .... 154 A7
　TON TN9 .... 147 K5
　WADH TN5 .... 188 B8
George Summers Cl *STRD* ME2 .. 50 A5
Georgian Dr *RMAID* ME17 .... 136 F2
Georgian Wy *RHAM* ME8 .... 84 E1
Gerald Av *CHAT* ME4 .... 66 B3
Gerald Rd *GVE* DA12 .... 32 A5
Gerdview Dr *RDART* DA2 .... 42 E1
Gerrard Av *ROCH* ME1 .... 65 M5
Gerrards Dr *SIT* ME10 .... 88 B3
Gertrude Rd *BELV* DA17 .... 12 C3
Ghyll Side Rd *RYE* TN31 .... 206 D6
Gibbet La *STPH/PW* TN12 .... 167 H7
Gibbetts *RRTW* TN3 .... 176 B2
Gibbons Rd *SIT* ME10 .... 70 D8
Gibbs HI *HDCN* TN27 .... 156 A8
　WBY/YAL ME18 .... 118 D8
Gibraltar Av *GILL* ME7 .... 50 C6
Gibraltar HI *CHAT* ME4 .... 4 C4
Gibraltar La *MAID/BEAR* ME14 .. 103 G5
Gibson Cl *GVW* DA11 .... 31 H8
Gibson Dr *E/WMAL* ME19 .... 118 B1
Gibson St *SIT* ME10 .... 88 A1
Giddyhorn La *MAIDW* ME16 .... 6 A1
　MAIDW ME16 .... 120 E1
Gideon Cl *BELV* DA17 .... 12 D3
Gifford Cl *GILL* ME7 .... 67 L1
Giffordside *CDH/CHF* RM16 .... 17 K4
Giggs HI *STMC/STPC* BR5 .... 40 E6
Gighill Rd *DIT/AY* ME20 .... 101 H2
Gilbert Cl *GILL* ME7 .... 67 J3
　SWCM DA10 .... 29 M4
Gilbert Rd *BELV* DA17 .... 12 C2
　CDH/CHF RM16 .... 15 L2
Gildenhill Rd *SWLY* BR8 .... 42 E4
Gill Av *STRD* ME2 .... 49 M2
Gill Crs *GVW* DA11 .... 31 H8
Gilletts La *E/WMAL* ME19 .... 101 J7
Gillies Rd *WBY/YAL* ME15 .... 60 A8
Gillingham Gn *GILL* ME7 .... 51 G7
Gillingham Rd *GILL* ME7 .... 5 K5
Gillmans Rd *STMC/STPC* BR5 .. 56 D1
Gill's Rd *EYN* DA4 .... 44 A5
The Gill *RTWE/PEM* TN2 .... 165 G5
Gilroy Wy *STMC/STPC* BR5 .... 56 D3
Gimble Wy *RTWE/PEM* TN2 .. 164 F5
Gingerbread La *HAWK* TN18 .. 198 B2
Ginsbury Cl *STRD* ME2 .... 4 A2
Gipps Cross La *RRTW* TN3 .. 176 B2
Gipsy La *GRAYS* RM17 .... 16 E5
The Glades *GVE* DA12 .... 46 F3
The Glade *SEV* TN13 .... 9 G2
　WALD ME5 .... 83 J3
Gladstone Dr *SIT* ME10 .... 88 C2
Gladstone Rd *CHAT* ME4 .... 4 B9
　DART DA1 .... 28 B4
　MAID/BEAR ME14 .... 103 J7
　STH/RUST TN4 .... 176 D1
　TON TN9 .... 147 K4
Gladwyn Cl *RHAM* ME8 .... 84 F1
Glamford Rd *STRD* ME2 .... 48 F8
Glamis Cl *WALD* ME5 .... 66 C8
Glanville Rd *GILL* ME7 .... 5 M4
　STRD ME2 .... 2 F3
Glassenbury Rd *CRBK* TN17 .. 192 A1
Glastonbury Cl *STMC/STPC* BR5... 56 E4
Gleaming Wood Dr
　MAID/BEAR ME14 .... 83 M5
Gleaners Cl *MAID/BEAR* ME14.. 122 A1
Glebe Cl *HDCN* TN27 .... 173 K3
The Glebefield *SEV* TN13 .... 8 C2
Glebelands *DART* DA1 .... 27 H2
　HDCN TN27 .... 186 B4
　RRTW TN3 .... 162 F2
　RTON TN11 .... 161 J2
Glebe La *MAIDW* ME16 .... 120 B4
　SEV TN13 .... 9 H9
　SIT ME10 .... 88 D3
Glebe Meadow *WBY/YAL* ME18 .. 118 F6
Glebe Pl *EYN* DA4 .... 43 L8
Glebe Rd *GILL* ME7 .... 67 G2
　GVW DA11 .... 31 H6
　RSEV TN14 .... 129 K2
The Glebe *RTWE/PEM* TN2 .. 164 F5

　STH/RUST TN4 .... 162 F2
　STRD ME2 .... 64 E3
Glebe Wy *ERITH* DA8 .... 13 G5
Gleeson Dr *ORP* BR6 .... 56 B8
Glenbrook Gv *SIT* ME10 .... 71 G6
Glencoe Rd *CHAT* ME4 .... 4 E9
Glendale *SWLY* BR8 .... 58 B1
Glendale Rd *ERITH* DA8 .... 12 E4
Glendale Wk *SEV* TN13 .... 9 H9
　GVW DA11 .... 46 A1
Glendower Crs *ORP* BR6 .... 56 C2
Gleneagles Dr
　MAID/SHEP ME15 .... 121 H4
Glengall Rd *BXLYHN* DA7 .... 26 A1
Glenhurst Av *BXLY* DA5 .... 26 B6
Glenmore Pk *RTWE/PEM* TN2 .. 177 H5
Glenrosa Gdns *GVE* DA12 .... 47 H2
Glentrammon Av *ORP* BR6 .... 73 H1
Glentrammon Cl *ORP* BR6 .... 73 H1
Glentrammon Gdns *ORP* BR6.. 73 H1
Glentrammon Rd *ORP* BR6 .... 73 H1
Glen Vw *GVE* DA12 .... 31 L6
Glenwood Cl *GILL* ME7 .... 67 H6
　MAIDW ME16 .... 102 E8
　TENT TN30 .... 196 D2
　WALD ME5 .... 66 E4
Glimpsing Gn *ERITHM* DA18 .. 12 A2
Glistening Gld *RHAM* ME8 .... 68 A7
Gload Crs *STMC/STPC* BR5 .... 56 F5
Globe La *CHAT* ME4 .... 4 C4
Gloucester Av *CDH/CHF* RM16 .. 16 E1
　TIL RM18 .... 18 E4
Gloucester Cl *RHAM* ME8 .... 68 C5
Gloucester Rd *BELV* DA17 .... 12 B4
　DART DA1 .... 27 K4
　GVE DA12 .... 46 E1
　MAID/SHEP ME15 .... 121 M5
　MEO DA13 .... 95 L3
Gloxinia Rd *MEO* DA13 .... 45 K3
Glyn Davies Cl *SEV* TN13 .... 95 C6
Glynde Rd *BXLYHN* DA7 .... 26 A1
Glyn Dr *SCUP* DA14 .... 40 D1
Goad Av *WALD* ME5 .... 83 K2
Goatsfield Rd *BH/WHM* TN16 .. 91 L6
Goddard Cl *CRBK* TN17 .... 192 D1
Godden Cl *RYE* TN31 .... 206 D5
Godden Rd *MAID/BEAR* ME14 .. 65 J2
Goddings Dr *ROCH* ME1 .... 65 K8
Goddington Cha *ORP* BR6 .... 56 E6
Goddington La *ORP* BR6 .... 56 E6
　RMAID ME17 .... 124 D7
Goddington Rd *STRD* ME2 .... 3 C1
Godfrey Evans Cl *TONN* TN10.. 132 B8
Godman Rd *CDH/CHF* RM16 .. 17 K2
Godstone Rd *OXTED* RH8 .... 108 E8
Godwin Cl *SIT* ME10 .... 71 G6
Goldace *GRAYS* RM17 .... 16 B5
Golden Sq *SEV* TN13 .... 196 D5
Golden Wood Cl *WALD* ME5 .... 83 M5
Goldfinch *DIT/AY* ME20 .... 101 J3
　ORP BR6 .... 56 C8
　STPH/PW TN12 .... 150 C8
Golding Cl *DIT/AY* ME20 .... 101 L4
Golding Gdns *STPH/PW* TN12.. 134 C7
Golding Rd *SEV* TN13 .... 95 L8
Goldings *STPH/PW* TN12 .... 150 A1
Goldings Cl *E/WMAL* ME19 .... 118 C3
The Goldings *RHAM* ME8 .... 67 L5
Goldsel Rd *SWLY* BR8 .... 42 A8
Goldsmid Rd *TON* TN9 .... 147 L6
Goldsmith *GRAYS* RM17 .... 16 B5
Goldsmith Ct *TENT* TN30 .... 196 D4
Goldsmith Rd *RHAM* ME8 .... 68 A8
Goldsmith Wk *WALD* ME5 .... 83 J4
Goldstone Wk *WALD* ME5 .... 83 J4
Gold St *GVE* DA12 .... 63 G1
Goldsworth Dr *STRD* ME2 .... 49 J4
Goldthorne Cl *MAID/BEAR* ME14... 7 L4
Golf Links Av *GVW* DA11 .... 46 D2
Golford Rd *CRBK* TN17 .... 184 B8
Gooch Cl *MAIDW* ME16 .... 102 F5
Goodall Cl *RHAM* ME8 .... 68 A8
Goodbury Rd *BGR/WK* TN15.. 76 D7
Goodley Stock Rd *EDEN* TN8 .. 110 D7
Goodmead Rd *ORP* BR6 .... 56 C3
Goodnestone Rd *SIT* ME10 .... 88 D2
Goods HI *TENT* TN30 .... 195 M5
Goods Station Rd *RTW* TN1 .. 11 G3
Goodwin Dr *MAID/BEAR* ME14.. 103 K5
Goodwin Rd *HOO/HM* ME3 .... 34 D6
Goodwood Cl *HOO/HM* ME3 .... 43 K4
　MAID/SHEP ME15 .... 122 B7
Goodwood Crs *GVE* DA12 .... 46 E3
Goodworth Rd *BGR/WK* TN15 .. 98 B2
Goose Cl *WALD* ME5 .... 83 B1
Goose Green Cl *STMC/STPC* BR5 .. 40 C6
Gooseneck La *HDCN* TN27 .... 155 L8
Gordon Av *OBOR* ME11 .... 55 J1
Gordon Cl *SIT* ME10 .... 88 E1
　TIL RM18 .... 18 F6
Gordon Pl *GVE* DA12 .... 31 L4
Gordon Rd *BELV* DA17 .... 12 E3
　CDH/CHF RM16 .... 17 G1
　CHAT ME4 .... 4 F9
　DART DA1 .... 27 M5
　GILL ME7 .... 50 C6
　GVW DA11 .... 31 G5
　HOO/HM ME3 .... 35 M8
　SEV TN13 .... 9 G6
　STH/RUST TN4 .... 163 L6
　TON TN9 .... 2 E2
Gordons Wy *OXTED* RH8 .... 108 F6
Gordon Ter *ROCH* ME1 .... 3 J9
Gorringe Av *EYN* DA4 .... 43 M6
Gorse Av *WALD* ME5 .... 83 G1
Gorse Crs *DIT/AY* ME20 .... 101 M5
Gorse Rd *RTWE/PEM* TN2 .. 164 A8
　SIT ME10 .... 71 L8
　STMC/STPC BR5 .... 57 G2
　STRD ME2 .... 2 D1
Gorse Wy *HART* DA3 .... 61 H1
Gorse Wood Rd *HART* DA3 .... 45 J8

Goss HI *SWLY* BR8 .... 42 E3
Gothic Cl *DART* DA1 .... 27 M8
Goudhurst Cl *MAIDW* ME16 .. 6 A1
Goudhurst Rd *CRBK* TN17 .. 183 M5
　RHAM ME8 .... 67 K2
　STPH/PW TN12 .... 152 D8
　STPH/PW TN12 .... 167 K8
Gouge Av *GVW* DA11 .... 31 G6
Gould Rd *WALD* ME5 .... 83 K2
Gover HI *WBY/YAL* ME18 .... 117 G7
Gover Wy *WBY/YAL* ME18 .... 117 G6
Gowers La *CDH/CHF* RM16 .. 17 H1
Grace Av *BXLYHN* DA7 .... 12 B8
Gracious La *SEV* TN13 .... 113 J8
Gracious Lane End *RSEV* TN14.. 113 H8
Grafton Av *ROCH* ME1 .... 66 A5
Grafton Rd *SIT* ME10 .... 88 B1
Grainey Fld *RSIT* ME9 .... 86 A1
Grain Rd *HOO/HM* ME3 .... 37 K2
　RHAM ME8 .... 84 E2
Grampian Cl *ORP* BR6 .... 56 B2
　RTWE/PEM TN2 .... 11 M2
Grampian Wy
　MAID/SHEP ME15 .... 122 C4
Granada St *MAID/SHEP* ME15.. 7 G5
Granary Cl *MAIDW* ME16 .... 6 A1
Granary *STPH/PW* TN12 .... 150 D7
Granary Cl *MAID/BEAR* ME14 .. 104 A8
　RHAM ME8 .... 68 B4
Granby Rd *GVE* DA12 .... 30 F4
Grandshore La *CRBK* TN17 .. 170 C8
Grandsire Gdns *HOO/HM* ME3.. 36 A7
Grand View Av *BH/WHM* TN16.. 91 L3
Grange Cl *BH/WHM* TN16 .. 110 F4
　E/WMAL ME19 .... 100 E3
　EDEN TN8 .... 142 E4
Grange Crs *RDART* DA2 .... 28 D4
Grange Gdns *STH/RUST* TN4.. 176 F1
Grange HI *BGR/WK* TN15 .... 116 A5
　WALD ME5 .... 5 H8
Grange La *HART* DA3 .... 61 K3
　MAID/BEAR ME14 .... 103 K4
Grange Rd *RYE* TN31 .... 206 D5
The Grange *BGR/WK* TN15 .... 77 H3
　E/WMAL ME19 .... 101 J6
　ROCH ME1 .... 43 M5
Grange Wy *ERITH* DA8 .... 13 K6
　HART DA3 .... 61 H2
　ROCH ME1 .... 65 L2
Grangeways Cl *GVW* DA11 .... 46 B1
Grangewood *BXLY* DA5 .... 26 B6
Grangewood Av *CDH/CHF* RM16 .. 17 G2
Grant Cl *GILL* ME7 .... 67 K4
Granton Rd *SCUP* DA14 .... 40 D3
Granville Ms *SCUP* DA14 .... 40 C1
Granville Rd *BH/WHM* TN16.. 110 E4
　GILL ME7 .... 51 G8
　GVW DA11 .... 31 H5
　MAID/BEAR ME14 .... 103 J7
　OXTED RH8 .... 109 H7
　RTW TN1 .... 11 J2
　SCUP DA14 .... 40 C1
　SEV TN13 .... 8 F5
Grapple Rd *MAID/BEAR* ME14.. 103 J6
Grasmere Gv *STRD* ME2 .... 49 L3
Grasmere Rd *BXLYHN* DA7 .... 12 E7
Grassington Rd *SCUP* DA14 .... 40 C1
Grasslands *RMAID* ME17 .... 139 G1
Grassmere *DIT/AY* ME20 .... 101 G4
Grassy Gld *GILL* ME7 .... 67 K7
Grassy La *SEV* TN13 .... 113 K5
Gravel HI *BXLYHS* DA6 .... 26 A6
Gravel Hill Cl *BXLY* DA5 .... 26 D4
　BXLYHS DA6 .... 26 D4
Gravelly Bottom Rd
　RMAID ME17 .... 139 K3
Gravelly Ways *STPH/PW* TN12.. 150 D7
Gravel Pit Wy *ORP* BR6 .... 56 C5
Gravel Rd *EYN* DA4 .... 43 K4
Gravel Wk *ROCH* ME1 .... 3 K8
Graveney Cl *HOO/HM* ME3 .... 34 E6
Graveney Rd *MAID/SHEP* ME15.. 122 B6
Gravesend Rd *BGR/WK* TN15 .. 79 F3
　GVE DA12 .... 48 B1
　HOO/HM ME3 .... 35 M8
　STRD ME2 .... 2 C2
Graylings Ct *SIT* ME10 .... 87 L3
Grayne Av *HOO/HM* ME3 .... 25 K8
Grays End Cl *CDH/CHF* RM16.. 16 C2
Grays Farm Rd *STMC/STPC* BR5... 40 D5
Grayshott Cl *SIT* ME10 .... 88 B2
Grays Rd *BH/WHM* TN16 .... 92 D7
Grazeley Cl *BXLYHS* DA6 .... 26 E3
Great Bounds Dr
　STH/RUST TN4 .... 163 G2
Great Brooms Rd
　STH/RUST TN4 .... 163 K5
Great Courtlands *RRTW* TN3 .. 176 C2
Great Elms *RTON* TN11 .... 133 G4
Great Footway *RRTW* TN3 .... 176 B1
Great Lines *GILL* ME7 .... 4 F3
Greatness La *RSEV* TN14 .... 95 L7
Greatness Rd *RSEV* TN14 .... 95 L7
Great Queen St *DART* DA1 .... 28 B4
Great South Av *CHAT* ME4 .... 66 C4
Great Till Cl *RSEV* TN14 .... 95 J2
Grebe Cl *HOO/HM* ME3 .... 37 L2
Grebe Crest *WTHK* RM20 .... 15 J3
Grecian Rd *RTW* TN1 .... 11 G7
Grecian St *MAID/BEAR* ME14 .. 7 H1
Greenacre *SWLY* BR8 .... 42 A1
　WALD ME5 .... 66 C3
Greenacres *OXTED* RH8 .... 109 L5
Greenbank *WALD* ME5 .... 66 D5
Green Bank Cl *GILL* ME7 .... 67 J3
Greenbanks *DART* DA1 .... 28 A7
Greenborough Cl
　MAID/SHEP ME15 .... 122 A7
Green Cl *ROCH* ME1 .... 65 M3
Greencourt Rd *STMC/STPC* BR5.. 56 A1

Green Court Rd *SWLY* BR8 .... 57 M1
Green Farm Cl *ORP* BR6 .... 56 B8
Green Farm La *GVE* DA12 .... 33 G8
Greenfield *EDEN* TN8 .... 142 F4
Greenfield Cl *DIT/AY* ME20 .... 82 C7
　STH/RUST TN4 .... 162 E1
Greenfield Rd *GILL* ME7 .... 5 M2
　RDART DA2 .... 41 M2
Greenfields *MAID/SHEP* ME15 .. 122 A5
Greenfields Cl *HOO/HM* ME3 .. 49 M2
Greenfinches *GILL* ME7 .... 67 H7
　HART DA3 .... 45 K7
Greenfrith Dr *TONN* TN10 .... 131 K6
Green Hedges *TENT* TN30 .. 196 D5
Green HI *MAID/SHEP* ME15 .. 122 D4
　ORP BR6 .... 72 A6
Green Hill La *RMAID* ME17 .. 140 F5
Greenhill Rd *GVW* DA11 .... 31 H7
　RSEV TN14 .... 95 L1
Greenhithe *MAID/SHEP* ME15 .. 6 F7
Greenlands *BGR/WK* TN15 .... 98 D6
Green Lands *GVE* DA12 .... 62 F1
Green La *CRBK* TN17 .... 194 E2
　E/WMAL ME19 .... 79 J8
　EDEN TN8 .... 127 L6
　HDCN TN27 .... 173 J4
　HOO/HM ME3 .... 20 D7
　HOO/HM ME3 .... 25 K7
　MEO DA13 .... 137 L2
　RMAID ME17 .... 138 B8
　RMAID ME17 .... 139 G2
　RMAID ME17 .... 141 H4
　RSIT ME9 .... 86 B4
　RSIT ME9 .... 88 D6
　STPH/PW TN12 .... 150 C8
　STPH/PW TN12 .... 152 A4
The Green La *RTON* TN11 .. 146 B4
Greenleas *RTWE/PEM* TN2 .. 164 E7
Greenleigh Av *STMC/STPC* BR5 .. 40 D8
Greenoak Ri *BH/WHM* TN16 .. 91 L4
Green Porch Cl *SIT* ME10 .... 71 H6
Green Rd *STPH/PW* TN12 .. 167 J8
Greensand Rd
　MAID/SHEP ME15 .... 122 C3
Green Sands *MAID/BEAR* ME14 .. 83 L3
Greensand Wy *EDEN* TN8 .... 110 E8
　EDEN TN8 .... 126 E1
　MAID/SHEP ME15 .... 136 A3
　OXTED RH8 .... 109 G4
　RMAID ME17 .... 137 L4
　RSEV TN14 .... 116 B8
　RTON TN11 .... 116 B8
　SEV TN13 .... 9 J2
　WBY/YAL ME18.. 134 C2
Greenside *BXLY* DA5 .... 26 A6
　MAID/SHEP ME15 .... 7 J6
　SWLY BR8 .... 41 M6
Green Sq *WADH* TN5 .... 188 B8
Green St *GILL* ME7 .... 5 J3
Green Street Green Rd
　RDART DA2 .... 28 E8
The Green *BH/WHM* TN16 .. 110 F4
　BXLYHN DA7 .... 12 C7
　CTHM CR3 .... 108 C1
　RDART DA2 .... 28 F7
　RRTW TN3 .... 176 A2
　RSIT ME9 .... 69 K2
　RTON TN11 .... 146 B4
　SCUP DA14 .... 40 C2
　SEV TN13 .... 95 M8
　STMC/STPC BR5 .... 40 D4
Greentrees *MAID* TONN TN10 .. 132 B8
Greenvale Gdns *RHAM* ME8 .. 67 K3
Green View Av *RTON* TN11 .. 146 C4
Greenview Crs *RTON* TN11 .. 147 G1
Green Wk *DART* DA1 .... 27 H2
Greenway *BH/WHM* TN16 .. 91 L6
　CRBK TN17 .... 192 D1
Green Wy *HART* DA3 .... 61 G1
　MAIDW ME16 .... 120 D2
　RTWE/PEM TN2 .... 164 A5
Greenway *WALD* ME5 .... 65 M7
Greenway Court Rd
　RMAID ME17 .... 124 B6
Greenway La *RMAID* ME17 .. 124 C6
Greenways *HART* DA3 .... 45 M7
　MAID/BEAR ME14 .... 104 D3
　SIT ME10 .... 88 D2
The Greenways
　STPH/PW TN12 .... 150 B8
Greenwich Cl *MAIDW* ME16 .. 6 A1
　WALD ME5 .... 83 K1
Greenwood Cl *STMC/STPC* BR5 .. 56 A2
Greenwood Rd *BXLY* DA5 .... 41 M1
Greenwood Wy *SEV* TN13 .... 8 D6
Greggs Wood Rd
　RTWE/PEM TN2 .... 164 A6
Gregory Cl *RHAM* ME8 .... 85 G1
　SIT ME10 .... 71 J5
Grenadier Cl *RHAM* ME8 .... 68 D3
Grenville Cl *MEO* DA13 .... 62 C6
Gresham Av *HART* DA3 .... 45 L8
　WARL CR6 .... 90 A4
Gresham Cl *BXLY* DA5 .... 26 A4
　OXTED RH8 .... 109 H7
　RHAM ME8 .... 68 B4
Gresham Rd *OXTED* RH8 .... 109 H7
　RMAID ME17 .... 136 F2
Greybury La *EDEN* TN8 .... 158 D2
Greyfriars Cl *MAIDW* ME16 .. 6 B3
Greyhound La *CDH/CHF* RM16 .. 17 J1
Greyhound Wy *DART* DA1 .... 27 G3
Greystone Pk *RSEV* TN14 .... 112 A3
Greystones Cl *RSEV* TN14 .... 96 A3
Greystones Rd
　MAID/SHEP ME15 .... 122 C3
Grey Wethers
　MAID/BEAR ME14 .... 103 G2
Gribble Bridge La *HDCN* TN27 .. 186 D6
Grieves Rd *GVW* DA11 .... 31 H8
The Griffins *CDH/CHF* RM16 .. 16 D1
Griffin Wk *GRH* DA9 .... 29 H3
Grifon Cl *CDH/CHF* RM16 .. 15 L2
Grifon Rd *CDH/CHF* RM16 .. 15 L2
Grigg La *HDCN* TN27 .... 156 F6
Griggs Wy *BGR/WK* TN15 .... 98 C8
Grizedale Cl *ROCH* ME1 .... 65 M5
Gromenfield *RRTW* TN3 .... 175 L6

Groombridge HI *RRTW* TN3 ...... 175 L5
Groombridge Rd *RRTW* TN3 ...... 175 J5
Groombridge Sq
 MAID/SHEP ME15 .... 122 B7 🔳
Grosvenor Av *ROCH* ME1.......... 4 A8
Grosvenor Br *STH/RUST* TN4 ..... 11 H1
Grosvenor Crs *DART* DA1 .... 27 M3
Grosvenor Pk *RTW* TN1 .... 10 F3
Grosvenor Rd *BELV* DA17 .... 12 B5
 GILL ME7 .... 67 H4
 RTW TN1 .... 10 F3
 STMC/STPC BR5 .... 56 A2
Grosvenor Wk *RTW* TN1 .... 10 F3 🔳
Grove Av *RTW* TN1 .... 10 F7
Grovebury Cl *ERITH* DA8 .... 12 F5
Grove Green La
 MAID/BEAR ME14 .... 104 A8
Grove Green Rd
 MAID/BEAR ME14 .... 104 B8
Groveherst Rd *DART* DA1 .... 28 B1
Grove Hill *RTW* TN1 .... 11 G7
Grove Hill Gdns *RTW* TN1 .... 11 G7
Grove Hill Rd *RTW* TN1 .... 11 G6
Grovehurst Av *SIT* ME10 .... 71 H4
Grovehurst La *STPH/PW* TN12 .... 167 L8
 SIT ME10 .... 71 G4
Grovelands Rd *STMC/STPC* BR5 .. 40 C4
Grovelands Wy *GRAYS* RM17 ...... 16 B4
Grove Park Av *SIT* ME10 .... 70 C8
Grove Rd *BELV* DA17 .... 12 B5
 BGR/WK TN15 .... 96 C8
 BH/WHM TN16 .... 91 L6
 BXLYHN DA7 .... 26 E2
 CHAT ME4 .... 5 H9
 EDEN TN8 .... 160 F4
 GILL ME7 .... 51 J7
 GRAYS RM17 .... 16 E5
 GVW DA11 .... 30 D3
 MAID/SHEP ME15 .... 121 L7
 RSEV TN14 .... 95 L7
 STRD ME2 .... 3 H2
 STRD ME2 .... 63 M8
Grover St *RTW* TN1 .... 11 H3
The Groves *SNOD* ME6 .... 81 H6
The Grove *BGR/WK* TN15 .... 77 H4
 BH/WHM TN16 .... 91 M4
 GVE DA12 .... 31 K5
 MAID/BEAR ME14 .... 122 C2
 RTWE/PEM TN2 .... 164 F5
 SCUP DA14 .... 41 G2
 SWCM DA10 .... 30 B3
 SWLY BR8 .... 42 B7 🔳
Grovewood Dr
 MAID/BEAR ME14 .... 121 M1 🔳
 MAID/BEAR ME14 .... 122 B1 🔳
Grub St *OXTED* RH8 .... 109 L7
Guardian Ct *RHAM* ME8 .... 67 L4
Guestwick *TONN* TN10 .... 132 B8
Guildables La *EDEN* TN8 .... 126 A6
 OXTED RH8 .... 126 A4
Guildford Gdns *STRD* ME2 .... 48 E7 🔳
Guildford Rd *RTW* TN1 .... 11 C7
Guild Rd *ERITH* DA8 .... 13 H6
Gullands *RMAID* ME17 .... 139 C1
Gumley Rd *WTHK* RM20 .... 15 M5
Gun Back La *STPH/PW* TN12 ..... 167 J8 🔳
Gundulph Rd *CHAT* ME4 .... 4 A5
Gundulph Sq *ROCH* ME1 .... 3 J6 🔳
Gunfleet Cl *GVE* DA12 .... 32 A5
Gun HI *TIL* RM18 .... 17 M5
Gunlands *STPH/PW* TN12 .... 167 J7
Gun La *STRD* ME2 .... 2 F7
Gunnis Rd *RHAM* ME8 .... 84 E1
Gunn Rd *SWCM* DA10 .... 30 A4
Guston Rd *MAID/BEAR* ME14 .... 7 L2
Gwynn Rd *GVW* DA11 .... 30 E7
Gybbon Ri *STPH/PW* TN12 .... 170 A2
Gybbons Rd *CRBK* TN17 .... 202 B2

H

Hackney Rd *MAIDW* ME16.......... 120 E3
Haddon Ct *STMC/STPC* BR5 .... 56 A2
Hadleigh Ct *GILL* ME7 .... 84 C2
Hadley Cl *MEO* DA13 .... 62 E5
Hadley Rd *BELV* DA17 .... 12 B3
Hadlow Pk *RTON* TN11 .... 133 G4
Hadlow Rd *MAID/BEAR* ME14........ 7 L2
 SCUP DA14 .... 40 C1
 TON TN9 .... 147 L3
 TONN TN10 .... 132 C8
Hadlow Stair Rd *TONN* TN10 .... 148 B1
Hadlow Wy *MEO* DA13 .... 46 A4 🔳
Haffenden Cl *STPH/PW* TN12 .... 152 F7
Haffenden Rd *TENT* TN30 .... 196 C4
Haig Av *CHAT* ME4 .... 65 M4
 GILL ME7 .... 67 C1
Haig Gdns *GVE* DA12 .... 31 L5
Haig Rd *BH/WHM* TN16 .... 92 A3
 CDH/CHF RM16 .... 17 J2
Haileybury Rd *ORP* BR6 .... 56 C7
Hailey Rd *ERITHM* DA18.......... 12 C1
Hailstone Rd *RTON* TN11 .... 133 G5 🔳
Halcot Av *BXLYHS* DA6 .... 26 D3
Haldane Gdns *GVW* DA11 .... 30 E6
Halden Cl *MAID/SHEP* ME15 ..... 122 B7
Haldon La *CRBK* TN17 .... 195 G4
Hale Ct *STPH/PW* TN12 .... 134 C6
Hale La *RSEV* TN14 .... 95 H3
Hale Oak Rd *EDEN* TN8 .... 145 G1
 RSEV TN14 .... 129 J4
Hale Rd *HOO/HM* ME3 .... 34 E6
Hales Cl *TENT* TN30 .... 196 D5
Hales Rd *SIT* ME10 .... 87 M4
Hale St *STPH/PW* TN12 .... 134 C6
Haleys PI *ROCH* ME1 .... 82 C5 🔳
Half Moon La *RTON* TN11 .... 130 F7
Halfpence La *GVE* DA12 .... 47 K6
Halfpenny Cl *MAIDW* ME16....... 120 C3
Halfway Ct *PUR* RM19 .... 14 C3
Halifax Cl *WALD* ME5 .... 66 D7
Hall Cl *SIT* ME10 .... 71 G7
Hall Crs *SOCK/AV* RM15 .... 14 E1
Hall DR *MAID/DART* DA1.......... 27 L4
Hall HI *BGR/WK* TN15 .... 114 D1
Hall Place Crs *BXLY* DA5........ 27 L3
Hall Rd *DART* DA1 .... 28 B2

 DIT/AY ME20 .... 102 B4
 GVW DA11 .... 30 F7
 HOO/HM ME3 .... 22 E7
 ROCH ME1 .... 81 L2
 SOCK/AV RM15 .... 14 E1
 WALD ME5 .... 83 L2
Hallsfield Rd *WALD* ME5 .... 82 F2
Hall's Hole Rd *RTWE/PEM* TN2 ... 11 M6
Hall Ter *SOCK/AV* RM15 .... 14 F1
Hallwards *STPH/PW* TN12 .... 170 A3
Hallwood Cl *RHAM* ME8.......... 67 M8
Halstead La *RSEV* TN14 .... 94 A1
Halstead Rd *ERITH* DA8 .... 13 G7
Halstow Cl *MAID/SHEP* ME15 .... 121 K8
Halt Dr *TIL* RM18 .... 18 C3
Halton Rd *CDH/CHF* RM16 .... 17 K2
Halt Robin Rd *BELV* DA17 .... 12 C3
Hambledon Ct *MAIDW* ME16 ..... 120 D2 🔳
Hamble Dr *TONN* TN10 .... 131 K8
Hambrook Wk *SIT* ME10 .... 71 H5
Hamelin Rd *GILL* ME7 .... 67 H5
Hamerton Rd *GVW* DA11 .... 30 D3 🔳
Hamfield Cl *OXTED* RH8 .... 108 E5
Hamilton Crs *SIT* ME10 .... 87 L2
Hamilton Rd *BFN/LL* DA15........ 40 C1
 BXLYHN DA7 .... 12 A8
 GILL ME7 .... 50 F6
Ham La *GILL* ME7 .... 84 A2
 RMAID ME17 .... 125 K8
Hamlin Rd *SEV* TN13 .... 95 G7
Hammonds *HAWK* TN18 .... 199 J3 🔳
Hammonds Sq *SNOD* ME6........... 81 J5
Hampden Rd *GRAYS* RM17 .... 16 D4
Hampshire Cl *WALD* ME5 .... 66 E6 🔳
Hampshire Drive Rd
 MAID/SHEP ME15 .... 121 L5
Hampson Wy *MAID/BEAR* ME14.... 122 C1
Hampstead La *WBY/YAL* ME18 .... 134 E4
Hampton Cl *WALD* ME5 .... 66 C8
Hampton Crs *GVE* DA12........... 32 A7
Hampton Rd *MAID/BEAR* ME14 ..... 7 L1
Hamptons Rd *RTON* TN11 .... 116 B8
Hamwick Gn *WALD* ME5 .... 83 L4
Hanbury Cl *WBY/YAL* ME18....... 119 G6
Hancock Cl *STRD* ME2 .... 49 K4
Handel Crs *TIL* RM18 .... 17 J6
Handel Wk *TONN* TN10 .... 132 B7 🔳
Hang Grove HI *ORP* BR6 .... 72 D7
Hanmer Wy *STPH/PW* TN12 .... 170 A3
Hanover Cl *SIT* ME10 .... 88 A3
Hanover Dr *RHAM* ME8 .... 84 E1
Hanover Rd *RMAID* ME17 .... 136 E2
 RTW TN1 .... 10 F4
Hansol Rd *BXLYHS* DA6 .... 26 A3
Hanway *RHAM* ME8 .... 67 J3
Harbex Cl *BXLY* DA5 .... 26 D5
Harbledown PI
 STMC/STPC BR5 .... 40 E8 🔳
Harbourland Cl
 MAID/BEAR ME14 .... 103 K5 🔳
Harbourne La *RASHW* TN26 ...... 197 G1
 TENT TN30 .... 196 F5
The Harbour *RMAID* ME17 .... 139 G8 🔳
Harcourt Gdns *RHAM* ME8 .... 85 G1
Harcourt Rd *BXLYHS* DA6 .... 26 A2
Harden Rd *GVW* DA11 .... 31 H7
Hardie Cl *E/WMAL* ME19 .... 101 H4 🔳
Hardinge Av *STH/RUST* TN4 ..... 163 G2
Hardinge Cl *RHAM* ME8 .... 84 E1
Harding Rd *BXLYHN* DA7 .... 12 B8
 CDH/CHF RM16 .... 17 J2
Hards Town *CHAT* ME4 .... 4 F6
Hardwick Crs *DART* DA1 .... 28 D4 🔳
Hardwick Rd *RTON* TN11 .... 131 G7
Hardy Av *GVW* DA11 .... 31 G7
Hardy Cl *WALD* ME5 .... 66 D7
Hardy Gv *DART* DA1 .... 28 C2
Hardy St *MAID/BEAR* ME14 .... 7 G1
Harebell Cl *MAID/BEAR* ME14 .. 104 A8 🔳
Haredale Cl *ROCH* ME1 .... 65 M6
Harescroft *RTWE/PEM* TN2 ...... 177 H6 🔳
Harfst Wy *SWLY* BR8 .... 41 L5
Hargate Ct *RTWE/PEM* TN2 ...... 177 H6
Harland Wy *STH/RUST* TN4 ...... 163 H2
Harlech Cl *STRD* ME2 .... 49 H4
Harley Gdns *ORP* BR6 .... 56 A7
Harlington Rd *BXLYHN* DA7 ...... 26 A1
Harman Av *GVW* DA11 .... 46 D2
Harmer Rd *SWCM* DA10 .... 30 B4
Harmer St *GVE* DA12 .... 31 L4
Harmony St *STH/RUST* TN4 ...... 176 F1
Harold Av *BELV* DA17 .... 12 B4
 GILL ME7 .... 67 G1
Harold Rd *RDART* DA2 .... 43 H1
 SIT ME10 .... 88 D1
 STRD ME2 .... 64 D2
Harold St *QBOR* ME1 .... 55 J1
Harp Farm Rd *MAID/BEAR* ME14 .. 83 L6
Harple La *MAID/BEAR* ME14 ..... 104 B4
Harptree Dr *WALD* ME5 .... 66 B8
Harrap Cha *GRAYS* RM17 .... 16 B4
Harrier Dr *SIT* ME10 .... 72 B5
Harries Rd *RTWE/PEM* TN2 ...... 163 M6
Harris Cl *GVW* DA11 .... 31 G8
Harrison Rd *HOO/HM* ME3 .... 36 A1
 RMAID ME17 .... 125 G7
Harrison Rd *BGR/WK* TN15 .... 98 B6
Harrisons Whf *PUR* RM19 .... 14 C4
Harrison Wy *SEV* TN13 .... 8 F1
Harris Rd *BXLYHN* DA7 .... 26 B1
Harrowby Gdns *GVW* DA11 .... 31 G7 🔳
Harrow Ct *RSIT* ME9 .... 85 M5
Harrow Gdns *ORP* BR6 .... 56 D7
 WARL CR6 .... 90 B2
Harrow Rd *GILL* ME7 .... 67 H7
 RSEV TN14 .... 94 A1
 WARL CR6 .... 90 B1
Harrow Wy *MAID/BEAR* ME14 .... 104 A8
Harrys Rd *RSIT* ME9 .... 89 L2
Hart Dyke Rd *STMC/STPC* BR5 ... 56 E4 🔳
 SWLY BR8 .... 42 B7
Hartfield Cl *TONN* TN10 .... 132 A8
Hartfield PI *GVW* DA11 .... 30 F5 🔳
Hartfield Rd *EDEN* TN8 .... 159 J1
Hartford Rd *BXLY* DA5 .... 26 C4
Hartington St *CHAT* ME4 .... 4 E7
Hartlake Rd *RTON* TN11 .... 148 E5
Hartlands *BXLY* DA5 .... 26 B4

Hartley Bottom Rd *HART* DA3 .... 61 K4
Hartley Cl *MAID/SHEP* ME15 .... 122 B7
Hartley Court Gdns
 CRBK TN17 .... 192 C2 🔳
Hartley HI *HART* DA3 .... 61 J4
Hartley Rd *BH/WHM* TN16 .... 110 F3
 CRBK TN17 .... 192 C3
 HART DA3 .... 45 G6
Hartlip HI *RSIT* ME9 .... 69 G6
Hartnokes *HAWK* TN18 .... 199 J3
Hartnup St *MAIDW* ME16 .... 120 E3
Hartpiece Cl *RHAM* ME8 .... 68 B3 🔳
Hart Shaw *HART* DA3 .... 45 K6
Hartshill Rd *GVW* DA11 .... 31 H7
Hartsland Rd *SEV* TN13 .... 9 K3
Hart St *MAIDW* ME16 .... 6 E7
Harty Av *RHAM* ME8 .... 84 D2
Harvel Av *STRD* ME2 .... 2 B3
Harvel Cl *CHST* BR7 .... 40 C7
Harvel La *MEO* DA13 .... 79 K2
Harvel Rd *MEO* DA13 .... 79 G6
Harvel St *MEO* DA13 .... 79 L2
Harvesters Cl *RHAM* ME8 .... 68 A7
Harvesters Wy
 MAID/BEAR ME14 .... 121 M1 🔳
Harvest Rdg *E/WMAL* ME19 ..... 100 F3
Harvest Rd *TONN* TN10 .... 131 M7
Harvest Wy *SWLY* BR8 .... 57 L3
Harvey Cl *CDH/CHF* RM16 .... 16 D1
Harvey Dr *SIT* ME10 .... 88 C3
Harvey Rd *RHAM* ME8 .... 68 A5
Harvill Rd *SCUP* DA14 .... 40 F2
Haslemere Rd *BXLYHN* DA7 .... 12 B8
Hasletts Cl *STH/RUST* TN4 ..... 163 K7
Haslewood Cl *HDCN* TN27 .... 173 K3 🔳
Hasted Cl *GRH* DA9 .... 29 L4
Hasted Rd *RSIT* ME9 .... 69 K6
Hasteds *RMAID* ME17 .... 137 J2
Haste Hill Cl *MAID/SHEP* ME15 . 137 J2
Haste Hill Rd *MAID/SHEP* ME15 . 137 J2
Hastings Cl *CRBK* TN17 .... 201 M4
 HAWK TN18...................... 199 H6
 MAID/SHEP ME15 .... 7 J6
 RTWE/PEM TN2 .... 164 F7
Hastings Rd *RTWE/PEM* TN2 ..... 165 H8
Hatches La *RTON* TN11 .... 133 M7
Hatfield Rd *STRD* ME2 .... 2 A6
Hatham Green La *BGR/WK* TN15 .. 77 M4
Hathaway Ct *ROCH* ME1 .... 3 H8
Hathaway Rd *GRAYS* RM17 .... 16 D2
Hatherall Rd *MAID/BEAR* ME14 ... 7 K1
Hatmill La *STPH/PW* TN12 ...... 166 C6
Hattersfield Cl *BELV* DA17 ...... 12 B3
Hatton Cl *CDH/CHF* RM16 .... 15 M2
 GVW DA11 .... 31 G8
Hatton Rd *WALD* ME5 .... 83 L2
Havelock Rd *BELV* DA17 .... 12 B3 🔳
 DART DA1 .... 27 K5
 GVW DA11 .... 31 H6
 TON TN9 .... 147 K2
Haven Cl *MEO* DA13 .... 46 B5
 ROCH ME1 .... 65 L3
 SCUP DA14 .... 40 E3
 SWLY BR8 .... 42 B6
Havengore Av *GVE* DA12.......... 32 A5
Haven HI *BGR/WK* TN15........... 78 C1
Haven PI *CDH/CHF* RM16......... 16 E1
Haven Rd *HOO/HM* ME3 .... 34 E8
Haven Wy *CHAT* ME4 .... 50 D4
Havering Cl *RTWE/PEM* TN2 ..... 164 B7
Haven Wy *RTWE/PEM* TN2 .... 164 B7
Havisham Rd *GVE* DA12........... 32 C6
Havock La *MAID/BEAR* ME14 .... 6 F4
Hawbeck Rd *RHAM* ME8 .... 84 E2
Hawden Cl *RTON* TN11 .... 147 H1
Hawden La *RTON* TN11 .... 147 H2
Hawden Rd *TON* TN9 .... 147 K3
Hawfield Bank *ORP* BR6 .... 56 F6 🔳
Hawkenbury Cl *RTWE/PEM* TN2 ... 11 L8
Hawkenbury Md
 RTWE/PEM TN2 .... 11 L9
Hawkenbury Rd
 RTWE/PEM TN2 .... 11 M9
 STPH/PW TN12 .... 154 E7
Hawkes Cl *GRAYS* RM17 .... 16 D5 🔳
Hawkes PI *SEV* TN13 .... 113 J5
Hawkes Rd *DIT/AY* ME20 .... 82 B8
Hawkhurst Rd *BUR/ETCH* TN5 ... 198 A3
 HAWK TN18 .... 192 B6
 RHAM ME8 .... 67 J2
Hawkins Av *GVE* DA12 .... 46 E1
Hawkins Cl *CHAT* ME4 .... 4 E2
 SIT ME10 .... 71 G7
Hawkwood *MAIDW* ME16 .... 102 D8 🔳
Hawkwood Cl *ROCH* ME1 .... 3 M8
Hawley Rd *DART* DA1 .... 28 A7
Hawser Rd *ROCH* ME1 .... 65 L4
Hawstead La *ORP* BR6 .... 57 H8
Hawthorn Cl *EDEN* TN8 .... 142 E5 🔳
 GVE DA12 .... 46 D1
Hawthorne Av *BH/WHM* TN16 ..... 91 M4
 RHAM ME8 .... 67 L3
Hawthorn PI *ERITH* DA8 .... 12 E4
Hawthorn Rd *BXLYHS* DA6 .... 26 B2 🔳
 DART DA1 .... 27 M7
 SIT ME10 .... 88 A1
 STRD ME2 .... 2 A6
Hawthorns *HART* DA3 .... 45 H8
 WALD ME5 .... 83 H4 🔳
The Hawthorns *DIT/AY* ME20 ... 102 A4
Hawthorn Wk
 RTWE/PEM TN2 .... 164 A5 🔳
 TONN TN10 .... 131 L6
Haydens Cl *STMC/STPC* BR5 ...... 56 E3
Haydens Ms *TON* TN9 .... 147 L2
The Haydens *TON* TN9 .... 147 L2
Hayes Cl *HOO/HM* ME3 .... 48 E2
 WTHK RM20 .... 15 L5
Hayesden La *RRTW* TN3 .... 162 C1
Hayes La *RSIT* ME9 .... 86 B7
Hayes Plat *RTW* TN1 .... 206 E8
Hayes Rd *RDART* DA2 .... 29 G5
Hayfield *E/WMAL* ME19 .... 100 F3
Hayfield Rd *STMC/STPC* BR5 ..... 56 C1
Hayfields *WALD* ME5 .... 83 M3
Hayle *TIL* RM18 .... 18 E2

Hayle Mill Rd *MAID/SHEP* ME15 . 121 H5
Hayle Rd *MAID/SHEP* ME15 .... 7 G7
Hayley Cl *STRD* ME2 .... 64 E3
Haymans HI *STPH/PW* TN12 ...... 167 K6
Haymen St *CHAT* ME4 .... 4 B8
Hayrick Cl *MAID/BEAR* ME14..... 104 A8
Haysel *SIT* ME10 .... 88 C3
Haywain Cl
 MAID/BEAR ME14 .... 122 B1 🔳
 MAID/SHEP ME15 .... 150 C8 🔳
The Haywain *OXTED* RH8 .... 108 F8
Hayward Av *STRD* ME2 .... 3 G2
Hayward Cl *DART* DA1 .... 26 F7
Haywood Ri *ORP* BR6 .... 56 A8
Hazel Av *HOO/HM* ME3 .... 50 F2
 MAIDW ME16 .... 102 E8
Hazelbank *RRTW* TN3 .... 176 B2 🔳
Hazelden Cl *BGR/WK* TN15 .... 77 J3
Hazel Dr *ERITH* DA8 .... 13 J7
Hazel End *SWLY* BR8 .... 58 A1 🔳
Hazel Gdns *CDH/CHF* RM16 .... 17 G2
Hazel Gv *WALD* ME5 .... 66 D5
Hazel Rd *DART* DA1 .... 27 M7
 ERITH DA8 .... 13 J7
Hazel Shaw *TONN* TN10 .... 131 L7
The Hazels *RHAM* ME8 .... 67 K8
Hazel Street Rd *RSIT* ME9 ...... 106 C1
Hazelwood Cl *RTWE/PEM* TN2 ... 163 M5
Hazelwood Dr *MAID/SHEP* ME16 . 120 D1
Hazelwood Rd *RSEV* TN14 .... 72 F6
Hazlemere Dr *GILL* ME7 .... 51 J8
Hazlitt Dr *MAIDW* ME16........... 6 A2
Headcorn Rd *HDCN* TN27 .... 172 B6
 RHAM ME8 .... 67 K1 🔳
 RMAID ME17 .... 141 C5
 STPH/PW TN12 .... 170 C1
Headingley Rd *MAIDW* ME16 .... 102 D7
The Head Race *MAID/SHEP* ME15 .. 6 B9
Healy Dr *ORP* BR6 .... 56 B6
Heansill La *HAWK* TN18 .... 199 C5
Heard Wy *SIT* ME10 .... 71 K8
Hearns Cl *RTWE/PEM* TN2 .... 167 K6
Hearns Rd *STMC/STPC* BR5 .... 40 E8
Heartenoak Rd *HAWK* TN18 ..... 199 J1
Hearts Delight Rd *RSIT* ME9 .... 87 K4
Heath Cl *STMC/STPC* BR5 .... 56 E2
 SWLY BR8 .... 42 A6 🔳
Heathclose Av *DART* DA1 .... 27 K5
Heathclose Rd *DART* DA1 .... 27 J5
Heathcote Cl *DIT/AY* ME20 ..... 102 B3
Heathdene Dr *BELV* DA17 .... 12 D3
Heathend Rd *BXLY* DA5 .... 27 G6
Heather Bank
 STPH/PW TN12 .... 150 D7 🔳
Heatherbank Cl *DART* DA1 .... 27 G4
Heather Cl *SIT* ME10 .... 88 C2
 WALD ME5 .... 83 H1
Heather Dr *DART* DA1 .... 27 J5
 MAID/SHEP ME15 .... 137 J2
 TENT TN30 .... 196 D2
Heather End *SWLY* BR8 .... 57 M1 🔳
The Heathers *CRBK* TN17 .... 192 C2
Heather Wk *TONN* TN10 .... 131 K7 🔳
Heatherwood Ri *RMAID* ME17 ... 140 A3 🔳
Heathfield *RMAID* ME17 .... 139 G1
Heathfield Av
 MAID/BEAR ME14 .... 103 L6
Heathfield Cl *MAID/BEAR* ME14 . 103 L6
 WALD ME5 .... 66 D6
Heathfield Rd *BXLYHS* DA6 ...... 26 B2
 MAID/SHEP ME15 .... 136 A1
 MAIDW ME16 .... 120 B2
 RMAID ME17 .... 139 G1
Heathside Av *BXLYHN* DA7 .... 12 A8
 RMAID ME17 .... 136 E1
Heath St *DART* DA1 .... 27 M5
The Heath *E/WMAL* ME19 .... 101 G8
Heathview Av *DART* DA1 .... 27 G4
Heathview Crs *DART* DA1 .... 27 J5
Heath View Gdns
 CDH/CHF RM16 .... 16 E1
Heath View Rd *CDH/CHF* RM16 ... 16 E1
Heath Wy *ERITH* DA8 .... 13 H6
Heathwood Gdns *SWLY* BR8....... 41 L6
Heathwood Wk *BXLY* DA5 .... 27 J2
Heaverham Rd *BGR/WK* TN15 ..... 96 D3
Hectorage Rd *TON* TN9 .... 147 L5
Hedge Place Rd *GRH* DA9 .... 29 G4
The Hedgerows *GVW* DA11 .... 31 G7
The Hedgerow
 MAID/BEAR ME14 .... 104 A8
The Hedges
 MAID/BEAR ME14 .... 103 J6 🔳
Hedley Av *WTHK* RM20 .... 15 L6
Hedley St *MAID/BEAR* ME14 .... 7 H3
Helen Cl *DART* DA1 .... 27 K5
Helen Thompson Cl *RSIT* ME9 ... 71 G1
Helleborine *GRAYS* RM17 .... 16 B4
Hellyar Ct *ROCH* ME1 .... 3 K9 🔳
 ROCH ME1 .... 65 L1 🔳
Hempstead La *RSIT* ME9 .... 89 G2
Hempstead Rd *GILL* ME7 .... 67 J7
Hempstead Valley Dr *GILL* ME7 . 67 J7
Hemsted Rd *ERITH* DA8 .... 13 G7
Henbane Cl
 MAID/BEAR ME14 .... 104 A8 🔳
Henderson Dr *DART* DA1 .... 28 C2
Hendley Dr *CRBK* TN17 .... 183 L8
Hendy Rd *SNOD* ME6 .... 81 K5
Henfield Cl *BXLY* DA5 .... 26 C4
Hengist Rd *ERITH* DA8 .... 12 E6
Hengrove Cl *BXLY* DA5 .... 26 A6 🔳
Henham Gdns *STPH/PW* TN12 .... 134 C2
Henhurst Rd *MEO* DA13 .... 46 F6
Heniker La *RMAID* ME17 .... 139 H8
Henley Cl *RHAM* ME8 .... 67 M5
 RTWE/PEM TN2 .... 11 L2

 WALD ME5 .... 66 C7
Henley Deane *GVW* DA11 .... 46 A1
Henley Flds *MAID/BEAR* ME14 .. 104 A7
 TENT TN30 .... 196 D3
Henley Mdw *TENT* TN30 .... 196 C3
Henley Rd *STPH/PW* TN12 ...... 150 C6
Henley St *MEO* DA13 .... 63 H2
Henry St *CHAT* ME4 .... 5 G8
 GRAYS RM17 .... 16 E5 🔳
 RHAM ME8 .... 68 C4
Henwood Green Rd
 RTWE/PEM TN2 .... 164 F6
Henwoods Crs *RTWE/PEM* TN2 .. 164 F7
Henwoods Mt *RTWE/PEM* TN2 ... 165 G7
Herbert Rd *BXLYHN* DA7 .... 12 A8
 CHAT ME4 .... 4 E8
 RHAM ME8 .... 68 A5
 SWCM DA10 .... 30 B4
 SWLY BR8 .... 42 B3
Herdsdown *HOO/HM* ME3 .... 35 M8
Hereford Rd *MAID/SHEP* ME15 .. 121 L6
Heritage Dr *GILL* ME7 .... 67 H4
Heritage Rd *WALD* ME5 .... 66 C7
Herman Ter *CHAT* ME4 .... 4 E7
Hermitage Ct *MAID/BEAR* ME14 . 102 B8
 MAIDW ME16 .... 102 B7
Hermitage La *DIT/AY* ME20 ..... 102 B6
 MAID/BEAR ME14 .... 104 D2
 MAIDW ME16 .... 102 B7
 RHAM ME8 .... 138 A7
Hermitage Rd *HOO/HM* ME3 ...... 48 C3
Herne Rd *RHAM* ME8 .... 67 L3
Herne Crs *SCUP* DA14 .... 40 A1
Herondale *MAID/SHEP* ME15... 138 C1
Herongate Rd *SWLY* BR8......... 42 A3
Heron HI *BELV* DA17 .... 12 B3
Heron Hill La *MEO* DA13 .... 79 K1
Heron Rd *DIT/AY* ME20 .... 101 H4
Herons Wy *RTWE/PEM* TN2 ...... 165 C5
Heron Wy *HOO/HM* ME3 .... 37 L1
 WALD ME5 .... 66 C7
 WTHK RM20 .... 15 K4
Herts Crs *MAID/SHEP* ME15 .... 137 H2 🔳
Herying Cl *STRD* ME2 .... 81 K1
Hesiers HI *WARL* CR6 .... 91 G3
Hesiers Rd *WARL* CR6 .... 91 G2
Hesketh Av *RDART* DA2 .... 28 D6
Heskett Pk *RTWE/PEM* TN2 ..... 165 G7
Hever Av *BGR/WK* TN15.......... 77 G1
Hever Cl *MAID/SHEP* ME15 ..... 122 B7
Hever Court Rd *GVE* DA12....... 46 E3
Hever Cft *STRD* ME2 .... 2 C7
Hever Gdns *MAIDW* ME16 .... 6 C7
Hever PI *SIT* ME10 .... 87 L2
Hever Rd *BGR/WK* TN15 .... 77 G1
 EDEN TN8 .... 143 J6
Heversham Rd *BXLYHN* DA7 ...... 12 C8
Hever Wood Rd *BGR/WK* TN15.... 77 G2
Hewett PI *SWLY* BR8 .... 41 M8
Hewitt Cl *GILL* ME7 .... 51 H7
Hewitts Rd *ORP* BR6 .... 74 B2
Hextable Cl *MAIDW* ME16 ...... 102 E6 🔳
Hibbs Cl *SWLY* BR8 .... 41 M6
Hibernia Dr *GVE* DA12 .... 32 B8
Hickory Dell *GILL* ME7 .... 67 J8
Higham Cl *MAID/SHEP* ME15 ...... 6 C9
Higham Gdns *TONN* TN10 .... 132 B8
Higham La *RTON* TN11 .... 132 A4
 RYE TN31 .... 206 C7
 TONN TN10 .... 132 B7
Higham Rd *HOO/HM* ME3 .... 34 C1
 HOO/HM ME3 .... 49 L2
Higham School Rd *TONN* TN10 .. 132 A7
High Ash Cl *TIL* RM18 .... 18 C2
High Bank *ROCH* ME1 .... 65 M3
High Banks *MAID/SHEP* ME15 ... 121 H8
High Beeches *ORP* BR6 .... 73 J1
 RTWE/PEM TN2 .... 163 H7
 SCUP DA14 .... 41 G2
Highberry *E/WMAL* ME19 .... 101 G3 🔳
High Brooms Rd *STH/RUST* TN4 . 163 L5
Highbury La *TENT* TN30 .... 196 C6
High Cross Rd *BGR/WK* TN15 ... 115 K4
Highcross Rd *MEO* DA13 .... 44 F3
High Dewar Rd *RHAM* ME8 .... 68 C5
High Dr *CTHM* CR3 .... 90 B8
High Elms *RHAM* ME8 .... 68 A3
High Elms Rd *ORP* BR6 .... 72 C7
Highfield Av *ERITH* DA8 .... 12 D5 🔳
 ORP BR6 .... 73 H1
Highfield Cl *HAWK* TN18 .... 199 J4
 RHAM ME8 .... 67 M6 🔳
 RTWE/PEM TN2 .... 164 F7
Highfield Gdns *CDH/CHF* RM16 .. 16 F1
Highfield Rd *BH/WHM* TN16...... 91 L3
 BXLYHS DA6 .... 26 B3
 DART DA1 .... 27 M5
 RHAM ME8 .... 67 M6
 RSEV TN14 .... 96 A2
 STH/RUST TN4 .... 163 L2
 STMC/STPC BR5 .... 40 B7
Highfield Rd South *DART* DA1 .. 27 M5
Highfields Rd *EDEN* TN8 .... 126 E8
High Firs *SWLY* BR8 .... 42 A8
Highgate HI *HAWK* TN18 .... 199 H4
Highgrove *RTWE/PEM* TN2 ...... 177 J5
Highgrove Rd *WALD* ME5 .... 66 C8
High Halden Rd *HDCN* TN27 .... 186 C4
High Hilden Cl *RTON* TN11..... 147 J1
High House La *CDH/CHF* RM16... 17 M2
 RTON TN11 .... 132 D4
Highland Rd *BXLYHS* DA6 .... 26 C2 🔳
 MAID/SHEP ME15 .... 122 A6
 RSEV TN14 .... 74 D5
Highlands Cl *STRD* ME2 .... 48 F7
Highlands HI *SWLY* BR8 .... 42 C6
Highlands Pk *BGR/WK* TN15 ..... 96 A7
Highlands Rd *STMC/STPC* BR5 ... 56 D3
High La *CTHM* CR3 .... 90 B5
 WARL CR6 .... 90 B4
High Meadow *RYE* TN31 .... 206 C6
High Oak HI *RSIT* ME9 .... 70 A5
High Pk *RYE* TN31 .... 206 C6
High Rdg *CRBK* TN17 .... 181 M6
Highridge *GILL* ME7 .... 67 H4 🔳
Highridge Cl *MAID/BEAR* ME14 . 104 B8
High Rd *RDART* DA2 .... 27 L8
High Rocks La *RRTW* TN3 ...... 176 E4
Highstead Crs *ERITH* DA8 ...... 13 G7

Highsted Rd RSIT ME9 88 B6
High St BGR/WK TN15 96 C3
BGR/WK TN15 96 B7
BGR/WK TN15 98 C2
BGR/WK TN15 98 B6
BH/WHM TN16 110 E5
BH/WHM TN16 111 L2
CHAT ME4 4 E6
CHAT ME4 4 C5
CRBK TN17 182 A5
CRBK TN17 192 E1
CRBK TN17 202 B2
DART DA1 28 A4
DIT/AY ME20 102 B2
E/WMAL ME19 100 D5
E/WMAL ME19 101 J7
EDEN TN8 142 E4
EDEN TN8 159 J8
EYN DA4 59 H2
EYN DA4 59 G5
GILL ME7 4 E1
GILL ME7 5 H2
GILL ME7 5 K3
GRAYS RM17 16 C4
GRH DA9 29 K2
GVE DA12 31 K4
GVW DA11 30 D4
HAWK TN18 198 F3
HDCN TN27 155 L8
HDCN TN27 173 J4
HDCN TN27 186 B4
HOO/HM ME3 25 K7
HOO/HM ME3 37 L1 3
MAID/BEAR ME14 6 F5
ORP BR6 56 C3
ORP BR6 72 C5
OXTED RH8 108 F8
OXTED RH8 109 K6
RDART DA2 29 K8
RHAM ME8 68 B5
RMAID ME17 139 G6
RMAID ME17 141 M1
ROCH ME1 3 M9
ROCH ME1 3 K6
ROCH ME1 81 L1
RRTW TN3 189 J1
RSEV TN14 75 H4
RSEV TN14 95 J2
RSIT ME9 69 K7
RTON TN11 133 G5
RTON TN11 146 A4
RTW TN1 10 F7
RTWE/PEM TN2 164 E7
SCUP DA14 40 C1
SEV TN13 9 J6
SEV TN13 94 E8
SIT ME10 71 G7
SNOD ME6 81 J5
STH/RUST TN4 162 E2
STMC/STPC BR5 40 E8
STMC/STPC BR5 56 E2
STPH/PW TN12 152 F7
STPH/PW TN12 166 D5
STPH/PW TN12 170 B2
STRD ME2 2 F3
STRD ME2 3 H4
STRD ME2 50 B3
SWCM DA10 30 B3
SWLY BR8 42 A7
TENT TN30 196 C6
TON TN9 147 L4
TONN TN10 147 L3
WADH TN5 188 A8
WBY/YAL ME18 135 H4
High Vw HOO/HM ME3 48 E1
Highview MEO DA13 79 K5
High View Av GRAYS RM17 16 E4
Highview Dr WALD ME5 65 M8
High View Gdns GRAYS RM17 16 E4
Highview Rd SCUP DA14 40 D1
The Highway ORP BR6 56 D8
High Weald Wk RRTW TN3 162 D6
RTON TN11 164 E2
RTWE/PEM TN2 178 A5
STH/RUST TN4 10 B8
STH/RUST TN4 163 L3
TON TN9 148 A6
Highwoods Cl HOO/HM ME3 48 E1 1
High Woods La RTWE/PEM TN2 11 M7
Hilary Gdns ROCH ME1 65 H3
Hilbert Cl RTW TN1 11 K2
Hilda May Av SWLY BR8 42 A7
Hilda Rd CHAT ME4 4 E8
Hilden Av RTON TN11 147 H1
Hildenborough Crs
MAIDW ME16 102 D6
Hildenborough Rd RTON TN11 131 H1
RTON TN11 146 C2
Hilden Dr ERITH DA8 13 K6
Hilden Park Rd RTON TN11 147 H1
Hilders Cl EDEN TN8 142 D1
Hilders La EDEN TN8 142 B1
Hillary Av GVW DA11 31 G8
Hillary Rd MAID/BEAR ME14 103 J6
Hillborough Av SEV TN13 9 M1
Hillborough Gv WALD ME5 83 J2
Hill Brow DART DA1 27 H4
MAID/BEAR ME14 104 C8
SIT ME10 87 M3
Hillbrow Cl BXLY DA5 41 M1
Hill Bunker's BELV DA17 12 C3
Hill Cha WALD ME5 83 G2
Hill Cl MEO DA13 46 A4
Hill Ct HOO/HM ME3 50 B1
Hill Crs BXLY DA5 26 E6
Hillcrest EDEN TN8 127 K8
Hill Crest SEV TN13 8 E1
STH/RUST TN4 163 K5
Hillcrest Av WTHK RM20 15 J5
Hillcrest Dr GRH DA9 29 J3
RTWE/PEM TN2 163 M6
STRD ME2 64 E3
Hillcrest Rd BH/WHM TN16 91 M2
CHAT ME4 4 C9
DART DA1 27 G5
EDEN TN8 142 E1
ORP BR6 56 C5
Hillden Shaw MAID/SHEP ME15 121 J5
Hill End ORP BR6 56 B5
Hill Farm Av STRD ME2 49 H4
Hillfield Rd SEV TN13 95 G6
Hill Fort Pitt CHAT ME4 4 A6
Hillgarth STH/RUST TN4 163 J5 1
Hill Green Rd RSIT ME9 85 L5
Hill House Rd RDART DA2 28 E5
Hillingdale BH/WHM TN16 91 K4
Hillingdon Av SEV TN13 95 L7
Hillingdon Ri SEV TN13 95 M8
Hillingdon Rd BXLYHN DA7 26 E1
GVW DA11 31 K7
Hill Ri RDART DA2 43 M2
Hill Rd DART DA1 28 A7
ROCH ME1 65 G8
ROCH ME1 65 J3
Hill Shaw HART DA3 61 H2
Hillshaw Crs STRD ME2 2 A7
Hillside EYN DA4 59 H3
GRAYS RM17 16 F3
RDART DA2 44 A2
TON TN9 147 J6
Hillside Av GVE DA12 31 M7
QBOR ME11 55 H2
STRD ME2 3 H1
Hillside Ct SWLY BR8 42 C8
WBY/YAL ME18 119 G6
Hillside Dr GVE DA12 31 M7
Hillside Rd BH/WHM TN16 92 A5
CHAT ME4 4 F6
DART DA1 27 J4
RSEV TN14 96 B3
SEV TN13 9 L2
The Hillside ORP BR6 73 K3
Hills La BGR/WK TN15 76 D6
Hill's Ter CHAT ME4 4 C7
Hill St RTW TN1 11 G2
The Hill CRBK TN17 192 F1
GVW DA11 30 E4
Hill Top CRBK TN17 169 G8
Hilltop MAID/SHEP ME15 135 M2
TON TN9 147 K6
Hilltop Gdns DART DA1 28 B3
ORP BR6 56 A5
Hilltop Rd STRD ME2 49 L4
WTHK RM20 15 J5
Hilltop Wk CTHM CR3 90 A6
Hill Vw BGR/WK TN15 98 C6
Hill View Cl BGR/WK TN15 98 C6
Hillview Crs ORP BR6 56 A4
Hill View Rd HART DA3 45 K7
ORP BR6 56 B4
RTON TN11 131 H8
STH/RUST TN4 176 E1
Hill View Wy WALD ME5 66 A8
Hillydeal Rd RSEV TN14 95 L1
Hillyfield Cl STRD ME2 49 H4 1
Hilton Dr SIT ME10 70 D7
Hilton Rd HOO/HM ME3 34 D6
Hind Crs ERITH DA8 12 E6
Hinde Cl SIT ME10 71 H6
Hinksden Rd CRBK TN17 200 B2
Hinton Crs GILL ME7 67 J7
Hitchen Hatch La SEV TN13 8 F3
Hither Chantlers RRTW TN3 176 C2
Hive La GVW DA11 30 D3
Hoath Cl GILL ME7 67 J6
Hoath La RHAM ME8 67 K6
Hoath Wy RHAM ME8 67 K6 1
Hobart Gdns SIT ME10 87 L1
Hobart Rd TIL RM18 17 J7
Hobbs La RYE TN31 207 M7
Hoblands End CHST BR7 40 A3
Hockenden La SWLY BR8 41 J7
Hockers Cl MAID/BEAR ME14 104 C5
Hockers La MAID/BEAR ME14 104 B6
Hoddesdon Rd BELV DA17 12 C4
Hodgson Crs SNOD ME6 81 J4 1
Hodsoll St BGR/WK TN15 78 F3
Hodson Crs STMC/STPC BR5 56 F1 1
Hogbarn La RMAID ME17 125 H3
Hogg La CDH/CHF RM16 16 C2
GRAYS RM17 16 C3
Hoghole La RRTW TN3 189 G3
Hog La MEO DA13 30 F8
Hognore La BGR/WK TN15 78 F7
Hogtrough Hl BH/WHM TN16 93 J8
Hogtrough La OXTED RH8 108 D6
Holborough Rd SNOD ME6 81 J5
Holcombe Cl BH/WHM TN16 110 F4
Holcombe Rd CHAT ME4 4 D9
ROCH ME1 65 L2
Holcote Cl BELV DA17 12 A2
Holden Cnr STH/RUST TN4 163 G4
Holden Park Rd STH/RUST TN4 163 H5
Holden Rd STH/RUST TN4 163 H4
Holder Cl WALD ME5 66 E7
Holding St RHAM ME8 68 A4
Hole La EDEN TN8 126 C7
Holford Rd CDH/CHF RM16 18 A2
TIL RM18 17 M3
Holford St TON TN9 147 K4 2
Holland Rd MAID/BEAR ME14 7 H3
WALD ME5 83 G1
Hollands Cl GVE DA12 48 A2
The Hollies GVE DA12 46 F3
HART DA3 45 L7
Hollin Cl STH/RUST TN4 10 C3
Hollingbourne Av BXLYHN DA7 12 B7
Hollingbourne Hl RMAID ME17 124 B1
Hollingbourne Rd RHAM ME8 67 L8
Hollingworth Rd
MAID/SHEP ME15 122 B8
Hollingworth Wy
BH/WHM TN16 110 F4 3
Hollis Pl GRAYS RM17 16 C2
Hollowfield Av GRAYS RM17 16 F3
Hollow La RSIT ME9 68 F8
SNOD ME6 81 H6
Hollow Trees Dr RTON TN11 146 C4
Holly Bank STPH/PW TN12 166 D5
Hollybush Cl SEV TN13 9 K4
Hollybush La ORP BR6 74 C1
Holly Bush La SEV TN13 9 K4
Hollybush Rd GVE DA12 31 L7
Holly Cl GILL ME7 51 G7
WALD ME5 66 E4
Hollydene Rd WADH TN5 188 B7
Holly Farm Rd
MAID/SHEP ME15 122 E7
Holly Hl MEO DA13 80 C3
Holly Hill Rd BELV DA17 12 D4
Holly Rd DART DA1 27 M6
ORP BR6 73 J2
STRD ME2 2 B6
Hollyshaw Cl RTWE/PEM TN2 11 J8
Hollytree Av SWLY BR8 42 A6
Holly Tree Cl RMAID ME17 140 A3
Hollytree Dr HOO/HM ME3 48 D2
Hollywood La BGR/WK TN15 77 H5
STRD ME2 49 L3
Hollywood Wy ERITH DA8 13 K7
Holmes Cl HOO/HM ME3 36 A2
Holmesdale Cl
MAID/SHEP ME15 137 H2
WADH TN5 188 A8 1
Holmesdale Hl EYN DA4 43 M5
Holmesdale Rd EYN DA4 43 L5
SEV TN13 9 L3
Holmewood Rdg RRTW TN3 176 B2
Holmewood Rd STH/RUST TN4 163 L6
Holmhurst Cl STH/RUST TN4 10 B4
Holmhurst Rd BELV DA17 12 D4
Holmleigh Av DART DA1 27 L2
Holm Mill La RMAID ME17 124 D7
Holmoaks MAID/BEAR ME14 7 M3
RHAM ME8 68 A3
Holmsdale Gv BXLYHN DA7 13 G8
Holmside GILL ME7 67 G3
Holt Wood Av DIT/AY ME20 101 M5
Holtwood Cl RHAM ME8 67 M8
Holtye Crs MAID/SHEP ME15 7 J9
Holyoake Ter SEV TN13 8 E4
Holyrood Gdns CDH/CHF RM16 17 L3
Holywell La RSIT ME9 69 H3
Homedean Rd SEV TN13 94 E8
Home Farm Cl RTON TN11 146 C2
Home Farm La RTWE/PEM TN2 164 A5
Homefield Cl STMC/STPC BR5 40 D8 2
SWLY BR8 42 B7
Homefield Dr RHAM ME8 68 D3
Homefield Ri ORP BR6 56 C4
Homefield Rd SEV TN13 8 B1
Home Gdns DART DA1 28 A4
Home Hl SWLY BR8 42 B4
Home Lea ORP BR6 56 B8
Home Mead Cl GVE DA12 31 K5
Homer Cl BXLYHN DA7 12 E7
Homesdale Rd ORP BR6 56 A3
Homestead Rd EDEN TN8 126 D8
ORP BR6 73 K2
The Homestead DART DA1 27 L4
RRTW TN3 175 L6 2
Homestead Vw RSIT ME9 87 K3
Homeview SIT ME10 88 D1 1
Homewards Rd HOO/HM ME3 23 K5
Homewood Av SIT ME10 87 M2
Homewood Crs CHST BR7 40 A3
Homewood Rd RRTW TN3 176 B2
TENT TN30 196 D4
Hone St STRD ME2 3 G2
Honeyball Wk RSIT ME9 89 L3
Honey Bee Gld RHAM ME8 68 A7 1
Honey Cl GILL ME7 67 J8
Honeycrock Hl RSIT ME9 86 B5
Honeyden Rd SCUP DA14 41 G3
Honey La MAID/SHEP ME15 122 D7
Honeypot Cl STRD ME2 3 H1
Honeypot La BGR/WK TN15 78 E3
BGR/WK TN15 96 E5
Honeysuckle Cl GILL ME7 84 B1 1
Honywood Rd RMAID ME17 125 L8
Hoo Common HOO/HM ME3 50 C1
Hood Av STMC/STPC BR5 56 D1
Hook Cl WALD ME5 66 A8
Hookfields GVW DA11 31 G8
Hook Green La RDART DA2 27 H8
Hook Green Rd MEO DA13 45 H4
Hook Hl WADH TN5 189 J7
Hook La RMAID ME17 124 E7
Hook Rd SNOD ME6 81 H5
Hookwood Cnr OXTED RH8 109 K6
Hookwood Rd ORP BR6 73 L5
Hoopers La HOO/HM ME3 23 H8
Hooper's Pl ROCH ME1 3 K9 3
Hooper's Rd ROCH ME1 3 K9
Hoo Rd STRD ME2 49 M2
Hope Av RTON TN11 133 G4
Hopehouse La CRBK TN17 201 H4
HAWK TN18 201 G6
Hope Rd SWCM DA10 30 B4
Hopes Gv RASHW TN26 187 M6
Hope St CHAT ME4 4 F8
MAID/BEAR ME14 6 F1
Hopewell Dr GVE DA12 47 H2
WALD ME5 66 E5
Hopgarden La SEV TN13 113 J6
Hopgarden Rd TONN TN10 131 M8
Hop Pocket Cl CRBK TN17 184 C5 1
Hop Pocket La STPH/PW TN12 150 B6
Hopwood Gdns STH/RUST TN4 163 J7
Horizon Cl STH/RUST TN4 163 K5
Horley Cl BXLYHS DA6 26 C3 1
Hornbeam Av RTWE/PEM TN2 163 M4
WALD ME5 83 K3 1
Hornbeam Cl DIT/AY ME20 101 K4
STPH/PW TN12 150 B8 2
Hornbeams MEO DA13 79 K5
Horns La WBY/YAL ME18 117 M3
Horns Lodge La RTON TN11 131 L5
Horn's Oak Rd MEO DA13 62 D7
Horns Rd HAWK TN18 198 F5
Horn Yd GVE DA12 31 K4 3
Horsa Rd ERITH DA8 12 E6
Horsecroft Cl ORP BR6 56 D4 1
Horsell Rd STMC/STPC BR5 40 C5
Horseshoe Cl GILL ME7 67 H8
MAID/BEAR ME14 104 A8 4
Horseshoes La RMAID ME17 138 F1
Horsfield Cl RDART DA2 28 E5 2
Horsham La RHAM ME8 68 F2
Horsham Rd BXLYHS DA6 26 B4
Horsley Rd ROCH ME1 3 H9
Horsmonden Cl ORP BR6 56 B3 1
Horsmonden Rd
STPH/PW TN12 166 E6
Horsted Av CHAT ME4 66 A4
Horsted Wy ROCH ME1 65 M6
Horton Downs
MAID/SHEP ME15 122 B4
Horton Pl BH/WHM TN16 110 F4
Horton Rd EYN DA4 43 L7
Hortons Cl CRBK TN17 193 M6
Hortons Wy BH/WHM TN16 110 F4
Horton Wy EYN DA4 59 H3
Horwood Cl ROCH ME1 65 K5 2
Hoselands Vw HART DA3 45 G8
Hosey Common La
BH/WHM TN16 111 G8
Hosey Common Rd
BH/WHM TN16 111 G7
Hosey Hl BH/WHM TN16 111 G5
Hoskins Rd OXTED RH8 109 G7
Hospital La ROCH ME1 4 A5 1
Hospital Rd RMAID ME17 124 A5
SEV TN13 95 L7
Hostier Cl STRD ME2 81 K1
Hotel Rd RHAM ME8 67 J3
Hotham Cl EYN DA4 43 J4
SWLY BR8 42 D5
Hothfield Rd RHAM ME8 68 B4
Hottsfield HART DA3 45 G7
Houghton Av GILL ME7 84 D2
Houselands Rd TON TN9 147 K3 1
Hove Cl GRAYS RM17 16 C5
Hovendens CRBK TN17 184 C5
Howard Av ROCH ME1 65 M2
SIT ME10 70 F7
Howard Dr MAIDW ME16 102 D7
Howard Gdns RTWE/PEM TN2 10 E9
Howard Rd CDH/CHF RM16 15 L2
DART DA1 28 C4
E/WMAL ME19 101 H5
Howbury La ERITH DA8 13 J8
Howbury Rd DART DA1 13 J8
Howells Cl BGR/WK TN15 77 G1 1
How Green La EDEN TN8 143 L4
Howick Cl DIT/AY ME20 102 B5
Howland Rd STPH/PW TN12 153 H7
Howlsmere Cl STRD ME2 81 K2
Hubbard's Hl SEV TN13 129 K1
Hubbard's La MAID/SHEP ME15 137 J2
Hubble Dr MAID/SHEP ME15 122 A6
Huckleberry Cl WALD ME5 83 K2 2
Hudson Cl RHAM ME8 67 L4
Hudson Rd BXLYHN DA7 12 B8
Hughes Dr STRD ME2 49 M3
Hughes Rd CDH/CHF RM16 17 J2
Hugh Price Cl SIT ME10 71 L8
Hulsewood Cl RDART DA2 27 K8
Humber Crs STRD ME2 2 D4
Humber Rd DART DA1 27 M3
Humboldt Ct RTWE/PEM TN2 11 L1
Hume Av TIL RM18 31 K1
Hume Cl TIL RM18 31 J1
Hungershall Pk STH/RUST TN4 10 A8
Hunsdon Dr SEV TN13 9 H3
Hunstanton Cl RHAM ME8 85 G2
Hunters Cl BXLY DA5 27 G8
Huntersfield Cl WALD ME5 83 L4 1
Hunters Wk RSEV TN14 74 A8
Hunters Wy GILL ME7 67 G4
RTWE/PEM TN2 177 H4
Hunters Wy West WALD ME5 66 F3
Huntingdon Wk
MAID/SHEP ME15 122 A6 1
Huntingfield Rd MEO DA13 62 C3
Huntington Cl CRBK TN17 192 F1 1
Huntington Rd RMAID ME17 136 D2
Huntley Av GVW DA11 30 D4
Huntleys Pk STH/RUST TN4 163 H7
Hunton Hl MAID/SHEP ME15 136 B4
Hunton Rd STPH/PW TN12 136 B8
Hunt Rd GVW DA11 31 G8
TONN TN10 132 A7
Hunts Farm Cl BGR/WK TN15 98 C6
Huntsman La BGR/WK TN15 99 G4
MAID/BEAR ME14 7 K4 1
Huntsmans Cl CHAT ME4 66 A4 1
Hunt St WBY/YAL ME18 135 G1
Hurlfield RDART DA2 27 L8
Hurlingham Rd BXLYHN DA7 12 B6
Huron Cl ORP BR6 73 H1 2
Hurricane Rd E/WMAL ME19 118 B2
Hurst Cl STPH/PW TN12 170 B1
TENT TN30 196 A6
WALD ME5 66 A7
Hurst Farm Rd RSEV TN14 129 K2
Hurst Hl WALD ME5 83 G3
The Hurstings MAIDW ME16 6 B8
Hurst La RSEV TN14 129 K3
SIT ME10 71 H4
Hurst Pl RHAM ME8 68 B5
Hurst Rd BXLY DA5 26 A6
ERITH DA8 12 E6
Hurst Springs BXLY DA5 26 A6
The Hurst RTWE/PEM TN2 164 A6
Hurst Wy MAIDW ME16 120 B3
SEV TN13 113 L5
Hurstwood WALD ME5 83 G1
Hurstwood Av BXLY DA5 26 A6
BXLYHN DA7 13 G7
Hurstwood La STH/RUST TN4 10 B4
Hurstwood Pk STH/RUST TN4 10 C5
Hurstwood Rd GILL ME7 84 D4
MAID/BEAR ME14 84 D6
Husheath Hl CRBK TN17 169 H7
Hutsford Cl RHAM ME8 67 M8 3
Hyacinth Rd STRD ME2 48 F7
Hybrid Cl ROCH ME1 65 M4
Hyde Dr STMC/STPC BR5 40 D8
Hyde Rd BXLYHN DA7 12 B8
MAIDW ME16 102 F6
Hyder Rd CDH/CHF RM16 17 L2
Hydes Orch HDCN TN27 156 A8 2
Hyperion Dr STRD ME2 49 H4 1
Hythe Av BXLYHN DA7 12 A6
Hythe Cl STH/RUST TN4 163 J4
STMC/STPC BR5 40 E8 2
Hythe Rd SIT ME10 70 F8
Hythe St DART DA1 28 A3

I

Ide Hill Rd RSEV TN14 128 B2
Iden Crs STPH/PW TN12 170 A3
Iden Rd STRD ME2 49 L4
Idenwood Cl RHAM ME8 67 M7
Idleigh Court Rd HART DA3 61 K5
Ifield Cl MAID/SHEP ME15 122 B5
Ifield Wy GVE DA12 46 F3
Ightham By-pass BGR/WK TN15 97 L7
Ightham Rd ERITH DA8 12 C6
RTON TN11 131 L2
Illustrious Cl WALD ME5 66 C8
Impala Gdns STH/RUST TN4 163 K7
Imperial Dr GVE DA12 47 H2
Imperial Rd GILL ME7 5 J8
Impton La WALD ME5 83 H5
Ingleby Rd CDH/CHF RM16 17 K2
Ingleden Cl SIT ME10 71 H5
Ingleden Park Rd TENT TN30 196 D4
Ingle Rd CHAT ME4 4 C9
Inglewood Rd BXLYHN DA7 26 F2
Ingoldsby Rd GVE DA12 32 A6
Ingram Rd DART DA1 28 A6
GILL ME7 51 G8
GRAYS RM17 16 E3
Institute Rd CHAT ME4 4 F6
Instone Rd DART DA1 27 M5
Invicta Ct SIT ME10 71 H6
Invicta Rd RDART DA2 28 D4
Iona Cl WALD ME5 83 M4
Iona Rd MAID/SHEP ME15 121 J6
Irene Rd ORP BR6 56 B3
Ireton Pl GRAYS RM17 16 C3
Iris Av BXLY DA5 26 A4
Iris Cl WALD ME5 83 J5
Iris Crs BXLYHN DA7 12 B5
Iron Mill La DART DA1 27 H2
Iron Mill Pl DART DA1 27 H2
Ironside Cl WALD ME5 66 C5
Ironstones RRTW TN3 176 D2 1
Irvine Rd HOO/HM ME3 48 D2
Irvine Wy ORP BR6 56 B3
Irving Wy SWLY BR8 41 M6
Island Wy East CHAT ME4 50 D4
Island Wy West CHAT ME4 50 D3
Islingham Rd HOO/HM ME3 49 L2
Ismays Rd BGR/WK TN15 115 K3
Istead Ri MEO DA13 46 B4
Ivens Wy RMAID ME17 124 F7
Iversgate Cl RHAM ME8 68 B3
Ives Rd TON TN9 147 H4
Ivy Bower Cl GRH DA9 29 K3
Ivy Cl DART DA1 28 C4
GVE DA12 46 E1
RMAID ME17 139 M3
Ivy House La SEV TN13 94 F3
Ivy La RSEV TN14 94 A2
Ivy St RHAM ME8 68 B5
Izane Rd BXLYHS DA6 26 B2

J

Jacklin Cl WALD ME5 83 H2
Jackson Av ROCH ME1 66 A5
Jackson Cl GRH DA9 29 H3
RHAM ME8 67 L4
Jacksons La TENT TN30 196 C6 1
Jacob's La HOO/HM ME3 36 D7
Jaggard Wy STPH/PW TN12 170 A2
Jagger Cl RDART DA2 28 E5
Jail La BH/WHM TN16 91 M1
James Rd DART DA1 27 J5
STRD ME2 64 D3
James St CHAT ME4 4 D6
GILL ME7 5 K2
MAID/BEAR ME14 7 G2
ROCH ME1 3 K9
James Watt Wy ERITH DA8 13 H5
James Whatman Wy
MAID/BEAR ME14 6 E2
Japonica Cl WALD ME5 83 L3 1
Jarrett Av STRD ME2 49 M3 1
Jarvis La CRBK TN17 182 C4
Jarvis Pl TENT TN30 196 D2
Jasmine Cl E/WMAL ME19 101 H5
Jasmine Rd E/WMAL ME19 101 H5
Jasper Av ROCH ME1 65 L3
Javelin Rd E/WMAL ME19 118 B2
Jefferson Dr RHAM ME8 67 L4
Jeffery St GILL ME7 5 J2
Jeffrey Cl STPH/PW TN12 170 A1
Jeffrey St MAID/BEAR ME14 7 H3
Jellicoe Av GVE DA12 31 L8
Jenkins' Dl CHAT ME4 4 D8
Jenkins Dr MAID/SHEP ME15 122 A8
Jenner Rd ROCH ME1 65 L1
Jenner Wy DIT/AY ME20 82 B7
Jenningtree Rd ERITH DA8 13 K6
Jenningtree Wy BELV DA17 12 E1
Jenton Av BXLYHN DA7 12 A7
Jerome Rd DIT/AY ME20 101 H1
Jersey Rd STRD ME2 2 E2
Jeskyns Rd MEO DA13 46 F6
Jessamine Pl RDART DA2 28 E5
Jessett Cl ERITH DA8 12 F3
Jessica Ms SIT ME10 71 G6
Jetty Rd HOO/HM ME3 36 F6
Jetty Wk GRAYS RM17 16 C5 1
Jewell Gv STPH/PW TN12 152 F8 1
Jeyes Rd GILL ME7 5 J6
Jezreels Rd GILL ME7 5 L8
Jiniwin Rd ROCH ME1 65 M6
Jockey La CRBK TN17 183 M8 1
Jodrell Wy WTHK RM20 15 H4
Johns Cl HART DA3 61 H1
Johnsdale OXTED RH8 109 H7
Johnson Av GILL ME7 50 E6
Johnson Cl GVW DA11 30 F8
Johnson Rd SIT ME10 87 M1
Johnsons Av RSEV TN14 74 D4
Johnsons Wy GRH DA9 29 L4 3
John's Rd BH/WHM TN16 91 M6
MEO DA13 62 B1
John St GRAYS RM17 16 E5
MAID/BEAR ME14 103 J7
ROCH ME1 3 K9
STH/RUST TN4 10 E1
Joiners Ct CHAT ME4 66 D3
Jonas Dr WADH TN5 188 A8
Jonas La WADH TN5 188 A8
Jordan Cl MAID/SHEP ME15 122 A8
Joslin Rd PUR RM19 14 E4
Joyce Cl CRBK TN17 192 E1
Joyce Green La DART DA1 13 M7
Joyden's Wood Rd BXLY DA5 41 M1 1

Joy Rd GVE DA12 31 L6
Jubilee Cl GRH DA9 29 L4
Jubilee Crs BGR/WK TN15 97 L7
GVE DA12 32 A7
Jubilee Fld TENT TN30 209 G1
Jubilee Ri BGR/WK TN15 96 B7
Jubilee Rd ORP BR6 74 C1
WTHK RM20 15 K5
Jubilee St SIT ME10 71 G8
Jubilee Ter GILL ME7 5 J1
Judd Rd TON TN9 147 K6
Judeth Gdns GVE DA12 47 G2
Judkins Cl WALD ME5 66 E7
Juglans Rd ORP BR6 56 C4
Julian Rd ORP BR6 73 J1
Julians Cl SEV TN13 113 J5
Julians Wy SEV TN13 113 J5
Juliette Wy PUR RM19 14 B1
Junction Rd DART DA1 27 M4
GILL ME7 5 M6
RBTBR TN32 204 C3
Juniper Cl BH/WHM TN16 92 A3
MAIDW ME16 102 D7
RTWE/PEM TN2 163 M4
WALD ME5 83 J1
Jury St GVE DA12 31 K4
Jutland Cl HOO/HM ME3 23 M6

K

Katherine Rd EDEN TN8 142 E5
Keary Rd SWCM DA10 30 B5
Keats Gdns TIL RM18 17 K8
Keats Rd BELV DA17 12 E2
DIT/AY ME20 101 H2
Kedleston Dr STMC/STPC BR5 56 B2
Keefe Cl WALD ME5 82 F4
Keel Gdns STH/RUST TN4 163 G5
Keith Av EYN DA4 43 K3
Kelchers La RTON TN11 133 H8
Kellaway Rd WALD ME5 83 J3
Kelly Dr GILL ME7 50 E6
Kelsey Rd STMC/STPC BR5 40 D6
Kelso Dr GVE DA12 47 H1
Kelvin Cl TONN TN10 131 M6
Kelvin Pde ORP BR6 56 A4
Kelvin Rd TIL RM18 17 J8
Kemble Cl RTWE/PEM TN2 164 A6
Kembleside Rd
BH/WHM TN16 91 L4
Kemp Cl WALD ME5 82 F1
Kempton Cl ERITH DA8 12 E5
WALD ME5 83 L2
Kemsing Cl BXLY DA5 26 A5
Kemsing Rd BGR/WK TN15 97 K3
Kemsley Cl GRH DA9 29 K4
GVW DA11 46 B1
Kemsley Rd BH/WHM TN16 91 M5
Kemsley Street Rd
MAID/BEAR ME14 84 E4
Kendal Dr TON TN9 147 L3
Kendale CDH/CHF RM16 17 K2
Kendal Pk STH/RUST TN4 10 A2
Kendal Wy RHAM ME8 67 M5
Kenilworth Ct SIT ME10 70 E8
Kenilworth Dr RHAM ME8 67 M7
Kenley Cl BXLY DA5 26 C5
CHST BR7 40 A7
Kennard Cl ROCH ME1 65 H3
Kennedy Gdns SEV TN13 9 L2
Kennel Barn Rd RSIT ME9 106 D1
Kennet Rd TONN TN10 131 L8
Kennington Cl
MAID/SHEP ME15 122 B5
RHAM ME8 67 K1
Kent Av MAID/SHEP ME15 121 L4
SIT ME10 87 M2
Kent Cl ORP BR6 73 G1
ROCH ME1 65 L5
STPH/PW TN12 150 C7
Kent Hatch Rd OXTED RH8 109 L8
Kentish Gdns RTWE/PEM TN2 177 G5
Kentish Rd BELV DA17 12 C3
Kent Rd DART DA1 27 M4
GRAYS RM17 16 E5
GVW DA11 31 J6
HART DA3 44 F6
SNOD ME6 81 J7
STH/RUST TN4 163 J7
STMC/STPC BR5 56 D2
STRD ME2 64 C7
Kent St WBY/YAL ME18 118 A3
Kent Ter RHAM ME8 68 E3
Kent Vw SOCK/AV RM15 14 E1
Kenward Ct RTON TN11 133 G5
Kenward Rd MAIDW ME16 102 E8
WBY/YAL ME18 135 G2
Kenwood Av HART DA3 45 L7
WALD ME5 83 J1
Kenwyn Rd DART DA1 27 M3
Kerry Av PUR RM19 14 B1
Kershaw Cl CDH/CHF RM16 15 L2
Kesteven Cl STRD ME2 64 C8
Kestrel Cl SIT ME10 88 C3
Kestrel Rd WALD ME5 83 L3
Keswick Cl TON TN9 147 L3
Keswick Dr MAIDW ME16 102 E8
Keswick Rd BXLYHN DA7 12 C8
ORP BR6 56 B4
SIT ME10 88 E2
Ketridge La WBY/YAL ME18 118 F3
Kettle La MAID/SHEP ME15 120 A7
Kettlewell Ct SWLY BR8 42 B6
Kevington Cl STMC/STPC BR5 40 B8
Kevington Dr CHST BR7 40 B8
Kewlands MAID/BEAR ME14 7 M1
Keycol Hl RSIT ME9 70 A8
Keyes Av CHAT ME4 66 B3
Keyes Gdns TON TN9 147 H6
Keyes Rd DART DA1 28 C2
Keymer Cl BH/WHM TN16 91 L2
Key St SIT ME10 70 C8
Keyworth Cl STPH/PW TN12 150 B7
Khartoum Rd CHAT ME4 4 D2
GILL ME7 4 E2
Khyber Rd GILL ME7 50 D6
Kibbles La STH/RUST TN4 163 G5
Killewarren Wy STMC/STPC BR5 56 E3
Killick Cl SEV TN13 95 G7
Killick Rd HOO/HM ME3 35 M8
Kiln Barn Rd DIT/AY ME20 101 L5
Kiln Cl SIT ME10 88 C2
Kilndown GVE DA12 46 E3
Kilndown Cl MAIDW ME16 102 E6
Kiln Fld TENT TN30 196 E6
Kiln La RTON TN11 146 B4
Kiln Wy GRAYS RM17 16 B4
STPH/PW TN12 150 C8
Kilnwood RSEV TN14 74 B7
Kimberley Rd GILL ME7 5 L7
Kincraig Dr SEV TN13 8 F3
King Arthur's Dr STRD ME2 49 J4
King Edward Av DART DA1 27 M4
King Edward Dr CDH/CHF RM16 17 G2
GRAYS RM17 17 G3
King Edward Rd CHAT ME4 4 C9
GILL ME7 51 H7
GRH DA9 29 J3
MAID/SHEP ME15 6 F8
ROCH ME1 3 J8
Kingfisher Cl RSIT ME9 71 G1
STMC/STPC BR5 40 F8
Kingfisher Dr WALD ME5 66 E6
Kingfisher Rd DIT/AY ME20 101 H3
King George Rd WALD ME5 83 G1
King George V Hl RTW TN1 11 J1
King George Vi Av TIL RM18 18 D3
King Henry Ms ORP BR6 56 B8
King Hl E/WMAL ME19 100 C8
Kings Acre MAID/SHEP ME15 122 C4
King's Av ROCH ME1 65 L2
King's Bastion GILL ME7 4 F4
Kings Cl DART DA1 27 G2
Kingsdown Cl GILL ME7 84 C1
GVE DA12 32 B6
MAIDW ME16 6 C4
Kings Dr GVE DA12 31 K8
Kingsferry Br RSIT ME9 55 J6
Kingsgate Cl BXLYHN DA7 12 A7
MAIDW ME16 120 E1
STMC/STPC BR5 40 E6
Kingsgate La TENT TN30 203 L8
Kings Hill Av E/WMAL ME19 118 C1
Kingshill Dr HOO/HM ME3 35 M7
Kingsingfield Cl
BGR/WK TN15 77 G2
Kingsingfield Rd BGR/WK TN15 77 G3
Kingsland Gv HDCN TN27 155 M8
Kings La STPH/PW TN12 151 L6
Kingsley Av DART DA1 28 C3
Kingsley Rd MAID/SHEP ME15 7 H6
ORP BR6 73 H1
Kingsley Wk CDH/CHF RM16 17 J3
Kingsmead BH/WHM TN16 91 M2
Kings Mill Cl SIT ME10 71 G8
Kingsnorth Rd RHAM ME8 67 L1
King's Orch ROCH ME1 3 K7
Kingsridge Gdns DART DA1 27 M4
Kings Rd BH/WHM TN16 91 L3
HDCN TN27 155 L8
ORP BR6 56 B7
TON TN9 147 L6
WALD ME5 66 F4
Kings Standing Wy
RTWE/PEM TN2 164 B3
Kings Toll Rd RTWE/PEM TN2 165 J7
Kingston Ct GVW DA11 30 D4
Kingston Crs WALD ME5 83 K1
Kingston Dr MAID/SHEP ME15 121 J5
King St CHAT ME4 4 E5
E/WMAL ME19 100 D5
GILL ME7 5 K3
GVE DA12 31 K4
MAID/BEAR ME14 7 H4
ROCH ME1 3 K9
SIT ME10 71 G8
Kingsway GILL ME7 67 G4
WALD ME5 66 F4
Kingswear Gdns STRD ME2 3 H4
Kingswood Av BELV DA17 12 B3
CHAT ME4 66 B3
SWLY BR8 42 B8
Kingswood Cl DART DA1 27 L4
RTWE/PEM TN2 11 K5
Kingswood Rd GILL ME7 5 L2
ROCH ME1 82 F5
RTWE/PEM TN2 11 K5
SEV TN13 95 G7
King William Rd GILL ME7 50 E6
Kinnings Rw TON TN9 147 L3
Kinross Cl WALD ME5 66 D6
Kipling Av TIL RM18 17 K7
Kipling Dr DIT/AY ME20 101 H1
Kipling Rd BXLYHN DA7 12 A7
DART DA1 28 D3
Kippington Cl SEV TN13 8 D4
Kippington Rd SEV TN13 8 E5
Kirby Cl CRBK TN17 192 F1
Kirby Rd HOO/HM ME3 35 G8
RDART DA2 28 E5
Kirkdale MAID/SHEP ME15 121 H8
Kirkdale Cl WALD ME5 83 M4
Kirkdale Rd MAID/SHEP ME15 121 H7
RTW TN1 11 H3
Kirkins Cl STPH/PW TN12 167 J7
Kitchener Av CHAT ME4 66 B4
GVE DA12 46 E1
Kitchener Rd HOO/HM ME3 50 B1
STRD ME2 2 F1
Kitchenour La RYE TN31 208 A8
Kite La STPH/PW TN12 166 C7
Kit Hill Av WALD ME5 83 G2
Knatts La BGR/WK TN15 77 G5
Knatts Valley Rd EYN DA4 76 E1
Knaves Acre HDCN TN27 155 M8
Knave Wood Rd RSEV TN14 96 A3
Knight Av GILL ME7 5 M1
Knighton Rd RSEV TN14 95 H3
Knightrider Ct
MAID/SHEP ME15 7 G6
Knightrider St
MAID/SHEP ME15 7 G6
Knight Rd STRD ME2 2 E7
TONN TN10 132 A7
Knightsbridge Cl STH/RUST TN4 10 C2
Knights Cl HOO/HM ME3 36 A8
RTWE/PEM TN2 164 F6
Knights Cft HART DA3 61 H6
Knightsfield Rd SIT ME10 70 F7
Knights Manor Wy DART DA1 28 B4
Knights Pk RTWE/PEM TN2 164 B4
Knights Rdg ORP BR6 56 D8
RTWE/PEM TN2 164 F6
Knights Rd HOO/HM ME3 35 M7
Knight's Wy HDCN TN27 155 M8
RTWE/PEM TN2 164 B5
Knockhall Cha GRH DA9 29 L3
Knockhall Rd GRH DA9 29 L4
Knockholt Rd RSEV TN14 74 B8
Knock Mill La BGR/WK TN15 77 J7
Knockwood Rd TENT TN30 196 E4
Knole La BGR/WK TN15 9 J8
Knole Rd DART DA1 27 J5
SEV TN13 9 L3
WALD ME5 83 L3
The Knole MEO DA13 46 A4
Knole Wy BGR/WK TN15 9 J6
Knoll Ri ORP BR6 56 B4
Knoll Rd BXLY DA5 26 C5
SCUP DA14 40 D2
Knott Ct MAID/BEAR ME14 103 J7
Knotts Pl SEV TN13 8 F5
Knowle Av BXLYHN DA7 12 A6
Knowle Cl RRTW TN3 176 A2
Knowle La STPH/PW TN12 166 E1
Knowle Rd MAID/BEAR ME14 103 J7
ROCH ME1 81 L1
STPH/PW TN12 166 F3
Knowles Gdns HDCN TN27 155 M8
Knowlton Gdns
MAIDW ME16 120 D3
Knowsley Wy RTON TN11 130 F7
Koonowla Cl BH/WHM TN16 91 M1
Kyetop Wk RHAM ME8 67 M7
Kynaston Rd STMC/STPC BR5 56 D3

L

Labour-in-vain Rd BGR/WK TN15 77 M7
Laburnum Av DART DA1 27 L6
SWLY BR8 41 M7
Laburnum Dr DIT/AY ME20 101 J3
Laburnum Gv GVW DA11 30 F5
Laburnum Pl SIT ME10 88 A1
Laburnum Rd STRD ME2 2 A7
Lacey Cl RMAID ME17 139 G1
Laceys La RMAID ME17 136 E6
Lacy Cl MAIDW ME16 102 F6
Ladds La SNOD ME6 81 J3
Ladds Wy SWLY BR8 41 M8
Ladham Rd CRBK TN17 182 C3
Ladyclose Av HOO/HM ME3 34 C6
Ladyfields GVW DA11 46 B1
WALD ME5 83 M3
Ladyfields Cl RSIT ME9 70 B8
Lady Oak La CRBK TN17 190 E5
Lady's Gift Rd STH/RUST TN4 163 H5
Ladywood Av STMC/STPC BR5 56 A1
Ladywood Rd RDART DA2 44 A2
STRD ME2 64 D3
Lagonda Wy DART DA1 27 L2
Laird Av CDH/CHF RM16 16 F1
Lake Dr HOO/HM ME3 33 L7
Lakelands MAID/SHEP ME15 121 J6
RMAID ME17 125 G7
Lake Ri WTHK RM20 15 J3
Lake Rd DIT/AY ME20 102 A5
STH/RUST TN4 10 A3
Laker Rd ROCH ME1 65 L7
Lakeside RTWE/PEM TN2 164 A7
SNOD ME6 81 H7
Lakeside Cl EDEN TN8 144 B1
Lakeview Cl SNOD ME6 81 J7
Lake View Rd SEV TN13 8 E2
Lakewood Dr RHAM ME8 67 L7
Lambarde Cl STRD ME2 81 J1
Lambarde Dr SEV TN13 8 E2
Lambarde Rd SEV TN13 8 E1
Lambardes HART DA3 61 H6
Lamb Cl TIL RM18 17 L8
Lamberhurst Cl
STMC/STPC BR5 56 F4
Lamberhurst Gn RHAM ME8 67 K3
Lamberhurst Rd
STPH/PW TN12 180 E4
Lambersart Cl
RTWE/PEM TN2 163 M4
Lambert Cl BH/WHM TN16 91 M2
Lambert Ms SNOD ME6 81 J5
Lamberts Pl STPH/PW TN12 167 K8
Lamberts Rd RTWE/PEM TN2 163 M5
Lambert's Yd TON TN9 147 K4
Lambeth Cl WALD ME5 83 K1
Lambfrith Gv GILL ME7 84 D2
Lambourne Dr E/WMAL ME19 118 B3
Lambourne Pl RHAM ME8 68 C3
Lambourn Wy RTWE/PEM TN2 177 M4
WALD ME5 83 L3
Lambs Bank TON TN9 147 K6
Lambsfrith Gv GILL ME7 84 D2
Lammas Dr SIT ME10 71 G7
Lamorna Av GVE DA12 31 M7
Lamorna Cl ORP BR6 56 C3
Lampington Rw RRTW TN3 176 A2
Lamplighters Cl DART DA1 28 B4
GILL ME7 84 B1
Lancashire Rd
MAID/SHEP ME15 122 A6
Lancaster Ct RHAM ME8 67 L6
Lancaster Wy E/WMAL ME19 118 B2
Lance Cl SIT ME10 71 H5
Lancelot Av STRD ME2 2 A4
Lancelot Cl STRD ME2 2 A5
Lances Cl MEO DA13 62 C3
Lancet La MAID/SHEP ME15 121 H7
Lancing Rd ORP BR6 56 D5
Landale Gdns DART DA1 27 L6
Landau Wy ERITH DA8 13 M4
Lander Rd GRAYS RM17 16 F4
Landor Ct GILL ME7 84 C2
Landrail Rd RSIT ME9 69 K2
Landseer Av GVW DA11 30 F8
Landseer Cl TONN TN10 132 A7
Landway BGR/WK TN15 96 B6
Land Wy HOO/HM ME3 33 M8
The Landway BGR/WK TN15 96 C3
BGR/WK TN15 98 B6
MAID/BEAR ME14 122 C1
STMC/STPC BR5 40 E7
Lane End BXLYHN DA7 26 D1
Lanes Av GVW DA11 31 H8
The Lane RRTW TN3 161 L8
Langafel Cl HART DA3 45 G6
Langdale Cl RHAM ME8 67 M4
Langdale Crs BXLYHN DA7 12 C7
Langdale Ri MAIDW ME16 102 E8
Langdon Shaw SCUP DA14 40 B2
Langham Gv MAIDW ME16 120 E1
Langholm Rd RRTW TN3 176 B2
Langlands Dr RDART DA2 44 A2
Langley Rd SIT ME10 71 H7
Langthorne Crs GRAYS RM17 16 E3
Langton Cl MAID/BEAR ME14 7 L3
Langton Rd RRTW TN3 162 C6
Langton Wy CDH/CHF RM16 17 L3
Langworth Cl RDART DA2 27 M8
Lankester Parker Rd
ROCH ME1 65 L7
Lansbury Crs DART DA1 28 C3
Lansdowne Av
MAID/SHEP ME15 121 L7
Lansdowne Rd CHAT ME4 66 A3
RTW TN1 11 H4
SEV TN13 9 L1
TON TN9 147 K3
TONN TN10 147 K2
Lansdowne Sq GVW DA11 31 H4
RTW TN1 11 H4
Lansdown Rd GVW DA11 31 H6
SIT ME10 88 E1
TIL RM18 17 H8
Lapins La WBY/YAL ME18 118 B3
Lapis Cl GVE DA12 32 D6
Lapwing Cl ERITH DA8 13 K6
Lapwing Dr RSIT ME9 69 K2
Lapwing Rd HOO/HM ME3 25 K8
Lapwings HART DA3 45 K7
Lapworth Cl ORP BR6 56 E5
Larch Cl DIT/AY ME20 101 K3
WARL CR6 90 A5
Larch Crs HOO/HM ME3 51 G2
TONN TN10 131 L7
Larchcroft WALD ME5 83 J1
The Larches HOO/HM ME3 48 E2
Larch Gv STPH/PW TN12 150 B7
Larch Rd DART DA1 27 M6
Larch Wood Cl WALD ME5 83 M4
Larkfield STPH/PW TN12 149 J6
Larkfield Av GILL ME7 67 G1
SIT ME10 71 G7
Larkfield Cl DIT/AY ME20 101 J4
Larkfield Rd DIT/AY ME20 101 J4
SEV TN13 112 E1
Larkfields GVW DA11 31 G8
Larkin Cl STRD ME2 49 K3
Larking Dr MAIDW ME16 102 F6
Larks Fld HART DA3 45 H8
Larkspur Cl E/WMAL ME19 101 J4
ORP BR6 56 E5
Larkspur Rd E/WMAL ME19 101 H4
WALD ME5 83 G1
Larkswood Cl ERITH DA8 13 J7
Larkwell La HART DA3 45 H8
Larner Rd ERITH DA8 13 G6
Laser Quay STRD ME2 3 M5
Latham Cl BH/WHM TN16 91 L2
Latham Rd BXLYHS DA6 26 C3
Latimer Pl GILL ME7 50 E6
Latona Dr GVE DA12 47 H2
Latymers RTON TN11 161 K1
Launder Wy MAID/SHEP ME15 6 C8
Laura Dr SWLY BR8 42 C4
Laura Pl ROCH ME1 65 H3
Laurel Av GVE DA12 31 L7
Laurel Bank STH/RUST TN4 163 K5
Laurel Cl DART DA1 27 L6
Laurel Gv RMAID ME17 139 M3
Laurel Rd GILL ME7 50 E6
RTWE/PEM TN2 163 M6
The Laurels HART DA3 45 L7
MAIDW ME16 120 E3
Laurie Gray Av WALD ME5 82 F4
Lavenda Cl GILL ME7 84 C1
Lavender Cl E/WMAL ME19 101 H5
Lavender Ct SIT ME10 88 C2
Lavender Hl SWLY BR8 41 M7
TON TN9 147 L5
Lavender Rd E/WMAL ME19 101 H5
Lavenders Rd E/WMAL ME19 100 E6
Lavernock Rd BXLYHN DA7 12 C8
Laverstoke Rd MAIDW ME16 102 E5
Lavinia Rd DART DA1 28 B4
Lawford Gdns DART DA1 27 L3
Lawn Cl CHAT ME4 66 D3
SWLY BR8 41 L6
TENT TN30 196 B6
Lawn Pk SEV TN13 113 K5
Lawn Rd GVW DA11 30 E4
TON TN9 147 K5
Lawns Crs GRAYS RM17 16 F5
The Lawns SCUP DA14 40 D1
STPH/PW TN12 166 D5
Lawrence Cl
MAID/SHEP ME15 121 J6
Lawrence Dr GVE DA12 47 J8
Lawrence Gdns TIL RM18 17 K6
Lawrence Hill Gdns DART DA1 27 L4
Lawrence Hill Rd DART DA1 27 L4
Lawrence Rd ERITH DA8 12 D6
TONN TN10 132 A7
Lawrence St GILL ME7 5 J4
Lawson Gdns DART DA1 27 M3
Lawson Rd DART DA1 27 M2
Laxey Rd ORP BR6 73 H1
Laxton Cl MAID/SHEP ME15 122 B2
Laxton Dr RMAID ME17 138 C4
Laxton Gdns STPH/PW TN12 150 A6
Laxton Wy SIT ME10 70 F7
Layfield Rd GILL ME7 51 H6
Laymarsh Cl BELV DA17 12 B2
Leafield La SCUP DA14 41 H1
Leafy Gld RHAM ME8 67 K7
Leafy La MEO DA13 79 J1
Lealands Av RTON TN11 146 C4
Lealands Cl RRTW TN3 175 L6
Leaman Cl HOO/HM ME3 36 A1
Leamington Av ORP BR6 56 A7
Leander Dr GVE DA12 47 H1
Leander Rd ROCH ME1 65 L6
Lea Rd CDH/CHF RM16 17 J4
SEV TN13 113 L5
Leas Gn CHST BR7 40 B3
Leaside SLH/COR SS17 19 J1
The Leas WADH TN5 188 C7
Leatherbottle Gn ERITHM DA18 12 B2
Leather Cl EDEN TN8 142 E5
Lea V DART DA1 26 F2
Lebanon Gdns BH/WHM TN16 91 M3
Leckwith Av ABYW SE2 12 A5
Leconfield Cl TON TN9 147 H6
Ledgers Rd WARL CR6 90 D5
Leechcroft Av SWLY BR8 42 B7
Leeds Cl ORP BR6 56 F5
Leeds Rd RMAID ME17 139 G2
Leeds Sq RHAM ME8 67 K2
Lee Gn STMC/STPC BR5 56 C1
Lee Green Rd HOO/HM ME3 49 M1
Lee Rd SNOD ME6 81 J5
Leesons Hl CHST BR7 40 A7
Leesons Wy STMC/STPC BR5 40 B6
Lees Rd WBY/YAL ME18 135 G6
Leet Cl GILL ME7 51 G7
Leeward Rd ROCH ME1 65 L4
Leewood Pl SWLY BR8 41 M8
Legge La E/WMAL ME19 80 F6
Leggs' La RRTW TN3 162 A8
Leicester Dr RTWE/PEM TN2 177 H5
Leicester Rd MAID/SHEP ME15 121 M6
TIL RM18 17 H7
Leigh Av MAID/SHEP ME15 121 K7
Leigh Rd GVW DA11 31 K7
HOO/HM ME3 49 L2
RTON TN11 146 F3
Leighton Cl STH/RUST TN4 163 J6
Leighton Gdns TIL RM18 17 J6
Leith Hl STMC/STPC BR5 40 C5
Leith Park Rd GVW DA11 31 K6
Lendon Rd BGR/WK TN15 98 B7
Leneda Dr RTWE/PEM TN2 177 G5
Leney Rd WBY/YAL ME18 119 G6
Lenfield Av MAID/BEAR ME14 7 K4
Lenham Heath Rd RMAID ME17 141 K2
Lenham Rd BXLYHN DA7 12 B5
HDCN TN27 156 C5
RMAID ME17 140 B3
Lenmore Av GRAYS RM17 16 E2
Lennard Rd SEV TN13 95 G6
Lennox Av GVW DA11 31 J4
Lennox Rd GVW DA11 31 H4
Lennox Rd East GVW DA11 31 J5
Lenor Cl BXLYHS DA6 26 A2
Lenside Dr MAID/SHEP ME15 122 C3
Lenthall Av GRAYS RM17 16 C1
Leonard Av RSEV TN14 95 K1
SWCM DA10 30 A5
Leonard Cl MAIDW ME16 102 D7
Leonard Rd CHAT ME4 5 H8
Leopold Rd CHAT ME4 4 E8
Lesley Cl BXLY DA5 26 D5
MEO DA13 46 B5
SWLY BR8 41 M7
Lesley Pl MAIDW ME16 6 D3
Leslie Crs TENT TN30 196 D3
Leslie Rd GILL ME7 50 F6
Lesney Pk ERITH DA8 12 F5
Lesney Park Rd ERITH DA8 12 F5
Lessness Pk BELV DA17 12 B4
Lested La RMAID ME17 138 D3
Lester Rd CHAT ME4 4 F7
Letchworth Av CHAT ME4 66 B4
Le Temple Rd STPH/PW TN12 150 D6
Letter Box La SEV TN13 113 L7
Lever Sq CDH/CHF RM16 17 J3
Leveson Rd CDH/CHF RM16 17 K2
Levett Cl HOO/HM ME3 25 K7
Levetts La RBTBR TN32 204 F4
Lewd La HDCN TN27 173 J1
Lewes Cl GRAYS RM17 16 C5
Lewing Cl ORP BR6 56 A4
Lewin Rd BXLYHS DA6 26 A2
Lewis Av RHAM ME8 67 K3
Lewis Court Dr RMAID ME17 137 K2
Lewis Rd MEO DA13 46 B5
SWCM DA10 30 A4
Leybank RTON TN11 147 G1
Leybourne Cl WALD ME5 83 J3
Leybourne Dell CRBK TN17 194 A7
Leybourne Rd STRD ME2 2 B2
Leybourne Wy DIT/AY ME20 101 H1
Leycroft Gdns ERITH DA8 13 K7
Leydenhatch La SWLY BR8 41 M5
Leyhill Cl SWLY BR8 58 A1
Leysdown Av BXLYHN DA7 26 E2
Leyton Av GILL ME7 67 G4
Leyton Cross Rd RDART DA2 27 H8
Leywood Rd MEO DA13 79 M2
Lezayre Rd ORP BR6 73 H1
Lidsing Rd GILL ME7 84 B3
MAID/BEAR ME14 103 L1
Lidwells La CRBK TN17 181 L4
Liege Cl SIT ME10 71 H4
Lilac Crs STRD ME2 2 A6
Lilac Gdns SWLY BR8 41 M7
Lilac Gn E/WMAL ME19 101 J5
Lilac Pl MEO DA13 62 D3
Lilac Rd STRD ME2 2 A7
Lila Pl SWLY BR8 42 A8
Lillechurch Rd HOO/HM ME3 34 B6
Lillieburn E/WMAL ME19 100 F3
Lillie Rd BH/WHM TN16 91 M4
Lime Av GVW DA11 30 F5
Lime Cl STPH/PW TN12 152 E7
Lime Ct RHAM ME8 84 E2
Lime Crs E/WMAL ME19 101 J6
Lime Gv SIT ME10 88 C1
WARL CR6 90 A5
Lime Hill Rd RTW TN1 10 F4
Lime Pit La RSEV TN14 94 E3
Lime Rd SWLY BR8 41 M7
Limes Cl TENT TN30 196 E6
Limes Gv HAWK TN18 192 B8
The Limes EDEN TN8 142 E4
PUR RM19 14 C4
Lime Tree Av GRH DA9 29 J6
Lime Tree Cl TON TN9 147 L3
Limetree Cl WALD ME5 66 D6

Lime Trees *STPH/PW* TN12 ...... 170 A1
Lime Tree Wk *SEV* TN13 .... 9 H7
Limewood Rd *ERITH* DA8 .... 12 E6
Limpsfield Rd *WARL* CR6 .... 90 C5
Linclon Cl *ERITH* DA8 .... 13 H8
Lincoln Green Rd
 STMC/STPC BR5 .... 56 B1
Lincoln Rd *ERITH* DA8 .... 13 H8
 MAID ME15 .... 121 L5
 SCUP DA14 .... 40 D2
Lincon Rd *GILL* ME7 .... 50 F6
Linden Av *DART* DA1 .... 27 L6
Linden Cha *SEV* TN13 .... 9 G1
Linden Cl *ORP* BR6 .... 56 C8
 PUR RM19 .... 14 E5
 RTWE/PEM TN2 .... 10 D8
 SIT ME10 .... 87 M2
 STPH/PW TN12 .... 150 C7
Linden Gdns *RTWE/PEM* TN2 .. 10 D9
Linden Gv *WARL* CR6 .... 90 A4
Linden Park Rd *RTWE/PEM* TN2 .. 10 D9
Linden Rd *GILL* ME7 .... 51 G8
 RMAID ME17 .... 136 E1
Linden Sq *SEV* TN13 .... 95 G8
The Lindens *DIT/AY* ME20 .... 102 A3
Lindisfarne Cl *GVE* DA12 .... 32 A7
Lindridge La *STPH/PW* TN12 .. 153 L8
Lineacre Cl *RHAM* ME8 .... 67 M7
Lines Ter *CHAT* ME4 .... 4 E5
Linford Rd *CDH/CHF* RM16 ...... 17 L4
Lingfield Av *RDART* DA2 .... 28 D5
Lingfield Rd *BGR/WK* TN15 ...... 98 C6
 EDEN TN8 .... 31 K7
 GVE DA12 .... 142 C5
Lingley Dr *STRD* ME2 .... 49 L1
Ling Rd *ERITH* DA8 .... 12 E5
Link Hill La *HDCN* TN27 .... 157 L3
The Links *E/WMAL* ME19 .... 100 A3
 WALD ME5 .... 66 D5
Links Vw *DART* DA1 .... 27 L6
Linkway *DIT/AY* ME20 .... 101 L4
 RSIT ME9 .... 70 F1
Link Wy *RTWE/PEM* TN2 .... 164 A5
Linley Cl *TIL* RM18 .... 18 F6
Linnet Av *STPH/PW* TN12 .... 150 C8
Linnet Wy *PUR* RM19 .... 14 D4
Linslade Rd *ORP* BR6 .... 73 J1
Linton Dann *HOO/HM* ME3 ...... 35 M7
Linton Gore *RMAID* ME17 .... 136 E2
Linton HI *RMAID* ME17 .... 137 C5
Linton Rd *MAID/SHEP* ME15 .... 137 H2
Linwood Av *STRD* ME2 .... 2 H2
Lionel Rd *TON* TN9 .... 147 J5
Lion Rd *BXLYHS* DA6 .... 26 A2
Liphook Wy *MAIDW* ME16 .... 102 E5
Lipscombe Rd
 RTWE/PEM TN2 .... 163 M7
Liptraps La *RTWE/PEM* TN2 .... 163 M6
Lipwell HI *HOO/HM* ME3 .... 35 K1
Lisle Cl *GVE* DA12 .... 32 D7
Lisle Pl *GRAYS* RM17 .... 16 C2
Lismore Rd *MAID/SHEP* ME15 .. 121 J6
Lister Cl *E/WMAL* ME19 .... 101 H5
Lister Rd *TIL* RM18 .... 17 J8
Listmas Rd *CHAT* ME4 .... 5 G8
Little Aly *EDEN* TN8 .... 142 D8
Little Boundes Cl
 STH/RUST TN4 .... 163 G2
Littlebourne Av *RHAM* ME8 ...... 67 K1
Littlebourne Rd
 MAID/BEAR ME14 .... 103 L7
Littlebrook Manor Wy *DART* DA1 .. 28 C3
Little Browns La *EDEN* TN8 .... 142 A1
Little Buckland Av *MAIDW* ME16 .. 6 B1
Littlecourt Rd *SEV* TN13 .... 8 E4
Littlecroft *MEO* DA13 .... 46 A4
Littlefield Rd *RHAM* ME8 .... 68 D3
Little Footway *RRTW* TN3 .... 176 B2
Little Glovers *SIT* ME10 .... 88 B2
Little Heath Rd *BXLYHN* DA7 .... 12 B7
Little John Av *WALD* ME5 .... 83 H3
Littlejohn Rd *STMC/STPC* BR5 .. 56 C2
Little Julians Wd *TIL* RM18 ...... 113 J5
Little Mallett *RRTW* TN3 .... 176 B2
Little Market Rw
 E/WMAL ME19 .... 101 C3
Little Mount Sion *RTW* TN1...... 10 F7
Little Oakham Ct
 HOO/HM ME3 .... 37 L1
Little Orch *RMAID* ME17 .... 136 F2
Little Oxley *DIT/AY* ME20 .... 101 C3
Little Pk *WADH* TN5 .... 188 A8
Little Queen St *DART* DA1 ...... 28 B5
Little Robhurst *RASHW* TN26 .. 187 M6
Little Wd *SEV* TN13 .... 95 L8
Little Wood Cl
 STMC/STPC BR5 .... 40 C5
Livesey St *WBY/YAL* ME18 ...... 119 H3
Livingstone Gdns *GVE* DA12 .... 46 F2
Livingstone Rd *GILL* ME7 .... 51 G8
 GVE DA12 .... 46 F2
Lloyds Gn *TENT* TN30 .... 208 F1
Loampits La *TON* TN9 .... 147 M2
Lobelia Cl *GILL* ME7 .... 51 G7
Locarno Av *RHAM* ME8 .... 67 J3
Lochat Rd *HOO/HM* ME3 .... 35 C7
Lochmere Cl *ERITH* DA8 .... 12 D5
Lockesley Dr *STMC/STPC* BR5 .. 56 A2
Lockington Gv *ROCH* ME1 ...... 3 J8
Lockington Gv *ROCH* ME1 .... 3 J8
Lockside *TON* TN9 .... 147 L3
Locksley Cl *WALD* ME5 .... 83 C3
Lock St *GILL* ME7 .... 5 J3
Lockswood *MAIDW* ME16 .... 102 F6
Lockyer Rd *PUR* RM19 .... 14 E4
Lockyers HI *MEO* DA13 .... 63 C8
Loddington La *RMAID* ME17 .... 137 J6
Loder Cl *RMAID* ME17 .... 125 K8
Lodge Av *DART* DA1 .... 27 L4
Lodge Cl *ORP* BR6 .... 56 D4
 WBY/YAL ME18 .... 118 F5
Lodge Ct *GVE* DA12 .... 48 A3
Lodge Crs *ORP* BR6 .... 56 D4
Lodge Gdns *RMAID* ME17 .... 140 B2
Lodge Hill La *HOO/HM* ME3 .... 35 M7
Lodge La *BH/WHM* TN16 .... 110 E5
 CDH/CHF RM16 .... 16 C1
 GRAYS RM17 .... 16 E2
 GVE DA12 .... 47 K8

Lodge Oak La *TON* TN9 .... 147 M5
Lodge Rd *MAID/BEAR* ME14 .... 103 M8
 STPH/PW TN12 .... 154 A8
 TON TN9 .... 147 K3
Loewen Rd *CDH/CHF* RM16 ...... 17 J2
Lomas La *HAWK* TN18 .... 201 J8
Lomas Rd *SIT* ME10 .... 88 F1
Lombard St *EYN* DA4 .... 43 L8
Lombardy Cl *GILL* ME7 .... 67 J7
Lombardy Dr *MAID/BEAR* ME14 .. 7 M4
London La *CRBK* TN17 .... 184 C3
London Rd *BGR/WK* TN15 .... 77 K4
 BH/WHM TN16 .... 110 F3
 DART DA1 .... 26 F3
 DIT/AY ME20 .... 101 K4
 E/WMAL ME19 .... 99 L4
 EYN DA4 .... 58 F2
 GRAYS RM17 .... 29 C4
 GRH DA9 .... 30 F4
 GVW DA11 .... 30 D8
 MAIDW ME16 .... 6 B3
 RDART DA2 .... 28 E5
 RHAM ME8 .... 68 C5
 RSEV TN14 .... 74 B3
 RSIT ME9 .... 69 H6
 RTON TN11 .... 147 J2
 SEV TN13 .... 8 D5
 SIT ME10 .... 70 C8
 SOCK/AV RM15 .... 14 C1
 STH/RUST TN4 .... 10 E7
 STRD ME2 .... 2 E3
 SWCM DA10 .... 30 A3
 SWLY BR8 .... 41 L6
 SWLY BR8 .... 42 A7
 TIL RM18 .... 17 K8
 TONN TN12 .... 147 K2
 WTHK RM20 .... 15 M5
London Road Purfleet
 PUR RM19 .... 14 D5
London Road Rocky HI
 MAIDW ME16 .... 6 D5
London Road West Thurrock
 WTHK RM20 .... 15 H5
Lonewood Wy *RTON* TN11 ...... 133 H3
Long Acre *STMC/STPC* BR5 ...... 56 F5
Long Barn Rd *RSEV* TN14 .... 129 K3
Longbury Cl *STMC/STPC* BR5 .. 40 D7
Longbury Dr *STMC/STPC* BR5.. 40 D7
Long Catlis Rd *RHAM* ME8........ 84 F1
Long Ct *PUR* RM19 .... 14 C3
Longfellow Rd *GILL* ME7 .... 5 J8
Longfield Av *HART* DA3 .... 45 L6
 HOO/HM ME3 .... 36 A1
Longfield Pl *MAID/SHEP* ME15 .. 121 K5
Longfield Rd *MEO* DA13 .... 62 A1
 RTWE/PEM TN2 .... 164 A5
Longfields Dr
 MAID/BEAR ME14 .... 104 C3
Longford Cl *RHAM* ME8 .... 68 C5
Longham Copse
 MAID/SHEP ME15 .... 122 B6
Long HI *CTHM* CR3 .... 90 A7
Longhill Av *GILL* ME7 .... 5 G7
Longhouse Rd *CDH/CHF* RM16.. 17 K2
Longhurst Dr *WALD* ME5 .... 83 H3
Long La *BXLYHN* DA7 .... 12 B8
 CDH/CHF RM16 .... 16 D1
 RMAID ME17 .... 137 M8
Longley Rd *RHAM* ME8 .... 68 B4
 ROCH ME1 .... 65 L2
Longmarsh Vw *EYN* DA4 .... 43 K5
Longmeadow *SEV* TN13 .... 94 F7
Long Meads *RRTW* TN3 .... 176 D2
Long Mead Wy *TONN* TN10 .... 131 K8
Longparish Cl
 MAID/SHEP ME15 .... 122 B2
Longreach Rd *ERITH* DA8 .... 13 K6
Long Rede La *MAIDW* ME16 .... 120 B2
Longridge *SIT* ME10 .... 88 D3
Longshaw Rd
 MAID/SHEP ME15 .... 138 B1
Long Slip *RRTW* TN3 .... 176 C2
Longview Wy *RTWE/PEM* TN2 .. 163 M5
Longwalk *MEO* DA13 .... 46 A5
Longwood *WALD* ME5 .... 83 K4
Lonsdale Crs *RDART* DA2 .... 28 E7
Lonsdale Dr *RHAM* ME8 .... 68 A7
 SIT ME10 .... 70 E8
Lonsdale Gdns *RTW* TN1 .... 10 F5
Lonsdale Rd *BXLYHN* DA7 ...... 12 B8
Loose Rd *MAID/SHEP* ME15 .... 7 J9
Lord Chatham's Ride *RSEV* TN14.. 93 L3
Lords Cl *RSIT* ME9 .... 89 C3
Lord St *GVE* DA12 .... 31 K5
Lordswood Cl *RDART* DA2 ...... 44 A1
Lords Wood Cl *WALD* ME5 ...... 83 K3
Lords Wood La *WALD* ME5 ...... 66 D8
Lorton Cl *GVE* DA12 .... 32 A7
Lossenham La *HAWK* TN18 .... 206 F1
Lotus Rd *BH/WHM* TN16 .... 92 B4
Louisville Av *GILL* ME7 .... 5 M6
Louvain Rd *RDART* DA2 .... 29 C5
Lovelace Cl *BGR/WK* TN15 ...... 77 C1
 RHAM ME8 .... 67 M8
Love La *BXLY* DA5 .... 26 C4
 HDCN TN27 .... 156 C8
 ROCH ME1 .... 3 J7
 SOCK/AV RM15 .... 14 E1
 TIL RM18 .... 18 E5
 WBY/YAL ME18 .... 118 F6
Lovers La *CRBK* TN17 .... 182 A4
 GRH DA9 .... 29 M2
Low Cl *GRH* DA9 .... 29 J3
Lower Bell La *DIT/AY* ME20 .... 101 K3
Lower Bloors La *RHAM* ME8 .... 68 A3
Lower Boxley Rd
 MAID/BEAR ME14 .... 6 F2
Lower Crs *SLH/COR* SS17 .... 18 C2
Lower Cft *SWLY* BR8 .... 42 B8
Lower Fant Rd *MAIDW* ME16 .... 6 E7
Lower Farm Rd *RMAID* ME17 .. 137 K7
Lower Gn *RTON* TN11 .... 146 B4
Lower Green Rd *RRTW* TN3 .... 162 E8
 RTWE/PEM TN2 .... 164 F7
 STH/RUST TN4 .... 176 E1
Lower Hartlip Rd *RSIT* ME9 .... 85 M1
Lower Haysden La *TON* TN9 .... 146 F5
Lower Higham Rd *GVE* DA12 .. 32 B6

Lower Park Rd *BELV* DA17 .... 12 C2
Lower Rainham Rd *GILL* ME7 .... 51 L6
 RHAM ME8 .... 68 D2
Lower Range Rd *GVE* DA12 ...... 32 A5
Lower Rd *BELV* DA17 .... 12 C2
 ERITH DA8 .... 12 F3
 GVE DA12 .... 33 G7
 GVW DA11 .... 30 C2
 MAID/SHEP ME15 .... 7 J8
 RMAID ME17 .... 139 G6
 RSIT ME9 .... 89 H2
 STMC/STPC BR5 .... 56 D7
 SWLY BR8 .... 42 D4
 TIL RM18 .... 31 J7
Lower Rochester Rd
 HOO/HM ME3 .... 33 M7
Lower Station Rd *DART* DA1 .... 27 G4
Lower Stone St *MAID/SHEP* ME15.. 7 G5
Lower St *RMAID* ME17 .... 123 J6
 RTON TN11 .... 130 C8
Lower Tovil *MAID/SHEP* ME15 .. 6 C9
Lower Twydall La *GILL* ME7 .... 67 L1
 RHAM ME8 .... 67 K1
Lower Warren Rd *WALD* ME5 .... 83 G7
Lower Woodlands Rd *GILL* ME7.. 51 H7
Lowfield St *DART* DA1 .... 28 A5
Low Meadow *STRD* ME2 .... 64 C8
Low Street La *TIL* RM18 .... 18 B4
Loxwood Cl *STMC/STPC* BR5 .. 56 F5
Lubbock Cl
 MAID/SHEP ME15 .... 122 A8
Lucas Rd *GRAYS* RM17 .... 16 C2
 SNOD ME6 .... 81 G6
Lucerne Rd *ORP* BR6 .... 56 B4
Lucerne St *MAID/BEAR* ME14 .. 7 H3
Lucilina Dr *EDEN* TN8 .... 142 E5
Lucknow Rd *STPH/PW* TN12 .... 150 D7
Lucks HI *E/WMAL* ME19 .... 100 F5
Lucks La *RMAID* ME17 .... 138 B7
 STPH/PW TN12 .... 150 C4
Lucks Wy *STPH/PW* TN12 .... 152 D7
Luddenham Cl *MAID/BEAR* ME14.. 7 M1
Luddesdon Rd *ERITH* DA8 .... 12 C6
Luddesdown Rd *MEO* DA13 .... 63 J4
Ludlow Pl *GRAYS* RM17 .... 16 D2
Lughorse La *WBY/YAL* ME18 .... 135 J3
Luilarook Cl *RHAM* ME8 .... 91 L2
Lullingstone Av *SWLY* BR8 ...... 42 B7
Lullingstone Cl *GILL* ME7 .... 68 A2
 STMC/STPC BR5 .... 40 D4
Lullingstone Crs
 STMC/STPC BR5 .... 40 C4
Lullingstone La *EYN* DA4 .... 58 E6
Lullingstone Rd *BELV* DA17 .... 12 B5
 MAIDW ME16 .... 102 E6
Lumley Cl *BELV* DA17 .... 12 C5
Lumsden Ter *CHAT* ME4 .... 4 B6
Lunar Cl *BH/WHM* TN16.......... 91 M2
Lunedale Rd *RDART* DA2 .... 28 E6
Lunghurst Rd *CTHM* CR3 .... 90 C7
Lunsford La *DIT/AY* ME20 .... 81 H8
 DIT/AY ME20 .... 101 H3
Lurkins Ri *CRBK* TN17 .... 181 M6
Lushington Rd
 MAID/BEAR ME14 .... 103 G6
Lusted Hall La *BH/WHM* TN16 .. 91 L6
Luton High St *WALD* ME5 .... 66 E3
Luton Rd *CHAT* ME4 .... 5 G7
Luxon Rd *ORP* BR6 .... 72 C6
Luxted Rd *ORP* BR6 .... 84 F1
Lyall Wy *RHAM* ME8 .... 67 M8
Lychfield Dr *STRD* ME2 .... 2 F1
Lych Gate Rd *ORP* BR6............ 56 C4
Lydbrook Cl *SIT* ME10 .... 87 L1
Lydd Rd *BXLYHN* DA7 .... 12 B6
 WALD ME5 .... 66 D8
Lydens La *EDEN* TN8 .... 143 H7
Lydia Rd *ERITH* DA8 .... 13 H5
Lyle Cl *STRD* ME2 .... 3 G1
Lyle Ct *MAIDW* ME16 .... 120 E1
Lyle Pk *SEV* TN13.................. 9 H2
 SCUP DA14 .... 40 B1
Lymington Ct
 MAID/SHEP ME15 .... 138 B1
Lynden Wy *SWLY* BR8 .... 41 L7
Lyndhurst Av *RHAM* ME8 .... 67 L6
Lyndhurst Cl *BXLYHN* DA7 .... 26 D1
Lyndhurst Dr *SEV* TN13 .... 8 B4
Lyndhurst Gv *SIT* ME10 .... 88 A3
Lyndhurst Rd *BXLYHN* DA7 .... 26 D1
 MAID/SHEP ME15 .... 121 L5
Lyndhurst Wy *MEO* DA13 .... 46 A5
Lyndon Rd *BELV* DA17 .... 12 C3
Lynette Av *STRD* ME2 .... 49 J4
Lyngs *WBY/YAL* ME18 .... 135 H5
Lynmead Cl *EDEN* TN8 .... 142 D1
Lynmouth Ri *STMC/STPC* BR5 .. 40 D8
Lynne Cl *ORP* BR6 .... 73 H1
Lynors Av *STRD* ME2 .... 49 J3
Lynsted Cl *BXLYHS* DA6 .... 26 D1
Lynsted La *RSIT* ME9 .... 89 K6
Lynsted Rd *RHAM* ME8 .... 68 A7
Lynton Av *STMC/STPC* BR5 ...... 40 D8
Lynton Dr *WALD* ME5 .... 83 K2
Lynton Rd *GVW* DA11 .... 31 J6
Lynton Rd South *GVW* DA11 .... 31 J6
Lyons Crs *TON* TN9 .... 147 L3
Lysander Rd *E/WMAL* ME19 .... 118 B2
Lytton Rd *CDH/CHF* RM16 ...... 17 J7

M

Mabel Rd *SWLY* BR8 .... 42 C3
Mabledon Rd *TON* TN9 .... 147 J5
Macaulay Cl *DIT/AY* ME20 .... 101 J1
Macdonald Rd *GILL* ME7 .... 5 L1
Mace La *RSEV* TN14 .... 72 F7
Mackenders Cl *DIT/AY* ME20 .... 82 B7
Mackenders La *DIT/AY* ME20 .... 82 C7
Mackenzie Wy *GVE* DA12 .... 46 F3
Mackerel HI *RYE* TN31 .... 208 B8
Macklands Wy *RHAM* ME8 ...... 68 C3
Macleod Cl *GRAYS* RM17 ...... 16 F3
Madan Rd *BH/WHM* TN16 ...... 110 F3
Madden Av *WALD* ME5 .... 66 A8

Madden Cl *SWCM* DA10 .... 30 A4
Maddocks Cl *SCUP* DA14 .... 40 F3
Madeira Pk *RTW* TN1 .... 10 F7
Madginford Cl
 MAID/SHEP ME15 .... 122 C1
Madginford Rd
 MAID/SHEP ME15 .... 122 B3
Madison Wy *SEV* TN13 .... 8 D2
Maesmaur Rd *BH/WHM* ME7 .. 91 M7
Mafeking Rd *WALD* ME5 .... 83 H2
Magdalen Cl *GILL* ME7 .... 84 C1
Magdelan Gv *ORP* BR6 .... 56 D7
Magnet Rd *WTHK* RM20 .... 15 L5
Magnolia Av *RHAM* ME8 .... 67 K8
Magnolia Dr *BH/WHM* TN16 .... 91 M2
Magpie Cl *DIT/AY* ME20 .... 101 J4
Magpie Hall Rd *CHAT* ME4 ...... 66 B5
Magpie La *MAID/BEAR* ME14 .. 85 H4
Magwitch Cl *ROCH* ME1 .... 65 K1
Maida Rd *BELV* DA17 .... 12 C2
Maida Vale Rd *DART* DA1 .... 27 G4
Maiden Erlegh Av *BXLYHS* DA6.. 26 A6
Maiden La *DART* DA1 .... 27 J1
Maidstone Rd *BGR/WK* TN15 .. 96 D3
 CHAT ME4 .... 4 C6
 GILL ME7 .... 84 D5
 GRAYS RM17 .... 16 C5
 HDCN TN27 .... 155 J4
 RHAM ME8 .... 84 E2
 RMAID ME17 .... 139 C3
 ROCH ME1 .... 65 L5
 RSIT ME9 .... 86 F2
 RTON TN11 .... 133 C5
 RTWE/PEM TN2 .... 164 E5
 SCUP DA14 .... 40 F3
 SEV TN13 .... 8 B1
 SIT ME10 .... 70 C7
 STPH/PW TN12 .... 134 C5
 SWLY BR8 .... 41 K5
 WBY/YAL ME18 .... 134 D3
The Mailyns *RHAM* ME8 .... 67 L6
Main Gate Rd *CHAT* ME4 .... 50 B6
Main Rd *BH/WHM* TN16 .... 91 M2
 EDEN TN8 .... 126 E4
 EYN DA4 .... 43 K3
 EYN DA4 .... 59 C2
 HART DA3 .... 45 C6
 HOO/HM ME3 .... 35 K8
 HOO/HM ME3 .... 36 F6
 HOO/HM ME3 .... 50 B1
 RDART DA2 .... 93 J4
 RSEV TN14 .... 94 E5
 RSEV TN14 .... 112 A2
 STMC/STPC BR5 .... 40 E7
 SWLY BR8 .... 42 B5
 SWLY BR8 .... 57 L2
Main Road Gorse HI *EYN* DA4.. 59 K4
Main St *RYE* TN31 .... 206 D3
Major York's Rd *STH/RUST* TN4 .. 10 B6
Malan Cl *BH/WHM* TN16 .... 92 A3
Malden Dr *MAID/BEAR* ME14 .. 103 H5
Mallard Cl *DART* DA1 .... 28 B3
Mallards Wy *MAID/SHEP* ME15.. 122 C4
Mallard Wy *HOO/HM* ME3 ...... 37 K1
Mallingdene Cl *HOO/HM* ME3 .. 34 D5
Malling Rd *DIT/AY* ME20 .... 81 C8
 SNOD ME6 .... 81 J6
 WBY/YAL ME18 .... 118 A4
Mallings Dr *MAID/BEAR* ME14 .. 122 E1
Mallings La *MAID/BEAR* ME14 .. 122 E1
Malling Ter *MAIDW* ME16.......... 120 E1
Mallow Cl *GVW* DA11 .... 46 A1
Mallow Ct *GRAYS* RM17 .... 16 F5
The Mallows *MAID/BEAR* ME14.. 103 G6
Mallys Pl *EYN* DA4 .... 43 L5
Malmaynes Hall Rd
 HOO/HM ME3 .... 36 E2
Malpas Rd *CDH/CHF* RM16 .... 17 L2
Malta Av *WALD* ME5 .... 66 C6
Malta Rd *TIL* RM18 .... 17 H8
Maltby Cl *ORP* BR6 .... 56 C4
Malthouse Cl *RMAID* ME17 .... 125 M8
Malthouse HI
 MAID/SHEP ME15 .... 137 H1
Malthouse La *GVE* DA12 .... 48 A2
Malt House La *TENT* TN30 ...... 208 E3
Malthouse Rd *BGR/WK* TN15 .. 78 B3
Maltings Cl *RTON* TN11 .... 133 C5
The Maltings
 MAID/BEAR ME14 .... 104 A8
 ORP BR6 .... 56 B4
 RHAM ME8 .... 68 C5
 RMAID ME17 .... 137 K1
Malton Wy *RTWE/PEM* TN2 .... 164 B7
Malus Cl *WALD* ME5 .... 83 J4
Malvern Av *BXLYHN* DA7 .... 12 A6
Malvern Rd *GILL* ME7 .... 17 C3
 GRAYS RM17 .... 16 D2
 ORP BR6 .... 56 D7
Malvina Av *GVE* DA12 .... 31 K7
Malyons Rd *SWLY* BR8 .... 42 B4
Mamignot Cl
 MAID/BEAR ME14 .... 104 B8
Manchester Cl *WALD* ME5 ...... 66 E7
Mangravet Av
 MAID/SHEP ME15 .... 121 L6
Manning Rd *STMC/STPC* BR5 .. 56 F1
Mannock Rd *DART* DA1 .... 28 B1
Mann Sq *TON* TN9 .... 147 M6
Manor Cl *DART* DA1 .... 26 F2
 GVE DA12 .... 32 D7
 MAID/BEAR ME14 .... 122 D2
 OBOR ME11 .... 55 H2
 RDART DA2 .... 27 J8
 STH/RUST TN4 .... 10 B4
 WARL CR6 .... 90 A3
Manor Ct *MAID/BEAR* ME14 .... 122 D2
 MEO DA13 .... 62 F1
Manor Dr *HART* DA3 .... 61 J2
Manor Fld *GVE* DA12 .... 48 A2
Manorfields Cl *CHST* BR7 .... 61 H6
Manor Forstal *HART* DA3 .... 61 H6
Manor Gdns *WALD* ME5 .... 83 H1
Manor Gv *SIT* ME10 .... 147 L2
Manor House Dr *MAIDW* ME16.. 6 A4
Manor House Gdns *EDEN* TN8 .. 142 H4
Manor La *HART* DA3 .... 60 E3

 HART DA3 .... 61 J2
 ROCH ME1 .... 65 H2
Manor Pk *STH/RUST* TN4.......... 10 B5
Manor Ri *MAID/BEAR* ME14 .... 122 E1
Manor Rd *BH/WHM* TN16 .... 92 A6
 BXLY DA5 .... 26 C6
 CHAT ME4 .... 4 C5
 DART DA1 .... 27 G2
 EDEN TN8 .... 142 D4
 ERITH DA8 .... 13 H5
 GRAYS RM17 .... 16 E5
 GVE DA12 .... 31 K4
 HART DA3 .... 61 L1
 MEO DA13 .... 62 E1
 QBOR ME11 .... 55 H2
 RSEV TN14 .... 111 M2
 STH/RUST TN4 .... 163 G4
 SWCM DA10 .... 29 M4
 TIL RM18 .... 17 J8
 WTHK RM20 .... 15 L5
Manor St *GILL* ME7 .... 5 H4
Manor Wy *BXLY* DA5 .... 26 C6
 BXLYHN DA7 .... 26 E6
 GRAYS RM17 .... 16 E6
 GVW DA11 .... 30 A2
 SWCM DA10 .... 30 A2
Mansel Dr *ROCH* ME1 .... 65 J1
Manse Wy *SWLY* BR8 .... 42 C8
Mansfield Cl *STMC/STPC* BR5 .. 56 F4
Mansfield Rd *SWLY* BR8.......... 42 A3
Mansion House Cl *HDCN* TN27 .. 186 B3
Mansion Rw *GILL* ME7 .... 4 F1
The Manwarings
 STPH/PW TN12 .... 167 J7
Manwood Cl *SIT* ME10 .... 88 B3
Maple Av *GILL* ME7 .... 51 C8
 MAIDW ME16 .... 102 E7
Maple Cl *DIT/AY* ME20 .... 101 J3
 RTWE/PEM TN2 .... 10 E9
 SWLY BR8 .... 42 A6
Maple Rd *DART* DA1 .... 27 L6
 GRAYS RM17 .... 16 E1
 GVE DA12 .... 46 E1
 HOO/HM ME3 .... 51 G2
 STRD ME2 .... 2 C5
Maplescombe La *EYN* DA4 ...... 59 J6
Maplesden Cl *MAIDW* ME16 .... 120 B2
The Maples *HART* DA3 .... 45 K7
Mapleton Rd *BH/WHM* TN16 .. 111 C8
 EDEN TN8 .... 127 J5
Maplins Cl *RHAM* ME8 .... 68 B4
Marathon Paddock *GILL* ME7 .. 5 M5
Marcellina Wy *ORP* BR6 .... 56 A6
Marcet Rd *DART* DA1 .... 27 L3
Marconi Rd *GVW* DA11 .... 30 F8
Marcus Rd *DART* DA1 .... 27 J5
Mardale Cl *RHAM* ME8 .... 68 C4
Marden Crs *BXLY* DA5 .... 26 E5
Marden Rd *STPH/PW* TN12 .... 153 J8
 STRD ME2 .... 49 L4
Margate Cl *GILL* ME7 .... 51 G7
Margetts La *ROCH* ME1 .... 81 M4
Margetts Pl *STRD* ME2 .... 50 C2
Marian Sq *STPH/PW* TN12 ...... 170 B1
Marina Dr *DART* DA1 .... 28 C6
 GVW DA11 .... 31 H5
Marine Ct *PUR* RM19 .... 14 B3
Marine Dr *HOO/HM* ME3.......... 51 G2
Marine Vw *CHAT* ME4 .... 50 D4
Marion Cl *WALD* ME5 .... 83 J3
Marion Crs *MAID/SHEP* ME15 .. 121 K4
 STMC/STPC BR5 .... 56 D1
Marisco Cl *CDH/CHF* RM16 .... 17 K3
Maritime Cl *GRH* DA9 .... 29 K3
 STRD ME2 .... 3 M1
Maritime Wy *CHAT* ME4 .... 50 C5
Mark Cl *BXLYHN* DA7 .... 12 A7
Market Buildings
 MAID/BEAR ME14 .... 6 F4
Market Meadow
 STMC/STPC BR5 .... 40 E8
Market Pl *BXLYHS* DA6 .... 26 C2
 DART DA1 .... 28 A5
Market Sq *BH/WHM* TN16 ...... 110 E5
Market St *DART* DA1 .... 28 A5
 MAID/BEAR ME14 .... 6 F4
 RTWE/PEM TN2 .... 10 E7
 STPH/PW TN12 .... 154 B8
Market Wy *BH/WHM* TN16 ...... 110 E4
Mark La *GVE* DA12 .... 32 A5
Marks Rd *WARL* CR6 .... 90 A4
Marks Sq *GVW* DA11 .... 46 B1
Marlborough Cl *CDH/CHF* RM16.. 16 E1
 ORP BR6 .... 56 B2
 STH/RUST TN4 .... 10 B4
Marlborough Crs *SEV* TN13 ...... 8 A4
Marlborough Rd *DART* DA1 ...... 27 L4
 GILL ME7 .... 5 H4
Marle Place Rd *STPH/PW* TN12 .. 166 D8
Marley La *HDCN* TN27 .... 172 E1
Marley Rd *HOO/HM* ME3.......... 35 M7
 RMAID ME17 .... 125 H7
Marley Wy *ROCH* ME1 .... 65 L3
Marlhurst *EDEN* TN8 .... 142 D1
Marlings *CHST* BR7 .... 40 A8
Marlings Park Av *CHST* BR7 .... 40 A8
Marling Wy *GVE* DA12 .... 47 G2
Marlow Av *PUR* RM19 .... 14 C3
Marlow Copse *WALD* ME5 ...... 83 H4
Marlowe Rd *DIT/AY* ME20 ...... 101 H2
The Marlowes *DART* DA1 .... 26 F2
Marlpit Cl *EDEN* TN8 .... 142 E1
The Marlpit *WADH* TN5 .... 188 A8
Marquis Dr *GILL* ME7 .... 84 D2
Marriott Rd *DART* DA1 .... 28 C5
Marsden Wy *ORP* BR6 .... 56 B7
Marshall Crs *QBOR* ME11 ...... 55 H2
Marshall Gdns *RTON* TN11 .... 133 C5
Marshall Rd *RHAM* ME8 .... 67 L4
Marshalls Land *TENT* TN30 .... 196 C4
Marsham Crs *RMAID* ME17 .... 138 D4
Marsham St *MAID/BEAR* ME14 .. 7 H4
Marsham Wy *STRD* ME2 .... 64 C8
Marsh Crs *RHAM* ME8 .... 36 M1
Marshfoot Rd *GRAYS* RM17 .... 17 H4
Marsh Green Rd *EDEN* TN8 .... 158 D1
Marshland Vw *HOO/HM* ME3 .. 23 L8
Marsh La *HOO/HM* ME3 .... 20 D7
Marsh Quarter La *HAWK* TN18 .. 205 L4
Marsh Rd *STRD* ME2 .... 64 D8

Marsh St *DART* DA1 .... 28 C1
STRD ME2 .... 3 H3
Marsh Wy *DIT/AY* ME20 ...... 101 J1
Marstan Cl *RSIT* ME9 .... 69 G3
Marston Cl *WALD* ME5 .... 83 C2
Marston Dr *MAID/BEAR* ME14 .. 7 K3
WARL CR6 .... 90 A4
Martens Av *BXLYHN* DA7 .... 26 E2
Martens Cl *BXLYHN* DA7 ...... 26 E2
Martin Ct *GILL* ME7 .... 84 C2 5
Martindale Av *ORP* BR6 ...... 56 C8
Martin Dene *BXLYHS* DA6 .... 26 B3
Martin Hardie Wy *TONN* TN10 .. 132 A8
Martin Ri *BXLYHS* DA6 .... 26 B3
Martin Rd *RDART* DA2 .... 27 L8
STRD ME2 .... 3 G2
Martins Cl *HOO/HM* ME3 ...... 33 M7
STMC/STPC BR5 .... 40 F7
TENT TN30 .... 196 C5
Martins La *STPH/PW* TN12 .. 134 C3
Martin Sq *DIT/AY* ME20 ...... 101 J4 5
Martin's Shaw *SEV* TN13 .... 94 E8
Marwell *BH/WHM* TN16 .... 110 D4
Mary Day's *CRBK* TN17 ...... 182 A6
Maryfield Cl *BXLY* DA5 .... 27 C8
Maryland Ct *RHAM* ME8 ...... 68 A8
Maryland Dr *MAIDW* ME16 .. 120 B3
Maryland Rd *RTWE/PEM* TN2 .. 11 L9
Mascall's Court La
STPH/PW TN12 .... 166 D1
Mascall's Court Rd
STPH/PW TN12 .... 166 D1
Mascalls Pk *STPH/PW* TN12 .. 150 B8
Masefield Cl *ERITH* DA8 ...... 13 H7
Masefield Rd *CDH/CHF* RM16 .. 17 C1
DART DA1 .... 28 D3
GVW DA11 .... 30 F8
Masefield Wy *TON* TN9 ...... 147 H5
Mason Cl *BXLYHN* DA7 .... 26 D1
Master Cl *OXTED* RH8 .... 109 C7
Masters La *E/WMAL* ME19 .... 80 D8
Masthead Cl *GRH* DA9 .... 28 E2
Matfield Crs *MAID/BEAR* ME14 .. 7 L2
Matfield Rd *BELV* DA17 ...... 12 C5
Matilda Cl *GILL* ME7 .... 67 K5
Matterdale Gdns *MAIDW* ME16 .. 120 A3
Matthews La *RTON* TN11 .... 133 H2
Mattinson Pl *RSIT* ME9 ...... 107 H6
Matts Hill Rd *RSIT* ME9 ...... 85 G3
Maude Rd *SWLY* BR8 .... 42 C3
Maunders Cl *WALD* ME5 ...... 66 E5 6
Maximfeldt Rd *ERITH* DA8 .... 13 C4
Maximilian Dr *STRD* ME2 .... 81 K1
Maxim Rd *DART* DA1 .... 27 C3
ERITH DA8 .... 13 C4
Maxton Cl *MAID/BEAR* ME14 .. 104 B8 5
Maxwell Dr *MAIDW* ME16 .... 102 D7
Maxwell Gdns *ORP* BR6 ...... 56 B6
Maxwell Rd *GILL* ME7 .... 4 E3
May Av *GVW* DA11 .... 31 H6
STMC/STPC BR5 .... 56 D1
Maybury Av *RDART* DA2 ...... 28 E6 3
Maycotts La *STPH/PW* TN12 .. 165 M4
Maycroft Av *GRAYS* RM17 .... 16 F4
Maycroft Gdns *GRAYS* RM17 .. 16 F4
Mayes Cl *SWLY* BR8 .... 42 C8
Mayfair *STRD* ME2 .... 49 L4 4
Mayfair Av *MAID/SHEP* ME15 .. 121 J5
Mayfair Rd *DART* DA1 .... 27 M3
Mayfield *BXLYHN* DA7 .... 26 D1
SWCM DA10 .... 30 A4 2
Mayfield Av *ORP* BR6 .... 56 B4
Mayfield Cl *RHAM* ME8 ...... 68 A3
WALD ME5 .... 83 J4
Mayfield Rd *BELV* DA17 ...... 12 E3
GVW DA11 .... 31 H6
STH/RUST TN4 .... 10 D4
Mayfields *CDH/CHF* RM16 .... 16 E1
Mayfly Cl *STMC/STPC* BR5 .. 40 F8 5
Mayford Rd *WALD* ME5 .... 83 M3
Maynard Cl *ERITH* DA8 ...... 13 H6
Maynard Pl *WALD* ME5 .... 5 M9
Maynards *STPH/PW* TN12 .... 152 E8
Maynard's La *STPH/PW* TN12 .. 166 A4
Mayplace Av *DART* DA1 ...... 27 J2
Mayplace Cl *BXLYHN* DA7 .... 26 D1
Mayplace Rd *BXLYHN* DA7 .. 26 E1
Mayplace Rd East *BXLYHN* DA7 .. 26 D1
Mayplace Rd West
BXLYHN DA7 .... 26 C2 3
Maypole Crs *ERITH* DA8 ...... 13 M5
Maypole La *CRBK* TN17 ...... 182 A5
Maypole Rd *GVE* DA12 .... 32 B6 6
ORP BR6 .... 74 B1
May Rd *GILL* ME7 .... 5 H5
RDART DA2 .... 43 H1
ROCH ME1 .... 65 L2
May St *SNOD* ME6 .... 81 K5
STRD ME2 .... 64 D3
May Ter *GILL* ME7 .... 50 C6 2
Maytham Rd *CRBK* TN17 .... 202 B3
Mayweed Av *WALD* ME5 ...... 83 G1
Mcalpine Crs *MAID/SHEP* ME15 .. 137 H2
Mccabe Ct *STPH/PW* TN12 .. 170 A3
Mccudden Rd *DART* DA1 ...... 28 B1
Mcdermott Rd *STMC/STPC* TN15 .. 14 B8
Mckenzie Cl *DIT/AY* ME20 .... 102 B5
Mc Kenzie Rd *WALD* ME5 .... 83 J2
Mead Cl *CDH/CHF* RM16 .... 16 D1
SWLY BR8 .... 58 C1 8
Mead Crs *DART* DA1 .... 27 M6
Meades Cl *STPH/PW* TN12 .. 152 D7
Meadfield Rd *MEO* DA13 .... 62 C5 8
Meadow Bank *E/WMAL* ME19 .. 100 E5
RTON TN11 .... 146 B4 8
Meadow Bank Cl
BGR/WK TN15 .... 77 H3 8
Meadowbank Rd *CHAT* ME4 .. 4 C7
Meadowbrook *OXTED* RH8 .. 108 E8
Meadow Cl *BXLYHS* DA6 ...... 26 B3
RSIT ME9 .... 70 F1 8
SEV TN13 .... 8 E2
SLH/COR SS17 .... 18 C2
STRD ME2 .... 81 G1
WALD ME5 .... 66 B8
Meadow Crs *STRD* ME2 ...... 81 G1

Meadowdown
MAID/BEAR ME14 .... 122 A1
Meadowdown Cl *GILL* ME7 .. 84 C1
Meadow Hill Rd *RTW* TN1 .. 11 G7
Meadowlands *BGR/WK* ME7 .. 96 B6
Meadow La *EDEN* TN8 .... 142 D1
MEO DA13 .... 79 H4
Meadow Ri *RSIT* ME9 .... 70 F1
Meadow Rd *GVW* DA11 ...... 30 E6
GVW DA11 .... 31 J7
RRTW TN3 .... 175 K6
RTW TN1 .... 10 F3
STH/RUST TN4 .... 163 H4
TON TN9 .... 147 J5
Meadowside *DART* DA1 ...... 28 A6 1
The Meadow *RTWE/PEM* TN2 .. 164 F5
Meadowview Rd *BXLY* DA5 .. 26 A4
Meadow View Rd *RMAID* ME17 .. 137 K2
Meadow Wk *MAID/SHEP* ME15 .. 7 J6
RDART DA2 .... 42 E1
SNOD ME6 .... 81 H6
Meadow Wy *RDART* DA2 ...... 28 E5
STPH/PW TN12 .... 152 F7
Mead Rd *DART* DA1 .... 27 M6
EDEN TN8 .... 142 F6
GVW DA11 .... 31 K7
The Meads Av *SIT* ME10 ...... 70 F6
Meadside Wk *WALD* ME5 .... 66 B7
The Meads *CRBK* TN17 ...... 192 B4
RTWE/PEM TN2 .... 11 K8
The Mead *E/WMAL* ME19 .... 101 G3
HART DA3 .... 61 G5
Mead Wall *HOO/HM* ME3 .... 19 M5
Meadway *GRAYS* RM17 ...... 16 F3
RSEV TN14 .... 74 B7
RTON TN11 .... 131 C8
SEV TN13 .... 8 D1
Meath Cl *STMC/STPC* BR5 .. 56 D1
Medbury Cl *GVE* DA12 .... 32 B6
Medhurst Crs *GVE* DA12 .... 32 B8
Medhurst Gdns *GVE* DA12 .. 32 B8
Medick Ct *GRAYS* RM17 ...... 17 G5
Medina Rd *DIT/AY* ME20 .... 101 L4
GRAYS RM17 .... 16 F4
TONN TN10 .... 131 L7 8
Medlar Cl *RSIT* ME9 .... 87 J7
Medlar Gv *GILL* ME7 .... 84 C1
Medlar Rd *GRAYS* RM17 ...... 16 F5
The Medlars *MAID/BEAR* ME14 .. 103 M7
MEO DA13 .... 62 C2 3
Medway Av *HOO/HM* ME3 .. 36 A1
WBY/YAL ME18 .... 135 H4
Medway Br *STRD* ME2 .... 65 G2
Medway Cl *SIT* ME10 .... 87 M1
Medway Gdns *CHAT* ME4 .... 50 B6
Medway Mdw *STPH/PW* TN12 .. 134 C7
Medway Rd *DART* DA1 .... 27 J1
GILL ME7 .... 50 D6
RTW TN1 .... 11 H1
Medway St *CHAT* ME4 .... 4 C4
MAID/BEAR ME14 .... 6 F5
Medway Valley Wk *DIT/AY* ME20 .. 81 M8
MAIDW ME16 .... 102 F1
ROCH ME1 .... 3 H7
STPH/PW TN12 .... 150 A2
WBY/YAL ME18 .... 119 J7
Medway Wharf Rd *TON* TN9 .. 147 L4
Meeres Court La *SIT* ME10 .. 71 L7
Meesons La *GRAYS* RM17 .. 16 B3
Meeting House La *CHAT* ME4 .. 4 D5
Megrims Hi *HAWK* TN18 .... 200 C7
Meirscourt Rd *RHAM* ME8 .. 85 G1
Melanie Cl *BXLYHN* DA7 .... 12 A7
Melba Gdns *TIL* RM18 .... 17 J6
Melbourne Cl *ORP* BR6 ...... 56 A3
Melbourne Rd *CHAT* ME4 .... 4 F8
TIL RM18 .... 17 G7
Meldrum Cl *STMC/STPC* BR5 .. 56 E2 2
Melford Dr *MAIDW* ME16 .... 120 D1
Melliker La *MEO* DA13 .... 62 B2
Mellor Rw *SIT* ME10 .... 71 H4 8
Melody Cl *RHAM* ME8 .... 84 E1
Melody Rd *BH/WHM* TN16 .. 91 L4
Melrose Cl *MAID/SHEP* ME15 .. 121 J6
Melrose Rd *BH/WHM* TN16 .. 91 L2
Melville Rd *MAID/SHEP* ME15... 7 H5
Mendip Rd *BXLYHN* DA7 .... 13 G7
Menin Rd *SIT* ME10 .... 71 H4
Mera Dr *BXLYHN* DA7 .... 26 C2
Mercer Dr *RMAID* ME17 ...... 125 H7
Mercers *HAWK* TN18 .... 199 J4
RRTW TN3 .... 176 C2
Mercers Cl *STPH/PW* TN12 .. 170 A3
Mercers Pl *WBY/YAL* ME18 .. 118 C3 8
Mercer St *RTW* TN1 .... 11 G2
Mercer Wy *RMAID* ME17 .... 138 D4 8
Merchant Pl *STPH/PW* TN12 .. 152 F7 8
Mercury Cl *ROCH* ME1 .... 65 J3
Meredith Rd *CDH/CHF* RM16 .. 17 J3
Meresborough La *RHAM* ME8 .. 68 C3
Meresborough Rd *RHAM* ME8 .. 85 H1
Merewood Rd *BXLYHN* DA7 .. 12 E8
Mereworth Cl *STH/RUST* TN4 .. 163 J7
WBY/YAL ME18 .... 117 L6
Merivale Gv *WALD* ME5 ...... 83 K1
Merleburgh Dr *SIT* ME10 .... 71 H5 8
Merlewood *SEV* TN13 .... 9 G2
Merlin Av *DIT/AY* ME20 ...... 101 H3
Merlin Cl *SIT* ME10 .... 88 C2
TONN TN10 .... 148 A1
Mermaid Cl *WALD* ME5 ...... 66 C7
Mermerus Gdns *GVE* DA12 .. 47 H1 8
Merrals Wood Rd *STRD* ME2 .. 48 F8
Merriments La *BUR/ETCH* TN19 .. 198 F8
Merrion Cl *STH/RUST* TN4 .. 163 J7
Merrion Wy *STH/RUST* TN4 .. 163 K6
Merry Boys Rd *HOO/HM* ME3 .. 34 D5
Merryfields *STRD* ME2 .... 49 J4
Merryfields *HART* DA3 .... 45 H8 2
Merryhills *BH/WHM* TN16 .. 91 M2
Merryweather Cl *DART* DA1 .. 28 B4 2

Mersey Rd *TONN* TN10 ...... 131 K8
Merton Av *HART* DA3 .... 45 G8
Merton Cl *WALD* ME5 .... 83 L1
Merton Pl *CDH/CHF* RM16 .. 17 J3
Merton Rd *MAID/SHEP* ME15 .. 122 B3
Mesne Wy *RSEV* TN14 .... 75 H6
Meteor Cl *SIT* ME10 .... 71 G5
Meteor Rd *E/WMAL* ME19 .. 118 B2
Methuen Rd *BELV* DA17 ...... 12 D3
BXLYHS DA6 .... 26 B2
Mewsend *BH/WHM* TN16 .... 91 M4
The Mews *RTWE/PEM* TN2 .. 164 E7
SIT ME10 .... 88 B2
STRD ME2 .... 2 D4
Meyer Rd *ERITH* DA8 .... 12 E5
Micawber Cl *WALD* ME5 ...... 83 J4 8
Michael Gdns *GVE* DA12 .... 47 G3
Michaels La *HART* DA3 .... 60 D5
Mickleham Cl *STMC/STPC* BR5 .. 40 B6
Mickleham Rd *STMC/STPC* BR5 .. 40 B5
Middle Fld *RTWE/PEM* TN2 .. 165 C5
Middlefields *RHAM* ME8 ...... 68 C5 8
Middle La *GVW* DA11 .... 31 M6
HOO/HM ME3 .... 34 D5
RSEV TN14 .... 74 D4
Middlesex Rd
MAID/SHEP ME15 .... 121 M6
Middle St *GILL* ME7 .... 4 E1
Middleton Av *SCUP* DA14 .... 40 E3
Middleton Cl *RHAM* ME8 .... 85 G1 8
Middletune Av *SIT* ME10 .... 71 G6
Middle Wk *RTWE/PEM* TN2 .. 164 A5
Middle Wy *SIT* ME10 .... 88 D2
Middlings Ri *SEV* TN13 .... 8 D8
Middlings Wd *SEV* TN13 ...... 8 D8
Midfield Av *BXLYHN* DA7 .... 26 E1
SWLY BR8 .... 42 C3
Midfield Wy *STMC/STPC* BR5 .. 40 D5
Midhurst Hi *BXLYHS* DA6 .... 26 C3
Midley Cl *MAIDW* ME16 ...... 102 E6
Midsummer Rd *SNOD* ME6 .. 81 G5
The Midway *STH/RUST* TN4 .. 176 F3
Mierscourt Cl *RHAM* ME8 .... 68 C5
Mierscourt Rd *RHAM* ME8 .. 68 B6
Milbourne Gv *SIT* ME10 ...... 71 G6
Milburn Rd *GILL* ME7 .... 50 E6
Mildenhall Rd *RHAM* ME8 .. 68 A8
Mildmay Pl *RSEV* TN14 ...... 75 H5
Mildred Cl *DART* DA1 .... 28 C4
Mildred Rd *ERITH* DA8 ...... 13 G4
Milebush La *STPH/PW* TN12 .. 152 F4
Mile La *CRBK* TN17 .... 182 D4
Mile Oak Rd *STPH/PW* TN12 .. 166 E3
Miles Pl *ROCH* ME1 .... 65 M2 8
Mile Stone Rd *RDART* DA2 .. 28 D4
Milford Cl *ABYW* SE2 .... 12 A5
MAIDW ME16 .... 102 E8
Military Rd *CHAT* ME4 .... 4 D4
Milk House Cottages
CRBK TN17 .... 184 C5
Milking La *ORP* BR6 .... 72 A6
Millais Pl *TIL* RM18 .... 17 J6
Mill Bank *HDCN* TN27 .... 155 L7
Millbro *SWLY* BR8 .... 42 C5 8
Millbrook Cl *MAID/SHEP* ME15 .. 100 F4
Mill Brook Rd *STMC/STPC* BR5 .. 40 E8
Mill Cl *RMAID* ME17 .... 141 L1
STRD ME2 .... 49 K4
Mill Crs *TON* TN9 .... 147 M3
Millcroft Rd *HOO/HM* ME3 .. 34 D1
Millen Rd *SIT* ME10 .... 71 C8
Miller Rd *SIT* ME10 .... 71 J5
Miller Rd *GVE* DA12 .... 32 C7
Millers Wk *MEO* DA13 .... 62 C5
Millfield *HART* DA3 .... 61 C5
RASHW TN26 .... 187 M6
SIT ME10 .... 88 B2
Millfield Dr *GVW* DA11 ...... 31 G7
Millfield La *HART* DA3 .... 61 C5
Millfield Rd *BGR/WK* TN15 .. 76 F1
Millfields *WALD* ME5 .... 83 M3
Millfields Cl *STMC/STPC* BR5 .. 40 D8
Millfordhope Rd *STRD* ME2 .. 48 E6
Millhall *DIT/AY* ME20 .... 101 M3
Mill Hall Rd *DIT/AY* ME20 .. 101 K2
Mill Hi *EDEN* TN8 .... 142 F6
Mill Hill La *GVE* DA12 .... 47 M2
Millhouse La *E/WMAL* ME19 .. 99 M2
Mill La *MAID/SHEP* ME15 .... 97 M8
BGR/WK TN15 .... 130 D2
BH/WHM TN16 .... 110 C5
CRBK TN17 .... 171 C6
CRBK TN17 .... 184 B5
EYN DA4 .... 59 C4
HDCN TN27 .... 173 H3
ORP BR6 .... 72 C4
OXTED RH8 .... 126 B1
RMAID ME17 .... 136 F2
RSEV TN14 .... 75 H4
RSEV TN14 .... 95 L7
RSIT ME9 .... 69 G7
RSIT ME9 .... 89 K8
RTON TN11 .... 130 D5
SNOD ME6 .... 81 K5
STPH/PW TN12 .... 167 K4
STPH/PW TN12 .... 170 C4
TENT TN30 .... 196 D4
TON TN9 .... 147 L3
WALD ME5 .... 66 C4
WALD ME5 .... 82 F4
WBY/YAL ME18 .... 118 F5
WBY/YAL ME18 .... 135 J7
WTHK RM20 .... 15 M4
Mill Pl *DART* DA1 .... 27 J2
Mill Pond Cl *SEV* TN13 ...... 95 M7
Millpond Cl *STRD* ME2 ...... 3 G1
Millpond La *HDCN* TN27 .... 195 K3
Mill Pond Rd *DART* DA1 .... 28 A4
Mill Rd *ERITH* DA8 .... 12 E6
GILL ME7 .... 5 J1
GVW DA11 .... 31 C5
PUR RM19 .... 14 D5
RDART DA2 .... 43 H1
STRD ME2 .... 95 G7
Mills Crs *BGR/WK* TN15 .... 96 B6
Mills Rd *DIT/AY* ME20 .... 102 A6
Mills Ter *CHAT* ME4 .... 4 F7
Mill Stone Cl *EYN* DA4 ...... 43 L6 8

Millstone Ms *EYN* DA4 ...... 43 L5
Millstream Cl *RRTW* TN3 .. 174 F3 8
Mill St *BH/WHM* TN16 ...... 110 F5
CRBK TN17 .... 200 E2
E/WMAL ME19 .... 101 H6
HAWK TN18 .... 200 D3
MAID/BEAR ME14 .... 6 F5
MAID/SHEP ME15 .... 7 G6
MAID/SHEP ME15 .... 121 H8 8
SIT ME10 .... 71 G8
SNOD ME6 .... 81 K5
Mill Vw *RTON* TN11 .... 132 F4
Mill Wk *MAIDW* ME16 .... 120 C2
Mill Wy *SIT* ME10 .... 71 H7
Millwood Rd *STMC/STPC* BR5 .. 40 E7
Milner Rd *GILL* ME7 .... 50 F6
Milroy Av *GVW* DA11 .... 31 C7
Milstead Cl *MAID/BEAR* ME14 .. 7 L3
Milsted Rd *RHAM* ME8 ...... 67 L3
Milton Av *GVE* DA12 .... 31 M6
HOO/HM ME3 .... 34 D3
RSEV TN14 .... 74 D4
Milton Dr *RTWE/PEM* TN2 .. 163 M6
Milton Gdns *TIL* RM18 ...... 17 K7
TON TN9 .... 147 H6
Milton Hall Rd *GVE* DA12 .. 31 M6
Milton Pl *GVE* DA12 .... 31 L4
Milton Rd *BELV* DA17 .... 12 C3
GILL ME7 .... 5 K7
GRAYS RM17 .... 16 D3
GVE DA12 .... 31 L4 8
SEV TN13 .... 95 G7
SIT ME10 .... 88 A1
SWCM DA10 .... 30 A4
Milton St *MAIDW* ME16 ...... 120 E3
SWCM DA10 .... 29 M4
Mimosa Cl *ORP* BR6 .... 56 E5 3
Mincers Cl *WALD* ME5 .... 83 L3 2
Minerva Cl *SCUP* DA14 ...... 40 A1
Minerva Rd *STRD* ME2 ...... 2 E3
Minster Rd *RHAM* ME8 ...... 67 L2 8
Minterne Av *SIT* ME10 ...... 87 L3
Minters Orch *BGR/WK* TN15 .. 98 D6
Miskin Rd *DART* DA1 .... 27 L5
HOO/HM ME3 .... 35 M8
Miskin Wy *GVE* DA12 .... 46 F3
Mitchell Av *CHAT* ME4 ...... 66 B3
GVW DA11 .... 30 F7
Mitchell Cl *BELV* DA17 ...... 12 E2
DART DA1 .... 28 A7
RMAID ME17 .... 125 L8
Mitchell Rd *E/WMAL* ME19 .. 118 B3
ORP BR6 .... 56 B7
Mitcham Cl *BGR/WK* TN15 .. 77 G2
Mitre Cl *TON* TN9 .... 147 L3
Mitre Rd *ROCH* ME1 .... 3 H9
Moat Cl *ORP* BR6 .... 73 H1
Moat Farm *RTWE/PEM* TN2 .. 177 J6
Moat Farm Rd *HOO/HM* ME3 .. 22 E7
Moat La *EDEN* TN8 .... 159 M6
ERITH DA8 .... 13 J7
Moat Rd *HDCN* TN27 .... 155 K8
Mockbeggar La *CRBK* TN17 .. 194 E1
Molash Rd *STMC/STPC* BR5 .. 40 F8
Molescroft Wy *TON* TN9 .... 147 H6
Moles Md *EDEN* TN8 .... 142 E3
Mollison Rd *GVE* DA12 ...... 47 G2
Molyneux Park Rd
STH/RUST TN4 .... 10 B3
Monarch Cl *TIL* RM18 .... 17 K8
WALD ME5 .... 66 C7
Monarch Rd *BELV* DA17 .... 12 C2
Monckton's Av
MAID/BEAR ME14 .... 103 G6
Monckton's Dr
MAID/BEAR ME14 .... 103 G6 2
Monckton's La
MAID/BEAR ME14 .... 103 G6
Monkdown
MAID/SHEP ME15 .... 122 C4 8
Monks La *WADH* TN5 .... 188 D6
Monks Orch *DART* DA1 ...... 27 L7
Monks Wk *MEO* DA13 .... 45 J3
Monks Wy *RYE* TN31 .... 206 D5
Monkton Rd *BGR/WK* TN15 .. 98 B6
Monkwood Cl *ROCH* ME1 .. 65 K5 3
Monmouth Cl *RHAM* ME8 .. 67 M3
Mons Cl *SIT* ME10 .... 71 H4
Monson Rd *RTW* TN1 .... 11 G4
Monson Wy *RTW* TN1 .... 11 G3
Montacute Gdns
RTWE/PEM TN2 .... 10 E9
Montacute Rd *RTWE/PEM* TN2 .. 10 E9
Montague Cl *SWLY* BR8 .... 42 B8
Montbretia Cl
STMC/STPC BR5 .... 40 E8 8
Monteith Cl *RRTW* TN3 ...... 176 C2
Monterey Cl *BXLY* DA5 ...... 26 E7
Montfort Dr *WBY/YAL* ME18 .. 118 C3
Montfort Rd *RSEV* TN14 .... 96 A3
STRD ME2 .... 2 F3
WALD ME5 .... 83 G3
Montgomery Av *WALD* ME5 .. 66 G6
Montgomery Rd *EYN* DA4 .. 43 M5
GILL ME7 .... 5 J7
STH/RUST TN4 .... 163 K6
Montpelier Ga *MAIDW* ME16 .. 102 D8 3
Montreal Rd *SEV* TN13 ...... 8 B2
TIL RM18 .... 31 J1
Montrose Av *WALD* ME5 .... 67 G3
Mont St Aignan Wy *EDEN* TN8 .. 142 E4
Monypenny *CRBK* TN17 .... 202 B3
Moonstone Dr *WALD* ME5 .. 83 K3 3
Moorden La *RTON* TN11 .... 145 J4
Moore Av *TIL* RM18 .... 17 K8
WTHK RM20 .... 16 A4
Moore St *STRD* ME2 .... 2 F1
Moorfield Rd *ORP* BR6 ...... 56 C3
Moorhen Cl *ERITH* DA8 ...... 13 K6 8
Moor Hi *HAWK* TN18 .... 199 H5
Moorhouse Rd *OXTED* RH8 .. 110 B8
Mooring Rd *ROCH* ME1 ...... 65 M4
Moor Park Cl *RHAM* ME8 .. 68 C5
The Moor Rd *RSEV* TN14 .. 95 K6
Moor St *RHAM* ME8 .... 68 D5
The Moor *HAWK* TN18 ...... 199 H5
Morant Cl *CDH/CHF* RM16 .. 17 K2
Morants Court Rd *RSEV* TN14 .. 94 E4

Morden St *ROCH* ME1 .... 3 J9
Morelands Av *CDH/CHF* RM16 .. 16 E1 8
Morel Ct *SEV* TN13 .... 9 H1
Morello Cl *RSIT* ME9 .... 89 L3 8
SWLY BR8 .... 41 M8
Morement Rd *HOO/HM* ME3 .. 35 M7
Morenco Ct *DART* DA1 ...... 27 G1
Morewood Cl *SEV* TN13 .... 8 D3
Morgan Dr *RDART* DA2 ...... 29 G5
Morgan Rd *STRD* ME2 ...... 2 F2 8
Morhen Cl *SNOD* ME6 .... 81 G6
Morland Av *DART* DA1 ...... 27 K3
Morland Dr *RRTW* TN3 ...... 180 D8
STRD ME2 .... 49 J4
Morley Dr *STPH/PW* TN12 .. 167 H7
Morley Rd *TON* TN9 .... 147 M4
Morley Sq *CDH/CHF* RM16 .. 17 J3
Morley's Rd *RSEV* TN14 .... 129 M3
Mornington Ct *BXLY* DA5 .. 26 F6
Morris Cl *E/WMAL* ME19 .. 101 H4 3
ORP BR6 .... 56 A6
Morris Court Cl *RSIT* ME9 .. 88 F3
Morris Gdns *DART* DA1 ...... 28 C3
Morry La *RMAID* ME17 ...... 139 M5
Mortimer Rd *ERITH* DA8 .... 12 F5
ORP BR6 .... 56 C4 8
Morvale Cl *DART* DA1 .... 12 B3 8
Moselle Rd *BH/WHM* TN16 .. 92 A4
Mosquito Rd *E/WMAL* ME19 .. 118 B2
Moss Bank *GRAYS* RM17 .. 16 C3
Mossbank *WALD* ME5 .... 83 J2 8
Mossdown Cl *BELV* DA17 .. 12 C3
Moss Wy *RDART* DA2 .... 43 M1
Mossy Gld *RHAM* ME8 .... 68 A7
Mostyn Rd *MAID/BEAR* ME14 .. 7 L4
Mosyer Dr *STMC/STPC* BR5 .. 56 F5
Mote Av *MAID/SHEP* ME15 .. 7 J6
MAID/SHEP ME15 .... 121 M2
Mote Rd *BGR/WK* TN15 .... 115 J6 8
MAID/SHEP ME15 .... 7 H6
Motherwell Wy *WTHK* RM20 .. 15 J4
Motney Hill Rd *RHAM* ME8 .. 68 C1
Moultain Hi *SWLY* BR8 ...... 42 C8
Mount Av *WBY/YAL* ME18 .. 135 J4
Mountbatten Av *HOO/HM* ME3 .. 48 E1
WALD ME5 .... 66 C6
Mount Cl *SEV* TN13 .... 8 D2
Mount Culver Av *SCUP* DA14 .. 40 F3
Mount Dr *MAID/BEAR* ME14 .. 122 D1 8
Mount Edgcumbe Rd
STH/RUST TN4 .... 10 E5
Mount Ephraim *RTW* TN1 .. 10 E4
STH/RUST TN4 .... 10 D5
Mount Ephraim Rd *RTW* TN1 .. 10 E4
Mountfield *BGR/WK* TN15 .. 98 C6
Mountfield Cl *MEO* DA13 .. 79 C3
Mountfield Gdns
RTWE/PEM TN2 .... 11 G6
Mountfield Pk *TON* TN9 .... 147 L5
Mountfield Rd *RTWE/PEM* TN2 .. 11 G6
Mountfield Wy *STMC/STPC* BR5 .. 40 E8
Mount Harry Rd *SEV* TN13 .. 8 F3
Mount La *MAID/BEAR* ME14 .. 122 D1
RSIT ME9 .... 85 M1
Mount Pleasant
BH/WHM TN16 .... 91 M3
DIT/AY ME20 .... 102 C2
RTON TN11 .... 130 F7
STPH/PW TN12 .... 150 B7 8
TENT TN30 .... 196 E5 8
WADH TN5 .... 188 A8 2
Mount Pleasant Av
RTWE/PEM TN2 .... 11 G5
Mount Pleasant Dr
MAID/BEAR ME14 .... 104 C8
Mount Pleasant La *RRTW* TN3 .. 180 B7
Mount Pleasant Rd *DART* DA1 .. 28 B4
RSEV TN14 .... 129 K3
RTWE/PEM TN2 .... 10 F7
Mount Rd *BXLYHS* DA6 .... 26 A3
CHAT ME4 .... 4 D8
DART DA1 .... 27 H4
ROCH ME1 .... 65 J3
Mountsfield Cl *MAIDW* ME16 .. 6 B2
Mounts Hi *CRBK* TN17 ...... 193 J6
Mount Sion *RTW* TN1 .... 10 F7
STH/RUST TN4 .... 10 E7
Mounts La *CRBK* TN17 ...... 202 C3
Mounts Rd *GRH* DA9 .... 29 K4
Mountview *RSIT* ME9 .... 87 K3
Mountview Rd *ORP* BR6 .... 56 C5
Moyle Cl *RHAM* ME8 .... 84 F1
Mozart Ct *CHAT* ME4 .... 4 B8
Muckingford Rd *TIL* RM18 .. 18 B5
Muir Rd *MAID/SHEP* ME15... 7 G7
Mulberry Cl *GILL* ME7 .... 84 C1
MEO DA13 .... 62 B2
RTWE/PEM TN2 .... 163 M4
Mulberry Dr *PUR* RM19 .... 14 B3
Mulberry Rd *GVW* DA11 .... 46 A1
Mulberry Wy *BELV* DA17 .. 12 E1
Mullein Ct *GRAYS* RM17 .... 16 F5
Multon Rd *BGR/WK* TN15 .. 77 G1
Munford Dr *SWCM* DA10 .. 30 B5
Mungo Park Rd *GVE* DA12 .. 46 F2
Mungo Park Wy
STMC/STPC BR5 .... 56 E3
Munn's La *RSIT* ME9 .... 69 G7
Munsgore La *RSIT* ME9 ...... 87 G3
Murrain Dr *MAID/SHEP* ME15 .. 122 C4
Murray Rd *STMC/STPC* BR5 .. 40 D7
STRD ME2 .... 49 L4
Murston Rd *SIT* ME10 .... 88 D2
Murton-neale Cl *HAWK* TN18 .. 199 J3 8
Museum St *MAID/BEAR* ME14 .. 6 F4
Musgrave Rd *SIT* ME10 .... 71 H7
Musket La *RMAID* ME17 .... 123 J3
Mussenden La *EYN* DA4 .... 59 J2
Mustang Rd *E/WMAL* ME19 .. 118 B2 8
Mynn Crs *MAID/BEAR* ME14 .. 7 L4
Myrtle Cl *ERITH* DA8 .... 13 G6
Myrtle Crs *WALD* ME5 .... 83 K3
Myrtle Gv *SOCK/AV* RM15 .. 14 E1
Myrtle Pl *DART* DA1 .... 28 F6
Myrtle Rd *DART* DA1 .... 27 M7

N

Nags Head La *ROCH* ME1 .... 3 M9 🔲
 ROCH ME1................................. 3 L9
Nansen Rd *GVE* DA12 .... 46 F1
Napier Cl *SIT* ME10 .... 12 B3
Napier Rd *BELV* DA17 .... 5 L7
 GILL ME7 .... 31 H6
 GVW DA11 .... 81 L1
 RTWE/PEM TN2 .... 11 L8
Napoleon Dr *STPH/PW* TN12 .. 152 F8 🔲
Napwood Cl *RHAM* ME8 .... 67 M7 🔲
Nares Rd *RHAM* ME8 .... 84 F1
Nash Bank *MEO* DA13 .... 46 B6
Nash Cl *WALD* ME5 .... 83 L3
Nash Cft *MEO* DA13 .... 46 A1
Nashenden La *ROCH* ME1 .... 65 H3
Nash St *MEO* DA13 .... 46 C6
Natal Rd *CHAT* ME4 .... 4 E9
Nativity Cl *SIT* ME10 .... 88 A1
Neale St *CHAT* ME4 .... 4 D9
Neal Rd *BGR/WK* TN15 .... 77 G1
Neills Rd *RRTW* TN3 .... 188 F3
Nellington Rd *RRTW* TN3 .... 176 D1
Nelson Av *TON* TN9 .... 147 J4
Nelson Cl *BH/WHM* TN16 .... 92 A3
Nelson Pl *SCUP* DA14 .... 40 C1
Nelson Belv *DA17* 12 B4
 DART DA1 .... 27 L4
 GILL ME7 .... 31 J5
 GVW DA11 .... 31 H7
 ROCH ME1 .... 81 L1
 RTWE/PEM TN2 .... 11 L8
 SCUP DA14 .... 40 C1 🔲
Nelson Ter *WALD* ME5 .... 66 E4
Nepicar La *BGR/WK* TN15 .... 98 E1
Neptune Cl *STRD* ME2 .... 50 A6
Neptune Wy *STRD* ME2 .... 4 B1
Nestor Ct *WBY/YAL* ME18 .... 119 J5
Nethern Court Rd *CTHM* CR3 ... 108 C1
Netley Rd *MAID/BEAR* ME14 .. 103 M7 🔲
Nettlestead La *WBY/YAL* ME18.. 118 C2
Nevell Rd *CDH/CHF* ME16 .... 17 K2 🔲
Nevill Cft *DART* DA1 .... 28 C4
 WALD ME5................................. 83 L2
Nevill Ct *E/WMAL* ME19 .... 100 E4
Neville Cl *BFN/LL* DA15 .... 40 B1
 MAID/BEAR ME14 .... 103 K5
Neville Rd *CHAT* ME4 .... 4 B9
Nevill Ga *RTWE/PEM* TN2 .... 177 K4
Nevill Pl *SNOD* ME6 .... 81 J6 🔲
Nevill Rdg *STH/RUST* TN4 .... 176 F2
Nevill Rd *SNOD* ME6 .... 81 J6
Nevill St *RTWE/PEM* TN2 .... 10 E8
Nevill Ter *RTWE/PEM* TN2 .... 10 D8
Newark Yd *RHAM* ME8 .... 2 G3
Newbarn La *RSEV* TN14 .... 92 F2
New Barn Rd *HART* DA3 .... 45 K7
 MEO DA13 .... 45 L2
 RMAID ME17 .... 155 G3
 SWLY BR8 .... 42 A5
New Barns Rd
 MAID/BEAR ME14 .... 103 J5
Newbery Rd *ERITH* DA8 .... 13 H7
Newbridge Av *SIT* ME10 .... 71 G6
Newbury Av *MAIDW* ME16 .... 102 F7
Newbury Cl *HOO/HM* ME3 ..... 34 D5 🔲
Newbury La *WADH* TN5 .... 188 E5
Newchurch Rd
 MAID/SHEP ME15 .... 121 J4
Newcomen Rd *STH/RUST* TN4 .. 10 E4
New Covenant Pl *ROCH* ME1 .... 3 M9 🔲
New Cut *CHAT* ME4 .... 4 C5
 MAID/SHEP ME15 .... 120 F6
New Cut Rd *MAID/BEAR* ME14 .. 103 M8
 MAID/BEAR ME14 .... 121 M1
Newenden Cl
 MAID/BEAR ME14 .... 103 M7 🔲
Newenden Rd *STRD* ME2 .... 49 L3
New England Rd
 STH/RUST TN4 .... 163 J6
New Gardens Rd *RSIT* ME9 .... 89 L3
New Hall Farm La *HOO/HM* ME3 .. 23 K7
New House La *GVW* DA11 .... 31 H8
New Hythe La *DIT/AY* ME20 ...... 101 J3
Newick Cl *BXLY* DA5 .... 26 D4
Newitt Rd *HOO/HM* ME3 .... 35 M8
Newland Green La *HDCN* TN27 .. 157 M5
Newlands *RRTW* TN3 .... 176 C1
Newlands Av *SIT* ME10 .... 87 K1
Newlands Farm Rd
 HOO/HM ME3 .... 22 D8
Newlands La *MEO* DA13 .... 79 H4
Newlands Ri *STH/RUST* TN4 .... 163 J7 🔲
Newlands Rd *STH/RUST* TN4 ... 163 K7
Newlands Wy *STH/RUST* TN4 .. 163 K6 🔲
New Lodge Dr *OXTED* RH8 .... 109 H6
Newlyn Dr *STPH/PW* TN12 ...... 154 B8
Newman Dr *SIT* ME10 .... 71 H5
Newman's Rd *GVW* DA11 .... 31 H7
New Mill Rd *STMC/STPC* BR5 .... 40 E5
Newnham Cl *RHAM* ME8 .... 67 L3 🔲
Newnham Pl *CDH/CHF* ME16 .. 17 J3 🔲
Newnham St *CHAT* ME4 .... 5 G7
New Pond Rd *CRBK* TN17 .... 193 L7
Newports *SWLY* BR8 .... 57 M3
New Pound La *WBY/YAL* ME18.. 117 L3
New Rd *CHAT* ME4 .... 4 C6
 CRBK TN17 .... 192 D1
 DIT/AY ME20 .... 101 L4
 E/WMAL ME19 .... 101 J4
 EYN DA4 .... 43 L6
 GRAYS RM17 .... 16 C5
 GVW DA11 .... 31 J4 🔲
 HDCN TN27 .... 155 M8
 HOO/HM ME3 .... 34 C1
 MEO DA13 .... 62 B1
 ORP BR6 .... 56 C5
 OXTED RH8 .... 109 K8
 RMAID ME17 .... 122 E8
 ROCH ME1 .... 3 M9
 ROCH ME1 .... 82 B5
 RSEV TN14 .... 111 M2
 RTON TN11 .... 161 J4
 STPH/PW TN12 .... 150 C7
 SWLY BR8 .... 42 B7
New Road Av *CHAT* ME4 .... 4 B5
New Road Hl *HAYES* BR2 .... 72 A4
New Stairs *CHAT* ME4 .... 4 C2
New St *BGR/WK* TN15 .... 78 F1

 BH/WHM TN16 .... 110 E5
 CHAT ME4 .... 4 B7
New Street Rd *BGR/WK* TN15.... 61 L6
Newton Abbot Rd *GVW* DA11 ... 31 H7
Newton Av *TONN* TN10 .... 131 M6
Newton Cl *MAIDW* ME16 .... 6 C7
 WALD ME5 .... 83 L3 🔲
Newton Gdns
 STPH/PW TN12 .... 150 B6 🔲
Newton Rd *RTW* TN1 .... 10 F4
 TIL RM18 .... 17 J8
Newton's Ct *GRH* DA9 .... 28 F2
Newton Willows *RRTW* TN3 ..... 175 L6
New Wharf Rd *TON* TN9 .... 147 K3
New Years La *RSEV* TN14 .... 93 H1
Nicholas Cl *MAIDW* ME16 .... 120 C2 🔲
Nicklaus Dr *WALD* ME5 .... 83 H1
Nickleby Cl *ROCH* ME1 .... 65 L3
Nickleby Rd *GVE* DA12 .... 32 C6
Nicolson Rd *STMC/STPC* BR5 .... 56 E3
Nightingale Cl *BH/WHM* TN16 .. 91 L1
 DIT/AY ME20 .... 101 H3
 GVW DA11 .... 46 A1 🔲
 RHAM ME8 .... 68 B6 🔲
Nightingale La *RSEV* TN14 .... 112 D8
Nightingale Rd *RSEV* TN14 .... 95 M3
The Nightingales *CRBK* TN17 ... 185 H5
Nightingale Wy *SWLY* BR8 .... 42 A7
Nile Rd *GILL* ME7 .... 5 K5
Nine Acres Rd *STRD* ME2 .... 64 C2
Nine Elms Gv *GVW* DA11 .... 31 J5
Ninehams Rd *BH/WHM* TN16 ..... 91 M7
Nineveh La *HAWK* TN18 .... 193 C7
Niven Cl *HOO/HM* ME3 .... 49 L2
Nizels La *RTON* TN11 .... 130 B6
Noah's Ark *BGR/WK* TN15 .... 96 D4
Nobel Ct *RSIT* ME9 .... 89 L3
Noble Tree Rd *RTON* TN11 .... 130 D7
The Nook *WBY/YAL* ME18 .... 135 H3
Norah La *HOO/HM* ME3 .... 48 D1
Nordenfeldt Rd *ERITH* DA8 .... 12 F4 🔲
Nore Cl *GILL* ME7 .... 67 G4
Norfield Rd *RDART* DA2 .... 41 L1
Norfolk Cl *DART* DA1 .... 28 C4
 WALD ME5.............................. 83 L2
Norfolk Gdns *BXLYHN* DA7 .... 12 B7
Norfolk Rd *GVE* DA12 .... 31 M4
 MAID/SHEP ME15 .... 121 L5
 RTW TN1 .... 11 G7
 TON TN9 .... 147 J4
Norheads La *BH/WHM* TN16 ..... 91 L2
Norman Cl *MAID/BEAR* ME14 .. 103 K7
 RHAM ME8 .... 84 D1
 RHAM ME8 .... 95 M3
 STRD ME2 .... 2 D9
Normandy Wy *ERITH* DA8 .... 13 J2
Normanhurst Rd *BGR/WK* TN15 .. 98 C6
 STMC/STPC BR5 .... 40 D6
Norman Ri *CRBK* TN17 .... 192 F1 🔲
Norman Rd *BELV* DA17 .... 12 D1
 DART DA1 .... 28 A6
 E/WMAL ME19 .... 11 H3
 RTW TN1 .... 81 J7
 SNOD ME6 ....
Normans Cl *GVW* DA11 .... 31 J5
Normans La *EDEN* TN8 .... 142 A5
Norman St *RSEV* TN14 .... 112 A8
Norreys Rd *RHAM* ME8 .... 68 A6
Norrington Rd
 MAID/SHEP ME15 .... 121 J7
Norris Wy *DART* DA1 .... 27 H1
Norstead Gdns *STH/RUST* TN4 .. 163 K6
Northail La *ORP* BR6 .... 73 K5
Northall Rd *BXLYHN* DA7 .... 12 E8
North Ash Rd *HART* DA3 .... 61 H6
North Bank Cl *STRD* ME2 .... 2 D7
Northbourne Rd *RHAM* ME8 ...... 45 M7
Northcote Rd *GVW* DA11 .... 31 H6
 SCUP DA14 .... 40 A1
 STRD ME2 .... 2 E4
 TON TN9 .... 147 K4 🔲
North Cray Rd *BXLY* DA5 .... 26 C7
 SCUP DA14 .... 41 G3
North Crs *RMAID* ME17 .... 136 F1
North Dane Wy *WALD* ME5 .... 66 E8
North Down *STPH/PW* TN12 ... 170 A1
Northdown Cl
 MAID/BEAR ME14 .... 103 K6
 STPH/PW TN12 .... 150 B7 🔲
Northdown Rd *GDST* RH9 .... 108 C3
 HART DA3 .... 45 G6
 RSEV TN14 .... 94 A6
North Downs Wy *BGR/WK* TN15 .. 98 A1
 MAID/BEAR ME14 .... 104 A1
 OXTED RH8 .... 109 J1
 RMAID ME17 .... 105 M7
 RMAID ME17 .... 125 M6
 SEV TN13 .... 94 F4
 STRD ME2 .... 64 B4
Northdown Vw *RMAID* ME17 ... 125 M5
Northdr *ORP* BR6 .... 56 A7
North End La *ORP* BR6 .... 72 D3
Northend Rd *ERITH* DA8 .... 13 H7
North Farm La *RTWE/PEM* TN2.. 163 M5
North Farm Rd *STH/RUST* TN4 .. 163 L6
Northfield *HART* DA3 .... 45 H7
Northfield Av *STMC/STPC* BR5 .. 56 E2
Northfields *GRAYS* RM17 .... 16 E3
 MAIDW ME16 .... 120 B3
 RRTW TN3 .... 162 C5
Northfleet Cl *MAID/BEAR* ME14 .. 7 M2
North Folly Rd
 MAID/SHEP ME15 .... 136 B2
Northgate *ROCH* ME1 .... 3 K6
Northgrove Rd *HAWK* TN18 .... 199 H3 🔲
North Hill Rd *HAWK* TN18 .... 198 E4
North Kent Av *GVW* DA11 .... 30 E4
North Kent Aveune *GVW* DA11 .. 30 E4
Northlands Av *ORP* BR6 .... 56 A7
Northleigh Cl *MAID/SHEP* ME15.. 121 J7
North Meadow *E/WMAL* ME19 .. 99 M6
Northolme Cl *CDH/CHF* ME16 .. 16 E2 🔲
Northolme Ri *ORP* BR6 .... 56 A5 🔲
North Pasley Rd *CHAT* ME4 .... 50 D6
North Pole Rd *WBY/YAL* ME18 .. 119 K3
Northridge *RYE* TN31 .... 206 C7
Northridge Rd *GVE* DA12 .... 31 L8
North Riding *HART* DA3 .... 45 M7
North Belv *DA17* 12 D2

 CHAT ME4 .... 50 D5
 CRBK TN17 .... 182 A4
 GILL ME7 .... 27 H4
 HOO/HM ME3 .... 20 D7
 PUR RM19 .... 14 E3
North St *BXLYHN* DA7 .... 26 C2
 DART DA1 .... 27 M5
 EDEN TN8 .... 31 K5 🔲
 GVE DA12 .... 31 K5 🔲
 HDCN TN27 .... 155 L8
 HDCN TN27 .... 186 C3
 MAIDW ME16 .... 120 A3
 RMAID ME17 .... 139 G6
 RTWE/PEM TN2 .... 11 J5
 SIT ME10 .... 71 G6
 STRD ME2 .... 3 G3
North Ter *HOO/HM* ME3 .... 35 H6
Northumberland Av *RHAM* ME8 .. 68 A4
Northumberland Cl
 ERITH DA8 .... 12 E6 🔲
Northumberland Rd
 MAID/SHEP ME15 .... 121 L6
 MEO DA13 .... 46 B4
 SLH/COR SS17 .... 18 B1
Northumberland Wy
 BXLYHN DA7 .... 12 E7
North Vw *MAID/SHEP* ME15 .... 121 K4
Northview *SWLY* BR8 .... 42 A6
North View Av *TIL* RM18 .... 17 J7
North View Cl *SEV* TN13 .... 95 L7
North Wy *MAID/BEAR* ME14 ... 103 K6
Northwood *CDH/CHF* ME16 .... 17 K1 🔲
Northwood Av *HOO/HM* ME3... 36 A1
Northwood Dr *SIT* ME10 .... 88 B3
Northwood Pl *ERITHM* DA18 ... 12 B2
Northwood Rd *TONN* TN10 ..... 131 K7
Norton Crs *RTON* TN10 .... 131 K6
Norton Gv *WALD* ME5 .... 83 G1
Norton Rd *RMAID* ME17 .... 138 E4
 SWLY BR8 .... 42 A6
Nortons La *TENT* TN30 .... 187 G8
Nortons Wy *STPH/PW* TN12 .... 149 J6
Norwich Av *TONN* TN10 .... 131 M8
Norwich Cl *STRD* ME2 .... 48 F7 🔲
Norwich Pl *BXLYHS* DA6 .... 26 C2
Norwood La *MEO* DA13 .... 62 D1
Nottidge Rd *STH/RUST* TN4 .... 176 F4 🔲
Nottingham Av
 MAID/SHEP ME15 .... 121 M7 🔲
Nouds La *RSIT* ME9 .... 89 M6
Nouds Rd *RSIT* ME9 .... 89 M5
Novar Cl *ORP* BR6 .... 56 B3
The Nower *RSEV* TN14 .... 93 H6
 RSEV TN14 .... 93 M2
Nuffield Rd *SWLY* BR8 .... 42 C3
Nunnery La *RTON* TN11 .... 161 H5
Nunns Wy *GRAYS* RM17 .... 16 F5
Nursery Av *BXLYHN* DA7 .... 26 B1
 MAID/BEAR ME14 .... 122 D2
 MAIDW ME16 .... 102 D7
Nursery Cl *ORP* BR6 .... 56 B3
 RDART DA2 .... 28 E5
 SEV TN13 .... 9 J1
 SWLY BR8 .... 41 L6 🔲
 TONN TN10 .... 148 A1
Nursery Gdns *HOO/HM* ME3 ... 36 A8 🔲
Nursery Pl *SEV* TN13 .... 94 F8
Nursery Rd *DIT/AY* ME20 .... 101 L4
 MEO DA13 .... 62 C1
 RHAM ME8 .... 67 M5
 STH/RUST TN4 .... 163 K5
The Nursery *ERITH* DA8 .... 13 H6
Nurstead Av *MAID/SHEP* ME15 .. 45 M7
Nurstead Church La *MEO* DA13.. 46 C8
Nurstead La *HART* DA3 .... 45 M8
Nurstead Rd *ERITH* DA8 .... 12 C6
Nutberry Av *CDH/CHF* ME16 ..... 16 C1 🔲
Nutberry Cl *CDH/CHF* RM16 .... 16 C1 🔲
 RSIT ME9 .... 89 M3
Nutfield Cl *WALD* ME5 .... 66 D5
Nutfields *BGR/WK* TN15 .... 115 K1
 SIT ME10 .... 88 D2
Nuthatch *HART* DA3 .... 45 K7
Nutley Cl *SWLY* BR8 .... 42 B5
Nutmead Cl *BXLY* DA5 .... 26 E6
Nut Tree Cl *ORP* BR6 .... 56 F6
Nutwood Cl
 MAID/BEAR ME14 .... 122 A1 🔲
Nuxley Rd *BELV* DA17 .... 12 B5

O

Oakapple La *MAIDW* ME16 .... 120 C2
Oak Av *GILL* ME7 .... 51 G7
 SEV TN13 .... 113 K6
Oak Cl *DART* DA1 .... 27 G2
 HOO/HM ME3 .... 51 G2 🔲🔲
Oakdale La *EDEN* TN8 .... 126 E3
Oakdale Rd *STH/RUST* TN4 .... 10 C3
Oakdene Av *ERITH* DA8 .... 12 E5
Oakdene Rd *SEV* TN13 .... 8 F1
 STMC/STPC BR5 .... 56 C2
Oak Dr *DIT/AY* ME20 .... 101 J3
 HOO/HM ME3 .... 48 D2
Oak End Cl *STH/RUST* TN4 ...... 163 J5
Oakenden La *EDEN* TN8 .... 160 D4
Oakenden Rd *MEO* DA13 .... 63 G4
Oak Farm Gdns *HDCN* TN27 ... 155 M7
Oak Farm La *BGR/WK* TN15 ...... 79 G4
Oakfield *HAWK* TN18 .... 199 H3
Oakfield Court Rd
 RTWE/PEM TN2 .... 11 H6
Oakfield La *RDART* DA2 .... 27 J7
Oakfield Park Rd *DART* DA1 ...... 27 M7
Oakfield Pl *DART* DA1 .... 27 M7
Oakfield Rd *EDEN* TN8 .... 142 D1
 STPH/PW TN12 .... 165 M5
Oakfields *SEV* TN13 .... 9 H9
 SIT ME10 .... 87 L2 🔲
Oakhill Rd *ORP* BR6 .... 56 B5
 PUR RM19 .... 14 D4
Oak Hill Rd *SEV* TN13 .... 8 E5
Oakhouse Rd *BXLYHS* DA6 .... 26 C3
Oakhurst Av *BXLYHN* DA7 .... 12 A6
Oakhurst Cl *WALD* ME5 .... 83 H2

Oakhurst Gdns *BXLYHN* DA7 ..... 12 A6
Oaklands Cl *BGR/WK* TN15 ...... 77 G1
 BXLYHS DA6 .... 26 B3
 STMC/STPC BR5 .... 56 A2
Oaklands La *BH/WHM* TN16 ...... 91 L1
Oaklands Rd *BXLYHS* DA6 .... 26 B2
 GVW DA11 .... 199 H4
 HAWK TN18 .... 28 D6
 RDART DA2 .... 175 K7
 RRTW TN3 .... 147 H1
Oaklands Wy *RTON* TN11 .... 155 M8
 RSIT ME9 .... 68 F4
 SEV TN13 .... 9 H9
Oaklea Rd *STPH/PW* TN12 .... 150 B7
Oakleigh Cl *SWLY* BR8 .... 42 A7
 WALD ME5 .... 83 G3
Oakleigh Gdns *ORP* BR6 .... 56 A7
Oak Lodge La *BH/WHM* TN16 .. 110 F3
Oakmead *MEO* DA13 .... 62 C5 🔲
 TONN TN10 .... 131 L7
Oakmore Gdns *STMC/STPC* BR5.. 40 E8
Oak Rd *BH/WHM* TN16 .... 110 F3
 ERITH DA8 .... 12 E6
 GRAYS RM17 .... 16 E5
 GRH DA9 .... 29 G4
 GVE DA12 .... 31 K8
 HOO/HM ME3 .... 51 G2 🔲
 ORP BR6 .... 163 M6
 RTWE/PEM TN2 .... 71 L8
 SIT ME10 .... 71 G6
 STPH/PW TN12 .... 149 K6
 STRD ME2 .... 2 B6
Oaks Dene *WALD* ME5 .... 83 H4
Oaks Forstal *HAWK* TN18 .... 200 E8
Oakshaw *OXTED* RH8 .... 108 F5
Oaks Rd *TENT* TN30 .... 196 D6
The Oaks *DIT/AY* ME20 .... 102 A4
 SWLY BR8 .... 42 A6
Oak Tree Avenue *GRH* DA9 .... 29 H5
Oak Tree Av *MAID/SHEP* ME15 .. 121 L6
Oak Tree Cl *RTW* TN1 .... 10 F9
 STPH/PW TN12 .... 152 F8 🔲
Oakum Ct *CHAT* ME4 .... 66 D3
Oak Vw *EDEN* TN8 .... 142 D3
Oakway Cl *BXLY* DA5 .... 26 A4
Oakwood Cl *DART* DA1 .... 28 D6
Oakwood Ct *MAIDW* ME16 .... 6 B6
Oakwood Dr *BXLYHN* DA7 .... 26 E2
 SEV TN13 .... 9 G3
Oakwood Ri *HART* DA3 .... 45 G2
 RTWE/PEM TN2 .... 164 A6
Oakwood Rd *MAIDW* ME16 ...... 120 E2
 STMC/STPC BR5 .... 163 M6
Oast Cl *RTWE/PEM* TN2 .... 88 A3
Oast Ct *SIT* ME10 .... 135 H4
Oast House Wy *STMC/STPC* BR5.. 40 D8
Oast La *RTON* TN11 .... 147 J1
Oastview *RHAM* ME8 .... 68 C5
Oast Vw *STPH/PW* TN12 .... 167 J7
Oast Wy *HART* DA3 .... 61 G2
Oatfield Cl *CRBK* TN17 .... 183 L8
Oatfield Dr *CRBK* TN17 .... 183 L8
Oatfield Rd *ORP* BR6 .... 56 B4
Ocelot Ct *CHAT* ME4 .... 5 H8 🔲
Ockham Dr *STMC/STPC* BR5 .... 40 C4 🔲
Ockley La *HAWK* TN18 .... 199 J1
Ockley Rd *HAWK* TN18 .... 199 J3
Octavia Cl *WALD* ME5 .... 83 K2 🔲
Odiham Dr *MAIDW* ME16 .... 102 E6
Offen's Dr *STPH/PW* TN12 .... 170 A2
Offham Rd *E/WMAL* ME19 .... 100 C6
Officers Ter *CHAT* ME4 .... 50 B6
The Old Bailey *RMAID* ME17 .. 125 G7 🔲
Old Barn Rd *BGR/WK* TN15 ...... 67 H7
 GILL ME7 .... 147 H5
 TON TN9 .... 100 F3
Old Barn Rd *E/WMAL* ME19 ...... 26 F2
Old Barn Wy *BXLYHN* DA7 .... 26 F7
Old Bexley La *BXLY* DA5 .... 26 F7
Oldbury Cl *STMC/STPC* BR5 ..... 40 F8
Oldbury La *BGR/WK* TN15 .... 97 K8
The Old Carriageway *GILL* ME7 .. 84 B2
 SEV TN13 .... 112 E1
Old Chapel Rd *SWLY* BR8 .... 57 L3
Old Chatham Rd *DIT/AY* ME20 .. 82 F7
 MAID/BEAR ME14 .... 103 G4
Old Church La *WBY/YAL* ME18 .. 118 A3
Old Church Rd *ROCH* ME1 .... 81 M4
 RTWE/PEM TN2 .... 164 F4
 WBY/YAL ME18 .... 117 M8
Old Coach Rd *BGR/WK* TN15 .... 78 A3
Old Dartford Rd *EYN* DA4 .... 59 H2
Old Downs *HART* DA3 .... 61 G1
Old Dr *MAID/SHEP* ME15 .... 121 H7
Old Farleigh Rd *WARL* CR6 .... 90 B1
Old Farm Gdns *SWLY* BR8 .... 42 B7 🔲
Old Ferry Rd *RSIT* ME9 .... 55 C7
Oldfield Cl *MAID/SHEP* ME15 .. 122 A4
 RHAM ME8 .... 67 M5
Oldfield Rd *BXLYHN* DA7 .... 12 A8
Old Forge La *EDEN* TN8 .... 106 B1
Old Forge Wy *SCUP* DA14 .... 40 D1
Old Gardens Cl *RTWE/PEM* TN2.. 177 K5
The Old Gdn *SEV* TN13 .... 112 F1
Old Hadlow Rd *TONN* TN10 .... 148 A1
Old Ham La *RMAID* ME17 .... 141 K1
Old Hl *ORP* BR6 .... 73 G1
Old House La *RRTW* TN3 .... 161 M8
Old House Rd *RSIT* ME9 .... 86 A1
Old Kent Rd *STPH/PW* TN12 .... 150 B7
Old Lain *RMAID* ME17 .... 125 H7
Old Ld La *BGR/WK* TN15 .... 115 K1
 BH/WHM TN16 .... 91 M7
 OXTED RH8 .... 109 H8
Old London Rd *BGR/WK* TN15 .. 98 B1
 RSEV TN14 .... 74 C4
 TONN TN10 .... 147 L2 🔲
Old Loose Hl *MAID/SHEP* ME15.. 137 H1
Old Maidstone Rd *SCUP* DA14 .. 41 H4
Old Manor Wy *BXLYHN* DA7 ..... 12 F8
Old Mill La *DIT/AY* ME20 .... 59 C4
Old Mill Rd *RMAID* ME20 .... 102 E2
 RMAID ME17 .... 123 H5
Old Orch *HAWK* TN18 .... 200 D8
Old Orchard La *E/WMAL* ME19 .. 100 F4
The Old Orch *RHAM* ME8 .... 68 C7
Old Otford Rd *RSEV* TN14 .... 95 K4
Old Pattens La *ROCH* ME1 .... 65 M3

Old Perry St *CHST* BR7 .... 40 A4
 GVW DA11 .... 31 G7
Old Regent Dr *CRBK* TN17 .... 202 A2
Old Rd *CHAT* ME4 .... 4 C6
 DART DA1 .... 26 F2
 STPH/PW TN12 .... 134 B7
 WBY/YAL ME18 .... 118 D6
Old Rd East *GVE* DA12 .... 31 M6
Old Rd West *GVW* DA11 .... 31 H6
Old School Cl *RMAID* ME17 .... 141 M1
Old School Ct *HOO/HM* ME3 ..... 50 B1 🔲
Old School La *E/WMAL* ME19 .. 100 B1
Old Soar Rd *BGR/WK* TN15 ...... 116 D5
Old Station Rd *WADH* TN5 .... 188 A7
Old Tannery Cl *TENT* TN30 ..... 196 B6 🔲
Old Terry's Lodge Rd
 BGR/WK TN15 .... 97 H2
Old Tovil Rd *MAID/SHEP* ME15 .. 6 F9
Old Trafford Cl *MAIDW* ME16 .. 102 D7
Old Tree La *RMAID* ME17 .... 137 L2
Old Tye Av *BH/WHM* TN16 .... 92 A2
The Old Wk *RSEV* TN14 .... 95 K3
Old Watling St *STRD* ME2 .... 48 D5
The Old Yews *HART* DA3 .... 45 K7
Oliver Cl *CHAT* ME4 .... 66 D3
 WTHK RM20 .... 15 H4
Oliver Crs *EYN* DA4 .... 59 H3
Olive Rd *DART* DA1 .... 27 M6
Oliver Rd *STPH/PW* TN12 .... 170 A2
 SWLY BR8 .... 41 M7
 WTHK RM20 .... 15 H5
Oliver Twist Cl *ROCH* ME1 .... 3 G9 🔲
Olivine Cl *WALD* ME5 .... 83 H3 🔲
Olliffe Cl *WALD* ME5 .... 83 H3 🔲
Onslow Rd *ROCH* ME1 .... 65 M2
Orache Dr *MAID/BEAR* ME14 .. 104 A3
Orange Court La *ORP* BR6 .... 72 C3
Orange Ter *ROCH* ME1 .... 3 L8
Orbit Cl *WALD* ME5 .... 83 J5
Orchard Av *BELV* DA17 .... 27 K5
 DART DA1 .... 102 A4
 DIT/AY ME20 .... 101 K8
 GVW DA11 .... 46 D2
 STRD ME2 .... 49 H4 🔲
Orchard Cl *BXLYHN* DA7 .... 12 A7
 EDEN TN8 .... 142 D5
 HART DA3 .... 45 K6
 RMAID ME17 .... 136 E2
 RMAID ME17 .... 139 G1
 RSEV TN14 .... 95 L7
 RTWE/PEM TN2 .... 163 M6
 STPH/PW TN12 .... 167 H7
Orchard Crs *STPH/PW* TN12 .... 167 J3
Orchard Dr *EDEN* TN8 .... 142 D3
 GRAYS RM17 .... 16 C1
 MEO DA13 .... 62 B1
 RSIT ME9 .... 69 J8
 TONN TN10 .... 132 A8
Orchard Gld *HDCN* TN27 .... 155 M8
Orchard Gn *ORP* BR6 .... 56 A5
Orchard Gv *DIT/AY* ME20 .... 101 K3
 ORP BR6 .... 56 B5
Orchard Hl *DART* DA1 .... 27 H7
Orchard Pl *MAIDW* ME16 .... 6 D6
 SIT ME10 .... 88 C2
Orchard Ri *RRTW* TN3 .... 175 K6
Orchard Rd *BELV* DA17 .... 12 C3
 GVW DA11 .... 30 F7
 MAID/BEAR ME14 .... 122 A1
 ORP BR6 .... 73 L3
 RSEV TN14 .... 95 H2
 SCUP DA14 .... 40 A1
 SEV TN13 .... 95 G8
 STPH/PW TN12 .... 134 C7
 SWCM DA10 .... 30 A3
 TENT TN30 .... 196 C2
Orchard St *DART* DA1 .... 28 A4
 MAID/SHEP ME15 .... 7 G7
 RHAM ME8 .... 68 B1
The Orchard *MAID/BEAR* ME14 .. 122 D1
 SEV TN13 .... 95 G7 🔲
 SWLY BR8 .... 41 M6 🔲
Orchard Vw *MAID/BEAR* ME14 .. 104 C5
 RSIT ME9 .... 89 L2
 TENT TN30 .... 196 E6
Orchard Wy *BGR/WK* TN15 ...... 96 C3
 CRBK TN17 .... 192 D1
 RDART DA2 .... 27 M8
 SNOD ME6 .... 81 H6
 STPH/PW TN12 .... 167 J7
Orchid Cl *STRD* ME2 .... 48 E7
Orchidhurst *RTWE/PEM* TN2 ... 163 M6 🔲
Orchis Gv *GRAYS* RM17 .... 16 B3
Ordnance St *CHAT* ME4 .... 4 B8
Ordnance Ter *CHAT* ME4 .... 4 B8
Oriel Wy *DIT/AY* ME20 .... 101 H3
Orion Rd *ROCH* ME1 .... 65 L6
Orlestone Gdns *ORP* BR6 .... 57 G8 🔲
Orlick Rd *GVE* DA12 .... 32 D7
The Orpines *WBY/YAL* ME18 ... 119 H6
Orpington By-pass *RSEV* TN14.... 74 C3
Orpington Rd *CHST* BR7 .... 40 A4
Orsett Heath Crs *CDH/CHF* RM16.. 17 J2
Orsett Rd *GRAYS* RM17 .... 16 C4
Orwell Cl *DIT/AY* ME20 .... 101 H2
Orwell Spike *E/WMAL* ME19 .... 100 C8
Osborne Rd *BELV* DA17 .... 12 B4
 GILL ME7 .... 5 K4
Osbourne Rd *RDART* DA2 .... 28 D4
Osgood Av *ORP* BR6 .... 56 B8
Osgood Gdns *ORP* BR6 .... 56 B8
Osmers Hl *WADH* TN5 .... 188 B6
Osney Wy *GVE* DA12 .... 32 B7
Osprey Av *WALD* ME5 .... 67 G3
Osprey Cl *SIT* ME10 .... 88 C7
Osprey Wk *DIT/AY* ME20 .... 101 H4
Ospringe Pl *RTWE/PEM* TN2 ... 164 B7
Osterberg Rd *DART* DA1 .... 28 B2
Ostlers Ct *SNOD* ME6 .... 81 J5 🔲
Otford Cl *BXLY* DA5 .... 26 C6
Otford La *RSEV* TN14 .... 74 B7
Otford Rd *RSEV* TN14 .... 95 K7
Otham La *MAID/SHEP* ME15 ... 122 E3
Otham St *MAID/SHEP* ME15 .... 122 E5
Otlinge Cl *STMC/STPC* BR5 ..... 40 F8 🔲
Ottawa Rd *TIL* RM18 .... 17 J7
Otterbourne Pl
 MAID/SHEP ME15 .... 122 A4 🔲
Otterden Cl *ORP* BR6 .... 56 A7 🔲

Otterham Quay La RHAM ME8...... 68 D5
Otteridge Rd MAID/BEAR ME14.. 122 C2
Otters Cl STMC/STPC BR5 .... 40 F8 5
Otway St CHAT ME4 .... 4 E8
Otway Ter CHAT ME4 .... 4 F7
Oval Gdns GRAYS RM17 .... 16 E2
The Oval HART DA3 .... 45 L7
Ovenden Rd RSEV TN14 .... 93 M6
Overcliffe GVW DA11 .... 31 J4
Overcliff Rd GRAYS RM17 .... 16 F4
Overdale RSEV TN14 .... 129 K3
Overmead SWLY BR8 .... 58 A1 3
Over Minnis HART DA3.......... 61 H6
Overy St DART DA1.......... 28 B4
Owen Cl E/WMAL ME19 .... 101 H5 2
Owens Wy GILL ME7.......... 51 J7
Oxenden Wood Rd ORP BR6 .... 73 K1
Oxenhill Rd RSEV TN14 .... 96 A3
Oxenhoath Rd RTON TN11 .... 132 E1
Oxford Av CDH/CHF RM16 .... 17 J3
Oxford Cl GVE DA12 .... 32 B7 1
Oxford Ms BXLY DA5 .... 26 C6
Oxford Rd GILL ME7 .... 5 M7
MAID/SHEP ME15 .... 121 M4
SCUP DA14 .... 40 D2
Oxford St SNOD ME6 .... 81 J5
Ox La TENT TN30.......... 196 D3
Ox Lea RRTW TN3.......... 176 C2
Oxley Shaw La E/WMAL ME19 .... 101 G3
Oyster Cl SIT ME10 .... 71 G7 5

P

Packer Pl WALD ME5 .... 66 C5
Packham Rd GVW DA11 .... 31 H8
Packhorse Rd SEV TN13 .... 112 E1
Padbrook OXTED RH8 .... 109 J7
Paddlesworth Rd SNOD ME6 .... 80 E4
Paddock Cl BGR/WK TN15.......... 98 E7
EYN DA4 .... 43 L5
RRTW TN3.......... 161 K8
Paddock Rd BXLYHS DA6 .... 26 A2
Paddocks Cl STMC/STPC BR5 .... 56 F5
The Paddocks EDEN TN8 .... 159 K6
GILL ME7 .... 67 J8
SEV TN13.......... 9 L4
STPH/PW TN12 .... 134 A7 1
The Paddock BH/WHM TN16 .... 110 E4
CHAT ME4 .... 4 C6
MEO DA13.......... 79 H6
RTON TN11 .... 133 G4
RTWE/PEM TN2 .... 164 E7
RYE TN31 .... 206 D6
Pad's Hl MAID/SHEP ME15 .... 7 H5
Padsole La MAID/SHEP ME15 ..... 7 H5 1
Pageant Cl TIL RM18 .... 17 L7
Page Cl RDART DA2 .... 29 L8
Page Crs ERITH DA8 .... 13 H6
Pagehurst Rd STPH/PW TN12 .... 169 L2
Paget St GILL ME7 .... 5 H4
Pagette Wy GRAYS RM17 .... 16 C4
Pagitt St CHAT ME4 .... 4 B9
Paiges Farm Cl RSEV TN14 .... 129 L3
Painters Ash La GVW DA11 .... 30 F8
Palace Av MAID/SHEP ME15 .... 7 G5
Palace Rd BH/WHM TN16 .... 92 C7
Palewell Cl STMC/STPC BR5 .... 40 D6
Palmar Crs BXLYHN DA7 .... 26 C1
Palmar Rd BXLYHN DA7.......... 12 C8
MAIDW ME16 .... 6 A1
Palmarsh Cl STMC/STPC BR5 ..... 40 F8 7
Palm Av SCUP DA14 .... 40 F3
Palmer Av GVE DA12 .... 46 F1
Palmer's Av GRAYS RM17 .... 16 E4
Palmers Brook RTON TN11.......... 133 H3
Palmers Dr GRAYS RM17 .... 16 E3
Palmers Green La
STPH/PW TN12 .... 166 F4
Palmers Orch RSEV TN14 .... 75 H5 1
Palmerston Gdns WTHK RM20.......... 15 M4
Palmerston Rd CHAT ME4.......... 66 B4
WTHK RM20 .... 15 M4
Pankhurst Rd HOO/HM ME3 .... 35 M7
Pannell Rd HOO/HM ME3 .... 25 J7
Panteny La RSIT ME9.......... 89 G3
Panter's SWLY BR8.......... 42 B4
The Pantiles BXLYHN DA7 .... 12 B6
RTWE/PEM TN2.......... 10 E8
Panton Cl WALD ME5.......... 83 L1
Papion Gv WALD ME5.......... 83 G3
The Parade STRD ME2 .... 2 B1
Parham Rd CHAT ME4 .... 4 D9 1
Park Av EDEN TN8 .... 142 D3
GILL ME7 .... 5 M8
GVE DA12 .... 31 L6
GVW DA11.......... 31 G6
MAID/BEAR ME14 .... 7 J1
ORP BR6 .... 56 C6
QBOR ME11 .... 55 K1
RMAID ME17.......... 137 G3
RTON TN11 .... 131 H8
SIT ME10.......... 88 A3
WTHK RM20 .... 15 J5
Park Barn Rd RMAID ME17 .... 123 K8
Park Corner Rd MEO DA13.......... 30 C7
Park Crs CHAT ME4.......... 66 B5
ERITH DA8.......... 12 F5
Park Dr HART DA3 .... 45 G7 1
SIT ME10.......... 87 M4
Parker Av TIL RM18 .... 17 L7
Parker Cl RHAM ME8 .... 68 A8
Parker Rd GRAYS RM17 .... 16 B4
Park Farm Rd E/WMAL ME19.......... 80 A6
Parkfield BGR/WK TN15 .... 114 B1
Parkfield Rd RHAM ME8 .... 68 B3
Parkfields STRD ME2 .... 48 E6
Park Gdns ERITH DA8.......... 12 F3
Parkgate Rd ORP BR6 .... 57 L7
Park Gv BXLYHN DA7 .... 26 E2
Park Hl MEO DA13.......... 46 A8
Parkhill Rd BXLY DA5.......... 26 B5
Park Hill Rd RSEV TN14 .... 96 A3
Park House Gdns
STH/RUST TN4 .... 163 J4
Parkhurst Gdns BXLY DA5 .... 26 C5 1
Parkhurst Rd BXLY DA5.......... 26 C5
Parkland Cl SEV TN13 .... 113 L7
Park La BGR/WK TN15 .... 96 C4
BGR/WK TN15 .... 114 C1
HAWK TN18.......... 191 M6
MAID/BEAR ME14 .... 103 H6
RMAID ME17.......... 137 M3
SEV TN13.......... 9 J4
SWLY BR8 .... 42 E6
Park Pl GVE DA12 .... 31 L4
SEV TN13.......... 112 F1
Park Rd DART DA1 .... 28 C5
E/WMAL ME19 .... 99 L2
E/WMAL ME19 .... 100 F2
GVW DA11.......... 31 K7
OXTED RH8.......... 109 H6
RTON TN11 .... 116 E8
SIT ME10.......... 88 A2
STH/RUST TN4 .... 11 G1
STMC/STPC BR5 .... 56 E2
STPH/PW TN12 .... 169 J2
SWCM DA10 .... 30 A4
SWLY BR8 .... 42 B8
WBY/YAL ME18.......... 118 B8
Parkside CDH/CHF RM16.......... 16 F2
HOO/HM ME3.......... 34 D6
RSEV TN14 .... 74 A7
Parkside Av BXLYHN DA7 .... 12 F8
TIL RM18 .... 17 K8
Parkside Cross BXLYHN DA7.......... 13 G8
Parkside Rd BELV DA17 .... 12 D3
Park St RTWE/PEM TN2.......... 11 J6
Park Ter GRH DA9.......... 29 K3
The Park SCUP DA14 .... 40 B2
Park Vw RYE TN31 .... 206 C7
Park View Cl EDEN TN8.......... 142 D3
Park View Gdns GRAYS RM17 ... 16 D4 3
Park View Rd CTHM CR3.......... 90 B8
Park Wallis GVW DA11 .... 30 D3
Park Wy BXLY DA5 .... 27 H8
MAID/SHEP ME15 .... 121 K4
RMAID ME17.......... 136 E2
Parkway ERITHM DA18 .... 12 A2
TONN TN10.......... 131 M8
Parkwood Cl RTWE/PEM TN2 .... 163 L7
Park Wood La STPH/PW TN12 .... 170 E3
Parkwood Rd BH/WHM TN16 .... 92 A7
BXLY DA5 .... 26 B5
Paroma Rd BELV DA17.......... 12 C2
Parr Av GILL ME7.......... 5 M1
Parrock Av GVE DA12.......... 31 L6
Parrock Rd GVE DA12 .... 31 L5
Parrock St GVE DA12 .... 31 K4 12
Parrs Haed Ms ROCH ME1 .... 3 K5 2
Parsonage Cl STH/RUST TN4 .... 162 D8 1
WARL CR6 .... 90 A2
Parsonage La EYN DA4 .... 43 K3
RRTW TN3.......... 180 D7
RSIT ME9.......... 70 C5
SCUP DA14 .... 41 H1
Parsonage Manorway
ERITH DA8.......... 12 C5
Parsonage Rd STH/RUST TN4.... 162 D8
WTHK RM20 .... 15 L5
Parsons La BGR/WK TN15 .... 78 A4 1
RDART DA2 .... 27 K8
Partridge Av DIT/AY ME20 .... 101 H2
Partridge Dr CHAT ME4 .... 50 D4 1
Pasley Rd GILL ME7 .... 50 C6
Pasley Rd East CHAT ME4 .... 50 C6
Pastime Cl SIT ME10 .... 71 G5 1
The Patch SEV TN13.......... 95 G8
Patrixbourne Av RHAM ME8 .... 67 L3
Pattenden Gdns
STPH/PW TN12 .... 134 C6
Pattenden La STPH/PW TN12 ..... 152 D5
Pattens La CHAT ME4.......... 66 A4
Patterdale Rd RDART DA2 .... 28 E6
Paulinus Cl STMC/STPC BR5 .... 40 E6
The Pavement TENT TN30 .... 196 C2
Pavilion Dr SIT ME10 .... 71 H4
Pavilion La WBY/YAL ME18 .... 118 C5
Paynesfield Rd BH/WHM TN16 ..... 91 L6
Payne's La MAID/SHEP ME15 .... 121 J6
Peach Cft GVW DA11 .... 31 G8
Peacock St GVE DA12 .... 31 L5
Peal Cl HOO/HM ME3.......... 36 A8
Peareswood Rd ERITH DA8 .... 13 H7
Pearman Cl RHAM ME8 .... 68 C4 1
Pearse Pl RRTW TN3 .... 180 C8
Pearsons Green Rd
STPH/PW TN12 .... 150 E8
STPH/PW TN12 .... 167 G1
Pearson Wy DART DA1 .... 28 B7
Pear Tree Av DIT/AY ME20 .... 101 L5
Pear Tree Cl BXLYHN DA7 .... 12 F7
CRBK TN17 .... 192 F2
SWLY BR8 .... 41 M6 3
Pear Tree La GILL ME7 .... 67 G6
MAID/SHEP ME15 .... 121 K7
Peartree La STRD ME2.......... 48 C3
Pease Hl BGR/WK TN15 .... 78 B1
Peasley La CRBK TN17.......... 181 M7
Peat Wy HOO/HM ME3 .... 24 F6
Peckham Cl STRD ME2.......... 3 J1
Peel Dr SIT ME10.......... 88 E1
Peel St MAID/BEAR ME14 .... 7 G1
Peens La RMAID ME17.......... 137 L6
Pegasus Ct GVE DA12 .... 31 L8
Peggoty Cl HOO/HM ME3 .... 48 D2
Pelham Rd BXLYHN DA7 .... 26 C1
GVW DA11.......... 31 H5
Pelham Rd South GVW DA11 .... 31 H6
Pelican Cl STRD ME2 .... 48 E7
Pell Cl WADH TN5 .... 188 C7
Pells La BGR/WK TN15 .... 77 J5
Pemberton Gdns SWLY BR8 .... 42 A7 2
Pemberton Sq STRD ME2 .... 3 K1 1
Pemble Cl STPH/PW TN12.......... 149 J6
Pembroke CHAT ME4.......... 50 C5
Pembroke Cl ERITH DA8 .... 12 F3 2
Pembroke Gdns RHAM ME8 .... 85 G1 2
Pembroke Pl EYN DA4 .... 43 K5 1
Pembroke Rd ERITH DA8 .... 12 E4
RMAID ME17.......... 136 E2
SEV TN13.......... 9 H6
TON TN9 .... 147 J4 1
Pembury Cl RTWE/PEM TN2 .... 164 F6 5
Pembury Crs SCUP DA14.......... 26 A7
Pembury Gdns MAIDW ME16 .... 6 B6
Pembury Gra RTWE/PEM TN2 .... 164 C7
Pembury Gv TON TN9 .... 147 L5 3
Pembury Hall Rd
RTWE/PEM TN2 .... 164 E2
Pembury Rd BXLYHN DA7 .... 12 A6
RTON TN11 .... 164 C2
RTWE/PEM TN2 .... 11 J5
TON TN9 .... 147 K5
Pembury St SIT ME10 .... 88 A1 5
Pembury Wks RTON TN11 .... 164 D3
Pembury Wy RHAM ME8 .... 68 A3 2
Pencroft Dr DART DA1.......... 27 L5
Penda Rd ERITH DA8 .... 12 D6
Pendennis Rd ORP BR6 .... 56 E5
SEV TN13.......... 9 H2
Penderel Ms TENT TN30 .... 196 D5
Penenden HART DA3 .... 61 H5
Penenden Heath Rd
MAID/BEAR ME14 .... 103 K6
Penenden St MAID/BEAR ME14 .... 7 G1
Penfold Cl MAID/SHEP ME15 ...... 122 A7
WALD ME5 .... 66 D6 2
Penfold Hl RMAID ME17 .... 123 K5
Penfolds Cl TONN TN10 .... 131 L8 1
Penfold Wy MAID/SHEP ME15 .... 121 H7
Penguin Cl STRD ME2 .... 48 F7 3
Penhurst Cl MAID/BEAR ME14 104 B8 4
Penlee Cl EDEN TN8.......... 142 E3
Pennant Rd ROCH ME1 .... 65 L6
Penn Cl SIT ME10 .... 88 D3
Penney Cl DART DA1 .... 27 M5
Pennine Wy BXLYHN DA7 .... 13 G7
GVW DA11.......... 31 G8
MAID/SHEP ME15 .... 122 C4 1
Pennington Pl STH/RUST TN4 ..... 163 K3
Pennington Rd STH/RUST TN4.... 163 J3
Penn La RSEV TN14 .... 112 A5
Penns Yd RTWE/PEM TN2.......... 164 E7
Pennyfields CRBK TN17 .... 192 F1 3
Penshurst Cl BGR/WK TN15 .... 77 G1 3
HART DA3 .... 45 M6 1
RHAM ME8 .... 67 M3
Penshurst Rd BXLYHN DA7 .... 12 B7
RTON TN11.......... 145 K5
RTON TN11.......... 161 M3
Penshurst Wy
STMC/STPC BR5 .... 40 E8 5
The Penstocks MAIDW ME16 .... 6 B9
Pen Wy TONN TN10 .... 132 A8
Pepingstraw Cl E/WMAL ME19 .... 99 M6
Pepper Hl GVW DA11 .... 30 E8
Pepys Cl GVW DA11 .... 30 F8
TIL RM18.......... 17 L7
Pepys Ri ORP BR6.......... 56 B4
Pepy's Wy STRD ME2.......... 2 D2
Perch La RRTW TN3.......... 179 M4
Percy Rd BXLYHN DA7 .... 12 A8
Percy St GRAYS RM17.......... 16 E5
Peregrine Dr SIT ME10.......... 88 C2
Peregrine Rd WBY/YAL ME18 .... 118 C3
Perimeter Rd DIT/AY ME20.......... 101 L2
Periwinkle Cl SIT ME10 .... 71 G8
Perkins Cl GRH DA9 .... 29 H3
Perran Cl HART DA3 .... 45 H8 3
Perryfield St MAID/BEAR ME14 ...... 6 F1
Perry Gv DART DA1 .... 28 C2
Perry Hall Cl ORP BR6 .... 56 C3
Perry Hall Rd ORP BR6 .... 56 B2
Perry Hl HOO/HM ME3.......... 34 E4
Perry Mnr CHST BR7 .... 40 A3
Perrys La ORP BR6 .... 73 K7
Perry St CHAT ME4 .... 4 A8
CHST BR7 .... 40 A3
DART DA1 .... 27 G1
GVW DA11.......... 31 G6
MAID/BEAR ME14 .... 6 F1
Perth Gdns SIT ME10 .... 87 L1 1
Pescot Av HART DA3 .... 45 J7
Pested Bars Rd RMAID ME17 .... 121 L8
Peter Av OXTED RH8 .... 108 F7
Petersfield RTWE/PEM TN2 .... 165 G6
Petersham Dr STMC/STPC BR5 .... 40 B6
Petersham Gdns
STMC/STPC BR5 .... 40 B6 1
Petham Gn RHAM ME8 .... 67 L3
Petten Cl STMC/STPC BR5.......... 56 F4
Petten Gv STMC/STPC BR5 .... 56 E4
Petteridge La STPH/PW TN12 .... 166 A7
Pett La RSIT ME9.......... 86 C5
Petworth Rd BXLYHS DA6.......... 26 C3
Peverel Dr MAID/BEAR ME14 .... 104 B8
Pheasant La MAID/SHEP ME15 .... 121 K6
Pheasant Rd CHAT ME4 .... 66 E3 3
Phelps Cl BGR/WK TN15 .... 77 G1
Phillip Av SWLY BR8 .... 41 M8
Phillippa Ct SIT ME10.......... 71 G6
Phillips Cl DART DA1 .... 27 K4
Phillips Ct RHAM ME8 .... 67 K3
Philpots La RTON TN11 .... 130 A7
Phoenix Dr WBY/YAL ME18.......... 119 G7
Phoenix Pl DART DA1.......... 27 M5
Phoenix Rd WALD ME5 .... 83 K3
Picardy Manorway BELV DA17 .... 12 D2
Picardy Rd BELV DA17 .... 12 C4
Picardy St BELV DA17 .... 12 C2
Pickering St MAID/SHEP ME15.... 121 J7
Pickford Cl BXLYHN DA7 .... 12 A8
Pickford La BXLYHN DA7 .... 12 A8
Pickford Rd BXLYHN DA7 .... 26 A1
Pickle's Wy HOO/HM ME3.......... 20 C7
Pickwick Crs ROCH ME1 .... 65 L3
Pickwick Gdns GVW DA11 .... 30 F8
Pier Approach Rd GILL ME7 .... 50 F6
Pierce Mill La RTON TN11 .... 133 K8
Pier Rd ERITH DA8 .... 13 G5
GILL ME7 .... 50 F6
GRH DA9 .... 29 K2
GVW DA11.......... 31 H4
Pigdown La EDEN TN8 .... 159 M1
Pigsdean Rd MEO DA13 .... 63 K3
Pikefish La STPH/PW TN12 .... 151 G4
Pikey La E/WMAL ME19.......... 100 F8
Pile La STPH/PW TN12.......... 170 C1
Pilgrims Ct DART DA1 .... 28 C3
Pilgrims Lakes RMAID ME17 .... 125 G7
Pilgrims La CDH/CHF RM16.......... 15 M3
OXTED RH8.......... 109 L2
Pilgrims Rd STRD ME2 .... 64 B6
SWCM DA10 .... 30 A3
Pilgrims Vw GRH DA9 .... 29 L4
MAID/BEAR ME14 .... 103 G2 1
Pilgrims Wy BGR/WK TN15.......... 98 B1
DART DA1 .... 28 D6
DIT/AY ME20.......... 82 D7
E/WMAL ME19 .... 79 H7
MAID/BEAR ME14 .... 103 L1
MAID/BEAR ME14 .... 104 D4
RMAID ME17.......... 124 B2
RMAID ME17.......... 125 H6
ROCH ME1 .... 82 A1
RSEV TN14 .... 96 A2
SNOD ME6.......... 80 D4
STRD ME2 .... 64 E2
STRD ME2 .... 80 F2
Pilgrims Wy East RSEV TN14 .... 95 L2
Pilgrims Wy West RSEV TN14.......... 95 H2
Pillar Box La RTON TN11 .... 116 F8
Pillar Box Rd BGR/WK TN15 .... 97 G8
Pilot Rd ROCH ME1.......... 65 L5
Pilots Pl GVE DA12.......... 31 L4
Pimpernel Cl
MAID/BEAR ME14 .... 122 D1 2
Pimpernel Wy WALD ME5 .... 83 G1 1
Pinchbeck Rd ORP BR6 .... 73 H1
Pincott Rd BXLYHS DA6.......... 26 C3
Pincroft Wd HART DA3 .... 45 L8
Pine Av GVE DA12.......... 31 M6
Pine Cl DIT/AY ME20.......... 101 J3
SWLY BR8 .... 42 B8 2
Pine Gv EDEN TN8 .... 142 D3
GILL ME7 .... 67 J8
MAID/BEAR ME14 .... 103 K7
Pinehurst RSEV TN14.......... 96 A7
Pineneedle La SEV TN13 .... 9 G2
Pine Pl MAID/SHEP ME15 .... 121 G4
Pine Rdg TONN TN10 .... 131 K7
Pine Ri MEO DA13.......... 62 C2
Pine Rd STRD ME2 .... 2 D6
Pinesfield La E/WMAL ME19.......... 79 K7
Pine Tree La BGR/WK TN15.......... 115 J3
Pine Vw BGR/WK TN15 .... 98 E6 1
Pinewood Av SEV TN13.......... 95 M7
Pinewood Cl STPH/PW TN12 .... 150 B7
TIL RM18 .... 18 D2 1
Pinewood Dr MAID/BEAR ME14.... 83 M5
ORP BR6 .... 56 A8
Pinewood Gdns STH/RUST TN4 .. 163 J4
Pinewood Rd RTWE/PEM TN2 ..... 11 L1
Pinkham STPH/PW TN12.......... 134 C8
Pinks Hl SWLY BR8.......... 58 A1
Pinnacle Hl BXLYHN DA7 .... 26 D2
Pinnacle Hl North BXLYHN DA7 .... 26 D1
Pinnock La STPH/PW TN12.......... 170 A4
Pinnock's Av GVW DA11 .... 31 K6
Pintail Cl HOO/HM ME3 .... 25 K7 3
The Pintails CHAT ME4.......... 50 D4
Pioneer Wy SWLY BR8 .... 42 A7
Piper's Green Rd
BH/WHM TN16.......... 111 J6
Pipers La BH/WHM TN16.......... 111 K5
Pippin Cl RMAID ME17 .... 136 D3
SIT ME10 .... 70 F7 1
Pippin Cft GILL ME7 .... 67 J7
Pippin Rd STPH/PW TN12 .... 134 B7
The Pippins MEO DA13.......... 62 C2
Pippin Wy WBY/YAL ME18.......... 118 C3
Pirbright Cl WALD ME5 .... 83 M3 4
Pirrip Cl GVE DA12.......... 32 B6
Pitchfont La OXTED RH8 .... 109 J4
Pitfield HART DA3.......... 45 H8
Pitfield Dr MEO DA13.......... 62 B6
Pit La EDEN TN8 .... 142 E1
Pittlesden TENT TN30 .... 196 C6
Pitt Rd MAIDW ME16 .... 120 D4
RMAID ME17.......... 139 J3
Pixot Hl STPH/PW TN12.......... 166 D4
Pix's La CRBK TN17.......... 202 B2
Pizien Well Rd WBY/YAL ME18 .... 118 C7
Place La RSIT ME9.......... 68 F8
Plain Rd STPH/PW TN12 .... 168 E2
Plains Av MAID/SHEP ME15 .... 121 K4
Plane Av GVW DA11 .... 30 F5
Plane Wk TONN TN10.......... 131 L6
Plantation Dr STMC/STPC BR5 ..... 56 F4
Plantation La
MAID/BEAR ME14 .... 122 C1
WARL CR6 .... 90 A5
Plantation Rd ERITH DA8 .... 13 J7
GILL ME7 .... 51 J7
SWLY BR8 .... 42 C4
Platt Common BGR/WK TN15 .... 98 E6
The Platters RHAM ME8 .... 67 L5
The Plat EDEN TN8.......... 142 F4
RYE TN31 .... 206 D7
Platt House La BGR/WK TN15.......... 78 E7
The Platt RMAID ME17.......... 139 G6
Plaxdale Green Rd
BGR/WK TN15 .... 77 M6
Plaxtol La BGR/WK TN15.......... 115 L5
Plaxtol Rd ERITH DA8 .... 12 C6
Playstool Cl RSIT ME9 .... 69 K7
Playstool Rd RSIT ME9.......... 69 J7
Pleasance Rd STMC/STPC BR5 ...... 40 D6
Pleasant Rw GILL ME7 .... 4 E1
Pleasant Valley La
MAID/SHEP ME15 .... 136 D1
Pleasant Vw ERITH DA8 .... 13 G4 1
Pleasure House Rd
RMAID ME17.......... 139 J6
Plomley Cl RHAM ME8 .... 84 F1
Plough Hl BGR/WK TN15.......... 116 B1
Ploughmans Wy RHAM ME8.......... 68 A7
WALD ME5.......... 83 J4
Plough Wents Rd RMAID ME17 .. 138 E3
Plover Cl WALD ME5.......... 83 M4
Plover Rd DIT/AY ME20 .... 101 H3
Plowenders Cl E/WMAL ME19 .... 99 M2
Pluckley Cl RHAM ME8.......... 67 L2
Pluckley Rd HDCN TN27 .... 173 K3
Plug La MEO DA13.......... 62 F8
Plummer La TENT TN30.......... 196 B7
Plumtree Gv GILL ME7 .... 84 C1
Plum Tree La RSIT ME9 .... 85 K5
Plumtree Rd HDCN TN27.......... 155 J5
Plumtrees MAIDW ME16 .... 120 C3
Plymouth Dr BGR/WK TN15 .... 9 J5
Plymouth Pk BGR/WK TN15 .... 9 K5
Plympton Cl BELV DA17 .... 12 A2 3
Poachers Cl WALD ME5 .... 66 E8
Podkin Wd WALD ME5.......... 83 H5
Polesden Rd RTWE/PEM TN2 .... 11 L8
Polesteeple Hl BH/WHM TN16 ...... 91 M3
The Poles RSIT ME9 .... 69 G1
Polhill RSEV TN14 .... 94 E1
Polhill Dr WALD ME5.......... 83 H3
Police Station Rd E/WMAL
ME19 .... 100 E5
Pollards Wood Hl OXTED RH8...... 109 J8
Polley Cl RTWE/PEM TN2 .... 164 F6
Pollyhaugh EYN DA4 .... 59 G6
Polperro Cl ORP BR6 .... 56 B2
Pond Dr SIT ME10 .... 88 C3
Pond Farm Rd RMAID ME17 .... 105 M4
RSIT ME9.......... 87 H4
Pondfield La GVE DA12 .... 48 A4
Pond Hl HOO/HM ME3.......... 20 D7
Pond La BGR/WK TN15 .... 115 G3
Pondwood Ri ORP BR6 .... 56 A3
Pontoise Cl SEV TN13.......... 8 D1
Pook La HDCN TN27.......... 186 E1
Poona Rd RTWE/PEM TN2 .... 11 H7
Pootings Rd EDEN TN8 .... 126 F5
Poot La RSIT ME9 .... 53 G7
Pope Dr STPH/PW TN12 .... 170 A1
Pope House La TENT TN30 .... 196 D1
Pope St MAIDW ME16 .... 120 E3
Poplar Av GVE DA12.......... 46 E1
Poplar Cl HOO/HM ME3.......... 51 G2
STRD ME2 .... 2 C7
Poplar Gv MAIDW ME16.......... 102 E8
Poplar Mt BELV DA17.......... 12 D3
Poplar Rd STRD ME2 .... 2 A8
TENT TN30 .... 208 F1
Poplars Cl HART DA3 .... 45 L7
Poplar Wk MEO DA13 .... 62 D2
Poplicans Rd STRD ME2 .... 64 D2
Poppy Cl GILL ME7 .... 51 G8
MAIDW ME16 .... 6 B7
Porchester Cl HART DA3 .... 45 H8
MAID/SHEP ME15 .... 121 J7
Porchfield Cl GVE DA12.......... 31 L7
Port Av GRH DA9.......... 29 K4
Port Cl MAID/BEAR ME14 .... 104 B8
WALD ME5 .... 83 K2 4
Porter Cl WTHK RM20 .... 15 L5
Porters Cl STPH/PW TN12.......... 166 B7
Porters Wk RMAID ME17 .... 139 G1
Port Hl ORP BR6.......... 73 K6
Portland Av GVE DA12.......... 31 K7
SIT ME10.......... 88 E1
Portland Pl SNOD ME6 .... 81 J5 3
Portland Rd GILL ME7 .... 51 G7
GVW DA11.......... 30 F4
ROCH ME1.......... 81 L1
Portland St CHAT ME4 .... 4 F9
Portman Cl BXLY DA5 .... 27 G6
BXLYHN DA7 .... 26 A1 2
Portman Pk TON TN9 .... 147 L2
Port Ri CHAT ME4 .... 4 C7
Portsdown Cl MAIDW ME16 .... 120 D3 3
Portsea Rd TIL RM18 .... 17 L7
Portsmouth Cl STRD ME2 .... 48 F7
Port Victoria Rd HOO/HM ME3 ..... 39 L2
Portway Rd HOO/HM ME3 .... 34 D5
Post Barn Rd CHAT ME4 .... 66 B3
Postern La TON TN9.......... 147 M3
Postley Rd MAID/SHEP ME15 .... 7 G8
Postmill Dr MAID/SHEP ME15.... 121 H4
Post Office Rd HAWK TN18 ...... 199 H3 2
Potash La BGR/WK TN15.......... 98 E7
Pot Kiln La RASHW TN26 .... 187 M2
Potter's La HAWK TN18.......... 192 C7
Pottery Rd BXLY DA5.......... 26 E7
HOO/HM ME3.......... 35 M8
Pound Bank Cl BGR/WK TN15 .... 77 H3 3
Poundfield Rd HAWK TN18.......... 200 D8
Pound La RSEV TN14 .... 93 M1
SEV TN13.......... 9 J4
Pound Rd STPH/PW TN12.......... 134 A7
Poundsbridge Hl RRTW TN3.......... 161 M7
Pounsley Rd SEV TN13 .... 95 G7
Pout Rd SNOD ME6 .... 81 H6
Poverest Rd STMC/STPC BR5.......... 56 B1
Povey Av STRD ME2 .... 49 L3
Powdermill Cl
RTWE/PEM TN2.......... 163 L5 1
Powder Mill La DART DA1 .... 28 A7
RTON TN11.......... 146 C3
STH/RUST TN4 .... 163 K6
Powell Cl DIT/AY ME20.......... 102 C2
Powerscroft Rd SCUP DA14 .... 40 E3
Powlett Rd STRD ME2 .... 49 L4
Poynder Rd TIL RM18 .... 17 K7
Poynings Cl ORP BR6 .... 56 E5 3
Poyntell Rd STPH/PW TN12 .... 170 B1
Prall's La STPH/PW TN12.......... 166 A3
Pratling St DIT/AY ME20 .... 102 D2
Premier Av CDH/CHF RM16.......... 16 E1
Premier Pl DIT/AY ME20 .... 102 A4
Prentis Cl SIT ME10.......... 70 E8
Prentis Quay SIT ME10 .... 71 G8 2
Prestley Dr TONN TN10 .... 131 M6
Preston Av GILL ME7 .... 67 G4
Preston Rd GVW DA11.......... 31 G6
TON TN9 .... 147 J4
Pretoria Rd GILL ME7.......... 5 L7
Prettymans La EDEN TN8.......... 143 J2
Pridmore Rd SNOD ME6 .... 81 H5 1
Priestfield Rd GILL ME7 .... 51 G8
Priestfields ROCH ME1.......... 65 K3
Priest Hl OXTED RH8 .... 109 K7
Priestley Dr DIT/AY ME20 .... 101 H1
Priestwood Rd MEO DA13 .... 79 K1
Primrose Av RHAM ME8 .... 67 K8
Primrose Cl ROCH ME1 .... 66 A6
Primrose Dr DIT/AY ME20 .... 101 M5
Primrose La RSIT ME9 .... 87 J7
Primrose Rd STRD ME2 .... 64 A8
Primrose Wk STPH/PW TN12 .... 150 C8
Prince Arthur Rd GILL ME7 .... 5 G1
Prince Charles Av EYN DA4.......... 43 M6
SIT ME10 .... 88 D3
WALD ME5.......... 83 K1
Princes Av RDART DA2.......... 28 D6
STMC/STPC BR5.......... 56 A1
WALD ME5.......... 66 E6
Princes Rd DART DA1 .... 27 K5
GVE DA12 .... 46 E1
RDART DA2 .... 28 E6
SWLY BR8 .... 42 C3
Princess Av TIL RM18.......... 18 E3
Princess Margaret Rd TIL RM18.... 18 D3

Princess Mary Av *CHAT* ME4 .... 50 D6
Princess St *BXLYHN* DA7 .... 26 B1
Princes St *CVW* DA11 .... 31 K4
  MAID/BEAR ME14 .... 7 H3
  ROCH ME1 .... 65 L2
  RTWE/PEM TN2 .... 11 J6
Princes Vw *DART* DA1 .... 28 C6
Princes Wy *MAID/BEAR* ME14 .... 104 C4
Prinys Dr *RHAM* ME8 .... 84 E1
Prior Cha *GRAYS* RM17 .... 16 B3
Priorsdean Crs *MAIDW* ME16 .... 120 A4
Priorsford Av *STMC/STPC* BR5 .... 40 C8
Prior's Wy *EDEN* TN8 .... 159 J7 ⓘ
Priory Cl *DART* DA1 .... 120 D5
  MAID/SHEP ME15 .... 120 D5
Priory Flds *EYN* DA4 .... 59 H5
Priory Gdns *DART* DA1 .... 27 M3
Priory Gv *DIT/AY* ME20 .... 101 M4
  TON TN9 .... 147 K5
Priory Hl *DART* DA1 .... 27 M4
Priory La *EYN* DA4 .... 59 H4
Priory Pl *DART* DA1 .... 27 M4
Priory Rd *DART* DA1 .... 27 M2
  MAID/SHEP ME15 .... 7 G6
  RHAM ME8 .... 67 J3
  STRD ME2 .... 2 E5
  TON TN9 .... 147 L5
Priory St *TON* TN9 .... 147 K5
Priory Wk *TON* TN9 .... 147 K5
Priory Wy *TENT* TN30 .... 196 E6
Pristling La *STPH/PW* TN12 .... 169 K5
Prospect Av *STRD* ME2 .... 3 H1
Prospect Cl *BELV* DA17 .... 12 C3 ⓘ
Prospect Gv *GVE* DA12 .... 31 M5
Prospect Pk *STH/RUST* TN4 .... 163 H4
Prospect Pl *DART* DA1 .... 28 A4
  GRAYS RM17 .... 16 D5 ⓘ
  GVE DA12 .... 31 M5
  MAIDW ME16 .... 6 C7
Prospect Rd *RTWE/PEM* TN2 .... 11 H6
  SEV TN13 .... 9 J2
  STH/RUST TN4 .... 163 H4
Prospect Rw *CHAT* ME4 .... 4 E7
  GILL ME7 .... 4 E2
Provender Wy
  MAID/BEAR ME14 .... 122 A1
Providence La *ROCH* ME1 .... 3 K7
Providence St *GRH* DA9 .... 29 J3
Puddingcake La *CRBK* TN17 .... 195 L8
Pudding La *MAID/BEAR* ME14 .... 6 F4
Pudding Rd *RHAM* ME8 .... 68 B5 ⓘ
Puddledock La *BH/WHM* TN16 .... 127 J2
  RDART DA2 .... 42 A2
Puffin Rd *HOO/HM* ME3 .... 25 K8 ⓘ
Pump Cl *E/WMAL* ME19 .... 100 F4
Pump La *GILL* ME7 .... 67 M2
  RHAM ME8 .... 67 L3
Punch Cft *HART* DA3 .... 61 G6
Purbeck Rd *CHAT* ME4 .... 66 A3
Purcell Av *TONN* TN10 .... 132 B7
Purfleet By-pass *PUR* RM19 .... 14 E4
Purser Wy *GILL* ME7 .... 50 E6
Puttenden Rd *RTON* TN11 .... 132 B3
Puttney Dr *SIT* ME10 .... 71 J5
Pym Pl *GRAYS* RM17 .... 16 C3
Pyrus Cl *WALD* ME5 .... 83 J5

Q

The Quadrant *PUR* RM19 .... 14 E3
Quaker Cl *SEV* TN13 .... 9 J3
Quaker Dr *CRBK* TN17 .... 183 M7
Quaker La *CRBK* TN17 .... 183 M7
Quakers Cl *HART* DA3 .... 45 H7
Quantock Rd *BXLYHN* DA7 .... 13 G8 ⓘ
Quantock Rd *BXLYHN* DA7 .... 13 G8 ⓘ
Quarry Bank *TON* TN9 .... 147 K6
Quarry Cl *OXTED* RH8 .... 109 C8
Quarry Hl *BGR/WK* TN15 .... 9 M2
  GRAYS RM17 .... 16 C4
Quarry Hill Rd *BGR/WK* TN15 .... 98 A7
  STH/RUST TN4 .... 147 J7
  TON TN9 .... 147 J7
Quarry Ms *PUR* RM19 .... 14 C3
Quarry Ri *TON* TN9 .... 147 J6
Quarry Rd *MAID/SHEP* ME15 .... 7 G9
  OXTED RH8 .... 109 C8
  RMAID ME17 .... 137 L1
  RTW TN1 .... 11 H2
Quarry Sq *MAID/BEAR* ME14 .... 7 G2
Quarry Wy *WTHK* RM20 .... 15 H5
Quay La *GRH* DA9 .... 29 K2
Quayside *CHAT* ME4 .... 50 D5
Quebec Av *BH/WHM* TN16 .... 110 F4
Quebec Rd *TIL* RM18 .... 17 J8
Quebec Sq *BH/WHM* TN16 .... 110 F4
Queen Anne Rd
  MAID/BEAR ME14 .... 7 J4 ⓘ
Queendown Av *RHAM* ME8 .... 67 M8
Queen Elizabeth Av *TIL* RM18 .... 18 E3 ⓘ
Queen Elizabeth Ii Br
  WTHK RM20 .... 15 C8
Queen Elizabeth Sq
  MAID/SHEP ME15 .... 121 M7
Queen Mary Av *TIL* RM18 .... 18 E5
The Queen Mother Ct
  ROCH ME1 .... 65 K1 ⓘ
  SNOD ME6 .... 81 J5
Queens Cottages *WADH* TN5 .... 188 A8
Queens Ct *HAWK* TN18 .... 199 J3
Queen's Dr *RSEV* TN14 .... 95 L6
Queen's Farm Rd *GVE* DA12 .... 33 G7
Queens Gdns *RDART* DA2 .... 28 D6
  STH/RUST TN4 .... 163 K7
Queens Rd *ERITH* DA8 .... 13 G5
  GILL ME7 .... 5 K5
  GVE DA12 .... 31 L3
  HAWK TN18 .... 199 J3
  MAIDW ME16 .... 6 A4
  SNOD ME6 .... 81 J5
  STH/RUST TN4 .... 10 F1
  WALD ME5 .... 66 H4
Queen St *BXLYHN* DA7 .... 26 B1
  CHAT ME4 .... 4 E5
  ERITH DA8 .... 13 G5 ⓘ
  GVE DA12 .... 31 K4 ⓘ

R

Rabbits Rd *EYN* DA4 .... 44 B6
Racefield Cl *GVE* DA12 .... 48 A3
Radleigh Gdns *CHAT* ME4 .... 66 A4 ⓘ
Radnor Cl *CHST* BR7 .... 40 A3
Raeburn Av *DART* DA1 .... 27 K3
Raeburn Cl *TONN* TN10 .... 132 A7 ⓘ
Ragge Wy *BGR/WK* TN15 .... 96 B6
Rag Hill Rd *BH/WHM* TN16 .... 91 M7
Raglan Rd *BELV* DA17 .... 12 B3
Ragstone Ct *DIT/AY* ME20 .... 101 L5
Ragstone Rd *MAID/SHEP* ME15 .... 122 C3
Railway Ap *TON* TN9 .... 147 K5
Railway Pl *BELV* DA17 .... 12 C2 ⓘ
  GVE DA12 .... 31 K4 ⓘ
Railway St *CHAT* ME4 .... 4 C6
  GILL ME7 .... 5 L3
  GVW DA11 .... 30 C3
Railway Ter *BH/WHM* TN16 .... 110 F3
Rainbow Rd *CDH/CHF* RM16 .... 15 L3
Rainham Rd *GILL* ME7 .... 13 H5
Raleigh *ERITH* DA8 .... 66 C7
  WALD ME5 .... 66 B8 ⓘ
Raleigh Ms *ORP* BR6 .... 56 B8 ⓘ
Ramillies Cl *WALD* ME5 .... 66 C8
Rammell Ms *CRBK* TN17 .... 192 F1
Rampion Cl *MAID/BEAR* ME14 .... 104 A8
Ramsden Cl *MAID/SHEP* ME15 .... 56 E4 ⓘ
Ramsden La *CRBK* TN17 .... 201 H1
Ramsden Rd *ERITH* DA8 .... 12 F6
  ORP BR6 .... 56 D3
  STMC/STPC BR5 .... 56 E4
Ramslye Rd *STH/RUST* TN4 .... 176 F4
Ramus Wood Av *ORP* BR6 .... 56 A8
Randall Cl *ERITH* DA8 .... 12 E5
Randall Hill Rd *BGR/WK* TN15 .... 98 B2
Randall Rd *CHAT* ME4 .... 66 A4
Randall St *MAID/BEAR* ME14 .... 6 F1
Randle's La *ORP* BR6 .... 73 M8
Randolph Cl *BXLYHN* DA7 .... 26 E1
Randolph Rd *GILL* ME7 .... 5 K4
Ranelagh Gdns *GVW* DA11 .... 31 H5
Range Rd *GVE* DA12 .... 31 M5
Rankine Rd *RTWE/PEM* TN2 .... 163 M6
Ranleigh Gdns *BXLYHN* DA7 .... 12 B6 ⓘ
Ranmore Pth *STMC/STPC* BR5 .... 40 C8
Ranscombe Cl *STRD* ME2 .... 48 F8
Ranters La *CRBK* TN17 .... 190 C1
Ranworth Cl *ERITH* DA8 .... 13 G8
Raphael Av *TIL* RM18 .... 17 J7
Raphael Rd *GVE* DA12 .... 31 M5
Rapier Cl *PUR* RM19 .... 14 B3
Rashleigh Wy *EYN* DA4 .... 43 L8
Raspberry Hill La *RSIT* ME9 .... 54 E7
Ratcliffe Hwy *HOO/HM* ME3 .... 36 C3
Rathmore Rd *GVW* DA11 .... 31 J5
Raven Cl *DIT/AY* ME20 .... 101 J4 ⓘ
Ravenbourne Rd *DART* DA1 .... 27 J1
Ravensbury Rd *STMC/STPC* BR5 .... 40 B8
Ravenscourt Rd
  STMC/STPC BR5 .... 40 C7
Ravens Dane Cl
  MAID/SHEP ME15 .... 122 C4 ⓘ
Ravenswood *BXLY* DA5 .... 26 A6
Ravenswood Av *RTW* TN1 .... 163 L7
  STRD ME2 .... 3 H1
Rawdon Rd *MAID/SHEP* ME15 .... 7 H7
Rawlings Cl *ORP* BR6 .... 56 B8
Rayfield Ct *SNOD* ME6 .... 81 J4
Rayford Ct *DART* DA1 .... 27 L3
Ray Lamb Wy *ERITH* DA8 .... 13 K5
Rayleigh Cl *MAIDW* ME16 .... 102 F6 ⓘ
Raymer Rd *MAID/BEAR* ME14 .... 103 K5
Rays Hl *EYN* DA4 .... 43 L8
Reader's Bridge Rd *TENT* TN30 .... 196 B1
Readers La *RYE* TN31 .... 209 H8
Readscroft Rd *RHAM* ME8 .... 67 M8
Read Wy *GVE* DA12 .... 46 F2
Recreation Av *SNOD* ME6 .... 81 J5 ⓘ
Recreation Cl *MAID/BEAR* ME14 .... 7 J1
Recreation Ground Rd
  TENT TN30 .... 196 D6
Rectory Cl *DART* DA1 .... 27 G2
  ROCH ME1 .... 64 E8
  SCUP DA14 .... 40 D1
  SNOD ME6 .... 81 J5
Rectory Dr *STH/RUST* TN4 .... 162 E2
Rectory Flds *CRBK* TN17 .... 183 M8 ⓘ
Rectory Gra *ROCH* ME1 .... 65 L3 ⓘ
Rectory La *BGR/WK* TN15 .... 97 L8
  BH/WHM TN16 .... 110 A1
  BH/WHM TN16 .... 111 L2
  MAIDW ME16 .... 120 C4
  RMAID ME17 .... 125 G8
  RMAID ME17 .... 138 E7
  RMAID ME17 .... 139 G6
  RYE TN31 .... 207 H8
  SCUP DA14 .... 40 D1
  SEV TN13 .... 9 J1
Rectory La North
  E/WMAL ME19 .... 100 F3
Rectory La South
  E/WMAL ME19 .... 101 G3
Rectory Meadow *MEO* DA13 .... 45 J3
Rectory Park Rd
  STPH/PW TN12 .... 181 J3
Rectory Rd *BGR/WK* TN15 .... 61 L8
  GRAYS RM17 .... 16 F2

HOO/HM ME3 .... 34 C3
SIT ME10 .... 88 D2
SWCM DA10 .... 30 A5
TIL RM18 .... 17 M5
Redbank *E/WMAL* ME19 .... 101 G3
Redbridge Cl *WALD* ME5 .... 66 E8 ⓘ
Red Cedars Rd *ORP* BR6 .... 56 A3
Redcliffe La *MAID/BEAR* ME14 .... 103 K6
Redding Cl *RDART* DA2 .... 29 C7
Reddy Rd *ERITH* DA8 .... 13 H5
Rede Court Rd *STRD* ME2 .... 2 A2
Rede Wood Rd *MAIDW* ME16 .... 120 A2
Redfern Av *GILL* ME7 .... 51 G8
Red Hl *WBY/YAL* ME18 .... 119 G5
Redhill Rd *BGR/WK* TN15 .... 61 G7
Redhill Wd *HART* DA3 .... 61 J7
Red House Gdns
  WBY/YAL ME18 .... 118 F5
Redhouse Rd *BH/WHM* TN16 .... 91 L7
Redland Shaw *CHAT* ME4 .... 66 A4
Redlands Rd *SEV* TN13 .... 8 D5
Redleaf Cl *BELV* DA17 .... 12 C5
  RTWE/PEM TN2 .... 163 M7
Red Lion Cl *STMC/STPC* BR5 .... 56 E1
Red Lodge Crs *BXLY* DA5 .... 26 F8
Red Lodge Rd *BXLY* DA5 .... 26 F8
Redmans La *RSEV* TN14 .... 75 H1
Red Oak *HAWK* TN18 .... 199 L5
Redpoll Wk *STPH/PW* TN12 .... 150 C8
Redsells Cl *MAID/SHEP* ME15 .... 122 C4 ⓘ
Redshank Rd *CHAT* ME4 .... 50 C4
Red St *MEO* DA13 .... 45 K3
Redvers Rd *CHAT* ME4 .... 4 E9
Redwall La *RMAID* ME17 .... 136 D6
Redwell La *BGR/WK* TN15 .... 115 K1
Redwing Rd *WALD* ME5 .... 66 D7
Redwings La *RTWE/PEM* TN2 .... 164 F3
Redwood Cl *WALD* ME5 .... 83 K3
Redwood Pk *RTON* TN11 .... 149 J8
Reed Av *ORP* BR6 .... 56 A6
Reedham Crs *HOO/HM* ME3 .... 34 E6
Reeds La *RTON* TN11 .... 116 A8
Reed St *HOO/HM* ME3 .... 20 D7
Reeves Cl *STPH/PW* TN12 .... 170 A1
Reeves Ct *DIT/AY* ME20 .... 101 J4
Reeves Cresent *SWLY* BR8 .... 41 M7
Reform Rd *CHAT* ME4 .... 5 G8
Regency Cl *BGR/WK* TN15 .... 77 G1
  RHAM ME8 .... 84 E2
Regency Ct *MAID/SHEP* ME15 .... 87 M1
Regent Cl *CDH/CHF* RM16 .... 16 E1
Regent Dr *MAID/SHEP* ME15 .... 121 J5
Regent Rd *GILL* ME7 .... 5 H5
Regent Sq *BELV* DA17 .... 12 D3
Regent St *CRBK* TN17 .... 202 A2
Reginald Av *STRD* ME2 .... 64 E2
Reginald Rd *MAIDW* ME16 .... 6 D7
Regis Crs *SIT* ME10 .... 71 H6
Reinden Gv *MAID/SHEP* ME15 .... 122 B4
Rembrandt Cl *TONN* TN10 .... 132 A7
Rembrandt Dr *GVW* DA11 .... 30 F8
Renown Rd *WALD* ME5 .... 83 L3
Renshaw Cl *BELV* DA17 .... 12 B5 ⓘ
Renton Dr *STMC/STPC* BR5 .... 56 F3
Repton Rd *ORP* BR6 .... 56 C7
Repton Wy *WALD* ME5 .... 83 H1
Resolution Cl *WALD* ME5 .... 66 C8
Restharrow Rd
  MAID/BEAR ME14 .... 122 A1
The Retreat *GRAYS* RM17 .... 16 D5 ⓘ
  ORP BR6 .... 73 K1
Revenge Rd *MAID/BEAR* ME14 .... 83 L5
  WALD ME5 .... 83 L4
Reynolds Cl *TONN* TN10 .... 132 A7
Reynolds Flds *HOO/HM* ME3 .... 33 L7
Reynolds La *STH/RUST* TN4 .... 163 H7
Rhode St *CHAT* ME4 .... 4 E6
Rhodewood Cl
  MAID/SHEP ME15 .... 122 C4
Rhododendron Av *MEO* DA13 .... 79 J2
Ribblesdale Av *STH/RUST* TN4 .... 163 J7
Ribston Gdns *STPH/PW* TN12 .... 150 A6
Richard's Cl *RTON* TN11 .... 145 H3
Richardson Cl *GRH* DA9 .... 29 H3
Richardson Rd *STH/RUST* TN4 .... 163 J7
Richard St *CHAT* ME4 .... 4 D6
  ROCH ME1 .... 65 L2
Richborough Cl
  STMC/STPC BR5 .... 40 F8 ⓘ
Richborough Dr *STRD* ME2 .... 49 J4
Richmond Cl *BH/WHM* TN16 .... 91 K5 ⓘ
  STRD ME2 .... 50 B4 ⓘ
  WALD ME5 .... 83 K1 ⓘ
Richmond Dr *SIT* ME10 .... 71 G6
Richmond Rd *GILL* ME7 .... 5 K1
  GRAYS RM17 .... 16 E4
Richmond Wy
  MAID/SHEP ME15 .... 121 J5
Ricketts Hill Rd *BH/WHM* TN16 .... 91 M4
Riddledale Av *STH/RUST* TN4 .... 163 J7
Riddles Rd *SIT* ME10 .... 87 L2
Ridge Av *DART* DA1 .... 27 H4
Ridgecroft Cl *BXLY* DA5 .... 26 E6
Ridgelands *RRTW* TN3 .... 162 E1
Ridge La *MEO* DA13 .... 79 J2
The Ridge *BXLY* DA5 .... 26 B5
Ridge Wy *DART* DA1 .... 27 H4
  EDEN TN8 .... 142 E1
Ridgeway *GRAYS* RM17 .... 17 G3
  RDART DA2 .... 44 A2
  RTWE/PEM TN2 .... 164 F6 ⓘ
Ridgeway Av *GVE* DA12 .... 31 K8
Ridgeway Crs *ORP* BR6 .... 56 A6
  TONN TN10 .... 147 M1
Ridgeway Crescent Gdns
  ORP BR6 .... 56 A6 ⓘ
The Ridgewaye *STH/RUST* TN4 .... 163 J4
The Ridgeway *CHAT* ME4 .... 66 A6
  GILL ME7 .... 50 E6 ⓘ
  GVE DA12 .... 48 A4
  TON TN9 .... 147 M1
Ridgewood *MEO* DA13 .... 45 L5
Ridgway *MAIDW* ME16 .... 120 D3
Ridham Av *SIT* ME10 .... 71 J4
Riding La *RTON* TN11 .... 130 F6
Riding Pk *RTON* TN11 .... 130 F6
The Ridings *BH/WHM* TN16 .... 92 A3
  RTWE/PEM TN2 .... 164 B7
  STPH/PW TN12 .... 150 C2

Ridlands Gv *OXTED* RH8 .... 110 A8
Ridlands Rd *OXTED* RH8 .... 110 A8
Ridlands Ri *OXTED* RH8 .... 110 A8
Ridley Rd *ROCH* ME1 .... 3 H9
Rigby Gdns *CDH/CHF* RM16 .... 17 K3
Ringden Av *STPH/PW* TN12 .... 150 A8
Ringlestone Crs
  MAID/BEAR ME14 .... 103 H5 ⓘ
Ringlestone Rd *RMAID* ME17 .... 124 E1
Ringshall Rd *CHST* BR7 .... 40 C7
Rings Hl *RTON* TN11 .... 146 C1
Ringwood Av *ORP* BR6 .... 73 L4
Ringwood Rd *RHAM* ME8 .... 67 M2 ⓘ
Ringwood Rd
  MAID/SHEP ME15 .... 121 L5
Ripley Rd *BELV* DA17 .... 12 C3
Ripon Cl *RHAM* ME8 .... 67 M2 ⓘ
Risden La *HAWK* TN18 .... 199 L6
Risedale Rd *BXLYHN* DA7 .... 26 E1
The Rise *DART* DA1 .... 27 H2
  GILL ME7 .... 84 C2
  GVE DA12 .... 47 G1
  ROCH ME1 .... 65 M2
  RSIT ME9 .... 87 K3
  SEV TN13 .... 113 L6
Ritch Rd *SNOD* ME6 .... 81 G6
River Cl *MAID/SHEP* ME15 .... 120 C6
Riverdale Rd *BXLY* DA5 .... 26 B5
  ERITH DA8 .... 12 F3
River Dr *STRD* ME2 .... 2 B4
Riverhead Cl *SIT* ME10 .... 87 L2
Riverhill *SEV* TN13 .... 130 A1
River Lawn Rd *TON* TN9 .... 147 K4
River Park Vw *ORP* BR6 .... 56 D3
Rivers Cl *WBY/YAL* ME18 .... 119 G6
Riversdale *GVW* DA11 .... 31 G7
Riverside *EDEN* TN8 .... 142 E4
  EYN DA4 .... 58 F5
Riverside Cl *STMC/STPC* BR5 .... 40 E6
Riverside Rd *SCUP* DA14 .... 26 A8
Riverside Wy *DART* DA1 .... 28 A3
Rivers Rd *RSIT* ME9 .... 89 M3
River St *GILL* ME7 .... 4 E1
River Vw *CDH/CHF* RM16 .... 17 J4
  GILL ME7 .... 67 M2
  MAID/SHEP ME15 .... 122 C3 ⓘ
  QBOR ME11 .... 55 H2
Riverview Rd *GRH* DA9 .... 29 J3 ⓘ
River Wk *DIT/AY* ME20 .... 101 J1
River Wy *DIT/AY* ME20 .... 101 J1
Roach St *STRD* ME2 .... 2 F4
Roan Ct *STRD* ME2 .... 2 C2 ⓘ
Roberts Cl *SIT* ME10 .... 70 F6
  STMC/STPC BR5 .... 56 E1 ⓘ
Roberts Orchard Rd
  MAIDW ME16 .... 120 A2
Roberts Rd *BELV* DA17 .... 12 C4
  RHAM ME8 .... 68 A5
  SNOD ME6 .... 81 H5
Robin Hood Gn *STMC/STPC* BR5 .... 56 C1
Robin Hood La *BXLYHS* DA6 .... 26 A3
  WALD ME5 .... 82 F4
Robin Hood La (Lower)
  WALD ME5 .... 83 G4
Robin Hood La (Upper)
  WALD ME5 .... 83 G4
Robinia Av *GVW* DA11 .... 30 F5
Robins Av *RMAID* ME17 .... 141 L4
Robins Cl *RMAID* ME17 .... 141 L4
Robin Wy *STMC/STPC* BR5 .... 40 D7
Robson Dr *DIT/AY* ME20 .... 101 M3
  HOO/HM ME3 .... 35 M8
Robyns Cft *GVW* DA11 .... 31 G8
Robyns Wy *EDEN* TN8 .... 142 F5
  SEV TN13 .... 95 H8
Rocfort Rd *SNOD* ME6 .... 81 J5
Rochdale Rd *RTW* TN1 .... 11 J1
Rochester Av *ROCH* ME1 .... 65 L1
Rochester Crs *HOO/HM* ME3 .... 35 M7
Rochester Dr *BXLY* DA5 .... 26 C5
Rochester Rd *DART* DA1 .... 102 C2
  DIT/AY ME20 .... 32 B7
  GVE DA12 .... 82 A2
  ROCH ME1 .... 64 F2
  STRD ME2 .... 2 C2
  TONN TN10 .... 147 M1
  WALD ME5 .... 82 A1
Rochester St *CHAT* ME4 .... 4 B9
Rochester Wy *DART* DA1 .... 27 G5
Rock Av *GILL* ME7 .... 5 K7
Rockdale Rd *SEV* TN13 .... 9 J4
Rockfield Rd *OXTED* RH8 .... 109 H8
Rock Hl *ORP* BR6 .... 74 D7
Rock Rd *BGR/WK* TN15 .... 98 B6
  MAID/BEAR ME14 .... 103 J6
  SIT ME10 .... 88 A1
Rocks Cl *E/WMAL* ME19 .... 101 J7
Rocks Hl *CRBK* TN17 .... 184 B4
  RBTBR TN32 .... 204 A7
The Rocks Rd *E/WMAL* ME19 .... 101 J7
Rock Villa Rd *RTW* TN1 .... 10 F4
Rodeo Cl *ERITH* DA8 .... 13 K7
Rodmell Rd *RTWE/PEM* TN2 .... 10 F8
Rodney Av *TONN* TN10 .... 148 A1
Roebuck Rd *ROCH* ME1 .... 3 J8
Roedean Cl *ORP* BR6 .... 56 D7
Roedean Rd *RTWE/PEM* TN2 .... 177 J4
Roehampton Cl *GVE* DA12 .... 32 A5
Roffen Rd *ROCH* ME1 .... 64 E4
Rogers Ct *SWLY* BR8 .... 42 C8 ⓘ
Rogers La *WARL* CR6 .... 90 B4
Rogersmead *TENT* TN30 .... 196 B6
Rogers Rd *GRAYS* RM17 .... 16 E3
Rogers Rough Rd *CRBK* TN17 .... 190 C2
Rogues Rough Rd *BGR/WK* TN15 .... 66 G7
Rogues Hl *RTON* TN11 .... 161 K1
Rokesley Rd *GRH* DA9 .... 29 K7
Rolvenden Av *RHAM* ME8 .... 67 J4
Rolvenden Dr *SIT* ME10 .... 70 D8
Rolvenden Hl *CRBK* TN17 .... 195 K8
Rolvenden Rd *STRD* ME2 .... 49 L3
Roman Cl *WALD* ME5 .... 82 F4
Roman Hts *MAID/BEAR* ME14 .... 103 L6
Roman Rd *EDEN* TN8 .... 142 F6
  GVW DA11 .... 30 E8
  RDART DA2 .... 29 K7
  SNOD ME6 .... 81 H5
Roman Sq *SIT* ME10 .... 88 B2
Roman Villa Rd *EYN* DA4 .... 43 L3
Roman Wy *DART* DA1 .... 27 C3

STRD ME2 .... 2 C9
Romany Rd *RHAM* ME8 .... 67 K3
Romford Rd *RTWE/PEM* TN2 .... 165 G6
Romney Cl *MAID/SHEP* ME15 .... 122 C2
Romney Ct *SIT* ME10 .... 70 F6
Romney Gdns *BXLYHN* DA7 .... 12 B7
Romney Pl *MAID/SHEP* ME15 .... 7 G5
Romney Rd *GVW* DA11 .... 31 G8
  WALD ME5 .... 66 D8
Romney Wy *TONN* TN10 .... 132 A8
Romsey Cl *STRD* ME2 .... 2 A1
Ronfearn Av *STMC/STPC* BR5 .... 56 F1
Roodlands La *EDEN* TN8 .... 127 M7
Rookery Cl *RSIT* ME9 .... 87 J7
Rookery Crs *HOO/HM* ME3 .... 20 D7
Rookery Gdns *STMC/STPC* BR5 .... 56 E1
Rookery Rd *ORP* BR6 .... 72 B4
The Rookery *WTHK* RM20 .... 15 J5
Rookery Vw *GRAYS* RM17 .... 16 F4
Rookesley Cl *RTWE/PEM* TN2 .... 56 F3
Rook La *RSIT* ME9 .... 70 B7
Rookley Cl *RTWE/PEM* TN2 .... 11 L7
Rooks Hl *BGR/WK* TN15 .... 114 E7
Rookwood Cl *GRAYS* RM17 .... 16 D5
Roonagh Ct *SIT* ME10 .... 88 A3
Roopers *RRTW* TN3 .... 162 C6
Roosevelt Av *WALD* ME5 .... 66 B6
Ropemakers Ct *CHAT* ME4 .... 66 C4
Roper Cl *RHAM* ME8 .... 84 E2
Roper Cl *RSIT* ME9 .... 89 M2
Roper's Green La *HOO/HM* ME3 .... 36 C5
Roper's La *HOO/HM* ME3 .... 36 B5
Rope Wk *CHAT* ME4 .... 4 D4
Ropewalk *CRBK* TN17 .... 183 J4
The Rope Wk *HAWK* TN18 .... 200 D8
Roseacre Gdns
  MAID/BEAR ME14 .... 122 C2 ⓘ
Roseacre La *MAID/BEAR* ME14 .... 122 C2
Rose Av *GVE* DA12 .... 32 A6
Rose Bank Cl *MAID/SHEP* ME15 .... 7 J5
Rosebank Gdns *GVW* DA11 .... 31 G6
Roseberry Gdns *DART* DA1 .... 27 L5
  ORP BR6 .... 56 A6
Rosebery Cl *SIT* ME10 .... 88 F1
Rosebery Ct *GVW* DA11 .... 31 H6
Rosebery Rd *CHAT* ME4 .... 66 A3
  GILL ME7 .... 5 M1
  GRAYS RM17 .... 16 A5
Rosecroft Cl *BH/WHM* TN16 .... 92 B4 ⓘ
  STMC/STPC BR5 .... 56 E2
Rosedale Cl *RDART* DA2 .... 28 D5
Rosedale Rd *GRAYS* RM17 .... 16 F4
Rosedene Cl *DART* DA1 .... 27 L5
Rosefield *SEV* TN13 .... 8 E5
Rosegarth *MEO* DA13 .... 46 A5
Rosehill Rd *BH/WHM* TN16 .... 91 L3
Rosehill Wk *RTW* TN1 .... 10 E5
Roseholme *MAIDW* ME16 .... 6 B8
Roselare Cl *BH/WHM* TN16 .... 110 F3
Roseleigh Av *MAIDW* ME16 .... 120 E1
Roseleigh Rd *SIT* ME10 .... 87 M4
Rosemary La *BGR/WK* TN15 .... 78 F3
  HDCN TN27 .... 157 G8
  WADH TN5 .... 190 C8
Rosemary Rd *E/WMAL* ME19 .... 101 H4
  MAID/SHEP ME15 .... 122 C2 ⓘ
Rosemount Cl
  MAID/SHEP ME15 .... 137 H1
Rosemount Ct *STRD* ME2 .... 49 J4 ⓘ
Rosenheath Cl *ORP* BR6 .... 73 K2
Rose St *GVW* DA11 .... 30 D4
  ROCH ME1 .... 65 M2
  TON TN9 .... 147 L5
Rosewood *RDART* DA2 .... 42 A4
Rose Yd *MAID/BEAR* ME14 .... 7 G4
Rosherville Wy *GVW* DA11 .... 31 G5
Rossdale *RTWE/PEM* TN2 .... 164 B6
Rosell Rd *TIL* RM18 .... 17 H8 ⓘ
Rossland Cl *BXLYHS* DA6 .... 26 C5
Rosslyn Gln *MAIDW* ME16 .... 102 D8 ⓘ
Ross Rd *DART* DA1 .... 27 J4
Ross St *ROCH* ME1 .... 3 J9
Rothermere Cl *CRBK* TN17 .... 194 A7
Rother Rd *TONN* TN10 .... 131 K8
Rother V *WALD* ME5 .... 83 L1
Rothley Cl *TENT* TN30 .... 196 D5
Rouge La *GVE* DA12 .... 31 K6
Roughetts Rd *E/WMAL* ME19 .... 100 B2
Roughway La *RTON* TN11 .... 116 D7
Round Ash Wy *HART* DA3 .... 61 G2
Roundel Ct *RSIT* ME9 .... 89 M3
The Roundel *SIT* ME10 .... 88 A3
Roundel Wy *STPH/PW* TN12 .... 152 E8
Roundhay *E/WMAL* ME19 .... 100 F4
Roundhill Rd *RTWE/PEM* TN2 .... 177 M4
Roundlyn Gdns *STMC/STPC* BR5 .... 40 D8
Round St *MEO* DA13 .... 46 E7
Roundwell *MAID/BEAR* ME14 .... 122 F1
Round Wood *WALD* ME5 .... 83 J4
Rover Rd *WALD* ME5 .... 83 K3
Rowan Cl *DIT/AY* ME20 .... 102 A4 ⓘ
  MEO DA13 .... 62 D2
  STPH/PW TN12 .... 150 B8
Rowan Crs *DART* DA1 .... 27 L6
Rowan Lea *WALD* ME5 .... 66 D5
Rowan Rd *BXLYHN* DA7 .... 26 A1
Rowans Cl *HART* DA3 .... 44 F6
Rowan Shaw *TONN* TN10 .... 131 M7
Rowan Tree Rd *RTWE/PEM* TN2 .... 10 B9
Rowbrocke Cl *RHAM* ME8 .... 84 F2
Rowdow La *RSEV* TN14 .... 95 M2
Rowhill Rd *RDART* DA2 .... 42 C2
Rowland Av *GILL* ME7 .... 67 G4
Rowland Cl *WALD* ME5 .... 82 E5
Rowlatt Cl *RDART* DA2 .... 42 E1
Rowley Hl *RTWE/PEM* TN2 .... 164 F4
Rowmarsh Cl *GVW* DA11 .... 30 F8
Rowzill Rd *SWLY* BR8 .... 42 B3
Royal Av *TON* TN9 .... 147 L5
Royal Cha *STH/RUST* TN4 .... 10 D3
Royal Eagle Cl *STRD* ME2 .... 50 A6
Royal Engineers' Rd
  MAID/BEAR ME14 .... 103 H7
Royal Oak La *BXLYHS* DA6 .... 26 B3
Royal Pier Rd *GVE* DA12 .... 31 K4
Royal Rd *DART* DA1 .... 43 J2
Royal Sovereign Av *CHAT* ME4 .... 50 D6
Royal West Kent Av
  TONN TN10 .... 147 M1

Roydon Hall Rd *WBY/YAL* ME18 .. 118 A8
Royston Rd *DART* DA1 .... 27 H4
  MAID/SHEP ME15 .... 122 C2
Roystons Cl *RHAM* ME8 .... 68 B3
Royton Av *RMAID* ME17 .... 125 M8
Ruckinge Wy *RHAM* ME8 .... 67 L2
Ruck La *STPH/PW* TN12 .... 181 C2
Rudge La *WALD* ME5 .... 83 M3
Rudland Rd *BXLYHN* DA7 .... 26 D1
Rugby Cl *HOO/HM* ME5 .... 36 A2
Ruggles Cl *HOO/HM* ME5 .... 36 A2
Ruins Barn Rd *RSIT* ME9 .... 107 L1
  SIT ME10 .... 88 A5
Rumstead La *MAID/BEAR* ME14.. 105 L3
  RSIT ME9 .... 85 M8
Rumstead Rd *RSIT* ME9 .... 105 M1
Runciman Cl *ORP* BR6 .... 73 L4
Runham La *RMAID* ME17 .... 141 C2
Rural V *GVW* DA11 .... 31 G5
Ruscombe Cl *STH/RUST* TN4 .. 163 H3 🔲
Rush Cl *WALD* ME5 .... 83 J2
Rushdean Wk *BH/WHM* TN16 ... 91 M3
Rushdene Wk *BH/WHM* TN16 ... 91 M3
Rushdon Cl *CDH/CHF* RM16 ..... 16 C2
Rushenden Rd *QBOR* ME11 ..... 55 J1
Rushet Rd *STMC/STPC* BR5 .... 40 C6
Rushetts *RRTW* TN3 .... 176 B1
Rushetts Rd *BGR/WK* TN15 .... 76 F2
Rushford Cl *HDCN* TN27 .... 155 L8
Rushlye Cl *RRTW* TN3 .... 178 B8
Rushmead Dr
  MAID/SHEP ME15 .... 121 J6
Rushmere Ct *BGR/WK* TN15 ... 97 M6
Rushmore Hl *ORP* BR6 .... 73 L4
  RSEV TN14 .... 73 M8
Rushymead *BGR/WK* TN15 ..... 96 C4
Ruskin Cl *E/WMAL* ME19 ...... 101 H5 🔲
Ruskin Dr *ORP* BR6 .... 56 A6
Ruskin Gv *DART* DA1 .... 28 C3
Ruskin Rd *BELV* DA17 .... 12 C3
  CDH/CHF RM16 .... 17 J3
Russell Cl *BXLYHN* DA7 .... 26 C2
  DART DA1 .... 27 J1
  SIT ME10 .... 87 L2
Russell Ct *CHAT* ME4 .... 5 G8
Russell Pl *EYN* DA4 .... 43 J5
Russell Rd *DIT/AY* ME20 .... 82 E6
  GVE DA12 .... 31 M4
  TIL RM18 .... 17 G7
Russells Av *RHAM* ME8 .... 68 C5
Russel Rd *GRAYS* RM17 .... 16 C3
Russet Cl *STRD* ME2 .... 2 A1
The Russets *MAID* ME16 .... 102 D8 🔲
  MEO DA13 .... 62 C2
Russett Cl *DIT/AY* ME20 .... 102 A5
  ORP BR6 .... 56 D8
Russett Rd *STPH/PW* TN12 ... 134 D7
Russett Wy *SWLY* BR8 .... 41 M6
Russet Wy *E/WMAL* ME19 ..... 118 B3
Rusthall Gra *STH/RUST* TN4 .. 176 F1 🔲
Rusthall High St *STH/RUST* TN4 .. 176 D1
Rusthall Rd *STH/RUST* TN4 ... 176 F2
Rustwick *STH/RUST* TN4 .... 176 F1
Rutherford Wy *TONN* TN10 ... 131 M6
Rutland Av *DART* DA1 .... 27 M5 🔲
Rutland Ga *BELV* DA17 .... 12 D4
Rutland Pl *RHAM* ME8 .... 84 E2
Rutland Wy *MAID/SHEP* ME15 .. 122 A5
  STMC/STPC BR5 .... 56 E2
Ruxley Cl *SCUP* DA14 .... 40 F3
Ruxton Cl *SWLY* BR8 .... 42 A7
Ruxton Ct *SWLY* BR8 .... 42 A7 🔲
Ryan Dr *MAID/SHEP* ME15 .... 122 C3
Ryarsh Crs *ORP* BR6 .... 56 A7
Ryarsh La *E/WMAL* ME19 ..... 100 D4
Ryarsh Rd *E/WMAL* ME19 ..... 80 D8
Rycault Cl *MAIDW* ME16 .... 6 C4
Rycaut Cl *RHAM* ME8 .... 84 F2
Rycroft La *RSEV* TN14 .... 113 G8
Rydal Cl *STH/RUST* TN4 .... 10 A3
Rydal Dr *BXLYHN* DA7 .... 12 C7
  STH/RUST TN4 .... 10 A2
Ryde Cl *WALD* ME5 .... 66 D5
Ryders *RRTW* TN3 .... 176 C1
Rye Cl *BXLY* DA5 .... 26 D4
Rye Crs *STMC/STPC* BR5 ...... 56 E4
Ryecroft *GVE* DA12 .... 47 G2 🔲
  HART DA3 .... 45 M8
Ryecroft Rd *RSEV* TN14 .... 95 J3
Ryedale Ct *SEV* TN13 .... 95 G7
Ryegrass Cl *WALD* ME5 ...... 66 E7 🔲
Rye La *RSEV* TN14 .... 95 H5
Rye Rd *HAWK* TN18 .... 199 M5
  TENT TN30 .... 209 J3
Rykhill *CDH/CHF* RM16 .... 17 K2
Rymers Cl *RTWE/PEM* TN2 ... 163 M6
Rysted La *BH/WHM* TN16 ..... 110 E4

Sabina Rd *CDH/CHF* RM16 .... 17 L3
Sackville Cl *SEV* TN13 .... 95 K8
Sackville Rd *DART* DA1 .... 27 M7
Saddington St *GVE* DA12 .... 31 K5
Saddlers Cl *MAID/BEAR* ME14 .. 104 A8
Saddler's Pk *EYN* DA4 .... 58 F6
Sadlers Cl *WALD* ME5 .... 82 F3
Saffron Cl *CDH/CHF* RM16 ..... 15 L3
Saffron Wy *SIT* ME10 .... 71 H6
Sage Rd *ROCH* ME1 .... 65 J2
Sailmakers Ct *CHAT* ME4 .... 66 D3
St Aidan's Wy *GVE* DA12 .... 32 A8
St Albans Cl *GILL* ME7 .... 51 G6
  GVE DA12 .... 31 M8
St Albans Gdns *GVE* DA12 ..... 31 M8
St Alban's Rd *DART* DA1 .... 28 B4
  STRD ME2 .... 48 E7
St Andrew Rd *GILL* ME7 .... 50 F6
St Andrew's Cl *MAIDW* ME16 .. 6 C4
  STPH/PW TN12 .... 150 C7 🔲
St Andrews Cl *STH/RUST* TN4 .. 163 J4 🔲
St Andrews Dr *ORP* BR6 .... 56 D2
St Andrews Park Rd
  STH/RUST TN4 .... 163 J4
St Andrews Rd *GVE* DA12 .... 31 K5 🔲
  MAIDW ME16 .... 120 C3
  STPH/PW TN12 .... 150 C7
St Andrews Wy *OXTED* RH8 .. 126 A1
St Anne Ct *MAIDW* ME16 .... 6 D4
St Ann's Green La
  STPH/PW TN12 .... 153 H5
St Aubyns Cl *ORP* BR6 .... 56 B6
St Aubyns Gdns *ORP* BR6 ...... 56 B5
St Audrey Av *BXLYHN* DA7 .... 12 C8
St Augustine Rd *CDH/CHF* RM16 .. 17 K3
St Augustine's Rd *BELV* DA17 .. 12 B3
St Barnabas La *GILL* ME7 .... 5 M7
  MAIDW ME16 .... 102 E5
  RTW TN1 .... 11 H2 🔲
St Bartholomew's La
  CHAT ME4 .... 4 A5 🔲
St Bartholomew's Ter
  ROCH ME1 .... 4 A5 🔲
St Benedict Rd *SNOD* ME6 ..... 81 G5
St Benedict's Av *GVE* DA12 .... 32 A8
St Benets Wy *TENT* TN30 ..... 196 D5
St Benjamins Dr *ORP* BR6 ...... 73 L3
St Bernards Rd *TONN* TN10 ... 131 L7
St Botolph Rd *GVW* DA11 .... 30 F8
St Botolph's Av *SEV* TN13 .... 8 F4
St Botolph's Rd *SEV* TN13 .... 9 G4
St Cecilia Rd *CDH/CHF* RM16 ... 17 K3
St Chad's Dr *GVE* DA12 .... 32 A8
St Chad's Rd *TIL* RM18 .... 17 J7
St Clair Cl *OXTED* RH8 .... 108 E8
St Clement's Av *WTHK* RM20 .. 15 J5
St Clements Cl *GVW* DA11 .... 31 H8 🔲
St Clements Ct *PUR* RM19 ..... 14 C3 🔲
St Clement's Rd *WTHK* RM20 .. 15 L6
St Clere Hill Rd *BGR/WK* TN15 .. 77 H6
St Columba's Cl *GVE* DA12 ..... 32 A8
St David's Crs *GVE* DA12 .... 31 M8
St David's Rd *HOO/HM* ME3 ... 23 M5
  STH/RUST TN4 .... 163 K7
  SWLY BR8 .... 42 B3
St Dunstan's Dr *GVE* DA12 ..... 32 A8
St Edith's Rd *BGR/WK* TN15 ... 96 C4
St Edmunds Rd *DART* DA1 ...... 28 B2
St Faith's La *MAID/BEAR* ME14 .. 122 D1
St Faith's St *MAID/BEAR* ME14 .. 6 F4
St Fidelis' Rd *ERITH* DA8 .... 12 F3
St Francis Av *GVE* DA12 .... 47 C1
St Francis Cl *ORP* BR6 .... 56 A2
St Francis Rd *MEO* DA13 .... 79 K2
St Francis Wy *CDH/CHF* RM16 .. 17 L3
St George's Av *GRAYS* RM17 .. 16 E3
St George's Ct *BGR/WK* TN15 .. 98 B2 🔲
St George's Crs *GVE* DA12 ..... 46 F1
St Georges Ms *TON* TN9 ...... 147 K5 🔲
St George's Pk *RTWE/PEM* TN2 .. 177 H5 🔲
St George's Rd *GILL* ME7 .... 5 K1
  SCUP DA14 .... 40 F3
  SEV TN13 .... 95 K8
  SWLY BR8 .... 42 B8 🔲
St George's Sq *MAIDW* ME16 .. 6 B6
St Gregory's Crs *GVE* DA12 ... 32 A7
St Helens La *MAID/SHEP* ME15.. 120 A5
St Helens Rd *HOO/HM* ME3 ... 20 D8
St Helier's Cl *MAIDW* ME16 ... 120 D3
St Hildas *BGR/WK* TN15 ...... 116 B5
St Hilda's Wy *GVE* DA12 .... 46 F1
St James' La *RDART* DA2 .... 29 G5
St James' Pk *RTW* TN1 .... 11 J2
  RTWE/PEM TN2 .... 11 K2
St James Pl *DART* DA1 .... 27 M4 🔲
  RTW TN1 .... 11 J3
St James's Av *GVW* DA11 ...... 31 J5
St James's Pl *GRAYS* RM17 . 16 E5 🔲
  SEV TN13 .... 95 K8
St James's St *GVW* DA11 .... 31 J4 🔲
St James Wy *SCUP* DA14 ..... 41 G2
St John's Av *SIT* ME10 .... 88 D2
St John's Cl *HOO/HM* ME3 ...... 48 E2
St John's Hl *SEV* TN13 .... 9 J1
St John's La *HART* DA3 .... 61 H2
St John's Pk *STH/RUST* TN4 .. 163 J5
St Johns Rd *CDH/CHF* RM16 ... 17 K4
  ERITH DA8 .... 12 F4
  GILL ME7 .... 5 J8
  GVE DA12 .... 31 M5
  HOO/HM ME3 .... 35 M7
  HOO/HM ME3 .... 48 E1
  RDART DA2 .... 28 E5
  SCUP DA14 .... 40 D1
  SEV TN13 .... 95 K8
  STH/RUST TN4 .... 163 J6
St Johns *ROCH* ME1 .... 65 J3
St Josephs Cl *ORP* BR6 ...... 56 B7 🔲
St Justin Cl *STMC/STPC* BR5 .. 40 F7
St Katherine's La *SNOD* ME6 .. 81 H6
St Kilda Rd *ORP* BR6 .... 56 B4
St Laurence Av *DIT/AY* ME20 .. 102 D5
St Laurence Ri *RSIT* ME9 .... 88 F3
  STMC/STPC BR5 .... 40 F7
St Lawrence Av *CHAT* ME4 .... 66 B3
St Leonards Av *CHAT* ME4 ..... 66 A7
St Leonards Ri *ORP* BR6 .... 56 A7
St Leonards Rd *MAIDW* ME16 .. 102 E5
St Leonard's La *E/WMAL* ME19 .. 100 D6
St Luke's Av *MAID/BEAR* ME14 .. 7 J3
St Lukes Cl *RDART* DA2 ...... 41 M6 🔲
  SWLY BR8 .... 42 B3
St Luke's Rd *MAID/BEAR* ME14.. 7 J2
  STH/RUST TN4 .... 163 K7
St Luke's Wy *HOO/HM* ME3 ... 23 M5
St Margaret's Banks *ROCH* ME1 .. 3 L8 🔲
  ROCH ME1 .... 3 M9 🔲
St Margarets Cl
  MAIDW ME16 .... 120 D3 🔲
  ORP BR6 .... 56 D7 🔲
  RDART DA2 .... 28 F7
St Margaret's Crs *GVE* DA12 .. 32 A8
St Margarets Dr *RHAM* ME8 ... 67 L8
St Margaret's Ms *ROCH* ME1 ... 3 J7
St Margaret's Rd *RHAM* ME8 .. 44 A4
St Mark's Av *GVW* DA11 .... 31 G5
St Marks Cl *DIT/AY* ME20 ..... 82 B7 🔲
St Mark's Rd *RTWE/PEM* TN2 .. 177 H6
St Martin's La *MAID/BEAR* ME14 .. 104 C4
St Martins Dr *EYN* DA4 .... 58 F6
St Martins Meadow
  BH/WHM TN16 .... 111 L1
St Martin's Rd *DART* DA1 ...... 28 B4
St Mary's Church Rd
  RSEV TN14 .... 112 A3

St Mary's Cl *BGR/WK* TN15 .... 98 E6
  GRAYS RM17 .... 16 F5 🔲
  GVE DA12 .... 31 L7
  OXTED RH8 .... 109 C7
  STMC/STPC BR5 .... 40 D6
  WBY/YAL ME18 .... 151 G1
St Mary's Ct *BH/WHM* TN16 .. 110 F4
St Mary's Dr *SEV* TN13 .... 8 B2
St Mary's Gdns *CHAT* ME4 ..... 50 D6
St Mary's Gn *BH/WHM* TN16 ... 91 L4
St Mary's Gv *RRTW* TN3 .... 91 L4
St Marys Rd *BGR/WK* TN15 ... 98 C3
  BXLY DA5 .... 26 B6
  CDH/CHF RM16 .... 17 K3
  GILL ME7 .... 5 K1
  GRH DA9 .... 29 C3
  STRD ME2 .... 3 G3
  SWLY BR8 .... 41 M8
  TON TN9 .... 147 K6
St Mary's Vw *RSIT* ME9 .... 69 L7
St Marys Wy *HART* DA3 .... 45 G7
St Matthews Rd *ROCH* ME1 .... 65 J3
St Matthew's Wy
  HOO/HM ME3 .... 23 M5 🔲
St Michael's Cl *CHAT* ME4 .... 4 C8
  DIT/AY ME20 .... 102 E2
St Michaels Gdns *RSEV* TN14 ... 3 H2 🔲
St Michaels Rd *CDH/CHF* RM16 .. 17 K4
  MAIDW ME16 .... 6 B6
  SIT ME10 .... 88 A1
  STH/RUST TN4 .... 163 K6
St Mildred's Cl *TENT* TN30 ... 196 C6 🔲
St Nicholas Dr *SEV* TN13 .... 9 J8
St Nicholas Gdns *STRD* ME2 .... 2 D2
St Patrick's Gdns *GVE* DA12 .... 46 F1
St Patrick's Pl *CDH/CHF* RM16 .. 17 K3
St Paul's Cl *STRD* ME2 .... 48 F8 🔲
  SWCM DA10 .... 30 A5
St Paul's Rd *ERITH* DA8 .... 12 E6
  SIT ME10 .... 71 G8 🔲
  STH/RUST TN4 .... 176 E1
St Paul's Wood Hl
  STMC/STPC BR5 .... 40 A6
St Peter's Br *MAIDW* ME16 ...... 6 E5
St Peters Cl *DIT/AY* ME20 ..... 101 K4
  SWCM DA10 .... 30 B5
St Peters Pl *DIT/AY* ME20 ...... 82 B7
St Peters Rd *CDH/CHF* RM16 ... 17 K3
  DIT/AY ME20 .... 101 K4
St Peters Rw *MAIDW* ME16 ...... 6 E3
  RTWE/PEM TN2 .... 11 K6
St Peter St *ROCH* ME1 .... 3 L9
St Philip's Wy *MAID/SHEP* ME15 .. 7 J7
St Ronan's Cl
  MAID/SHEP ME15 .... 121 L6 🔲
St Saviours Rd
  MAID/SHEP ME15 .... 121 M7
Saints Hl *RTON* TN11 .... 161 J4
St Stephen's Sq *MAID/SHEP* ME15.. 6 D9
St Stephen's St *TON* TN9 ..... 147 K5
St Stephons Ct *RTW* TN1 ..... 11 H2 🔲
Saint's Wk *CDH/CHF* RM16 .... 17 L3
St Teresa Wk *CDH/CHF* RM16 .. 17 K3
St Thomas Ct *BXLY* DA5 .... 26 C5
St Thomas Rd *BELV* DA17 ...... 12 E1
  GVW DA11 .... 31 G6 🔲
St Thomas's Av *GVW* DA11 .... 31 K7
St Thomas's Pl *GRAYS* RM17 .. 16 E5 🔲
St Vincents La *E/WMAL* ME19 .. 99 K3
St Vincents Rd *DART* DA1 ...... 28 C4
St Welcume's Wy *RMAID* ME17.. 125 C7
St Werburgh Crs *HOO/HM* ME3 .. 35 M8
St William's Wy *ROCH* ME1 .... 65 M2
St Winifred's Rd *BH/WHM* TN16 .. 92 B4
Saladin Dr *PUR* RM19 .... 14 C3
Salcote Rd *GVE* DA12 .... 47 G2 🔲
Salem Pl *GVW* DA11 .... 30 F5 🔲
Salem St *MAID/SHEP* ME15 ..... 7 H7
Salisbury Av *RHAM* ME8 .... 67 M5
  SWLY BR8 .... 42 C8
Salisbury Cl *SIT* ME10 .... 88 E1
Salisbury Rd *BXLY* DA5 .... 26 C6
  CHAT ME4 .... 4 F7
  DIT/AY ME20 .... 82 E5
  GRAYS RM17 .... 16 E5
  GVW DA11 .... 31 H6
  MAID/BEAR ME14 .... 7 H1
  RDART DA2 .... 28 A5
  RRTW TN3 .... 176 B2
  STH/RUST TN4 .... 163 L5
  TONN TN10 .... 147 M1
Salix Rd *GRAYS* RM17 .... 16 F5
Sallows Shaw *MEO* DA13 .... 62 E1
Sally Port *GILL* ME7 .... 4 F1
Sally Port Gdns *GILL* ME7 .... 4 F2
Salmon Rd *BELV* DA17 .... 12 C4
  DART DA1 .... 28 B1
Saltford Cl *ERITH* DA8 .... 13 G4
Saltings Rd *SNOD* ME6 .... 81 J6
Salt La *HOO/HM* ME3 .... 34 B1
Salt's Av *MAID/SHEP* ME15 ... 137 H2
Salts La *MAID/SHEP* ME15 .... 137 J1
Saltwood Cl *STMC/STPC* BR5 .. 56 E7
Saltwood Rd *MAID/SHEP* ME15 .. 121 H6
Samara Cl *WALD* ME5 .... 83 H1
Samphire Cl *MAID/BEAR* ME14 .. 122 A1
Samphire Ct *GRAYS* RM17 ..... 17 G5
Sanctuary Cl *DART* DA1 .... 27 L4
Sanctuary Rd *RHAM* ME8 .... 67 J2
Sandbanks Hl *RDART* DA2 ..... 44 E3
Sandbourne Dr
  MAID/BEAR ME14 .... 103 H4
Sandcliff Rd *ERITH* DA8 .... 12 F3
Sandersons Av *RSEV* TN14 ... 74 C4 🔲
Sanderson Wy *TON* TN9 ...... 148 A4
Sanderstead Rd
  STMC/STPC BR5 .... 56 D2 🔲
Sandfield Rd *RTON* TN11 ...... 161 H6
Sandford Rd *BXLYHS* DA6 ..... 26 A2
  SIT ME10 .... 70 D8
Sandgate Ct *RHAM* ME8 .... 85 H1
Sandhill La *MAID/BEAR* ME14 .. 33 M7
Sandhurst Av *RTWE/PEM* TN2 .. 165 G7
Sandhurst Rd *RHAM* ME8 ... 67 L2 🔲
  RTWE/PEM TN2 .... 163 L6

Sandhurst Pk *RTWE/PEM* TN2 .. 163 M7
Sandhurst Rd *CRBK* TN17 ..... 201 K4
  ORP BR6 .... 56 C6
  RTWE/PEM TN2 .... 163 M6
  TIL RM18 .... 17 L8
Sandilands *SEV* TN13 .... 94 F8
Sand La *CRBK* TN17 .... 171 J7
Sandling La *MAID/BEAR* ME14 .. 6 F1
Sandling Rd *MAID/BEAR* ME14 .. 6 F1
Sandown Cl *RTWE/PEM* TN2 .. 164 B7
Sandown Dr *RHAM* ME8 .... 67 M6
Sandown Gv *RTWE/PEM* TN2.. 164 B7
Sandown Pk *RTWE/PEM* TN2.. 164 B8
Sandown Rd *E/WMAL* ME19 .. 100 D5
  GVE DA12 .... 46 E3
Sandpiper Dr *ERITH* DA8 .... 13 K6
Sandpiper Rd *WALD* ME5 .... 83 L3
The Sandpipers *GVE* DA12 .... 31 M7
Sandpiper Wy *STMC/STPC* BR5 .. 40 B8
Sandringham Rd *RHAM* ME8 .. 85 G1
Sand Rd *RRTW* TN3 .... 189 J1
Sandrock Rd *RTWE/PEM* TN2 .. 11 K3
Sandstone Dr *SIT* ME10 .... 71 G5
Sandstone Ri
  MAID/BEAR ME14 .... 83 L5 🔲
Sandway Rd *RMAID* ME17 .... 141 J2
  STMC/STPC BR5 .... 40 E8
Sandy Bank Rd *GVE* DA12 ..... 31 K6
Sandycroft Rd *STRD* ME2 .... 49 H4 🔲
Sandy Dell *GILL* ME7 .... 84 C2
Sandy La *BGR/WK* TN15 .... 99 H4
  BGR/WK TN15 .... 115 K3
  BH/WHM TN16 .... 110 F3
  CDH/CHF RM16 .... 17 K5
  E/WMAL ME19 .... 100 C4
  MAID/BEAR ME14 .... 103 L4
  MAID/BEAR ME14 .... 104 D8
  MEO DA13 .... 45 G1
  ORP BR6 .... 56 C3
  OXTED RH8 .... 108 E7
  OXTED RH8 .... 109 K5
  RDART DA2 .... 29 M8
  SEV TN13 .... 9 K2
  SNOD ME6 .... 81 G7
  STMC/STPC BR5 .... 40 F7
  TENT TN30 .... 196 D6
  WTHK RM20 .... 15 K5
Sandy Mt *MAID/BEAR* ME14 .. 104 D8
Sandy Rdg *BGR/WK* TN15 ..... 98 C6
Sapho Pk *GVE* DA12 .... 47 H1
Saracen Cl *GILL* ME7 .... 67 J4
Saracen Flds *WALD* ME5 .... 83 K5
Sara Crs *GRH* DA9 .... 29 J2
Sara Pk *GVE* DA12 .... 47 G1 🔲
Sare Hts *WALD* ME5 .... 83 H4
Sarsens Cl *WALD* ME5 .... 47 H7 🔲
Sassoon Cl *DIT/AY* ME20 ..... 101 J1
Satis Av *SIT* ME10 .... 71 G6
Saunders Cl *GVW* DA11 .... 31 G7
Saunders Rd *STH/RUST* TN4 .. 177 C4
Saunders St *GILL* ME7 .... 5 J1
Saunders Wy *DART* DA1 .... 28 B7
Savage Rd *WALD* ME5 .... 83 K2
Savoy Rd *DART* DA1 .... 27 L3
Sawyers Ct *CHAT* ME4 .... 66 D3
Saxbys Rd *BGR/WK* TN15 ...... 96 F8
Saxby Wd *RTON* TN11 .... 146 B4
Saxon Cl *GVW* DA11 .... 30 E8
  RSEV TN14 .... 95 H3
  STRD ME2 .... 49 H4
  WBY/YAL ME18 .... 118 B3
Saxon Pl *EYN* DA4 .... 59 L1
Saxon Rd *RDART* DA2 .... 43 G1
Saxons Dr *MAID/BEAR* ME14 .. 103 K7
Saxon Shore Wy *GILL* ME7 .... 51 L7
  GVE DA12 .... 31 L4
  HOO/HM ME3 .... 33 J2
  ROCH ME1 .... 3 K6
  RSIT ME9 .... 54 E4
  STRD ME2 .... 50 A5
Saxton St *GILL* ME7 .... 5 J4
Saxville Rd *STMC/STPC* BR5 .. 40 D7
Sayer Cl *GRH* DA9 .... 29 J3
Sayes Court Rd *STMC/STPC* BR5 .. 40 C7
Scabharbour Rd *RSEV* TN14 .. 129 L3
Scadbury Gdns *STMC/STPC* BR5 .. 40 C6
Scads Hill Cl *ORP* BR6 .... 56 B2
Scarborough Cl *BH/WHM* TN16 .. 91 L4
Scarborough La *ROCH* ME1 .... 81 M4
Scarlet Cl *STMC/STPC* BR5 .. 40 D8 🔲
Scholars Ri *STRD* ME2 .... 48 E6
Scholey Cl *STRD* ME2 .... 81 K1
School Ap *BGR/WK* TN15 .... 98 B6
School Av *GILL* ME7 .... 67 G1
School Cl *DART* DA1 .... 27 H2
  MEO DA13 .... 62 C3 🔲
School Fld *EDEN* TN8 .... 142 E3
Schoolfield Rd *WTHK* RM20 .... 15 J5
School Hl *RRTW* TN3 .... 180 D7
School House La
  STPH/PW TN12 .... 167 M6
School La *BGR/WK* TN15 .... 77 H5
  BGR/WK TN15 .... 96 B7
  E/WMAL ME19 .... 79 J8
  EYN DA4 .... 60 B2
  HOO/HM ME3 .... 33 L7
  HOO/HM ME3 .... 48 E1
  MAID/SHEP ME15 .... 122 A6
  MEO DA13 .... 79 J3
  RDART DA2 .... 29 L8
  RMAID ME17 .... 139 C6
  RMAID ME17 .... 141 H3
  ROCH ME1 .... 64 F8
  RSIT ME9 .... 69 K3
  RSIT ME9 .... 69 K6
  RSIT ME9 .... 70 E2
  RSIT ME9 .... 87 H2
  RSIT ME9 .... 88 F3
  RTON TN11 .... 116 A7
  RTON TN11 .... 133 C5
  SWLY BR8 .... 42 B4
School Rd *RTWE/PEM* TN2 ... 177 H4 🔲
School Rd *GVE* DA12 .... 31 L3
  SIT ME10 .... 88 C1
School Ter *HAWK* TN18 .... 199 H3
Schooner Ct *GRH* DA9 .... 28 E2
Scimitar Cl *GILL* ME7 .... 67 J4
Scords La *BH/WHM* TN16 ..... 127 L2
Scotby Av *WALD* ME5 .... 83 K1

Scotland La *GVE* DA12 .... 47 J5
Scotsdale Cl *CHST* BR7 .... 40 A8
Scotshall La *WARL* CR6 .... 90 E1
Scott Av *MAID* ME4 .... 68 C5
Scott Crs *ERITH* DA8 .... 13 H7
Scotteswood Av *CHAT* ME4 .... 66 B3
Scott Rd *CDH/CHF* RM16 .... 17 J3
  GVE DA12 .... 46 F2
  TON TN9 .... 147 H5 🔲
Scott's Ter *CHAT* ME4 .... 4 C8
Scott St *MAID/BEAR* ME14 ...... 6 F1
Scotts Wy *RTWE/PEM* TN2 ... 177 G5
  SEV TN13 .... 95 G8
Scragged Oak Rd
  MAID/BEAR ME14 .... 84 D7
Scraps Hl *RSIT* ME9 .... 89 L1
Scratchers La *EYN* DA4 .... 59 M6
Scratton Flds *GVE* DA12 .... 62 F1
Scudders Hl *HART* DA3 .... 60 E2
Seaborough Rd *CDH/CHF* RM16 .. 17 L2
Seabrook Rd *RTON* TN11 ..... 147 J2
Seagull Rd *STRD* ME2 .... 48 F7
Seal Dr *BGR/WK* TN15 .... 96 B7
Seal Hollow Rd *SEV* TN13 .... 9 L4
Seal Rd *SEV* TN13 .... 95 M7
Seaton Rd *DART* DA1 .... 27 J5
  GILL ME7 .... 67 G2
Seaview *HOO/HM* ME3 .... 25 K8
Seaview Rd *GILL* ME7 .... 5 K5
Second Av *GILL* ME7 .... 67 G2
  QBOR ME11 .... 55 H2
  WALD ME5 .... 66 E4
  WTHK RM20 .... 15 J5
Secretan Rd *ROCH* ME1 .... 65 K4
Sedcombe Cl *SCUP* DA14 .... 40 E3 🔲
Sedge Crs *WALD* ME5 .... 83 G1
Sedley *MEO* DA13 .... 45 J2
Sedley Cl *DIT/AY* ME20 .... 102 A3
  HOO/HM ME3 .... 34 E6
  RHAM ME8 .... 84 E2
Sefton Cl *STMC/STPC* BR5 .... 40 B8
Sefton Rd *STMC/STPC* BR5 ... 40 B8
Selah Dr *SWLY* BR8 .... 41 L5
Selborne Av *BXLY* DA5 .... 26 A6
Selborne Rd *SCUP* DA14 .... 40 D1
Selbourne Cl *HART* DA3 .... 45 M8
Selbourne Rd *GILL* ME7 .... 50 F6
Selbourne Wk
  MAID/SHEP ME15 .... 122 B7
Selby Rd *MAID/SHEP* ME15 .. 138 B1
Selkirk Dr *ERITH* DA8 .... 13 G7
Selstead Cl *RHAM* ME8 .... 67 K4
Selwyn Rd *TIL* RM18 .... 17 H8
Semper Rd *CDH/CHF* RM16 .. 17 L1 🔲
Senacre La *MAID/SHEP* ME15 .. 122 A7
Senacre Sq *MAID/SHEP* ME15.. 122 A7
Sequoia Gdns *ORP* BR6 ...... 56 B3 🔲
Sermon Dr *SWLY* BR8 .... 41 L7
Serpentine Ct *SEV* TN13 .... 9 L1
Serpentine Rd *SEV* TN13 .... 9 L2
Setford Rd *WALD* ME5 .... 66 E4
Settington Av *WALD* ME5 .... 66 E4
Seven Acres *SWLY* BR8 .... 57 M2
Seven Mile La *BGR/WK* TN15 .. 99 H5
  RTON TN11 .... 134 A1
Sevenoaks Rd *BGR/WK* TN15 .. 98 A6
  ORP BR6 .... 56 B7
  RSEV TN14 .... 74 B3
Sevenoaks Wy *STMC/STPC* BR5.. 40 E6
Severn *TIL* RM18 .... 18 D2
Severn Cl *TONN* TN10 .... 131 L8
Severn Rd *WALD* ME5 .... 66 E4
Sevington Pk
  MAID/SHEP ME15 .... 121 H7
Sexton Rd *TIL* RM18 .... 17 H7 🔲
Seymour Rd *CDH/CHF* RM16 .. 15 L2
  GVW DA11 .... 31 H6
  RHAM ME8 .... 68 E5
  TIL RM18 .... 17 H7
  TON TN9 .... 5 G7
Seymour Wk *SWCM* DA10 ..... 30 A5
Shacklands Rd *RSEV* TN14 ..... 74 B5
Shackleton Cl *WALD* ME5 .... 66 D7 🔲
The Shades *STRD* ME2 .... 48 D6
Shaftesbury Cl *E/WMAL* ME19 .. 101 H4 🔲
Shaftesbury Dr *MAIDW* ME16.. 120 E1
Shaftesbury La *DART* DA1 ...... 28 D2
Shaftesbury Rd *STH/RUST* TN4 .. 163 J7
Shakespeare Av *TIL* RM18 ..... 17 K8
Shakespeare Farm Rd
  HOO/HM ME3 .... 23 H6
Shakespeare Rd *BXLYHN* DA7 .. 12 A7
  DART DA1 .... 28 C2
  GILL ME7 .... 5 J7
  SIT ME10 .... 88 C1
  TON TN9 .... 147 H5
The Shambles *SEV* TN13 .... 9 J1
Shamrock Rd *GVE* DA12 .... 32 A5
Shandon Cl *RTWE/PEM* TN2 .. 11 K4
Shanklin Cl *WALD* ME5 .... 66 E5
Sharfleet Dr *STRD* ME2 .... 48 D6
Sharland Rd *GVE* DA12 .... 31 L7
Sharman Ct *SCUP* DA14 .... 40 C1
Sharnal La *SNOD* ME6 .... 81 J6
Sharnal St *HOO/HM* ME3 .... 36 C4
Sharon Crs *WALD* ME5 .... 83 H1
Sharp's Fld *HDCN* TN27 .... 156 A8
Sharps Gn *GILL* ME7 .... 51 M8
Sharp Wy *DART* DA1 .... 28 B1
Sharsted Wy *GILL* ME7 .... 84 C2
  MAID/BEAR ME14 ...... 104 D8 🔲
Shaw Cl *HOO/HM* ME3 .... 34 D6
Shaw Crs *TIL* RM18 .... 17 K7
Shaw Rd *BH/WHM* TN16 .... 91 L6
Shawstead Rd *WALD* ME5 ..... 66 E6
Shaws Wy *ROCH* ME1 .... 65 K7
The Shaw *RTWE/PEM* TN2 ..... 11 K8
Sheafe Dr *CRBK* TN17 .... 183 L8
Sheal's Crs *MAID/SHEP* ME15 .. 7 H9
Shearers Cl *MAID/BEAR* ME14 .. 122 A1
Shearwater *HART* DA3 .... 45 K7
  MAIDW ME16 .... 102 B7 🔲
Shearwater Cl *STRD* ME2 .... 48 E6 🔲
Shearwood Cresent *DART* DA1 .. 27 M1
Sheen Rd *STMC/STPC* BR5 .... 40 B8
Sheepcote La *STMC/STPC* BR5 .. 41 K8
Sheephurst La *STPH/PW* TN12 .. 151 M8
Sheerstone *RSIT* ME9 .... 70 F2
Sheet Glass Rd *QBOR* ME11 ... 55 J2

Sheet HI *BGR/WK* TN15 .... 115 M4
Sheffield Rd *STH/RUST* TN4 .... 163 H3
The Sheilings *BGR/WK* TN15 .... 96 B6
Shelden Dr *RHAM* ME8 .... 68 B5
Sheldon Rd *BXLYHN* DA7 .... 12 B7
Sheldon Wy *DIT/AY* ME20 .... 101 J2
Shellbank La *RDART* DA2 .... 44 D2
Shelldrake Cl *HOO/HM* ME3 .... 25 K8 ▣
Shelley Cl *ORP* BR6 .... 56 A6
Shelley Pl *TIL* RM18 .... 17 K7
Shelley Rd *MAIDW* ME16 .... 120 E3
Shelleys La *RSEV* TN14 .... 93 J2
Shelton Cl *SEV* TN13 .... 113 L6
Shenden Cl *SEV* TN13 .... 113 L6
Shenden Wy *SEV* TN13 .... 113 L6
Shenley Gv *MAID/BEAR* ME14 ... 103 H3
Shenley Rd *DART* DA1 .... 28 C4
Shepherds Cl *ORP* BR6 .... 56 B6 ▣
Shepherds Ga *GILL* ME7 .... 67 H8
Shepherds Gate Dr
    MAID/BEAR ME14 .... 104 A8
Shepherdsgrove La
    EGRIN RH19 .... 158 B8
Shepherds La *DART* DA1 .... 27 J6
Shepherd St *GVW* DA11 .... 30 F5
Shepherds Wk *RTWE/PEM* TN2 ... 11 L4
Shepherds Wy *HOO/HM* ME3 ..... 37 L1
    RMAID ME17 .... 139 G1
Shepperton Cl *WALD* ME5 .... 83 L1 ▣
Sheppey Cl *ERITH* DA8 .... 13 K6
Sheppey Rd *MAID/SHEP* ME15 .. 121 H6
Sheppey Wy *IOS* ME12 .... 55 M2
    RSIT ME9 .... 55 J6
    SIT ME10 .... 70 C8
Sheppy Pl *GVE* DA12 .... 31 K5
Sheraton Ct *WALD* ME5 .... 83 H4
Sherborne Rd *STMC/STPC* BR5 ... 56 B1
Sherbourne Cl *BGR/WK* TN15 ..... 77 G1
Sherbourne Dr *MAIDW* ME16 ... 120 D3
    STRD ME2 .... 49 J4 ▣
Sherbrooke Cl *BXLYHN* DA7 .... 26 C2 ▣
Sherenden La *STPH/PW* TN12 ... 168 E5
Sherenden Rd *RTON* TN11 .... 148 C4
Sherfield Rd *GRAYS* RM17 .... 16 D5
Sheridan Cl *MAID/BEAR* ME14 ... 103 H5
    WALD ME5 .... 66 E6
Sheridan Ct *DART* DA1 .... 28 C2
Sheridan Rd *BELV* DA17 .... 12 C3
    BXLYHN DA7 .... 26 A1
Sheriff Dr *WALD* ME5 .... 83 J3
Sherlies Av *ORP* BR6 .... 56 A5
Sherman Cl *GILL* ME7 .... 67 K4
Shernden La *EDEN* TN8 .... 142 E6
Shernolds *MAID/SHEP* ME15 ..... 121 K6
Sherway Rd *HDCN* TN27 .... 156 A8
Sherway Rd *HDCN* TN27 .... 156 F6
Sherwood Av *WALD* ME5 .... 83 J3
Sherwood Pl *RRTW* TN3 .... 176 A2 ▣
Sherwood *RTWE/PEM* TN2 ..... 11 M1
Sherwood Wy *RTWE/PEM* TN2 .. 163 M7
The Shieling *MEO* DA13 .... 79 H4
Shillingheld Cl
    MAID/BEAR ME14 .... 104 B8
Shingle Barn La *WBY/YAL* ME18.. 135 K1
Shinglewell Rd *ERITH* DA8 .... 12 C6
Shipbourne Rd *RTON* TN11 ...... 131 M3
    TON TN9 .... 147 L1
    TONN TN10 .... 147 L2
Ship Field Cl *BH/WHM* TN16 ..... 91 L7
Ship HI *BH/WHM* TN16 .... 91 M7
Ship La *EYN* DA4 .... 43 G5
    ROCH ME1 .... 4 A5
    SOCK/AV RM15 .... 14 F1
    SWLY BR8 .... 42 F5
Shipley Hills Rd *MEO* DA13 .... 62 B4
Shipwrights Av *CHAT* ME4 .... 66 C3
Shirehall Rd *RDART* DA2 .... 42 F2
Shire La *ORP* BR6 .... 72 B2
The Shires *STPH/PW* TN12 ...... 150 C6
Shirley Cl *DART* DA1 .... 27 L2
    GVE DA12 .... 32 D7 ▣
Shirley Gdns *STH/RUST* TN4 ... 176 E1 ▣
Shirley Gv *STH/RUST* TN4 .... 162 F8
Shirley Wy *MAID/SHEP* ME15 ... 122 C2
Sholden Gdns *STMC/STPC* BR5 .. 56 E1
Sholden Rd *STRD* ME2 .... 49 L4 ▣
Shorefields *RHAM* ME8 .... 68 C3
Shoregate La *RSIT* ME9 .... 53 H7
Shoreham La *ORP* BR6 .... 74 C1
    RSEV TN14 .... 74 C6
    TENT TN30 .... 196 C2
Shoreham Pl *RSEV* TN14 .... 75 J4
Shoreham Rd *RSEV* TN14 .... 95 K1
    STMC/STPC BR5 .... 40 D5
Shorehill La *BGR/WK* TN15 ...... 96 C1
The Shore *GVW* DA11 .... 30 E3
Shorne Cl *STMC/STPC* BR5 .... 40 F4 ▣
Shorne Ifield Rd *GVE* DA12 ...... 47 K3
Shortlands Cl *BELV* DA17 .... 12 B2
Shortlands Rd *SIT* ME10 .... 88 C1
Short St *CHAT* ME4 .... 5 G8
Shorts Wy *ROCH* ME1 .... 65 J3
Shottenden La *GILL* ME7 .... 50 F6
Showfields Rd *RTWE/PEM* TN2 .. 177 H4
Shropshire Ter
    MAID/SHEP ME15 .... 122 A6
Shrubbery Av *EYN* DA4 .... 43 M5
    GVE DA12 .... 32 C7 ▣
Shrubcote *TENT* TN30 .... 196 E6 ▣
Shrubsole Dr *MAID/BEAR* ME14.. 103 G2
Shurland Av *SIT* ME10 .... 88 F4
Shurlock Av *SWLY* BR8 .... 41 M6
Shuttlemead *BXLY* DA5 .... 26 B5
Shuttle Rd *DART* DA1 .... 27 J1
Sibley Cl *BXLYHS* DA6 .... 26 A3
Sidcup By-pass Rd *SCUP* DA14 .. 40 C4
Sidcup HI *SCUP* DA14 .... 40 D2
Sidcup Pl *SCUP* DA14 .... 40 C2
Sidmouth Rd *STMC/STPC* BR5 .. 56 D1 ▣
Sidney Gdns *RSEV* TN14 .... 177 G4
Sidney Rd *GILL* ME7 .... 50 E6
    ROCH ME1 .... 65 J3
Sidney St *MAIDW* ME16 .... 120 E3
Silchester Ct *MAID/BEAR* ME14 .. 103 L6
Silecroft Rd *BXLYHN* DA7 .... 12 C7
Silkham Rd *OXTED* RH8 .... 108 F5
Silk Mills Cl *RSEV* TN14 .... 95 J7
Silver Bank *WALD* ME5 .... 66 C7
Silver Birch Av *MEO* DA13 .... 79 H4

Silver Birch Cl *RDART* DA2 .... 42 A1
Silver Birches *WALD* ME5 .... 83 J2
Silver Cl *TON* TN9 .... 147 K7
Silverdale *HART* DA3 .... 45 H8 ▣
    MAIDW ME16 .... 120 B3
Silverdale Dr *RHAM* ME8 .... 68 A6
Silverdale Gv *SIT* ME10 .... 87 L2
Silverdale La *HAWK* TN18 .... 205 H1
    STH/RUST TN4 .... 163 K7
Silverdale Rd *BXLYHN* DA7 ...... 12 D8
    STH/RUST TN4 .... 163 K7
Silver HI *CHAT* ME4 .... 4 D7
    ROCH ME1 .... 65 H3 ▣
    TENT TN30 .... 196 D4
Silver Hill Gdns *CHAT* ME4 .... 4 D7
Silverhurst Dr *TONN* TN10 ...... 131 L7
Silverlocke Rd *GRAYS* RM17 ..... 16 F5
Silver Rd *GVE* DA12 .... 32 A7
Silverspot Cl *RHAM* ME8 .... 68 B6
Silver Spring *ERITH* DA8 .... 12 D5
Silversted La *BH/WHM* TN16 ..... 92 F7
Silver St *RSIT* ME9 .... 87 H8
Silver Tree *WALD* ME5 .... 83 J4
Silverweed Rd *WALD* ME5 .... 66 B8
Silwood *RTWE/PEM* TN2 .... 164 A6
Simmonds La
    MAID/SHEP ME15 .... 122 D7
Simpson Rd *SIT* ME10 .... 70 E8
    SNOD ME6 .... 81 J7
Sinclair Cl *RHAM* ME8 .... 68 A8 ▣
Sinclair Wy *RDART* DA2 .... 43 M1
Singapore Dr *GILL* ME7 .... 4 F3
Single's Cross La *RSEV* TN14 ..... 93 L1
Single St *BH/WHM* TN16 .... 92 D1
Singlewell Rd *GVW* DA11 .... 31 K8
Sirdar Strd *GVE* DA12 .... 47 H2
Sir David's Pk *STH/RUST* TN4 ... 163 G4
Sir Evelyn Rd *ROCH* ME1 .... 65 K5
Sir John Hawkins Wy *CHAT* ME4 .. 4 C5
Sir Thomas Longley Rd
    STRD ME2 .... 4 A1
Siskin Gdns *STPH/PW* TN12 .... 150 C8 ▣
Sissinghurst Dr *MAIDW* ME16 ... 120 B3
Sissinghurst Rd *CRBK* TN17 .... 184 F5
    HDCN TN27 .... 185 K3
Sittingbourne Rd
    MAID/BEAR ME14 .... 7 K2
Six Bells La *SEV* TN13 .... 9 J8
Six Bells Ms *RYE* TN31 .... 206 E8
Six Fields Pth *TENT* TN30 .... 196 C6
Six Penny Cl *EDEN* TN8 .... 142 E5
Skeet Hill La *STMC/STPC* BR5 ... 57 H5
Skene Cl *RHAM* ME8 .... 68 C4
Skeynes Rd *EDEN* TN8 .... 142 D4
Skibbs La *ORP* BR6 .... 57 G6
Skid Hill La *WARL* CR6 .... 91 H1
Skinner Gdns *CRBK* TN17 ...... 184 C5
Skinners Cl *DIT/AY* ME20 .... 82 C7
Skinners La *DIT/AY* ME20 .... 82 C7
Skinners La *DIT/AY* ME20 .... 142 F3
Skinner St *CHAT* ME4 .... 4 D7
    GILL ME7 .... 5 J2
Skinner's Wy *RMAID* ME17 ...... 139 G1
Skinney La *GVW* DA11 .... 43 M7
Skippers Cl *GRH* DA9 .... 29 K3 ▣
Skye Cl *MAID/SHEP* ME15 ...... 121 J6
Slade Cl *WALD* ME5 .... 83 K3
Slade Gdns *ERITH* DA8 .... 13 H7
Slade Green Rd *ERITH* DA8 .... 13 H7
The Slade *RRTW* TN3 .... 189 J2
    TON TN9 .... 147 K3
Slaney Rd *STPH/PW* TN12 ...... 170 B1
Slatin Rd *STRD* ME2 .... 2 F1
Sleepers Farm Rd
    CDH/CHF RM16 .... 17 K1
Sleepers Stile Rd *WADH* TN5 ... 188 E4
Slicketts HI *CHAT* ME4 .... 4 E6 ▣
Slines Oak Rd *CTHM* CR3 .... 90 C5
Slip Mill Rd *HAWK* TN18 .... 199 G5
The Slip *BH/WHM* TN16 .... 110 E4
Small Bridge Rd
    STPH/PW TN12 .... 181 K3
Small Grains *HART* DA3 .... 60 D6
Smallhythe Rd *TENT* TN30 ..... 196 B6 ▣
Small Profits *WBY/YAL* ME18 ... 135 J1
Smarden Cl *BELV* DA17 .... 12 C4
Smarden Rd *HDCN* TN27 .... 172 A1
    HDCN TN27 .... 186 C1
Smarts HI *RTON* TN11 .... 161 J4
Smarts Rd *GVE* DA12 .... 31 K8
Smeed Cl *SIT* ME10 .... 88 D1 ▣
Smetham Gdns *STRD* ME2 .... 49 K4 ▣
Smithers Cl *RHAM* ME8 .... 133 G4
Smithers La *STPH/PW* TN12 .... 134 C6
Smithfield Rd *HOO/HM* ME3 .... 25 L8
Smith Rd *WALD* ME5 .... 83 K2
Smith's HI *MAID/SHEP* ME15 ... 135 L1
Smiths La *EDEN* TN8 .... 126 C3
Smiths Orch *RSIT* ME9 .... 87 H8
Smith St *STRD* ME2 .... 2 E5
Smugglers Ms *HAWK* TN18 ..... 199 J4
Smugglers Whf *GRH* DA9 .... 29 K3
Smythe Cl *STH/RUST* TN4 ...... 163 G2
Smythe Rd *EYN* DA4 .... 43 M5 ▣
Snag La *RSEV* TN14 .... 72 F6
Snatts HI *OXTED* RH8 .... 109 H7
Snelling Av *GVW* DA11 .... 31 H7
Snipe Cl *ERITH* DA8 .... 13 K6
    RTWE/PEM TN2 .... 165 L3
Snoad La *STPH/PW* TN12 .... 169 J5
Snodhurst Av *WALD* ME5 .... 66 A8
Snodland Rd *E/WMAL* ME19 ..... 80 F6
Snoll Hatch Rd *STPH/PW* TN12 .. 134 B8
Snowdon Av *MAID/BEAR* ME14 .. 7 K3
Snowdon Cl *WALD* ME5 .... 66 B6 ▣
Snughorne La *HDCN* TN27 ...... 172 E5
Solefields Rd *SEV* TN13 .... 113 K6
Soleoak Dr *SEV* TN13 .... 113 K5
Sole St *MEO* DA13 .... 62 F1
Solomon Rd *RHAM* ME8 .... 68 B4
Solomons Rd *CHAT* ME4 .... 4 D5
Solway *TIL* RM18 .... 18 E2
Somerden Rd *STMC/STPC* BR5 .. 56 F1
Somerfield Cl *MAIDW* ME16 ..... 6 B4 ▣
Somerfield La *MAIDW* ME16 ..... 6 B4
Somerfield Rd *MAIDW* ME16 ..... 6 B4
Somerhill Rd *TON* TN9 .... 147 M5
Somerset Cl *SIT* ME10 .... 87 L1
    WALD ME5 .... 83 K4 ▣
Somerset Rd *DART* DA1 .... 27 K4

Somersham Rd *BXLYHN* DA7 ..... 12 A8
Somerton Gdns *STH/RUST* TN4... 10 D4
Somerville Rd *DART* DA1 .... 28 B4 ▣
Somner Wk *MAID/SHEP* ME15 .. 138 B1 ▣
Soper's La *HAWK* TN18 .... 198 F1
Sophurst La *STPH/PW* TN12 ... 165 L8
Sopwith Cl *BH/WHM* TN16 .... 91 M2
Sorrell Rd *WALD* ME5 .... 83 H1
Sorrell Wy *GVW* DA11 .... 46 A1 ▣
Sortmill Rd *SNOD* ME6 .... 81 K6
Sounds Ldg *SWLY* BR8 .... 57 L2 ▣
South Ash Rd *BGR/WK* TN15 ..... 78 A1
South Av *RHAM* ME8 .... 67 J3
    SIT ME10 .... 88 C2
South Bank *BH/WHM* TN16 ..... 110 F4
    HOO/HM ME3 .... 34 D3
    RMAID ME17 .... 139 G6
    STPH/PW TN12 .... 170 A3
Southbourne Gv *WALD* ME5 ..... 83 J3 ▣
South Bush La *RHAM* ME8 .... 68 D7
South Crs *RMAID* ME17 .... 136 E2
Southcroft Rd *ORP* BR6 .... 56 A6
Southdene *RSEV* TN14 .... 74 B7
Southdown Rd *CTHM* CR3 .... 90 B8
South Dr *ORP* BR6 .... 56 A8
South Eastern Rd *STRD* ME2 ..... 3 H3
South Ena Rd *GRAYS* RM17 ...... 16 E5
Southernden Rd *HDCN* TN27 ... 156 C4
Southern Pl *SWLY* BR8 .... 41 M8 ▣
Southey Wk *TIL* RM18 .... 17 K7
Southey Wy *DIT/AY* ME20 ...... 101 H1
Southfield Rd *CHST* BR7 .... 163 J7
    STH/RUST TN4 .... 65 K2
Southfields *ROCH* ME1 .... 162 C6
    WADH TN5 .... 188 B7
Southfields Shaw *MEO* DA13 ..... 79 K4
Southfields Rd *BGR/WK* TN15 ... 77 H2
    CTHM CR3 .... 108 D1
    GDST RH9 .... 108 D3
South Ga *PUR* RM19 .... 14 E3
Southgate Rd *TENT* TN30 .... 196 E6
South Green La *RSIT* ME9 .... 86 B6
South Gv *RTW* TN1 .... 10 F7
South Hall Cl *EYN* DA4 .... 59 H3
South Hill Rd *GVE* DA12 .... 31 K6
Southill Rd *CHAT* ME4 .... 4 C8
South Kent Av *GVW* DA11 .... 30 E4
Southlands Av *ORP* BR6 .... 56 A7
Southlands La *RMAID* ME17 .... 139 G7
Southlees La *RSIT* ME9 .... 106 B3
South Pk *SEV* TN13 .... 9 G7
South Park Rd
    MAID/SHEP ME15 .... 121 K4
South Rd *ERITH* DA8 .... 13 H5
    GILL ME7 .... 50 C6
    STPH/PW TN12 .... 153 G7
South St *GVE* DA12 .... 31 K5
    MAIDW ME16 .... 120 A5
    MEO DA13 .... 62 B7
South Street Rd *RSIT* ME9 .... 86 A5
South View Av *TIL* RM18 .... 17 J7
South View Cl *BXLY* DA5 .... 26 B4
Southview Rd *SWLY* BR8 .... 42 C8 ▣
South View Rd *RDART* DA2 .... 27 M8
    STH/RUST TN4 .... 163 K5
    WADH TN5 .... 188 B7
    WTHK RM20 .... 15 L5
Southwark Rd *STRD* ME2 .... 48 F7
South Wy *PUR* RM19 .... 15 G2
Southways *RMAID* ME17 .... 139 G6 ▣
Southwell Rd *STRD* ME2 .... 48 E7
South Wharf Rd *GRAYS* RM17 ... 16 B5
Southwold Rd *BXLY* DA5 .... 26 D4 ▣
Southwood *MAIDW* ME16 .... 120 B5
Southwood Av *STH/RUST* TN4 .. 163 J7
Southwood Rd *STH/RUST* TN4 .. 162 D8
Sovereign Bvd *GILL* ME7 .... 67 G3
Sovereigns Wy *STPH/PW* TN12 .. 152 D7
Sovereign Wy *TON* TN9 .... 147 L4
Spade La *RSIT* ME9 .... 68 E7
Spar Cl *RTON* TN11 .... 133 H4
Sparepenny La *EYN* DA4 .... 59 G3
Sparkeswood Av *CRBK* TN17 ... 202 A1
Spearhead Rd
    MAID/BEAR ME14 .... 103 H6
Speedgate HI *HART* DA3 .... 60 C5
Speedwell Av *WALD* ME5 .... 83 G1
Speedwell Cl *GILL* ME7 .... 51 G8
    MAID/BEAR ME14 .... 104 A8 ▣
Spekes Rd *GILL* ME7 .... 67 J7
Spelow Wy *MAID/SHEP* ME15 ... 83 J5 ▣
Spenny La *STPH/PW* TN12 ...... 151 L7
Speyside *TONN* TN10 .... 131 K8 ▣
Spielman Rd *DART* DA1 .... 28 B2
The Spillway *MAID/SHEP* ME15.. 6 B9
Spindle Gld *MAID/BEAR* ME14 ... 7 M2
Spindles *TIL* RM18 .... 17 J6
Spindlewood Cl *WALD* ME5 ...... 83 K2 ▣
Spinners Cl *HDCN* TN27 .... 186 B3
The Spinney *MAID/SHEP* ME15 .. 7 K8
    SCUP DA14 .... 41 G2
    SWLY BR8 .... 42 A6
    TON TN9 .... 147 L2
    WADH TN5 .... 83 K4 ▣
Spinney Wy *RSEV* TN14 .... 72 F5
Spire Cl *GVE* DA12 .... 31 K6 ▣
The Spires *DART* DA1 .... 27 M7

MAIDW ME16 .... 6 A4
    STRD ME2 .... 48 F8
Spital St *DART* DA1 .... 27 M4
Spitfire Cl *WALD* ME5 .... 66 D7
Spitfire Rd *E/WMAL* ME19 ...... 118 B2
Spode La *EDEN* TN8 .... 159 J5
Sponden La *HAWK* TN18 .... 200 B5
Spongs La *CRBK* TN17 .... 184 C4
Sportsfield *MAID/BEAR* ME14 .... 7 K2
Spot La *MAID/SHEP* ME15 .... 122 C3
Spout La *EDEN* TN8 .... 126 E4
    STPH/PW TN12 .... 166 D8
Spray HI *RRTW* TN3 .... 189 K1
The Sprig *MAID/BEAR* ME14 ... 122 C1
Springcroft *HART* DA3 .... 61 J2
Spring Cross *HART* DA3 .... 61 J6
Springett Cl *DIT/AY* ME20 .... 82 B7
Springett Wy *RMAID* ME17 ..... 136 F1
Springfield *OXTED* RH8 .... 108 F8
Springfield Av
    MAID/BEAR ME14 .... 103 G7
    SWLY BR8 .... 42 B8 ▣
    TENT TN30 .... 196 D3
Springfield Rd *BXLYHN* DA7 ..... 26 D1
    CDH/CHF RM16 .... 17 G1
    DIT/AY ME20 .... 101 H1
    EDEN TN8 .... 142 D4
    GILL ME7 .... 51 G7
    SIT ME10 .... 70 F8
    STH/RUST TN4 .... 163 H4
Springfield Wy *STMC/STPC* BR5.. 40 C7
Spring Gdns *BH/WHM* TN16 ..... 91 L4
    RTWE/PEM TN2 .... 11 M1
Spring Gv *GVE* DA12 .... 31 K6
Springhead Rd *BGR/WK* TN15 ... 96 B3
Springhead Rd *ERITH* DA8 .... 13 H5
    GVW DA11 .... 30 E5
Spring HI *RTON* TN11 .... 161 J7
    RYE TN31 .... 206 D6
Springholm Cl *BH/WHM* TN16 ... 91 L4
Spring La *BGR/WK* TN15 .... 97 K8
    STH/RUST TN4 .... 162 F2
Spring Shaw Rd *STMC/STPC* BR5.. 40 C5
Spring V *BXLYHN* DA7 .... 26 D1
    GRH DA9 .... 29 L4
    MAIDW ME16 .... 6 D5
Springvale *RHAM* ME8 .... 67 L7
    RSIT ME9 .... 70 F1
Spring Vale *SWLY* BR8 .... 42 B4
Spring V North *DART* DA1 .... 27 M4 ▣
Spring V South *DART* DA1 .... 27 M3 ▣
Springwell Rd *TON* TN9 .... 147 K5
Springwood Rd *MAIDW* ME16 .. 120 C2
Sprotshill Cl *SIT* ME10 .... 71 G7
Spruce Cl *DIT/AY* ME20 .... 101 J3
Sprucedale Cl *SWLY* BR8 .... 42 A6
Spruce Rd *BH/WHM* TN16 .... 91 M2
Spurrell Av *RDART* DA2 .... 41 M1
Spur Rd *ORP* BR6 .... 56 C5
Spurway *MAID/BEAR* ME14 ..... 122 C1
Square HI *MAID/SHEP* ME15 ..... 7 J5 ▣
The Square *BH/WHM* TN16 ...... 91 L6
    RMAID ME17 .... 125 M8
    RTON TN11 .... 133 C5
Squeryes Mede
    BH/WHM TN16 .... 110 E5 ▣
Squires Cl *STRD* ME2 .... 48 D6
Squires Fld *SWLY* BR8 .... 42 C5
Squires Wy *RDART* DA2 .... 41 M1
Squirrel's Cha *CDH/CHF* RM16 .. 17 J1 ▣
Squirrel Wy *RTWE/PEM* TN2 ... 164 A8
Stable Cl *WALD* ME5 .... 66 E3 ▣
Stabledene Wy
    RTWE/PEM TN2 .... 164 F7 ▣
Stace Cl *TENT* TN30 .... 196 E5
Stacey Cl *GVE* DA12 .... 47 G2
Stacey Rd *RTON* TN11 .... 147 J2
Staceys St *MAID/BEAR* ME14 .... 6 F2
Stacklands Cl *BGR/WK* TN15 ..... 77 G1 ▣
Stack La *HART* DA3 .... 61 H1
Stack Rd *EYN* DA4 .... 43 M8
Stadium Wy *DART* DA1 .... 27 G4
    SIT ME10 .... 71 L7
Staffa Rd *MAID/SHEP* ME15 ... 121 J6
Stafford Cl *CDH/CHF* RM16 ..... 15 L3
    GRH DA9 .... 29 H3 ▣
    SLH/COR SS17 .... 18 C2
Stafford Rd *RTWE/PEM* TN2 ... 178 A1
    SCUP DA14 .... 40 A1
    TON TN9 .... 147 K3
Stafford St *GILL* ME7 .... 5 J4
Stafford Wy *SEV* TN13 .... 113 L5
Stag Rd *RTWE/PEM* TN2 .... 163 M4
    WALD ME5 .... 66 E8
Stagshaw Cl *MAID/SHEP* ME15 .. 7 G9
Stainer Rd *TONN* TN10 .... 132 B7
Stairfoot La *SEV* TN13 .... 94 E8
Stair Rd *TONN* TN10 .... 148 B1
Stake La *STRD* ME2 .... 64 C7
Staleys Rd *BGR/WK* TN15 .... 98 A6
Stalham Ct *GILL* ME7 .... 84 D1 ▣
Stalin Av *WALD* ME5 .... 66 D5
The Stampers *MAIDW* ME16 ..... 6 B9
Stanam Rd *RTWE/PEM* TN2 ... 165 G8
Stanbridge Rd *EDEN* TN8 .... 142 D5
Stanbrook Rd *GVW* DA11 .... 31 H6
Standard Rd *BELV* DA17 .... 12 C4
    BXLYHS DA6 .... 26 A2
    ORP BR6 .... 72 C4
Standen Cl *RHAM* ME8 .... 85 C1
Standen St *CRBK* TN17 .... 200 D5
    HAWK TN18 .... 201 J5
    STH/RUST TN4 .... 10 E1
Stanford Dr *MAIDW* ME16 ..... 120 E2 ▣
Stanford La *RTON* TN11 .... 133 L3
Stanford Rd *CDH/CHF* RM16 .... 17 G1
Stanford Wy *STRD* ME2 .... 64 E3
Stangate Rd *E/WMAL* ME19 ..... 80 D7
    STRD ME2 .... 48 E6
Stangrove Rd *EDEN* TN8 .... 142 D4
Stanham Pl *DART* DA1 .... 27 J2
Stanham Rd *DART* DA1 .... 27 J3
Stanhope Av *SEV* TN13 .... 88 C2
Stanhope Cl *MAID/BEAR* ME14.. 103 G8
Stanhope Rd *BFN/LL* DA15 ...... 40 C1
    BXLYHN DA7 .... 12 A8
    RTW TN1 .... 11 J1

STRD ME2 .... 2 F3
SWCM DA10 .... 30 B3
Stanhopes *OXTED* RH8 .... 109 K6
Stanhope Wy *SEV* TN13 .... 94 F8
Stan La *WBY/YAL* ME18 .... 117 J6
Stanley Av *OBOR* ME11 .... 29 G3
Stanley Cr *GRH* DA9 .... 29 G3
    STPH/PW TN12 .... 169 M1
Stanley Crs *GVE* DA12 .... 46 F2
Stanley Rd *GILL* ME7 .... 5 K1
    GRAYS RM17 .... 16 B4
    ORP BR6 .... 56 B4
    RTW TN1 .... 11 H2
    SWCM DA10 .... 30 B4
    WALD ME5 .... 66 E7
Stanley Wy *STMC/STPC* BR5 ..... 56 D1
Stanmore Rd *BELV* DA17 .... 12 E3
Stansted Cl *MAIDW* ME16 ...... 102 E6
Stansted HI *BGR/WK* TN15 ...... 78 C4
Stansted La *BGR/WK* TN15 ...... 77 K4
Stanton Cl *STMC/STPC* BR5 ..... 56 E3
Staple Cl *BXLY* DA5 .... 26 F5
    SIT ME10 .... 71 G7
Staple Dr *STPH/PW* TN12 ...... 170 B2
Stapleford Ct *SEV* TN13 .... 8 D3
Staplehurst Rd *RHAM* ME8 ...... 67 K2
    SIT ME10 .... 70 E7
    STPH/PW TN12 .... 153 K2
Staplers Ct *MAID/BEAR* ME14 .. 103 K3 ▣
Stapleton Rd *BXLYHN* DA7 ...... 12 B6
    ORP BR6 .... 56 B6
Stapley Rd *BELV* DA17 .... 12 C4
Starboard Av *GRH* DA9 .... 29 K4 ▣
Starborough Rd *EDEN* TN8 ..... 158 A1
Star HI *DART* DA1 .... 27 L8
    ROCH ME1 .... 3 J9
Star Hill Rd *RSEV* TN14 .... 94 B3
Star La *GILL* ME7 .... 67 H5
    STMC/STPC BR5 .... 40 E5
Starling Cl *HART* DA3 .... 45 K7
Star Mill La *WALD* ME5 .... 66 F3
Starveacre La *RSIT* ME9 .... 87 L3
Station Ap *BGR/WK* TN15 .... 98 B6 ▣
    BXLYHN DA7 .... 12 A8
    BXLYHN DA7 .... 12 E8
    DART DA1 .... 28 A4
    EDEN TN8 .... 142 D4
    MAIDW ME16 .... 6 E6
    ORP BR6 .... 56 B5
    ORP BR6 .... 56 B6
    OXTED RH8 .... 109 G7
    RSEV TN14 .... 95 L2
    STMC/STPC BR5 .... 40 D8
    STPH/PW TN12 .... 150 C6 ▣
    STPH/PW TN12 .... 154 A8
    STRD ME2 .... 64 C8 ▣
    SWLY BR8 .... 42 A8
Station Approach Rd *TIL* RM18 .. 31 J2
Station Ct *BGR/WK* TN15 .... 98 B6
Station HI *RTON* TN11 .... 145 H4
Station Rd *BELV* DA17 .... 12 C2
    BGR/WK TN15 .... 98 B6
    BH/WHM TN16 .... 111 K1
    BXLYHN DA7 .... 26 A1
    CRBK TN17 .... 181 L6
    CTHM CR3 .... 90 A8
    DART DA1 .... 27 H4
    DIT/AY ME20 .... 101 J2
    DIT/AY ME20 .... 102 B3
    EDEN TN8 .... 126 D3
    EDEN TN8 .... 142 E2
    EYN DA4 .... 43 K6
    EYN DA4 .... 58 F7 ▣
    GRH DA9 .... 29 J3
    GVW DA11 .... 30 D4
    HART DA3 .... 45 G2
    HDCN TN27 .... 155 M8
    HOO/HM ME3 .... 34 C2
    HRTF TN7 .... 174 D8
    MAID/BEAR ME14 .... 6 F3
    MAID/SHEP ME15 .... 120 C5
    MEO DA13 .... 45 H1
    MEO DA13 .... 62 C1
    ORP BR6 .... 56 B5
    RHAM ME8 .... 68 C3
    RMAID ME17 .... 124 F7
    RRTW TN3 .... 175 L6
    RSEV TN14 .... 74 B5
    RSEV TN14 .... 75 J3
    RSEV TN14 .... 95 K2
    RSIT ME9 .... 69 K7
    RSIT ME9 .... 89 L3
    RYE TN31 .... 206 D5
    SEV TN13 .... 95 G6
    STMC/STPC BR5 .... 40 E8 ▣
    STPH/PW TN12 .... 150 B6
    STPH/PW TN12 .... 154 B8
    STRD ME2 .... 3 H4
    STRD ME2 .... 64 E3 ▣
    SWLY BR8 .... 42 A8 ▣
    TENT TN30 .... 196 C6
    TIL RM18 .... 18 D2
    WBY/YAL ME18 .... 134 E4
Station Rd East *OXTED* RH8 .... 109 G7
Station Rd North *BELV* DA17 ... 12 D2
Station Rd West *OXTED* RH8 ... 109 G7
Station St *SIT* ME10 .... 88 B1
Steadman Cl *HOO/HM* ME3 ..... 33 L8
Stede HI *RMAID* ME17 .... 125 H5
Stedman Cl *BXLY* DA5 .... 27 G8
Steele Av *GRH* DA9 .... 29 J3
Steele's La *MEO* DA13 .... 62 B7
Steele St *STRD* ME2 .... 2 F1
Steep Cl *ORP* BR6 .... 73 H1
Steeple Heights Dr
    BH/WHM TN16 .... 91 M3
Steerforth Cl *ROCH* ME1 .... 65 L3 ▣
Steers Pl *RTON* TN11 .... 133 L3
Stella Cl *STPH/PW* TN12 .... 152 F8 ▣
Stelling Rd *ERITH* DA8 .... 12 F6
Stenning Av *TIL* RM18 .... 18 D3
Stephen Cl *ORP* BR6 .... 56 B6
Stephen Rd *BXLYHN* DA7 .... 26 E1
Stephenson Av *TIL* RM18 .... 17 J7
Stephen's Rd *STH/RUST* TN4 ... 163 J7
Stepneyford La *CRBK* TN17 ..... 194 E4
Steps Hill Rd *RSIT* ME9 .... 85 M7
Step Style *SIT* ME10 .... 88 D3
Sterling Av *MAIDW* ME16 .... 102 E8
Sterling Rd *SIT* ME10 .... 87 M4

Sterndale Rd DART DA1 ...... 28 B5
Stevens Cl BXLY DA5 ...... 41 M1
  RDART DA2 ...... 44 A2
  SNOD ME6 ...... 81 J5
Stevenson Cl ERITH DA8 ...... 13 K6
  MAID/SHEP ME15 ...... 6 F7
Stevenson Wy DIT/AY ME20 ...... 101 H1
Stevens Rd STH/RUST TN4 ...... 163 L6
Steynton Av BXLY DA5 ...... 26 A7
Stickens La E/WMAL ME19 ...... 101 C7
Stickfast La RMAID ME17 ...... 155 M1
  RSIT ME9 ...... 70 C4
Stickland Rd BELV DA17 ...... 12 C3
Stilebridge La RMAID ME17 ...... 137 J8
  STPH/PW TN12 ...... 153 C2
Stiles Cl ERITH DA8 ...... 12 D4
Still La STH/RUST TN4 ...... 163 H3
Stirling Cl RHAM ME8 ...... 85 C1
  ROCH ME1 ...... 65 J3
Stirling Dr ORP BR6 ...... 56 D7
Stirling Rd E/WMAL ME19 ...... 118 B2
Stockbury Dr MAIDW ME16 ...... 102 F6
Stockenbury STPH/PW TN12 ...... 134 B7
Stockers Brow RSIT ME9 ...... 88 C6
Stockers Hl RSIT ME9 ...... 88 C6
Stockett La RMAID ME17 ...... 136 E2
Stock Hl BH/WHM TN16 ...... 91 M2
Stockland Green Rd RRTW TN3 .. 162 E5
Stocks Green Rd RTON TN11 ...... 130 E8
Stocks Rd TENT TN30 ...... 209 C2
Stockton Rd MAID/BEAR ME14 ...... 103 K5
Stoddards La RTN31 ...... 207 C8
Stoke Rd HOO/HM ME3 ...... 23 L8
  HOO/HM ME3 ...... 36 D6
Stoneacre Cl RHAM ME8 ...... 67 M8
Stoneacre La MAID/SHEP ME15 .. 122 D7
Stonebridge Rd GVW DA11 ...... 30 C3
Stone Court La RTWE/PEM TN2.. 165 C5
Stonecroft MEO DA13 ...... 79 J5
Stonecroft Rd ERITH DA8 ...... 12 E6
Stonecross Lea WALD ME5 ...... 66 D4
Stonefield Rd RMAID ME17 ...... 26 C1
Stonegate Cl STMC/STPC BR5 ...... 40 E7
Stonehorse La HOO/HM ME3 ...... 49 J2
Stonehouse La ORP BR6 ...... 73 M3
  PUR RM19 ...... 15 C4
Stonehouse Rd ORP BR6 ...... 73 M3
Stoneings La RSEV TN14 ...... 94 C6
Stoneleigh Rd OXTED RH8 ...... 110 A8
Stoneness Rd WTHK ME20 ...... 15 K5
Stone Pit La HAWK TN18 ...... 201 C8
Stone Place Rd GRH DA9 ...... 29 C3
Stones Cross Rd SWLY BR8 ...... 54 F1
Stonestile Rd HDCN TN27 ...... 155 J6
Stone St CRBK TN17 ...... 183 M8
  GVE DA12 ...... 31 K4
  RTW TN1 ...... 11 H3
Stone Street Rd BGR/WK TN15 .. 114 E2
Stoneswood Rd OXTED RH8 ...... 109 K8
Stonewall Park Rd RRTW TN3 .. 176 B2
Stonewood RDART DA2 ...... 29 L8
Stonewood Rd ERITH DA8 ...... 13 G4
Stoney Bank GILL ME7 ...... 67 H4
Stony Cnr HART DA3 ...... 46 A8
Stony La ROCH ME1 ...... 65 K8
Stopford Rd GILL ME7 ...... 5 K6
Stornaway Strd GVE DA12 ...... 47 H1
  TONN TN10 ...... 131 K8
Stour Cl STRD ME2 ...... 2 C4
Stour Rd CDH/CHF RM16 ...... 17 J4
  DART DA1 ...... 27 J1
Stour Valley Wk RMAID ME17 .. 141 M1
Stowe Rd ORP BR6 ...... 56 D7
Stowting Rd ORP BR6 ...... 56 A7
Strand Approach Rd GILL ME7 .. 51 C6
Strand Cl MEO DA13 ...... 62 C3
Strand Rd RTW TN1 ...... 11 J1
Stratford Av RHAM ME8 ...... 67 M5
Stratford La RHAM ME8 ...... 68 B5
Stratford Rd E/WMAL ME19 ...... 100 C5
Stratford St RTW TN1 ...... 11 J1
Strathmore TIL RM18 ...... 18 E3
Stratton Cl BXLYHN DA7 ...... 26 A1
Stratton Rd BXLYHN DA7 ...... 26 A1
Stratton Ter RHAM ME8 ...... 110 E5
Strawberry Cl RRTW TN3 ...... 177 C5
Strawberry Flds RYE TN31 ...... 206 C6
  SWLY BR8 ...... 42 A6
Strawberry V TON TN9 ...... 147 L4
Straw Mill Hl MAID/SHEP ME15 .. 121 C4
Stream La HAWK TN18 ...... 199 H6
Stream Pit La HAWK TN18 ...... 200 D8
Streamside DIT/AY ME20 ...... 101 K4
Stream Side TONN TN10 ...... 131 M6
The Stream DIT/AY ME20 ...... 101 K4
Stream Wy BELV DA17 ...... 12 C5
Streatfield EDEN TN8 ...... 142 F4
Street End Rd WALD ME5 ...... 66 D5
Streetfield RMAID ME17 ...... 140 B6
Streetfield Rd RHAM ME8 ...... 68 B4
The Street BGR/WK TN15 ...... 61 C8
  BGR/WK TN15 ...... 116 B6
  CRBK TN17 ...... 171 G7
  CRBK TN17 ...... 184 C5
  CRBK TN17 ...... 193 M3
  E/WMAL ME19 ...... 79 J8
  E/WMAL ME19 ...... 100 B1
  EYN DA4 ...... 43 K8
  GILL ME7 ...... 84 D1
  GVE DA12 ...... 47 J8
  GVE DA12 ...... 48 A2
  HOO/HM ME3 ...... 36 A2
  MAID/BEAR ME14 ...... 103 L2
  MAID/BEAR ME14 ...... 104 C3
  MAID/BEAR ME14 ...... 122 E1
  MEO DA13 ...... 62 C4
  RMAID ME17 ...... 140 B6
  RSIT ME9 ...... 69 L1
  RSIT ME9 ...... 69 K2
  RSIT ME9 ...... 71 C1
  RSIT ME9 ...... 85 M1
  RSIT ME9 ...... 87 J3
  RSIT ME9 ...... 87 H8
  RSIT ME9 ...... 89 J7
  RSIT ME9 ...... 89 C2
  RSIT ME9 ...... 107 H6
  TENT TN30 ...... 208 F3
  WBY/YAL ME18 ...... 117 M5

WBY/YAL ME18 ...... 119 J6
Strettitt Gdns STPH/PW TN12 .. 134 B8
Strickland Av DART DA1 ...... 28 B2
Strickland Wy ORP BR6 ...... 56 B7
Strover St GILL ME7 ...... 50 E6
Strumer Ct WBY/YAL ME18 ...... 118 C3
Struttons Av RSEV TN14 ...... 31 H7
Stuart Cl MAID/BEAR ME14 ...... 7 L1
  RTWE/PEM TN2 ...... 177 H5
  SWLY BR8 ...... 42 B4
Stuart Mantle Wy ERITH DA8 .. 12 F6
Stuart Rd GILL ME7 ...... 5 M8
  GRAYS RM17 ...... 16 D4
  GVW DA11 ...... 31 J4
Stubbs Hl ORP BR6 ...... 73 L7
Studley Ct SCUP DA14 ...... 40 D2
Studley Crs HART DA3 ...... 45 L6
Sturdee Av GILL ME7 ...... 67 G1
Sturla Rd CHAT ME4 ...... 4 E9
Sturry Wy RHAM ME8 ...... 67 L3
Styants Bottom Rd
  BGR/WK TN15 ...... 97 H8
Style Cl RHAM ME8 ...... 85 C1
Styles Cl EDEN TN8 ...... 127 K8
Suffolk Av RHAM ME8 ...... 68 B4
Suffolk Cl DART DA1 ...... 28 A4
  GVE DA12 ...... 31 M4
  MAID/SHEP ME15 ...... 121 M5
  SCUP DA14 ...... 40 D3
Suffolk Wy BGR/WK TN15 ...... 9 J6
Sullivan Cl DART DA1 ...... 27 K4
Sullivan Rd TIL RM18 ...... 17 J7
  TONN TN10 ...... 132 A8
Sultan Rd MAID ME5 ...... 83 L3
Summer Cl TENT TN30 ...... 196 E4
Summerhill HDCN TN27 ...... 155 J7
Summerhill Av
  STH/RUST TN4 ...... 163 H4
Summerhill Cl ORP BR6 ...... 56 A7
Summerhill Rd DART DA1 ...... 27 M5
  STPH/PW TN12 ...... 153 K5
Summerhouse Dr RDART DA2 .. 41 M2
Summervale Rd STH/RUST TN4 .. 10 A9
Sunburst Cl STPH/PW TN12 ...... 152 F8
Sun Ct ERITH DA8 ...... 13 H8
Sunderland Cl ROCH ME1 ...... 65 J2
Sunderland Dr RHAM ME8 ...... 68 C5
Sundridge Cl DART DA1 ...... 28 C4
Sundridge Dr WALD ME5 ...... 83 J1
Sundridge Hl RSEV TN14 ...... 93 L4
  STRD ME2 ...... 64 E3
Sundridge La RSEV TN14 ...... 93 K3
Sundridge Rd RSEV TN14 ...... 94 C6
Sun Hl HART DA3 ...... 60 C5
Sunland Av BXLYHS DA6 ...... 26 A2
Sun La GVE DA12 ...... 31 L7
Sunningdale Cl RHAM ME8 ...... 67 M7
Sunningdale Dr RHAM ME8 ...... 67 M7
Sunninghill TIL RM18 ...... 31 G7
Sunningvale Av BH/WHM TN16 .. 91 M1
Sunningvale Cl BH/WHM TN16 .. 91 M2
Sunny Bank SIT ME10 ...... 71 K8
  WARL CR6 ...... 90 A3
Sunnyfields Cl RHAM ME8 ...... 68 A5
Sunnymead Av GILL ME7 ...... 51 C8
Sunnyside Rd STH/RUST TN4 .. 176 E1
Sun Rd SWCM DA10 ...... 30 B4
Sunset Cl ERITH DA8 ...... 13 K6
Superior Dr ORP BR6 ...... 73 H1
Surrenden Rd STPH/PW TN12 .. 170 A2
Surrey Cl RTWE/PEM TN2 ...... 177 H5
Surrey Rd MAID/SHEP ME15 ...... 121 K5
Susan's Hl RASHW TN26 ...... 197 M3
Sussex Border Pth EDEN TN8 .. 158 E5
  HAWK TN18 ...... 199 J7
  RRTW TN3 ...... 174 F1
  TENT TN30 ...... 208 F6
Sussex Cl RTWE/PEM TN2 ...... 11 J9
Sussex Dr WALD ME5 ...... 83 J1
Sussex Ms RTWE/PEM TN2 ...... 10 E8
Sussex Rd DART DA1 ...... 28 C5
  ERITH DA8 ...... 12 D6
  MAID/SHEP ME15 ...... 121 M4
  SCUP DA14 ...... 40 D2
  STMC/STPC BR5 ...... 56 E2
  TON TN9 ...... 147 J5
Sutherland Av BH/WHM TN16 .. 91 M3
  STMC/STPC BR5 ...... 56 B2
Sutherland Cl GVE DA12 ...... 32 D7
  RTW TN1 ...... 11 G7
Sutherland Rd BELV DA17 ...... 12 C2
Sutton Baron Rd RSIT ME9 ...... 87 H5
Sutton Cl RHAM ME8 ...... 68 C5
Sutton Ct STPH/PW TN12 ...... 152 E8
Sutton Forge STPH/PW TN12 .. 152 F8
Sutton Rd MAID/SHEP ME15 ...... 121 K5
  MAID/SHEP ME15 ...... 138 E1
Sutton St MAID/BEAR ME14 ...... 122 E1
Swadelands Cl RMAID ME15 ...... 125 L8
Swaffield Rd SEV TN13 ...... 95 L8
Swain Cl STRD ME2 ...... 2 A1
Swain Rd RHAM ME8 ...... 67 K7
  TENT TN30 ...... 196 D2
Swaisland Rd DART DA1 ...... 27 K3
Swaislands Dr DART DA1 ...... 27 H3
Swale Av QBOR ME11 ...... 55 H2
Swaledale Rd RDART DA2 ...... 28 E6
Swale Rd DART DA1 ...... 27 J1
  STRD ME2 ...... 48 E6
Swallow Cl BXLYHN DA7 ...... 13 G7
  CDH/CHF RM16 ...... 15 L3
  GRH DA9 ...... 29 H3
Swallow Dr RTWE/PEM TN2 ...... 164 B7
Swallow Ri WALD ME5 ...... 66 C8
Swallow Rd DIT/AY ME20 ...... 101 H3
Swallowtail Cl
  STMC/STPC BR5 ...... 40 F8
Swanbridge Rd BXLYHN DA7 .. 12 C7
Swan Cl SIT ME10 ...... 88 D1
  STMC/STPC BR5 ...... 40 C7
Swan Cottages TENT TN30 ...... 208 F2
Swanland Dr TON TN9 ...... 147 H6
Swanmead Wy TON TN9 ...... 147 M3
Swan La CRBK TN17 ...... 182 B2
  DART DA1 ...... 27 H5
  EDEN TN8 ...... 142 E1
Swanley La SWLY BR8 ...... 42 B7
Swanley Village Rd SWLY BR8 .. 42 D5
Swan Rdg EDEN TN8 ...... 142 F3

Swanscombe St SWCM DA10 ...... 30 B4
Swanstree Av SIT ME10 ...... 88 D3
Swan St E/WMAL ME19 ...... 100 E5
  TENT TN30 ...... 208 D2
Swanton Rd ERITH DA8 ...... 12 C6
  WBY/YAL ME18 ...... 117 H6
Swanzy Rd RSEV TN14 ...... 95 L6
Sward Rd STMC/STPC BR5 ...... 56 C2
Swattenden La CRBK TN17 ...... 192 D3
Swaylands Rd BELV DA17 ...... 12 C5
Swaynesland Rd OXTED RH8 .. 126 B4
Sweeps Hill Cl
  RTWE/PEM TN2 ...... 164 F6
Sweeps La STMC/STPC BR5 ...... 56 F1
Sweetings La RRTW TN3 ...... 188 F4
Sweets La E/WMAL ME19 ...... 119 J1
Sweyne Rd SWCM DA10 ...... 30 A4
Swift Cl DIT/AY ME20 ...... 101 J3
Swift Crs WALD ME5 ...... 66 D7
Swifts Rd CDH/CHF RM16 ...... 15 L3
Swifts Vw CRBK TN17 ...... 183 M7
Swiller's La GVE DA12 ...... 48 A2
Swinburne Gdns TIL RM18 ...... 17 K8
Swingate Av HOO/HM ME3 ...... 20 D8
Swingate Cl WALD ME5 ...... 83 K3
Swinton Av HOO/HM ME3 ...... 35 H8
Sycamore Cl GVE DA12 ...... 31 M5
  TIL RM18 ...... 17 H7
Sycamore Crs MAIDW ME16 ...... 102 E8
Sycamore Dr DIT/AY ME20 ...... 102 A4
  SWLY BR8 ...... 42 A7
Sycamore Gdns
  STPH/PW TN12 ...... 150 B8
Sycamore Rd DART DA1 ...... 27 M5
  STRD ME2 ...... 2 B8
Sychem La RTON TN11 ...... 149 J3
Sychem Pl STPH/PW TN12 ...... 149 J6
Sydney Cl SIT ME10 ...... 87 L1
Sydney Rd CHAT ME4 ...... 4 E1
  SCUP DA14 ...... 40 A1
Sylewood Cl ROCH ME1 ...... 65 K5
Sylvan Cl CDH/CHF RM16 ...... 16 A3
  OXTED RH8 ...... 109 K7
Sylvan Gld WALD ME5 ...... 83 J5
Sylvan Rd RHAM ME8 ...... 68 C5
Sylvestre Cl STRD ME2 ...... 81 J1
Symmonds Dr SIT ME10 ...... 71 J8
Symonds Cl BGR/WK TN15 ...... 60 A8
Symonds La WBY/YAL ME18 ...... 135 G6
Symonds Rd HOO/HM ME3 ...... 34 C2
Symons Av CHAT ME4 ...... 4 E9

T

Tadburn Gn WALD ME5 ...... 83 K1
Taddington Wood La WALD ME5 .. 83 G3
Taillour Cl SIT ME10 ...... 71 H6
The Tail Race MAID/SHEP ME15 .. 6 C8
Tainter Rd RTON TN11 ...... 132 F4
Talbot Pk RTWE/PEM TN2 ...... 11 L2
Talbot Rd HAWK TN18 ...... 199 H5
  MAIDW ME16 ...... 102 E7
Tallents Cl EYN DA4 ...... 43 K4
Tall Trees Cl RMAID ME17 ...... 139 M3
Tally Rd OXTED RH8 ...... 126 A1
Talus Cl PUR RM19 ...... 14 F3
Tamar Dr STRD ME2 ...... 2 C5
Tamarind Cl GILL ME7 ...... 84 C1
Tamar Rd TONN TN10 ...... 131 K8
Tamesis Strd GVE DA12 ...... 47 G2
Tandridgehill La GDST RH9 ...... 108 B6
Tangier La RRTW TN3 ...... 177 K7
Tanglewood Cl RHAM ME8 ...... 67 L7
Tangmere Cl GILL ME7 ...... 51 H8
Tanker Hl RHAM ME8 ...... 67 M7
Tank Hill Rd PUR RM19 ...... 14 C3
Tank La PUR RM19 ...... 14 C3
Tanners Md EDEN TN8 ...... 142 E4
Tannery Rd TON TN9 ...... 147 J5
Tanyard HAWK TN18 ...... 200 D8
Tanyard La GVE DA12 ...... 48 A3
Tan Yard La BXLY DA5 ...... 26 C5
Tanyard La STH/RUST TN4 ...... 163 H4
The Tanyard CRBK TN17 ...... 192 F1
Tarragon Rd MAIDW ME16 ...... 120 D2
Tasker Cl MAID/SHEP ME15 ...... 122 D2
Tasker Rd CDH/CHF RM16 ...... 17 K2
Tassell Cl E/WMAL ME19 ...... 101 J4
Taswell Rd RHAM ME8 ...... 68 C4
Tates HAWK TN18 ...... 199 J4
Tates Orch HART DA3 ...... 61 H2
Tatler Cl WALD ME5 ...... 83 M3
Tatsfield La BH/WHM TN16 ...... 92 B7
Tattlebury La CRBK TN17 ...... 182 B5
Tattlebury Rd HDCN TN27 ...... 155 K6
Taunton Cl BXLYHN DA7 ...... 26 F1
  MAID/SHEP ME15 ...... 122 B7
Taunton Rd GVW DA11 ...... 30 C3
Taunton V GVE DA12 ...... 31 M8
Taveners Rd RHAM ME8 ...... 67 M6
Tavern Cl BGR/WK TN15 ...... 98 B6
Tavistock Cl RHAM ME8 ...... 68 A6
  SIT ME10 ...... 87 M1
Tay Cl WALD ME5 ...... 66 D8
Taylor Cl ORP BR6 ...... 56 B7
  RMAID ME17 ...... 124 F7
Taylor Rd SNOD ME6 ...... 81 H6
Taylor Rw RDART DA2 ...... 27 L8
Taylors Cl SCUP DA14 ...... 40 B2
Taylors La E/WMAL ME19 ...... 79 H7
  HOO/HM ME3 ...... 33 K8
  HOO/HM ME3 ...... 48 E2
Taylor St STH/RUST TN4 ...... 163 H5
Tea Garden La RRTW TN3 ...... 176 D4
Teal Av STMC/STPC BR5 ...... 40 F8
Teal Cl HOO/HM ME3 ...... 25 K8
Teapot La DIT/AY ME20 ...... 102 A3
Teasaucer Hl MAID/SHEP ME15 .. 121 H5
Teasel Cl MAID/BEAR ME14 ...... 122 D1
Tebbs Wy BGR/WK TN15 ...... 115 L2
Tedder Av WALD ME5 ...... 66 C6
Tedder Rd STH/RUST TN4 ...... 163 K6
Teesdale Rd RDART DA2 ...... 28 E6

Telegraph Hl HOO/HM ME3 ...... 48 E2
Telscombe Cl ORP BR6 ...... 56 A5
Telston Cl RSEV TN14 ...... 95 H3
  SEV TN13 ...... 95 G3
Tempest Rd E/WMAL ME19 ...... 118 B2
Templar Dr GVW DA11 ...... 46 C2
Temple Gdns SIT ME10 ...... 88 D2
Temple Hl DART DA1 ...... 28 B3
Temple Hill Sq DART DA1 ...... 28 B3
Templer Av CDH/CHF RM16 ...... 17 J3
Temple Wy E/WMAL ME19 ...... 101 H5
Ten Acre Wy RHAM ME8 ...... 68 D4
Tenchley's La OXTED RH8 ...... 126 A3
Tennyson Av GRAYS RM17 ...... 34 D6
  HOO/HM ME3 ...... 34 D6
Tennyson Rd DART DA1 ...... 28 C3
  GILL ME7 ...... 5 J7
Tennyson Wk GVW DA11 ...... 30 F8
  TIL RM18 ...... 17 K8
Tensing Av GVW DA11 ...... 31 C8
Tenterden Rd CRBK TN17 ...... 202 B1
  HDCN TN27 ...... 186 C5
  HDCN TN27 ...... 195 H2
  WALD ME5 ...... 66 D8
Terence Cl CHAT ME4 ...... 66 C3
  GVE DA12 ...... 32 B7
Terminus Rd MAIDW ME16 ...... 120 C3
Tern Crs STRD ME2 ...... 48 E7
Terrace Rd MAIDW ME16 ...... 6 D5
  SIT ME10 ...... 88 D2
Terrace St GVE DA12 ...... 31 K4
The Terrace RDART DA2 ...... 28 E5
Terrace St GVE DA12 ...... 31 K4
The Terrace GVE DA12 ...... 31 K4
  ROCH ME1 ...... 3 K8
  SEV TN13 ...... 94 F8
Terry's Lodge Rd BGR/WK TN15.. 77 L8
Terry Wk DIT/AY ME20 ...... 101 G3
Teston La MAID/SHEP ME15 ...... 119 L6
Teston Rd E/WMAL ME19 ...... 99 K5
Teynham Gn RHAM ME8 ...... 67 J1
Thackeray Av TIL RM18 ...... 17 K7
Thackeray Rd DIT/AY ME20 ...... 101 H3
Thames Av HOO/HM ME3 ...... 36 A1
  RHAM ME8 ...... 68 A5
Thames Dr CDH/CHF RM16 ...... 17 J4
Thames Ga DART DA1 ...... 28 C3
Thames Rd DART DA1 ...... 27 J1
  GRAYS RM17 ...... 16 D6
  TONN TN10 ...... 131 L8
Thames Vw GRAYS RM17 ...... 17 J4
  HOO/HM ME3 ...... 34 E6
Thames Wy GVW DA11 ...... 30 F6
Thamley PUR RM19 ...... 14 C3
Thanet Rd BXLY DA5 ...... 26 C5
  ERITH DA8 ...... 13 G6
Thatch Barn Rd HDCN TN27 ...... 155 M7
Thatcher Rd DART DA1 ...... 170 A4
Thatchers La HOO/HM ME3 ...... 20 D8
The Thatchers MAIDW ME16 ...... 102 D8
Thelma Cl GVE DA12 ...... 47 H2
Theobalds Av GRAYS RM17 ...... 16 E4
Theodore Cl RTWE/PEM TN2 ...... 164 A6
Theodore Pl GILL ME7 ...... 5 J3
Thicketts SEV TN13 ...... 9 J3
Third Av CHAT ME4 ...... 66 E4
  GILL ME7 ...... 67 G2
  WTHK ME20 ...... 15 J5
Third St RRTW TN3 ...... 176 B2
Thirlemere Cl MAIDW ME16 ...... 102 F5
Thirlmere Cl GILL ME7 ...... 51 J8
  STRD ME2 ...... 49 L4
Thirlmere Rd BXLYHN DA7 ...... 12 E8
  STH/RUST TN4 ...... 10 A2
Thirza Rd DART DA1 ...... 28 B4
Thistlebank WALD ME5 ...... 83 J2
Thistledown
  MAID/BEAR ME14 ...... 122 B1
Thistledown Cl GILL ME7 ...... 84 C1
Thistle Rd GVE DA12 ...... 32 A5
Thomas Bata Av TIL RM18 ...... 18 D3
Thomas Dr GVE DA12 ...... 31 M7
Thomas Rd SIT ME10 ...... 88 D1
Thomas St ROCH ME1 ...... 65 L2
  STH/RUST TN4 ...... 10 A2
Thompson Cl RHAM ME8 ...... 68 C5
Thomson Cl SNOD ME6 ...... 81 J4
Thong La BGR/WK TN15 ...... 98 A8
  GVE DA12 ...... 32 C7
Thorn Cl WALD ME5 ...... 82 F4
Thorndale Cl WALD ME5 ...... 65 M8
Thornden La CRBK TN17 ...... 202 C5
Thorndike Cl CHAT ME4 ...... 66 B5
Thorndon Cl STMC/STPC BR5 ...... 40 B6
Thorndon Rd STMC/STPC BR5 ...... 40 B6
Thorne Cl ERITH DA8 ...... 12 D5
Thornfield Gdns
  RTWE/PEM TN2 ...... 164 B8
Thornham Rd RHAM ME8 ...... 67 L2
Thornhill Pl MAID/BEAR ME14 ...... 7 L1
Thorn Rd STPH/PW TN12 ...... 169 H2
Thorn's Meadow
  BH/WHM TN16 ...... 111 L1
Thornton Rd BELV DA17 ...... 12 D3
Thorold Rd CHAT ME4 ...... 5 G7
Thorpe Av TONN TN10 ...... 131 L8
Thorpe Cl ORP BR6 ...... 56 A5
Thorpe Wk RHAM ME8 ...... 84 E2
Thrale Wy RHAM ME8 ...... 85 C1
Three Corners BXLYHN DA7 ...... 12 D8
Three Elm La TONN TN10 ...... 132 D7
Three Gates Rd HART DA3 ...... 60 C3
Threshers Dr MAID/BEAR ME14 .. 103 M8
The Thrift RDART DA2 ...... 29 L8
Thrush Cl WALD ME5 ...... 66 D6
Thurloe Wk GRAYS RM17 ...... 16 F5
Thurrock Park Wy GRAYS RM17 .. 16 F6
Thursland Rd SCUP DA14 ...... 41 G2
Thurston Dr STRD ME2 ...... 48 E7
Thwaite Cl ERITH DA8 ...... 12 E5
Thyssel La RYE TN31 ...... 206 D7
Tibbs Court La STPH/PW TN12.. 166 B6
Ticehurst Cl STMC/STPC BR5 ...... 40 C4
Tichborne Cl MAIDW ME16 ...... 102 E7
Tickham La RSIT ME9 ...... 89 M7
The Tideway ROCH ME1 ...... 65 L5
Tilbury Cl STMC/STPC BR5 ...... 40 D6
Tilbury Gdns TIL RM18 ...... 31 J2
Tilbury Rd RHAM ME8 ...... 68 C3
Tilden Cl RASHW TN26 ...... 187 M6

Tilden Gill Rd TENT TN30 ...... 196 E6
Tilden La STPH/PW TN12 ...... 152 E5
Tilden Rd HDCN TN27 ...... 156 A3
Tilebarn Cnr TONN TN10 ...... 148 A1
Tile Flds RMAID ME17 ...... 123 M3
Tile Kiln La BXLY DA5 ...... 26 F7
Tilghman Wy SNOD ME6 ...... 81 K4
Till Av EYN DA4 ...... 59 H3
Tillingbourne Gn
  STMC/STPC BR5 ...... 40 C8
Tilmans Md EYN DA4 ...... 59 H3
Tilsden La CRBK TN17 ...... 193 G2
Tilton Rd BGR/WK TN15 ...... 98 B6
Timber Bank MEO DA13 ...... 79 H5
Timberbank WALD ME5 ...... 66 C7
Timbertop Rd BH/WHM TN16 ...... 91 L4
Timber Tops WALD ME5 ...... 83 M5
Timothy Cl BXLYHS DA6 ...... 26 A3
Tinker Pot La BGR/WK TN15 ...... 77 C7
Tinkerpot Ri BGR/WK TN15 ...... 76 E8
Tintagel Gdns STRD ME2 ...... 2 C4
Tintagel Rd STMC/STPC BR5 ...... 56 E5
Tintern Rd MAIDW ME16 ...... 102 E6
Titan Rd GRAYS RM17 ...... 16 C4
Titchfield Rd MAID/SHEP ME15 .. 122 B7
Titsey Hl OXTED RH8 ...... 109 K2
  WARL CR6 ...... 109 H2
Titsey Rd OXTED RH8 ...... 109 K5
Tobruk Wy WALD ME5 ...... 66 B7
Toby Gdns RTON TN11 ...... 133 G5
Todd Crs SIT ME10 ...... 71 J5
Toddington Crs WALD ME5 ...... 82 F4
Toft Av GRAYS RM17 ...... 16 F3
Tolgate La STRD ME2 ...... 3 G4
Tolgate Wy MAID/BEAR ME14 ...... 103 G2
Tolhurst Rd STPH/PW TN12 ...... 149 J6
Toll GRH DA9 ...... 28 E2
Tolsey Md BGR/WK TN15 ...... 98 C5
Tom Joyce Cl SNOD ME6 ...... 81 J5
Tomlin Cl SNOD ME6 ...... 81 J5
  STPH/PW TN12 ...... 170 A1
Tonbridge By-pass RSEV TN14.. 130 A3
  RTON TN11 ...... 130 C5
Tonbridge Rd BGR/WK TN15 ...... 115 L3
  MAIDW ME16 ...... 120 B3
  RTON TN11 ...... 130 F7
  RTWE/PEM TN2 ...... 164 D6
  SEV TN13 ...... 113 L5
  WBY/YAL ME18 ...... 118 A5
Tonge Rd SIT ME10 ...... 88 D1
Tong La STPH/PW TN12 ...... 180 D2
Tong Rd STPH/PW TN12 ...... 166 D8
Tongswood Dr HAWK TN18 ...... 199 L4
Tooley St GVW DA11 ...... 30 F5
Top Dartford Rd SWLY BR8 ...... 42 C3
Torbay Rd STPH/PW TN12 ...... 134 D3
Toronto Rd GILL ME7 ...... 67 G1
  TIL RM18 ...... 17 J3
Torrens Wk GVE DA12 ...... 47 G2
Torrington Cl WBY/YAL ME18 .. 117 M5
Tovil Gn MAID/SHEP ME15 ...... 6 C9
Tovil Hl MAID/SHEP ME15 ...... 121 C4
Tovil Rd MAID/SHEP ME15 ...... 6 E9
Tower Cl GVE DA12 ...... 47 G2
  ORP BR6 ...... 56 B5
Tower Gdns MAID/BEAR ME14 .. 122 D2
Tower Hl E/WMAL ME19 ...... 99 M6
Tower La MAID/BEAR ME14 ...... 122 C1
Tower Rd BELV DA17 ...... 12 E3
  BXLYHN DA7 ...... 26 C2
  DART DA1 ...... 27 L5
  ORP BR6 ...... 56 B5
Towers Rd GRAYS RM17 ...... 16 E4
Towers Wd EYN DA4 ...... 43 M5
Tower Vw E/WMAL ME19 ...... 118 D1
Town Acres TON TN9 ...... 147 L1
Townfield Cnr GVE DA12 ...... 47 G2
Town Hl E/WMAL ME19 ...... 100 E4
  RRTW TN3 ...... 189 J1
Town Hill Cl E/WMAL ME19 ...... 100 E4
Townland Rd HDCN TN27 ...... 186 C4
Townley Rd BXLYHS DA6 ...... 26 B3
Town Rd HOO/HM ME3 ...... 34 C7
Townsend Rd SNOD ME6 ...... 81 G4
Townshead Cl SCUP DA14 ...... 40 D3
Toy's Hl BH/WHM TN16 ...... 127 L1
  EDEN TN8 ...... 127 L1
The Tracies RSIT ME9 ...... 69 L7
Tradescant Dr MEO DA13 ...... 62 D2
Trafalgar Rd DART DA1 ...... 28 A7
  GVW DA11 ...... 31 J5
  ROCH ME1 ...... 81 L1
Trafalgar St GILL ME7 ...... 5 J4
Tramways CHAT ME4 ...... 66 E3
Tranquil Ri ERITH DA8 ...... 13 G4
Transfesa Rd STPH/PW TN12 ...... 150 C6
Trapfield Cl MAID/BEAR ME14 .. 122 E1
Trapfield La MAID/BEAR ME14 .. 122 E1
Trapham Rd MAIDW ME16 ...... 6 A3
Travers Gdns STRD ME2 ...... 87 H8
Travertine Rd WALD ME5 ...... 83 K4
Trebble Rd SWCM DA10 ...... 30 A4
Trebilco Cl RTWE/PEM TN2 ...... 163 M6
Tredegar Rd RDART DA2 ...... 27 J8
Treebourne Rd BH/WHM TN16 .. 91 L3
Tree La BGR/WK TN15 ...... 116 A5
Treetops BGR/WK TN15 ...... 96 C3
  GVE DA12 ...... 46 E2
  TON TN9 ...... 147 K6
Treetops Cl ABYW SE2 ...... 12 A4
Trelawn Crs WALD ME5 ...... 83 K3
Trellyn Cl MAIDW ME16 ...... 120 B3
Trench Rd TONN TN10 ...... 131 K7
Trent TIL RM18 ...... 18 E3
Trentham Dr STMC/STPC BR5 ...... 40 D6
Trenton Cl MAIDW ME16 ...... 102 D6
Trevale Rd ROCH ME1 ...... 65 K4
Trevelyan Cl DART DA1 ...... 28 E2
Trevereux Hl OXTED RH8 ...... 126 C2
Trevino Dr WALD ME5 ...... 83 H3
Trevithick Dr DART DA1 ...... 28 B2
Trevor Dr MAIDW ME16 ...... 102 D8
Trewin Cl DIT/AY ME20 ...... 101 M3
Tribune Dr SIT ME10 ...... 71 H7
Trident Cl STRD ME2 ...... 50 A6

Trinity CI *RTWE/PEM* TN2 ..... 11 L4
Trinity Gdns *DART* DA1 ..... 27 M4
Trinity PI *BXLYHS* DA6 ..... 26 B2
Trinity Rd *GILL* ME7 ..... 5 K1
  GVE DA12 ..... 31 L5
  SIT ME10 ..... 71 H6
Tristan Gdns *STH/RUST* TN4 ..... 176 F6
Trivett CI *GRH* DA9 ..... 29 J3
Triumph CI *CDH/CHF* RM16 ..... 15 L3
Trolling Down HI *MAID/BEAR* ME14 ..... 103 H5
Trosley Av *GVW* DA11 ..... 31 K7
Trosley Rd *BELV* DA17 ..... 12 C5
Trottiscliffe Rd *E/WMAL* ME19 ..... 99 L2
Trotts La *BH/WHM* TN16 ..... 110 E5
Trotwood CI *WALD* ME5 ..... 83 J5
Troy La *EDEN* TN8 ..... 142 B1
Troys Md *RMAID* ME17 ..... 123 M3
Trubridge Rd *HOO/HM* ME3 ..... 35 M8
Truro CI *RHAM* ME8 ..... 67 M2
Truro Rd *GVE* DA12 ..... 31 M8
Truro Wk *TONN* TN10 ..... 131 M8
Trycewell La *BGR/WK* TN15 ..... 97 M7
Tubbenden CI *ORP* BR6 ..... 56 A5
Tubs HI *SEV* TN13 ..... 8 F4
Tudeley La *RTON* TN11 ..... 148 D5
  TON TN9 ..... 147 M6
Tudeley Rd *TON* TN9 ..... 148 A6
Tudor Av *MAID/BEAR* ME14 ..... 103 K7
Tudor CI *DART* DA1 ..... 27 K4
  GVW DA11 ..... 31 G6
Tudor Ct *RTWE/PEM* TN2 ..... 177 G4
  SWLY BR8 ..... 57 L3
Tudor Crs *RSEV* TN14 ..... 95 L3
Tudor Dr *RSEV* TN14 ..... 95 L2
Tudor Gv *HOO/HM* ME3 ..... 50 B1
  RHAM ME8 ..... 68 A5
Tufa CI *WALD* ME5 ..... 83 K4
Tufnail Rd *DART* DA1 ..... 28 B4
Tufton Rd *RHAM* ME8 ..... 68 B4
Tufton St *MAID/BEAR* ME14 ..... 7 H4
Tulip Tree CI *TON* TN9 ..... 147 J5
Tumblefield Rd *BGR/WK* TN15 ..... 78 B5
Tumblers HI *RMAID* ME17 ..... 139 H6
Tunbury Av *WALD* ME5 ..... 83 H2
Tunbury Av South *WALD* ME5 ..... 83 H4
Tunnel Rd *RTW* TN1 ..... 11 G3
Tunstall CI *ORP* BR6 ..... 56 A7
Tunstall Rd *RSIT* ME9 ..... 87 L5
Tunstock Wy *BELV* DA17 ..... 12 A2
Tupman Rd *ROCH* ME1 ..... 3 G9
Turgis CI *RMAID* ME17 ..... 139 G1
Turnbull Rd *RDART* DA2 ..... 29 C5
Turnden Rd *CRBK* TN17 ..... 192 C2
Turner Av *CRBK* TN17 ..... 192 F2
Turner CI *SIT* ME10 ..... 71 J6
Turner Ct *DART* DA1 ..... 27 L3
Turner Rd *RDART* DA2 ..... 29 K8
  TONN TN10 ..... 132 A8
Turners Av *TENT* TN30 ..... 196 D5
Turners Gdns *SEV* TN13 ..... 113 L6
Turners Green Rd *WADH* TN5 ..... 188 B7
Turners Green Rd *WADH* TN5 ..... 188 B6
Turner's Oak Shaw *HART* DA3 ..... 61 G5
Turner St *HOO/HM* ME3 ..... 20 D8
Turnpike Dr *ORP* BR6 ..... 73 L3
Turnpike La *CDH/CHF* RM16 ..... 17 M4
Turnstone Rd *WALD* ME5 ..... 83 L3
The Turnstones *GVE* DA12 ..... 31 M7
Turp Av *CDH/CHF* RM16 ..... 16 E1
Turpin La *ERITH* DA8 ..... 13 L5
Tuscan Dr *WALD* ME5 ..... 83 L4
Tutsham Wy *STPH/PW* TN12 ..... 150 B7
Tuxford St *STH/RUST* TN4 ..... 162 D8
Tweed *TIL* RM18 ..... 18 E3
Tweed Rd *TONN* TN10 ..... 131 L8
Twigg CI *ERITH* DA8 ..... 13 C6
Twisden Rd *E/WMAL* ME19 ..... 101 H5
Twisleton Ct *DART* DA1 ..... 27 M4
Twitton La *RSEV* TN14 ..... 95 C2
Twitton Mdw *RSEV* TN14 ..... 95 C2
Two Gates HI *HOO/HM* ME3 ..... 34 B8
Twydall Gn *RHAM* ME8 ..... 67 K2
Twydall La *RHAM* ME8 ..... 67 K3
Twyford CI *RHAM* ME8 ..... 68 C3
Twyford Rd *RTON* TN11 ..... 133 C4
Tydeman Rd *MAID/SHEP* ME15 ..... 122 B3
Tyeshurst CI *ABYW* SE2 ..... 12 A4
Tyland La *MAID/BEAR* ME14 ..... 103 H2
Tyler CI *E/WMAL* ME19 ..... 101 H5
Tyler Dr *RHAM* ME8 ..... 85 C1
Tylers Green Rd *SWLY* BR8 ..... 57 L2
Tyne CI *WALD* ME5 ..... 66 D8
Tynedale CI *RDART* DA2 ..... 28 F6
Tyne Rd *TONN* TN10 ..... 131 K8
Typhoon Wy *E/WMAL* ME19 ..... 118 B2
Tyron Wy *SCUP* DA14 ..... 40 A1
Tyrrells Hall CI *GRAYS* RM17 ..... 16 F5

U

Uckfield La *EDEN* TN8 ..... 143 L8
Ufton CI *MAID/SHEP* ME15 ..... 122 A4
Ufton La *SIT* ME10 ..... 88 A2
Ulcombe HI *RMAID* ME17 ..... 140 B4
Ulcombe Rd *HDCN* TN27 ..... 155 L1
  RMAID ME17 ..... 139 C2
Ulstan CI *CTHM* CR3 ..... 108 C1
Underdown Av *CHAT* ME4 ..... 66 B4
Underlyn La *STPH/PW* TN12 ..... 152 E5
Underriver House Rd
  RTON TN11 ..... 130 E2
Underwood CI *MAID/SHEP* ME15 ..... 6 F8
Unicorn Wk *GRH* DA9 ..... 29 H3
Unicumes La *MAIDW* ME16 ..... 120 E3
Union St *CHAT* ME4 ..... 4 E6
  MAID/BEAR ME14 ..... 7 G3
  ROCH ME1 ..... 3 K8
Unity St *SIT* ME10 ..... 88 A2
University Gdns *BXLY* DA5 ..... 26 B5
University Wy *DART* DA1 ..... 27 M1
Unwin CI *DIT/AY* ME20 ..... 102 C2
Upbury Wy *CHAT* ME4 ..... 4 F6
Upchat Rd *HOO/HM* ME3 ..... 50 A1
Updale Rd *SCUP* DA14 ..... 40 B1
Upland Rd *BXLYHN* DA7 ..... 26 B1
  CTHM CR3 ..... 90 C6

Uplands CI *SEV* TN13 ..... 8 D3
  STRD ME2 ..... 48 F7
Uplands Rd *ORP* BR6 ..... 56 D4
Uplands Wy *SEV* TN13 ..... 8 C2
Upnor Rd *STRD* ME2 ..... 3 M1
Upper Abbey Rd *BELV* DA17 ..... 12 B3
Upper Austin Lodge Rd
  EYN DA4 ..... 58 F8
Upper Av *MEO* DA13 ..... 46 A5
Upper Barn HI
  MAID/SHEP ME15 ..... 136 A2
Upper Britton PI *GILL* ME7 ..... 5 H4
Upper Bush Rd *STRD* ME2 ..... 64 B3
Upper Court Rd *CTHM* CR3 ..... 108 C1
Upper Cumberland Wk
  RTW TN1 ..... 11 G9
Upper Dr *BH/WHM* TN16 ..... 91 L4
Upper Dunstan Rd
  STH/RUST TN4 ..... 163 K7
Upper Fant Rd *MAIDW* ME16 ..... 120 E3
Upper Field Rd *SIT* ME10 ..... 71 K8
Upper Green Rd *RTON* TN11 ..... 115 L8
Upper Grosvenor Rd *RTW* TN1 ..... 10 F3
Upper Grove Rd *BELV* DA17 ..... 12 B5
Upper Haysden La
  STH/RUST TN4 ..... 146 F7
Upper Holly Hill Rd *BELV* DA17 ..... 12 D4
Upper Hunton HI
  MAID/SHEP ME15 ..... 136 C2
Upper Luton Rd *WALD* ME5 ..... 5 J8
Upper MI *WBY/YAL* ME18 ..... 118 F5
Upper Nellington *RRTW* TN3 ..... 176 D1
Upper Park Rd *BELV* DA17 ..... 12 D3
Upper Profit *RRTW* TN3 ..... 176 C2
Upper Rd *MAID/SHEP* ME15 ..... 7 J8
Upper Sheridan Rd
  BELV DA17 ..... 12 C3
Upper Spring La *MAID/SHEP* ME15 ..... 7 H6
Upper Stephens *RRTW* TN3 ..... 176 C2
Upper Stone St *MAID/SHEP* ME15 ..... 7 H6
Upper St *RMAID* ME17 ..... 123 H8
  RMAID ME17 ..... 124 A2
Upperton Rd *SCUP* DA14 ..... 40 B2
Upton CI *BXLY* DA5 ..... 26 B4
Upton Quarry *RRTW* TN3 ..... 176 B2
Upton Rd *BXLYHS* DA6 ..... 26 A2
Upton Rd South *BXLY* DA5 ..... 26 B4
Uptons *HDCN* TN27 ..... 155 L7
Uridge Crs *TONN* TN10 ..... 147 L1
Uridge Rd *TONN* TN10 ..... 147 L1
Urquhart CI *WALD* ME5 ..... 66 C8
Usborne Rd *STPH/PW* TN12 ..... 170 A2
Uvedale Rd *OXTED* RH8 ..... 109 H7

V

Vale Av *RTW* TN1 ..... 10 F6
  STH/RUST TN4 ..... 163 H4
Vale Dr *WALD* ME5 ..... 65 M8
Valence Rd *ERITH* DA8 ..... 12 F6
Valenciennes Rd *SIT* ME10 ..... 88 A2
Valentine Av *BXLY* DA5 ..... 26 A7
Valentine CI *GILL* ME7 ..... 67 J4
Valentine Dr *HOO/HM* ME3 ..... 36 A2
Valentine Rd
  MAID/SHEP ME15 ..... 122 A6
Valerian CI *WALD* ME5 ..... 83 L1
Vale Ri *TON* TN9 ..... 147 M4
Vale Rd *DART* DA1 ..... 27 K6
  GVW DA11 ..... 30 F5
  HAWK TN18 ..... 199 H2
  MAID/SHEP ME15 ..... 137 C1
  RTW TN1 ..... 10 F6
  STH/RUST TN4 ..... 163 H4
  TON TN9 ..... 147 K4
  TON TN9 ..... 147 M4
Valetta Wy *ROCH* ME1 ..... 3 H9
Valiant Rd *WALD* ME5 ..... 83 L3
The Vallance *RSIT* ME9 ..... 89 J7
Valley CI *DART* DA1 ..... 27 H4
Valley Dr *GVE* DA12 ..... 46 F1
  MAID/SHEP ME15 ..... 121 H7
  RTON TN11 ..... 133 H3
  SEV TN13 ..... 9 H7
Valley Forge CI *TONN* TN10 ..... 148 B1
Valley Gdns *GRH* DA9 ..... 29 K4
Valley La *BGR/WK* TN15 ..... 78 E3
  MEO DA13 ..... 79 J3
Valley Ri *WALD* ME5 ..... 83 H3
Valley Rd *DART* DA1 ..... 27 H4
  ERITH DA8 ..... 12 E3
  GILL ME7 ..... 67 C1
  HART DA3 ..... 60 D4
  STH/RUST TN4 ..... 176 F1
  STMC/STPC BR5 ..... 40 D5
The Valley *RMAID* ME17 ..... 136 F2
Valley Vw *BH/WHM* TN16 ..... 91 L4
  GRH DA9 ..... 29 K4
  STH/RUST TN4 ..... 163 J3
Valley View Rd *ROCH* ME1 ..... 65 K4
Vanburgh CI *ORP* BR6 ..... 56 A4
Vancouver Dr *RHAM* ME8 ..... 67 L4
Vanessa CI *BELV* DA17 ..... 12 C4
Vanessa Wk *GVE* DA12 ..... 47 H2
Vanessa Wy *BXLY* DA5 ..... 26 F8
Vange Cottage Ms *ROCH* ME1 ..... 3 H9
Vanguard Wy *EDEN* TN8 ..... 126 C4
  EGRIN RH19 ..... 158 B8
  LING RH7 ..... 158 C5
  OXTED RH8 ..... 109 H3
  WARL CR6 ..... 90 C1
Vanity La *RMAID* ME17 ..... 136 F5
Vanquisher Wk *GVE* DA12 ..... 32 B8
Varnes St *DIT/AY* ME20 ..... 82 B7
Vaughan Av *TONN* TN10 ..... 132 A7
Vaughan Dr *SIT* ME10 ..... 71 H5
Vauxhall CI *DART* DA1 ..... 28 B4
Vauxhall CI *GVW* DA11 ..... 31 H5
Vauxhall Crs *SNOD* ME6 ..... 81 J7
Vauxhall Gdns *TON* TN9 ..... 147 L6
Vauxhall La *RTON* TN11 ..... 147 M7
Vauxhall PI *DART* DA1 ..... 28 A5
Vectis Dr *SIT* ME10 ..... 71 H5
Veles Rd *SNOD* ME6 ..... 81 H7
Venners CI *BXLYHN* DA7 ..... 13 G8
Ventnor CI *WALD* ME5 ..... 66 E5
Venture CI *BXLY* DA5 ..... 26 A5
Vermont Rd *STH/RUST* TN4 ..... 176 E1

Vernon CI *BGR/WK* TN15 ..... 77 H3
  STMC/STPC BR5 ..... 40 D7
Vernon Rd *RTW* TN1 ..... 163 L7
  SWCM DA10 ..... 30 B4
Veroan Rd *BXLYHN* DA7 ..... 12 A8
Verona Gdns *GVE* DA12 ..... 47 G1
Veryan Ct *STMC/STPC* BR5 ..... 40 E8
Vesper Ct *HDCN* TN27 ..... 173 J4
Vestry Rd *RSEV* TN14 ..... 95 L5
Vexil CI *PUR* RM19 ..... 14 F3
Via Romana *GVE* DA12 ..... 32 D6
Vicarage CI *DIT/AY* ME20 ..... 102 B2
  ERITH DA8 ..... 12 E5
  HOO/HM ME3 ..... 37 J2
  STRD ME2 ..... 64 C8
Vicarage Dr *GVW* DA11 ..... 30 E4
Vicarage HI *BH/WHM* TN16 ..... 110 F4
Vicarage La *GVE* DA12 ..... 32 C7
  HOO/HM ME3 ..... 51 J1
  MAID/SHEP ME15 ..... 120 D6
  RSIT ME9 ..... 69 L2
Vicarage Rd *BXLY* DA5 ..... 26 D6
  GILL ME7 ..... 5 H4
  SIT ME10 ..... 70 F6
  STH/RUST TN4 ..... 163 H3
  STRD ME2 ..... 3 H2
  STRD ME2 ..... 64 A8
  WBY/YAL ME18 ..... 135 J4
Vicarage Sq *GRAYS* RM17 ..... 16 C5
Vicary Wy *MAIDW* ME16 ..... 6 A2
Vickers Rd *ERITH* DA8 ..... 12 F4
Victoria Av *CDH/CHF* RM16 ..... 16 E1
Victoria CI *CDH/CHF* RM16 ..... 16 E1
  RMAID ME17 ..... 141 G6
Victoria Dr *EYN* DA4 ..... 43 M6
  WBY/YAL ME18 ..... 118 B3
Victoria Gdns *BH/WHM* TN16 ..... 91 L1
Victoria Hill Rd *SWLY* BR8 ..... 42 B5
Victoria Rd *BXLYHS* DA6 ..... 26 C3
  CHAT ME4 ..... 5 G9
  DART DA1 ..... 27 M3
  EDEN TN8 ..... 142 E5
  ERITH DA8 ..... 13 G5
  GVW DA11 ..... 31 H6
  RTON TN11 ..... 133 H7
  RTW TN1 ..... 11 G3
  SEV TN13 ..... 9 H6
  SIT ME10 ..... 87 M1
  STMC/STPC BR5 ..... 40 D5
  STH/RUST TN4 ..... 163 G4
  WALD ME5 ..... 83 G3
Victoria St *BELV* DA17 ..... 12 B4
  DIT/AY ME20 ..... 82 B7
  GILL ME7 ..... 5 K3
  MAIDW ME16 ..... 6 C6
  ROCH ME1 ..... 3 K8
  STRD ME2 ..... 3 H3
Victoria Ter *ROCH* ME1 ..... 65 J5
Victory Wy *GRH* DA9 ..... 28 E2
Vidgeon Av *HOO/HM* ME3 ..... 35 M7
View CI *BH/WHM* TN16 ..... 91 J2
Viewlands Av *BH/WHM* TN16 ..... 93 G6
View Rd *HOO/HM* ME3 ..... 34 D6
The View *ABYW* SE2 ..... 12 A4
Vigerons Wy *CDH/CHF* RM16 ..... 17 K3
Vigilant Wy *GVE* DA12 ..... 47 H2
Vigo Rd *BGR/WK* TN15 ..... 78 F6
Viking Rd *GVW* DA11 ..... 30 E8
Viking Wy *BELV* DA17 ..... 12 E2
Villa CI *GVE* DA12 ..... 32 D7
Village Green Av *BH/WHM* TN16 ..... 92 A3
Village Green Rd *DART* DA1 ..... 27 J2
Village Green Wy
  BH/WHM TN16 ..... 92 A3
Villa Rd *HOO/HM* ME3 ..... 48 D2
Vincent Rd *DIT/AY* ME20 ..... 82 E6
  SIT ME10 ..... 88 E2
Vine Av *SEV* TN13 ..... 9 H4
Vine Court Rd *SEV* TN13 ..... 9 J4
The Vineries *GILL* ME7 ..... 51 G8
Vine Rd *ORP* BR6 ..... 73 H1
Viners CI *SIT* ME10 ..... 88 A4
Vines La *ROCH* ME1 ..... 3 J7
  RTON TN11 ..... 130 E4
The Vine *SEV* TN13 ..... 9 J4
Vine Wk *STPH/PW* TN12 ..... 170 A2
Vineyard Crs *RHAM* ME8 ..... 68 D4
Viney's Gdns *TENT* TN30 ..... 196 E4
Vinson CI *ORP* BR6 ..... 56 C4
Vinters Rd *MAID/BEAR* ME14 ..... 7 K4
Vintners Wy
  MAID/BEAR ME14 ..... 122 A1
Violet CI *WALD* ME5 ..... 83 J5
Virginia Rd *GILL* ME7 ..... 50 E6
Vixen CI *WALD* ME5 ..... 66 E7
Volante Dr *SIT* ME10 ..... 71 G6
Volante Wy *GVE* DA12 ..... 47 G1
Vulcan CI *WALD* ME5 ..... 66 D6
The Vyne *BXLYHN* DA7 ..... 26 D1

W

Wade Av *STMC/STPC* BR5 ..... 56 F3
Wadeville CI *BELV* DA17 ..... 12 C4
Wadham Rd *PUR* RM19 ..... 14 F3
Wadlands Rd *HOO/HM* ME3 ..... 20 D8
Waghorn Rd *SNOD* ME6 ..... 81 J5
Waghorn St *CHAT* ME4 ..... 5 G9
Wagoners CI
  MAID/BEAR ME14 ..... 122 A1
Wagon La *STPH/PW* TN12 ..... 150 E4
Wagtail Wy *STMC/STPC* BR5 ..... 40 F8
Waid CI *DART* DA1 ..... 28 B4
Wainscott Rd *STRD* ME2 ..... 49 M3
Wainscott Wk *STRD* ME2 ..... 49 M2
Wakefield Rd *GRH* DA9 ..... 29 L3
Wakehurst Rd *RMAID* ME17 ..... 136 D2
Wakeley Rd *RHAM* ME8 ..... 68 C4
Wakely Rd *BH/WHM* TN16 ..... 91 L4
Wake Rd *ROCH* ME1 ..... 65 L5
Waldeck Rd *DART* DA1 ..... 28 B5
Walden CI *ERITH* DA8 ..... 12 B4
Waldenhurst Rd
  STMC/STPC BR5 ..... 56 F3
Waldens CI *STMC/STPC* BR5 ..... 56 F3
Waldens Rd *STMC/STPC* BR5 ..... 57 G2
The Waldens *RMAID* ME17 ..... 140 A3

Walderslade Rd *WALD* ME5 ..... 66 B7
Walderslade Woods *WALD* ME5 ..... 82 F3
Waldon *TIL* RM18 ..... 18 D3
Waldrist Wy *ERITH* DA18 ..... 12 B1
Walker CI *MAID/SHEP* ME15 ..... 121 H7
Walker CI *DART* DA1 ..... 27 H1
Walkhurst Rd *CRBK* TN17 ..... 194 A6
Walkley Rd *DART* DA1 ..... 27 K3
Wallace CI *RTWE/PEM* TN2 ..... 177 J5
Wallace Gdns *SWCM* DA10 ..... 30 A4
Wallace Rd *GRAYS* RM17 ..... 16 C3
  ROCH ME1 ..... 66 A5
Wallbridge La *RHAM* ME8 ..... 68 F2
Wall CI *HOO/HM* ME3 ..... 35 M6
Waller HI *CRBK* TN17 ..... 170 D8
Wallers *RRTW* TN3 ..... 162 C6
Wallhouse Rd *ERITH* DA8 ..... 13 L6
Wallis Av *MAID/SHEP* ME15 ..... 122 A8
Wallis CI *RDART* DA2 ..... 27 J8
The Wall *SIT* ME10 ..... 71 G8
Walmer Gdns *SIT* ME10 ..... 70 F8
Walmers Av *HOO/HM* ME3 ..... 48 C1
Walnut CI *STPH/PW* TN12 ..... 150 C7
  WALD ME5 ..... 66 D5
Walnut Hill Rd *MEO* DA13 ..... 46 A7
Walnuts Rd *ORP* BR6 ..... 56 C4
Walnut Tree Av *DART* DA1 ..... 28 A7
  MAID/SHEP ME15 ..... 121 J8
Walnut Tree Ct *DIT/AY* ME20 ..... 101 K4
Walnut Tree Dr *SIT* ME10 ..... 87 M1
Walnut Tree La
  MAID/SHEP ME15 ..... 121 J8
Walnut Tree Rd *ERITH* DA8 ..... 13 G4
Walnut Wy *RTWE/PEM* TN2 ..... 163 M5
  SWLY BR8 ..... 41 M6
Walpole CI *E/WMAL* ME19 ..... 101 H5
  GRAYS RM17 ..... 16 E3
Walsby Dr *SIT* ME10 ..... 71 J5
Walsham Rd *WALD* ME5 ..... 83 H4
Walsingham CI *RHAM* ME8 ..... 62 C2
Walsingham Rd *STMC/STPC* BR5 ..... 40 D5
Walsingham Wk *BELV* DA17 ..... 12 C5
Walter Burke Av *ROCH* ME1 ..... 64 E8
Walter's Farm Rd *TON* TN9 ..... 147 L4
Walters Green Rd *RTON* TN11 ..... 161 G1
Walters Rd *HOO/HM* ME3 ..... 36 A7
Waltham CI *DART* DA1 ..... 27 J4
  STMC/STPC BR5 ..... 40 F8
Waltham Rd *RHAM* ME8 ..... 67 K2
Walton Rd *TONN* TN10 ..... 132 B7
Wanden La *HDCN* TN27 ..... 157 K4
Wansbury Wy *SWLY* BR8 ..... 58 C1
Wansunt Rd *BXLY* DA5 ..... 26 E6
Warblers CI *STRD* ME2 ..... 2 F3
Ward Av *GRAYS* RM17 ..... 16 D3
Ward CI *ERITH* DA8 ..... 12 F5
  WADH TN5 ..... 188 A8
Warden CI *MAIDW* ME16 ..... 120 E1
Warden Mill CI *WBY/YAL* ME18 ..... 118 F6
Warden Rd *ROCH* ME1 ..... 65 L2
Wardwell La *RSIT* ME9 ..... 69 L3
Ware St *MAID/BEAR* ME14 ..... 104 C8
Warham Rd *RSEV* TN14 ..... 95 K2
Waring CI *ORP* BR6 ..... 73 H1
Waring Dr *ORP* BR6 ..... 73 H1
Waring Rd *SCUP* DA14 ..... 40 E3
Warland Rd *BGR/WK* TN15 ..... 77 H3
Warlingham CI *RHAM* ME8 ..... 68 C4
Warmlake Rd *RMAID* ME17 ..... 138 D4
Warner St *CHAT* ME4 ..... 4 D8
Warnford Gdns
  MAID/SHEP ME15 ..... 121 J5
Warnford Rd *ORP* BR6 ..... 56 B8
Warren Av *ORP* BR6 ..... 56 B8
Warren CI *BXLYHS* DA6 ..... 26 C3
  SIT ME10 ..... 88 D3
Warren Ct *BGR/WK* TN15 ..... 9 J6
Warren Dr *ORP* BR6 ..... 56 D8
Warren Gdns *ORP* BR6 ..... 56 C8
Warren La *CDH/CHF* RM16 ..... 15 M3
  RSIT ME9 ..... 85 L2
Warren Rd *BXLYHS* DA6 ..... 26 C3
  DART DA1 ..... 28 A8
  MEO DA13 ..... 45 K2
  MEO DA13 ..... 63 L2
  ORP BR6 ..... 56 B8
  WALD ME5 ..... 82 F5
The Warrens *HART* DA3 ..... 61 H2
The Warren *GVE* DA12 ..... 46 F1
  RTON TN11 ..... 161 J1
Warren Vw *GVE* DA12 ..... 48 A3
Warren Wood Rd *ROCH* ME1 ..... 65 J3
Warrington Rd *STPH/PW* TN12 ..... 150 B7
Warrior Av *GVE* DA12 ..... 46 E1
Warwick CI *BXLY* DA5 ..... 26 B5
  SIT ME10 ..... 70 E8
Warwick Crs *ROCH* ME1 ..... 65 H3
Warwick Gdns *MEO* DA13 ..... 62 C5
Warwick Pk *RTW* TN1 ..... 10 F8
  RTWE/PEM TN2 ..... 177 K4
Warwick PI *GVW* DA11 ..... 30 D3
  MAIDW ME16 ..... 6 C6
Warwick Rd *RTW* TN1 ..... 10 F7
  SCUP DA14 ..... 40 D2
Washneys Rd *ORP* BR6 ..... 73 J7
Washpond La *WARL* CR6 ..... 90 K4
Wassall La *CRBK* TN17 ..... 202 A6
Watchmans Ter *MAID/BEAR* ME14 ..... 66 E3
Watercress Dr *RSEV* TN14 ..... 95 L6
Watercroft Rd *RSEV* TN14 ..... 74 B4
Waterdales *GVW* DA11 ..... 30 F6
Waterdown Rd *STH/RUST* TN4 ..... 176 F4
Waterfield CI *BELV* DA17 ..... 12 C2
Waterhead CI *ERITH* DA8 ..... 13 C6
Wateringbury CI
  STMC/STPC BR5 ..... 40 D7
Wateringbury Rd
  E/WMAL ME19 ..... 119 H2
Waterlakes *EDEN* TN8 ..... 142 E5
Water La *E/WMAL* ME19 ..... 100 E5
  HAWK TN18 ..... 192 C6
  HAWK TN18 ..... 171 J1
  HDCN TN27 ..... 173 C3
  MAID/BEAR ME14 ..... 105 G8
  MAID/SHEP ME15 ..... 135 M7
  OXTED RH8 ..... 109 J4
  PUR RM19 ..... 14 C3

  RMAID ME17 ..... 140 B2
  RSEV TN14 ..... 75 H6
  SCUP DA14 ..... 26 B8
Waterloo PI *TON* TN9 ..... 147 K5
Waterloo Rd *CRBK* TN17 ..... 183 M8
  GILL ME7 ..... 5 J5
  SIT ME10 ..... 70 F8
  TON TN9 ..... 147 K5
Waterloo St *GVE* DA12 ..... 31 L5
  MAID/SHEP ME15 ..... 7 H7
Waterlow Rd *MAID/BEAR* ME14 ..... 7 H1
  MEO DA13 ..... 79 J6
Waterman's La *STPH/PW* TN12 ..... 166 D2
  GILL ME7 ..... 67 H7
Watermeadow CI *ERITH* DA8 ..... 13 K7
Watermill CI *MAIDW* ME16 ..... 102 D8
  STRD ME2 ..... 3 J1
Water Mill Wy *EYN* DA4 ..... 43 K6
Watermint CI
  STMC/STPC BR5 ..... 40 F8
Waters Edge *MAID/SHEP* ME15 ..... 6 E8
Waterside *DART* DA1 ..... 27 G3
  MAID/BEAR ME14 ..... 6 E3
Waterside La *GILL* ME7 ..... 51 H6
Waterside Ms *WBY/YAL* ME18 ..... 118 F7
Water Slippe *RTON* TN11 ..... 132 F4
Waterson Rd *CDH/CHF* RM16 ..... 17 K3
Waters PI *GILL* ME7 ..... 67 J7
Waterton Av *GVE* DA12 ..... 32 A5
Watery La *BGR/WK* TN15 ..... 96 F6
  SCUP DA14 ..... 40 D3
Watkins CI *STPH/PW* TN12 ..... 154 A8
Watling Av *WALD* ME5 ..... 5 L9
Watling PI *SIT* ME10 ..... 88 C2
Watling St *BXLYHS* DA6 ..... 26 D2
  DART DA1 ..... 28 D5
  GVE DA12 ..... 47 J5
  GVW DA11 ..... 46 D2
  MEO DA13 ..... 30 D8
  STRD ME2 ..... 2 D3
  STRD ME2 ..... 2 D3
  WALD ME5 ..... 5 M9
Watson Av *WALD* ME5 ..... 65 M8
Watson CI *WTHK* RM20 ..... 15 J7
Watson's HI *SIT* ME10 ..... 71 G8
Watt's Av *ROCH* ME1 ..... 3 J9
Watts CI *SNOD* ME6 ..... 81 K5
Watts Crs *PUR* RM19 ..... 14 E3
Watt's Cross Rd *RTON* TN11 ..... 130 D8
Watts' St *CHAT* ME4 ..... 4 B7
Wat Tyler Wy *MAID/SHEP* ME15 ..... 7 J5
Waveney Rd *TONN* TN10 ..... 131 K8
Waverley CI *RMAID* ME17 ..... 136 E3
  WALD ME5 ..... 83 M3
Waverley Dr *RTWE/PEM* TN2 ..... 164 B7
Waverley Gdns *CDH/CHF* RM16 ..... 16 C1
Wayfaring Gn *GRAYS* RM17 ..... 16 B3
Wayfield Rd *WALD* ME5 ..... 66 B6
Waylands *SWLY* BR8 ..... 42 B8
Waylands CI *RSEV* TN14 ..... 94 A1
Wayne CI *ORP* BR6 ..... 56 B6
Wayside *TENT* TN30 ..... 196 D3
Wayside Av *TENT* TN30 ..... 196 D2
Wayside Dr *EDEN* TN8 ..... 142 F2
Wayville Rd *DART* DA1 ..... 28 D5
Weald CI *MAID/SHEP* ME15 ..... 121 L7
  MEO DA13 ..... 46 A4
  RSEV TN14 ..... 129 K3
Weald Ct *RTON* TN11 ..... 130 F7
  SIT ME10 ..... 71 H5
Wealden Av *TENT* TN30 ..... 196 D3
Wealden CI *RTON* TN11 ..... 131 G8
Wealden Wy *DIT/AY* ME20 ..... 102 A5
Weald Rd *SEV* TN13 ..... 113 K6
Weald Vw *STPH/PW* TN12 ..... 166 F4
  WADH TN5 ..... 188 B7
Weald View Rd *TON* TN9 ..... 147 K6
Wealdway *E/WMAL* ME19 ..... 99 J3
  HRTF TN7 ..... 174 C8
  MEO DA13 ..... 46 D5
  RRTW TN3 ..... 161 M7
  STPH/PW TN12 ..... 133 M3
  TON TN9 ..... 148 B2
  WBY/YAL ME18 ..... 116 F3
Weardale Av *RDART* DA2 ..... 28 E7
Weare Rd *STH/RUST* TN4 ..... 163 L5
Weatherly CI *ROCH* ME1 ..... 3 K9
Weavering St *STRD* ME2 ..... 49 K3
Weavering St
  MAID/BEAR ME14 ..... 122 A1
Weavers CI *GVW* DA11 ..... 31 J6
  STPH/PW TN12 ..... 170 B1
Weavers La *RSEV* TN14 ..... 95 L7
The Weavers *HDCN* TN27 ..... 186 C4
  MAIDW ME16 ..... 120 D1
Webb CI *HOO/HM* ME3 ..... 35 M7
Webber CI *ERITH* DA8 ..... 13 K6
Webster Rd *RHAM* ME8 ..... 68 B4
Wedgewood CI
  MAIDW ME16 ..... 102 D8
Wedgewood Dr *WALD* ME5 ..... 82 F3
Wedgwoods *BH/WHM* TN16 ..... 91 L7
Weeds Wood Rd *WALD* ME5 ..... 83 H1
Weeks La *HDCN* TN27 ..... 172 C8
Week St *MAID/BEAR* ME14 ..... 6 F3
Weird Wd *HART* DA3 ..... 45 L7
Weir Rd *BXLY* DA5 ..... 26 D5
Welbeck Av *STH/RUST* TN4 ..... 163 L5
Weld CI *STPH/PW* TN12 ..... 170 B1
Welland Rd *TONN* TN10 ..... 147 K1
Well CI *RTON* TN11 ..... 146 B4
Wellcome Av *DART* DA1 ..... 28 A2
Weller Av *ROCH* ME1 ..... 65 M3
Weller Rd *STH/RUST* TN4 ..... 176 E1
Wellers CI *BH/WHM* TN16 ..... 110 E4
Well Fld *HART* DA3 ..... 45 H8
Well HI *ORP* BR6 ..... 57 K8
Well Hill La *ORP* BR6 ..... 74 D2
Wellington Cottages
  HAWK TN18 ..... 199 G1
Wellingtonia Wy *EDEN* TN8 ..... 142 E3
Wellington PI *MAID/BEAR* ME14 ..... 6 F7
Wellington Rd *BELV* DA17 ..... 12 B4
  DART DA1 ..... 27 L4
  GILL ME7 ..... 5 K6
  SIT ME10 ..... 70 D8
  STMC/STPC BR5 ..... 56 D2
  TIL RM18 ..... 31 J1
Wellington St *GVE* DA12 ..... 31 L5
Wellington Wy *E/WMAL* ME19 ..... 118 B2

Wellmeade Dr SEV TN13 ..... 113 K5
Well Penn Rd HOO/HM ME3 ..... 34 D1
Well Rd MAID/BEAR ME14 ..... 7 G2
  RSEV TN14 ..... 95 L3
Wells CI RTW TN1 ..... 10 E5
  TENT TN30 ..... 196 C5
  TON TN9 ..... 147 M1
Wells Rd STRD ME2 ..... 48 F8
Well St E/WMAL ME19 ..... 101 G7
  MAID/SHEP ME15 ..... 137 C1
Well Winch Rd SIT ME10 ..... 70 F8
Welton CI TON TN9 ..... 147 H6
Wemmick CI ROCH ME1 ..... 65 M6 [8]
Wendover CI STRD ME2 ..... 64 D8 [2]
Wendover Wy ORP BR6 ..... 56 C2 [2]
Wents Wd MAID/BEAR ME14 ..... 104 B8
Wentworth CI GVW DA11 ..... 46 C2 [2]
  ORP BR6 ..... 56 A8 [2]
Wentworth Dr DART DA1 ..... 27 J5
  HOO/HM ME3 ..... 34 D5
  RHAM ME8 ..... 68 A6 [2]
  SIT ME10 ..... 70 E8 [2]
Wentworth PI CDH/CHF RM16 .. 16 F2 [2]
Wenvoe Av BXLYHN DA7 ..... 12 D8
Wesley CI MAIDW ME16 ..... 120 B2
  STMC/STPC BR5 ..... 40 E7
Wessex Dr ERITH DA8 ..... 13 G8
Westbourne St SIT ME10 ..... 71 G8
Westbrook Dr STMC/STPC BR5 .. 56 F4
Westbrooke CI CHAT ME4 ..... 66 C3 [3]
Westbury Ter BH/WHM TN16 .. 110 E4
Westcott Av GVW DA11 ..... 31 J8
Westcourt St CHAT ME4 ..... 4 D1
West Crescent Rd GVE DA12 ... 31 K4
West Cross TENT TN30 ..... 196 B6
West Cross Gdns TENT TN30 .. 196 B6
West Dr RMAID ME17 ..... 139 K6
  WALD ME5 ..... 65 M8
Wested La SWLY BR8 ..... 58 C3
West End BGR/WK TN15 ..... 96 B3
  BH/WHM TN16 ..... 111 K3
Westergate Rd ABYW SE2 ..... 12 A5
  STRD ME2 ..... 49 H4
Westerham CI RHAM ME8 ..... 67 K1
Western Av HAWK TN18 ..... 199 H3
Westerham HI BH/WHM TN16 .. 92 D8
Westerham Rd BH/WHM TN16 .. 111 J3
  OXTED RH8 ..... 109 J7
  RSEV TN14 ..... 112 C1
  SIT ME10 ..... 87 L2
Westerhill Rd RMAID ME17 .. 136 E4
Western Av HAWK TN18 ..... 199 H3
Western Cross CI GRH DA9 ..... 29 L4
Western Rd BGR/WK TN15 ..... 98 B6
  HAWK TN18 ..... 199 H3
  MAIDW ME16 ..... 120 E2
  RTW TN1 ..... 11 J4
  STH/RUST TN4 ..... 163 H4
  WADH TN5 ..... 188 B7
Westfield SEV TN13 ..... 95 L8
Westfield CI GVE DA12 ..... 46 E3
Westfield Rd BXLYHN DA7 ..... 26 E1
Westfield Sole Rd
  MAID/BEAR ME14 ..... 83 M5
Westfield Ter CRBK TN17 ..... 192 B4
Westgate Rd DART DA1 ..... 27 M4
West Gn SIT ME10 ..... 71 H4
Westharold SWLY BR8 ..... 41 M7 [7]
West Heath CI DART DA1 ..... 27 H4 [1]
West Heath La SEV TN13 ..... 113 K6
West Heath Rd DART DA1 ..... 27 H4
West HI DART DA1 ..... 27 M4
  ORP BR6 ..... 72 B6
  OXTED RH8 ..... 108 F8
West Hill Bank OXTED RH8 .. 108 F8
Westhill CI GVE DA12 ..... 31 K6
West Hill Dr DART DA1 ..... 27 L4
West Hill Ri DART DA1 ..... 27 M4
West Holme ERITH DA8 ..... 12 E7
Westholme ORP BR6 ..... 56 A3
West Kent Av GVW DA11 ..... 30 E4
Westlands Av SIT ME10 ..... 87 K1
Westlands Wy OXTED RH8 ..... 108 F5
West La HOO/HM ME3 ..... 25 J7
  SIT ME10 ..... 88 C1
Westmarsh CI
  MAID/SHEP ME15 ..... 122 B6
Westmead DIT/AY ME20 ..... 101 L1 [1]
West Mill DIT/AY ME20 ..... 101 L1
Westmoreland Dr RSIT ME9 ..... 69 K2
Westmore Rd BH/WHM TN16 .. 91 L7
Westmorland CI
  MAID/SHEP ME15 ..... 122 A6
Westmorland Gn
  MAID/SHEP ME15 ..... 122 A6
Westmorland Rd
  MAID/SHEP ME15 ..... 122 A6
West Motney Wy RHAM ME8 .. 68 B2
Westmount Av CHAT ME4 ..... 4 C6
Weston Av WTHK RM20 ..... 15 H3
Weston Rd STRD ME2 ..... 2 E3
West Park Av STH/RUST TN4 .. 163 J4
West Park Rd
  MAID/SHEP ME15 ..... 7 K8 [1]
Westree Rd MAIDW ME16 ..... 6 D6
West Rdg SIT ME10 ..... 87 M3
Westrise TON TN9 ..... 147 J6
West Rd CRBK TN17 ..... 182 A5
  GILL ME7 ..... 50 C6
West Shaw HART DA3 ..... 44 F6
West St BGR/WK TN15 ..... 98 B2
  BXLYHN DA7 ..... 26 B2
  E/WMAL ME19 ..... 100 D5
  ERITH DA8 ..... 12 F3
  GILL ME7 ..... 5 L2
  GRAYS RM17 ..... 16 C5
  GVW DA11 ..... 31 J4
  MAID/SHEP ME15 ..... 136 A5
  RMAID ME17 ..... 124 E7
  SIT ME10 ..... 88 A1
West Thurrock Wy WTHK RM20.. 15 J3
West View Rd DART DA1 ..... 28 B4
  SWLY BR8 ..... 57 M2 [2]
Westway WK MAIDW ME16 ..... 120 D2
Westways BH/WHM TN16 ..... 110 E4
  EDEN TN8 ..... 142 E3
  RTWE/PEM TN2 ..... 164 F6
Westwell CI STMC/STPC BR5 .. 56 F4
Westwell Ct TENT TN30 ..... 196 B6

Westwood Rd
  MAID/SHEP ME15 ..... 121 J6
  MEO DA13 ..... 45 G2
West Wood Rd RSIT ME9 ..... 85 K6
Westwood Wy STH/RUST TN4.. 162 D8 [2]
  STPH/PW TN12 ..... 134 A7
West Woodside BXLY DA5 ..... 26 A6 [2]
Westwood Wy SEV TN13 ..... 8 D1
Wetheral Dr MAID ME5 ..... 83 K1
Weybridge CI WALD ME5 ..... 83 L1
Wey CI WALD ME5 ..... 66 E8
Weyhill CI MAID/BEAR ME14 .. 103 L7 [1]
Wharfedale Rd RDART DA2 ... 28 E6 [3]
Wharf La HOO/HM ME3 ..... 20 D7
Wharf Rd GILL ME7 ..... 50 E6 [2]
  GRAYS RM17 ..... 16 B5
  GVE DA12 ..... 32 A4
  MAID/SHEP ME15 ..... 6 C8
Whatman CI
  MAID/BEAR ME14 ..... 103 L7 [2]
Wheatcroft CI SIT ME10 ..... 88 D1
Wheatcroft Gv RHAM ME8 ..... 68 B6
Wheatear Wy WALD ME5 ..... 66 D6 [2]
Wheatfield E/WMAL ME19 ..... 101 G4
Wheatfield CI CRBK TN17 ..... 183 L5
Wheatfield Dr CRBK TN17 ..... 183 L8
Wheatfield Lea CRBK TN17 ... 183 L8
Wheatfields
  MAID/BEAR ME14 ..... 121 M1 [2]
  WALD ME5 ..... 83 M3
Wheatley Wy CRBK TN17 ..... 183 L8
Wheatley CI GRH DA9 ..... 29 J3 [3]
Wheatley Terrace Rd ERITH DA8.. 13 H5
Wheatsheaf CI
  MAID/SHEP ME15 ..... 121 K5
Wheatsheaf HI RSEV TN14 ..... 74 B3 [4]
  RSEV TN14 ..... 128 B1
Wheatsheaf Wy TONN TN10.. 131 M7
Wheeler Av OXTED RH8 ..... 108 F7
Wheeler's La RMAID ME17 ... 136 F5
The Wheelers RHAM ME8 ..... 67 K7
Wheeler St HDCN TN27 ..... 155 M8
  MAID/BEAR ME14 ..... 7 H3
Whenman Av BXLY DA5 ..... 26 E7
Whetsted Rd STPH/PW TN12 .. 149 L5
Whiffen's Av CHAT ME4 ..... 4 D4
Whiffen's Avenue W CHAT ME4.. 4 D4 [4]
Whimbrel CI SIT ME10 ..... 71 H5
Whimbrel Gn DIT/AY ME20 .. 101 H4
The Whimbrels CHAT ME4 ..... 50 D4 [2]
Whinfell Wy GVE DA12 ..... 31 K8
Whippendell CI STMC/STPC BR5 .. 40 D5
Whippendell Wy
  STMC/STPC BR5 ..... 40 D5
Whistler Rd TONN TN10 ..... 131 M6
Whitby CI BH/WHM TN16 ..... 91 K5
  GRH DA9 ..... 29 J3
Whitchurch CI MAIDW ME16.... 6 C4
Whitcombe CI WALD ME5 ..... 83 L1
White Av GVW DA11 ..... 31 H8
Whitebeam Dr RMAID ME17 .. 136 D2
White Bear Pas
  STH/RUST TN4 ..... 10 F7 [3]
Whitebine Gdns
  STPH/PW TN12 ..... 134 C7
Whitebread La RYE TN31 ..... 206 F5
White Cottage Rd TONN TN10.. 131 L7
Whitecroft SWLY BR8 ..... 42 A6 [2]
Whitefield CI STMC/STPC BR5 .. 40 E7 [2]
Whitefield Rd STH/RUST TN4 .. 10 E1
White Friars SEV TN13 ..... 113 J5
Whitegate CI RHAM ME8 ..... 163 H5
Whitegates Av BGR/WK TN15 .. 77 G1 [2]
Whitehall Dr RMAID ME17 ... 139 M2
Whitehall La ERITH DA8 ..... 13 H8
  GRAYS RM17 ..... 16 E5
  MAID/BEAR ME14 ..... 105 J7
  SIT ME10 ..... 88 A3
White Hart CI SEV TN13 ..... 113 L6
White Hart Rd ORP BR6 ..... 56 C3
White Hart Wd SEV TN13 ..... 113 L7
Whitehead Ct RDART DA2 ..... 27 L8
Whiteheads La
  MAID/BEAR ME14 ..... 122 D1
Whitehill BGR/WK TN15 ..... 98 D2
Whitehill La GVE DA12 ..... 31 M8
Whitehill Pde GVE DA12 ..... 31 L8
Whitehill Rd DART DA1 ..... 27 J3
  GVE DA12 ..... 31 L7
  HART DA3 ..... 44 F6
White Hill Rd MAID/BEAR ME14.. 84 F4
Whitehill Rd MEO DA13 ..... 44 F4
  MEO DA13 ..... 62 D6
Whitehorse HI WALD ME5 ..... 5 H8
White Horse La
  MAID/SHEP ME15 ..... 122 C6
White Horse Rd MEO DA13.... 79 M4
Whitehouse CI HOO/HM ME3.. 51 G1 [1]
White House Crs ROCH ME1 .. 82 C5
White House Rd RSEV TN14 .. 113 H8
Whitelake Rd TONN TN10 ..... 131 L8
White La BH/WHM TN16 ..... 109 K1
Whiteleaves Ri STRD ME2 ..... 64 D3
White Lodge CI SEV TN13 ..... 9 H3
White Oak CI TON TN9 ..... 147 K6 [2]
White Post HI EYN TN4 ..... 59 J3
White Post La MEO DA13 ..... 46 D8
Whitepost La MEO DA13 ..... 79 H3
White Rd CHAT ME4 ..... 66 C4
White Rock Ct MAIDW ME16.... 6 D6
White Rock PI MAIDW ME16.... 6 D6
Whites CI GRH DA9 ..... 29 L4
White's La HAWK TN18 ..... 199 K3
Whitewall Rd STRD ME2 ..... 3 M3
Whitewall Wy STRD ME2 ..... 3 M3
Whitewebbs Wy
  STMC/STPC BR5 ..... 40 B5
Whitewood Cottages
  BH/WHM TN16 ..... 91 L6
Whitfield Rd BXLYHN DA7 ..... 12 B6
Whitmore St MAIDW ME16 ... 120 E3
Whitney Wk SCUP DA14 ..... 41 G3
Whittaker St CHAT ME4 ..... 4 E6
Whybourne Crest
  RTWE/PEM TN2 ..... 11 K9
Whyman Av CHAT ME4 ..... 66 C4
Wichling CI STMC/STPC BR5 ... 56 F4 [1]
Wickenden Rd SEV TN13 ..... 9 K1
Wickham CI RSIT ME9 ..... 69 K7

Wickham Gdns STH/RUST TN4 .. 162 F8
Wickham Rd CDH/CHF RM16 .. 17 L1
Wickham St ROCH ME1 ..... 65 M2
Wickhams Wy HART DA3 ..... 61 H1 [1]
Wickhurst Rd RSEV TN14 ..... 129 H2
Wicksteed CI BXLY DA5 ..... 26 F8
Widbury CI RRTW TN3 ..... 176 B2 [2]
Widgeon Rd ERITH DA8 ..... 13 K6
  STRD ME2 ..... 48 F7
Wierton HI RMAID ME17 ..... 137 M6
Wierton La RMAID ME17 ..... 138 A3
Wierton Rd RMAID ME17 ..... 138 A4
Wigmore Rd RHAM ME8 ..... 67 K8
Wihtred Rd RSIT ME9 ..... 88 F3
Wilberforce Rd RMAID ME17 .. 136 F2
Wilberforce Wy GVE DA12 ... 46 F2
Wilde CI TIL RM18 ..... 17 K8
Wilderness Gdns RYE TN31.... 206 C6
Wilderness Rd OXTED RH8 ... 109 G8
Wilde Rd ERITH DA8 ..... 12 D6
Wildfell CI MAID/BEAR ME14.... 83 L5
Wildland CI RHAM ME8 ..... 84 F7
Wildwood Rd RMAID ME17 ... 140 A3
Wildwood Gld GILL ME7 ..... 67 J8
Wilfred St GVE DA12 ..... 31 K4 [16]
Wilks Av DART DA1 ..... 28 B7
Wilks CI RHAM ME8 ..... 68 D3
Will Adams Wy GILL ME7 ..... 67 H4
  RHAM ME8 ..... 67 H2
Willesley Gdns CRBK TN17 ... 183 M7 [2]
Willett CI STMC/STPC BR5 ..... 56 A2
Willetts La RRTW TN3 ..... 174 E1
William Judge CI TENT TN30.. 196 F6
William Luck CI
  STPH/PW TN12 ..... 134 A7 [2]
William Rd STRD ME2 ..... 64 E3 [7]
  GVE DA12 ..... 31 K5
  RHAM ME8 ..... 68 C3
  SIT ME10 ..... 88 A2
  STH/RUST TN4 ..... 10 E1
Willington Gn
  MAID/SHEP ME15 ..... 122 A6
Willington St MAID/SHEP ME15.. 122 A6
Willis Rd ERITH DA8 ..... 12 E3
Willow Av HOO/HM ME3 ..... 51 G2 [16]
  SWLY BR8 ..... 42 B8
Willowbank Dr HOO/HM ME3 .. 36 A1
Willowby Gdns RHAM ME8 ... 85 G1
Willow CI BXLY DA5 ..... 26 B4
  STMC/STPC BR5 ..... 56 D2
Willow Crs STPH/PW TN12 ... 149 J6
  STPH/PW TN12 ..... 154 B8
Willow La STPH/PW TN12 ..... 151 G5
Willow Lea TONN TN10 ..... 131 L6
Willowmead DIT/AY ME20.... 101 C3
Willow Pk RSEV TN14 ..... 95 H3
Willow Ri MAID/SHEP ME15 .. 122 B4
Willow Rd DART DA1 ..... 27 L6
  DIT/AY ME20 ..... 101 H2
  ERITH DA8 ..... 13 J7
  STRD ME2 ..... 2 B6
Willowside SNOD ME6 ..... 81 J4
The Willows GRAYS RM17 ..... 16 F5
  RHAM ME8 ..... 68 A3
  RSIT ME9 ..... 69 K7
  SIT ME10 ..... 71 H4 [2]
Willow Tree Rd
  RTWE/PEM TN2 ..... 10 B9
Willow Wk MEO DA13 ..... 79 H2
  RTWE/PEM TN2 ..... 164 A5
Willow Wy MAID/SHEP ME15 ... 7 K7
Willow Wents WBY/YAL ME18 .. 117 L4
Wilman Rd STH/RUST TN4..... 163 H5
Wilmar Wy BGR/WK TN15 ..... 96 B6
Wilmington Av ORP BR6 ..... 56 E5
Wilmington Court Rd
  RDART DA2 ..... 27 J8
Wilmington Wy RHAM ME8 ... 67 K3
Wilmot Rd DART DA1 ..... 27 K3
Wilson Av ROCH ME1 ..... 65 M4
Wilson CI MAID/SHEP ME15 .. 122 A6
  RTON TN11 ..... 131 G8
Wilson La EYN DA4 ..... 44 B6
Wilson Rd TONN TN10 ..... 132 A8
Wilsons La MAID/SHEP ME15 .. 136 C1
Wilsons Wy MEO DA13 ..... 79 H2
Wilton Dr DIT/AY ME20 ..... 101 K5
Wiltshire CI RDART DA2 ..... 28 F5
  WALD ME5 ..... 66 E5
Wiltshire Rd ORP BR6 ..... 56 C3
Wiltshire Wy
  MAID/SHEP ME15 ..... 122 A6 [1]
  RTWE/PEM TN2 ..... 163 M6
Wimborne Av STMC/STPC BR5.. 40 B7
Wimbourne Dr RHAM ME8 ... 67 M7
Winch CI CRBK TN17 ..... 192 F2
Winchelsea Av BXLYHN DA7 .. 12 B6
Winchelsea Rd WALD ME5 ..... 66 D8
Winchester Av MAID ME5 ..... 83 H1
Winchester Crs GVE DA12 ..... 31 M8
Winchester Gv SEV TN13 ..... 9 G3
Winchester Gv HAWK TN18.. 199 J3
  ORP BR6 ..... 56 E7
  TONN TN10 ..... 147 M1
Winchester Wy RHAM ME8 ... 67 K8
Winch's Garth STPH/PW TN12 .. 154 B8 [1]
Wincliff Rd TON TN9 ..... 147 K5
Windermere CI DART DA1 ..... 27 K6
Windermere Dr RHAM ME8 ... 67 M6
Windermere Gv SIT ME10 ..... 87 M2
Windermere Rd BXLYHN DA7 .. 12 E8
Windhover Wy GVE DA12 ..... 47 G1
Windmill CI STRD ME2 ..... 64 K4
Windmill La East
  E/WMAL ME19 ..... 100 D7
Windmill La West
  E/WMAL ME19 ..... 100 C7
Windmill Pk BGR/WK TN15 ... 98 F6
Windmill Rd GILL ME7 ..... 5 J7
  SEV TN13 ..... 113 K8

  SIT ME10 ..... 70 F7
  RTWE/PEM TN2 ..... 11 K6
  STRD ME2 ..... 49 K4
Windsor Av CDH/CHF RM16 .. 16 D1
  CHAT ME4 ..... 4 D9 [1]
Windsor Dr DART DA1 ..... 27 J4
  ORP BR6 ..... 73 J1
  SIT ME10 ..... 87 M3
Windsor Rd BXLYHS DA6 ..... 26 A2
  GILL ME7 ..... 5 M3
  GVE DA12 ..... 46 D1
Windward Rd ROCH ME1 ..... 65 L4
Windyridge GILL ME7 ..... 67 G4
Winfield La BGR/WK TN15 ..... 116 A3
Winford Ms ROCH ME1 ..... 65 J3
Wingate Rd SCUP DA14 ..... 40 E2
Wingfield GRAYS RM17 ..... 16 B4
Wingfield Rd GVW DA11 ..... 31 K5
Wingham CI MAID/SHEP ME15.. 122 B6
  RHAM ME8 ..... 67 L2
Wingrove Dr MAID/BEAR ME14.. 104 B3
  STRD ME2 ..... 3 K3
Winifred Rd DART DA1 ..... 27 K3
  ERITH DA8 ..... 13 G4
  MAID/SHEP ME15 ..... 122 B2
Winnipeg Dr ORP BR6 ..... 73 H1
Winser Rd CRBK TN17 ..... 202 C4
Winston CI GRH DA9 ..... 29 H4
Winston Dr STRD ME2 ..... 49 M5
Winstone Scott Av
  RRTW TN3 ..... 176 A1 [1]
Winston Rd STRD ME2 ..... 48 F8
Winterfield La E/WMAL ME19.. 101 G5
Wireless Rd BH/WHM TN16 ... 91 M1
The Wirrals WALD ME5 ..... 83 J1
Wiseacre RRTW TN3 ..... 189 J7
Wise's La BGR/WK TN15 ..... 78 A4 [1]
  RSIT ME9 ..... 87 J2
Wisley Rd STMC/STPC BR5 ... 40 C4
Wisteria Gdns SWLY BR8 ..... 41 M6
Witches La SEV TN13 ..... 112 F1
Witham Wy STRD ME2 ..... 2 D4
Withens CI STMC/STPC BR5 ... 40 E8 [7]
Withyham Rd RRTW TN3 ..... 175 J7
Wittersham CI RHAM ME8 ..... 66 D8
Wittersham Rd CRBK TN17 ... 207 M1
  RYE TN31 ..... 209 K8
  TENT TN30 ..... 209 K2
Wivenhoe CI RHAM ME8 ..... 68 C3
Wodehouse CI DIT/AY ME20 .. 101 H1 [1]
Wodehouse Rd DART DA1 ..... 28 C2
Wokindon Rd CDH/CHF RM16.. 17 K2
The Wold CR3 ..... 90 C8
Wolfe Rd MAIDW ME16 ..... 120 D3
Wolf's Rd OXTED RH8 ..... 108 A4
Wollaston CI RHAM ME8 ..... 84 F2
Wolseley Rd STH/RUST TN4 .. 163 L6
Wolsey Ms ORP BR6 ..... 56 B8
Wolsley CI DART DA1 ..... 27 J3
Wombwell Gdns GVW DA11 .. 30 F7
Wood Av PUR RM19 ..... 14 E3
Woodberry Dr SIT ME10 ..... 88 D2
Woodberry Gv BXLY DA5 ..... 26 F8
Woodbridge Dr
  MAID/SHEP ME15 ..... 121 G4
Woodbury CI BH/WHM TN16 .. 92 B4
Woodbury La TENT TN30 ..... 196 C6
Woodbury Park Gdns
  STH/RUST TN4 ..... 11 G1
Woodbury Park Rd
  STH/RUST TN4 ..... 10 F2
Woodbury Rd HAWK TN18 ... 199 J2
  WALD ME5 ..... 83 G4
Woodchurch CI WALD ME5 ... 66 D8 [8]
Woodchurch Crs RHAM ME8 .. 67 L3
Woodchurch Rd TENT TN30 .. 196 L5
Wood CI BXLY DA5 ..... 27 G8
  DIT/AY ME20 ..... 102 A5
Woodcock La CRBK TN17 ..... 200 F2
Woodcocks HDCN TN27 ..... 155 M8 [8]
Woodcourt CI SIT ME10 ..... 88 A3
Woodcut MAID/BEAR ME14 .. 103 J5
Woodcutters Av
  CDH/CHF RM16 ..... 16 E1 [1]
Wood Dr SEV TN13 ..... 8 D8
Wood End SWLY BR8 ..... 41 L8 [8]
Woodfall Dr DART DA1 ..... 27 H2
Woodfield Av GVW DA11 ..... 31 K7
  RTON TN11 ..... 131 G8
Woodfield Rd TON TN9 ..... 147 K5
Woodfields SEV TN13 ..... 112 F1
Woodfield Wy HOO/HM ME3 .. 49 M1
Woodford Rd MAIDW ME16 .. 120 D3
Woodgate La RSIT ME9 ..... 88 E4
Woodgate Rd E/WMAL ME19 .. 99 M1
Woodgate Wy TON TN9 ..... 147 M6
Woodgers Gv SWLY BR8 ..... 42 B6 [1]
Woodhead Dr ORP BR6 ..... 56 A6
Woodhill Pk RTWE/PEM TN2 .. 164 E7
Woodhurst WALD ME5 ..... 82 F1
Woodhurst CI STRD ME2 ..... 64 D3
Woodhurst Pk OXTED RH8 ... 109 G8
Woodland Av HART DA3 ..... 61 H1
Woodland CI E/WMAL ME19 .. 100 C5
  HART DA3 ..... 45 L7
  STH/RUST TN4 ..... 163 K6
Woodland Ct OXTED RH8 ..... 108 F6
Woodland Dr EDEN TN8 ..... 142 F2
Woodland Ri BGR/WK TN15 .. 96 B8
  OXTED RH8 ..... 109 G8
Woodland Rd STH/RUST TN4 .. 163 L6
Woodlands RMAID ME17 ..... 136 D2
  RTWE/PEM TN2 ..... 165 H6
  STPH/PW TN12 ..... 150 B6
  WALD ME5 ..... 83 J3
Woodlands Av SNOD ME6 ..... 81 H5 [2]
Woodlands CI CDH/CHF RM16 .. 17 H2
  MAID/BEAR ME14 ..... 103 K6 [1]
  SWLY BR8 ..... 42 B6 [2]
  WBY/YAL ME18 ..... 119 J5
Woodlands La GVE DA12 ..... 47 M4
Woodlands Pk BXLY DA5 ..... 41 L1
Woodlands Ri SWLY BR8 ..... 42 B6 [2]
Woodlands Rd BXLYHN DA7 .. 26 A1
  DIT/AY ME20 ..... 101 L4
  GILL ME7 ..... 67 H3

  ORP BR6 ..... 73 J1
  SIT ME10 ..... 88 D2 [2]
  TON TN9 ..... 147 J7
The Woodlands ORP BR6 ..... 73 K1
Woodland Vw TENT TN30 ..... 209 G1
Woodland Wy GRH DA9 ..... 29 J3
  MAID/BEAR ME14 ..... 103 K6
  STH/RUST TN4 ..... 162 F2
Wood La CRBK TN17 ..... 194 E2
  RDART DA2 ..... 29 H8
Woodlark Rd CHAT ME4 ..... 50 C4
Woodlea DIT/AY ME20 ..... 101 G3
  HART DA3 ..... 45 L7
Woodleas MAIDW ME16 ..... 120 B3
Woodley Rd ORP BR6 ..... 56 E5
Woodmount SWLY BR8 ..... 57 M3
Woodpecker Gld RHAM ME8 .. 67 L7
Woodpecker Rd DIT/AY ME20 .. 101 H4
Wood Rd BH/WHM TN16 ..... 91 L4
Woodruff CI RHAM ME8 ..... 68 F1
Woodrush PI CHAT ME4 ..... 50 C4
Woodsgate Wy
  RTWE/PEM TN2 ..... 164 D7 [2]
Woodside MEO DA13 ..... 79 H5
  ORP BR6 ..... 56 C8
  RHAM ME8 ..... 67 K7
Woodside CI BXLYHN DA7 ..... 26 F2
  RTWE/PEM TN2 ..... 165 G7
Woodside Dr RDART DA2 ..... 42 A1
Woodside Gdns SIT ME10 ..... 87 M3
Woodside Rd BXLYHN DA7 ... 26 F2
  MAID/SHEP ME15 ..... 121 L6
  RSEV TN14 ..... 111 M2
  RTWE/PEM TN2 ..... 165 G7
  SEV TN13 ..... 9 H3
  STH/RUST TN4 ..... 176 F1
  TON TN9 ..... 147 K6
Woodstock CI BXLY DA5 ..... 26 B6
Woodstock Rd SIT ME10 ..... 88 A4
  STRD ME2 ..... 2 D4
Wood St GILL ME7 ..... 4 F1
  GRAYS RM17 ..... 16 E5
  RSIT ME9 ..... 89 H5
  RTW TN1 ..... 11 H3
  STRD ME2 ..... 64 D3
  SWLY BR8 ..... 42 E5
Wood Vw GRAYS RM17 ..... 17 G3
Wood View CI STH/RUST TN4.. 77 G2 [2]
Woodview Ri STRD ME2 ..... 49 H4
Woodview Rd SWLY BR8 ..... 41 L6
Woodville PI GVE DA12 ..... 31 H6
Woodville Rd MAID/SHEP ME15.. 7 H8
Woodward CI GRAYS RM17 .. 16 D3
Woodward Hts GRAYS RM17 .. 16 D3
Woodward Ter GRH DA9 ..... 29 G4
Woolaston CI
  MAID/SHEP ME15 ..... 121 H4 [2]
Wooldeys Rd RHAM ME8 ..... 68 B3
Woolett Rd SIT ME10 ..... 70 D8
Woollett CI DART DA1 ..... 27 J2
Woollett St MAID/BEAR ME14 .. 7 G3
Woolley CI STH/RUST TN4 ... 163 H4 [2]
Woolley Rd MAID/SHEP ME15 .. 122 B5
  STH/RUST TN4 ..... 163 H4
Woolwich CI WALD ME5 ..... 66 C6
Woolwich Rd ABYW SE2 ..... 12 A5
  BELV DA17 ..... 12 B4 [4]
  BXLYHN DA7 ..... 26 C1
Wopsle CI ROCH ME1 ..... 65 M6
Worcester Av E/WMAL ME19 .. 118 C3
Worcester CI GRH DA9 ..... 29 K3
  MEO DA13 ..... 46 B4
  STRD ME2 ..... 2 B1
Worcester Dr SIT ME10 ..... 70 F7
Worcester Rd
  MAID/SHEP ME15 ..... 121 M6
Wordsworth CI TIL RM18 ..... 17 L8 [3]
  WALD ME5 ..... 66 E6
Wordsworth Rd
  MAID/BEAR ME14 ..... 103 K6
Wordsworth Wy DART DA1 ... 28 C2
  DIT/AY ME20 ..... 101 J1
Workhouse La
  MAID/SHEP ME15 ..... 136 E1
Workhouse Rd E/WMAL ME19.. 80 A8
  RMAID ME17 ..... 139 J5
Worlds End La ORP BR6 ..... 73 J2
Wormdale HI RSIT ME9 ..... 86 D2
Wormdale Rd RSIT ME9 ..... 86 C1
Worships HI SEV TN13 ..... 8 A2
Worth CI ORP BR6 ..... 56 A7
Wotton CI MAID/SHEP ME15 .. 122 A8 [2]
Wotton Gn STMC/STPC BR5 .. 40 F8
Wouldham Rd ROCH ME1 ..... 64 E7
  WTHK RM20 ..... 16 A5
Wrangleden CI
  MAID/SHEP ME15 ..... 122 A8 [2]
Wrangleden Rd
  MAID/SHEP ME15 ..... 121 M8
Wrangling La MEO DA13 ..... 63 J8
Wren CI DIT/AY ME20 ..... 101 H4
  STMC/STPC BR5 ..... 40 F7
Wrens Ct RSIT ME9 ..... 87 J5
Wrens Rd RSIT ME9 ..... 87 H7
Wren Wk TIL RM18 ..... 17 K6
Wren Wy WALD ME5 ..... 66 D7 [2]
Wright CI RHAM ME8 ..... 67 L3
Wrights CI TENT TN30 ..... 196 C5 [2]
Wrotham Hill Rd BGR/WK TN15.. 78 B7
Wrotham Rd BGR/WK TN15 ... 98 B6
  GVW DA11 ..... 31 J8
  MEO DA13 ..... 46 B6
Wrotham Water La
  E/WMAL ME19 ..... 98 F1
Wrotham Water Rd
  E/WMAL ME19 ..... 98 F1
Wulfred Wy BGR/WK TN15 ... 96 D4
Wyatt CI BGR/WK TN15 ..... 96 B6
Wyatt PI STRD ME2 ..... 2 E4
Wyatt Rd DART DA1 ..... 27 H1
Wyatt St MAID/BEAR ME14 .... 7 H4
Wybourne Ri RTWE/PEM TN2.. 177 K4
Wybournes La HOO/HM ME3 .. 35 L2
Wycliffe Rw GVW DA11 ..... 31 H6
Wye CI ORP BR6 ..... 56 B3
Wye Rd BGR/WK TN15 ..... 98 C5
  GVE DA12 ..... 31 M7
  TONN TN10 ..... 131 L8

Wykeham Cl *GVE* DA12 .... 47 C3
QBOR ME11 .... 55 H2 🔢
Wykeham Gv *RMAID* ME17 ... 123 J6
Wykeham Rd *SIT* ME10 .... 88 D1
Wykeham St *STRD* ME2 .... 3 G2
Wyke Manor Rd
  MAID/BEAR ME14 .... 7 G4
Wyles Rd *CHAT* ME4 .... 66 A3
Wyles St *GILL* ME7 .... 5 J1
Wylie Rd *HOO/HM* ME3 .... 36 A7
Wyndham Av *RTON* TN11 ... 146 B4
Wyndham Cl *RTON* TN11 ... 146 B4
Wyndham Rd *CHAT* ME4 .... 66 A3
Wynford Gv *STMC/STPC* BR5 ... 40 D7
Wynford Pl *BELV* DA17 .... 12 C5 🔢
The Wytchlings *RMAID* ME17 ... 139 M3

Wytherling Cl
  MAID/BEAR ME14 .... 104 B8 🔢
Wyvern Cl *DART* DA1 .... 27 L5
  ORP BR6 .... 56 D6
  SNOD ME6 .... 81 J6
Wyvill Cl *RHAM* ME8 .... 68 A8

Yarnton Wy *ERITHM* DA18 .... 12 B2
Yarrow Ct *MAID/BEAR* ME14 ... 104 B8 🔢
Yarrow Rd *WALD* ME5 .... 83 G1
Yaugher La *RSIT* ME9 .... 85 K2
Yeates Dr *SIT* ME10 .... 71 J5
Yelsted La *MAID/BEAR* ME14 ... 83 M6
  RSIT ME9 .... 85 J4
Yelsted Rd *RSIT* ME9 .... 85 J6
Yeoman Dr *GILL* ME7 .... 67 H4
Yeoman Gdns *STPH/PW* TN12 ... 150 A7
Yeoman La *MAID/BEAR* ME14.... 122 D2
Yeoman's Mdw *SEV* TN13 .... 8 E8
Yeoman Wy *MAID/SHEP* ME15 ... 122 D3
Yeovil Cl *ORP* BR6 .... 56 A5
Yew Rd *HOO/HM* ME3 .... 51 G2 🔢
The Yews *GVE* DA12 .... 31 M7
Yew Tree Cl *DIT/AY* ME20 .... 102 A4

HART DA3 .... 45 M7
SEV TN13 .... 112 F1
WALD ME5 .... 83 M4
Yew Tree Green Rd
  STPH/PW TN12 .... 167 J4
Yew Tree Rd *STH/RUST* TN4 ... 163 J5
Yopps Gn *BGR/WK* TN15 ... 116 A4
York Av *GILL* ME7 .... 5 H5
  WALD ME5 .... 83 G2
York Hl *WALD* ME5 .... 5 J9
York Pde *TONN* TN10 .... 131 L7
York Pl *GRAYS* RM17 .... 16 C5 🔢
York Ri *ORP* BR6 .... 56 A4
York Rd *BH/WHM* TN16 .... 91 K5
  DART DA1 .... 28 B5
  GVE DA12 .... 31 L8
  GVW DA11 .... 30 F5

MAID/SHEP ME15 .... 7 K9
ROCH ME1 .... 65 L2
RTW TN1 .... 10 E4
TONN TN10 .... 131 M8
York Ter *ERITH* DA8 .... 12 E7
Ypres Dr *SIT* ME10 .... 71 H4

Zambra Wy *BGR/WK* TN15 .... 96 B6
Zealand Rd *STMC/STPC* BR5 ... 56 D3
Zetland Av *GILL* ME7 .... 67 G3
Zillah Gdns *RHAM* ME8 .... 67 K7
Zion Pl *GVE* DA12 .... 31 K5 🔢

Y

Z

Yalding Cl *STMC/STPC* BR5 ... 40 F8 🔢
  STRD ME2 .... 49 K4
Yalding Hl *WBY/YAL* ME18.... 135 J2
Yantlet Dr *STRD* ME2 .... 48 E6
Yardley Cl *TON* TN9 .... 147 M2
Yardley Park Rd *TON* TN9 ... 147 L2

Index - featured places

The Abbey Clinic
  BELV DA17 .... 12 B4
Abbey Court Special School
  STRD ME2 .... 2 B1
A B C Cinema
  GVE DA12 .... 31 K4
A B C Cinema
  RTW TN1 .... 10 F5
Acorn Business Centre
  MAIDW ME16 .... 120 E3
Acorn Industrial Park
  DART DA1 .... 27 J3
Acorn Trading Centre
  WTHK RM20 .... 15 M5
Airport Industrial Estate
  BH/WHM TN16 .... 91 M1
Alan Carter Gallery
  OXTED RH8 .... 109 G7
Albany Clinic
  BFN/LL DA15 .... 40 C1
Albion Surgery
  BXLYHS DA6 .... 26 C2
Alexandra Hospital
  WALD ME5 .... 83 H5
Allhallows & Stoke CP School
  HOO/HM ME3 .... 23 L8
Allington CP School
  MAIDW ME16 .... 102 D6
All Saints C of E Primary School
  CHAT ME4 .... 4 F8
All Saints C of E Primary School
  MAID/SHEP ME15 .... 7 G6
Alwin Gallery
  STH/RUST TN4 .... 10 E7
Amherst County Junior School
  SEV TN13 .... 112 F1
Anchor Business Park
  SIT ME10 .... 71 K7
Anchorians All Weather
  Sports Club
  RHAM ME8 .... 68 B4
Angel Indoor Bowling
  TON TN9 .... 147 L4
Angley School
  CRBK TN17 .... 183 K8
Anthony Roper County Primary
  School
  EYN DA4 .... 59 C5
Archbishops Palace
  MAID/SHEP ME15 .... 6 F5
Arden Business Centre
  STRD ME2 .... 50 A6
Arden Junior School
  GILL ME7 .... 5 L1
Arden Junior School
  GILL ME7 .... 50 F6
Argent Business Park
  QBOR ME11 .... 55 J3
The Artisan Gallery
  GRH DA9 .... 29 H5
Ascot Hever Golf Club
  EDEN TN8 .... 143 M4
Ashford Borough Council
  TENT TN30 .... 196 D5
The Ashworth Practice
  ORP BR6 .... 56 D3
Assembly Hall Theatre
  RTW TN1 .... 11 G5
Astor of Hever School
  MAIDW ME16 .... 120 E2
The Atman Clinic
  STH/RUST TN4 .... 163 J7
Avenue Theatre
  SIT ME10 .... 88 B2
Avicenna Medical Centre
  E/WMAL ME19 .... 101 G3
Axton Chase School
  HART DA3 .... 45 H7
Aylesford CP School
  DIT/AY ME20 .... 101 M4
Aylesford St Marks
  C of E Primary School
  DIT/AY ME20 .... 82 B7
Aylesford St Peters
  C of E Primary School
  DIT/AY ME20 .... 102 C2
Aylesford Secondary School
  DIT/AY ME20 .... 101 M4
Bad Apple Theatre Co
  RTWE/PEM TN2 .... 11 J3
Balfour CP Infant School
  CHAT ME4 .... 66 A4
Balfour Junior School
  CHAT ME4 .... 4 A9
Balfour Medical Centre
  GRAYS RM17 .... 16 E3
Ballard Business Park
  STRD ME2 .... 2 D8
Ballater Surgery
  ORP BR6 .... 56 B3
Balmoral Clinic
  GILL ME7 .... 5 K3
Bapchild & Tonge C of E
  Primary School
  SIT ME10 .... 88 F2
Barming CP School
  MAIDW ME16 .... 120 B3
Barnehurst Junior School
  BXLYHN DA7 .... 12 E7
Barnes Cray Primary School
  DART DA1 .... 27 J2

Barnsole CP Infant School
  GILL ME7 .... 67 G1
Barnsole Junior School
  GILL ME7 .... 67 G1
Barrow Grove CP School
  SIT ME10 .... 87 M1
The Barry Clinic
  STH/RUST TN4 .... 163 J7
Bata Medical Centre
  TIL RM18 .... 18 E3
Beacon Hill Industrial Estate
  PUR RM19 .... 14 D3
Bean Primary School
  RDART DA2 .... 44 E1
Bearsted Golf Club
  MAID/BEAR ME14 .... 104 D8
Bearsted Green
  Business Centre
  MAID/BEAR ME14 .... 104 E8
Beaverwood School for Girls
  CHST BR7 .... 40 A3
Bedensfield Clinic
  SCUP DA14 .... 41 G2
Bedgebury Junior School
  CRBK TN17 .... 191 G4
Bedonwell Clinic
  ABYW SE2 .... 12 A5
Bedonwell Medical Centre
  BELV DA17 .... 12 B4
Bedonwell Primary Junior
  & Infant School
  BELV DA17 .... 12 A5
Beechcroft Farm
  Industrial Estate
  BGR/WK TN15 .... 60 F6
Beechings Industrial Centre
  RHAM ME8 .... 67 J1
Bell Shopping Centre
  SIT ME10 .... 88 B1
Bell Wood CP Infant School
  MAID/SHEP ME15 .... 122 M4
Bellwood CP Junior School
  MAID/SHEP ME15 .... 122 M4
Belmont Primary School
  BXLYHN DA7 .... 12 C6
Belvedere C of E (Aided)
  Trinity School
  BELV DA17 .... 12 D3
Benenden C of E Primary
  School
  CRBK TN17 .... 193 M7
Benenden Girls School
  CRBK TN17 .... 193 M5
Benenden Hospital
  CRBK TN17 .... 194 E2
Benenden School
  CRBK TN17 .... 193 L5
Bennett Memorial
  Diocesan School
  STH/RUST TN4 .... 163 G7
Bentley Street Industrial Estate
  GVE DA12 .... 31 L4
Bethany School
  CRBK TN17 .... 168 D8
Bexley College
  BELV DA17 .... 12 E3
Bexley Cricket Club
  BXLY DA5 .... 26 C6
Bexley Erith Technical
  Boys School
  BXLY DA5 .... 26 C4
Bexleyheath Centre
  BXLYHS DA6 .... 26 A2
Bexleyheath School
  BXLYHN DA7 .... 26 C1
Bexley Hospital
  BXLY DA5 .... 27 G7
Bexley Rugby Club
  BXLY DA5 .... 26 C5
Bidborough Primary School
  STH/RUST TN4 .... 162 F2
Biddenden Club House
  HDCN TN27 .... 186 A5
Biggin Hill Business Park
  BH/WHM TN16 .... 91 M1
Biggin Hill Junior School
  BH/WHM TN16 .... 92 A2
Birchwood County
  Primary School
  SWLY BR8 .... 41 M5
Bishops Down CP School
  STH/RUST TN4 .... 10 A2
Blacklands County
  Junior School
  E/WMAL ME19 .... 101 H6
Black Lion Leisure Centre
  GILL ME7 .... 5 H1
Blackshots Leisure Centre
  CDH/CHF RM16 .... 16 F1
Blackthorn Medical Centre
  MAIDW ME16 .... 120 C2
Blenheim Junior
  & Infant School
  ORP BR6 .... 56 E5
Bligh Way CP School
  STRD ME2 .... 48 E6
Blubery House
  Cranbrook School
  CRBK TN17 .... 183 M8
Bobbing CP School
  RSIT ME9 .... 70 D6

Bodiam Castle (NT)
  RBTBR TN32 .... 205 H5
Bodiam Manor School
  RBTBR TN32 .... 205 G5
Bodiam Primary School
  RBTBR TN32 .... 205 G5
Borden C of E Primary School
  RSIT ME9 .... 87 H2
Borden Grammar School
  SIT ME10 .... 88 B2
Borough Green Medical Centre
  BGR/WK TN15 .... 98 B6
Borough Green Primary School
  BGR/WK TN15 .... 98 C6
Borstal Manor County
  Junior School
  ROCH ME1 .... 65 H3
Borstal Village Surgery
  ROCH ME1 .... 65 H3
Bough Beech Sailing Club
  EDEN TN8 .... 144 D1
Boughton Monchelsea County
  Primary School
  RMAID ME17 .... 137 K3
Bower Grove School
  MAIDW ME16 .... 120 D3
The Bower Mount Clinic
  MAIDW ME16 .... 6 B5
Bowes Industrial Centre
  MEO DA13 .... 62 B7
Bowls Centre
  MAID/BEAR ME14 .... 7 H4
Boxmend Industrial Estate
  RMAID ME17 .... 138 C2
Boyd Business Centre
  STRD ME2 .... 3 M3
Bradbourne School
  RSEV TN14 .... 95 J7
Bradfields School
  WALD ME5 .... 66 C7
Braeside Surgery
  EYN DA4 .... 59 J3
Branbridges Industrial Estate
  STPH/PW TN12 .... 134 C8
Brasted Surgery
  BH/WHM TN16 .... 111 L3
Brattle Farm Museum
  STPH/PW TN12 .... 169 M4
Bredgar C of E Primary School
  RSIT ME9 .... 87 J8
Bredhurst C of E School
  GILL ME7 .... 84 D4
Brenchley & Matfield
  C of E Primary School
  STPH/PW TN12 .... 166 C5
Brent CP School
  RDART DA2 .... 28 E5
Brickmakers Industrial Estate
  SIT ME10 .... 71 K7
Bridge Industrial Centre
  MAIDW ME16 .... 6 C8
Bridge View Industrial Estate
  WTHK RM20 .... 15 J5
Brittania Business Park
  DIT/AY ME20 .... 102 A5
Broadwater CP School
  RTWE/PEM TN2 .... 177 H5
Broadway Shopping Centre
  MAIDW ME16 .... 6 E5
Bromley Hospitals N H S Trust
  ORP BR6 .... 56 B7
Bromley Museum
  ORP BR6 .... 56 D3
Brompton Medical Centre
  GILL ME7 .... 4 E1
Brompton Westbrook CP School
  GILL ME7 .... 4 F4
Brookfield County
  Infant School
  DIT/AY ME20 .... 101 J3
Brookfield CP Junior School
  DIT/AY ME20 .... 101 H3
Brookhurst Surgery
  ORP BR6 .... 56 C5
The Brook Theatre Arts &
  Entertainment Ltd
  CHAT ME4 .... 4 D4
Broomhill Bank School
  RRTW TN3 .... 162 E7
Brunswick House Clinic
  MAIDW ME16 .... 6 D3
Brunswick House CP School
  MAIDW ME16 .... 6 C3
Bryony School
  RHAM ME8 .... 67 L6
Bryony School
  RHAM ME8 .... 68 B8
Burnham Trading Estate
  DART DA1 .... 27 M2
Burrswood Medical Centre
  RRTW TN3 .... 175 J5
Bursted Woodprimary School
  BXLYHN DA7 .... 12 D8
Bursted Wood Surgery
  BXLYHN DA7 .... 12 D8
Burwood School
  ORP BR6 .... 56 F5
Business Centre
  WBY/YAL ME18 .... 119 K5

The Butts County
  Infants School
  SIT ME10 .... 71 G7
Byron CP School
  GILL ME7 .... 5 K7
Byron House Surgery
  GILL ME7 .... 5 J7
Cage Green County
  Primary School
  TONN TN10 .... 131 M8
Canal Industrial Park
  GVE DA12 .... 31 M4
Cannock House School
  SIT ME10 .... 57 H8
Canterbury Road CP School
  SIT ME10 .... 88 D2
Capel CP School
  RTON TN11 .... 149 H6
Capital Industrial Estate
  BELV DA17 .... 12 D3
Cascades Leisure Centre
  GVE DA12 .... 47 J1
Castleacres Industrial Park
  SIT ME10 .... 71 K7
Castle View Business Centre
  ROCH ME1 .... 3 L5
Cecil Road County
  Primary School
  GVW DA11 .... 31 H6
The Cedans School
  ROCH ME1 .... 65 L1
Central Business Park
  STRD ME2 .... 50 A6
Central Theatre
  CHAT ME4 .... 4 D5
Chadwell St Mary
  Primary School
  CDH/CHF RM16 .... 17 J3
The Chafford Hundred
  Medical Centre
  CDH/CHF RM16 .... 16 A2
Chalklin Business Park
  RTWE/PEM TN2 .... 164 A5
Chantry Medical Practice
  SEV TN13 .... 9 H7
Chapter School
  STRD ME2 .... 48 F6
Charles Darwin School
  BH/WHM TN16 .... 92 B1
Chart Hills Golf Club
  HDCN TN27 .... 172 C7
Chatham Grammar
  School for Boys
  CHAT ME4 .... 66 B4
Chatham Grammar
  School for Girls
  WALD ME5 .... 5 K9
Chatham South School
  CHAT ME4 .... 66 B5
Chaucer Business Park
  BGR/WK TN15 .... 96 F5
Chelsfield Park Hospital
  ORP BR6 .... 57 H8
Chelsfield Primary School
  ORP BR6 .... 57 G8
Chequers Shopping Centre
  MAID/SHEP ME15 .... 7 G5
Chevening Primary School
  RSEV TN14 .... 94 D8
Chiddingstone C of E School
  EDEN TN8 .... 144 E6
Child Health Centre
  STRD ME2 .... 2 A6
Chinese Medical Centre
  DART DA1 .... 28 A4
Church House Surgery
  TON TN9 .... 147 L3
Churchill Business Park
  BH/WHM TN16 .... 110 F4
Churchill Clinic
  WALD ME5 .... 66 C6
Churchill Gallery
  BH/WHM TN16 .... 110 E5
Churchill School
  BH/WHM TN16 .... 110 E3
Church Road Business Centre
  SIT ME10 .... 71 L7
Church Trading Estate
  ERITH DA8 .... 13 J6
Cinema
  MAID/SHEP ME15 .... 7 H5
Civic Centre
  DART DA1 .... 28 A4
Civic Centre
  GVW DA11 .... 31 K5
Clanricarde Medical Centre
  RTW TN1 .... 10 F5
Claremont CP School
  RTW TN1 .... 11 H7
Clearways Industrial Estate
  BGR/WK TN15 .... 77 G2
Cliffe Woods County
  Primary School
  HOO/HM ME3 .... 34 E5
Cliffe Woods Surgery
  HOO/HM ME3 .... 34 D5
The Clinic
  GVE DA12 .... 31 L8
Clock House Gallery
  TON TN9 .... 147 L2

The Club House
  MAID/BEAR ME14 .... 7 J3
Cobham CP School
  GVE DA12 .... 47 J8
Cobtree Medical Centre
  RMAID ME17 .... 138 F5
Colebrook Industrial Estate
  RTWE/PEM TN2 .... 164 A4
College
  SIT ME10 .... 87 L2
The College Practice
  MAID/SHEP ME15 .... 7 G7
Colliers Green Primary School
  CRBK TN17 .... 183 H3
Collingwood Industrial Estate
  RMAID ME17 .... 139 G3
Colyers Lane Medical Centre
  BXLYHN DA7 .... 12 F7
Combe Bank School
  RSEV TN14 .... 112 A1
Compass Centre
  CHAT ME4 .... 50 D5
The Computer Surgery
  MAIDW ME16 .... 102 E6
Connections Business Park
  RSEV TN14 .... 95 K6
Conquest Industrial Estate
  STRD ME2 .... 2 E7
Copperfields Shopping Centre
  DART DA1 .... 28 A4
Corinthian Sports Club
  HART DA3 .... 60 F2
Cornwallis School
  MAID/SHEP ME15 .... 137 H2
Cottage Industrial Estate
  DIT/AY ME20 .... 102 D3
Council Offices
  CRBK TN17 .... 183 L8
Council Offices
  MAIDW ME16 .... 6 D6
Council Offices
  SEV TN13 .... 9 G6
County Hall
  MAID/BEAR ME14 .... 7 G2
County Primary Infant School
  RHAM ME8 .... 68 A5
Court View Surgery
  STRD ME2 .... 2 D5
Coward Industrial Estate
  CDH/CHF RM16 .... 17 K4
Coxheath CP School
  RMAID ME17 .... 136 E2
Cranbrook Clinic
  CRBK TN17 .... 183 M8
Cranbrook Golf Club
  CRBK TN17 .... 193 M1
Cranbrook Primary School
  CRBK TN17 .... 183 M7
Cranbrook Rugby
  Football Club
  CRBK TN17 .... 183 M7
Cranbrook School
  CRBK TN17 .... 183 M8
The Crane Surgery
  CRBK TN17 .... 183 M8
Crayfield Industrial Park
  STMC/STPC BR5 .... 40 E6
Crayfields Business Park
  STMC/STPC BR5 .... 56 E1
Crayford Industrial Estate
  DART DA1 .... 27 H3
Crayford Leisure Centre
  & Greyhound Stadium
  DART DA1 .... 27 G4
Crayford Medical Centre
  DART DA1 .... 27 H3
Crayside Industrial Estate
  DART DA1 .... 27 J1
Crayside Industrial Estate
  DART DA1 .... 27 K1
Crescent Surgery
  STMC/STPC BR5 .... 56 E1
Crest Industrial Estate
  STPH/PW TN12 .... 152 E7
Crockenhill CP School
  SWLY BR8 .... 57 L7
Crockham Hill C of E
  Primary School
  EDEN TN8 .... 126 E3
Crosshall Surgery
  STMC/STPC BR5 .... 40 E8
Crowden House
  Cranbrook School
  CRBK TN17 .... 184 A1
Crown & County Courts
  MAIDW ME16 .... 6 E5
Crown Court Clinic
  ROCH ME1 .... 3 L8
Cudham School
  BH/WHM TN16 .... 92 C4
Culverstone Gm
  Primary School
  MEO DA13 .... 79 G2
Cuxton County Infant School
  STRD ME2 .... 64 D3
Cuxton CP Junior School
  STRD ME2 .... 64 D3
Cuxton Industrial Estate
  STRD ME2 .... 64 E3
Cygnet Leisure Centre
  GVW DA11 .... 31 G7

Dajen Business Park
CHAT ME4 .... 66 E4
Danecourt School
RHAM ME8 .... 67 J3
Darenth CP School
RDART DA2 .... 44 B3
Dartford Borough Council
DART DA1 .... 27 M6
Dartford County Court
DART DA1 .... 28 A4
Dartford FC
EYN DA4 .... 43 J5
Dartford FC
RDART DA2 .... 28 D6
Dartford Golf Club
DART DA1 .... 27 K7
Dartford Grammar School
DART DA1 .... 27 L4
Dartford Grammar
School for Girls
DART DA1 .... 27 L5
Dartford Hospital School
HART DA3 .... 45 J7
Dartford Magistrates Court
DART DA1 .... 27 M4
Dartford Natural
Health Centre
DART DA1 .... 28 A5
Dartford West Boys School
DART DA1 .... 27 M5
Dartford West Health Centre
DART DA1 .... 27 L4
Dartford West High
School for Girls
DART DA1 .... 27 L5
Deacon Industrial Estate
DIT/AY ME20 .... 102 C3
Deacon Trading Centre
STRD ME2 .... 2 F5
Delce Junior School
ROCH ME1 .... 65 L3
Deneholm CP School
CDH/CHF ME16 .... 16 E1
Detling C of E Primary School
MAID/BEAR ME14 .... 104 C4
Ditton C of E Junior School
DIT/AY ME20 .... 101 L4
Ditton Infant School
DIT/AY ME20 .... 101 L4
Dolphin Yard Sailing
Barge Museum
SIT ME10 .... 71 J8
Dominoes Health Centre
GRAYS RM17 .... 16 C5
Dorton College
of Further Education
BGR/WK TN15 .... 96 A8
Douglas Moat Practice
RTW TN1 .... 10 F7
Douglas Moat Practice
STH/RUST TN4 .... 10 E8
Dover Road Primary School
GVW DA11 .... 31 G6
Downe Primary School
ORP BR6 .... 72 C5
Down Ho
ORP BR6 .... 72 C6
Downsview Junior School
SWLY BR8 .... 42 C7
Downs Way School
OXTED RH8 .... 109 G5
Dr Ali Surgery
CHAT ME4 .... 4 D6
D2 Trading Estate
SIT ME10 .... 71 K7
Dulwich College
Preparatory School
CRBK TN17 .... 193 J1
Dunton Green County
Primary School
SEV TN13 .... 95 G6
Durgates Industrial Estate
WADH TN5 .... 188 A8
East Borough CP School
MAID/BEAR ME14 .... 7 K3
East Farleigh CP School
MAID/SHEP ME15 .... 120 C7
East Peckham Primary School
STPH/PW TN12 .... 134 B6
East Tilbury Surgery
TIL RM18 .... 18 D3
Edenbridge CP School
EDEN TN8 .... 142 E4
Edenbridge & District
War Memorial Hospital
EDEN TN8 .... 142 E6
Edenbridge Golf
& Country Club
EDEN TN8 .... 142 C3
Edenbridge Leisure Centre
EDEN TN8 .... 142 D3
The Edenbridge
Medical Centre
EDEN TN8 .... 142 E4
Eden Valley School
EDEN TN8 .... 142 E3
Education Centre
MAIDW ME16 .... 6 F4
Elaine CP School
STRD ME2 .... 2 B4
Elbourne Trading Estate
BELV DA17 .... 12 D2
Elm House Gallery
EDEN TN8 .... 127 K8
The Elms Medical Centre
HOO/HM ME3 .... 35 M8
The Elms Medical Practice
HOO/HM ME3 .... 23 M4
English Martyrs
Catholic Primary School
STRD ME2 .... 3 H1
Erith & Belvedere Football Club
BELV DA17 .... 12 D2
Erith & District Hospital
ERITH DA8 .... 12 F5
Erith Health Centre
ERITH DA8 .... 13 G5
Erith Library & Museum
ERITH DA8 .... 13 G4
Erith School
ERITH DA8 .... 12 E6
Erith Small Business Centre
ERITH DA8 .... 13 H5
Erith Theatre Guild
ERITH DA8 .... 13 H4
Essex County Council
GRAYS RM17 .... 16 D4

Essex County Council
TIL RM18 .... 17 J8
Eurolink Industrial Centre
SIT ME10 .... 71 J1
Eurolink Industrial Centre
SIT ME10 .... 88 C1
Europa Trading Estate
ERITH DA8 .... 12 F4
Europa Trading Estate
WTHK RM20 .... 15 M4
Eye Hospital
MAID/BEAR ME14 .... 7 G4
Eynsford Castle
EYN DA4 .... 59 G5
Eynsford Cricket Club
EYN DA4 .... 59 G5
Fairfax Gallery
RTW TN1 .... 10 E8
Fairfield Pool & Leisure Centre
DART DA1 .... 28 A5
Fairview Schools
RHAM ME8 .... 67 L8
The Family Medical Centre
WALD ME5 .... 83 L3
Farleigh Rovers F C
WARL CR6 .... 90 B1
Farrington School
CHST BR7 .... 40 A4
Fawkham Manor Hospital
HART DA3 .... 60 E4
Fawkham Primary School
HART DA3 .... 60 C4
Featherby CP School
RHAM ME8 .... 67 J2
Featherby Junior School
RHAM ME8 .... 67 J2
Fleetdown Infants School
RDART DA2 .... 28 E6
Fleetdown Junior School
RDART DA2 .... 28 E7
Fleetway Sports Club
GVE DA12 .... 31 L6
Fondu Sports Club
PUR RM19 .... 14 E3
Fordcombe C of E
Primary School
RRTW TN3 .... 161 K8
Forge Lane CP School
SIT ME7 .... 51 G7
Fort Luton Museum
CHAT ME4 .... 66 C4
Fort Pitt Grammar School
CHAT ME4 .... 4 A6
Fossebank New School
RTON TN11 .... 131 G6
Four Elms CP School
EDEN TN8 .... 127 K8
Friends of Orpington Hospital
ORP BR6 .... 73 G1
Frittenden Primary School
CRBK TN17 .... 171 G7
Fulston Manor School
SIT ME10 .... 88 B3
Furness School
SWLY BR8 .... 42 B3
Furness Swanley Football Club
SWLY BR8 .... 41 M8
Gads Hill House School
STRD ME2 .... 48 E3
The Gallery at Lakeside
WTHK RM20 .... 15 K3
The Gallery
CRBK TN17 .... 183 M8
The Gallery
MAID/SHEP ME15 .... 7 G5
The Gallery
ORP BR6 .... 56 C3
The Gallery
STH/RUST TN4 .... 163 J3
Galley Hill Industrial Estate
SWCM DA10 .... 30 A3
Gaza Trading Estate
RTON TN11 .... 129 M6
Geoffrey Whitworth Theatre
DART DA1 .... 27 H2
The Gillingham College
GILL ME7 .... 67 H1
Gillingham Football Club
GILL ME7 .... 51 G8
Gillingham Golf Club Ltd
GILL ME7 .... 67 G3
Gillingham Medical Centre
GILL ME7 .... 67 H1
The Glade Business Centre
WTHK RM20 .... 15 H4
Glencoe CP Junior School
CHAT ME4 .... 4 E9
Globe Industrial Estate
GRAYS RM17 .... 16 E5
Globe Works Industrial Estate
GRAYS RM17 .... 16 F4
Godden Green Clinic
BGR/WK TN15 .... 114 D3
Goldsmiths College
Sports Ground
SCUP DA14 .... 26 B8
Golf Centre
STMC/STPC BR5 .... 40 F5
Gordon CP Junior School
SEV TN13 .... 2 E2
Gore Court Cricket Club
SIT ME10 .... 70 D8
Goudhurst & Kilndown
C of E Primary School
CRBK TN17 .... 182 B5
Graham Gallery
STH/RUST TN4 .... 10 E7
Grange Park College
E/WMAL ME19 .... 100 E3
The Granville School
SEV TN13 .... 8 F3
Gravel Hill Primary School
BXLYHS DA6 .... 26 D3
Gravesend County Court
GVE DA12 .... 31 K4
Gravesend Cricket Club
GVW DA11 .... 31 J5
Gravesend Grammar
School for Boys
GVE DA12 .... 31 M5
Gravesend Grammar
School for Girls
GVW DA11 .... 31 J6
Gravesend Museum
GVW DA11 .... 31 K4

Gravesend & Northfleet
Football Club Ltd
GVW DA11 .... 30 E4
Gravesend & North
Kent Hospital
GVW DA11 .... 31 J4
Gravesend Rowing Club
GVE DA12 .... 31 L4
Gravesend Yacht Club
GVE DA12 .... 31 M4
Gravesham Borough Council
GVW DA11 .... 30 E6
Gravesham Borough Council
GVW DA11 .... 31 K5
Grays Athletic Football Club
SNOD ME6 .... 81 J6
Grays Business Centre
GRAYS RM17 .... 16 E2
Grays Convent High School
GRAYS RM17 .... 16 D3
Grays County Court
GRAYS RM17 .... 16 C5
Grays Farm Primary School
STMC/STPC BR5 .... 40 D5
The Grays Gm School
GRAYS RM17 .... 16 D2
Grays Health Centre
GRAYS RM17 .... 16 C4
Great Comp Garden
BGR/WK TN15 .... 99 G7
Great Hollenden
Business Centre
RTON TN11 .... 130 E3
Greenacres Dental
Health Centre
DIT/AY ME20 .... 102 A4
Greenhithe Health Clinic
GRH DA9 .... 29 K3
Green Street Primary School
ORP BR6 .... 73 H1
Greenvale Infant School
CHAT ME4 .... 66 C3
Grosvenor Medical Centre
RTW TN1 .... 10 F3
Grove Dairy Farm
Business Centre
RSIT ME9 .... 70 C7
Grovehurst Surgery
SIT ME10 .... 71 C4
Grove Park CP School
SIT ME10 .... 70 D7
Guardian Industrial Estate
STPH/PW TN12 .... 152 E6
Guelder Rose Medical Centre
STPH/PW TN12 .... 170 B1
The Guildhall Museum
ROCH ME1 .... 3 K6
Guru Nanak Sports Club
GVE DA12 .... 31 L5
Hadlow College
RTON TN11 .... 132 F5
Hadlow CP School
RTON TN11 .... 133 G5
Halling County Primary School
STRD ME2 .... 81 K2
Halstead Place School
RSEV TN14 .... 74 A6
Halstead Primary School
RSEV TN14 .... 74 B6
Hamlet International
Industrial Estate
ERITH DA8 .... 12 F4
Harenc School
SCUP DA14 .... 40 E2
Harrietsham Primary School
RMAID ME17 .... 125 G7
Hartley CP School
HART DA3 .... 61 G2
Haslemere Industrial Estate
MAID/SHEP ME15 .... 122 B8
Haslemere Trading Estate
MAID/SHEP ME15 .... 122 B8
Hawkhurst C of E
Primary School
HAWK TN18 .... 199 H5
Hawkhurst Squash Club
HAWK TN18 .... 199 G3
Hawkwell Business Centre
RTWE/PEM TN2 .... 165 H3
Hayesbrook School
TON TN9 .... 147 J5
Hazlitt Theatre
MAID/BEAR ME14 .... 6 F4
Headcorn CP School
HDCN TN27 .... 155 L7
The Headcorn Gallery
HDCN TN27 .... 155 L8
Helen Alison School
MEO DA13 .... 62 C3
Hempstead Infant School
GILL ME7 .... 67 J8
Hempstead Junior School
GILL ME7 .... 84 C1
Henley Business Park
STRD ME2 .... 3 M4
Herringham County
Infant School
CDH/CHF RM16 .... 17 K3
Herton Court School
SCUP DA14 .... 40 E1
Hever C of E Primary School
EDEN TN8 .... 143 M7
Hever Golf Club
EDEN TN8 .... 143 M4
Hever Golf Clubhouse
EDEN TN8 .... 143 M4
Hextable Comprehensive
School
SWLY BR8 .... 42 B5
Hextable CP School
SWLY BR8 .... 42 B3
Higham CP School
HOO/HM ME3 .... 33 L8
High Elms Golf Course
ORP BR6 .... 72 E2
High Firs CP School
SWLY BR8 .... 42 B8
High Halstow Primary School
HOO/HM ME3 .... 35 M2
Highsted School for Girls
SIT ME10 .... 88 B3
The Highways Primary School
ORP BR6 .... 56 E8
Hildenborough Primary School
RTON TN11 .... 130 E7
Hilden Oaks School
TONN TN10 .... 147 K1

Hill School
BH/WHM TN16 .... 110 D1
Hills Surgery
RHAM ME8 .... 67 M7
Hilltop Primary School
STRD ME2 .... 49 L8
Historical Society Museum
CHAT ME4 .... 4 C3
Historic Vehicles Collection
CRBK TN17 .... 202 A2
Hollingbourne County
Primary School
RMAID ME17 .... 123 M3
Holmesdale Community School
SNOD ME6 .... 81 J6
Holmewood House School
RRTW TN3 .... 176 C3
Holy Family Catholic
Primary School
RMAID ME17 .... 138 A1
Holy Innocents RC
Primary School
ORP BR6 .... 56 B6
Holy Trinity C of E
Primary School
DART DA1 .... 27 L3
Holy Trinity C of E School
GVE DA12 .... 31 L5
Homefarm Estate
DIT/AY ME20 .... 102 B4
Homeopathic Hospital
RTW TN1 .... 10 E5
Homewood School
TENT TN30 .... 196 D4
Honeycrest Industrial Park
STPH/PW TN12 .... 154 A8
Hoo St Werburgh C P School
HOO/HM ME3 .... 35 M8
Horsmonden CP School
STPH/PW TN12 .... 167 J7
Horsted CP Junior
& Infants School
WALD ME5 .... 65 M8
Horsted Retail Park
WALD ME5 .... 65 M7
Horton Kirby C of E
Primary School
EYN DA4 .... 43 L7
Horton Kirby & South
Darenth Parish Council
EYN DA4 .... 43 L6
Horton Kirby Trading Estate
EYN DA4 .... 43 L6
Hospital
HAWK TN18 .... 198 F3
Hospital Barn Farm
MAID/SHEP ME15 .... 136 B1
Howard School
RHAM ME8 .... 67 M5
Hugh Christie School
TONN TN10 .... 131 M7
The Hundred of Hoo School
HOO/HM ME3 .... 35 L8
Hunton CP School
MAID/SHEP ME15 .... 135 M6
Hylands Clinic
MAID/BEAR ME14 .... 7 G5
Ide Hill School
RSEV TN14 .... 128 A1
Ifield School
GVE DA12 .... 46 E2
Ightham County
Primary School
BGR/WK TN15 .... 97 K7
Imperial Retail Park
GVW DA11 .... 31 J4
The Industrial Estate
EDEN TN8 .... 142 D2
Invicta Grammar School
MAID/BEAR ME14 .... 7 L4
Invicta Sports Club
DART DA1 .... 27 M3
Istead Rise CP School
MEO DA13 .... 46 A5
Ivy Bower Surgery
GRH DA9 .... 29 K3
Iwade CP School
RSIT ME9 .... 70 F1
Jarvis Great Danes
Hotel & Country Club
RMAID ME17 .... 123 K4
John Fisher Sports Club
WARL CR6 .... 90 A4
John Goodhew Medical Centre
SIT ME10 .... 71 G4
John Mayne C of E
Primary School
HDCN TN27 .... 186 B4
Joyce Green Hospital
DART DA1 .... 14 B8
Joydens Wood CP School
BXLY DA5 .... 42 A1
The Judd School
TON TN9 .... 147 J5
Kemsing CP School
BGR/WK TN15 .... 96 C3
Kemsing Parish Council
BGR/WK TN15 .... 96 C3
Kenden Business Park
STRD ME2 .... 3 M1
Kent College for Girls
RTWE/PEM TN2 .... 164 F2
Kent County Council
DART DA1 .... 27 M4
Kent County Council
GVW DA11 .... 31 G3
Kent County Council
GVW DA11 .... 31 G8
Kent County Council
MAID/BEAR ME14 .... 7 G2
Kent County Council
MAIDW ME16 .... 102 F4
Kent County Council
MEO DA13 .... 79 G5
Kent County Council
RDART DA2 .... 42 E1
Kent Kraft Industrial Estate
GVW DA11 .... 30 B2
Kent Kraft Industrial Estate
SWCM DA10 .... 30 B3
Kents Potters Gallery
MAID/BEAR ME14 .... 7 G4
Kent & Sussex Hospital
STH/RUST TN4 .... 10 E4
The Kent Youth Theatre
WALD ME5 .... 83 M4

Kestner Industrial Estate
GRH DA9 .... 29 J2
Kevington CP School
STMC/STPC BR5 .... 56 F1
Kincade Gallery
GRH DA9 .... 29 H5
Kingfisher CP School
WALD ME5 .... 66 D6
Kingsdown Industrial Estate
DIT/AY ME20 .... 101 K5
The Kings Family Practice
CHAT ME4 .... 4 F7
The Kings Family Practice
CHAT ME4 .... 50 D3
Kings Farm Infant School
GVE DA12 .... 46 E2
Kings Farm Junior School
GVE DA12 .... 46 E1
Kings Hill Golf Club
E/WMAL ME19 .... 118 C3
Kings Hill Primary School
E/WMAL ME19 .... 100 C7
Kings Hill Primary School
E/WMAL ME19 .... 118 C2
Kings Preparatory School
ROCH ME1 .... 3 J8
Kings Road Clinic
WALD ME5 .... 66 F4
Kings School Rochester
ROCH ME1 .... 3 J7
Kingstanding Business Park
RTON TN11 .... 164 B3
King Street Surgery
MAID/SHEP ME15 .... 7 H5
Kingswood CP School
RMAID ME17 .... 140 A1
Kingswood Surgery
RMAID ME17 .... 139 M3
Kingswood Surgery
RTWE/PEM TN2 .... 11 K5
Kit's Coty House
DIT/AY ME20 .... 82 E7
Klondyke Industrial Estate
QBOR ME11 .... 55 H1
Knights Park Industrial Estate
STRD ME2 .... 2 E6
Knockholt School
RSEV TN14 .... 93 K3
Laddingford Farm
Industrial Estate
WBY/YAL ME15 .... 150 F1
Lady Boswell C of E School
BGR/WK TN15 .... 9 K6
Lakeside Shopping Centre
WTHK RM20 .... 15 K2
Lamberhurst C of E School
RRTW TN3 .... 180 D7
Lamberhurst Golf Club
RRTW TN3 .... 180 D7
Lamberhurst Surgery
RRTW TN3 .... 180 C8
Langafel C of E Primary School
HART DA3 .... 45 J7
Langton Green CP School
RRTW TN3 .... 176 A1
Lansdowne County
Primary School
TIL RM18 .... 17 H8
Lansdowne CP School
SIT ME10 .... 88 E2
Lansdowne Road Clinic
RTW TN1 .... 11 H4
Larkfield Leisure Centre
DIT/AY ME20 .... 101 J2
Larkfield Trading Estate
DIT/AY ME20 .... 81 K8
Larkfield Trading Estate
DIT/AY ME20 .... 101 K1
Lawn CP School
GVW DA11 .... 30 E4
Leeds & Broomfield
C of E School
RMAID ME17 .... 123 J6
Leeds Castle
RMAID ME17 .... 123 L6
Leesons Infant School
STMC/STPC BR5 .... 40 C7
Leigh City Technology College
DART DA1 .... 28 C6
Leigh Green Industrial Estate
TENT TN30 .... 197 G7
Leigh Primary School
RTON TN11 .... 146 B4
Lesney Park Primary School
ERITH DA8 .... 12 F5
Lessness Heath CP School
BELV DA17 .... 12 C4
Leybourne Business Centre
E/WMAL ME19 .... 101 G3
Leybourne C of E
Primary School
E/WMAL ME19 .... 101 G3
Limpsfield Chart Golf Club
OXTED RH8 .... 109 L7
Limpsfield C of E School
OXTED RH8 .... 109 K7
Limpsfield Grange School
OXTED RH8 .... 109 J5
Limpsfield Lawn Tennis Club
OXTED RH8 .... 109 J6
Liongate Clinic
STH/RUST TN4 .... 10 F1
Littlebrook Business Centre
DART DA1 .... 28 E1
Little Thurrock County
Primary School
GRAYS RM17 .... 16 F2
Livingstone Hospital
DART DA1 .... 28 B5
Loaland Business Centre
STRD ME2 .... 3 M1
London Beach Golf Club
TENT TN30 .... 196 C1
London Road Trading Estate
SIT ME10 .... 87 M1
Long Mead CP Junior
& Infant School
RTON TN11 .... 131 K8
Loose Junior School
MAID/SHEP ME15 .... 121 J7
Lordswood Health Centre
WALD ME5 .... 83 L4
Lordswood Industrial Estate
WALD ME5 .... 83 L4
Lordswood Leisure Centre
WALD ME5 .... 83 L2

Lower Halston CP School
RSIT ME9............................ 69 K3
Lowfield Medical Centre
DART DA1............................ 28 A5
Lullingstone Castle
EYN DA4............................ 58 D8
Lunsford CP School
DIT/AY ME20........................ 101 J3
Luton CP Junior School
CHAT ME4............................ 66 E3
Luton Infant School
CHAT ME4............................ 66 E3
Luton Medical Centre
WALD ME5............................ 66 E4
Lynsted CP School
RSIT ME9............................ 89 J6
Madginford Park CP
Junior School
MAID/SHEP ME15.................... 122 C3
Madginford Park
Infant School
MAID/SHEP ME15.................... 122 B3
Magnet Estate
WTHK RM20.......................... 15 L4
Maidstone Grammar School
MAID/SHEP ME15.................... 7 J8
Maidstone Grammar
School for Girls
MAIDW ME16........................ 6 D2
Maidstone Hospital
MAIDW ME16........................ 120 C1
Maidstone Industrial Centre
MAIDW ME16........................ 6 E3
Maidstone Lawn Tennis Club
MAIDW ME16........................ 102 E8
The Malling School
E/WMAL ME19....................... 101 K5
Manford Industrial Estate
ERITH DA8.......................... 13 K5
Manor Gallery
GVE DA12........................... 31 K5
Manor Way Industrial Estate
GRAYS RM17......................... 16 E6
Manzoori Clinic
SWLY BR8........................... 42 B4
The Maplesden Noakes School
MAIDW ME16........................ 6 C1
Marden CP School
STPH/PW TN12....................... 152 D8
Marden Medical Centre
STPH/PW TN12....................... 152 E7
Mardyke Surgery
PUR RM19.......................... 14 C3
Marlborough House School
HAWK TN18......................... 199 G3
Marlowe Park Medical Centre
STRD ME2........................... 48 F8
Marshlands Medical Practice
HOO/HM ME3......................... 48 E2
Mascalls Secondary School
STPH/PW TN12....................... 166 C1
Matrix Business Centre
DART DA1........................... 28 A3
Maundene CP School
WALD ME5.......................... 66 C8
May Avenue Industrial Estate
GVW DA11.......................... 31 H6
Mayplace Primary School
BXLYHN DA7......................... 26 F2
Maypole Community School
BXLY DA5.......................... 27 G7
Meadows Memorial School
STH/RUST TN4....................... 163 H3
The Mead School
RTWE/PEM TN2....................... 10 E9
Medway Community College
CHAT ME4.......................... 66 C4
Medway Little Theatre
ROCH ME1.......................... 3 L8
Medway Maritime Hospital
GILL ME7........................... 5 H7
Medway Rugby Football Club
ROCH ME1.......................... 65 K3
Medway Towns Rowing Club
ROCH ME1.......................... 65 J2
Medway Trading Estate
MAIDW ME16........................ 6 E7
Medway Yacht Club
HOO/HM ME3......................... 50 D2
Meopham CP School
MEO DA13.......................... 62 C3
Meopham Medical Centre
MEO DA13.......................... 62 C5
Meopham Parish Council
MEO DA13.......................... 62 B6
Meopham School
MEO DA13.......................... 62 C5
Meredale CP Infant School
RHAM ME8.......................... 68 C4
Mereworth CP School
WBY/YAL ME18....................... 117 M5
Middlesex Hospital
Sports Ground
CHST BR7.......................... 40 B2
Midfield Primary School
CHST BR7.......................... 40 C4
Mid Kent Business Park
SNOD ME6.......................... 81 K5
Mid Kent College of
Higher & Further Education
MAIDW ME16........................ 120 D2
Mid Kent College of
Higher & Further Education
ROCH ME1.......................... 65 M7
Mid Kent College of
Higher & Further Education
ROCH ME1.......................... 65 M2
Mid Kent School
MAID/BEAR ME14.................... 7 H3
Mid Kent Shopping Centre
MAIDW ME16........................ 102 E6
Mierscourt Primary School
RHAM ME8.......................... 68 B6
Milehams Industrial Estate
PUR RM19.......................... 14 C2
Milestone School
HART DA3.......................... 61 H4
Millside Industrial Estate
DART DA1.......................... 27 M2
Milton Road Business Park
GVE DA12.......................... 31 L5
Minterne CP School
SIT ME10.......................... 87 M3
Mole Hill Copse CP School
MAID/SHEP ME15.................... 121 M6
More Park R C Primary School
E/WMAL ME19....................... 100 F5

Moreton Industrial Estate
SWLY BR8.......................... 42 D8
Morley Business Centre
TON TN9........................... 147 M4
Mote Cricket Club
MAID/SHEP ME15.................... 7 K7
Mote Medical Practice
MAID/SHEP ME15.................... 121 K6
Mote Park Sailing Club
MAID/SHEP ME15.................... 122 A2
Motorway Industrial Estate
DIT/AY ME20....................... 102 E3
Murray Business Centre
STMC/STPC BR5...................... 40 D7
Murston County
Primary Infant School
SIT ME10.......................... 71 K8
Murston CP Junior School
SIT ME10.......................... 71 K8
Museum & Art Gallery
MAID/BEAR ME14.................... 6 F3
The Museum
CRBK TN17......................... 183 M8
Music School
MAID/SHEP ME15.................... 6 F6
Napier Road Junior School
GILL ME7.......................... 5 L5
Napier Road Secondary School
GILL ME7.......................... 5 M5
Neptune Industrial Estate
STRD ME2.......................... 4 B1
Nevill Golf Club
RTWE/PEM TN2....................... 177 M6
New Ash Green
County Primary School
HART DA3.......................... 61 H5
New Beacon School
SEV TN13.......................... 113 H5
New Grove Green Surgery
MAID/BEAR ME14.................... 104 B8
New Hythe Business Park
DIT/AY ME20....................... 81 L8
Newington C of E
Primary School
RSIT ME9.......................... 69 K6
Newington Industrial Estate
RSIT ME9.......................... 69 H7
New Road CP School
CHAT ME4.......................... 4 E7
New Road Surgery
CHAT ME4.......................... 4 C6
New Surgery
BH/WHM TN16....................... 91 L7
New Swan Valley
Community School
SWCM DA10......................... 30 B5
Nizels Hotel Golf
& Leisure Club
RTON TN11......................... 130 A4
The Noble Clinic
STPH/PW TN12....................... 166 D5
Normandy Primary School
BXLYHN DA7......................... 12 F7
North Borough CP
Junior School
MAID/BEAR ME14.................... 103 H6
Northcourt County
Primary School
GVE DA12.......................... 32 A6
North Cray Primary School
SCUP DA14......................... 41 G3
North Downs Business Park
RSEV TN14......................... 94 E2
North Downs Golf Club
GDST RH9.......................... 108 C3
Northend CP School
ERITH DA8......................... 13 H7
North Farm Industrial Estate
RTWE/PEM TN2....................... 164 A4
Northfleet Boys School
GVW DA11.......................... 30 F6
Northfleet Industrial Estate
GVW DA11.......................... 30 C2
Northfleet School for Girls
GVW DA11.......................... 30 F7
Northiam Primary School
RYE TN31.......................... 206 D8
North Kent Magistrates Court
CHAT ME4.......................... 4 D4
Northumberland
Heath Medical Centre
ERITH DA8......................... 12 F6
Northumberland
Heath Primary School
ERITH DA8......................... 12 D6
North West Kent College
GVE DA12.......................... 32 B6
North West Kent College of
Technology
DART DA1.......................... 27 M7
Nugent Industrial Park
STMC/STPC BR5...................... 40 E8
Oakfield CP Junior School
DART DA1.......................... 27 M7
Oakland Primary School
BH/WHM TN16....................... 91 L2
Oaklands CP Junior
& Infant School
WALD ME5.......................... 83 H1
Oaklands Junior School
BH/WHM TN16....................... 91 L2
Oaks County Infant School
SIT ME10.......................... 87 M3
Oak Trees CP School
MAID/SHEP ME15.................... 121 L6
Oakwood Hospital
MAIDW ME16........................ 120 C2
Oakwood Park
Grammar School
MAIDW ME16........................ 120 E2
Oasthouse Theatre
RHAM ME8.......................... 68 B5
Offham CP School
E/WMAL ME19....................... 99 M5
Offham Cricket Club
E/WMAL ME19....................... 99 M6
Old Bexley Business Park
BXLY DA5.......................... 26 D5
Old Bexley C of E
Primary School
BXLY DA5.......................... 26 B6
Oldborough Manor Community
School
MAID/SHEP ME15.................... 121 K6
Old Elthamians Sports Club
CHST BR7.......................... 40 A3

The Old Guild Theatre
GVW DA11.......................... 30 F6
Old Judd Rugby Club
TON TN9........................... 147 K3
Orchard Business Centre
MAIDW ME16........................ 102 E5
Orchard Business Centre
RTWE/PEM TN2....................... 163 M5
Orchard Business Centre
TON TN9........................... 147 M5
Orchard Industrial Estate
MAID/SHEP ME15.................... 138 B2
Orchard Medical Centre
RMAID ME17........................ 136 E3
Orchard Place Business Centre
E/WMAL ME19....................... 99 J7
The Orchard Theatre
DART DA1.......................... 28 A4
Orpington College of Further
Education
ORP BR6........................... 56 C4
Orpington Mental
Health Centre
ORP BR6........................... 56 B6
Orpington Retail Park
STMC/STPC BR5...................... 40 E8
Orpington Sports Centre
ORP BR6........................... 56 C4
Orpington Superbowl
ORP BR6........................... 56 C4
Otford County Primary School
RSEV TN14......................... 95 J2
Otford Medical Practice
RSEV TN14......................... 95 K1
Our Lady of Hartley RC School
HART DA3.......................... 61 H1
Our Ladys RC Primary School
DART DA1.......................... 27 L4
Oxleas NHS Trust
BXLY DA5.......................... 27 G7
Oxleas NHS Trust
ORP BR6........................... 56 D3
Oxted County School
OXTED RH8......................... 109 H1
Oxted Gallery
OXTED RH8......................... 109 G7
Oxted Health Centre
OXTED RH8......................... 109 H7
Oxted & Limpsfield Hospital
OXTED RH8......................... 108 F5
Paddock Wood
Business Centre
STPH/PW TN12....................... 150 C6
Paddock Wood CP School
STPH/PW TN12....................... 150 C7
Paddock Wood Town Council
STPH/PW TN12....................... 150 B7
Painters Ash Primary School
GVW DA11.......................... 30 F8
Palace Industrial Estate
MAID/SHEP ME15.................... 138 B1
Palace Wood County
Junior School
MAIDW ME16........................ 102 F7
Palmers College
GRAYS RM17........................ 17 H3
Parker Industrial Centre
RDART DA2......................... 28 E5
Park Road Industrial Estate
SWLY BR8.......................... 42 B7
Park Way CP School
MAID/SHEP ME15.................... 121 K4
Parkway Primary School
ERITHM DA18....................... 12 A2
Parkwood Hall School
SWLY BR8.......................... 42 D7
Parkwood Industrial Estate
MAID/SHEP ME15.................... 138 C1
Parkwood Infant School
RHAM ME8.......................... 68 A8
Parkwood Junior School
RHAM ME8.......................... 67 M8
Parrock Street Surgery
GVE DA12.......................... 31 K4
Pedham Place Industrial Estate
SWLY BR8.......................... 58 C1
Pegasus Gallery
SEV TN13.......................... 9 H6
Pelham Primary School
BXLYHN DA7......................... 26 C1
Pembury Hospital
RTWE/PEM TN2....................... 164 C6
Pembury Primary School
RTWE/PEM TN2....................... 164 F5
Penhurst Place
RTON TN11......................... 161 K1
Penshurst C of E
Primary School
RTON TN11......................... 161 J1
Perry Hall School
ORP BR6........................... 56 B2
Phoenix Industrial Estate
STRD ME2.......................... 3 L3
Phoenix Surgery
ROCH ME1.......................... 82 C5
Pickford Land Medical Centre
BXLYHN DA7......................... 12 A7
Platt C of E Primary School
BGR/WK TN15....................... 98 E6
Platt Industrial Estate
BGR/WK TN15....................... 98 E5
Plaxtol CP School
BGR/WK TN15....................... 116 A6
Police Station
& Magistrates Court
RTW TN1........................... 11 G5
Postley Industrial Centre
MAID/SHEP ME15.................... 7 H9
Poultwood Golf Club
RTON TN11......................... 132 B4
Poverest Primary School
STMC/STPC BR5...................... 56 C1
Power Industrial Estate
ERITH DA8......................... 13 J7
Pratts Bottom Primary School
ORP BR6........................... 73 L5
Premier Business Park
CHAT ME4.......................... 66 D4
Preston Hall Hospital
DIT/AY ME20....................... 102 B4
Princes Park Medical Centre
WALD ME5.......................... 66 D7
Princess Christian's Hospital
RTON TN11......................... 131 G3
Priory School
STMC/STPC BR5...................... 56 E4

Purfleet Primary School
PUR RM19.......................... 14 C3
Quarry Hill County
Junior School
GRAYS RM17........................ 16 D4
Quarry Wood
Industrial Estate
DIT/AY ME20....................... 102 A6
Queenborough
Business Centre
QBOR ME11......................... 55 J2
Queen Marys Hospital
SCUP DA14......................... 40 C2
Queen Victoria
Cottage Hospital
RTON TN11......................... 147 L7
Railway Street
Industrial Estate
GILL ME7.......................... 5 M2
Rainham Mark
Grammar School
RHAM ME8.......................... 67 M3
Rainham School for Girls
RHAM ME8.......................... 67 L5
Ravensquay Business Centre
STMC/STPC BR5...................... 56 D1
Raynehurst CP School
GVE DA12.......................... 32 B8
Rectory Business Centre
SCUP DA14......................... 40 D1
Rectory Paddock School
STMC/STPC BR5...................... 40 E6
Regional Sports Centre
TIL RM18.......................... 17 K8
Regis Manor County
Primary School
SIT ME10.......................... 71 G6
Reynolds Health Centre
DART DA1.......................... 27 M4
Richmond County
Infants School
GILL ME7.......................... 5 K1
Ridge View School
TONN TN10......................... 131 M8
Riding School
E/WMAL ME19....................... 119 K1
Riverhead County
Infant School
SEV TN13.......................... 8 C1
Riverside Business Centre
TON TN9........................... 147 K4
Riverside Industrial Estate
DART DA1.......................... 28 A3
Riverside Medical Practice
STRD ME2.......................... 81 K1
Riverside Retail Park
RSEV TN14......................... 95 L5
Riverside Swimming Centre
ERITH DA8......................... 13 G4
Riverview Clinic
GVE DA12.......................... 47 H2
Riverview Park Surgery
GVE DA12.......................... 47 G1
Riverview Primary School
GVE DA12.......................... 47 G1
The Robert Napier School
GILL ME7.......................... 67 G2
Rochester Airport
Industrial Estate
ROCH ME1.......................... 65 L7
Rochester Castle
ROCH ME1.......................... 3 H8
Rochester Grammar
School for Girls
ROCH ME1.......................... 65 L3
Rochester Health Centre
ROCH ME1.......................... 65 M2
The Rochester
Mathematical School
ROCH ME1.......................... 65 K4
Rochester Museum
ROCH ME1.......................... 3 L7
Rochester Tutors Independent
College
ROCH ME1.......................... 3 L9
Rodmersham CP School
RSIT ME9.......................... 88 D6
Rodmersham Squash Club
RSIT ME9.......................... 88 C7
Rolvenden Primary School
CRBK TN17......................... 202 A2
Roseacre Junior School
MAID/BEAR ME14.................... 122 C1
Rose Cottage Surgery
STPH/PW TN12....................... 170 B2
Rose Hill School
STH/RUST TN4....................... 10 A1
Rosherville C of E School
GVW DA11.......................... 31 G4
Rowhill School
RDART DA2......................... 42 E1
Royal Park Primary School
SCUP DA14......................... 26 A8
Royal Victoria Place
Shopping Centre
RTW TN1........................... 11 G3
RSPB
IOS ME12.......................... 55 M7
Rusthall Medical Centre
STH/RUST TN4....................... 176 D1
Ruxley Corner Industrial Estate
SCUP DA14......................... 40 F3
Ryarsh CP School
E/WMAL ME19....................... 100 C1
Sackville School
RTON TN11......................... 130 E7
Sacred Heart School
RTWE/PEM TN2....................... 178 A1
St Albans CP School
DART DA1.......................... 28 B4
St Andrews Medical Centre
STH/RUST TN4....................... 163 J4
St Andrews School
ROCH ME1.......................... 3 J8
St Anselms RC Primary School
DART DA1.......................... 28 C3
St Augustine Junior School
BELV DA17......................... 12 B3
St Augustine Primary School
BELV DA17......................... 12 B2
St Augustine RC
Primary School
RHAM ME8.......................... 84 F2
St Augustine School
STH/RUST TN4....................... 163 J6

St Barnabas C of E
Primary School
RTW TN1........................... 11 H1
St Bartholomews Hospital
ROCH ME1.......................... 4 A5
St Bartholomews Hospital
SWLY BR8.......................... 42 B7
St Bartholomews RC
Primary School
SWLY BR8.......................... 42 A7
St Bartholomews School
SIT ME10.......................... 71 H6
St Barts Hospital Sports
Ground
CHST BR7.......................... 40 A3
St Benedicts School
WALD ME5.......................... 83 L3
St Botolphs C of E
Primary School
GVW DA11.......................... 30 F5
St Catherines RC Girls School
BXLYHS DA6........................ 26 D3
St Chads School
TIL RM18.......................... 17 J7
St Columbas RC Boys School
BXLYHS DA6........................ 26 D3
St Fidelis RC Primary School
ERITH DA8......................... 12 E5
St Francis RC Primary School
MAID/BEAR ME14.................... 7 G3
St Georges C of E
County Primary School
BGR/WK TN15....................... 98 B2
St Georges C of E School
GVW DA11.......................... 31 J7
St Georges School
RTWE/PEM TN2....................... 164 C8
St Gregorys RC School
STH/RUST TN4....................... 163 J6
St Helens C of E
Primary School
HOO/HM ME3........................ 20 D8
St Hilarys School
SEV TN13.......................... 9 G1
St James C of E Primary School
HOO/HM ME3........................ 25 K7
St James CP School
E/WMAL ME19....................... 101 H5
St James's Junior
& Infant School
RTWE/PEM TN2....................... 11 J4
St John Fisher Catholic School
CHAT ME4.......................... 4 C9
St John Fisher RC
Primary School
ERITHM DA18....................... 12 A2
St John Fisher RC
Secondary School
CHAT ME4.......................... 4 A7
St Johns C of E Infant School
CHAT ME4.......................... 4 B7
St Johns C of E Primary School
MAID/BEAR ME14.................... 121 M1
St Johns Hill Surgery
SEV TN13.......................... 95 L8
St Johns Infant School
STH/RUST TN4....................... 10 E1
St Johns Primary School
STH/RUST TN4....................... 163 K6
St Johns RC
Comprehensive School
GVE DA12.......................... 31 M6
St Johns RC Primary School
GVE DA12.......................... 31 M6
St Joseph RC School
DART DA1.......................... 27 G2
St Josephs
Preparatory School
GVE DA12.......................... 31 L7
St Josephs RC School
GVW DA11.......................... 30 F5
St Katherines CP School
SNOD ME6.......................... 81 H6
St Lukes School
STH/RUST TN4....................... 163 L6
St Margaret Clitherow
RC Primary School
RTON TN11......................... 131 J7
St Margarets at Troy Town
C of E Primary School
ROCH ME1.......................... 3 K9
St Margarets C of E
Junior School
RHAM ME8.......................... 68 A5
St Margarets Old School
BGR/WK TN15....................... 114 D8
St Marks C of E
Primary School
STH/RUST TN4....................... 176 F4
St Marys Abbey
E/WMAL ME19....................... 100 E5
St Mary & St. Josephs
RC School
SCUP DA14......................... 40 B2
St Marys C of E Primary School
SWLY BR8.......................... 42 A8
St Marys CP School
STRD ME2.......................... 3 G2
St Marys Infant School
GILL ME7.......................... 5 M2
St Marys Island Church of England
Aided Primary School
CHAT ME4.......................... 50 D4
St Marys Medical Centre
STRD ME2.......................... 3 H2
St Marys Middle School
OXTED RH8......................... 109 G6
St Marys RC County
Primary School
TIL RM18.......................... 17 H8
St Matthews C of E
Infant School
ROCH ME1.......................... 65 J3
St Michaels C of E
Primary Junior School
MAIDW ME16........................ 6 C3
St Michaels C of E
Primary School
TENT TN30......................... 196 D3
St Michaels CP School
HRTF TN7.......................... 174 D8
St Michaels RC Primary School
CHAT ME4.......................... 4 C8
St Nicholas School
STRD ME2.......................... 2 F3
St Olaves Grammar School
ORP BR6........................... 56 D6

St Paulinus C of E
Primary School
DART DA1 .... 27 G2
St Pauls C of E Infant School
RRTW TN3 .... 176 D1
St Pauls C of E Junior School
STH/RUST TN4 .... 176 D1
St Pauls C of E School
SWLY BR8 .... 42 D5
St Pauls County Infant School
MAID/SHEP ME14 .... 103 J6
St Pauls Cray C of E
Primary School
STMC/STPC BR5 .... 40 E7
St Pauls Cray Health Clinic
STMC/STPC BR5 .... 40 C6
St Peter Chanel RC School
SCUP DA14 .... 40 E2
St Peters County Infant School
ROCH ME1 .... 65 L2
St Peters Primary School
RTWE/PEM TN2 .... 11 J6
St Peters RC Primary School
SIT ME10 .... 87 M2
St Philomenas RC
Primary School
STMC/STPC BR5 .... 56 E3
St Saviours Surgery
MAID/SHEP ME15 .... 121 M7
St Simon Stock RC
Comprehensive School
MAIDW ME16 .... 120 E1
St Stephens C of E
Infant School
MAID/SHEP ME15 .... 6 D9
St Stephens CP School
TON TN9 .... 147 M5
St Thomas C of E
Primary School
RRTW TN3 .... 175 L7
St Thomas More RC
Primary School
BXLYHN DA7 .... 12 B8
St Thomas More RC
Primary School
WALD ME5 .... 83 J1
St Thomas of
Canterbury Primary School
RHAM ME8 .... 67 K3
St Thomas RC Primary School
GRAYS RM17 .... 16 D3
St Thomas School
SIT ME10 .... 88 E3
St Werburgh CP Junior School
HOO/HM ME3 .... 35 L8
St Werburgh Medical Centre
HOO/HM ME3 .... 36 A7
St Werburgh Medical Practice
HOO/HM ME3 .... 25 K8
St William of Perth RC
Primary School
ROCH ME1 .... 65 K3
Sandhurst CP School
HAWK TN18 .... 200 E8
Sandling CP School
MAID/BEAR ME14 .... 103 K5
Sandown Court School
RTWE/PEM TN2 .... 164 A7
Schooling Licensed
Conveyancers
GRAYS RM17 .... 16 D4
School of Health
RDART DA2 .... 28 D4
Seal St Lawrence
Primary School
BGR/WK TN15 .... 115 G2
Sedleys C of E Primary School
MEO DA13 .... 45 J2
Seikh Temple
GILL ME7 .... 5 M4
Senacre Technology School
MAID/SHEP ME15 .... 121 M7
Senacre Wood CP School
MAID/SHEP ME15 .... 122 B6
Sessions House
MAID/BEAR ME14 .... 7 G2
Sevenoaks Business Centre
RSEV TN14 .... 95 K6
Sevenoaks CP School
SEV TN13 .... 9 G1
Sevenoaks Hospital
SEV TN13 .... 95 L7
Sevenoaks School
BGR/WK TN15 .... 9 J9
Sevenoaks Swimming Centre
BGR/WK TN15 .... 9 K6
Sevenoaks Town Council
SEV TN13 .... 95 K8
Sevenoaks Way
Industrial Estate
STMC/STPC BR5 .... 40 E7
Shamel Business Centre
STRD ME2 .... 3 K3
Shawcroft School
STMC/STPC BR5 .... 57 G1
Shears Green CP School
GVW DA11 .... 31 H8
Shears Green Infant School
GVW DA11 .... 31 H8
Sheldon Business Centre
STRD ME2 .... 3 M1
Shenstone School
DART DA1 .... 26 F3
Shepway County Primary
Junior Mixed School
MAID/SHEP ME15 .... 122 A5
Shepway CP Infants School
MAID/SHEP ME15 .... 122 A5
Sheridale Business Centre
STRD ME2 .... 2 E6
Sherwin Knight County Junior
& Infant School
STRD ME2 .... 2 B7
Sherwood Park Infant School
RTWE/PEM TN2 .... 163 M7
Sherwood Park Primary
School
RTWE/PEM TN2 .... 163 M7
Shipbourne CP School
RTON TN11 .... 115 L8
Shopping Arcades
MAID/BEAR ME14 .... 6 F4

Shoreham County Primary
School
RSEV TN14 .... 75 H5
Shorne C of E Primary School
GVE DA12 .... 48 A2
Sidcup Hill Primary School
SCUP DA14 .... 40 D2
Sidcup Sports Club
SCUP DA14 .... 40 B1
Sikh Temple
BELV DA17 .... 12 C2
Sikh Temple
DART DA1 .... 27 M5
Sikh Temple
GVE DA12 .... 31 K6
Sikh Temple
STRD ME2 .... 2 F1
Singlewell CP School
GVE DA12 .... 46 F3
Siri Guru Ravidass Temple
STRD ME2 .... 3 H2
Sissinghurst Primary School
CRBK TN17 .... 184 C5
Sittingbourne Industrial Park
SIT ME10 .... 70 E8
Sittingbourne Industrial Park
SIT ME10 .... 71 H8
Sittingbourne Memorial
Hospital
SIT ME10 .... 88 B2
Sittingbourne & Milton
Regis Golf Club
RSIT ME9 .... 86 D2
Sittingbourne Sports Centre
SIT ME10 .... 88 C2
The Skinners School
STH/RUST TN4 .... 163 J7
Skinner Street CP School
GILL ME7 .... 5 J2
Ski Slope
STMC/STPC BR5 .... 40 F5
Slade CP School
TON TN9 .... 147 K3
Slade Green Football Club
ERITH DA8 .... 13 K7
Slade Green Infant School
ERITH DA8 .... 13 J6
Smarden CP School
HDCN TN27 .... 173 J4
Snodland Clinic
SNOD ME6 .... 81 J5
Snodland CP School
SNOD ME6 .... 81 H5
Solefield School House
SEV TN13 .... 113 K5
Solefields School
SEV TN13 .... 113 L5
The Somerfield Hospital
MAIDW ME16 .... 6 B3
South Avenue County
Infant School
SIT ME10 .... 88 C2
South Aylesford Retail Park
DIT/AY ME20 .... 102 A5
South Borough CP School
MAID/SHEP ME15 .... 7 H9
Southfields School
GVE DA12 .... 46 E2
Southlands Surgery
ORP BR6 .... 56 A6
Spa Industrial Park
RTWE/PEM TN2 .... 164 A5
Speldhurst Primary School
RRTW TN3 .... 162 C6
Spinners Acre County
Junior School
WALD ME5 .... 83 M4
Sports Centre
ERITH DA8 .... 13 G5
Spotlites Theatre Company Ltd
CHAT ME4 .... 4 F6
Springfield Industrial Estate
HAWK TN18 .... 199 H2
Stag Theatre
SEV TN13 .... 9 H7
Stalham Business Centre
OBOR ME11 .... 55 J2
Stansted C of E Primary School
BGR/WK TN15 .... 78 B4
Staplehurst CP School
STPH/PW TN12 .... 170 A2
Stifford County Primary School
GRAYS RM17 .... 16 A4
Stocks Green CP School
RTON TN11 .... 131 G8
Stonecross Surgery
WALD ME5 .... 66 E4
Streete Court School
GDST RH9 .... 108 A8
Strood Swimming Pool
STRD ME2 .... 2 D3
Strood Yacht Club
STRD ME2 .... 2 F6
Sundridge Primary School
RSEV TN14 .... 112 A3
Super Bowl
BXLYHS DA6 .... 26 B2
Surex Swimming Pools
BH/WHM TN16 .... 91 M1
Sussex Road CP School
TON TN9 .... 147 J5
Sutton at Hone C of E
Primary School
EYN DA4 .... 43 J4
Sutton at Hone
& Hawley Parish Council
EYN DA4 .... 43 K3
Sutton Valence CP School
RMAID ME17 .... 138 F6
Sutton Valence School
RMAID ME17 .... 139 G6
Swan Business Park
DART DA1 .... 27 M2
Swanley School
SWLY BR8 .... 41 M7
Swanley Town Council
SWLY BR8 .... 42 A7
Swanley White Oak
County Primary School
SWLY BR8 .... 42 A6
Swanscombe Business Centre
SWCM DA10 .... 30 A3

Sweyne CP Junior School
SWCM DA10 .... 30 B5
Swingate County Infant School
WALD ME5 .... 83 L4
Target Business Centre
MAID ME15 .... 138 B1
Tatsfield Primary School
BH/WHM TN16 .... 91 M7
Teardrop Industrial Park
SWLY BR8 .... 58 E1
Temple Hill County
Infant & Primary School
DART DA1 .... 28 C3
Temple School
STRD ME2 .... 49 K4
Tennis Club
GILL ME7 .... 67 G2
Tenterden C of E Junior School
TENT TN30 .... 196 C6
Tenterden County
Primary School
TENT TN30 .... 196 D6
Tenterden Golf Club
TENT TN30 .... 196 F4
Tenterden Leisure Centre
TENT TN30 .... 196 D6
Teynham Medical Centre
RSIT ME9 .... 89 L3
Teynham Parochial C of E
(Controlled) Primary School
RSIT ME9 .... 89 L3
Thames Gateway NHS Trust
RDART DA2 .... 28 E5
Thameside County Infant School
GRAYS RM17 .... 16 E5
Thameside Theatre
GRAYS RM17 .... 16 C4
Thameslink Healthcare
Services N H S Trust
RDART DA2 .... 28 E4
Thamesmead Community
College
ERITHM DA18 .... 12 A1
Thames View CP School
RHAM ME8 .... 67 M3
Thamesview School
GVE DA12 .... 32 B8
The Thomas Aveling School
ROCH ME1 .... 65 L5
Thornhills Medical Centre
DIT/AY ME20 .... 101 J4
Thurrock Borough Council
GRAYS RM17 .... 16 D5
Thurrock Business Centre
WTHK RM20 .... 15 H5
Thurrock College
CDH/CHF RM16 .... 17 H3
Thurrock Council
PUR RM19 .... 14 B3
Thurrock Council for Voluntary
Services
GRAYS RM17 .... 16 D4
Thurrock Council Office
GRAYS RM17 .... 16 D4
Tilbury Fort
TIL RM18 .... 31 L2
Tilbury Manor Infant School
TIL RM18 .... 17 K6
Tilbury Surgery
TIL RM18 .... 17 J8
Titan Industrial Estate
GRAYS RM17 .... 16 C3
Tonbridge Football Club
RTON TN11 .... 131 K8
Tonbridge Grammar
School for Girls
TON TN9 .... 147 L6
Tonbridge Hillview School
TON TN9 .... 147 M5
Tonbridge Market
TON TN9 .... 147 K3
Tonbridge Oast Theatre
RTON TN11 .... 147 H1
Tonbridge School
TONN TN10 .... 147 K2
Tonbridge Town Sailing Club
RTON TN11 .... 146 E5
Torells County Secondary
School for Girls
CDH/CHF RM16 .... 17 H1
Tovil Green Business Park
MAID/SHEP ME15 .... 121 G4
Tower Industrial Estate
BGR/WK TN15 .... 77 M8
Townley Grammar School
for Girls
BXLYHS DA6 .... 26 B4
Town Medical Centre
SEV TN13 .... 9 H7
Toy & Model Museum
RRTW TN3 .... 180 E6
Trading Estate
WTHK RM20 .... 15 J4
Treetops School
GRAYS RM17 .... 16 B1
Trenchwood Medical Centre
TONN TN10 .... 131 L8
Trinity Theatre
& Arts Association
RTW TN1 .... 10 F5
Trinity Trading Estate
SIT ME10 .... 71 H7
Trottiscliffe C of E
Primary School
E/WMAL ME19 .... 79 J8
Tudor Court CP School
CDH/CHF RM16 .... 16 B1
Tudor Hotel Golf
& Country Club
MAID/BEAR ME14 .... 122 F2
Tunbridge Wells
Borderers Sports Club
RTWE/PEM TN2 .... 177 J5
Tunbridge Wells Centre
RTW TN1 .... 11 G4
Tunbridge Wells Golf Club
STH/RUST TN4 .... 10 A1
Tunbridge Wells Grammar
School for Boys
STH/RUST TN4 .... 163 J5

Tunbridge Wells Grammar
School for Girls
STH/RUST TN4 .... 163 H7
Tunbridge Wells Hockey Club
RTW TN1 .... 11 H9
Tunbridge Wells
Independent Hospital
RRTW TN3 .... 175 K2
Tunbridge Wells Museum
& Art Gallery
RTW TN1 .... 10 F4
Tunbridge Wells Nuffield
Hospital
RTWE/PEM TN2 .... 11 K5
Tunbridge Wells Sports Centre
STH/RUST TN4 .... 163 J6
Tunbury Avenue Surgery
WALD ME5 .... 83 H3
Tunbury CP School
WALD ME5 .... 83 H4
Tunnel Industrial Estate
WTHK RM20 .... 15 H3
Tunnel Industrial Estate
WTHK RM20 .... 15 H5
Tunstall C of E Primary School
RSIT ME9 .... 87 L5
Twenty Twenty
Industrial Estate
MAIDW ME16 .... 102 E5
Twydall Health
& Welfare Clinic
RHAM ME8 .... 67 K2
Twydall Infant School
RHAM ME8 .... 67 K3
Twydall Junior School
RHAM ME8 .... 67 K3
Tyrwitt Drake Museum
of Carriages
MAID/SHEP ME15 .... 7 G6
U C I Cinema
WTHK RM20 .... 15 H3
Ulcombe C of E
Primary School
RMAID ME17 .... 140 B7
Underhill School
RMAID ME17 .... 138 E6
Underling Industrial Estate
STPH/PW TN12 .... 153 H3
Union Mill
CRBK TN17 .... 192 F1
University of Greenwich
CHAT ME4 .... 50 D5
University of Greenwich
DART DA1 .... 27 L7
University of Greenwich
DART DA1 .... 28 B7
University of Greenwich
E/WMAL ME19 .... 118 C2
Upbury Manor School
GILL ME7 .... 5 G5
Upchurch Primary School
RSIT ME9 .... 69 G2
Upland Junior School
BXLYHN DA7 .... 26 B1
Upnor Castle
RSIT ME9 .... 50 B3
Upton Day Hospital
BXLYHS DA6 .... 26 A2
Upton Primary School
BXLY DA5 .... 26 A3
Upton Road School
BXLYHS DA6 .... 26 A3
Valence School
BH/WHM TN16 .... 111 H4
Valley Park
Community School
MAID/BEAR ME14 .... 7 M4
Vestry Industrial Estate
RSEV TN14 .... 95 K5
Vigo CP School
MEO DA13 .... 79 J5
Vigo Rugby Club
MEO DA13 .... 79 L4
The Vine Medical Centre
MAIDW ME16 .... 120 E2
Wadhurst C of E
Primary School
WADH TN5 .... 188 B8
Wainscott CP School
STRD ME2 .... 49 M3
Wakeley CP School
RHAM ME8 .... 68 C4
Walderslade CP School
WALD ME5 .... 83 J2
Walderslade Medical Centre
WALD ME5 .... 66 C7
Walnuts Leisure Centre
ORP BR6 .... 56 C4
Warders Medical Centre
TON TN9 .... 147 J3
Warlingham Park Hospital
WARL CR6 .... 90 C2
Warlingham Park School
WARL CR6 .... 90 C2
Warlingham Rugby
Football Club
WARL CR6 .... 90 B3
Warner Brothers Cinema
WTHK RM20 .... 15 J2
Warren Primary School
CDH/CHF RM16 .... 15 L2
Warren Road Primary School
ORP BR6 .... 56 B7
Warren Wood CP School
ROCH ME1 .... 65 L5
Warsop Trading Estate
EDEN TN8 .... 142 F5
Wayfield CP School
WALD ME5 .... 66 C6
Weald CP School
RSEV TN14 .... 129 K3
Weald Gallery
RSEV TN14 .... 111 M4
Weald of Kent Golf Club
HDCN TN27 .... 155 J4
Weald of Kent School
for Girls
TON TN9 .... 147 M6
Weald Sports Centre
CRBK TN17 .... 183 L7

Wentworth County
Infant School
DART DA1 .... 27 H5
Wentworth CP Junior School
DART DA1 .... 27 J5
West Borough
County Primary School
MAIDW ME16 .... 120 D2
West Borough
Secondary School
MAIDW ME16 .... 120 D2
West Borough Sports Centre
MAIDW ME16 .... 120 E2
Westcourt County
Primary School
GVE DA12 .... 32 A7
Westgate CP School
DART DA1 .... 27 M5
West Heath School
SEV TN13 .... 113 K7
West Hill County
Primary School
DART DA1 .... 27 K4
West Hill Hospital
DART DA1 .... 27 M4
West Kent College
TON TN9 .... 147 K5
West Kent College of Further
Education
STH/RUST TN4 .... 163 J6
West Kent College of Further
Education
TON TN9 .... 147 J5
West Kingsdown
Industrial Estate
BGR/WK TN15 .... 77 G3
West Kingsdown
Medical Centre
BGR/WK TN15 .... 77 H3
Westlands Secondary School
SIT ME10 .... 87 K1
West Lane Trading Estate
SIT ME10 .... 71 J8
West Malling C of E
Primary School
E/WMAL ME19 .... 100 D5
West Malling Golf Club
E/WMAL ME19 .... 99 L3
West Malling Group Practice
E/WMAL ME19 .... 100 D5
West Malling Industrial Park
E/WMAL ME19 .... 100 A3
West Thurrock CP School
WTHK RM20 .... 15 J5
West View Hospital
TENT TN30 .... 196 A7
Wheelbarrow Park Estate
STPH/PW TN12 .... 152 D6
Whitehill House Surgery
DART DA1 .... 27 J3
Whitehill Junior School
GVE DA12 .... 31 L8
The White House Gallery
BH/WHM TN16 .... 110 F4
Wildernesse Golf Club
BGR/WK TN15 .... 96 C8
Wilderness School
BGR/WK TN15 .... 96 A7
Wilderness Sports Centre
BGR/WK TN15 .... 96 A7
Wilmington Grange
Grammar School for Girls
RDART DA2 .... 27 K7
Wilmington High School
RDART DA2 .... 27 K8
Wilmington Parish Council
DART DA1 .... 27 M7
Wilmington Primary School
RDART DA2 .... 27 K8
Windmill Business Centre
MEO DA13 .... 62 B6
Winterton Surgery
BH/WHM TN16 .... 110 F5
Wish Valley Surgery
HAWK TN18 .... 199 H5
Wittersham Primary School
TENT TN30 .... 208 F3
Woldingham School
GDST RH9 .... 108 A3
Woodfalls Business Centre
WBY/YAL ME18 .... 134 F7
Woodlands CP Junior School
TONN TN10 .... 132 A7
Woodlands CP School
GILL ME7 .... 67 H1
Woodlands Health Centre
STPH/PW TN12 .... 150 B6
Woodlea Primary School
CTHM CR3 .... 90 B8
Woodside County
Primary School
CDH/CHF RM16 .... 17 H2
Woodside School
BELV DA17 .... 12 D3
Wren Industrial Estate
MAID/SHEP ME15 .... 138 B1
Wrotham Parish Council
BGR/WK TN15 .... 78 A4
Wrotham Road CP School
GVW DA11 .... 31 K5
Wrotham Road Health Clinic
GVW DA11 .... 31 K6
Wrotham Secondary School
BGR/WK TN15 .... 98 C4
Yalding C of E Primary School
WBY/YAL ME18 .... 135 J4
Yardley Court
Preparatory School
RTON TN11 .... 148 B6
Yew Tree Industrial Estate
DIT/AY ME20 .... 101 M3
York Road CP School
DART DA1 .... 28 B5
Zobel College
SEV TN13 .... 9 H5

Page 12

F3
1 Corinthian Rd
2 Pembroke Cl

F4
1 Nordenfeldt Rd

Page 16

D5
1 Bradbourne Rd
2 Darnley Rd
3 Hawkes Cl
4 Prospect Pl
5 The Retreat

F2
1 Wentworth Pl

Page 31

H7
1 Greenhill Rd

H8
1 Garden Rw
2 St Clements Cl

J4
1 Barrack Rw
2 Darnley Rd
3 New Rd
4 St James's St

J6
1 Weavers Cl

K4
1 Bank St
2 Bath St
3 Berkley Rd
4 Bernard St
5 Brewhouse Yd
6 Chase Sq
7 Garrick St
8 Horn Yd
9 Jury St
10 Manor Rd
11 New Swan Yd
12 Parrock St
13 Railway Pl
14 Wilfred St

L5
1 Albert Murray Cl
2 Blenheim Gv
3 Christ Church Rd
4 Cumberland Av
5 Waterloo St

M7
1 Evesham Rd

Page 40

E8
1 Harbledown Pl
2 Hythe Cl
3 Market Meadow
4 Montbretia Cl
5 Penshurst Wy
6 Station Rd
7 Withens Cl

F8
1 Admiral Cl
2 Buttermere Rd
3 Kingfisher Cl
4 Mayfly Cl
5 Ottinge Cl
6 Otters Cl
7 Palmarsh Cl
8 Richborough Cl
9 Swallowtail Cl
10 Watermint Cl
11 Yalding Cl

Page 49

H4
1 Hillyfield Cl
2 Hyperion Dr
3 Orchard Av
4 Sandycroft Rd

J5
1 Morgan Rd

J6
1 Stanhope Rd

L4
1 Mayfair
2 Thirlmere Cl

L7
1 Acorn Wharf Rd
2 Epaul La
3 George La
4 Gundulph Sq
5 Northgate
6 Pars Haed Ms

M2
1 Greenfields Cl

Page 50

C7
1 Barfleur Manor
2 Flaxmans Ct
3 Mansion Rw
4 River St

E6
1 Augusta Cl
2 Exmouth Rd
3 King William Rd
4 Latimer Pl
5 The Ridgeway
6 Virginia Rd
7 Wharf Rd

E7
1 Arden St
2 Chatsworth Rd
3 Cornwall Rd
4 Dalton St
5 High St
6 Jubilee Ter
7 Stanley Rd

F8
1 Avondale Rd
2 Balmoral Rd
3 Buckingham Rd
4 Connaught Rd
5 Edinburgh Rd
6 Glanville Rd
7 Osborne Rd

Page 51

G2
1 Aster Rd
2 Bay Cl
3 Beech Rd
4 Berry Rd
5 Cherry Rd
6 Clover Rd
7 Cypress Av
8 Damson Dr
9 Elder Cl
10 Elm Rd
11 Larch Crs
12 Maple Rd
13 Marine Dr
14 Oak Cl
15 Oak Rd
16 Willow Av
17 Yew Rd

Page 56

A3
1 Berkeley Cl

A4
1 Lewing Cl
2 Vanburgh Cl

A5
1 Northolme Rl

A6
1 Cromford Cl
2 Ridgeway Crescent Gdns

A7
1 Dymchurch Cl
2 Otterden Cl

A8
1 Downsway
2 Wentworth Cl

B2
1 Cotswold Rl
2 Marlborough Cl

B3
1 Horsmonden Cl
2 Sequoia Gdns

B6
1 Ambrose Cl
2 Bishop Butt Cl
3 Shepherds Cl

B7
1 St Josephs Cl
2 Strickland Wy

B8
1 Freesia Cl
2 Raleigh Ms

C2
1 Coleridge Wy
2 Wendover Wy

C3
1 Aynscombe Angle
2 Deakins Ter
3 Devonshire Rd
4 Lamorna Cl

C4
1 Mortimer Rd

C8
1 Atkinson Cl
2 Foxbury Cl

D1
1 Cross Rd
2 Sidmouth Rd

D2
1 Sanderstead Rd

D3
1 Brookmead Cl

D4
1 Horsecroft Rd

D7
1 St Margarets Cl

D8
1 Knights Rdg

E1
1 Burwash Cl
2 Copper Beech Cl
3 Roberts Cl

E2
1 Boswell Cl
2 Meldrum Cl

E4
1 Hart Dyke Rd
2 Ramsden Cl

E5
1 Larkspur Cl
2 Mimosa Cl
3 Poynings Cl

E7
1 Ampleforth Cl

F1
1 Hodson Crs

F4
1 Finglesham Cl
2 Lamberhurst Cl
3 Wichling Cl

F6
1 Hawfield Bank

Page 65

K1
1 Churchfields Ter
2 Magwitch Cl
3 Mitre Rd
4 The Queen Mother Ct
5 Vange Cottage Ms

L2
1 Dombey Cl

Page 66

A1
1 Hamond Hl
2 Lumsden Ter
3 Ordnance Ter
4 St Bartholomew's La
5 St Bartholomew's Ter

A2
1 Chilham Cl
2 Mozart Ct

A4
1 Huntsmans Cl
2 Radleigh Gdns

B1
1 Cambridge Ter
2 James St
3 Rhode St
4 Sir John Hawkins Wy

B2
1 Armada Wy
2 Claremont Wy
3 Silver Hill Gdns
4 Warner St

B3
1 Athelstan Rd
2 Freeman Gdns
3 Hillcrest Rd
4 Kingswood Av
5 Parham Rd
6 Pretoria Rd

B4
1 Underdown Av

B5
1 Thorndike Cl

B7
1 Walderslade Rd

B8
1 Bradfields Av West

C1
1 Church St
2 Hillside Rd
3 Meadowbank Rd
4 Rope Wk
5 Slicketts Hl
6 Union St

C2
1 Chalk Pit Hl
2 Hope St
3 Melbourne Rd

C3
1 Damiem Cl
2 Terence Cl
3 Westbrooke Cl

C6
1 Flamingo Cl
2 Goose Cl

C7
1 Timberbank

C8
1 Greenacre Cl
2 Urquhart Cl

D2
1 Bank St
2 Constitution Hl
3 Leonard Rd
4 Ocelot Ct
5 Short St
6 Whitehorse Hl

D3
1 Chamberlain Rd
2 Waghorn St

D5
1 Cameron Cl
2 Greenbank

D6
1 Kinross Cl
2 Penfold Cl
3 Snowdon Cl
4 Wheatear Wy

D7
1 Defoe Cl
2 Shackleton Cl
3 Wren Wy

D8
1 Lydd Rd
2 Tenterden Rd
3 Woodchurch Cl

E3
1 Chickfield Gdns
2 Coronation Rd
3 Pheasant Rd
4 Watchmans Ter
5 York Hl

E4
1 Durrell Gdns

E5
1 Maunders Cl

E6
1 Hampshire Cl

E7
1 Allen Cl
2 Judkins Cl
3 Manchester Cl
4 Ryegrass Cl

E8
1 Redbridge Cl
2 Stable Cl

F1
1 Marathon Paddock

Page 67

L3
1 Newnham Cl

Page 68

B4
1 Caversham Cl
2 Gresham Cl
3 Maplins Cl
4 Streetfield Rd

D3
1 Caldecote Cl
2 Littlefield Rd

D5
1 Bramley Cl

Page 81

J5
1 Charles Cl
2 Del Gdns
3 Lambert Ms
4 Ostlers Ct
5 Portland Pl
6 Recreation Av
7 Stevens Cl
8 Tomlin Cl
9 Waghorn Rd

Page 83

J4
1 Cinnabar Cl
2 Galena Cl
3 Goldstone Wk
4 Micawber Cl

K3
1 Hornbeam Av
2 Moonstone Dr

M4
1 Dogwood Cl

Page 102

D8
1 Fordingbridge Cl
2 Hawkwood
3 Montpelier Ga
4 Rosslyn Gn
5 The Russets
6 Shearwater
7 The Thatchers
8 Watermill Cl
9 Wedgewood Cl

Page 103

J8
1 Camden St
2 Cromwell Rd
3 Lucerne St
4 Princes St
5 Wheeler St
6 Woollett St

L8
1 Birchington Cl
2 Cowden Rd
3 Milstead Cl
4 Northfleet Cl

Page 120

D3
1 Burghclere Dr
2 Knowlton Gdns
3 Portsdown Cl
4 St Margarets Cl

Page 121

G4
1 The Quern

H1
1 Havock La
2 Market Buildings
3 Museum St
4 Pudding La
5 St Faith's St

H3
1 Barfreston Cl
2 River Vw
3 Underwood Cl

H4
1 Avington Cl
2 Woolaston Cl

H8
1 Church St
2 Mill St

J1
1 Brooks Pl
2 Church St
3 Gabriel's Hl
4 Granada St
5 Pad's Hl
6 Rose Yd
7 Wyke Manor Rd

J2
1 Brunswick St
2 Greenhithe
3 Knightrider Ct
4 Salem St

M7
1 Nottingham Av

Page 122

A4
1 Otterbourne Pl

A8
1 Brishing Cl
2 Disraeli Cl
3 Felderland Cl
4 Felderland Dr
5 Felderland Rd
6 Lubbock Cl
7 Wotton Cl
8 Wrangleden Cl

B7
1 Betsham Rd
2 Cheltenham Cl
3 Chiddingstone Cl
4 Chislehurst Cl
5 Doncaster Cl
6 Epsom Cl
7 Fontwell Cl
8 Goodwood Cl
9 Groombridge Sq
10 Taunton Cl

Page 177

H2
1 Clanricarde Rd

H4
1 Cobbett's Ride
2 The Goodwins
3 School Rl

H5
1 Broadmead Av
2 Devonshire Cl
3 Leicester Dr

H6
1 Harescroft

J1
1 Belgrave Rd
2 Clarence Rw
3 Culverden St
4 Dudley Rd
5 Grosvenor Wk
6 Hanover Rd
7 Lime Hill Rd
8 Mount Ephraim Rd
9 Rock Villa Rd

J2
1 Clanricarde Gdns
2 Clarence Rd
3 Lonsdale Gdns
4 Rosehill Wk
5 Vale Av
6 Wells Cl

J3
1 Berkeley Rd
2 Castle St
3 Cumberland Yd
4 Grove Av
5 Little Mount Sion
6 Market St
7 The Pantiles
8 South Gv
9 Sussex Ms
10 White Bear Pas

K1
1 Calverley Rd
2 The Ferns
3 Garden Rd
4 Garden St
5 Lansdowne Sq
6 Monson Rd
7 Monson Wy
8 Newton Rd
9 Victoria Rd

K3
1 Cambridge Gdns
2 Clifton Pl
3 Farmcombe Cl
4 Grecian Rd
5 Madeira Pk
6 Norfolk Rd

L2
1 Bucklers Cl
2 Calverley Ct
3 Cambridge St
4 Oakfield Court Rd
5 Park St
6 Prince's St
7 St Peter's St
8 Windmill St

L3
1 Camden Hl
2 Hollyshaw Cl

L5
1 Cypress Gv

M1
1 Shepherds Wk
2 Sherwood Rd

M3
1 Camden Pk
2 Hawkenbury Cl
3 Polesden Rd
4 Rookley Cl

M4
1 Hawkenbury Mead

Notes